With Eagles to Glory

The storming of Eggmühl (22 April). Württemberg Jägers break into the Eggmühl manor to clear the way for Napoleon's advance from Landshut. (Author)

WITH EAGLES TO GLORY

Napoleon and his German Allies in the 1809 Campaign

JOHN H. GILL

GREENHILL BOOKS, LONDON
PRESIDIO PRESS, CALIFORNIA

With Eagles to Glory first published 1992 by Greenhill Books,
Lionel Leventhal Limited, Park House, 1 Russell Gardens, London NW11 9NN
and
Presidio Press, P.O. Box 1764, Novato, Ca. 94948, USA

British Library Cataloguing in Publication Data
Gill, John
With Eagles to Glory: Napoleon and His
  German Allies in the 1809 Campaign
I. Title
940.2

ISBN 1-85367-130-4

Library of Congress Cataloging-in-Publication Data available

Produced via DAG Publications Limited, London, and Typesetters
(Birmingham) Limited, Warley.
Quality printing and binding by Butler & Tanner Ltd, Caxton Road, Frome,
Somerset, England.

Contents

List of Maps

List of Tables

Foreword

One of the most common misconceptions concerning the Napoleonic wars is the fact that Napoleon's armies are sometimes regarded as having been generally, or even exclusively, French in composition. Up to and including the campaign of Austerlitz in 1805, and even the Jena-Auerstädt campaign of 1806, there is reasonable justification for describing his forces as 'French'; but thereafter, until the final collapse of French influence in Germany, Napoleon's armies were truly multi-national, and unquestionably his most ambitious operations would not have been feasible without the support of his allied troops. The level of this contribution may be gauged from the participation of 'foreign' troops in the Grande Armée for the 1812 campaign: although due to different strengths of units the comparison can be deceptive, to 327 French battalions or cavalry regiments, the allied forces contributed some 330, with a further 53 foreign units serving as part of the French army.

Chief among these allies were the contingents of the Rheinbund, the 'Confederation of the Rhine' established in 1806, an organization of principally German satellite states. Their forces, although mostly maintaining independent establishments, collaborated with and formed an integral part of Napoleon's armies: while the territory of the states served as a buffer between the French empire itself and those nations ultimately intent upon its overthrow.

Valuable as was the military contribution of the Rheinbund, in other than German-language sources it has often failed to receive its due credit for its part in Napoleon's campaigns. To some extent this is due to unjustified prejudice against the foreign troops of the Grande Armée, which was common throughout the French parts of the army and certainly extended as high as the Emperor himself. Napoleon's own attitude is demonstrated by a remark reportedly made during the Battle of Borodino, when by a brilliant cavalry charge the Russian Raevsky Redoubt was captured, due in no small measure to Saxon, Westphalian and Polish cuirassiers. Observing the astonishing effect of the charge, Marshal Berthier exclaimed excitedly that the Saxon cuirassiers were inside the redoubt. Napoleon, in a reply taken to demonstrate his lack of willingness to recognize the German contribution, remarked that as he could see blue jackets, 'they must be my cuirassiers'.

Redressing the prejudiced view of the Rheinbund forces is long overdue, and *With Eagles to Glory* achieves the object splendidly, at the same time proving the most detailed account yet to appear in English of their operations in the crucial campaign of 1809. As a result, the importance of the troops of the Confederation of the Rhine will be recognized for the valuable contribution it was. Referring to the Hessian contingent, one force which did receive some praise from the Emperor, Marshal Davout remarked that Napoleon could not have been better served than by these troops: given that they loyally supported a cause not their own, and followed a leader often less than generous in his treatment, a similar comment is justified in regard to the entire force.

Philip Haythornthwaite

This book is dedicated to
Anne,
steady in the Cannon's roar,
and
Grant,
a source of Joy and more.

Official Bulletin

The fire of Heaven, which punishes the ungrateful, the unjust, the disloyal, has struck the Austrian Army.

It has been ground into dust, all its corps crushed. More than 20 generals have been killed or wounded; an Archduke is dead, two are wounded. More than 30,000 prisoners have been taken, a wealth of flags, cannon, munitions captured. From this army, which had dared to challenge the French, only a small remainder will return over the Inn. It is clear that here, as at Jena, the dread burden of war has fallen principally on those who began it. The Prince of Liechtenstein, one of the most outrageous, is mortally wounded.

The Emperor commanded personally yesterday, surrounded by 40,000 troops of the Confederation.

His Majesty addressed these troops and they demonstrated the greatest enthusiasm.

Rohr, between Landshut and Regensburg, 21 April 1809

Key to the Tables

Unit Function

⊠	INFANTRY
⊡	CAVALRY
•	ARTILLERY
◥	HORSE ARTILLERY

Unit Size

XXX	CORPS
XX	DIVISION
X	BRIGADE
(X)	HESSIAN *BRIGADE*
III	REGIMENT
II	BATTALION or SQUADRON
I	COMPANY or BATTERY

Preface

Ihave undertaken to write this book to fill a perceived gap in the military history of the Napoleonic era: the lack of a comprehensive history of Napoleon's German troops in the English language. The troops provided by the Confederation of the Rhine (Rheinbund) played a major role in Napoleon's campaigns, fighting and dying under the Imperial Eagle from Spain's arid hills to the ice-crowned walls of the Kremlin. Loyal or treacherous, valiant or cowardly, they contributed to the great victories and were often blamed for the great defeats. Yet, despite the innumerable volumes published about the great Emperor and his time, the historian who seeks to know something of the German contingents of the Grande Armée will find endless frustration. Works by German authors are often full of fascinating detail, but tend to focus on the deeds of their specific countrymen (Kraft's *Die Württemberger in den Napoleonischen Kriegen* for example), leaving the reader wishing for a broader perspective. As might be expected, archival material and regimental histories are equally narrow in scope. The Austrian General Staff officers who compiled the 'official' Habsburg history of the 1809 campaign mention this problem while describing the engagement at Riedau on 1 May. In that combat, Baden and Württemberg cavalry regiments overwhelmed an Austrian rear guard; naturally, both units filed post-action reports, but 'the very detailed reports are remarkable in one regard, that neither has a single word to say about the participation of the other contingent'.[1]

If German chroniclers are too narrow, French military historians often pay little attention to the contributions of their German allies. The loquacious Marbot formed an extraordinarily negative impression of the Bavarian and Baden troops: the former, though 'brave enough before the enemy', were 'slack when it was necessary to work' (1812), while the latter were 'miscreants' and 'notorious for cowardice' (1813).[2] Pelet is accused of neglecting the contributions of the Badeners because of a dispute over booty during the early stages of the 1809 campaign.[3] Sauzey, though sympathetic, commits some egregious mistakes. Even careful observers, such as Buat, often err when describing the German contingents. Differences in doctrine provide further barriers to understanding. The peculiarities of Hessian organization, for example, where a *'Brigade'* was the functional equivalent of a regiment, seem to have caused endless confusion for both Napoleon's staff officers and subsequent historians. Attempts to render German unit titles into French compound the problem. Two Württemberg cavalry regiments, the *Jäger Regiment zu Pferd König* and the *Leib-Chevauxlegers-Regiment*, are often confused, since both are 'light horse' and both have titles that can be related to the 'Roi'.

English language books dealing with the soldiers of the Rheinbund are rather a rare species. Those that do exist tend to emphasize the arcana of 'uniformology' rather than the quality of the soldiery or their battle record: the knowledge that a contingent took part in the 1809 campaign does little to elucidate their actual performance. As a result, it is often easier to discover the colour of Hessian infantry sabre knots than it is to determine which units of the Grand Duchy's contingent fought and bled at Aspern.

Why 1809? Napoleon's German allies participated in many campaigns that were grander, longer, more decisive (and more bloody). The campaign against Austria in 1809, however, formed a watershed in the career of Napoleon and Imperial France. Not only did the 'Emperor of Battles' suffer his first serious reverse (Aspern), but the victory that was finally achieved on the blood-soaked Marchfeld (Wagram) did not encompass the utter eradication of the enemy's army; it was not a stunning, crushing blow to compare with the glories that crowned the campaigns of 1805, 1806 and 1807. Moreover, the Emperor himself was beginning to show signs of the pernicious weaknesses that would grow more prominent in 1812 and 1813: over-estimation of his own abilities; dangerous contempt for the foe; unwillingness to tolerate contrary opinions; and even simple physical fatigue. Nor was the French army of 1809 equal to its glorious predecessors; sapped by the brutal struggle in Spain, the power of the French military had declined while that of its enemies had increased.

The grinding war in Spain also meant that Napoleon had to rely heavily on his German allies as hostilities with Austria threatened in 1808—9; nearly 100,000 Rheinbund troops would take part in the campaign. When combat eventually opened, the contingents from these states, relegated to siege and security duties in previous campaigns, found themselves in the thick of the action. Incorporated into French divisions (e.g., the Baden and Hessian contingents) or organized into their own Corps (e.g., the Bavarian and Württemberg forces), they played crucial roles in the great battles of the campaign: Abensberg, Eggmühl, Ebelsberg, Aspern, Wagram and Znaim. At Linz, the Württembergers and Saxons fought a key battle on their own, with no French troops in the vicinity, and the Bavarians bore the brunt of the cruel war against the Tyrolian insurgency. If the performance of certain contingents was somewhat less than glorious, others fully earned their battle honours, demonstrating courage, loyalty, endurance and tactical skill under trying circumstances. The Austrian campaign of 1809 is thus the first time the soldiers of the Rheinbund performed a major combat role. Initiating a trend that would grow through 1812 and 1813, Napoleon's German allies ceased to be mere auxiliaries and found steady employment in the centre of the battle line. Finally, 1809 was a year of glory for the German soldiers under Napoleon. Whereas the Russian and Saxon campaigns were months of gruelling struggle culminating in disaster, even ignominy, the war with Austria shines brightly in the annals of the Rheinbund contingents: 'all breathed vitality, ardour and activity, all were filled with the will to victory, the will of the Emperor'.[4] It was indeed 'the most glorious campaign'.[5]

This book, then, aims to provide a battle history of the Rheinbund troops in

1809. It is not a guide to the dress, equipment or armaments of the day. Some information on uniforms is included to depict the basic colours of each contingent (blue and white predominated), but those seeking details of buttons, buckles and busbies are referred to the efforts of uniform specialists such as the Knötels. Nor is this a history of the 1809 campaign. The first chapter provides an overview of operations to paint the broad picture and assist the reader in placing the actions of the German contingents in proper context, but details of French and Austrian operations, Marmont's march up from Dalmatia, Napoleon's decision-making process, Archduke Charles's relationship with his brother the Emperor and a host of other fascinating issues are excluded from this study. Rather, in the pages that follow, it is hoped that the reader will find a comprehensive account of the organization and combat operations of each of the German contingents that fought under Napoleon's eagles in 1809.

The reader will note that most chapters briefly address the social and political structures of the Rheinbund states. While researching this book, it became evident that an understanding of the spirit of the German soldiers in 1809 and their actions on the campaign's battlefields could only arise from a grounding in the sociopolitical environments pervading the kingdoms, duchies and principalities of early 19th-century Germany. The book thus attempts to outline the factors that shaped the soldiers and commanders: their societies, their sovereign rulers and their previous experiences with the Napoleonic military phenomenon. Furthermore, it is important to place the German contingents in the context of European military development. The very nature of war was changing as the calendar turned from the era of Frederick to that of Napoleon and the reflection of that change can be seen in the armies of France's German allies as they evolved from dynastic into national forces. This was particularly true in 1809, before French desires for political hegemony and military uniformity had erased many of the peculiarities of these small armies. From progressive Bavaria and Württemberg to stodgy Saxony (at best a reluctant participant in the nineteenth century), the Rheinbund presents a spectrum of modernizing armies, tough and professional, but altering as the norms of conflict assume new shapes.

To facilitate study (and pleasure!), the book is organized into chapters, with each chapter describing the operations of one contingent. This permits the reader to concentrate on one German ally at a time, from its background and preparations for war to the conclusion of the armistice. However, each chapter is further subdivided chronologically into sections that correspond with the principal phases of the campaign. The reader may thus proceed from chapter to chapter, phase to phase, to gain an appreciation of the operations of all the Rheinbund forces at any particular stage of the campaign. Additionally, a matrix at the beginning of the book provides a quick overview of the operations and battle participation of each contingent. You may chose the reading method that best suits your needs or inclinations.

A word about conventions. To deliver an account with the maximum accuracy and clarity, the following conventions have been adopted:

- titles of German regiments are presented in German, or in their most common contemporary German form (light horse regiments are thus referred to as

'Chevauxlegers' as that is the spelling most often used by German historians);

- to minimize confusion between individuals and units, those units which were known by the names of their *Inhaber* ('patrons') or commanders are presented in italics (for example, Oberst von Neuffer commanded Jäger-Bataillon *von Neuffer*), and, to preserve the flavour of the age, units are often described in the text by both their number and their name (the Bavarian 4th Chevauxlegers are also the *Bubenhofen* Chevauxlegers);

- battalions or squadrons of a regiment are designated by Roman numerals (thus II/10 indicates the 2nd Battalion of the 10th Regiment);

- German and French rank titles are preserved insofar as this is feasible and convenient; a table at the end of the volume relates these to current US and British ranks and lists my abbreviations (e.g., Oberst von Neuffer equates to Colonel von Neuffer);

- in addition, the term 'Rheinbund' is used throughout to refer to the Confederation of the Rhine (e.g., 5th Rheinbund Regiment);

- the terms 'Allied' and 'Allies', when capitalized, refer to the French and their German confederates;

- in most cases, modern German/Austrian spellings have been used for geographical names so the reader can locate these on a present-day map or road sign (e.g., Eggmühl for Eckmühl), however, conventional Austrian names have been retained for terrain features and towns in Czechoslovakia and Hungary to minimize confusion (e.g., Raab rather than Györ, Pressburg rather than Bratislava);

- finally, in those situations where the details of an action are not clear, I will generally present the results of my own analysis in the main text and provide principal divergent views in endnotes.

This work has been a labour of love, completed with the kind assistance of many others, and I hope that you will enjoy reading it as much as I enjoyed writing it.

NOTES

1   *Krieg 1809,* prepared by the staff of the K. und K. Kriegsarchiv as part of the series *Kriege unter der Regierung des Kaisers Franz,* Wien: Seidel & Sohn, 1907-1910, vol. III, p. 268.

2   Jean-Baptiste-Antoine-Marcelin Marbot, *The Memoirs of Baron de Marbot,* Arthur J. Butler, trans., London: Longmans, Green, and Co., 1905, vol. II, pp. 560 and 652.

3   This rather petty dispute revolved around the rights to an Austrian supply convoy (particularly the horses) captured on 23 April; everyone's pride was injured and the affair even came to the notice of the Corps commander, Marshal Massena. It is described in great detail in Karl von Zech and Friedrich von Porbeck, *Geschichte der Badischen Truppen 1809 im Feldzug der Französischen Hauptarmee gegen Osterreich,* Rudolf von Freydorf, ed., Heidelberg: Winter, 1909, pp. VII, 48-51.

4   Rudolf von Xylander, 'Zum Gedächtnis des Feldzugs 1809 in Bayern', *Darstellungen aus der Bayerischen Kriegs- und Heeresgeschichte,* Heft 18, München: Lindauer, 1909, p. 23.

5   Marcus Junkelmann, *Napoleon und Bayern,* Regensburg: Pustet, 1985, p. 235.

Acknowledgements

A great many people on both sides of the Atlantic have contributed to the preparation of this work and I would like to take a moment to express my heartfelt thanks. In Germany, Herr Alfred Umhey allowed me access to his voluminous files and helped clarify several points of detail. Frau Sabina Hermes provided invaluable assistance guiding me through the rich collection of German regimental histories and other works at the Wehrgeschichtliches Museum in Rastatt. Without her help, this project could never have gotten off the ground. The museum has a fine collection of militaria from throughout Germany's history and is well worth a visit on any trip to the continent. Another good collection is in the Bayerisches Armeemuseum at Ingolstadt and here I must thank the director, Herr Dr. Ernst Aichner, and the librarian, Herr Gerhard Robold, for their kind assistance. Similarly, Herr Dr. Klaus-Ulrich Keubke was most helpful in obtaining for me several unusual articles on the forces of the two Mecklenburg Duchies; Herr Karl Schröder generously did the same for the troops of Berg. Dr. Paul Sauer of the Stuttgart Stadtarchiv supplied extremely useful guidance. The staff of Heidelberg University Library was tireless in pursuing a host of obscure sources, and the staffs of numerous other German archives and libraries were most helpful; in particular, I am indebted to those of Bavaria (Dr. Braun), Bremen (Dr. Müller), Hesse (Dr. Degreif and others), Oldenburg (Herr Udo Elerd), Saxony, Sigmaringen, Württemberg (Dr. Theil and staff), Ysenburg, the Bundeswehr (Herr Köster) and the Military History Research Office (Herr Köhler). In Austria, I am indebted to the National Library as well as the libraries of Linz and Innsbruck. Thanks are also due to the Austrian Kriegsarchiv for supplying otherwise unlocatable cartographic products and to Dr. Manfried Rauchensteiner for kind advice and help with several recondite references.

In France, Dr. Ferdinand Beaucour of the Centre d'Etudes Napoléoniennes and M. Comault of the Carnet de la Sabretache provided encouragement, sources and counsel. The Service Historique of the Armée du Terre has also been helpful. I reserve especial thanks for my classmate, Commandant Eric de Stabenrath, French Army (a descendant of St. Hilaire's brigadier, Général de Brigade Jean de Stabenrath), for his thoughtful help with translations.

The mother country was equally supportive. Mr. Richard Brown of Ken Trotman Books, Ltd. was courteous enough to forward the initial scraps of manuscript to Greenhill Books. Professor David Chandler provided much-needed encouragement; his *Campaigns of Napoleon* has accompanied me on my travels for the past twenty-five years. Philip Haythornthwaite has not only been a consistently reliable source of advice, support and good humour, but has also been gracious enough to prepare the Foreword that enhances these pages and introduces the reader to the diversity and complexity of the Confederation of the Rhine. Needless to say, Mr. Lionel Leventhal and his staff at Greenhill have been more than helpful.

On this side of the Atlantic, I owe a debt of gratitude to Dr. Christopher Gabel of the Combat Studies Institute in Fort Leavenworth, Kansas, for his good advice, wry wit, and editorial sagacity. Also at Fort Leavenworth, Mary Jo Nelson and others at the Combined Arms Research Library have, through their diligence, given me access to a wealth of material. Farther east, Professor Gunther Rothenberg supplied insight and support in the early stages of this enterprise. Among my comrades in uniform, I wish to mention all those who participated in the staff ride to the Regensburg area in September 1989, particularly Colonel (retd) Stephen Gerlach and Lieutenant Colonel Arthur Fournier.

For illustrations, I am greatly indebted to the following individuals and institutions: the Anne S. K. Brown Collection (Mr. Peter Harrington), Philip Haythornthwaite, Alfred Umhey, and the Württembergische Landesbibliothek (for the 'official bulletin'). Graphic realization of my maps was the result of much hard work by the Geografik Design Group, Inc. of Alexandria, Virginia.

Finally, I must thank my family: my parents for opening my eyes to frailties in the text; my aunt, Mrs. Susan Bradman, for introducing me to Dr. Beaucour; my son, Grant, for his understanding; and my wife, Anne Rieman, for patience, proofing, patience, innumerable good ideas and patience.

ILLUSTRATION CREDITS

I owe a debt of gratitude to the following for their generous support in locating the engravings, paintings and drawings that accompany the text: Mr. Peter Harrington of the Anne S. K. Brown Military Collection at Brown University (ASKB), Mr. Philip J. Haythornthwaite (PH) and Herr Alfred Umhey (AU). Their cheerful assistance in supplying a host of rare illustrations has greatly enriched this work. Note that while some of the cartouches were selected from my own resources, most have been provided courtesy of the Anne S. K. Brown Collection.

Part I
THE CAMPAIGN IN THE
DANUBE VALLEY

CHAPTER 1:

Introduction:
Clash of Empires

E arly on the morning of 10 April 1809, shivering Bavarian cavalry pickets peered across the murky River Inn to see Austrian horsemen looming out of the fog on the far bank. They were the outriders of a huge host, 120,000 warriors of the Habsburg Empire whose twisting columns stretched along muddy roads twenty-five kilometres to the east. The Bavarian troopers did not wait to be accosted but spurred their mounts and sped west with news of the invasion. The War of 1809 had begun.

It was to be a clash of empires: ancient, reactionary Austrian and brash, revolutionary French, in no little part occasioned by the desire in both Vienna and Paris to control the destiny and resources of the multitude of states that made up central Germany. In 1809, however, those states, bound together in a political entity called the Confederation of the Rhine, were allies of Napoleon and their armies fought alongside Imperial eagles. Optimistic Habsburg courtiers might hope to rouse the Germans against their French Emperor, but they were to be bitterly disappointed: as Austrian pioneers struggled to bridge the broad Inn, 100,000 soldiers of the Confederation, Napoleon's German allies, were burnishing their bayonets and preparing for war.

THE CONFEDERATION OF THE RHINE

One of the principal political aims of Imperial France was the expansion of French influence in central Germany at the expense of the Austrian and Prussian monarchies. As French relations with Germany evolved, a number of schemes were developed to achieve this goal, but in their basic outlines all envisioned the establishment of a union of German states under French protection to replace the decrepit Holy Roman Empire and formalize Napoleon's influence in Germany. In addition to extending French power across the Rhine, this plan was also intended to provide for the security of France itself. Given the violent nature of the age and the sustained opposition to Napoleon's imperial pretensions, the safety of Napoleonic France was a key consideration in Paris and the German policy included an important military component that would serve to enhance French security in several ways. First, it would increase the French Empire's military strength *vis-à-vis* its chief enemies. Not only would anti-French coalitions be deprived of key military resources, particularly the manpower provided under the aegis of the Holy Roman Empire, but it was hoped that these same resources would produce allied armies to augment France's own forces in the field. Second, although the wars of the Revolutionary and Consular periods had pushed France's borders to the Rhine, its numerous opponents to the east still stirred great concern in the French leadership. A belt of friendly German states east of the Rhine (a *marche militaire*), armed and trained by the victorious Grande Armée and integrated into its command structure, would create a comfortable buffer between the borders of *la Patrie* and its foes. Moreover, the creation of French dependencies in Germany would establish a firm foundation upon which France might build for the future, a framework through which French cultural, political, social, and above all, military norms might be infused into central Germany. The multitude of princes across the Rhine would thus identify their interests with those of Paris and abjure the threats and blandishments of Vienna, Berlin and St. Petersburg. Finally, the establishment of a series of loyal allied monarchies whose ruling families had deep roots in

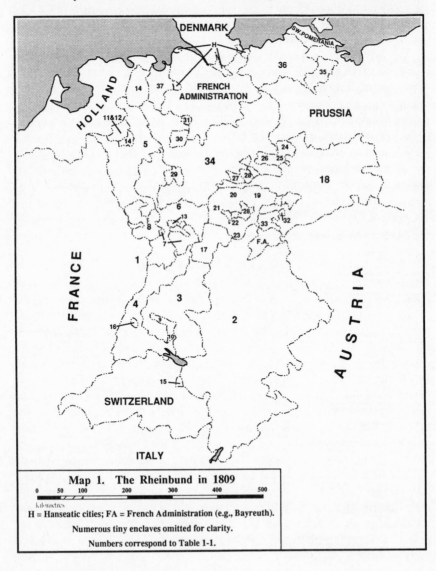

Map 1.   The Rheinbund in 1809

0   50   100   200   300   400   500

kilometres

H = Hanseatic cities; FA = French Administration (e.g., Bayreuth).

Numerous tiny enclaves omitted for clarity.

Numbers correspond to Table 1-1.

Europe's aristocratic past would serve to legitimize the upstart Napoleonic dynasty in France and lay the groundwork for its continued existence.[1]

The first major step toward the implementation of Napoleon's German policy came in 1805 when Bavaria, Württemberg and Baden signed bilateral agreements with France to supply auxiliary troops for the Grande Armée. The thunderous victory in that campaign gave the Emperor the power and prestige he needed to reshape Germany according to his own designs and established the preconditions for the further expansion of French hegemony over the 'Third Germany,' a rubric embracing the small states caught between Austria and Prussia. Work on the German union began in earnest that winter and culminated in July 1806 with the signature of the 'constitutional act' of the Confederation of the Rhine (Rheinbund) by Napoleon and fifteen German sovereigns. Although broad in scope, this act in practice was basically a military alliance and most of its subsidiary provisions were never exercised or developed (e.g., legislative and judicial features). Each member state was thus required to supply a contingent of troops in case of war, the contingents varying in size according to the population of the state; Bavaria, for example, as the largest German member, agreed to put an army of 30,000 into the field, whereas the Prince von der Leyen was called upon to commit only 29 of his subjects. Napoleon, as the 'Protector' of the Confederation, obligated France to provide 200,000 men for the common defence.

The campaign of 1806—7 against Prussia and Russia saw the first test of the new alliance and most of the member nations eventually contributed troops to the Grande Armée. Some of the original signatories were able to mobilize their

Table 1-1: Rheinbund States and Contingents

Original Member States (July 1806)	Populations	Contingents required by treaty	Actually participated in 1809 campaign (approx.)**
1. Empire of France	1. 36,559,000	1. 200,000	1. over 210,000 * [plus Italian formations]
2. Kingdom of Bavaria	2. 3,231,000	2. 30,000	2. 47,000
3. Kingdom of Württemberg	3. 1,211,000	3. 12,000	3. 19,700
4. Grand Duchy of Baden	4. 924,000	4. 8,000	4. 7,600 *
5. Grand Duchy of Berg	5. 931,000	5. 7,000	5. 2,500 *
6. Grand Duchy of Hesse-Darmstadt	6. 541,000	6. 4,000	6. 4,800 *
7. State of the Prince Primate	7. 170,000	7. 1,680	7. 600 *
8. Duchy of Nassau	8. 272,000	8. 1,680	8. 1,550 *
9. Principality of Hohenzollern-Hechingen	9. 14,000	9. 97	9. 181 *
10. Principality of Hohenzollern-Sigmaringen	10. 36,000	10. 193	10. [included with Hechingen]
11. Principality of Salm-Salm	11. 30,000	11. 323	11. [troops provided by Nassau]
12. Principality of Salm-Kyrburg	12. 19,000	12. [included with Salm-Salm]	12. [troops provided by Nassau]
13. Principality of Isenburg-Birstein	13. 43,000	13. 350	13. 200 *
14. Duchy of Aremberg	14. 58,600	14. 379	14. [troops provided by Nassau]
15. Principality of Liechtenstein	15. 5,000	15. 40	15. [troops provided by Nassau]
16. Principality of Hohengeroldseck (von der Leyen)	16. 4,500	16. 29	16. [troops provided by Nassau]
Joined September 1806			
17. Grand Duchy of Würzburg	17. 285,000	17. 2,000	17. 220 *
Joined December 1806			
18. Kingdom of Saxony	18. 1,987,000	18. 20,000	18. 23,380 [plus Polish formations]
[Grand Duchy of Warsaw added in 1807]			
19. Duchy of Sachsen-Weimar	19. 109,000	19. 800	19. 2,506
20. Duchy of Sachsen-Gotha-Altenburg	20. 180,000	20. 1,100	20. [included with Weimar]
21. Duchy of Sachsen-Meiningen	21. 48,000	21. 300	21. [included with Weimar]
22. Duchy of Sachsen-Hildburghausen	22. 33,000	22. 200	22. [included with Weimar]
23. Duchy of Sachsen-Koburg-Saalfeld	23. 59,000	23. 400	23. [included with Weimar]
Joined in April 1807			
24. Duchy of Anhalt-Bernburg	24. 35,000	24. 240	24. 840
25. Duchy of Anhalt-Dessau	25. 53,000	25. 350	25. [included with Bernburg]
26. Duchy of Anhalt-Köthen	26. 28,800	26. 210	26. [included with Bernburg]
27. Principality of Schwarzburg-Sondershausen	27. 45,000	27. 325	27. 460 *
28. Principality of Schwarzburg-Rudolstadt	28. 52,000	28. 325	28. [included with Sondershausen] *
29. Principality of Waldeck	29. 47,800	29. 400	29. 250 *
30. Principality of Lippe-Detmold	30. 70,500	30. 500	30. 520 *
31. Principality of Schaumburg-Lippe	31. 20,000	31. 150	31. [included with Detmold] *
32. Possessions of the senior Princes of Reuß	32. 26,000	32. 450	32. 254 *
33. Possessions of the junior Princes of Reuß	33. 56,000	33. [included with senior Princes]	33. [included with senior Princes] *
34. Kingdom of Westphalia	34. 1,942,000	34. 25,000 [part provided by France]	34. 8,000 *
Joined February 1808			
35. Duchy of Mecklenburg-Strelitz	35. 70,000	35. 400	35. 320
36. Duchy of Mecklenburg-Schwerin	36. 328,600	36. 1,900	36. 1,400
Joined October 1808			
37. Duchy of Oldenburg	37. 159,500	37. 800	37. 600

* Indicates this state also had elements of its contingent in Spain.
** All figures approximate to indicate magnitude of each monarchy's contribution. Where second line troops played
a role in the campaign, their numbers are counted in the total (e.g., Bavaria, Baden, Württemberg, Saxony).

forces in time for the autumn fighting of 1806, but most found themselves unprepared for the pace of Napoleonic warfare and were unable to field effective contingents before the onset of winter. Winter and spring, however, saw a host of Rheinbund contingents in Prussia and Poland, principally involved in securing Napoleon's long lines of communication or prosecuting the multitude of sieges against Prussian and Swedish fortresses holding out behind the main French army. Even the newest members of the Confederation, states like Saxony and the tiny Saxon Duchies that had been Prussian allies up to the Jena—Auerstädt débâcle, sent men to the front under French command, the Saxon cavalry being one of the few Allied contingents to participate in the grand battles of 1807. The campaign demonstrated the viability of the alliance and the value of the German troops (at least for rear area duties), but also highlighted some significant problems. Chief among these was the outdated structure of most of the German contingents and the resultant difficulty of integrating them into the modern French military machine. Over the next several years, therefore, most of Napoleon's German allies, either independently or under French pressure, embarked upon programmes of rapid military reform and, over time, most of the Allied armies took on an increasingly French complexion.[2]

Napoleon's juggernaut will dragged thousands of these German troops into the war with Spain starting in 1808 and only the largest Rheinbund states, such as Bavaria, Württemberg and Saxony, were able to evade the onerous responsibility of hurling their young men into the Iberian cauldron.[3] When war with the Habsburg Empire came in the spring of 1809, many of the German contingents would thus be incomplete, large portions of their armies having been swallowed by the insatiable Spanish conflict. The requirements of that dreadful struggle, however, also occupied the majority of France's veteran troops and Napoleon's Rheinbund Allies would therefore assume an unprecedented first line role in the grand battles of the 1809 campaign against Austria.

THUNDER ON THE DANUBE - THE 1809 WAR WITH AUSTRIA

For many in Austria, the spring of 1809 seemed to offer a clear opportunity to reassert Habsburg influence in Germany and avenge the humiliations Napoleon had inflicted on the ancient dynasty in 1797, 1800 and 1805. With most of the French Army and the dreaded Emperor of Battles himself off in the wilds of Spain, bogged down in a guerrilla quagmire, the military situation seemed propitious.[4] The political landscape appeared equally promising. In Germany, a host of patriots more zealous than realistic were anxious to persuade Vienna that the entire Teutonic population was ready to rise up and throw off the Napoleonic 'yoke'. The Tyrol, too, chafing under Bavarian rule, was restive and leaders of its fiercely independent inhabitants were already in contact with Austrian agents. To the east, quiet assurances from St. Petersburg indicated that the huge Russian Army would intervene slowly, if at all, should war come (despite the promises given to Napoleon by the Tsar at Erfurt the previous autumn). In Vienna, then, the war party slowly gained dominance and by February 1809 the lumbering Habsburg military machine, over the objections of its generalissimo, the Archduke Charles, was irrevocably committed to war.

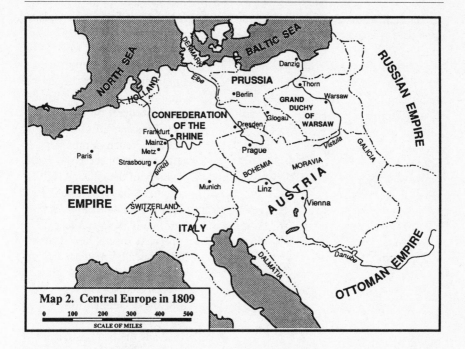

Map 2. Central Europe in 1809

0   100   200   300   400   500
SCALE OF MILES

APRIL: THE WAR OPENS AND THE TIDE TURNS

Austrian strategy in 1809 was offensive and an army of invasion was committed to each area where the Habsburg Empire bordered on the territory of France and its vassal states. The main effort would be made in the Danube valley, where Archduke Charles would invade Napoleon's largest German ally, Bavaria, at the head of eight army corps (I to VI, plus I and II Reserve). Several strategic options for the employment of this large host were considered, but the Habsburg military pundits eventually settled on a plan which sent six of the Main Army's (*Hauptarmee*) corps across the River Inn in the general direction of Landshut in the hopes of catching the French by surprise and destroying their scattered units one by one. In the meantime, the remaining two corps (I and II under the overall command of General der Kavallerie Graf Bellegarde) would debouch from Bohemia and approach the Danube from the north to pin French forces in that

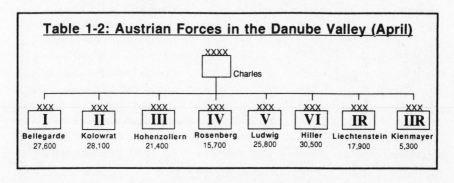

Table 1-2: Austrian Forces in the Danube Valley (April)

			XXXX				
			Charles				

XXX	XXX	XXX	XXX	XXX	XXX	XXX	XXX
I	**II**	**III**	**IV**	**V**	**VI**	**IR**	**IIR**
Bellegarde	Kolowrat	Hohenzollern	Rosenberg	Ludwig	Hiller	Liechtenstein	Kienmayer
27,600	28,100	21,400	15,700	25,800	30,500	17,900	5,300

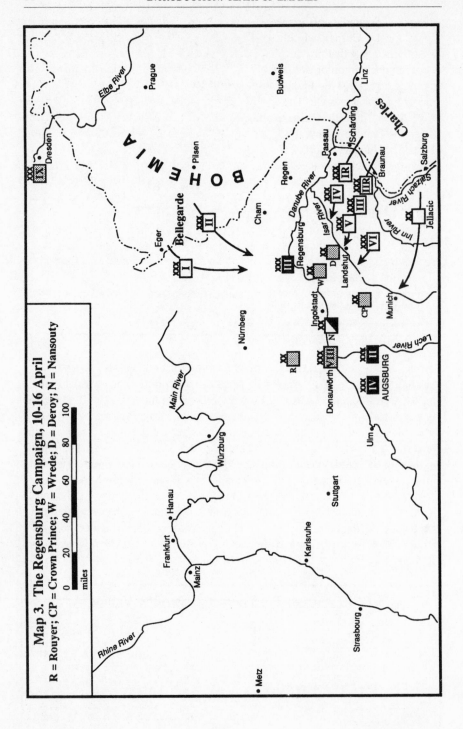

Map 3. The Regensburg Campaign, 10-16 April
R = Rouyer; CP = Crown Prince; W = Wrede; D = Deroy; N = Nansouty

direction. Secondary efforts were to be mounted in Poland (VII Corps) and Italy (VIII and IX Corps), while a small detachment pushed into the vales of the Tyrol to support that province's insurrection. Meanwhile, it was hoped that the Austrian declaration of war would rouse the peoples of Germany to a nationalistic struggle against the French and thereby force Napoleon to cope with a major uprising in his rear area. The war would thus span Europe from the Baltic to the Adriatic and from the Rhine to the Vistula with five principal theatres of operations: the Danube valley; the Tyrol and the Vorarlberg; the southern front (Italy, Dalmatia, Hungary); north-central Germany; and Poland.

On the French side, the situation was somewhat tense but not dire. Napoleon had long recognized Austria's belligerent intentions and even while campaigning in Spain, he had taken steps to concentrate the French troops dispersed in garrisons all across the face of Germany. With a large proportion of his men still tied down south of the Pyrenees, however, the Emperor realized that he would have to lean heavily on his German allies in any conflict with the Habsburgs. On 15 January, he had therefore sent a series of letters to the Rheinbund monarchs, directing them to put their contingents on a war footing and await further orders. Two days later, he left Spain for Paris. As a result of these orders, a large army was assembling in southern Germany by early April: Davout's huge III Corps was moving on Regensburg (Ratisbonne), Massena was slowly collecting a two-corps force along the River Lech (his own IV Corps and II Corps temporarily under Général de Division Oudinot), and the Guard was making the uncomfortable journey from Spain in hurriedly requisitioned wagons.[5] In addition, more than 58,000 Rheinbund troops were already along the Danube or en route: the three Bavarian divisions (Lefebvre's VII Corps) stretched in a thin screen from Munich to Straubing; the Württembergers (VIII

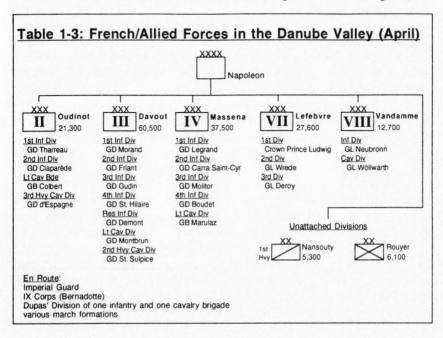

Table 1-3: French/Allied Forces in the Danube Valley (April)

Corps, Vandamme) around Heidenheim; the Baden and Hessian Brigades with Massena's Corps; and Rouyer's German Division gathering at Würzburg. Another 19,000 (Saxon IX Corps under Bernadotte) were soon to follow and 25,000 more Confederation soldiers (many under King Jerome's X Corps) were being organized to secure French and Rheinbund interests within the bounds of Germany itself. Napoleon, confident that the Austrians would not attack prior to 15 April, remained in Paris, leaving the immediate direction of affairs in the hands of his Chief of Staff, Marshal Alexander Berthier.

THE DANUBE VALLEY: INVASION AND REPULSE

10-17 April (Austrian): To the French Emperor's surprise, Charles launched his offensive on 10 April, crossing the Inn with IV Corps and I Reserve Corps on the right at Schärding, III Corps in the centre, and the remaining three corps at Braunau on the left; yet further to the left, a detached division under Feldmarschall-Leutnant (FML) Jellacic advanced on Munich from Salzburg (total strength of the Main Army, including Jellacic, about 128,000). With the Allied Army still concentrating, the invaders faced no real resistance, but their advance was painfully slow and the leading corps did not reach the Isar until the morning of the 16th. At Landshut, the main Austrian column attempted to cross but was delayed for several hours by the skilful defence of General-Leutnant (GL) Deroy's outnumbered 3rd Bavarian Division. Deroy, however, isolated and exposed, was forced to withdraw when he learned that Austrian forces had pushed over the river on both his northern (IV Corps near Dingolfing) and southern (VI Corps at Moosburg) flanks. Charles spent the following day bringing his army across the Isar and the evening of the 17th found him disposed with three of the regular corps (III, IV, V) and both reserve corps concentrated along the roads leading north and north-west from Landshut. All seemed to be going well for the Austrians, but the army's command structure was proving clumsy, movements were torpid and Charles was already beginning to weaken himself by detachments. On the extreme right of the main body, for example, General-Major (GM) Vécsey probed toward Regensburg with his brigade, while another detached command (albeit mostly second-rate Landwehr) remained behind to blockade the Bavarian fortress at Passau. On the left, FML Hiller's VI Corps was held at Moosburg to shield the army's southern flank and Jellacic's command capped its progress with an unopposed entrance into the Bavarian capital. The seizure of Munich seemed to typify Austrian operations: it discomfited Bavaria's King Max but did nothing to support Charles's larger plans and only served to deprive the main army of 9,300 men in the coming battles. Finally, Bellegarde's two corps (49,400) north of the Danube, slow, cautious and dispersed about the countryside, were equally useless, doing almost nothing to pin Davout's forces or divert French attention.

10-17 April (French): Despite these weaknesses on the Austrian side, Berthier's actions in the first week of the invasion had thrown the French army into even greater confusion and Charles stood on the threshold of a rare opportunity to defeat the isolated Allied forces in detail. Napoleon's invaluable Chief of Staff was over his head as the *de facto* army commander. The French and their

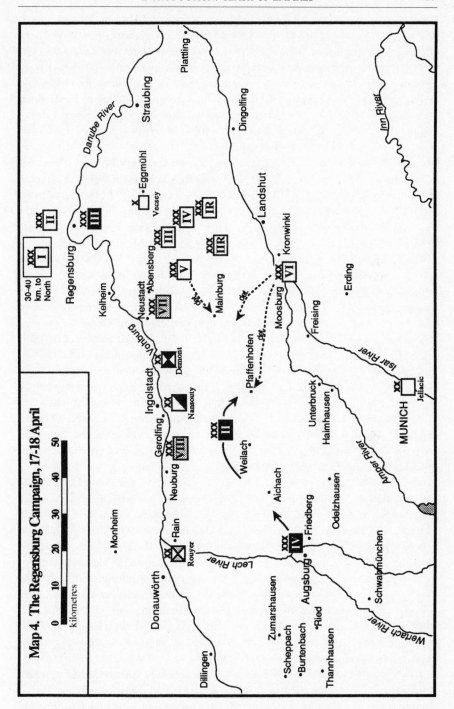

Map 4. The Regensburg Campaign, 17-18 April

Allies thus spent the early days of the campaign marching and countermarching with no clear picture of the enemy situation or their own leader's intentions.[6] As a result, the army that had been scattered from Munich to Nuremberg when the enemy crossed the Inn was still divided seven days into the campaign. Specifically, Berthier's oft-changed directions had brought the army to the following positions by 17 April: Massena, on the far right, was slowly assembling his two corps (II and IV) on the Lech around Augsburg; Lefebvre's Bavarians (VII Corps) were just south of the Danube, moving on Ingolstadt; the Württembergers and Rouyer's men were collecting in the vicinity of Donauwörth; and Davout (III Corps) was in and around Regensburg.[7] Davout's situation was thus critical. Dangerously exposed at Regensburg with a good day's march separating him from the nearest support (the VII Corps' elements approaching Vohburg), he might be cut off and hurled into the Danube if the Austrians moved swiftly. This was the situation when Napoleon reached Donauwörth on 17 April.

17-18 April: The appearance of the Emperor brought an abrupt shift in French operations and a flood of messages immediately began to issue from Imperial headquarters. As harried couriers splashed through the wretched April weather with decisive orders to concentrate and march, word of Napoleon's arrival spread and a palpable thrill seemed to course through the entire army, French and German alike. Infused with an offensive spirit, these men were now set on the road according to the plan Napoleon was rapidly developing. Although this plan would change in the ensuing days as new information came into headquarters, in its general outlines, it remained the same. It consisted of two basic components. First, Davout was to slip to the west from Regensburg, join Lefebvre and Vandamme near Abensberg and then strike south towards Landshut. Second, Massena and Oudinot were directed to march on the same town with all speed in an effort to cut the Austrian lines of communication and trap Charles' Army against the Danube.

During the night and throughout the 18th, French forces hastened to comply with the master's will: Davout brought his entire Corps south of the Danube at Regensburg and prepared to move west; Lefebvre's men turned about at Vohburg and headed for Abensberg, Vandamme close behind; and Massena belatedly got his two corps moving on the afternoon of the 18th.

19 April (Engagements at Teugn and Arnhofen): Davout's Corps began moving toward Abensberg early on the 19th and collided with elements of the Austrian III and IV Corps probing cautiously north toward the Danube. The ensuing struggle, focused principally around the ridges between Teugn and Hausen, was sanguinary, but by the end of the day, the French clearly held the advantage. Davout, the Iron Marshal, had once again demonstrated his tactical mastery and the initiative was already beginning to slip from Charles's hands.

While III (Hohenzollern) and IV (Rosenberg) Corps were trading musket balls with Davout, the Austrian flanks were also in motion. On the right, Liechtenstein led an *ad hoc* force toward Regensburg's walls. On the left, Hiller's VI Corps was now generally around Mainburg, still some distance from the main body, and Archduke Ludwig with V and II Reserve Corps moved up to the east bank of the River Abens. Two small commands connected Ludwig on the Abens with Hohenzollern at Hausen: one at Bachl under GM Pfanzelter, the other, commanded by GM Thierry, had detachments at Kirchdorf and Gaden. The latter now came into contact with Lefebvre's troops as the Bavarian VII Corps moved up through Abensberg to link with Davout. Thierry thus clashed with the Bavarian 1st Division between Abensberg and Arnhofen (the Austrians taking the worst of the encounter), while Ludwig's gunners engaged in an inconsequential cannonade with Wrede's 2nd Division at Biburg.

Farther south and west, Oudinot overpowered a detachment of Hiller's Corps at Pfaffenhofen as Massena drove his men east by forced marches towards Landshut.

By 19 April, therefore, the preconditions for Napoleon's subsequent operations had been established: Davout had been linked to Lefebvre, the centre of the army had been fairly well concentrated west of the Abens, Massena was en route for the Isar, and the initiative was rapidly swinging to the French.

20 April (Battle of Abensberg): Operations over the next four days can be viewed as taking place along the arms of a great 'V': starting at Abensberg, the top of the left leg, Napoleon's offensive would initially take him to the base of the 'V' at Landshut, where he achieved a clearer understanding of Austrian dispositions and turned north up the right leg toward Regensburg. The 20th opened with an attack by the Bavarian 1st Division, supported on their right by a pair of Württemberg light battalions. Directed from Abensberg due east toward Thierry's position at Offenstetten, the attack was intended to connect with a French provisional corps under Marshal Lannes (newly arrived from Spain) driving through Bachl to Rohr.[8] The well-conducted Bavarian attack was very successful and Thierry's little brigade, attempting to retreat to Bachl was trapped between the two Allied columns and destroyed. The Bavarian infantry remained at Bachl for the night while the French continued through Rohr to the Laaber at Rottenburg, where they were halted by Hiller's men, moving up the stream from Mainburg. On the Allied right, Bavarians and Württembergers under Wrede and Vandamme gradually pushed Ludwig back some 15 kilometres to Pfeffenhausen, which Wrede entered in a dramatic midnight charge. By the first dark hours of the 21st, therefore, the Austrian left wing (V, VI, and II Reserve Corps) had been severely battered and Napoleon had closed on the Laaber with major elements of three corps ready to resume the pursuit with the dawn.

Action on Davout's front had been limited. Charles had swung the Austrian III Corps back toward the Laaber so that his main line now ran almost north to south from Regensburg to Leierndorf, but the French marshal's men had only followed this movement and no serious fighting occurred. Unfortunately for the French, the 20th also saw the fall of Regensburg, the city's garrison (65th Ligne) having been forced to surrender when threatened by Liechtenstein from the south and Kolowrat (part of II Corps) from the north. Most of Bellegarde's two corps (more than 40,000 men), however, spent the day far north of the Danube, tying down about 1,500 French troops (an infantry battalion and a chasseur regiment).

21 April (Landshut and Schierling): The locus of action stayed with

Napoleon's right on the 21st as he pursued the bewildered Austrian left to Landshut. While he led Lannes' Corps and a host of French and Bavarian cavalry south on the road from Rottenburg, Vandamme and Wrede pushed towards the Isar along the Pfeffenhausen route. Desperate fighting by the Austrian rear guard delayed the Allies briefly on the plains north of the city, but the Habsburg troops were soon scattered and French grenadiers stormed a burning bridge into Landshut itself, followed by cheering Bavarians and Württembergers. Hiller beat a hasty retreat to Neumarkt, making better time than he had during his advance a week earlier, but delays on the part of Massena's command had limited the scope of the French victory. The veteran marshal had indeed arrived on Hiller's left south of the Isar in the early afternoon, but his subordinates had initially refrained from launching a determined attack into the Austrian flank and the opportunity for a crushing blow quickly slipped away. None the less, it was a significant triumph and Napoleon could be justly proud of the performance of his French, Bavarian and Württemberg soldiers.

To the north, the day had seen Davout push his left wing south to the Laaber, link with Deroy's 3rd Bavarian Division, and drive north-east along the stream toward Schierling. That village duly fell to the Allies, but the rest of the day was spent pinning the Austrians in place, Davout hesitating to continue his attack against the numerically superior Habsburg forces. Bellegarde's command remained north of the Danube.

22 April (Battle of Eggmühl): Napoleon had been convinced that the force fleeing before him at Landshut was the main Austrian army, but at about 2 a.m. on the 22nd, fresh messages from Davout opened his eyes to the real Habsburg dispositions. He consequently issued orders for the bulk of the army to head north immediately. By dawn, a long column of muddy figures was surging up the Regensburg highway from Landshut, while Marshal Bessières (like Lannes, recently arrived from Spain) led Wrede's and Marulaz's Divisions in the pursuit of Hiller. The crack Württemberg Light Brigade led Napoleon's main body, reaching and storming the tiny village of Eggmühl in mid-afternoon as the rest of the army deployed on the heights south of the Laaber. Arriving on this dominant high ground, the Emperor surveyed Rosenberg's IV Corps on the hills to north and gave the signal for a general advance. Davout instantly sent his men against the Austrian right, while Lannes threw his two divisions across the stream at Rosenberg's left; in the centre, a mass of several thousand Allied horsemen pressed towards the key to Rosenberg's position, a battery of sixteen guns above Eggmühl. The white-coated battalions resisted bravely, but their situation was hopeless and, as the Bavarian, French and Württemberg cavalry overran his central battery, Rosenberg ordered a rapid retreat. The jubilant Allies quickly took up the pursuit, French cuirassiers and Württemberg light horse crushing a Habsburg mounted brigade at Alteglofsheim as the moon rose. The chase was finally brought to a halt by night, French exhaustion, and Austrian reserves (II Corps had finally been brought south of the Danube that morning), but the Habsburg Main Army had clearly suffered a major reverse and Charles had little choice but to continue the withdrawal the next morning.

23 April (Storming of Regensburg): The final battle of the Regensburg

Campaign was fought on the 23rd as Charles attempted to extricate his army from the trap south of the Danube. An enormous cavalry struggle surged back and forth across the fields south of the old Imperial capital that morning as the Austrian horsemen sacrificed themselves to gain time for the rest of the army to escape. In the end, despite the extraordinary heroics of Lannes' and Davout's men, Charles managed to get most of his troops across the river safely, destroying the bridges behind him and retreating toward the Bohemian mountains.

The attack at Regensburg had occupied only a portion of Napoleon's army however: IV Corps marched to Straubing where it might be in a position to outflank the Austrians north of the river; the Bavarian 1st Division headed for Landshut; and Bessières continued his pursuit of Hiller, reaching Neumarkt on the River Rott by nightfall.

24-30 April (Pursuit): The final week of April was generally characterized by Austrian retreat and French pursuit. Davout thus followed Charles north of the Danube as the Habsburg Main Army withdrew into Bohemia, but Napoleon had apparently decided to drive on Vienna and the bulk of the Allied host marched east for the crossings over the Inn and the Salzach. Hiller, ignorant of the Main Army's defeat, checked Bessières' progress briefly when he turned and struck the 2nd Bavarian Division at Neumarkt on the 24th, but quickly headed east again when the true situation became clear. Napoleon moved his army in three principal columns: on the left, Massena's IV Corps marched along the southern bank of the Danube from Straubing toward Passau; Lefebvre took the bulk of VII Corps (1st and 3rd Divisions) through Landshut and Munich on the right to expel Jellacic from Bavaria; and the Emperor himself led the central column through Landshut to Burghausen on the Inn (II Corps, Württembergers and most of the cavalry).[9] Wrede was an exception to this general pattern; Napoleon sent him south from Neumarkt toward Salzburg in an effort to trap Jellacic. That Austrian general, however, had finally departed Munich on the 26th and was able to stay just ahead of the pursuing Bavarians. None the less, Lefebvre united his Corps in Salzburg on the last day of the month and Jellacic, exhausted and badly outnumbered, was compelled to retire into the mountains south of the city. The other two Allied columns were also along the Inn—Salzach line as the month closed: Napoleon at Burghausen and Braunau, Massena at Schärding and Passau. Davout, once it was obvious that Charles no longer posed a serious threat, was brought back south of the Danube and, by the 30th, he had reached Plattling on the Isar with his lead elements.

This initial phase of the 1809 campaign was a signal success for Napoleon: at a cost to his army of 16,300 killed, wounded and missing, he had speedily evicted the Austrians from Bavaria, gained the strategic initiative, inflicted some 44,700 casualties on his foes, and captured 73 of their guns. Still, the Habsburg Main Army had not been destroyed and Kaiser Franz remained as determined as ever to prosecute the war.

THE TYROL: INITIAL INSURGENT SUCCESS
Napoleon's triumph around Regensburg was an ominous sign for the Tyrolian rebels, enjoying a degree of self-government after evicting the hated Bavarians

from their mountainous land. On 10 April, as Charles crossed the Inn, the Tyrolians rose against their Bavarian overlords and, by the 13th, some 4,000 Bavarians and 2,000 Frenchmen together with all their guns and equipment were in the hands of the jubilant insurgents. The only bright spot on the gloomy landscape was the stout resistance offered by the little fortress of Kufstein. Though shocked and embarrassed by the sudden disaster, the Bavarians could do almost nothing in response; the outcome of the war would not be decided in the Tyrol but in the Danube valley and every available soldier was committed against the Austrian Main Army. Meanwhile in Innsbruck, the chief Tyrolian leader, a determined innkeeper named Andreas Hofer, now supported by a small detachment of Austrian regulars and Landwehr, vowed to keep his country free. With the Austrian Main Army in full retreat, however, Marshal Lefebvre was free to gather his VII Corps at Salzburg in preparation for the reconquest of the Tyrol.

THE FRENCH RESERVE CORPS

The threat posed to his lines of communications by the Tyrolian, and later the Vorarlberg, rebels, as well as the possibility of Austrian probes from Bohemia, led Napoleon to create a Reserve Corps in Germany under old Marshal Kellermann. Centred around Hanau, this corps was located in a position to respond to threats from the south and east, to assist in the repression of insurrection in central Germany (e.g., Westphalia), and to oppose the anticipated English landing on the North Sea coast. Its organization changed many times during the campaign, but it generally consisted of the following:

1. A division of five provisional dragoon regiments and some stray infantry detachments (French and Bavarian) under Général de Division (GD) Beaumont; this division was headquartered at Augsburg and had its principal combat elements around Kempten under Général de Brigade (GB) Picard; Beaumont also had nominal authority over Württemberg and Baden forces north of Lake Constance.

2. Two reserve infantry divisions (GD Rivaud and GD Despeaux) around Hanau with a sixth provisional dragoon regiment and twelve guns; only Rivaud's was ever sufficiently organized to participate in combat operations.

3. The small Berg contingent (a battery plus one regiment each of infantry and cavalry).

Almost all these units were composed of inexperienced conscripts and depot troops, but they took part in actions throughout the main army's rear area: around Lake Constance, across southern Bavaria, around Bayreuth, in the brief Saxon campaign and in Westphalia.[10]

THE SOUTHERN FRONT: AUSTRIA INVADES ITALY AND DALMATIA

Archduke Johann, one of Charles's younger brothers, commanded in this theatre, leading VIII and IX Corps through difficult mountain passes into northern Italy as his sibling invaded Bavaria. The opposing French and Italian forces under Napoleon's step-son, Eugène de Beauharnais, the Viceroy of Italy, were initially forced to withdraw, Eugène suffering a fairly severe reverse at Sacile on the 15th and 16th. Rallying on the Adige, Eugène turned on his pursuer and the two armies fought a series of inconclusive battles from the 28th to the 30th. By that time, however, word of Charles's defeat in Bavaria had arrived together with orders for Johann to effect a complete evacuation of Italy as soon as possible.

Along with the invasion of Italy, a small Austrian detachment advanced into Dalmatia to free that former Habsburg province from the French army of occupation under GD Marmont (soon to be redesignated XI Corps). Marmont fell back before the invaders, but the Austrians were slow to follow and no fighting of consequence occurred in this distant theatre of war until mid-May.

POLAND: THE FALL OF WARSAW

Austria's other diversionary attack was launched into Poland by VII Corps under Archduke Ferdinand d'Este (about 30,000 men). His rather grandiose mission was to knock Poland (existing at that time as the 'Grand Duchy of Warsaw' under the sceptre of the King of Saxony) out of the war and then turn west to strike across the Elbe into the French rear, perhaps in combination with Prussian forces. Delayed by inclement weather, Ferdinand did not cross the border until 15 April to begin a cautious advance on the Polish capital. Prince Poniatowski, the future French marshal, commanded the defenders, a small army of newly raised Polish troops reinforced by a detachment of Saxons under GM von Dyherrn. Poniatowski, unwilling to give up Warsaw without a fight, set his green troops in a solid position at Raszyn south of the capital and awaited the Austrians. A short, sharp battle duly occurred on the 19th, the Poles performing gallantly despite their inexperience. The result was an Austrian victory, however, and Poniatowski was compelled to evacuate Warsaw the following day, retiring over the Vistula to the east as the Saxons headed north to return to their kingdom. Poles and Austrians clashed several times east of the river during the second half of April, but the Poles were principally concerned with getting their new army on its feet and nothing of importance resulted from these skirmishes.

GERMANY: INSURRECTION IN WESTPHALIA

Behind the lines, two abortive insurrections broke out in Westphalia: one near Magdeburg and Stendal (2-3 April) before hostilities had opened and the other around Kassel (23-24 April) before news of Napoleon's victories in Bavaria had been circulated. Both fizzled out quickly, their leadership fleeing to Bohemia to join other disgruntled German expatriates.

MAY: ADVANCE AND REPULSE

May witnessed dramatic French advances on all fronts. In the Danube valley, the Emperor and the main army pressed rapidly toward Vienna (which fell on the 13th) but suffered a severe repulse at Aspern-Essling in the first attempt to cross the Danube. Despite this check, French and Allied forces in Italy, Dalmatia and Poland gained the initiative and made significant progress against their Habsburg opponents. The month thus concluded with an operational stalemate in the centre (around Vienna) and continuing Allied drives on both strategic flanks.

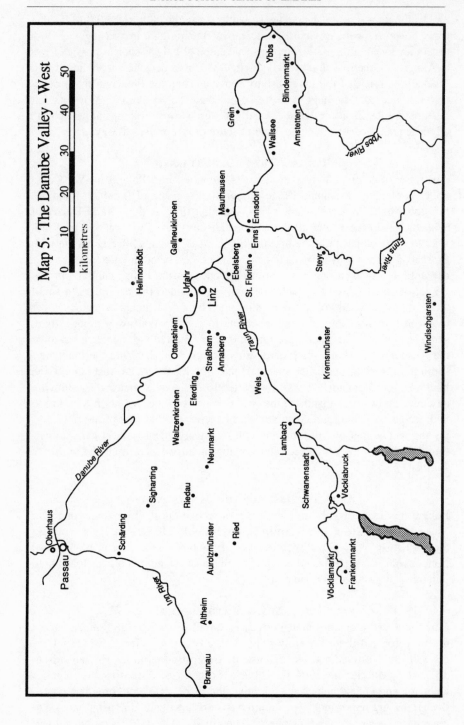

Map 5. The Danube Valley - West

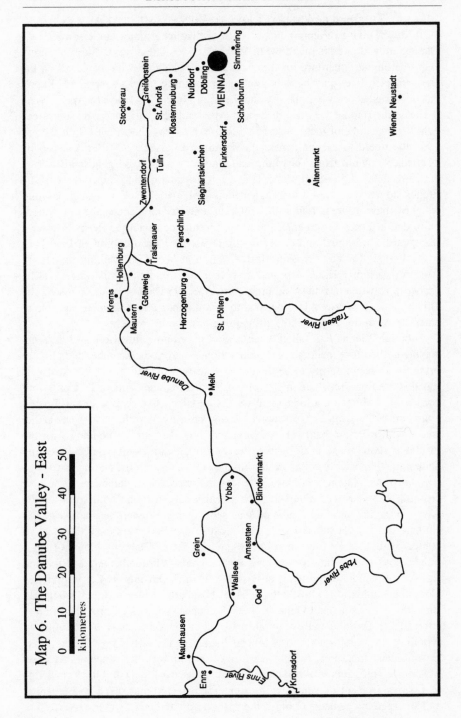

Map 6. The Danube Valley - East

The Danube Valley: Drive to Vienna, Check at Aspern

1-20 May (Drive to Vienna): Napoleon, anticipating a major battle south of the Danube, now drove his men toward Vienna at a relentless pace. Massena, however, waiting at Schärding for the main army to catch up with his Corps on the Inn—Salzach line, may have missed an opportunity to trap several of Hiller's isolated brigades between the Inn and the Traun in the final days of April. None the less, the pursuit was resumed on 1 May and after a number of sharp rear guard actions, one of these brigades, Schustekh's, was almost cut off on the 3rd as it attempted to escape across the Traun at Ebelsberg. Hiller, pressed by Massena's column from Schärding and Napoleon's from Burghausen/Braunau, hoped to delay the French at the Traun, but the rapidity and impetuosity of the French advance shattered his vague plans. Massena's subordinates, possibly stung by their failure at Landshut, sent their men storming across the long wooden bridge at Ebelsberg to enter the town intermingled with the fleeing Austrian rear guard. In a cruel and costly battle, IV Corps gained control of Ebelsberg while Lannes forced a crossing farther south at Wels, outflanking the strong Austrian position. Hiller now had no choice but to continue his retreat and he headed downstream, finally slipping north over the Danube near Krems on the 7th and 8th. This retreat left the road to Vienna open and Napoleon was able to enter the Austrian capital on the 13th after a brief bombardment.

Although Vienna had fallen, Charles and his Main Army were still at large. Napoleon therefore made hurried preparations to cross the Danube, intending to bring the Habsburg army to battle and to destroy it. On the 13th, the Austrians repelled the first French attempt north of Vienna, but elements of IV Corps succeeded in establishing a lodgement on Lobau Island five days later and French engineers were soon at work constructing a series of bridges to connect the island with the right bank. Hastily erected, however, and contending with the turbulent river, these bridges were never sturdy and, bombarded by floating debris, they repeatedly collapsed during the crucial days of the coming battle.

Meanwhile, Napoleon took steps to concentrate his army and secure the new crossing site at Kaiser Ebersdorf. A cavalry screen fanned out south of the Austrian capital and GD Lauriston was sent toward Wiener Neustadt with GB Colbert's Light Cavalry Brigade and most of the Baden infantry to establish contact with Viceroy Eugène at the Semmering Pass. The army's line of communications was to be protected by Vandamme's Württembergers at Linz and Rouyer's Rheinbund regiments at Passau, allowing Davout, his Corps stretched along the southern bank of the Danube, to hasten to Vienna. More distant still, Bernadotte's Saxons and Dupas's small French division (IX Corps) had finally entered the Danube valley, reaching Linz in time to assist Vandamme in repelling an attack on the bridgehead by Kolowrat's III Corps on 17 May. Despite these measures, Napoleon's army was still not fully concentrated when Massena's voltigeurs splashed on to Lobau. None the less, with little knowledge of Charles's recent movements, the Emperor believed that speed was essential and he urged his pioneers to finish the spans across the rapidly rising river.

21-22 May (Battle of Aspern-Essling): On the left bank of the Danube lies a broad, flat plain known as the Marchfeld. Covered with fields of grain and dotted with tiny villages, the Marchfeld spreads east from the great river some twelve kilometres to a small stream called the Russbach. The Russbach, flowing between steep banks and lined with heavy vegetation, is narrow and fordable by infantry, but impassable to cavalry and artillery except at bridges. Above the brook, the Russbach Heights, though low, dominate the plains toward the Danube and afford the defender a formidable position. North and south, the Marchfeld is bounded by the Bisamberg and River March respectively, while the Danube and its tangled network of twistings, turnings and subsidiary channels form the eastern marge of the plain. It was here, along this eastern edge of the Marchfeld, that the two armies would clash on 21 and 22 May.

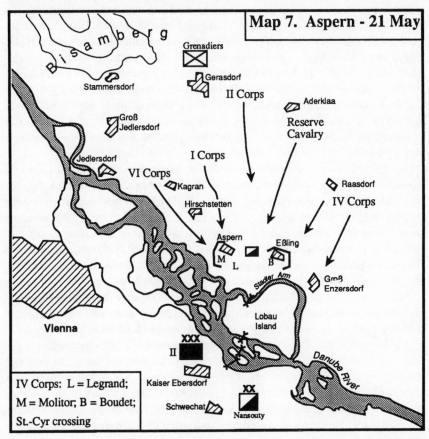

Map 7. Aspern - 21 May

Late on the 20th, the leading elements of Napoleon's army debouched from Lobau Island on to the Marchfeld to establish a bridgehead across the Stadtler Arm of the Danube. Austrian resistance was light and, by early evening, Massena's men (GD Molitor's 3rd Division) had a firm lodgement in the Mühlau. Napoleon, with little information on the Austrian Main Army, now pushed Lasalle's Division of light horse across to reconnoitre. In a brief cavalry fight at sunset, however, the French troopers were repulsed by the numerically superior Habsburg horse and the Emperor gained almost no new intelligence; his army had only encountered small infantry and cavalry formations thus far and he feared these were merely rear guards designed to cover the retreat of Charles's army into Moravia. Observations that night did little to clarify the situation: enemy camp fires were indeed to be descried to the north, but these were insufficient for an army and Napoleon chose to hasten his cavalry over the river lest Charles escape his grasp.

Charles had arrived at the Marchfeld by a roundabout route. Retreating into Bohemia after the disaster in Bavaria, he had rested and reorganized his battered army as Napoleon pushed through the fertile valley to the south. He formulated several concepts to oppose the French along the Danube, but the speed of Napoleon's advance ground all his plans to dust and he was left with no choice but to turn south-east towards the Marchfeld and unite with Hiller's column north of the river. Leaving Feldzeugmeister (FZM) Kolowrat behind with III Corps to threaten French communications, Charles gathered his forces in the north-eastern corner of the plain in the days immediately preceding Napoleon's assault crossing: four line corps (I, II, IV and VI) and Liechtenstein's I Reserve Corps of cavalry and grenadiers.[11] Now, on the night of 20/21 May, most of this host began to move, leaving no camp fires for the anxious French to see as the white-coated columns stumbled forward through the darkness to their designated attack positions.

The French were also on the move during the night and three of Massena's divisions were deployed on the edge of the Marchfeld as dawn broke on 21 May: Molitor at Aspern, Legrand (with one Baden infantry regiment) behind Essling, and Boudet facing Gross-Enzersdorf. Lasalle's Division provided a wide arc of outposts around the bridgehead and part of the Guard served as reserve. As more French and German cavalry (Marulaz's Division with the Baden and Hessian mounted regiments) became available on the north bank (at about noon), Napoleon sent patrols toward Hirschstetten and Breitenlee in search of the presumedly retiring Austrians. The Allied troopers soon discovered, however, that Austrian intentions were offensive and that several massive columns of all arms were bearing down on the weakly held French bridgehead.

The First Day (21 May): The German cavalry patrols had bumped into the right-most element of Charles's army, Hiller's VI Corps, pushing along the river toward Aspern. To Hiller's left, the rest of the Habsburg host advanced in a great semi-circle: Bellegarde (I Corps) and Hohenzollern (II Corps) approaching Aspern from the north; Liechtenstein with the cavalry reserve opposite the gap between the latter village and Essling; Rosenberg (IV Corps) swinging wide to move on Essling from the north and east.[12] Farther to the rear, the grenadiers were held in reserve just north of Gerasdorf. Although his initial understanding of Napoleon's dispositions was faulty, Charles quickly recognized the critical importance of the two villages, Aspern and Essling, the twin supports of Napoleon's position. If the Austrians could seize them, the French forces north of the Danube would be doomed.

Napoleon also understood that his army's fate depended upon firm possession of the twin villages, and he hastily redeployed his few available forces as Charles's attack plan became clear. Massena was thus entrusted with the defence of Aspern and the Gemeinde-Au on the right with Molitor's Division (Legrand slightly to the rear), while Lannes on the left was given Boudet's regiments to hold Essling; in the absence of additional infantry (the earlier decision to hasten the arrival of mounted units now became regrettable), the cavalry would have to cover the dangerous interval between these two strongpoints.

At about 2 p.m., Hiller launched a concerted attack on Aspern and the battle began in earnest. Combat on the first day thus opened on the French left and spread to the centre and right as afternoon turned to evening and evening to night. Aspern was the scene of bitter fighting between Hiller, later (about 5 p.m.) reinforced by Bellegarde, and Massena. Repeatedly taken by the Austrians and retaken by the French, the village was a flaming ruin by dusk but the struggle continued with unabated ferocity until deep into the night. Although greatly outnumbered by the two Austrian corps, Massena committed most of Molitor's and Legrand's Divisions to the fray and these men still clung to the south-western edges of the town when the fighting finally concluded. The duel on the French right had been equally hot but much less successful from the Austrian perspective. Rosenberg's repeated attacks on Essling were conducted with great determination, but they were poorly co-ordinated and Lannes, his men ensconced in the town granary (a veritable fortress), was able to repel assault after assault. Lannes, however, did not content himself with defensive success and attempted to exploit the confusion in Rosenberg's ranks with a cavalry charge in the gathering evening. Despite tremendous heroism, however, GD d'Espagne's cuirassiers and Lasalle's light troopers (including a Württemberg regiment) were repulsed with considerable loss at about 6 p.m.. The charge at Essling was the last of many French cavalry attacks on 21 May. The French horsemen and their German Allies (Baden and Hessian) had been in action in the centre throughout the hot afternoon. Battling first with Liechtenstein's cavalry reserve and later with Hohenzollern's II Corps, the Allied troopers had suffered painful losses but had been unable to break the stolid Austrian infantry. More charges were launched in the late afternoon as Bellegarde's Corps deployed north of Aspern, but the results were the same: temporary success followed by eventual retreat in the face of steady enemy fire. None the less, they had kept the Austrians at bay and thereby succeeded in their principal mission of protecting Napoleon's vulnerable centre.

Both commanders were confident at day's end. Charles mistakenly believed that he had held the entire French army in check and hoped for further victory on the 22nd. Napoleon was satisfied to have held his position against greatly superior numbers despite the repeated collapse of the crucial Danube bridges. Above all, he had won sufficient room to deploy for a true attack into the Marchfeld and he spent a busy, if frustrating, night bringing more forces across the river. The last of Massena's divisions, Carra Saint-Cyr's (including the Hessian Brigade), had already arrived on the evening of the 21st and, by the next morning, the whole of Lannes' II Corps plus Demont's Division and more elements of the Guard were safely on the north bank. With these reinforcements, supplemented by Davout's veterans (to be brought across the Danube), the Emperor planned to crack the Austrian centre and roll up both of Charles' flanks. The only worry was the tenuous connection to Ebersdorf.

The Second Day (22 May): To implement his plan, Napoleon had to have undisputed control of Aspern and he accordingly issued orders to Massena to attack in the pre-dawn hours of 22 May. The marshal's first attack was thrown back, but he immediately led his men forward a second time and the town was

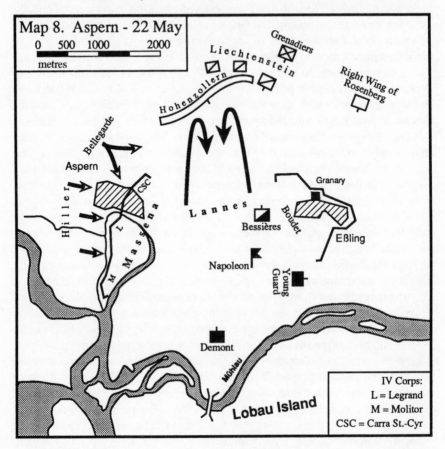

Map 8. Aspern - 22 May

0   500   1000   2000

metres

IV Corps:
L = Legrand
M = Molitor
CSC = Carra St.-Cyr

soon in French hands. Meanwhile, on the right flank, Lannes had pushed back Rosenberg and news arrived that the critical bridges had again been restored to operation, so that by 7 a.m., the preconditions for Napoleon's decisive central attack had been attained. Drums rolling, Lannes' Corps advanced to the attack at about 7:30, supported by the French light and heavy cavalry. The assault made considerable initial progress, but Charles steadied his men through personal example and eventually Lannes could go no farther without reinforcement. The arrival of his courier at Napoleon's headquarters, however, coincided with the appearance of a rider from Lobau Island bearing the news that the bridges had suffered yet another devastating break. Napoleon held Lannes' men in place for several hours, hoping for better news from his engineers, but with Austrian pressure increasing on Massena and only grim reports from the river, at about 11 a.m., he gave II Corps the order to withdraw.

The withdrawal initially proceeded in good order, but Napoleon's situation soon worsened. On his left, the fight for Aspern had intensified and, despite the commitment of three Young Guard battalions, Hiller was soon pressing Massena out of the village yet again. In the centre, the young conscripts of II Corps were wavering under a brutal artillery barrage and the Old Guard had to be ordered forward to steady the line. The crisis was reached when Liechtenstein, cobbling together a co-ordinated attack on the Austrian left, finally succeeded in evicting the French from Essling. Only Boudet's men in the granary still held out and Napoleon issued orders to initiate a retreat on to Lobau Island. Part of his plan was for Generals Rapp and Mouton to attack toward Essling with several Guard battalions so as to relieve pressure from that quarter and facilitate the French withdrawal. These two stalwarts, however, exceeded their orders and, to the surprise of French and Austrians alike, charged into the village and expelled its Habsburg defenders. Rosenberg retired to Enzersdorf to regroup and Charles, stung by the sudden reversal of fortunes, decided to pull back in the centre as well. Fighting continued around Aspern for a time, but by 4 p.m. the battle was over and Napoleon could order his withdrawal in relative safety. The Emperor of Battles had suffered his first serious repulse.

Despite this major setback and heavy losses (about 20,000 including the irreplaceable Lannes), Napoleon immediately began preparations for further offensive action. While the weary survivors of Aspern licked their wounds, the Emperor developed comprehensive plans for the next crossing of the Danube: Lobau was to be fortified; newer, stronger bridges were to be constructed with pilings to shield them from Austrian fire barges; the flank threat of Archduke Johann's Army in Hungary was to be eliminated; and all possible forces were to be collected at Vienna in time for the titanic struggle. Despite several miserable days of deprivation, work began on the fortifications and bridges even while most of the army was withdrawing from the island (by the end of the month, only IV Corps was left as garrison on Lobau). Meanwhile, Eugène was directed to turn south into Johann's flank and the corps along the army's line of communications in the Danube valley were slowly shifted eastward. This latter measure necessitated a complex series of related movements. First to move were those elements of Davout's command still guarding the south bank of the Danube around Melk; as they marched off to the Austrian capital, they were replaced by Vandamme's Württembergers, VIII Corps itself having been relieved at Linz by the Saxons of Bernadotte's IX Corps. The Saxons were the next to head east, marching for St. Pölten on the last day of the month; their duties at the Linz bridgehead were assumed by the Bavarians of Lefebvre's VII Corps (1st and 2nd Divisions only) brought north from the Tyrol.

Despite its success, the Austrian army passed the remainder of May in relative peace. The army's heavy losses (roughly equal to those of the French) were partially replaced, weapons were cleaned and equipment repaired, but nothing was done to capitalize on the advantage gained at Aspern. Although numerous plans for crossing the Danube were mooted, debated and scrutinized, Charles remained in place on the Marchfeld, indecisively considering his options as the days slipped away.

THE TYROL AND THE VORARLBERG: THE FIRST ALLIED OFFENSIVE, INSURGENTS RESURGENT

On 10 May the First Offensive into the Tyrol opened with GL Wrede leading his 2nd Division toward the Inn valley from Salzburg while GL Deroy's 3rd Division approached from the fortress of Kufstein; Crown Prince Ludwig's 1st Division remained in the vicinity of Salzburg. Battles were characterized by great determination and cruelty on both sides, but the Bavarians overcame all resistance and occupied Innsbruck, the capital of the Tyrol, on the 19th. Other Bavarian forces had been organized under Oberst Arco in late April to defend the homeland against frequent Austro—Tyrolian incursions; these now also entered the dangerous mountains, coming down from the north to link with the troops in Innsbruck.

The Bavarians were only in Innsbruck for ten days before Hofer and the Austrians renewed the struggle. A major battle was fought at Bergisel on the 29th and Deroy (in command since Wrede's departure for the Danube on the 23rd) knew that he could not maintain his force in its exposed position any longer. On the 30th he began a retreat down the Inn, reaching the protective walls of Kufstein on the last day of the month. The Tyrol had freed itself for a second time.

Rebellion had also broken out in the Vorarlberg in the final days of April and local dissatisfaction with Bavarian rule soon manifested itself in raids into Bavarian, Württemberg and Baden territory around Lake Constance. Events in the Vorarlberg tended to ebb and flow in sympathy with those in the Tyrol and the rebels were generally quiet in mid-May as VII Corps marched into Innsbruck. The recrudescence of Tyrolian fervour, however, also inspired their neighbours and the Vorarlbergers surged north again, throwing the mixed Allied forces out of their land by the end of the month.

THE SOUTHERN FRONT: THE AUSTRIANS RECOIL

Archduke Johann began his retreat from Italy on 1 May, but Eugène followed closely and won a neat victory over the Austrians at the River Piave on the 8th. Continuing the pursuit, the Viceroy forced the alpine passes and pressed into southern Austria. He then divided his command, sending half to follow Johann through Graz while taking the remainder himself through St. Michael toward the Semmering Pass and Vienna. At St. Michael on the 25th, he caught Jellacic's exhausted Division trying to retreat from the Tyrol and utterly destroyed the hapless Austrian force. The next day brought him into contact with the outposts of the main French Army and by the end of the month his other column had entered the important communications centre of Graz. Archduke Johann, meanwhile, retired toward Körmend in Hungary, his army in a state of considerable disarray.

The Austrians had also withdrawn from Dalmatia by the end of May. After a series of unsuccessful fights and in view of the generally unfavourable strategic situation, the small Austrian detachment slipped away to the north. Taking a different route, Marmont marched to effect a union with Eugène.

POLAND: THORN AND GALICIA

The Poles became more active in May, capturing an Austrian bridgehead on the east bank of the Vistula near Warsaw in a brilliant night assault before driving south into Galicia to unsettle the Austrian high command. Ferdinand, on the other hand, launched a foray to the north, attempting unsuccessfully to seize the fortress of Thorn from its Polish defenders. The threat in Galicia could not be ignored, however, and the end of the month saw Ferdinand sending significant forces south to counter the energetic Poles.

GERMANY: SCHILL'S RAID

In May, Westphalia, already shaken by the April insurrections, had to undergo a new trial. A renegade Prussian major named Schill illicitly marched his regiment of hussars out of Berlin on 28 April, told them he intended to free Germany from French occupation and proceeded to invade Saxony and Westphalia. Rebuffed by the Saxons at Wittenberg on 1 May, he turned north for Magdeburg and won a little victory against a Franco—Westphalian force south of that fortress on the 5th. The garrison was clearly too strong for his tiny band, however, and he was not receiving the popular response he had expected, so he continued north toward the coast with vague hopes of obtaining support from the Royal Navy. Reaching the Duchy of Mecklenburg—Schwerin, he seized the miniature fortress of Dömitz on the 15th and handily smashed a Schwerin battalion at Damgarten on the 24th. The following day, after a bitter fight with the tiny French garrison, he captured Stralsund and prepared to put the city in a state of defence. Unfortunately for Schill and his men, GD Gratien was rapidly approaching with a combined corps of Dutch and Danish troops. Gratien's men successfully stormed Stralsund on the 31st, capturing or dispersing the raiders and killing Schill himself. Order was soon restored and Gratien returned to Westphalia to rejoin King Jerome's X Corps with his Dutch Division while the Danes retired on Hamburg.

JUNE: CALM BEFORE THE STORM

June was a month of French preparation in the face of Austrian indecision. While Charles and his advisers pondered how to take advantage of the success they had won at Aspern, Napoleon acted, completing his thorough plans for a second crossing of the Danube while Eugène removed the threat of Johann's army in Hungary.

THE DANUBE VALLEY: A TIME OF WAITING

It was a hectic month for the planners and engineers of the French army. Napoleon was determined not to repeat the mistakes that had resulted in the Aspern repulse and he sought to cover every possible contingency before his next contest with Charles. Stout bridges were constructed, Lobau Island fortified with tens of guns drawn from the great arsenals of Vienna, and precisely detailed plans were composed to co-ordinate the coming operation.

As he reviewed his own preparations, Napoleon also considered Charles' options and devised a strategy to foil any Austrian attempt to interfere with his own plans. A key concern was the possibility that Charles would be able to effect a juncture with his brother Johann and that the two combined might then attempt to break out from the Austrian bridgehead opposite Pressburg. To preclude this eventuality, Napoleon ordered Davout to invest and eradicate the bridgehead at Engerau while supporting Eugène's operations against Johann in Hungary. With Gudin's Division, Lasalle's light cavalry and the two Hessian fusilier battalions, the Iron Marshal attacked the bridgehead on 1 and 3 June, but failed to eliminate it completely despite the heroic efforts of the French and Hessian troops. He thus settled in for a miniature siege while Lasalle roved far to the south with his light horse and the 'indefatigable Hessians'. Clearing the Schütt islands in the Danube, Lasalle's command linked with Eugène's left to seal the ring around the little fortress of Raab and remained in place until the garrison capitulated on the 22nd. By this time, preparations for the great battle were almost complete and the entire army was being recalled to Kaiser Ebersdorf. Lasalle and his Hessians accordingly returned to the north to meet their respective fates on the field of Wagram.

Troops were also being called in from the northern segment of the Danube valley. Bernadotte and his IX Corps thus inched toward Vienna as June drew to a close and Wrede at Linz headed east by forced marches on the last day of the month, having received an 'invitation' to join the army on Lobau Island.

The Austrian Main Army remained quiescent, its only significant activity being the erection of a series of small redoubts stretching from Enzersdorf through Aspern around the northern aspect of Lobau Island.

THE TYROL AND THE VORARLBERG: FREE TYROL

June saw the Allies on the defensive in southern Bavaria, Baden and Württemberg as the insurgents, encouraged by their successes, launched numerous raids into the lowlands. In broad terms, the Allied defence was organized into several sectors: in the east, an odd collection of Bavarian regular, reserve and irregular troops under GL Deroy and Oberst Arco protected the direct routes to Munich; further west, GD Beaumont commanded *ad hoc* French and Allied units around Kempten through GB Picard and exercised at least nominal control over the forces north of Lake Constance (Württemberg, Baden and French troops). The entire Allied command structure was creaky and inefficient, but it was sufficiently well assembled to hold the equally disorganized rebels at bay; even when Deroy's Division was called away to the Danube valley at the end of the month to join the 1st and 2nd Bavarian Divisions at Linz, the insurgents were slow to take advantage of the decrease in Allied strength.

THE SOUTHERN FRONT: VICTORY IN HUNGARY

Napoleon in Vienna, relieved to have established communications with Eugène's Army of Italy, now determined to eliminate the threat posed to his strategic right by Archduke Johann's forces in Hungary. He accordingly sent Eugène south toward the River Raab in an effort to cut off and destroy Johann's corps at Körmend. This complex operation sent Eugène, reinforced by GD Lauriston and most of the Baden Brigade, south-east from Wiener Neustadt through Oedenburg while GD MacDonald pushed due east from Graz; simultaneously, strong cavalry forces under Lasalle, Montbrun and Marulaz (including Hessians and Badeners) struck toward the lower Raab from the area between the Neusiedler See and the Danube. Eugène crossed the Raab at Sarvar on 9 and 10 June, linked with Montbrun and turned north to engage successfully Johann's rear guard at Papa on the 12th. The Habsburg Archduke, the size of his force increased by the addition of several thousand untrained Hungarian militia (these hastily raised troops were known by their antique title: the Hungarian 'Insurrection'), took a stand outside the little fortress of Raab at the confluence of the Raab and Danube. Some preliminary skirmishing occurred on the 13th, and the following day the Viceroy inflicted a serious defeat on Johann, forcing him to retreat on Komorn. The small fortress of Raab was thus uncovered and Eugène quickly besieged it with Lauriston's Badeners and Lasalle's mixed French and Hessian force. Raab capitulated on 22 June and Eugène's units began to shift north toward Vienna in preparation for the second crossing of the Danube.

Marmont was brought north to Graz in the latter part of June to combine with GD Broussier's Division, left near the city by Eugène. Austrian attempts to relieve the garrison of the Graz citadel led to several sharp engagements around the city from the 25th to the 26th, but the French retained the upper hand. The close of the month thus found Marmont and Broussier still in control of Graz with the exception of the citadel, where a stubborn Austrian force continued to hold out.

POLAND: WARSAW REGAINED

Sporadic fighting continued in the Galicia, but the threat in Galicia forced Ferdinand to abandon Warsaw and the Poles re-entered their capital on 7 June. Russian forces finally entered the war zone on about the 10th; they seem to have carefully avoided any earnest contact with the Austrians and generally caused more worries for Poniatowski (who feared a Russian land-grab at the expense of Polish aspirations) than Ferdinand. None the less, by the end of the month, the Austrians had been completely expelled from Poland and had lost their hold on much of Galicia.

GERMANY: AUSTRIAN INCURSIONS INTO SAXONY

Some small skirmishes had occurred along the Bohemian border between Austrian and Saxon forces in late May, but in June, Charles, buoyed by the success at Aspern, decided to launch a diversionary attack into Saxony itself. Two small Austrian divisions were to enter Saxony from Bohemia: one, under GM Am Ende, pushed due north towards Dresden, while a second, commanded by FML Radivojevich, aimed for Bayreuth and northern Bavaria. Am Ende's force, including small free corps from Braunschweig and Hesse—Kassel, crossed the border on 10 June, captured Dresden and slowly advanced on Leipzig. The Saxon defenders, led by an energetic colonel named Thielmann and reinforced by GM von Dyherrn's force recently arrived from Poland, were greatly outnumbered and forced to fall back before the torpid Austrian advance.

Westphalia's King Jerome marched to Saxony's aid at the head of X Corps and was able to unite with Thielmann east of Leipzig on the 23rd; the Allied forces now took the offensive and Thielmann led the Corps' advance guard into Dresden on the 30th. Meanwhile Radivojevich had pushed into Germany, entering Bayreuth and was pushing raiding parties out to Bamberg and Nuremberg. Napoleon, concerned about his line of communications, sent reserve forces from Hanau and Passau to counter the Austrian threat and these succeeded in forcing the evacuation of Nuremberg toward the end of the month.

JULY: THE STORM BREAKS

July opened with tremendous violence and closed with tenuous peace. Napoleon crossed on to the Marchfeld on the 4th and, after the gruelling two-day struggle at Wagram, pursued Charles' army into Moravia, imposing an armistice on the Habsburg generalissimo on the battlefield at Znaim (12 July). This act naturally set the tone for the other theatres of war and combat came to a halt except for the Duke of Braunschweig's bold foray in Germany and the grim conflict in the Tyrol.

THE DANUBE VALLEY: BLOOD AT WAGRAM, PEACE AT ZNAIM

During the first four days of July, Napoleon completed his final preparations for the second crossing of the Danube. From west and south, thousands of French and Allied troops streamed toward Kaiser Ebersdorf and passed over on to

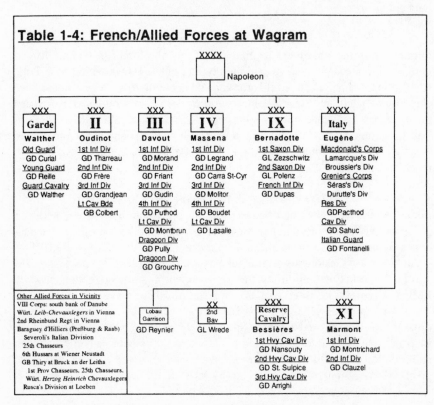

Table 1-4: French/Allied Forces at Wagram

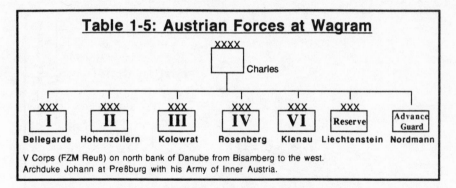

Table 1-5: Austrian Forces at Wagram

XXXX — Charles

XXX	XXX	XXX	XXX	XXX	XXX	
I	**II**	**III**	**IV**	**VI**	Reserve	Advance Guard
Bellegarde	Hohenzollern	Kolowrat	Rosenberg	Klenau	Liechtenstein	Nordmann

V Corps (FZM Reuß) on north bank of Danube from Bisamberg to the west.
Archduke Johann at Preßburg with his Army of Inner Austria.

Lobau Island: Eugène and Lasalle from Hungary, Davout from Pressburg, Marmont and Broussier from Graz, Bernadotte from St. Pölten, and Wrede from distant Linz. Ultimately, the Emperor's efforts would bring some 188,000 men and 488 guns on to the battlefield to oppose approximately 136,000 Austrians with 446 guns.[13]

But Napoleon's mind was nothing if not comprehensive and, in addition to turning Lobau into a great armed camp, his planning encompassed the protection of his army's strategic flanks. GD Baraguey d'Hilliers of the Army of Italy commanded French and Allied forces south of the Austrian capital: a small garrison in the tiny fortress of Raab, GD Filippo Severoli's Italian Division opposite Pressburg, a provisional cavalry brigade (including a Württemberg regiment) under GB Thiry at Bruck an der Leitha, and GD Jean Rusca's Division near the Semmering Pass. Vienna itself and its potentially restive population were entrusted to Vandamme's Württembergers, who were also responsible for watching the southern banks of the Danube as far as Melk.[14] Further downstream, the army's line of communications was guarded by Rouyer's German Division at Passau and the 1st Bavarian Division at Linz. Napoleon, always focused on his principal strategic objective, even ordered Deroy's 3rd Bavarian Division to march on Linz from southern Bavaria, leaving only a few *ad hoc* units to shield his primary German ally against Tyrolian incursions.

5 July (Battle of Wagram, First Day): Under the cover of a terrific thunderstorm and the roar of more than 100 guns, the Grande Armée crossed from Lobau on to the Marchfeld on the night of 4/5 July. Several days earlier (30 June), GD Legrand had established a lodgement in the Mühlau (site of the bridgehead during the Battle of Aspern—Essling), but this was a deception and the actual assault was launched from the eastern face of the island. Advance detachments from Oudinot's II Corps on the far right were the first to paddle across the Stadtler Arm, followed by similar detachments from Massena's command.[15] These picked troops quickly secured the far bank, and before long, hustling French pioneers had emplaced a series of prefabricated bridges to span the narrow body of water. Although the construction of bridges continued throughout the day, the army's advance did not stay upon their completion and by midday a huge force of more than 150,000 men was arrayed in glittering splendour under the brilliant sunshine that had succeeded the night's tumult. Massena's

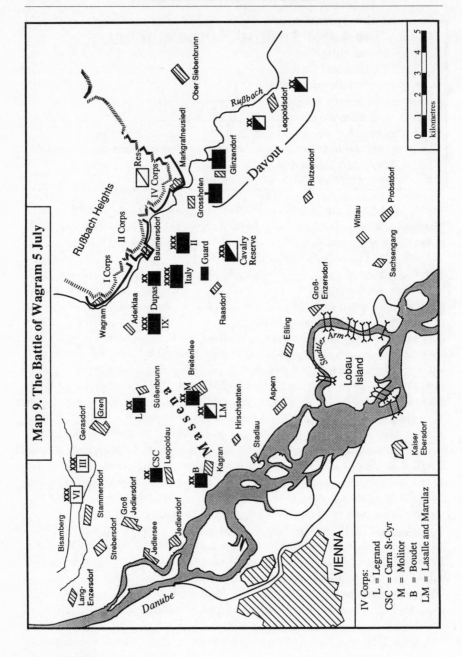

Map 9. The Battle of Wagram 5 July

troops had already stormed and seized Enzersdorf, outflanking the line of Austrian redoubts and enabling Napoleon to order his great host in two lines of battle from that village to Probstdorf. Their formations bristling with guns, Massena, Oudinot and Davout (from left to right) constituted the first of these lines, followed by Bernadotte, the Guard and the Army of Italy; swarms of light cavalry and dragoons ranged ahead of this mass and the army's iron men, the cuirassiers, were approaching the bridges to the rear. One hour after noon, the great army began to move.

Throughout the hot afternoon, the French army fanned out across the plain, artillery and cavalry leading, infantry following behind. Its progress was imposing, almost stately, as it seized Raasdorf and rolled up the line of Austrian redoubts at Aspern, but there was little serious fighting and Napoleon began to worry that Charles had withdrawn into Moravia, leaving only a rear guard behind.[16] As evening drew on and the army approached the Russbach Heights, however, it became clear that the Archduke meant to fight.

Charles had arranged his army to take advantage of the strong position on the Russbach Heights: General der Kavallerie (GdK) Liechtenstein's reserve cavalry and FML Rosenberg's IV Corps on the left around Markgrafneusiedl, FML Hohenzollern's II Corps in the centre with a detachment in Baumersdorf, and GdK Bellegarde's I Corps holding the right to include the town of Wagram.[17] The rest of the Main Army was deployed farther to the right between Wagram and the river: the grenadiers north of Gerasdorf, III Corps (FZM Kolowrat) and VI Corps (FML Klenau) north-east and north of Stammersdorf.[18] On the extreme right flank, FML Reuss's V Corps was posted from Bisamberg to the north-west to shield the northern bank of the Danube. Finally, Charles planned to position his brother Johann's command on the far left of the line around the Siebenbrunns as soon as it arrived from Pressburg.

Closing on the Russbach, Napoleon thus faced the three corps of the Austrian left supported by Liechtenstein's massed squadrons. His own army's front had expanded as it had progressed across the Marchfeld and it was now arrayed with Davout on the right opposite Markgrafneusiedl, Oudinot on his left facing Baumersdorf, and Bernadotte's Saxons around Aderklaa. Dupas's Division and elements of the Army of Italy were moving up to fill the gap between Bernadotte and Oudinot, while the Guard and heavy cavalry remained in reserve near Raasdorf. Massena's IV Corps protected the long front from Süssenbrunn to the Danube, with Boudet at Kagran especially charged with covering the approaches to Lobau Island. GD Reynier commanded the Allied garrison on the island itself, a collection of odd infantry detachments (including Saxons and Badeners) and numerous heavy guns confiscated from the Vienna arsenal. Satisfied with these dispositions and hoping to pin the Austrians in place, Napoleon decided to test the strength and determination of the Austrians on the Russbach Heights. At around 7 p.m., he issued orders for an immediate attack and sweating couriers dashed across the plain to launch the army toward the heights.

Although the entire French line was to advance against the Austrians on the high ground, no real effort was made to co-ordinate the actions of the various corps and divisions. As a result, this concerted attack quickly degenerated into a series of isolated assaults which the Austrians were able to repel in sequence. Oudinot's men were the first to advance, striking Hohenzollern's II Corps between Baumersdorf and Markgrafneusiedl. While part of the French corps attempted to wrest Baumersdorf from its defenders, two of the army's finest regiments, the 10th Léger and 57th Ligne, managed to get on to the heights. With no support at hand, however, they were soon forced back south of the Russbach by the overwhelming numbers of Habsburg units and the attack in this sector was called off. On Oudinot's left, Dupas's French and Saxon troops also enjoyed initial success. Wading the stream and clambering up the heights, they hit the seam between two Austrian corps and made admirable progress as some of Eugène's troops pushed up on their right. Unfortunately, a supporting column from the Army of Italy mistook Dupas's white-coated Saxons for Austrians in the darkness and fired upon them from the rear. This shock, combined with renewed Austrian counter-attacks, boldly led by Charles himself, sufficed to snap the cohesion of Dupas's Division and its battalions were soon streaming down the slopes in disordered retreat, carrying many of Eugène's men with them. The rest of the Army of Italy's troops were put to flight by Hohenzollern's reserves and they fell back across the Russbach in great confusion.

Two Allied attacks had already been repulsed in bloody disarray, when Bernadotte finally ordered his Saxons to seize Wagram. It was now after 9 p.m., however, and darkness made effective command almost impossible, so that the Saxons, despite repeated efforts, were unable to advance beyond the centre of the blazing town. The lead battalions were already wavering when they were mistakenly fired upon by their supports in the gloom. The same misfortune that had stunned Dupas's troops thus broke the will of Bernadotte's men at Wagram and the Saxons fled into the sheltering darkness. It was nearly midnight.

On the French right, Davout's attack never really got started and the Iron Marshal recalled his men after a brief desultory exchange between opposing skirmishers. In the words of a surgeon in the Baden Brigade: 'Night fell, spreading its sombre wings over the two armies. The silence of death reigned over all'.[19]

Thus ended the first day of the Battle of Wagram. Although his unco-ordinated evening attacks had been roughly handled, Napoleon had succeeded in executing a brilliant assault crossing from Lobau Island on to the Marchfeld and had held his adversary in his grasp. The climactic battle was at hand and, with more reinforcements en route (Marmont, Broussier, Pachtod, Wrede), he could look forward to the coming struggle with confidence. On the other side of the field, Charles too had reason for satisfaction. His men had stood well against the French assaults and were encouraged by their success and the strength of their position above the Russbach. Over half of his army had not even been engaged on the first day and there was every reason to expect that Archduke Johann would bring an additional 12,000 men on to the field on the morrow.[20] Harbouring a fairly sanguine outlook, he set in motion a bold offensive against Napoleon's army.

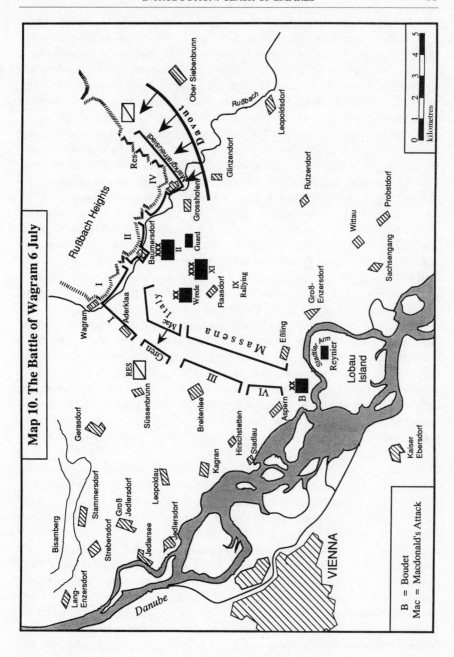

Map 10. The Battle of Wagram 6 July

B = Boudet
Mac = Macdonald's Attack

6 July (Battle of Wagram, Second Day): The second day of battle opened early with a general Austrian attack against both French flanks. Rosenberg was to strike Davout while the Reserve Corps (Liechtenstein had moved the cavalry west of Wagram during the night), Bellegarde, Kolowrat, and Klenau marched against Napoleon's left from Aderklaa to Kagran. Hohenzollern's II Corps, charged with defending the army's centre, was initially withheld from the attack and Reuss's Corps was inexplicably left idle on the Austrian extreme right.

The action began on the left flank shortly after sunrise as Rosenberg lumbered toward Davout's positions. A lively firefight was soon in progress and Napoleon, thinking that Johann had arrived on the field, rode to III Corps' support with several heavy cavalry regiments and part of the Guard. Rosenberg's white-coats had already begun to attack Davout's men at Glinzendorf and Grosshofen, when, much to the surprise of the French, the Austrian battalions began to retire. This unexpected action resulted from the inefficiencies of the Austrian command system. Although the entire army was to be in motion by 4 a.m., the transmission of orders to the right wing (especially III and VI Corps) had been badly delayed and Rosenberg, almost unique in attacking on schedule, was in danger of exposing himself to the attentions of the entire French army. To protect his IV Corps and bring the army's movements back in line with his plans, Charles thus ordered Rosenberg back into defensive positions until the right wing could begin its advance. Napoleon was unaware of his opponent's predicament, but it was quickly obvious that the attack on Davout had dissolved and that Johann was nowhere near the battlefield. Leaving the affairs of his right in Davout's capable hands, the Emperor rode back toward the centre and left of his army where an unpleasant surprise awaited him: the Austrians had occupied the key village of Aderklaa.

The other Austrian element to advance on time was Bellegarde's I Corps. Already stirring at 3 a.m., Bellegarde's scouts poked into Aderklaa shortly after 4 a.m. to discover that Bernadotte's IX Corps had departed several hours previously. The Austrian general, thrilled to win this prize so easily, immediately occupied the village and deployed his corps to engage the Saxons, now posted several hundred metres east of Aderklaa.[21] A deadly artillery duel opened, the Saxons on the plain suffering greatly under the converging fire of Bellegarde's guns to the west at Aderklaa and north on the Russbach Heights. To retrieve the situation on his left-centre, Napoleon directed Massena to seize Aderklaa at once. Massena, bringing three of his divisions up from their night's bivouacs (Boudet was left west of Aspern to shield Lobau), gave this mission to GD Carra Saint-Cyr's Division of French and Hessian troops, but the general moved too slowly for the marshal's taste and one of military history's more unusual scenes ensued. Injured in a fall from his horse several days earlier, Massena was unable to mount and was commanding his corps from a calèche drawn by a brace of white horses. Annoyed by Saint-Cyr's delays, he drove forward among the assault columns and ordered the drummers to beat the charge. His men responded to this peculiar spectacle with tremendous enthusiasm and swept into Aderklaa with loud cheers of 'Vive l'Empereur!' Unfortunately, they went too far, were caught by a powerful Austrian counter-attack and ejected from the village before it could be placed in a state of defence. The Saxons and Dupas to Massena's right suffered a similar fate and the area east of Aderklaa was soon crowded with a mass of disorganized French and Allied soldiery, vulnerable to Austrian exploitation. His left wing in disorder, Napoleon faced a perilous situation.

Nor was this the only bad news from the left. The Austrian III and VI Corps had finally made their appearance and were advancing into the gap just vacated by Massena. The movement of Klenau's VI Corps along the Danube was particularly dangerous and, by 10 a.m. it had succeeded in seizing Boudet's artillery and pushing the lone French division back into the Mühlau. The rest of Charles's right had also moved forward and the main Habsburg battle line now ran almost due south from Wagram to Aspern. Klenau's advance guard had even reached Essling, completely outflanking the French left and threatening Lobau Island itself. It was the crisis of the battle. Klenau, however, with no further orders, chose to halt his advance while Napoleon made military history.[22] Posting himself east of Aderklaa at the hinge in his line, he issued orders in rapid succession. First, he turned Massena's entire IV Corps ninety degrees and sent it on an incredible flank march toward Essling across the front of the Austrian position.[23] To fill the huge hole thus created, he resorted to an expedient, gathering up more than 100 guns and forming them into a grand battery east of Raasdorf. But even this extraordinary measure was insufficient, so he shifted the Army of Italy to its left: two of its divisions facing Wagram and Aderklaa while Macdonald's small Corps and Séras' Division assembled behind the Grand Battery. In addition, he committed much of the heavy cavalry on this wing to cover the army's complex deployments with sacrificial charges and ordered Wrede's Bavarian Division up from the reserve to provide further support to Macdonald. By late morning the situation had stabilized and the Emperor could tell Massena 'the battle is won'.

His optimism was well-founded because the key to French success lay on the opposite end of the battlefield and here Davout was making encouraging progress. Swinging his huge corps far to the right, the Iron Marshal gradually forced Rosenberg back on to the plateau north-west of Markgrafneusiedl. The Austrian left wing was beaten and when Oudinot's men began to scale the Russbach Heights around Baumersdorf, Charles had no choice but to retreat. Observing the progress of his right, Napoleon ordered a general advance and hurled Macdonald toward Süssenbrunn in an effort to crack the Austrian centre and complete the destruction of Charles' army. But the white-coated battalions held and the defeated Archduke was able to conduct his retreat in good order, withdrawing north into Moravia under the cover of night.

It had been an horrific struggle, immobile wounded burning to death when the grain around them caught fire, and both sides had paid a heavy price. French losses exceeded 37,000 for 5 and 6 July, while their Habsburg foes suffered more than 41,000 dead, wounded, missing and captured. It had been no Austerlitz, no Jena—Auerstädt, but that it was a major Napoleonic victory was very clear at least in Charles's mind and he headed north by multiple routes to find a sheltered spot where he might rest and refit his battered army.

7-9 July (Pursuit): There now followed what one Austrian commentator has chosen to call 'the feeble pursuit'.[24] Certainly, compared to the heady days following Jena, the pursuit after Wagram was lame indeed, none the less, the pressure on the Austrians was maintained and Charles was eventually brought to battle on 10 July. In part, Napoleon's delay in launching a rapid, violent pursuit was caused by the exhaustion of his own army and the lack of information about the enemy's. His first tasks were thus to reorganize his own forces and gather reliable intelligence about the armies of Charles and Johann. To ward off any threat from the latter, he reinforced Eugène's Army of Italy with the Saxons and Württembergers and gave his stepson a new mission: with Vandamme's men south of the Danube and the rest of his command to the north, the Viceroy was to protect the main army's rear and clear all Austrian units from the west bank of the River March.[25] The Emperor also considered his line of communications in the Danube valley but changed little along this vital avenue. Vandamme thus maintained his outposts along the river as far as Göttweig, the Bavarian 1st and 3rd Divisions remained at Linz, and Rouyer's Division continued to garrison Passau. With the remainder of the army, Napoleon intended to follow Charles and he pushed his men north on three separate routes: Massena toward Hollabrunn, Marmont (including the 2nd Bavarian Division) toward Staatz, and Davout toward Nikolsburg. Oudinot, the Guard and the cuirassiers followed Marmont and Davout. Unfortunately, the Emperor was on the wrong scent. Most of the Austrian army (I, II, III, V, VI and Reserve Corps) was heading north west toward Znaim and the only major formation on the road due north was Rosenberg's mangled IV Corps. When Marmont and Massena finally caught up with Charles at Znaim, therefore, a large part of the French army would be out of immediate supporting distance.

Chasing the bulk of the Austrian forces, Marshal Massena fought a series of sharp rear guard actions against VI and V Corps from the 7 through 9 July. The Austrians conducted themselves commendably, however, and the French were unable to gain a significant advantage over their quarry. Still, Charles was in no position to halt his retreat and Massena's IV Corps reached Hollabrunn on the evening of the 9th. Marmont, meanwhile, had also crossed sabres with Austrian rearguard elements on his drive north and the evening of the 9th found his main body at Staatz with a forward detachment at Laa.

The appearance of French forces at Laa forced Charles to alter his plans. Instead of defending in a position along the Pulkau as he had originally intended, he decided to continue his retreat to the north, holding the defiles around Znaim long enough for his numerous and cumbersome trains to escape.

10-11 July (Battle of Znaim): On the morning of 10 July, General Marmont turned his corps north-west and headed up the River Thaya toward the defile at Znaim.[26] He encountered Habsburg pickets east of Klein Tesswitz at about 11 a.m. and, believing the force ahead to be no more than a rear guard, deployed his corps to attack. Confident of success, Marmont sent the Bavarians toward Tesswitz and Clauzel toward Zuckerhandel, Claparède forming behind the other two infantry divisions as the corps reserve and Montbrun's horsemen swinging wide to the right with the mission of cutting the main road behind the presumedly small Austrian force. As his men cleared the heights east of Tesswitz, however, the French general realized that he had miscalculated. Thousands of white-coated soldiers were deployed across the hills to his front and a huge mass of wagons, men and horses was slowly making its way north along the main road. The Bavarians managed to seize Tesswitz and Clauzel took Zuckerhandel, but Montbrun was repulsed by a host of Austrian squadrons and forced to retire. Now estimating the enemy at 40,000, Marmont sent urgent messages to Davout and the Emperor but decided to maintain his exposed position as long as he could to fix the Austrians in place.

Marmont was initially opposed by the grenadiers and cavalry of the Austrian Reserve Corps, but the rest of Charles's army was en route and Marmont's situation grew increasingly dangerous as the afternoon wore on. The focus of the battle was the tiny village of Tesswitz. Stormed and lost several times by each side, Tesswitz cost the Bavarians more than 900 casualties, but Marmont committed elements of his reserve division to the fray and when darkness fell the village was firmly in Allied hands. The French and Bavarians, now facing five enemy corps (I, II, III, VI, and Reserve), settled in for the night, hopeful that dawn would bring the Emperor and reinforcements.[27]

Napoleon was indeed headed for Znaim in all haste with the remainder of the army. The evening of 10 July found Massena's column at Guntersdorf, about 22 kilometres from Znaim with Reuss's V Corps still blocking the road north. Napoleon was some 26 kilometres to the east of Znaim at Laa with Oudinot's II Corps, the Guard and part of the heavy cavalry; while Davout was yet further north and east around Nikolsburg (20 kilometres from Laa). In accordance with the Emperor's emphatic orders, these forces started for Znaim at about 2 a.m. on the 11th.

During the night, Charles pulled all his troops north of the Thaya and established a defensive position to protect the army's train, still struggling north into Moravia. He arrayed his forces in a great fish hook from Winau in the north to the Thaya just west of Tesswitz and then curving around along the water course to the high ground north-west of Znaim: reserve cavalry west and north of Winau on the extreme left; III Corps between Winau and Brenditz; I Corps on the ridge from Brenditz to opposite Zuckerhandel; V Corps on the right of the line from opposite Tesswitz to Klosterbruck and thence to Znaim. Both the grenadiers and II Corps were positioned behind the left wing in reserve, while VI Corps was several kilometres to the north-west along the highway.

Napoleon could thus observe a formidable army when he arrived on the heights above Tesswitz at about 10 a.m. on 11 July. Although he brought with him a large body of cavalry and horse artillery, he could not consider any serious offensive operations until Davout's and Oudinot's hard-marching infantry was at hand. These weary battalions, however, would not reach the battlefield until the morning of the 12th at the earliest and the Emperor consequently limited the actions of his army on the 11th. Napoleon may also have felt himself constrained by the possibility that an armistice agreement would soon be reached. Tentative contacts had been under way for several days and GM Maximilian Freiherr Wimpffen, Charles's Chief of Staff, arrived at Imperial headquarters that afternoon.

There was nothing constrained, however, about the attack Massena launched when his lead division, Legrand's, appeared on the heights south of the Thaya at 10 a.m. Seizing the main bridge intact, Legrand's French and Baden light troops stormed across the little river and, by 2 p.m., Klosterbruck and Altschallersdorf were in Allied hands. Legrand reordered his formations and renewed the advance at about 4 p.m., moving directly up the road on Znaim itself. This was a threat Charles could not ignore and he sent two grenadier brigades to reinforce V Corps. A counter-attack by one of these brigades, made under the cover of a violent thundershower, initially succeeded in throwing the French and Badeners back toward the Thaya in great disorder. A brilliantly executed charge by the 10th Cuirassiers restored the situation, however, decimating a grenadier battalion and capturing two guns. Carra Saint-Cyr was now on the scene and Massena had resumed his advance on Znaim when French and Austrian staff officers rode between the lines to announce that a ceasefire had been declared. Although the surprised soldiers did not yet know it, the campaign of 1809 was over.

Negotiations continued throughout the night of 11/12 July and, to Charles's relief, a six-week's armistice was announced the following morning. If Charles, convinced that peace was vital to the survival of the army and thus the Habsburg dynasty, was pleased by the armistice, his brother the Kaiser was furious. Franz considered the terms of the agreement too harsh, particularly the requirement to withdraw all Austrian forces from the Tyrol. Having recently issued a proclamation in which he pledged never to abandon the Tyrolians, Franz was loath to abjure his promise, but his own emissary could procure no better terms and, much to the enduring disgust of the sturdy Tyrolians, the vile medicine of armistice was swallowed for the larger good of the monarchy. By the end of the month, both armies had withdrawn behind their respective demarcation lines; they would not face each other again in 1809.[28]

THE TYROL AND THE VORARLBERG:
THE SECOND ALLIED OFFENSIVE BEGINS

The departure of Deroy's Division left the Allies seriously weak along the Tyrolian border and early July was consequently characterized by renewed insurgent raiding into Bavaria and Württemberg, culminating in a series of powerful attacks lasting from the 13th to the 17th. Although pressed on a broad arc from Lindau to Tölz, the Allies proved equal to the challenge, and the rebels were repulsed at all points with heavy losses.[29] The stage was thus set for the Allies to resume the offensive.

The conclusion of the armistice allowed Napoleon to turn his attention to the Tyrolian problem, and two Bavarian divisions (1st and 3rd) were soon on the way from Linz to Salzburg. Joined by GD Rouyer's Division from the minor German states (arriving from Passau), Marshal Lefebvre launched the Second Offensive on 27 July and marched up the Inn valley to enter Innsbruck on the 30th, encountering almost no resistance. Other Allied forces entered the region from the north. GB Montmarie (with Arco's men) crossed over the mountains and met Lefebvre in the Inn valley on the 29th and GD Beaumont took a force over the border before swinging west to outflank the Vorarlberg rebels. Finally, Deroy, taking a more southerly route through the Lueg Pass, met the other two divisions in the Tyrolian capital on 1 August. The Tyrol seemed secure.

THE SOUTHERN FRONT: MINOR OPERATIONS

As the day appointed for the second crossing of the Danube approached, Napoleon brought Marmont and Broussier north to participate in the climactic event of the campaign. The two divisions left Graz on 1 July and reached the Marchfeld in time for the second day of the Battle of Wagram. The Austrians were thus able to reoccupy Graz on the 3rd, but this and other minor operations in Hungary, southern Austria and Dalmatia earned them no significant advantages and most of their forces were required to withdraw under the terms of the armistice signed at Znaim.

POLAND: FINAL ADVANCES

The Poles continued to push south and west into Austrian territory and were in a position to threaten Moravia and northern Hungary when the armistice was concluded.

GERMANY: THE BLACK CORPS HEADS NORTH

The reserves Napoleon had committed to oppose Radivojevich in northern Bavaria were under GD Junot, who had assumed command of the Reserve Corps at Hanau in late June. Arriving at Bamberg on 5 July with GD Rivaud's Division, he immediately advanced against the Austrians around Bayreuth and brought them to battle at Gefrees on the 8th. Unfortunately for Junot, Radivojevich was reinforced during the course of the engagement and the day ended with a clear defeat for the French. Junot retired into Bavaria. The Austrian reinforcements had come from Am Ende's force around Dresden and were led west by the new Habsburg commander in Saxony, FML Kienmayer. Having beaten Junot, Kienmayer now planned to turn on Jerome and attack him. Jerome had personally entered Dresden on 1 July, but made no effort to move west and join Junot until the 4th. When he finally confronted Kienmayer in western Saxony, however, he felt himself inferior to the aggressive Austrian and retreated to the north, reaching Jena by the 15th where he learned of the armistice; his Corps was soon making its way hastily back to Westphalia. Austrian forces around Dresden (reoccupied by Am Ende on the 13th) and in western Saxony returned to Bohemia in accord with the terms of the armistice.

Although Austria had accepted the armistice, the Duke of Braunschweig, dispossessed of his lands by Napoleon in 1806, refused to lay down his arms. At the head of 2,000 followers, known as the 'Black Corps' because of the colour of their uniforms, he turned his back on Austria and marched north toward his homeland. He skirmished briefly with a Saxon cavalry detachment near Leipzig on the 26th, but quickly passed through that realm and into Westphalia. Here he managed to evade his pursuers and trap a Westphalian infantry regiment in the town of Halberstadt on 29 July. The inexperienced regiment was eradicated after tough resistance and Braunschweig continued north, his strength increased by some 300 Westphalian deserters.

AUGUST-DECEMBER: THE WAR WINDS DOWN

Although the possibility of renewed hostilities led both belligerents to reorganize their forces in the late summer and early autumn, the war of 1809 was over—at least as far as the main armies were concerned. In the Tyrol, however, the brutal guerrilla struggle continued with unabated fury, its last embers only dying out with the snows of early December.

THE DANUBE VALLEY: ARMISTICE AND PEACE

From August to October, both armies trained, reorganized and remained prepared for a renewal of combat operations. But the war was truly over. Although the initial agreement had only stipulated a six-week's armistice, the period was repeatedly extended as negotiations for a final settlement dragged on. In the end, however, Kaiser Franz had no choice but to sign yet another humiliating peace with France and the Treaty of Schönbrunn was duly promulgated on 14 October. By the terms of this document, the Habsburg monarchy was once again reduced in size, ceding huge territories to France and its allies for a loss of three and a half million inhabitants. Furthermore, the old empire was forced to join Napoleon's Continental System, accept a limit on the size of its armed forces (150,000 men), and pay France a significant indemnity. The War of 1809 thus came to an official conclusion and it only remained for Napoleon to suppress the intransigent insurgents in Germany and the Tyrol.

THE TYROL: A LAST DESPERATE STRUGGLE

The Second Allied Offensive proved too much for the rebels in the Vorarlberg. By 7 August, Beaumont's force coming out of the Tyrol had united in the Vorarlberg capital with a Württemberg detachment marching from the north. All serious resistance came to an end and the Allies were soon able to pull most of their troops out of the region.

The story in the Tyrol was vastly different, and Rouyer's men, marching south to link with French forces coming up out of Italy, saw ominous signs that the rebels were preparing to renew the fight. Attempting to press ahead, Rouyer encountered heavy resistance and suffered a bloody repulse at the tiny hamlet of Oberau on 4 and 5 August. Lefebvre brought up Bavarian reinforcements but could not force a passage through the narrow valley to the south and finally elected to retire on Innsbruck. Once again, Bergisel was the site of the decisive battle for the Tyrol. The insurgents attacked on the 13th and the Bavarians, poorly provisioned, tired and demoralized, were forced to retreat or face the danger of being completely cut off. By the 20th, the entire Bavarian command had again been expelled from the Tyrol, Deroy taking a position at Kufstein and Lefebvre assembling the rest of his Corps at Salzburg.

But the Tyrolian triumph was not to last. With no outside support, the mountaineers were at Napoleon's mercy and their cause was practically hopeless. Hofer ruled from Innsbruck until early October, but the signing of the Treaty of

Schönbrunn spelled the end of the insurgency. By mid-October French troops were pressing into the Tyrol from the east and south while VII Corps, now under GD Drouet d'Erlon, launched a well-co-ordinated assault from the north and north-west. The Bavarian attack was completely successful and Innsbruck was occupied by a detachment on the 28th. Opposition continued to be stiff for a time, but a final battle at Bergisel on 1 November was a one-sided victory for Drouet and convinced most Tyrolians that further struggle was pointless. There were still a number of insurgent bands to subdue, but when the Bavarians established contact with the French forces at Brixen on the 11th, the fate of Hofer and his last comrades was sealed. Support for the insurgency now evaporated quickly and by the first days of December the dreadful guerrilla war had ended.

GERMANY: THE BLACK CORPS ESCAPES

The Duke of Braunschweig reached his father's old capital on the last day of July, but found himself in a precarious position: the population had not risen in revolt as he had hoped and enemy forces were now closing in on him from north and south. He clashed with GD Reubell's Westphalian and Berg troops at Oelper on 1 August, but the result was unsatisfactory and he made up his mind to march for the coast and eventual rescue by the Royal Navy. Outrunning the inept Reubell, Braunschweig embarked his men on the 7th and reached the open sea two days later; even his rear guard, which had skirmished with Reubell's greatly superior forces on the 6th, was able to escape. The Black Corps would soon go to the Iberian Peninsula to continue its fight against Napoleon.

WALCHEREN: THE BRITISH DISASTER

One of the last acts of the 1809 campaign was the British landing on the coast of Holland. This operation, long hoped for by Austrian leaders and German patriots, had a variety of objectives: capture or destruction of French vessels at Antwerp; closure of the Scheldt estuary; demonstration of support for the Habsburg and German national causes; diversion of Napoleon's attention from the Danube theatre. None of these objectives was achieved. About 40,000 English troops indeed landed on Walcheren Island starting on 11 August, but they were soon bottled up by a hodgepodge Franco—Dutch force (initially commanded by Bernadotte, later by Bessières) and their own incompetent leadership. The English remained on the coast for several weeks, suffering greatly from the miasmas of the area and accomplishing little. Having lost some 4,000 men to disease and 106 to combat action, the tragic expedition was evacuated on 30 September.

The war of 1809 had come to an end and Napoleon seemed to stand at the height of his power. But it was to be 'the last success'; the rot had already set in. Despite his triumph over the Habsburgs, Napoleon's strategic situation did not improve: the Spanish ulcer continued to fester, Britain remained defiant and France became estranged from Russia. Two years after their return from Vienna, the soldiers of the Rheinbund would find themselves on the dreadful road to Moscow.

NOTES:

1: The complex diplomatic manoeuvrings involved in this process and the role of the controversial Talleyrand are beyond the scope of this essentially military history.

2: Some states, such as Bavaria and Württemberg, had already begun to modernize their militaries by 1806; others, like Baden, would succumb to tremendous French pressure after the Prussian campaign, and at least one, Saxony, would remain immersed in the stultifying traditions of the Frederickian era until after the war with Austria. It should also be noted that reforms were by no means limited to the military arena and most Rheinbund states also instituted manifold changes in their social and political structures, either on their own or as a result of demands from Paris. Many of these institutions would long outlast Napoleon and his empire and some would help sow the seeds of his defeat: the spirit of nationalism that the French carried on their bayonets and inculcated in their German allies would help to awaken a corresponding feeling of nationalism in thousands of German hearts.

3: By the autumn of 1808, when the Duchy of Oldenburg joined the Confederation, its membership had risen to thirty-six and included every German monarchy with the exception of Prussia and Austria (also excluding the Hanseatic city-states and various regions still under direct French administration).

4: Germans frequently referred to Napoleon as the *Schlachtenkaiser* or 'Emperor of Battles'.

5: Davout had commanded French forces in Germany (titled the 'Army of Germany') while Napoleon was in Spain and the troops now under his orders included four veteran infantry divisions, a small reserve division and two large cavalry divisions (one heavy and one light). Most of Massena's men, on the other hand, had come from locations deep within France. Oudinot held command of II Corps pending the arrival of Marshal Jean Lannes, hastening up from Spain.

6: There were problems in the line of communications between Paris and Donauwörth and some of Berthier's orders arrived in the wrong sequence. Furthermore, the harried marshal seriously misinterpreted the somewhat less than precise wording of one key order.

7: Davout's Reserve Division (Demont) and Nansouty's cuirassiers were also along the Danube between Ingolstadt and Donauwörth.

8: Lannes' Provisional Corps included two of Davout's infantry divisions (Morand and Gudin) as well as Jacquinot's light cavalry and some of St. Sulpice's cuirassiers.

9: Lannes had now taken his proper place as commander of II Corps.

10: Control of the Reserve Corps was a constant source of tension between Jerome Bonaparte and Marshal Kellerman.

11: Austrian units and commanders had been considerably reshuffled during the retreat from Bavaria and the halt in Bohemia (among other changes, the hapless Archduke Ludwig had been removed from command and II Reserve Corps had been dissolved); the reorganized army on the Marchfeld thus consisted of: I Corps (GdK Bellegarde), II Corps (FML Hohenzollern-Hechingen), IV Corps (FML Rosenberg), VI Corps (FML Hiller), I Reserve Corps (GdK Liechtenstein). III Corps (FZM Kolowrat) was in Bohemia and V Corps (FZM Reuss) was scattered on both distant flanks of the main army (elements at Krems and Pressburg, for example).

12: In typical Austrian fashion (that is, reminiscent of the eighteenth century), Charles divided his army into five 'columns' for the attack rather than using the more modern corps command structure. In actuality, however, most of the 'columns' were composed of one corps and the corps designations are used here for clarity and brevity: 1st Column = VI Corps; 2nd Column = I Corps; 3rd Column = II Corps; 4th Column = part of IV Corps; 5th Column = remainder of IV Corps. The cavalry reserve and the grenadiers were not assigned to a 'column'.

13: The strengths of the opposing armies at Wagram is a topic frequently debated by historians. This figure includes all of the forces the French fielded (5 and 6 July) and is taken from Manfried Rauchensteiner, *Die Schlacht bei Deutsch Wagram am 5. und 6. Juli 1809,* Militärhistorische Schriftenreihe Heft 36, Wien: Bundesverlag, 1977, pp. 9, 17, 22. For a vastly different appraisal, see Carl Bleibtreu, *Die Grosse Armee,* volume 2, Stuttgart: Krabbe, 1907.

14: The Nassau infantry regiment from Rouyer's Division and a Württemberg cavalry regiment were also part of the Vienna garrison, but not under Vandamme's command.

15: Command of the corps had devolved upon GD Nicolas Oudinot after Lannes was mortally wounded at Aspern-Essling.

16: The seriousness of the fighting on the afternoon of the 5th was relative: given the French numerical superiority, the Austrian Advance Guard under FML Nordmann could offer little resistance. None the less, Nordmann's force was almost eradicated and the general himself was killed as the French rolled forward on the afternoon of the 5th.

17: Baumersdorf is now called Parbasdorf.

18: Hiller had left command of VI Corps under a cloud a few days earlier. Kolowrat's III Corps had joined the Main Army from Bohemia, leaving only a small force to watch the Bavarians at Linz.

19: Quote from the memoirs of a surgeon in the Baden Brigade, cited in Captaine Veling, *Nos Alliés Allemands,*

Paris: Frères, 1909, p. 263.

20:    The march of Archduke Johann from Pressburg to Wagram has been much debated and many have laid the Austrian defeat at his door. It seems unlikely, however, that the appearance of this small corps would have altered the ultimate outcome of the battle (despite the uproar on the evening of the 6th).

21:    Bernadotte's withdrawal from Aderklaa forms one of the many controversies surrounding the Battle of Wagram: his detractors say he acted out of disloyalty or spite, his advocates claim he was following Napoleon's orders to close in on the centre of the army.

22:    Paraphrased from the Austrian historian Manfried Rauchensteiner: 'But Klenau stood still. He had no further orders and had probably understood Charles's operational intention to be that which had been written into the attack orders: a general attack by the entire army with neither finesse nor deep objectives...No one exploited the apparently unexpected situation. What did Napoleon do? He made military history!'

23:    Lasalle's and Marulaz's cavalry led Massena's march column, followed by Legrand (including the Baden Brigade), Carra Saint-Cyr (including the Hessian Brigade), and Molitor.

24:    Maximilian Ritter von Hoen, *Wagram,* vol. 8 of *Das Kriegsjahr 1809 in Einzeldarstellungen,* Wien: Stern, 1909, p. 112.

25:    Immediately after Wagram, Bernadotte was relieved of command and IX Corps dissolved. The Saxons were now under GD Reynier.

26:    Many of the towns that featured in this part of the campaign are now in Czechoslovakia. Modern Czech names of the principal places are given in parentheses: Nikolsburg (Mikulov), Znaim (Znojmo), Kukrowitz (Kucharovice), Zuckerhandel (Suchohrdly), Tesswitz (Dobsice), Thaya (Dyje), Oblass (Oblekovice), Schallersdorf (Saldorf), Pumlitz (Bohumilice).

27:    From north to south, the Austrians were deployed as follows by nightfall: III Corps on the left between Brenditz and Winau, I Corps from Brenditz to opposite Zuckerhandel, reserve cavalry west of Brenditz, grenadiers and one brigade of I Corps opposite Klein Tesswitz, II Corps south of the Thaya around Pumlitz, VI Corps north-west on the road north. II Corps was soon drawn north of the river and V Corps also crossed the Thaya to the north art about 11 p.m. from its rearguard position in front of Massena .

28:    Injured by his imperial brother's condemnations and the enmity at court, Charles resigned his command ten days after the conclusion of the armistice.

29:    For a brief period, the Allied forces around Lake Constance came under the direct orders of King Friedrich of Württemberg, further complicating Beaumont's chores as the local French commander.

CHAPTER 2

Bravoure, Bavière

Maximilian I. Joseph of Bavaria provided Napoleon with the largest Rheinbund contingent in 1809. From a population of 3.2 million, Bavaria fielded a mobile force of 32,100 in April, and had more than 47,000 men under arms at the conclusion of the campaign. Despite French arrogance and a chronically strained exchequer, Bavaria was a relatively willing ally. It had gained much from its association with Napoleonic France—Napoleon elevated Max Joseph from Elector to King in 1806 and increased his realm by more than 25,000 square kilometres and almost one million citizens from 1803 to 1808—and it feared Austria's hegemonistic desires in southern Germany. Moreover, for some Bavarians, such as the influential and opportunistic GL Carl Philipp Freiherr von Wrede, service under Napoleon provided scope for personal advancement. Of course, there were many who harboured anti-French and anti-Napoleon sentiments, the most notable among this group being Max's son and heir, Ludwig, but the greater part of the army regarded the alliance with France as beneficial and thrilled at thoughts of the glory to be won under the eagles of Mars' greatest captain.[1]

The army that responded to Napoleon's summons in early 1809 was much improved over that which Max had inherited a decade earlier. Fighting on the side of France's enemies in the early Wars of the Revolution, the Bavarian soldier proved himself courageous but poorly prepared for combat. Unable to react to unexpected situations, lacking fire discipline and with no knowledge of skirmishing tactics, the Bavarians were no match for the armies of revolutionary France. As with most states at this time, Bavaria drew its common soldiery from the very lowest elements of society; discipline was harsh and young men of any means purchased exclusion from military service. The procurement of supplies and replacement equipment was inadequate in garrison and catastrophic in the field: the soldiers of Bavaria often turned out in rags and barefoot, starving and unpaid. The officer corps did little to ameliorate the plight of the common soldier. Having purchased their commissions, many officers had no prior military training or experience; they were generally unable to provide the drive and leadership necessary to overcome the deficiencies in training and administration. The artillery was in sad condition, much of the cavalry was unmounted ('providing the cavalry with boots in addition to shoes was an unnecessary expenditure') and the white Rumford uniform was generally despised. As one contemporary commented, 'Bavarians no longer consider it an honour to serve, it has become almost a dishonour'.[2] It was the army of the monarch, but not of the nation.

Max Joseph was a man of little military experience, but he recognized the fundamental flaws in his state's armed forces. Shortly after succeeding to his father's throne in February 1799, he forbade the purchase of officers' commissions, thus laying the foundation for later improvements in the officer corps. He also did away with the unpopular Rumford uniform, returning to traditional Bavarian blue and introducing the Raupenhelm which would be the characteristic headgear of the Bavarian army for many years to come. Further military reforms were delayed by renewed war with France, but in 1804—5, he and his advisers introduced a broad series of measures which transformed the Bavarian army into a modern, national force.[3] Key to these reforms was the announcement of general conscription in 1804. Although the lower classes continued to supply most of Bavaria's soldiers, the recruiting base was considerably enlarged, resulting in an army that was more representative of its nation. Previously, it had not been uncommon for criminals to be sentenced to the army; now, service to King and Country became the duty of each citizen. To make the army more attractive, increase its effectiveness and raise its standing in the public eye, conditions for both officers and common soldiers were significantly improved. Under Max's paternal eye, steps were also taken to modernize the army's administration, organization and medical services. Corporal punishment was not abolished, but its impact was palliated and channels were established through which soldiers could raise complaints of maltreatment. A new, more liberal relationship between officers and their men was encouraged. Soldiers were no longer simply mercenaries or criminals (or both), but citizens in the service of their country; officers were no longer merely young nobles who received responsibility by virtue of their wealth, but men of proven military ability who attained their ranks by merit.

In initiating these reforms the Bavarian government consciously followed the French model. French influence was particularly evident in the realm of tactics. The Bavarians adopted small, flexible columns to enhance battlefield manoeuvrability and introduced skirmishing as a standard element of the tactical commander's repertoire. The principal architect of the new infantry regulations, GL Bernhard Graf von Deroy, thus effected the transition in the Bavarian infantry from the stiff, linear forms of eighteenth-century combat to the fast, adaptable tactics of the Napoleonic age.[4] The organization, training and equipment of the artillery was also significantly improved by borrowing from the French. This was chiefly the work of Jakob Graf von Manson, an expatriate Frenchman and student of the renowned Gribeauval. He formed his guns into permanent batteries, increased the number of artillerists, reintroduced light (or horse) artillery and promoted the tactical employment of guns in mass. In addition, a train battalion was raised in 1806 to provide greater mobility in the field. First tried in the 1806—1807 campaign, these innovations greatly improved the effectiveness of the Bavarian artillery, but Manson's exertions would bear their best fruit in the 1809 campaign.[5]

The impulse to transmogrify the army along French lines came from internal and external sources. Internally, Bavaria was energized by a natural desire to emulate the victorious armies of revolutionary France and overcome the martial weaknesses of the past. An effective military also meant that Bavaria could bargain with France rather than simply submit to Napoleon's desires.[6] Furthermore, reform in the army was just one piece of a larger restructuring effort that was sweeping through the entire structure of Bavarian state and society as Max strove to bring Bavaria out of the eighteenth century and into the nineteenth.[7] Externally, Napoleon demanded that Bavaria maintain an army of 30,000 men and required his Rheinbund allies conform to certain French standards.[8] From the pressure of these demands and the heat of combat in the cam-

Table 2-1: The Bavarian Army in April 1809

Line Infantry Regiments

Organization: two battalions per regiment; one grenadier company, four fusilier companies per battalion (one fusilier company per battalion served as depot); company strength 180 men.
Uniform: cornflower-blue coat with distinctive colour on collar, lapels, cuffs; white breeches; white belting; Raupenhelm.

Number	Title (Inhaber)	Distinctive Colour
1	Leib-Regiment (Max I. Joseph)	red
2	Kronprinz	red
3	Prinz Karl	red
4	none in 1809 (formerly Salern)	yellow with white piping
5	Preysing	pink with red piping
6	Herzog Wilhelm	red with white piping
7	Fürst Löwenstein	pink
8	Herzog Pius	yellow with red piping
9	Ysenburg	yellow with red piping
10	Junker	yellow with red piping
11	Kinkel	green with red piping
13	none in 1809	black with red piping
14	none in 1809	black with red piping

Light Infantry Battalions

Organization: five companies each (one of which served as battalion depot).
Uniform: dark-green coat with distinctive colour on collar; turnbacks red; lapels and cuffs black edged in red; grey breeches, black belting; Raupenhelm.

Number	Commander	Distinctive Colour
1	Oberstlieutenant Baron Habermann	red
2	Oberstlieutenant Wreden	red
3	Oberstlieutenant von Bernclau	black with red piping
4	Oberstlieutenant Baron Donnersberg	black with red piping
5	Oberstlieutenant Graf Butler	yellow with red piping
6	Oberstlieutenant von La Roche	yellow with red piping
7	Oberstlieutenant von Günther	light-blue with red piping

Cavalry Regiments

Organization: six squadrons per regiment (two served as depot); squadron strength 125 men.
Uniform: white (dragoons) or light-green (chevauxlegers) coat with distinctive colour on collar, lapels, cuffs; white breeches; white belting; Raupenhelm. Chevauxlegers changed to a dark-green coat in November 1809.

Regiment	Title (Inhaber)	Distinctive Colour
1st Dragoons	none in 1809 (formerly Minucci)	scarlet
2nd Dragoons	Taxis	scarlet
1st Chevauxlegers	Kronprinz	crimson with red piping
2nd Chevauxlegers	König	red
3rd Chevauxlegers	Leiningen	red
4th Chevauxlegers	Bubenhofen	black with red piping

Artillery

Organization: Artillery Regiment of four battalions, each of five companies; company strength 100 men.
Artillery uniform: dark-blue coat with black facings trimmed in red; dark-blue breeches; Raupenhelm. Train uniform: grey coat with light-blue collar and cuffs; grey breeches; Raupenhelm.

paigns of 1805, 1806 and 1807, a new Bavarian army was forged; it would fight the first and last battles of the 1809 campaign, winning the recognition of friend and foe alike for its battlefield performance.

In January 1809, Max Joseph's army comprised thirteen regiments of line infantry, seven light infantry battalions, six cavalry regiments, sixteen artillery batteries[9] and a garrison regiment.[10] A variety of reserve, national guard and other units were also raised during the war; these are covered in Chapter 7. The line infantry regiments were numbered sequentially from 1 to 11, to which were added the 13th and 14th Regiments. This anomalous situation was the result of a mutiny by the 12th Regiment in 1806; to reflect the dishonour brought upon the army by this incident, the regiment was disbanded and its very number stricken from the rolls of the Bavarian army, never to be given to another unit (the number was actually reinstated in 1814).[11]

The infantry uniform was unusual in two respects. First, in an era when most German troops wore dark-blue or white, King Max issued his men a coat in the traditional cornflower-blue of Bavaria. Second, the uniform was crowned with the Raupenhelm, a tall black leather helmet with a black caterpillar crest. Although this headgear pleased Bavarian sartorial tastes and warded off sabre blows, it was heavy, ungainly and the fur crest soaked up water like a sponge in the rain. It did, however, provide NCOs a convenient storage place for their notebooks.

All thirteen line regiments were organized on the same structure: two battalions, each of five companies. Two companies (one per battalion) normally served as the depots of the regiment; they remained behind to perform administrative and training functions (principally accepting new recruits and preparing them to join the battalions in the field) when the other companies marched to the sound of the guns. Each company numbered 180 men, including 20 Schützen (trained skirmishers supposedly armed with rifles), giving the battalion in the field an authorized strength of 720 bayonets plus officers, musicians and specialists. The average regiment thus embarked on the 1809 campaign with about 1,600 officers and men in its ranks and from 300 to 500 in the regimental depot. [12]

In March, just before the campaign opened, this organization changed slightly. To improve the infantry's ability to implement skirmishing tactics, the number of Schützen was increased to one-fifth of each company's strength, ideally resulting in a total of 36 Schützen per company (only seven of whom were armed with rifles). To fill these new positions, particularly active, intelligent soldiers were selected from the ranks of the company's fusiliers and given the honour of wearing the Schützen insignia, a light green plume on the left side of the Raupenhelm.[13]

The light infantry battalions were organized along similar lines; each battalion was composed of five 180-man companies (including Schützen), with the fifth being the depot or reserve company. The total strength of each light battalion thus reached approximately 800 at the start of the war.

Unlike the line regiments, the light battalions did not have Inhaber, but were named after their commanders (Habermann, Bernclau, etc.).[14] In keeping with the norms of Jäger fashion, they wore dark-green and grey. Despite the designation 'light', however, they too were burdened with the weighty Raupenhelm. Only the 7th Light Infantry escaped the heavy helmet, its soldiers wearing a black shako with a blue and white Bavarian cockade.[15]

The Bavarian mounted arm comprised six regiments in 1809, two of dragoons and four of chevauxlegers. Each regiment contained six squadrons, divided into three divisions of two squadrons each. Four squadrons (two divisions) deployed with the field army while the other two performed depot and internal duties. The field squadrons counted 125 sabres each in 1809, the depot squadrons generally somewhat less.[16]

Bavaria's Artillery Regiment was composed of twenty companies, each company capable of manning one battery of guns. At the start of hostilities, thirteen of these companies were assigned to batteries in Bavaria's mobile corps and one to the command in the Tyrol; the remaining six companies provided fortress garrisons and established the artillery depot. The field batteries assigned to the corps were of three types: light, line and reserve. The light and line batteries each mustered four 6-pounders and two howitzers, the chief distinction being that all of the soldiers in a light battery rode horses or the unit's limbers, whereas the men of the line batteries had to walk. The three reserve batteries each had four 12-pounders and two howitzers. Together with one of the light batteries, these were initially designated as the Corps' artillery reserve. Consistent with the strenuous work of a gunner, the better recruits of 1809 were assigned to the artillery as the army scrambled to fill gaps in the ranks just before the campaign. Thus a regimental order of 10 March stated that 'a large man of good appearance who has no front teeth will none the less probably meet the needs of the artillery because of his size and development'.[17]

The Train Battalion (Fuhrwesensbataillon) supplied the drivers and conductors for the army's artillery and ammunition vehicles. Recently militarized (1806), the train personnel were proud of their artillery-style swords (first issued in 1808) and the Raupenhelms they had in common with the rest of the artillery.

Bavaria organized these field forces into three divisions, each composed of two infantry brigades and one cavalry brigade. The infantry brigades each consisted of two line regiments and a light battalion; the cavalry brigades of two mounted regiments. Furthermore, each division was provided with four artillery batteries: one light, two line (6-pounders) and one reserve (12-pounders). This order of battle was first exercised in the summer of 1808 when Napoleon, spurred by incontrovertible evidence of Austrian rearmament, commanded the Bavarians to mobilize. Under the slim pretext of normal manoeuvres, a Bavarian observation corps was established to warn Vienna against any rash action. By autumn, however, Napoleon and Tsar Alexander had met at Erfurt, the war scare had subsided, and Bavaria demobilized in the aura of peace that followed the emperors' conclave.[18] But, given Austria's rearmament, this peaceful interlude could only be short-lived and, in January, Napoleon once again ordered his Bavarian allies to hold themselves in readiness. Actual mobilization followed on 25 February with the recall of furloughed soldiers and the requisition of draft animals. Three days later, the Bavarian army marched out to embark upon its most glorious campaign.[19]

Whereas the dispositions of the previous summer had served the interests of Napoleon the statesman by demonstrating resolve, the movements of the Bavarian forces in early 1809 were commanded by Napoleon the general. The Bavarian Ministry of War initially ordered its three divisions to occupy a line generally running from Munich—Landshut—Straubing—Regensburg; they were thus relatively well concentrated along the principal Austrian avenue of

Table 2-2: VII Corps in early April 1809
commander: Marshal Lefebvre, Duke of Danzig

staff cavalry (*Stabsreiter*) attached from V/1st Dragoons on 23 May

Note: Each *Stabsreiter* unit equaled about one half squadron.

1st Division - GL Crown Prince Ludwig
staff company (*Stabskompanie*) from 2nd Infantry depot
staff cavalry from V/1st Chevauxlegers
  1st Brigade - GM von Rechberg
    1st Leib Infantry Regiment
    2nd Infantry Regiment *Kronprinz*
    1st Light Battalion *Habermann*
  2nd Brigade - GM Stengel
    4th Infantry Regiment
    8th Infantry Regiment *Herzog Pius*
  Cavalry Brigade - GM von Zandt
    1st Dragoon Regiment (-)
    1st Chevauxlegers Regiment *Kronprinz*
  Artillery - Major Halder
    Line (Foot) Batteries: Wagner, Hofstetten
    Light (Horse) Battery: Regnier

2nd Division - GL von Wrede
staff company from 3rd Infantry depot
staff cavalry from V/2nd Chevauxlegers
  1st Brigade - GM von Minucci
    3rd Infantry Regiment *Prinz Karl*
    13th Infantry Regiment
    6th Light Battalion *La Roche*
  2nd Brigade - GM von Beckers
    6th Infantry Regiment *Herzog Wilhelm*
    7th Infantry Regiment *Löwenstein*
  Cavalry Brigade - GM von Preysing
    2nd Chevauxlegers Regiment *König*
    3rd Chevauxlegers Regiment *Leiningen*
  Artillery - Major von Zoller
    Line (Foot) Batteries: Dorn, Berchem
    Light (Horse) Battery Caspers

3rd Division - GL von Deroy
staff company from 13th Infantry depot
staff cavalry from V/4th Chevauxlegers
  1st Brigade - GM von Vincenti
    9th Infantry Regiment *Ysenburg*
    10th Infantry Regiment *Junker*
    5th Light Battalion *Butler*
  2nd Brigade - GM von Siebein
    5th Infantry Regiment *Preysing*
    14th Infantry Regiment
    7th Light Battalion *Günther*
  Cavalry Brigade - GM von Seydewitz
    2nd Dragoon Regt *Thurn und Taxis*
    4th Chevauxlegers Regt *Bubenhofen*
  Artillery - Major Tausch
    Line (Foot) Batteries: Peters*, Roys
    Light (Horse) Battery: Gotthardt

*Peters replaced by Pamler on 1 June

Corps Artillery - Major Göschl
  Reserve (12-pdr.) Batteries:
    von Dietrich, Dobl**, Leiningen
  Light (Horse) Battery: van Douwe

    Later distributed to the Divisions:
    Leiningen - 1st
    Dobl - 2nd
    von Dietrich - 3rd

**Dobl later replaced by Ulmer

In the Tyrol under GL von Kinkel:
    11th Infantry Regiment
    2nd Light Battalion *Wreden*
    3rd Light Battalion *Bernclau* (detached from 2nd Brigade, 1st Division)
    4th Light Battalion *Donnersberg* (detached from 2nd Brigade, 2nd Division)
    Two squadrons of the 1st Dragoon Regiment (detached from 1st Division)
    Line (Foot) Battery Binder (non-standard battery with a mix of 6-pdrs, 3-pdrs and howitzers)

Strength at the Outbreak of Hostilities:
VII Corps - 27,600 [Includes 1st Division (8,780), 2nd Division (8,940), 3rd Division (9,750) and Corps troops]
Kinkel's command - 4,560
Fortress Garrisons - 3,430

approach and prepared to operate in any direction. Before this position could be assumed, however, a new royal order was promulgated on 3 March. The Bavarian army was now to assemble around Munich (1st Division), Augsburg (2nd Division) and Altdorf bei Nürnberg (3rd Division). These new locations had barely been reached when revised orders, direct from the Emperor, arrived in Munich on 10 March. The 3 March deployment, principally the work of Wrede, was quickly discarded and the troops were sent trudging off to almost the same positions designated in their original instructions.[20] Despite some needless countermarching, which doubtless caused the men to grumble under the leaden March skies, this temporary confusion neither disadvantaged the Bavarians *vis-à-vis* the slowly approaching Austrians, nor hindered the overall mobilization effort. Indeed, thanks to early warning and its recent experiences (1806 and 1808), Bavaria's mobilization proceeded with considerable speed and efficiency in 1809; by 20 March, all three divisions were deployed along the Isar from Munich to the Bohemian border as the strategic avant-garde of Napoleon's gathering army.[21]

APRIL - THE OPENING GUNS

When Marshal Lefebvre arrived on 25 March to take command of the Bavarian mobile forces, now designated VII Corps, he found them well established in their respective positions: the 1st Division near Munich, the 2nd around Straubing and the 3rd about Landshut.[22] Napoleon's choice of François Joseph Lefebvre, the Duke of Danzig, to command the Bavarian Corps displeased Max Joseph. The King had hoped to see his son, Ludwig, at the head of the Corps, but the Emperor was adamant that all his army's senior leaders be battle-tested Frenchmen who owed their loyalty to him. The passionate and obstinate Crown Prince, however, was known to detest Napoleon ('If Satan were to take human form, he would, I feel sure, be Napoleon') and his 22 years were almost completely innocent of military experience. Ludwig thus hardly appeared an appropriate candidate for corps command, and the Emperor rather brusquely replied to Max's concern:

> I must speak to you frankly. The Crown Prince, whatever advantages he may have by nature, has never learned or made war, he cannot know it. You give me the privilege of utilizing your 40,000 men, but not of putting at their head a man who is sure and firm. I have named as commander the Duke of Danzig who is an old soldier. The Bavarian troops are too numerous and the situation is too grave for me to conceal my thoughts from Your Majesty. If the Crown Prince had been through six or seven campaigns at all levels, then he could command them.[23]

The sullen Ludwig was therefore assigned the 1st Division with a steady veteran, GM Clemens von Raglovich, as his Chief of Staff, while Wrede took the 2nd Division and Deroy the 3rd. Nor was Lefebvre a poor choice for this command. A native of Alsace, he spoke German (albeit with a strong accent) and had a solid military record; he was not, perhaps, the most imaginative or inspiring of

France's Marshals, but he was a competent, reliable leader who easily out-matched most of his Austrian contemporaries. Napoleon further reinforced the Corps' leadership by assigning the talented and experienced GD Jean-Baptiste Drouet, Comte d'Erlon as Lefebvre's Chief of Staff.

Although Lefebvre's appointment as Corps commander was the most visible evidence of Napoleon's intrusion into the Bavarian military, French dominance also manifested itself in all manner of small quotidian matters. All correspon-dence between the division commanders and their King was conducted in French, as were the communications exchanged among the generals. At the bayonet level, pickets and guards were instructed to use the French parole '*Qui vive?*' rather than the German 'Wer da?' (Who goes there?). Even the official seals of the three divisions showed the arms of Bavaria surmounted by the words 'première, deuxième, troisième division bavaroise'. Some of these mea-sures were simply practical expedients in a composite, multilingual army (the use of a common parole, for example, especially when the opposing army's lan-guage was also German), but they still rankled, injuring German pride. But, the Bavarians were still Bavarians, and Lefebvre understood. The history of the 6th Regiment relates the following tale:

> The French Marshal devoted his full attention to the condition of the troops under his command. During the inspection of the 1st and 3rd Divisions, he observed that soldiers were collapsing from exhaustion as they manoeuvred; he deduced from this, and not incorrectly, that the provi-sions were inadequate. In the investigation that followed, it was discovered that the victuals provided by the villages and hamlets in which our regiment had been quartered were very poor and, in particular, that the beer was unpalatable and thinned with water. This also explained the high number of sick (39) suffered by our regiment in contrast to that experienced by other units.[24]

March 1809 also saw the belated introduction of several tactical changes. First, as previously mentioned, the number of Schützen per company was increased to enhance the infantry's skirmishing capability. Second, the infantry was now to form in three-rank rather than two-rank lines, the new third rank being com-posed of the Schützen. This return to a three-rank order of battle (abandoned in 1801) was intended to improve the battalion's firepower by allowing the third rank to reload muskets while the front two ranks maintained a steady series of volleys. Generals Wrede, Deroy and Siebein were to suggest alterations to the drill regulations that would account for this new tactical arrangements, but hos-tilities began before their proposals could be evaluated. As a result, the Bavarian infantry had to adapt to a new formation while en route to battle and it devolved upon unit commanders to ensure that consistency was maintained within their own organizations.[25]

The army organization established by royal order of 11 March was basically unchanged when the Austrians crossed the Inn on 10 April (Table 2-2).[26] Lefebvre, however, had changed his corps' dispositions slightly: the 1st

Division, which had been guarding the roads from Braunau and Salzburg, was pulled back from Haag to Anzing, closer to Munich; the bulk of the 3rd Division shifted from Landshut to Freising.[27] The two divisions were linked by a detachment under GM Kurt Graf von Seydewitz posted at Pliening.[28] The 2nd Division remained around Straubing, responsible for an L-shaped line running from Dingolfing to Regen and then to Cham. The greater part of the division was held south of the Danube, with only the 6th Light Battalion, 13th Infantry and 2nd Chevauxlegers deployed north to cover the Bohemian border. Alarums and excursions seem to have been the order of the day in the 2nd Division. Worried about the breadth of his area of responsibility and the openness of his left flank, Wrede sent urgent appeals to Munich claiming Austrian attack was imminent and asking for support. His requests were received coolly by the War Ministry, however, and the only result of his rather overheated zeal was the infusion of a certain nervousness within the division through continual alerts and patrols.[29] Nevertheless, both Napoleon and Max were well served by the Bavarian cavalry and civil service in the weeks leading up to war.

General Deroy had a different problem with his division: unauthorized beards. Inspecting his troops on 5 April, the general was disturbed to note that

> ...numerous officers of the infantry, artillery and dragoons have allowed themselves to grow beards, which is against the current regulations and the royal wishes of His Majesty the King, according to which only the chevauxlegers officers should wear beards. For all other officers these are forbidden and those who have grown one shall have it removed.[30]

Despite Wrede's anxiety and Deroy's annoyance, the army was well positioned and ready when the invasion came on 10 April. Weeks earlier, Bavarian cavalry pickets had been posted along the Inn to observe the border and gather intelligence. In concert with local civil authorities, they had performed these classic cavalry tasks well and now fell back before the Austrian invaders without offering any resistance. The Austrians, hoping to coax Max out of his alliance with Napoleon, were under orders not to treat the Bavarians as enemies until the latter took hostile action. Despite Charles's proclamations and the restrained behaviour of his army, however, the Bavarians evinced no inclination to betray their King. They continued to withdraw before the advancing Austrians as the two armies jockeyed for position.[31]

The campaign thus opened with manoeuvre, the two armies blundering towards each other in the quiet Bavarian countryside. Neither Allied nor Austrian cavalry was performing adequately, consequently both Marshal Berthier and Archduke Charles received only the vaguest impressions of their enemies' locations and activities.[32] This was a period of frustration for Lefebvre and his soldiers. Poorly informed about the enemy's whereabouts and uncomfortable in command, Berthier issued a bewildering stream of contradictory orders, ultimately leaving Lefebvre unsure about his mission. The movements of the Bavarian divisions from 14 to 17 April illustrate Lefebvre's predicament. In the welter of confusing directives, the 1st Division was brought from Anzing to Freising on the 14th and sent on to Au the following day, where it lost contact with the enemy. As the division moved north, a detachment of about 50 troopers from the 1st Chevauxlegers skirmished with the *Liechtenstein* Hussars near Haag on the 14th. Under the command of French Chef d'Escadron Montégélier (one of Lefebvre's staff officers), the Bavarians were attacked and driven off by advancing Austrians from GM Armand von Nordmann's flank guard; eighteen men of *Kronprinz* fell into the hands of the hussars and Montégélier barely escaped capture. Deroy's 3rd Division was also set in motion on the 14th; it was ordered to hold the bridge-head at Landshut, where it arrived at 5 a.m. on 15 April. The 4th Chevauxlegers had a brief brush with Austrian cavalry (also *Liechtenstein* Hussars) near Erding on the 14th as von Seydewitz's detachment pulled back to Freising. The next day, they too were en route for Landshut. A company of the 10th Infantry and a gun, left behind to watch the Moosburg bridge, retired toward Pfeffenhausen upon the appearance of a detachment from FML Johann von Hiller's VI Corps under a Major Karl von Scheibler.[33]

Wrede's men spent much of their time marching about in response to the conflicting orders: their commander was not only receiving instructions from Lefebvre, he also got messages directly from Berthier. Moved north-west from Straubing toward Abensberg on the 9th and 10th, the 2nd Division spent the next three days between Vohburg and Langquaid. Ordered to return to Straubing on the 14th, Wrede marched as far as Eggmühl and sent a cavalry patrol to Dingolfing.[34] After repeated changes in orders, he was again sent toward Abensberg on the 15th, leaving his cavalry brigade between Pfeffenhausen and Rottenburg to support Deroy at Landshut.

THE FIRST ENGAGEMENT AT LANDSHUT (16 APRIL)

At Landshut, a long, narrow island divides the river into two channels, thus creating a double problem for any army aiming to cross. To the south, the land rises steeply to form high bluffs which completely dominate the town and its bridges. On the opposite bank, however, the river is flanked by flat, marshy meadows that stretch lazily on for 3 to 4 kilometres before rolling up into the buttressing hills to the north. This was the position Deroy's 9,700 men occupied on the morning of 16 April. His 1st Brigade with one battery was placed in the northern suburbs of the city: I/10 in Am Rennwege, II/10 in the meadows behind St. Nicolaus, II/9 at Kloster Seligenthal, I/9 behind the paper mill, and the 5th Light Battalion on the island in the river directly outposting the two partly dismantled bridges.[35] The 2nd Brigade guarded the defile at Altdorf. The 5th Infantry's 1st Battalion occupied the village itself and the heights to the west; a Schützen detachment of II/5 extended the line as far as Gündlkofen to maintain contact with another detachment at Bruckberg. The rest of the brigade deployed on the long slopes to the north-east together with two batteries and four cavalry squadrons: II/5 on the right, 14th Infantry in the centre and Seydewitz's horsemen on the left toward Ergolding. Of the remaining cavalry, three squadrons

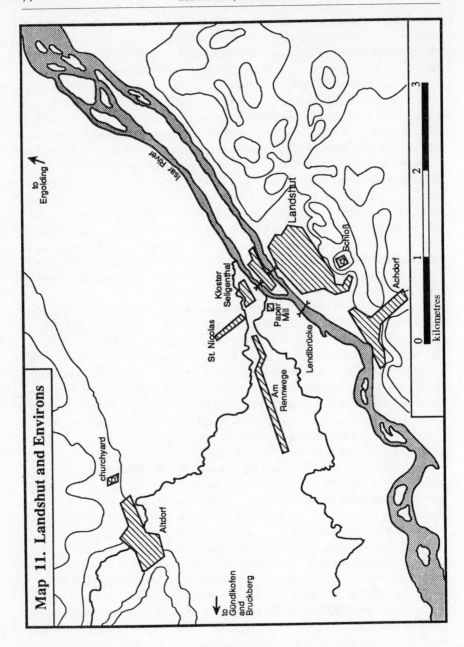

Map 11. Landshut and Environs

(one from 2nd Dragoons and two out of 4th Chevauxlegers) were posted between Altdorf and St. Nicolaus, and one squadron (2nd Dragoons) was held at Pfettrach with two companies of the 7th Light and a gun. Finally, the other two companies of 7th Light were detached out to Gammelsdorf to guard the Division's right flank.[36]

Austrian patrols from FML Archduke Ludwig's V Corps had arrived in Landshut on the night of the 15th.[37] Finding the city evacuated and the bridge unusable, they awaited the arrival of the corps advance guard under GM Josef Graf Radetzky. This general moved into the city early on the 16th and immediately sent one of his staff officers to negotiate passage of river and repair of the bridge with the Bavarians. The attempt met only Deroy's determination, however, and a subsequent effort at 10 a.m. was rebuffed by Oberstlieutenant Butler commanding the 5th Light. By this time, Archduke Charles had arrived on the scene. With the rest of V Corps (18,300) coming up to join Radetzky (2,900) and FML Friedrich Franz Fürst von Hohenzollern-Hechingen's III Corps also on the way with another 26,300 men, the Austrians heavily outnumbered Deroy's defenders. To this powerful force could be added the I and II Reserve Corps, both of which were marching up the Braunau highway. Moreover, IV and VI Corps were also in the process of crossing the Isar, outflanking the Bavarians to the east (Dingolfing) and west (Moosburg) respectively. Confident of his strength, Charles ordered Radetzky to 'drive the Bavarian pickets from the far bank and re-establish the bridges'.[38]

In contrast to the dismal rain of the preceding several days, the 16th was clear and sunny, providing the Bavarian light infantrymen with a clear view of the Austrian pioneers who now set to work to restore the two bridges. A lively engagement was soon ignited across the turbid waters of the Isar. The soldiers of the 5th Light, in their first battle, proved tenacious defenders, making good use of the buildings on the north bank to direct heavy musket fire on the struggling pioneers. The gunners of Peters' Battery were not so fortunate. Although they bravely served their pieces, they were quickly overpowered by the larger and more numerous Austrian cannon. The four pieces covering the westernmost bridge (Lendlbrücke or Ländbrücke) were particularly exposed and soon had to be withdrawn to less effective but more protected positions. The withdrawal of these few guns left Butler's men alone to face the growing Austrian pressure, but they courageously maintained their positions amongst the smoke-filled streets and burning buildings until ordered to withdraw shortly after 2 p.m. Deroy, having learned of the Austrian crossings at Dingolfing and Moosburg and facing mounting Austrian strength to his front, wisely decided to pull his division back from the river before it was cut off. The withdrawal began at about 2.30 p.m., with the two infantry regiments leading, followed by the 5th Light. Collecting itself in the St. Nicolaus suburb, the battalion retreated under the cover of two companies from I/10. At almost the same time, the Austrians began to cross the Lendlbrücke.

The Austrians did not immediately pursue the 1st Brigade with any great vigour. Small elements followed the retiring Bavarians, but it was late afternoon before major units of V Corps were formed on the north bank. Deroy's men, withdrawing with parade-ground precision across the soggy fields, thus experienced little difficulty in reaching Altdorf, although the commander of the 10th Infantry suffered a slight wound when he was ridden over by several retreating cavalrymen. Under little pressure, the 1st Brigade was thus able to continue its withdrawal through Altdorf and to the north, protected by parts of the 2nd Brigade and the now united cavalry. Additionally, reports of Major Scheibler's Austrian force were now beginning to filter in and Deroy sent the little detachment from Pfettrach west to Furth as further protection for his road north.

Blocking the mouth of the valley which was Deroy's only route of retreat, Altdorf was key to the survival of the 3rd Division; if the Austrians could seize the town and punch through the Bavarian rear guard, Deroy might be destroyed before help could arrive. The old veteran thus disposed his rear guard to shield the remainder of the Division as disturbing numbers of Habsburg troops assembled in the ground below. He supported his infantry on firm defensive posts, placing a detachment of the 14th in Altdorf's isolated churchyard and securing the village itself by giving I/5 orders to hold it until the detachment from Gündlkofen was successfully recovered. On the heights slightly to the northeast, von Seydewitz deployed his seven available squadrons in two lines *en echequier*, four squadrons of *Bubenhofen* in the first line and three of *Taxis* in the second.[39] Two batteries unlimbered in the open ground near the cavalry brigade where they could engage the Austrians attempting to debouch on to the broad meadows.

As Austrian strength built up on the north shore, Radetzky began to press the Bavarians. At about 4 p.m., just after the last of Deroy's infantry had passed through von Seydewitz's lines, Radetzky's horsemen fell upon the Bavarians. Oberstlieutenant Johann Heinrich Graf Hardegg had swung east and north of Altdorf with 180 Uhlans (from *Erzherzog Karl*, Nr. 3) to outflank the Bavarian cavalry. Although outnumbered, he launched a sudden charge into the left of the *Taxis* Dragoons and sent that regiment flying. A confused and free-wheeling cavalry battle ensued. Although his second line was broken and fleeing toward the Altdorf-Pfettrach road, von Seydewitz, with great presence of mind, turned the 4th Chevauxlegers about and charged north into the now disordered lancers. Fired on by rapidly deploying elements of the 14th Infantry on the northern edge of Altdorf and overwhelmed by the Bavarian light horse, Hardegg's men were recoiling when two squadrons of *Kienmayer* Hussars threw themselves into the mêlée and again restored the situation for the Austrians. However, the Bavarian dragoons had now reformed and they hit the right wing of the hussars, rolling them up and pressing them back on their supporting guns until the Austrian Uhlans, also reformed, returned to the roiling fray with the rest of their regiment.[40] With the outcome favouring the Austrians, von Seydewitz, elected to break off the struggle. Seeing that the Bavarian infantry had pulled back safely and concerned about the menacing advance of the Habsburg foot soldiers, he adroitly extricated his troopers from the engagement and retired toward Pfettrach.

In the swirling cavalry fight, Dragoon Wolf wounded and captured an Austrian Uhlan officer. When Wolf was himself wounded by three pistol balls, the Austrian retrieved a sword and struck a heavy blow to Wolf's right arm, rendering the limb useless. The cool Wolf took up his sword in his left hand and swung two ferocious cuts at his opponent, knocking him to the ground, dead. Despite his injuries, he joined his comrades chasing the Uhlans, killed or wounded three more of them and rescued a fellow dragoon before finally retiring. He was awarded the Bavarian Silver Medal for Bravery.[41]

The Bavarians continued their retreat in a masterly fashion. While the main body proceeded north in excellent order, the rear guard, composed of the cavalry, I/5 Infantry, the 14th Regiment's Schützen and the light battery, repeatedly halted to delay the pursuit. Exhibiting fine coolness and control, the various arms supported one another closely as they backed up the valley, allowing Radetzsky's Austrians no opportunities to interfere. I/5 Infantry, for example, calmly held on to Altdorf until the detachment in Gündlkofen had slipped past; it then made its own harrowing but successful withdrawal, covered by Seydewitz's troopers. From Altdorf, the battalion fell back on Pfettrach and held the village until about 5 p.m., when Austrian shells set the houses afire and forced the Bavarians to evacuate. The Schützen of the 5th Light held Arth briefly to let the cavalry disengage, and then, as night came on, withdrew to the division's next position near Weihmichl. With night falling, Deroy decided to discourage to his Austrian pursuers and unlimbered all his guns across a low ridge while the Division's combined Schützen deployed in the low ground to the front. Radetzky's force thus met with heavy artillery and musket fire as it pushed up the road, and the Austrian commander, already 7 kilometres in front of his Corps' main body, decided to terminate the pursuit. The enemy pressure eased, Deroy's men marched the night away, passing through Wrede's positions at Pfeffenhausen between 4 and 6 a.m. on the 17th, and moving on to bivouac behind the Abens near Siegenburg.

Casualties in the engagement at Landshut were not great: Austrian losses were about 90, and the Bavarian total of dead, wounded and missing barely exceeded 160. Of the Bavarian figure, however, about one fourth were soldiers listed as missing from the 7th Light Battalion. As the battalion was only on the periphery of the combat, it can be assumed that most of these were Tyrolians who took advantage of the confusion of battle to desert the Bavarian flag; this problem would grow steadily worse, and, by 25 April, the entire battalion would number only 158 soldiers. Aside from the incipient treachery of the 7th Light, the performance of Bavarian arms at Landshut had been superb. Under Deroy's cool and competent leadership, the 3rd Division conducted a difficult operation against overwhelming odds. The infantry proved itself firm under fire and deployed swiftly, as if on parade, even in tense situations, while von Seydewitz and his brigade earned Deroy's especial praise for their conduct during the retrograde from Altdorf to Weihmichl.[42]

The other two Bavarian divisions continued their general withdrawal toward the Danube on the 16th, Wrede's cavalry fighting two small skirmishes as they pulled back: at Postau on their left flank and Gammelsdorf on their right. The former was a brief brush between a squadron of the 3rd Chevauxlegers and the lead elements of the Austrian IV Corps, the *Stipsicz* Hussars. The two sides

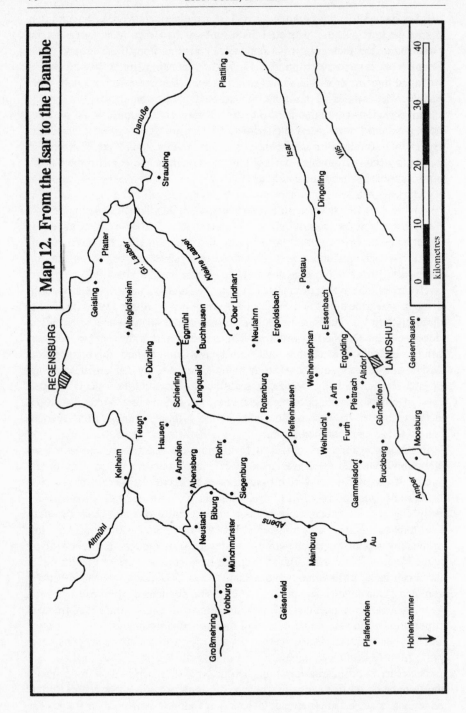

Map 12. From the Isar to the Danube

were in contact for about four hours, and the encounter ended with the Bavarians falling back to join the rest of their regiment at Neufahrn (one squadron) and Rottenburg (the remaining two squadrons). To the west, the energetic Major Scheibler with a patrol from the *Rosenberg* Chevauxlegers captured several Bavarian troopers near Gammelsdorf and probed almost to Pfeffenhausen before turning back at the sight of the *König* Chevauxlegers. In both cases, losses were insignificant. Night found the infantry of the 2nd Division split between Pfeffenhausen (1st Brigade) and Biburg (2nd Brigade). Farther west, the Crown Prince's Division, still out of contact with the enemy, moved to Pfaffenhofen, outposting a line from Mainburg to Hohenkammer. FML Franz von Jellacic's Austrian division occupied Munich.

ASSEMBLY ON THE ABENS (17-18 APRIL)

The 17th of April saw more skirmishing as the advanced guard of the Austrian V Corps probed toward the Abens. A small force of lancers (two squadrons of *Erzherzog Karl*) and infantry (two companies of *Gradiscaner* Grenzer) pushed north-west from Pfeffenhausen. Bavarian cavalry pickets spotted the Austrians as they approached Hornbach and notified GM Maximilian von Preysing, commander of Wrede's Cavalry Brigade; Preysing sent three squadrons of the 2nd Chevauxlegers to attack the Austrians south of Schweinbach. The Bavarian troopers overthrew the first batch of Austrians they encountered, but were themselves struck in the flank and routed by a small Austrian security patrol before they could fully deploy. The Bavarians were chased through Schweinbach to Irlach before the 3rd Chevauxlegers and the remaining squadron of *König* forced the Austrians to turn back. Preysing's initial attempts to return to Schweinbach were deterred by the musket fire of the Grenzer, but the Austrians abandoned the village in the late afternoon when the Bavarians threatened to outflank it.[43]

In the larger scheme of things, Berthier's confusing directions had pulled the Bavarians generally back toward the River Lech via Ingolstadt. The Crown Prince was to remain south of the Danube while the other two divisions marched north of the river to gain the city. Ludwig therefore drew in his outposts and took his division to Reichertshofen, sending cavalry patrols to reconnoitre towards Geisenfeld. Deroy's men spent most of the 17th west of the Abens, resting from their exertions of the previous day. Late in the afternoon, the division was assembled and pushed off toward Vohburg, crossed the Danube and arrived at Großmehring at about 3 a.m. on the 18th. Wrede's Division was also instructed to fall back on Ingolstadt and, leaving some cavalry patrols to screen its movement, it departed its positions behind the Abens at 10 p.m. on the 17th. Trudging through the damp darkness, the head of the division's march column passed through Neustadt and began to cross the great river at Vohburg. Suddenly there was shouting, stumbling and cursing as the long lines halted in the midst of their passage: new orders had appeared directing the 2nd Division to return to the heights above the Abens and prepare for battle. It was 2 a.m., and considerable confusion ensued as the tired men were turned round and marched back to a position just south of Neustadt. But the air was also full of decision and expectancy: Napoleon had arrived and there would be no more retreats.

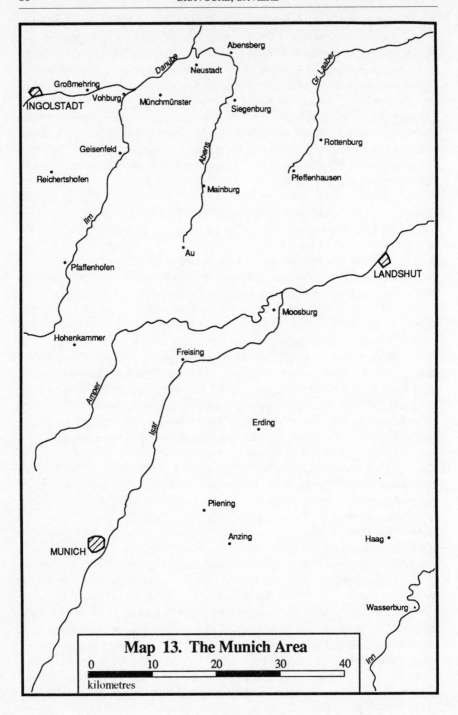

Map 13. The Munich Area

kilometres

In the dawn hours of 18 April, Lefebvre received orders from the Emperor directing the Marshal to attack the Austrian left flank and fix an Austrian force as least as large as his own VII Corps: 'Tell the Bavarians what I expect of them ... let all understand the urgency of the situation.'[44] Wrede's Division was therefore ordered out of its temporary encampment at Neustadt and sent back down the Landshut road to Siegenburg.[45] The division's advance guard, composed of the 13th Infantry, the Cavalry Brigade and Caspers' battery, found Austrians already over the Abens, the Bavarian cavalry patrols having done nothing to prevent the Austrians from crossing. These were troops from Radetzky's force; they had exchanged fire off and on with Preysing's retiring troopers earlier in the day and subsequently pushed across the Abens a detachment of *Erzherzog Karl* Uhlans and *Gradiscaner* Grenzer. This little force now occupied the woods south-east of Mühlhausen along the road to Siegenburg and they greeted the approaching Bavarians with a lively musketry. It was about 4:30 p.m. Wrede's advance guard immediately deployed Schützen from I/13, brought up a gun and sent the Leib squadron of the 2nd Chevauxlegers forward to the left of the road. The chevauxlegers chased off some of the Grenzer and threatened the right flank of the lancers, while Oberlieutenant Gravenreuth unlimbered his cannon in the middle of the road to blast the Austrian horsemen with canister. The Uhlans wisely withdrew and the Bavarians, pressing on to the Abens, found the bridge guarded by Grenzer. The Bavarian infantry (I/13) deployed and, supported by Caspers' battery, advanced on the well-posted Grenzer and drove them back over the stream. With the bulk of his division encamped around Dürnbuch, Wrede established outposts to watch the line of the Abens from Abensberg to Siegenburg and garrisoned these two towns with the 6th and 13th Infantry Regiments respectively.[46]

The other two divisions of VII Corps were also ordered toward the Abens on the 18th. The 1st Division marched via Ingolstadt and Vohburg[47] to reach Neustadt at about 4 p.m.; it took up a position south-east of the town in three lines facing Abensberg. One battalion (II/1) was left in Vohburg to guard the bridge and main ammunition reserve. The 3rd Division departed Großmehring after a few hours' rest (about 8 a.m.) and returned to the south bank of the Danube at Vohburg. Arriving about one hour before (*c.* 3 p.m.) the Crown Prince's columns, Deroy's men bivouacked to the south and south-west of Neustadt. Two battalions, two guns and 40 cavalry from the 3rd Division were posted near Münchmünster to watch the road toward Geisenfeld. With his Corps finally united, Lefebvre was to hold the line of the Abens, threaten the Austrian left and facilitate Davout's dangerous flank march from Regensburg to Abensberg. As half the French troops (Massena's and Oudinot's Corps) were still several marches away, the Bavarians were destined to play a pivotal role in the dramatic battles around Regensburg.[48]

ENGAGEMENT AT ARNHOFEN AND CANNONADE AT BIBURG (19 APRIL)

The turning-point in the Regensburg phase of the 1809 campaign came on 19 April. In the bloody encounter at Hausen—Teugn and the engagement at Arnhofen, Charles lost his best opportunity to destroy Davout's vulnerable corps and strike a decisive blow against the separated Allied forces; from this point on, the initiative was firmly in Napoleon's hands.

When Davout's III Corps collided with the Austrian III Corps between Hausen and Teugn at about 9 a.m. on the 19th, the Bavarians were still in the general area of their encampments. The 1st Division had moved forward of Mühlhausen, but the 2nd remained along the Abens and the 3rd near Neustadt. Napoleon's orders to Lefebvre instructed the Marshal to 'press the enemy vigourously as soon as the head of the Duke of Auerstädt's Corps is in your area'. When the dull and plangent beat of guns began to roll across the grey April hills, Lefebvre therefore concluded it was time to cross the Abens and attack. The 1st Division was ordered to Abensberg and the 3rd brought up to Mühlhausen, leaving its detachment at Münchmünster. Wrede's Division assumed a combat posture along the stream, with the 6th Infantry near Abensberg, the 7th at Biburg and GM Franz von Minucci's Brigade west of Siegenburg. Additional urgency was leant to these movements as troops of the Austrian V Corps began to appear on the bluffs east of the Abens and Thierry's brigade of III Corps became visible in the woods south of Arnhofen (Seeholz). GM Ludwig von Thierry was to form a link between V Corps, holding the Austrian left flank, and III Corps, now engaged in a desperate struggle with the deadly Davout. Arriving on the heights above Kirchdorf, however, Thierry could see numerous Bavarians in the valley of the Abens, some of whom seemed to be moving north-east along the Regensburg road. With no idea of the enemy's strength, he decided it was his duty to halt or slow this movement and set his force in motion to the north; leaving large detachments at Hörlbach and Bruckhof, his men (two battalions, four squadrons, four guns) began to debouch from the Seeholz at about 10.30 a.m.[49]

At that hour, the main body of the Crown Prince's Division was en route to Abensberg, preceded by its Cavalry Brigade and Regnier's battery as advance guard. The jangling troopers and gunners had already passed through Abensberg and turned north up the road to Arnhofen, their movement screened by a set of low hills. To the Austrian commander peering west from the fringes of the Seeholz, therefore, the 1st Division's advance troops on the road to Arnhofen were invisible; the only Bavarians he could see were a few cavalry vedettes on the high ground between the two villages. These pickets seeming to be the single obstacle between the Seeholz and Arnhofen, he set his brigade in motion across the fields to occupy the town. The Crown Prince's scouts naturally lost no time in reporting the approach of Thierry's little force and Lefebvre immediately ordered the avant-garde forward at the trot. In response, the *Kronprinz* Chevauxlegers executed a right turn and advanced up the low rise that had shielded them from Habsburg eyes. The unexpected appearance of an entire regiment of green-coated chevauxlegers surprised the *Levenehr* Dragoons advancing from the Seeholz and they halted momentarily while the Bavarians sent mounted skirmishers forward to contest any further Austrian advance. Thierry quickly deployed his four 6-pounders and opened up on the chevauxlegers, but Bavarian guns were also on the way and, favoured by a well-placed knoll, Regnier's battery gave the Austrians a second unpleasant surprise

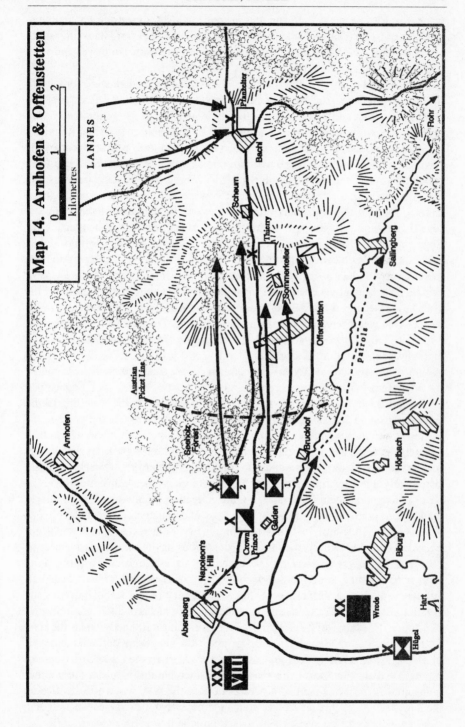

Map 14. Armhofen & Offenstetten

when it suddenly pounded up and unlimbered to the left of the cavalry regiment. The arrival of this battery boded ill for the Austrians: fifteen minutes after coming into action, the Bavarian gunners had disabled two Austrian pieces and were happily shelling the rest under Regnier's enthusiastic direction.

To ease the pressure on their brigade, the Austrian dragoons rode forward to the attack, but the first two squadrons were turned back by fire from the Bavarian battery. Undeterred, the other two spurred up the gentle slope after covering the withdrawal of their comrades. Despite canister fire from Regnier's sweating men, the white-coated horsemen drove into the flank and rear of the Bavarian chevauxlegers. The Bavarians, considering the ground too steep for a countercharge, chose to receive the Austrian charge from a stationary posture, defending themselves with a volley of carbine fire at short range. The dragoons charged through this fire, caught their foemen at the halt, disordered them and sent them fleeing to the rear. This turn of events made life dangerous for Regnier's men. Desperately trying to limber and displace, they would almost certainly have been overrun had the two squadrons of the 1st Dragoons not galloped up to conduct a timely counter-attack. Sent into the fray by the Crown Prince, these squadrons chased off the Austrian horse and provided time for the 1st Chevauxlegers to reorganize and return to the battle. The threat of enemy cavalry removed, Regnier reoccupied his position and resumed a lively fire, now aimed not only at the Austrian guns, but also at the infantry battalions deployed on the western rim of the Seeholz.

While this spirited cavalry engagement was in progress, Lefebvre had ordered the 6th Infantry to attack the Seeholz from the west. Thierry, justly concerned for his left flank, had placed his two battalions of *Kaiser* in the woodline facing Abensberg and a hot struggle ensued as the men of *Herzog Wilhelm* assaulted this position, the regiment in line following its deployed Schützen. This attack having failed, the Second Battalion made two attempts to push its skirmishers forward to the left of the First and into the forest; both efforts were beaten back. Fortunately, the Bavarian cavalry near Arnhofen held the Austrian dragoons in check, preventing them from charging the retreating infantry. A fourth attack, made in column behind a reinforced screen of Schützen and volunteers, was finally successful, but Austrians reinforcements (Thierry's detachment from Bruckhof) quickly evicted the 6th from the woods again and restored Thierry's position. By now, however, the 1st Brigade of the 1st Division was up and the *Kronprinz* Infantry went into action to the right of *Herzog Wilhelm*. Together, the two regiments managed to seize the western edge of the Seeholz, driving the Austrians to the east and taking a gun. Further to the right, 1st Light and Hofstetten's battery, followed by I/1, were advancing cautiously down the road from Abensberg to Offenstetten (the Ochsenstrasse) and soon outflanked the left of Thierry's increasingly perilous position. He ordered a retreat to Offenstetten.

The Austrian withdrawal was made in considerable disorder, despite a rather uninspired Bavarian pursuit. The energetic Regnier was an exception. Seeing the Austrians wavering, he shouted to his gunners: 'Now, boys, just shoot, balls, canister, whatever you've got, don't waste time aiming, just shoot, shoot!' An experienced officer, he knew that most soldiers, once they began to run, only needed the encouragement of whistling lead to keep running; the rounds did not have to strike anything, the psychological effect of their sound was enough. His battery was manhandling its guns forward when a violent thunderstorm brought combat to an end.

The Bavarians, having lost 227 men in the engagement, camped in the woods they had won. Thierry pulled his shaken command together around Offenstetten but decided against further retreat when he was promised support from detachments at Bachl and Rohr.[50]

While the 1st Division was slowly pressing Thierry back through the woods, Wrede was engaged in a desultory cannonade at Biburg. The 2nd Division had been quiescent until about 2 p.m., when a few shells were tossed at small detachments of Austrian infantry and artillery that appeared across the Abens north-east of Biburg. At about 3 p.m., however, Wrede decided to advance across the stream and move towards Thierry's weak left flank. Fortunately for the Austrian general, reinforcements from V Corps were on the way, coming up from the south in the form of GM Friedrich von Bianchi's Brigade.[51] Just as the Bavarian 3rd Infantry and half of Caspers' battery were debouching from the eastern edge of Biburg, Bianchi's men arrived to their right front. Deploying on the heights east and south-east of the village, the Austrians opened a heavy fire on the men of *Prinz Karl*, causing Wrede to withdraw them almost immediately. The Bavarian guns stayed in position, however, and were joined by the rest of their battery. Supported from north of Biburg by Dobl's battery and half of Dorn's, they held their position for almost two hours against a superior number of Austrian pieces, before lack of ammunition forced them to retire across the Abens. Farther south, at Siegenburg, V Corps opened a diversionary bombardment on the rest of Wrede's Division, but achieved little beyond the wounding of about ten unfortunate Bavarian infantrymen.[52] If militarily insignificant, this cannonade none the less made a dramatic impression on young soldier Mändler of the 6th Light:

This engagement was the beginning of my experience in war and combat, and the first moment in which I stood opposite those deadly gun barrels. I freely admit that these first kisses filled me — if only temporarily — with a terrible dread which I could not ward off. A similar feeling occurs to all at their first meeting with the enemy or battle, as no honest warrior or comrade will deny. It is particularly awkward for the soldier when he stands, as we did here, on the edge of a wood to protect a battery, does nothing else, merely serves, so to speak, as a target for the enemy; and, without being able to avenge himself, can and does hear every enemy ball. Then the attitude of even the most hearty man will be different from when he marches on to the parade field or manoeuvre area. It is better in actual battles and the tumult of combat; the soldier, occupied and tense with the loading and firing of his musket, neither hears the whistle of the balls nor notes the devastation they work in the ranks.[53]

The 3rd Division remained in its reserve position near Mühlhausen all day, but a few men were injured as cannon balls crashed through the trees overhead so that limbs and branches rained down on the troops. This division's inactivity, Wrede's late and feeble effort to cross the Abens and the Crown Prince's cautious pursuit of Thierry all indicate that Lefebvre was not acting in the offensive spirit of Napoleon's orders. The Bavarian success on the 19th was thus limited in scope. Still, Thierry had been roughly handled and Wrede's brief foray had prevented Bianchi from linking with Thierry's brigade; above all, the Bavarian left was now in contact with Davout's men and the grave danger for the French III Corps had been temporarily averted. Moreover, the Austrians were shaken and disjointed by the day's events; the deployments of III Corps and V Corps lacked cohesion. Only tenuously connected by Thierry's dispirited men at Offenstetten and GM Josef von Pfanzelter's weak force at Bachl, their situation invited attack. It was an invitation Napoleon was preparing to accept.

THE BATTLE OF ABENSBERG (20 APRIL)

Napoleon arrived at Abensberg at about 9 a.m. on the grey and drizzly 20th of April and quickly distributed orders for an immediate attack. The VII Corps' offensive was generally to proceed along two axes, a northern and a southern. The Crown Prince was to co-operate with Marshal Jean Lannes' provisional corps and aim for Rohr via the northern route through Offenstetten and Bachl; on the southern axis, Wrede would attack east through Biburg; Deroy's men were to follow the 1st Division's line of attack as reserve.[54] Before the attack was launched, however, the 1st and 3rd Divisions were drawn up around a small knoll east of Abensberg and the officers were called forward to hear an address from Napoleon.

> Bavarian soldiers! I stand before you not as the Emperor of France but as the protector of your country and the Rheinbund. Bavarians! Today you fight alone against the Austrians. Not a single Frenchman is in the first line, they are in the reserve and the enemy is unaware of their presence. I have complete faith in your bravery. I have already expanded the borders of your land; I see now that I have not yet gone far enough. I will make you so great that you will not need my protection in any future war with Austria. For 200 years, the Bavarian flag, supported by France, has fought heroically against Austria. We will march to Vienna, where we will punish it for all the evil it has caused your fatherland. They want to divide your nation and enroll you in the Austrian regiments! Bavarians! This war shall be the last you fight against your enemies. Attack them with the bayonet and destroy them![55]

If the physical appearance of the sodden little man on his white Arabian was unimpressive ('no one would think this person to be the Great Emperor, the victor of Austerlitz and Jena'), the impact of his words and presence was electric. Formed in an open square around the Emperor, the Bavarian officers responded enthusiastically as the Crown Prince translated Napoleon's speech. When the officers repeated the address to their units, the troops broke into loud and pro-

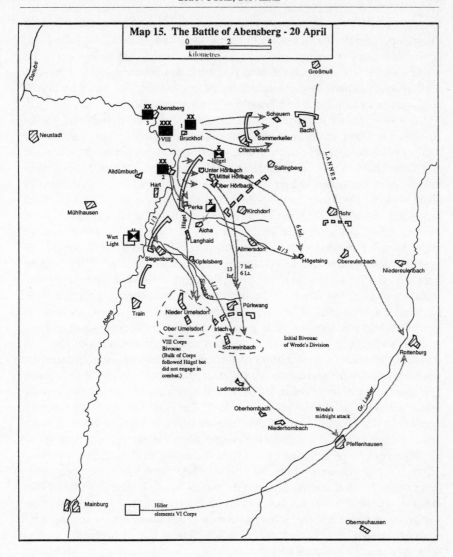

Map 15. The Battle of Abensberg - 20 April

0   2   4
kilometres

longed cheering. Even the Crown Prince was enthralled. Feeling the 'power of
the presence and personality of the Emperor,' he wrote, 'Could it have been otherwise than that the enemy, whom we instantly attacked, was thrown out of his
strong positions?'[56] Despite the dreary weather and the imminence of combat,
the Bavarian soldiers, further inspired by the distribution of a double ration of
beer, marched east infused with Napoleon's 'relentless will'.[57]

The Crown Prince moved directly from Abensberg on Offenstetten, his 1st
Brigade advancing along the Ochsenstrasse and his 2nd probing through the
damp Seeholz north of the road. Rain dripped from the branches as the
Schützen from his four line regiments led the way, clearing the Austrian skirmishers from the woods and pushing out into the fields west of Offenstetten by
about 10 a.m. Deploying to the right of the road, I/1 evicted a weak Austrian
detachment from the village while II/1 swung further to the right;[58] the 1st Light
and Hofstetten's battery moved straight up the road. The *Leib* Regiment's initial
efforts to move up the slope beyond the town were blocked by an Austrian company in a walled farmstead known locally as the 'Sommerkeller'. The Austrian
company, left by Thierry to cover his withdrawal, resisted several attempts to
storm its bastion, but finally fled when the persistent Bavarians threatened to
surround it completely. As pressure on the Sommerkeller was increasing, the
Levenehr Dragoons attacked I/1 to gain time for the farm's defenders to escape.
Although surprised by the sudden onset of the enemy, the men of the *Leib*
Regiment, in a fine demonstration of tactical competence, instantly formed a
square and coolly delivered a deadly volley at fifteen paces to shatter the charge.
The dragoons suffered further losses as they attempted to retreat through the
woods south-east of the Sommerkeller. Bold Bavarian Schützen, who had proceeded into the woods ahead of their formed units, took the Austrian cavalry
under fire and captured several in the close confines of the forest. Likewise, on
the Bavarian left, the Schützen of GM Karl von Stengel's Brigade bore the brunt
of the fighting. Emerging from the Seeholz, they crossed over the open, dewy
meadows to the east and pushed into the woods beyond, preceding the formed
elements of the 4th and 8th Infantry Regiments. Although ejected from the
woodline several times, the Schützen overcame Habsburg resistance and were
pressing through the ribbon of trees near Scheuern as the 1st Brigade surged up
the slopes past the Sommerkeller.[59]

Thierry, now in full retreat before the unfolding momentum of the 1st
Division's advance, had hoped to find support from Pfanzelter's little brigade
near Bachl. Unfortunately, Lannes had already forced Pfanzelter to evacuate
Bachl and Thierry found himself in the middle of the French corps as he left the
woods east of Offenstetten at about noon. His guns taken, his cavalry scattered,
Thierry ordered his men to fall back through the woods to FML Emanuel von
Schustekh's force at Rohr. The retreat was soon a full rout, ending with the
utter destruction of the Austrian brigade and Thierry's capture when the French
caught them at Rohr. GM Friedrich von Zandt's Cavalry Brigade, having
approached via Sallingberg, also made an appearance at Rohr, his troopers participating in the final eradication of Thierry's and Schustekh's commands and
the ensuing pursuit to the Laaber.[60]

The 1st Division bivouacked just north of Rohr, the 3rd near Bachl. Deroy's men had spent the day following the Crown Prince as reserve. Once arrived around Bachl, the 10th Infantry cleared some Austrians (probably stragglers) from the woods south of the village, and the 14th captured a few errant *Levenehr* dragoons trying to find their way back to their regiment. Napoleon, concerned about reports of enemy activity toward Großmuß, posted the two light battalions and the cavalry brigade near that village to secure his left flank and maintain the link with Davout. That night, the outposts of the 5th Light were able to capture two entire companies which had apparently lost their way in the darkness. Later in the evening, a detachment from the division was sent to reconnoitre towards Langquaid. Consisting of I/5, the consolidated Schützen of the 5th Infantry, a tiny cavalry element and one gun, the force probed into the town and took two captives, but roused the Austrian camp there in the process. Rather than face a night battle against a superior force, the Bavarians withdrew and returned to Bachl.[61]

For the Bavarians of the 1st Division, 19 and 20 April were thus crowned with success. For a loss of some 439 men over the two days, they had played a key role in the destruction of Thierry's brigade (it lost 3,000—4,000 men during the two days) and had helped to drive a deep wedge into the centre of the Archduke's army; the Crown Prince could justly report to his father that the 20th would be 'one of the most celebrated days' in his army's history: 'Nothing could withstand our troops,' he wrote.[62] If perhaps less energetic than other Allied soldiers, the Bavarians had demonstrated a fine mastery of tactical skills. At the small unit level, the infantry performed manoeuvres with cool precision, even under the pressure of immediate cavalry attack; the Schützen proved themselves courageous and aggressive despite minimal opportunity to practise their techniques. The artillery was particularly flexible and consistently well handled. At the brigade and division levels, the senior Bavarian generals displayed solid ability and personal valour; GM Raglovich's deployments of the 1st Division on both days are worthy of note for their aptness and the ease with which they were executed. Finally, it is interesting to observe the extraordinary effect of Napoleon's personality on the Germans. News of his arrival spread throughout the army like wildfire and the reaction of the Bavarians to his well-chosen words on the 20th at least partially belies the contention that France's German allies only fought under duress.

While the 1st and 3rd Divisions were attacking along the northern axis, Wrede's 2nd Division was involved in a confusing series of engagements on the southern axis. Wrede was an interesting character. Energetic and ambitious, he was a competent general who usually performed very well at the tactical level but lacked a sure grasp of grand tactics and strategy. He drove himself hard in this campaign, pursuing the enemy with vigour and demanding great exertions from his troops. It may have been this intelligent ambition which called him to Napoleon's attention, for he certainly basked in the Napoleonic sun, frequently receiving orders directly from army headquarters and enjoying an independence almost equal to that of the corps commanders. His high estimation of himself and reluctance to obey the orders of any but the Emperor trammelled co-operation with the similarly haughty Vandamme at Abensberg and led to considerable friction with Lefebvre throughout the campaign.[63]

In the proximity of the Emperor, Wrede opened his attack in the late morning of 20 April. His Schützen began skirmishing with Bianchi's men at about 10 a.m., and towards noon, with the little bridge repaired, the Bavarian general felt ready to cross the brook. Placing himself at the head of his brigade, GM Karl von Beckers led the way over the Abens, sending the 7th Infantry due east into the centre of the Austrian position supported by the 6th Light. The 13th Infantry aimed for the heights about Perka, the 6th received the Hörlbach villages as its objective, and the 3rd marched south along the right bank of the stream in the direction of Siegenburg. The cavalry and the light battery followed, their march temporarily interrupted by a break in the bridge.[64] Wrede's entire division was thus thrown across the brook and immediately committed to the attack against the Austrian V Corps.

Initially, the attacks proceeded successfully. On the left, the 6th Infantry stormed into the Hörlbachs against weak resistance and the Schützen of the 13th lodged themselves firmly in the woods north of Perka on the right. In the centre, the capable and determined Caspers provided excellent support to the 7th Infantry's advance with half his battery; the Austrian infantry obligingly withdrew when Caspers' well-directed fire made the area too hot for their supporting guns. Bianchi, however, was merely pulling his men back to a better position on the heights west of Kirchdorf. Here he was supported by two more battalions (*Beaulieu*) under FML Heinrich XV Fürst Reuß-Plauen, and Wrede, with a force approximately equal to the Austrians, could make no headway. By now, however, the sound of heavy gunfire from Rohr had convinced the V Corps commander, Archduke Ludwig, that his only salvation lay in retreat on Pfeffenhausen. At 2 p.m., Bianchi and Reuß thus received orders to pull back and by 3 p.m. the Austrians were withdrawing in good order south of Kirchdorf. Even then, Bianchi's and Reuß's rear guards held the 2nd Division at Kirchdorf until almost 5 p.m.

As these rear guards were preparing to pull out, Wrede's cavalry brigade finally had a chance to enter the action. Frustrated by the hilly and wooded terrain, the 2nd and 3rd Chevauxlegers had chafed under inaction all day, but in the late afternoon they were able to employ a clever tactic. As three Austrian companies were evacuating Aicha, the two regiments rode forward as if to charge them. The Austrian infantry hastily formed into a tightly packed mass to repel the approaching horsemen. At the last moment, the regiments neatly split, *König* swinging right and *Leiningen* left, to unmask a battery which proceeded to pour a merciless fire onto the surprised Austrians.[65] Despite small successes of this nature, the Austrian rear guards were able to fall back virtually uninjured to Pürkwang and Irlach, where their further withdrawal was covered by Radetzky's men. Wrede followed with the 7th Infantry, 6th Light, Preysing's cavalry and the light battery.

Radetzky had been pushed off the heights above Siegenburg by the combined efforts of the Bavarians and Württembergers. The 2nd Battalion, 3rd Infantry had advanced through Perka and up the heights to its south to threaten

Radetzky's right. Held in check for a time by Austrian cavalry, its attack received new impetus with the arrival of GM von Hügel with two battalions of the Württemberg Light Brigade. In the meantime, I/3 had captured Siegenburg and had combined with the other two Württemberg light battalions to strike Radetzky's left. The 13th Infantry was also beginning to make its presence felt, coming up on Radetzky's right from the direction of Aicha. Sweeping up the wet slopes, the Germans pushed Radetzky's men back after a brief fight and paused to reorganize. On the hillside near Kipfelsberg, GM von Minucci pulled together three of his battalions (13th and I/3) and two batteries. GD Vandamme asserted his authority as senior general to assume command of Minucci's Bavarians and sent them toward Irlach on the north side of the Siegbach while his own Württembergers (GM von Hügel's men) paralleled them to the south. Threatened by both Vandamme and Wrede (although the two made no effort to co-operate), Radetzky again withdrew, this time to a new position near Ludmannsdorf. With ammunition short and darkness falling, Wrede halted his pursuit at Schweinbach and camped for the night. Minucci remained at Irlach and the Württembergers bivouacked at Umelsdorf.[66]

It remains to account for the rest of the 2nd Division. In the mid-afternoon, Wrede had ordered the 6th Infantry to support the 7th, but the former regiment was apparently detained by Vandamme, much to Wrede's irritation. It was left without orders for some time (Vandamme having departed) and pushed off on its own toward Rohr at dusk in the hopes of locating the rest of the division. During its 'adventurous march', it encountered II/3 near Högetsing south-west of Rohr. After the engagement at Kipfelsberg, this battalion had followed various isolated Austrian detachments (probably from Radetzky's command) through Allmersdorf to the east. With no idea of where their superior headquarters might be found, these two units settled into a bivouac between Ober Eulenbach and Rohr.[67]

A damp night thus brought an end to the multitude of engagements that constituted the Battle of Abensberg. With Rheinbund troops carrying the brunt of the combat, the Austrian left wing had been pushed back some 14 kilometres from Biburg to Ludmannsdorf and many of its units were in considerable disorder. The Bavarians, in particular, had prevailed in an attack against an equal foe occupying an excellent defensive position. If the Austrian retreat was occasioned as much by Napoleon's advance on Rohr as by the pressure from Wrede's Division, the latter's men nevertheless demonstrated the same courage, tirailleur talent and tactical adaptability as their comrades under the Crown Prince. The artillery once again displayed its high quality and its co-operation with the cavalry provided a nasty surprise for the Austrians.

None the less, the victory was truncated by the Allies' poor command and control practices. Where a strong, centralized command might have dealt a crippling blow to the Austrian V Corps, the debilitating lack of overall direction on the Allied side splintered the attack and lamed the pursuit. The difficult terrain was an important factor, as was Napoleon's absence from the southern axis, and the presence of two strong-willed and ambitious commanders in Vandamme and Wrede, but Wrede himself must also share much of the blame. Directed to carry the attack against the Austrian left, he allowed his regiments to become separated and left some units without orders for most of the afternoon. He appears to have concerned himself more with matters appropriate to a brigade commander, leaving his division without unified leadership. As a result, some units contributed little to achieving the division's objectives on the 20th and three battalions were left isolated and useless until the night of the 21st.

If Wrede's span of command was overstretched during the 20th, he displayed the best of his leadership qualities the same night. At about 10 p.m., after only a few hours' rest, Wrede received new orders from Napoleon instructing him to seize Pfeffenhausen that night. Although he and his men were exhausted from their exertions during the day, Wrede soon had the 6th Light, a squadron of *König* Chevauxlegers and II/7 on the road toward the Laaber. Scattering a few Austrian pickets as they left Ludmannsdorf, the Bavarians proceeded slowly and carefully, hauling stragglers out of the dark, dank woods. Cavalry were sent forward to investigate a host of campfires above Ober Hornbach while the foot soldiers poked quietly through the solemn trees; the fires were found to be deserted, but the infantry brought in a few prisoners and the advance continued. Just beyond Nieder Hornbach there was a brief skirmish with the tail-end of the Austrian rear guard under Oberstlieutenant Hardegg (five companies of Grenzer and two squadrons of Uhlans). But Hardegg soon withdrew and Wrede pressed on to Pfeffenhausen, where the streets were crammed with horses, men, transport wagons and confusion.

Observing the pandemonium in the town, Wrede silently deployed *La Roche* in long, thin lines on both sides of the road and ordered the drummers to beat the charge at a given signal. A Schützen officer from the battalion was sent forward with a detachment to take the bridge but halted to skirmish with some Austrians and thereby gave the rear guard time to set the bridge aflame. Wrede, furious with the officer's actions, ordered the drums beaten and sent another company toward the town. Accompanied by all the dramatic military noise the battalion's drums, horns and lungs could produce, the company fell upon the bridge's defenders, overthrew them and stormed over the burning span into the village on the heels of the fleeing enemy. It was midnight. Illuminated by the flickering bridge, the chaos in the town was absolute. As panicked Austrians struggled to escape the apparently overwhelming enemy attack, the tiny Bavarian force captured horses and wagons by the score along with ammunition, stores and other booty of war; one of Ludwig's adjutants was included in the haul and several Austrian generals were fortunate to escape. In the early hours of 21 April, the 6th Light and chevauxlegers established pickets beyond the town as the last Austrians were brought in and the fire on the bridge was extinguished. The 7th Infantry, along with the 13th and I/3, were brought up from their rearward positions to bivouac for a few precious hours on the west side of the Laaber.[68]

In recognition of the Bavarian contribution at the Battles of Landshut and Abensberg, Napoleon established *'Bravoure et Bavière'* as the Army's parole for the 21st.

BATTLE AT LANDSHUT AND ENGAGEMENT AT SCHIERLING (21 APRIL)

The weary Bavarian foot soldiers would probably have preferred the honour of a few more hours' rest. In the early morning hours, Wrede received orders to march on Landshut via the Altdorf road with his entire division.[69] The 2nd Division, with Vandamme's VIII Corps, thus comprised the right wing of Napoleon's pursuit force; the Emperor himself was headed for the city over the road from Rottenburg to Ergolding with Lannes, St. Sulpice, Nansouty and von Zandt. It appears the Württembergers led the way south from Pfeffenhausen, but Bavarian cavalry also participated in the skirmishes with the Austrian rear guard at Altdorf. As the Austrians retired on Landshut, a swirling cavalry battle ensued on the plains north of the city. Both von Zandt's brigade from Ergolding and Preysing's from Altdorf contributed to the Allied attacks that finally broke the Austrian horsemen and drove them from the field. Von Zandt's troopers spurred to the attack next to Jacquinot's men, first overwhelming the *Hessen-Homburg* Hussars and then destroying a hastily-formed infantry square. Closer to Altdorf, Wrede led the 1st Squadron, 3rd Chevauxlegers in the chase, captured eleven Austrian guns and, according to legend, personally served a moment as a gunner to turn a piece against its former owners. The Allied infantry was not far behind the horsemen, Wrede's five battalions advancing on the west side of the Altdorf road, Vandamme and Lannes to their left. Before long, the island in the Isar was in Allied hands and French, Bavarians and Württembergers steeled themselves to cross the smouldering bridge into Landshut itself. Von Zandt fell here at the head of his brigade, waiting to storm over the river. Wrede was more fortunate: when French grenadiers charged over the span and broke in the city's gate with axes, he was close behind them, leading a squadron of *Leiningen* Chevauxlegers. In an elated rush, French, Württembergers and Bavarians vied with one another to reach Landshut. The 7th Infantry crossed, followed by I/3; both were soon involved in confused street-fighting amidst the detritus of the retreating Austrian left wing. With the Allies in Landshut and Massena pressing his left flank, Hiller had no choice but to withdraw as quickly as possible. The reliable Radetzky was left to hold off pursuit, and the day ended with Wrede leading the 1st Division of *Leiningen* to outflank the Austrian's rear guard position at Geisenhausen. Here the pursuit came to a halt in the early evening. Hiller continued his retreat, reaching Neumarkt between 1 and 2 a.m. in considerable disorder.[70]

In another finely calculated leadership move, Napoleon acknowledged Bavarian valour by according the *Kronprinz* Chevauxlegers the honour of bearing the day's trophies and leading his cavalcade when he entered Landshut that afternoon. In addition, GM Preysing was sent toward Munich to reconnoitre Austrian positions and bring news of the victory to Max's capital. With the 2nd Chevauxlegers and two squadrons from the 3rd, Preysing departed Landshut at about 4 p.m.; he got as far as Moosburg before halting his brigade for the night. Although most of his cavalry was now out of immediate reach, Wrede could take comfort in the return of his lost infantry battalions; the 6th Regiment and II/3 arrived in Landshut after a long day's wandering at 11 p.m. on the 21st.[71]

While Wrede's and Zandt's men were gathering laurels under the Emperor's

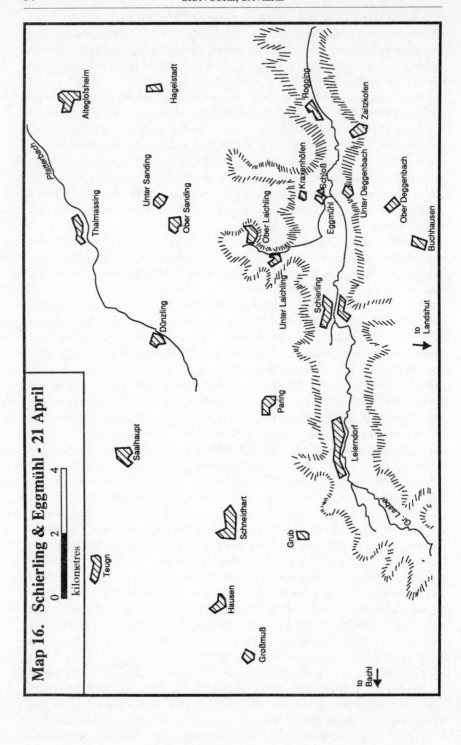

Map 16. Schierling & Eggmühl - 21 April

eyes at Landshut, Deroy's battalions spent the 21st in a long combat with the Austrian III and IV Corps. Davout and Lefebvre were instructed to follow Charles as he pulled his army back to the east. Breaking camp at Bachl at about 5 a.m., Lefebvre proceeded along the north bank of the Laaber with Deroy's and Demont's Divisions; Davout advanced on the Bavarians' left.[72] By 8:30 a.m., the division had reached Langquaid and linked with Davout's right at Grub. Both Allied Corps now turned east, paralleling the course of the Laaber to maintain pressure on Charles' main army. While Davout occupied the Austrian IV Corps between Laichling and Sanding, Lefebvre was to hold the right end of the Allied line and seek contact with Lannes' Corps towards Landshut.[73] The Austrians were retiring on both sides of the Laaber and fire from III Corps' artillery south of the stream caused some casualties in Deroy's advance guard (the two light battalions) as the Bavarians moved on Schierling. The rain of cannon and musket balls increased as the light infantry approached the town, which was occupied by an Austrian battalion. To remove this nuisance and secure a solid anchor for his right, Lefebvre sent the 7th Light forward to seize Schierling. Oberstlieutenant Günther's men quickly succeeded in taking the northern half of the town, but continued on, pushing out into the open ground toward Unter Laichling. Raked by canister from IV Corps to its north and charged by the *Vincent* Chevauxlegers, the battalion was immediately put to flight. Its casualties were so heavy and its behaviour so suspect, that it was taken out of the line and saw no further combat on the 21st.[74] The Austrians reoccupied Schierling.

Determined to take the important village, Deroy ordered the 5th Light to attack. With exemplary fortitude, the battalion stormed into Schierling from the north to evict the Austrian defenders. Rapidly clearing the northern half of the town, Butler left some of his men to hold their gains and resumed his attack across the Laaber into the southern half. The Austrians ceded Schierling to the ferocious Bavarians, but Butler's repeated attempts to push skirmishers beyond the village failed in the face of canister shot and the vigilant troopers of the *Vincent* Chevauxlegers. In the meantime, Bavarian gunners had succeeded in chasing the III Corps' artillery off the hills above Schierling, thereby removing the danger to Deroy's right flank. North of the Laaber, however, the Bavarian artillery was unable to make an impression on IV Corps despite a cannonade that lasted all afternoon. Although both sides nearly exhausted their ammunition in this duel, the net effect was to cause casualties in the unfortunate cavalry and infantry regiments whose duty it was to cover the guns.[75] There were ample opportunities for bravery, however, and two Bavarian cannoneers displayed tremendous courage and coolness when they pulled burning bits of wood and wadding from an ammunition wagon that had been struck by an Austrian shell.[76]

Deroy was prepared to support Davout as the threat to the south diminished, but most of the fighting was over and his assistance was no longer required.[77] The 3rd Division settled into an uncomfortable bivouac north of Schierling as darkness spread across the fields. It was neither a pleasant nor a restful night. Not only was there a general lack of bread, but the April night was bitterly cold;

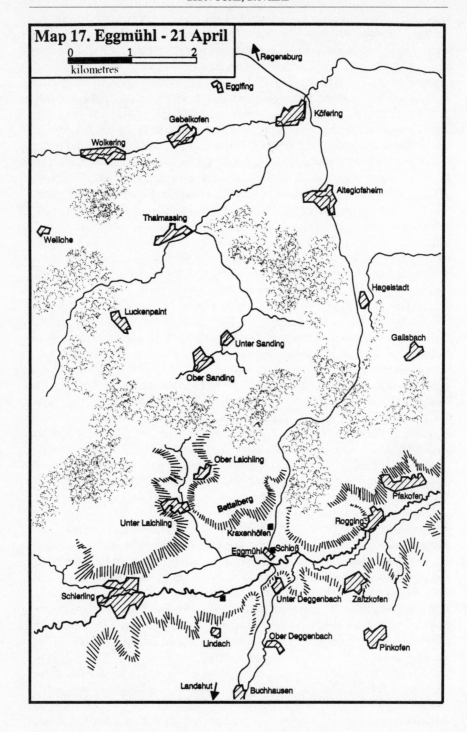

Map 17. Eggmühl - 21 April

0   1   2
kilometres

Regensburg

Egglfing

Köfering

Gebelkofen

Wolkering

Alteglofsheim

Thalmassing

Weillohe

Hagelstadt

Luckenpaint

Gailsbach

Unter Sanding

Ober Sanding

Ober Laichling

Pfakofen

Bettalberg

Unter Laichling

Rogging

Kraxenhöfen

Eggmühl   Schloß

Schierling

Unter Deggenbach   Zaitzkofen

Lindach

Ober Deggenbach

Pinkofen

Landshut   Buchhausen

the huddled infantrymen, trying to sleep on the ground, woke to find themselves covered with rime.[78]

Held back as a central reserve by Napoleon, the Crown Prince's infantry engaged in no fighting on the 21st. Marched from Rohr toward Landshut, it had reached Weihenstephan when it was ordered back to Rottenburg. It spent the frozen night here, prepared to move on Landshut or Schierling as required.[79]

THE BATTLES OF EGGMÜHL AND REGENSBURG (22-23 APRIL)

The frosty morning of 22 April thus found the Bavarian divisions scattered at Schierling, Rottenburg and Landshut, with Preysing's cavalry detachment approaching Freising. They had borne much of the fighting thus far in the campaign and this day would be no exception, for early on the 22nd, Napoleon finally realized his misapprehension: the main Austrian army under Archduke Charles's personal command was still intact, only the enemy's left wing had been defeated. Detailing Bessières to pursue the shaken Austrian left (V, VI and II Reserve Corps), the Emperor turned north to strike a hammer blow at Charles's flank near Eggmühl.

On the previous evening, Napoleon had ordered a squadron of the 1st Chevauxlegers to Essenbach on the road to Regensburg. Temporarily commanded by an Imperial officier d'ordonance, Captain de Montesquiou, the Bavarians were sent to probe towards Ergoldsbach when French and Württemberg cavalry began to file into Essenbach at about 1.30 a.m. on the 22nd.[80] The Württembergers moved ahead to form the advance guard of the great column now beginning to march north from Landshut. Although they followed the lead elements closely, the Bavarian brigade (now commanded by Oberst Anton Baron Vieregg of the 1st Dragoons) was not engaged in the initial skirmish at Buchhausen; instead, the dragoons swung left to form the link between Napoleon's column and Deroy's troops at Schierling, while the chevauxlegers were assigned to escort the Emperor. Below the Laaber, Vieregg's men met with their comrades from Seydewitz's Brigade who had been pushed south to locate Napoleon's approaching force.[81] The troopers were also reunited with the 1st Division, which arrived on the heights south of Schierling at about 2 p.m.

At approximately the same time, combat was opened all along the Allied line. On the left, Deroy's line infantry came at Unter Laichling from the south, while GD Louis Le Blond, Comte de St. Hilaire's Division (Davout's Corps) attacked from the north-west. Gotthardt's battery was posted on the hill just north of Schierling to provide supporting fire. Led by their division commander, the 14th Infantry advanced 'with varying manoeuvres according to the situation of the terrain, moving from one position to another in columns, deployed in line or spread out *en eventaille*'.[82] The assault was successful. The Austrian defenders were thrown out of the little village and the tiny woods above it, leaving two companies to be captured in the churchyard by the French. Unfortunately, the Allied infantry pursued too far and was set upon by Austrian chevauxlegers as they tried to debouch from the copse. Fleeing from the cavalry, they lost part of the wood to the reformed Austrian infantry.

At almost the same time that the 14th was being repulsed, a dramatic cavalry battle was raging in the centre of the Austrian position. The object of the struggle was a battery of sixteen guns, the centrepiece of the Austrian defence, deployed in a long, semi-circular line on the heights between Unter Laichling and Kraxenhöfen where they were clearly visible to Napoleon and his staff on the opposite bluffs.[83] The battery commanded the entire valley of the Laaber and casualties from its fire were mounting steadily; the Bavarians north of Schierling were particularly exposed and suffered accordingly. When a staff officer requested permission for the Bavarian cavalry to retire to a more protected position, Napoleon replied, 'If something is bothering us, let's get rid of it!' This almost offhand comment was taken as an order and soon passed to GM von Seydewitz. That general is said to have told Napoleon's courier, 'Ride and tell your Emperor that the battery is taken!'[84]

Seydewitz's brigade was posted on a small hill south-west of Unter Laichling; it had occupied this point with Gotthardt's battery in mid-morning when the Austrians pulled back behind the Laichlings. Seydewitz now (2.30 p.m.) took his troopers down the hill, crossed the little stream just south of Unter Laichling and headed for the guns. A stretch of dead ground ran along the base of the heights where the Austrian guns were deployed. Taking advantage of this fold in the terrain, Seydewitz quickly moved his $6^1/2$ squadrons east until they were below and just left of the batteries, swung into line and charged up the slope. With *Bubenhofen* on the right and *Taxis* on the left, the troopers were met with a storm of canister, but they galloped ahead and were soon happily sabring the scrambling Austrian gunners. Five pieces were already in Bavarian hands when GM Karl von Stutterheim counter-attacked with eight Austrian squadrons (four each of *Vincent* and *Stipsicz*). Disordered by their charge and weakened by losses, the Bavarians retreated down the hill but reformed rapidly among the other Allied cavalry gathered in the low ground west of Eggmühl. The pursuing Austrian squadrons threatened Gotthardt's battery, but were brought to a halt by well-delivered fire from the battery and nearby infantry squares.

This first attack had been repelled, but pressure on the Austrian centre did not ease. With the Württembergers forming on their left and GD Raymond de Bonardi, Comte de St. Sulpice's cuirassiers coming up on their right, the Bavarians stormed forward again at about 3.30. Now there was no time for clever manoeuvring, the brigade rode straight for the guns, reached them, but was again repulsed by a cavalry counter-attack (four squadrons of *Vincent*, three of *Stipsicz*). While still engaged with the Bavarians, however, the Austrian horsemen were hit by the Württemberg regiments. This support allowed Seydewitz to disengage and hastily reorder his ranks for yet another assault. To throw back the Württembergers, the last Austrian reserves (the remaining five squadrons of *Stipsicz*) were now committed into the swirling fury on the hillside, but the French heavies were trotting up and the Bavarians were ready to charge again. St. Sulpice's stately troopers rode over the Austrian hussars and the Allied cavalry spurred up the slope in unison. Breaking upon the enemy centre like a great wave, they scattered the remaining Austrians and took off in pursuit. This was the third charge for Seydewitz's men, but their courage was by no means exhausted. Lieutenant Joseph von Spengel of the 4th Chevauxlegers, for example, with only five fellow Bavarians, captured three Austrian cannon and participated in the seizure of two others. In all, twelve of the sixteen Austrian pieces were taken by the Allies, in large part due to the valour of von Seydewitz's troopers. They paid a heavy price. Some 164 Bavarians were dead or wounded, but they had seized the enemy's battery, broken his centre and covered themselves with glory under the eyes of the Emperor. Napoleon personally rode forward to praise the Bavarians and the Crown Prince, deeply moved, embraced Seydewitz in recognition of the brigade's bravery and sacrifice.

In the meantime, a brutal, bloody fight had developed in the little copse above Unter Laichling. As Seydewitz was suffering his first repulse, St. Hilaire's Division and the Bavarian 14th Infantry undertook a second assault on the wood. The French bore the brunt of the battle, St. Hilaire's 10th Léger's casualties exceeding 600 in the struggle for the town and wood, but the 14th's—more than 200—were also high. The little clump of trees was soon in Allied hands for a second time, but the skirmishers who swarmed out on to the plateau were again scattered by Stutterheim's cavalry. Fortunately for the Bavarians, Deroy had ordered Lieutenant Widnmann's guns to support the 14th's assault. Although he was only able to get one gun into action in the low ground on the regiment's right, his rapid canister fire checked the enemy pursuit and gave the Schützen a chance to rally on his lone cannon. About this time, the Allied cavalry was launching its final series of attacks on the Austrian centre and Rosenberg's Corps was soon in full retreat.

As the Allies organized to pursue the fleeing Austrians, Deroy relieved the 14th Infantry with the combined Schützen of the division. These detachments, reinforced by some sections of grenadiers, led the Bavarian division as it advanced through the woods and draws to Hagelstadt and Alteglofsheim; the Bavarian light battalions and Demont's men moved on the right of Deroy's line regiments and the 1st Division followed slowly in reserve. Isolated groups of Austrians were encountered, but the combined efforts of the Bavarian Schützen and artillery quickly overcame their incoherent resistance. In one of these combats, an Austrian shot tore the head from Major Lamey's horse. The unfortunate animal collapsed on its rider, but the major, despite his injuries, dragged himself from the wreckage and continued directing the fire of his guns. Although Seydewitz's Brigade and the 1st Chevauxlegers were present for the great moonlight cavalry battle at Alteglofsheim, they remained in reserve and did not actively participate in the destruction of Schneller's Austrian cuirassier brigade. As night fell, the 1st and 3rd Divisions with their cavalry bivouacked around Alteglofsheim, where Crown Prince Ludwig was almost burned to death when fires set by looting soldiers ignited the house where he was sleeping.[85]

While the Crown Prince was escaping the flames, the common Bavarian soldiers were searching for food. Poorly fed for several days, the men were famished, but the area around Alteglofsheim had already been over-foraged and there was little provender to be found. The 5th Light, however, experienced particular good fortune. The men were just settling in for another hungry night's rest 'when suddenly an ox sprang over the fence in front of the battalion's bivouac, threw off two Frenchmen who had been hanging on to its tail and, within moments, found itself slaughtered and distributed to our stewpots'.[86]

Next day Ludwig's men (minus Vieregg's Cavalry Brigade) left their encampment at about 2 p.m. for Ergoldsbach, continuing on to Landshut which they entered with much fanfare on the 24th. One battalion (II/8) trailed behind, escorting a convoy of 3,000 prisoners; it would not rejoin its regiment until the 25th. Vieregg's troopers apparently participated in the great cavalry battles south of Regensburg on the 23rd, rejoining their division at Landshut on the 24th.[87] Deroy's troops were up early, leaving their cook fires at 6 a.m. to form the reserve for Napoleon's assault on Regensburg. The only 3rd Division unit actually to engage the enemy that day, however, was von Dietrich's battery of 12-pounders. It was combined with a French battery of similar calibre at about 1 p.m. to attempt a breach in the city walls. The breach was not achieved, but the battery set a number of structures aflame, thereby contributing to the general misfortune of this much-battered city. Having spent the night outside Regensburg, the 3rd Division decamped for Landshut and points south on the 24th, reaching Ergoldsbach that evening.

THE PURSUIT OF HILLER AND JELLACIC (22-30 APRIL)

While Napoleon was ejecting Charles's main army from the area around Regensburg, Marshal Jean Bessières was given command of an *ad hoc* corps (Wrede's and Molitor's infantry divisions, Marulaz's cavalry division, Jacquinot's cavalry brigade) to pursue Hiller's force. The morning of the 22nd found Bessières in Geisenhausen with two squadrons of the 3rd Chevauxlegers under Major Harscher and the rest of the 2nd Division around Landshut. Attaching the French 2nd Chasseurs-à-Cheval to Wrede, the Marshal sent the Bavarians off to Neumarkt. En route, Beckers' Brigade was detached at Vilsbiburg to pursue three battalions of Vienna Volunteers who were retreating down the Vils. Beckers marched as far as Frontenhausen, but had no significant contact with the enemy and returned to the division at Neumarkt the next day. The division was granted the 23rd as a rest day, but the cavalry conducted some patrolling and the 6th Light was sent with the 2nd Chasseurs to support Marulaz along the River Isen. Major Harscher's two squadrons attacked a small Austrian detachment at Eggenfelden, capturing 50 soldiers, several wagons and, most importantly, more than 150 cattle. GM Preysing, with the other six squadrons of the division, arrived in Neumarkt on the evening of the 23rd. Having reached Freising on the morning of the 22nd, he had scouted toward Munich and had been prepared to undertake more serious action when recall orders arrived; his brigade had marched for Neumarkt that night (22nd). From Bessières's perspective, all was proceeding well.

Hiller, however, had managed to instil some order in his 31,000 men and was determined to counter-attack. As a prelude, he sent an advance guard toward Erharting on the evening of the 23rd to ease the next day's deployment from behind the Inn. This Austrian force pushed back GB Marulaz's cavalry screen and advanced through the darkness toward the 6th Light's positions above the Isen. Alerted by the fleeing Frenchmen, the Bavarians were anxious but prepared when a group of horsemen loomed up out of the night. Their challenge answered by a Hungarian curse, the men of the 6th coolly poured heavy volleys into the ranks of the surprised Austrian hussars. As the Bavarians tried to withdraw, however, they were charged and lost about 40 casualties before they could take cover behind nearby hedges. Despite its losses, the 6th Light had performed admirably, shielding the withdrawal of the Allied cavalry and earning Marulaz's gratitude: 'The retreat was supported by a Bavarian battalion which comported itself with extreme valour.' Marulaz pulled his squadrons back to Neumarkt under the cover of darkness to gain the protection of Wrede's Division; the Bavarian light troops also closed on their parent formation, moving

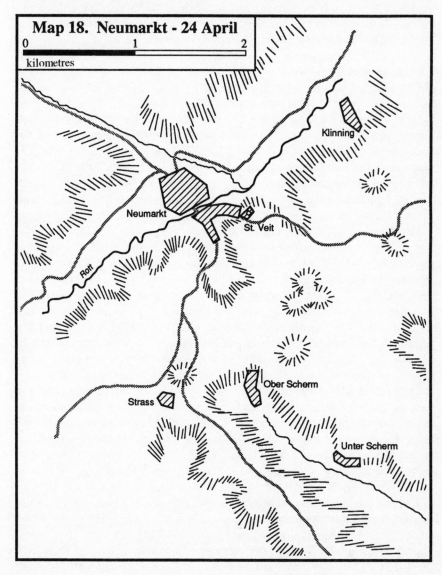

Map 18. Neumarkt - 24 April

0   1   2

kilometres

Klinning

Neumarkt

St. Veit

Rott

Ober Scherm

Strass

Unter Scherm

north to establish a line of pickets across the main road about five kilometres south of the town.[88]

THE BATTLE OF NEUMARKT (24 APRIL)

The principal Austrian attack columns encountered these pickets as Hiller advanced on Neumarkt in the early hours of the 24th. Skirmishing began around 7 a.m. and Wrede immediately alerted his troops north of the Rott. Although considerably surprised by the Austrian attack, Bessières was confident of victory and ordered Wrede to form his division on the hills south of Neumarkt. Wrede was less sanguine. In his eyes, the situation was dangerous: the unfordable Rott was spanned by only one bridge and that bridge could only be approached through the twisting and narrow alleys of the town; if withdrawal became necessary, he feared congestion, confusion and heavy losses. Bessières none the less ordered the Bavarians south of the stream and Wrede brought the 3rd, 6th and 7th Infantry Regiments across the Rott to join the 13th Infantry and 6th Light already engaged with the enemy. As the hilly terrain afforded little opportunity for cavalry action, Preysing's cavalry was left north of the stream with Marulaz's men. By 9 a.m., the 2nd Division was thus deployed as follows: 13th Infantry astride the main road from the south with two batteries; on its left, the 6th Light; north of the light battalion, the 3rd Infantry with Berchem's battery.[89] Major Harscher with his two squadrons was posted south of the Rott, but further downstream, about three kilometres west of Eggenfelden. Of Bessières's French troops, Jacquinot's brigade covered the approaches west of the 13th and Molitor's Division was en route from Vilsbiburg.

The Austrians opened the battle with attacks against the 13th Infantry. The Bavarians, however, with excellent support from their artillery, resisted vigourously and the Austrian made almost no progress. Unfortunately for Wrede, GM Bianchi attacked through a wood that formed the seam between the 13th and the 6th Light. Despite a determined defence on the part of the Bavarians, the Austrians were able to advance quickly; by 10 a.m. they had seized the village of Ober Scherm which anchored the 13th's left flank. Quickly perceiving the danger to the integrity of his defence, Wrede wasted no time in restoring the situation. The 6th Infantry was ordered forward and took the village by storm at about 10.30. Almost immediately, however, a new danger threatened. While an Austrian column on Wrede's left succeeded in pushing back the 3rd Infantry, another advanced against his weak right. With most of his reserve committed and ever-increasing numbers of Austrian appearing over the hills, Wrede realized his only hope for salvation lay in withdrawal. Bessières agreed; having just learned that a force under Radetzky was moving up the Rott from Eggenfelden to endanger the Allied left, the Marshal was anxious to extract Wrede's men while there was still time.

The order for withdrawal was given at about noon and Bavarian troops were soon headed back for the single bridge over the Rott. All Wrede's coolness and tactical skill was required to extricate his division from this difficult situation. The approaches to the bridge through the town's winding alleys were quickly clogged by retiring Bavarians, and the French 2nd Ligne, trying to cross south to cover the Bavarian withdrawal, only made matters worse. To the hard-pressed men of the 7th Infantry, however, whom Wrede had entrusted with the task of protecting the retreat, the arrival of the French regiment, rapidly reinforced by three voltigeur companies from the 16th Ligne, represented a welcome assistance. Supported by elements of the 13th, six companies of *Löwenstein* held the enemy at bay outside the village while the other two companies defended the monastery of St. Veit.[90] Wrede was everywhere, giving orders, directing movements, inspiring his men by his presence and competence. He repeatedly led the 7th forward to gain time for the rest of his division to escape. In one of these counter-attacks, Oberst Friedrich Graf von Thurn und Taxis, who had only commanded the 7th Regiment for five days, was killed and numerous other officers wounded. Wrede, his hat was pierced by a musket ball so that 'the feathers flew about like snow flakes', left the battle unscathed.

Just as the Bavarian general had feared, the scene in Neumarkt was almost chaotic. The narrow alleys were crammed with men, horses, guns and wagons, all under the fire of Austrian artillery and skirmishers. In the tense confusion, mistakes were made. Thus someone left GB Charles Jacquinot's cavalrymen at the end of the march column; unable to defend themselves in the town, they suffered severely when Austrian infantry broke into the streets.[91] With Austrian pressure mounting minute by minute, the last three companies of the 6th Infantry found themselves crossing the bridge under fire from Austrian skirmishers who had crept to within 30 metres of the span. The men of the 6th were able to escape to the north, but the 13th was not so lucky; about 100 of its soldiers were taken prisoner near the bridge. Sergeant Schmidt of the 7th Infantry, trapped in the congestion at the little bridge, only saved the regimental standard by leaping into the river and swimming to the opposite bank. Gathered on the north bank of the Rott at about 3 p.m., the Bavarians fell back on Vilsbiburg, covered by GD Gabriel Molitor's regiments.

Major Harscher brought back one bit of good news when he and his two squadrons rejoined the division that evening. Posted during the day to watch the Allied left west of Eggenfelden, they had fought a delaying action against Radetzky's Austrians throughout the afternoon. Although they had lost some 80 head of cattle, they and four companies of Molitor's infantry had managed to capture about 150 Austrians before they received word of Bessières's withdrawal and broke off the engagement.

The battle at Neumarkt was an irritating setback for the Allies and a costly one for the Bavarian 2nd Division. Bessières's insistence on fighting south of the Rott with a difficult defile to the rear cost the Bavarians almost 900 casualties, and it was only thanks to Wrede's personal courage and the steadfastness of the Bavarian and French soldiers that the figure was not higher.[92] Once again, the Bavarians had shown themselves to be reliable, dedicated soldiers. Tenacious in defence, they also demonstrated tactical flexibility and performed well in skirmish order. The skill and determination of the artillery was particularly noteworthy, as was the relative order with which the difficult withdrawal through Neumarkt was conducted.[93]

Hiller was unable to exploit his success at Neumarkt. During the night he received word of the defeats Napoleon had inflicted upon Archduke Charles and, early the next morning, his columns were headed back south toward the Inn. Bessières, chastened by the events of the 24th and confused by the contradictory reports he received, kept his force in the vicinity of Vilsbiburg throughout the 25th and the morning of the 26th.[94] The arrival of the fiery Lannes early on the 26th appears to have inspired greater activity and Wrede set forth from Vilsbiburg at about 11.30 a.m.[95] He reached Mühldorf at about 8 p.m. and immediately set about restoring the bridge. While the 6th Light drove off a few Austrian pickets, an energetic lieutenant of the engineers named Hazzi, with the help of local inhabitants, began work on the partially destroyed span. Although slightly wounded, he had the bridge in usable condition by the morning of the 27th and Wrede's Division crossed over at 6 a.m. to continue its march in the direction of Garching on the Alz. Napoleon visited Wrede while the crossing was under way and ordered him to cross the Salzach in the hopes of intercepting Jellacic's Austrian division, which Lefebvre would be pursuing from Munich. As he had been prior to the Battle of Abensberg, Wrede was again treated as an independent commander, no longer part of Bessières group and not yet returned to Lefebvre's command. Arriving at Garching that evening, the 2nd Division found no means to cross the river and marched through the night for Trostberg. This town was reached at 6 a.m. on the 28th after a wearing march, and a momentary skirmish sufficed to chase off a weak enemy cavalry outpost. Wrede's troops were headed over the Alz just two hours later, Hazzi having repaired the slightly damaged bridge in short order. Reaching Tittmoning at 1 p.m., the footsore infantry was granted a brief respite while yet another bridge was restored; Rittmeister Bernhard's squadron of *Leiningen* rode to Laufen to report on the status of the crossing there.

On the way to Laufen, Bernhard's men overthrew an outpost of *O'Reilly* Chevauxlegers at Fridolfing (about halfway from Tittmoning to Laufen), capturing a number of the Austrian troopers. Based on information from these prisoners, Wrede decided that there was still a chance to catch Jellacic; he immediately sent Preysing south to Laufen with the cavalry brigade. The bridge was already in flames when Preysing's men reached the town at about 9 p.m., but they were in time to rescue a number of salt boats from destruction. While GM Beckers with the 6th Light and 6th Infantry crossed the Salzach by boat at Tittmoning (1 a.m. on the 29th), Lieutenant Hazzi was sent to Laufen to put the bridge in order. En route, the alert engineer spotted numerous half-sunken boats along the right bank of the river. Crossing over in a punt with one chevauxleger, he roused the locals and, with their help, floated and repaired the boats; in no time, he was leading a little convoy upstream to Laufen, where three hours sufficed for the construction of a floating bridge. Wrede was thus able to send the 7th Infantry, Caspers' battery and the cavalry brigade across the river to join Beckers' column. By noon, this force was marching south on Salzburg.

Seven kilometres south of Laufen, Preysing's Brigade was attacked by six squadrons of *O'Reilly*, but quickly defeated the Austrian chevauxlegers and pressed on toward the city (1 p.m.). The Bavarians encountered more serious resistance at Bergheim where Jellacic's infantry held up Preysing's cavalry and

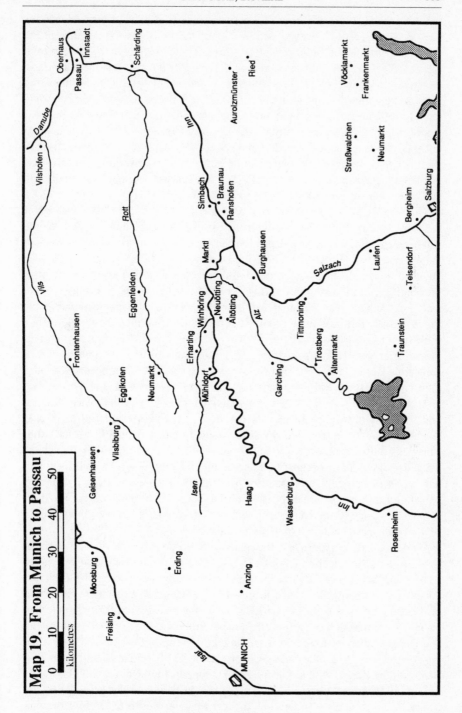

Map 19. From Munich to Passau

the 6th Light (arrived at about 3 p.m.) for several hours. As more Bavarians arrived on the scene, however, fire from Caspers' guns and the advance of the 6th Infantry with the Schützen of the 7th persuaded the Austrians to retreat again. A last defence was attempted at the gates of the city, but the Bavarians, employing canister fire at close quarters to devastating effect, threw their foe back and entered the city at about 5 p.m. The bulk of Jellacic's division had already retreated into the mountains and the remaining elements of the rear guard followed, hard pressed by the Bavarians. Most of them escaped as night fell, but Austrian losses exceeded 500 for the day against a Bavarian casualty figure of some thirteen men and two horses.[96] Wrede, satisfied with possession of the city, quickly informed Napoleon of his success but made no attempt to pursue Jellacic up the valley of the Salzach.[97]

The VII Corps was temporarily reunited in Salzburg on 30 April when Lefebvre marched into the city with the 1st and 3rd Divisions. While Wrede had been enjoying his semi-independent status, the Crown Prince and Deroy had manoeuvred east of Munich in a vain attempt to entrap Jellacic. The 1st Division departed Landshut on the morning of the 25th and spent the night in Freising.[98] The following day, Crown Prince Ludwig and his division were met with great jubilation as they marched into the capital with twelve captured guns. The men were left little time to enjoy the pleasures of Munich, however, as they took to the road again on the 27th, detaching Chef d'Escadron Gabriel Montélégier with II/4, a squadron of the 1st Dragoons and one gun to relieve Kufstein. Deroy's Division had followed the same route, halting at Moosburg (25th) and Freising (26th).[99] From the latter town, they marched to Wasserburg on the 27th to be reunited with the 1st Division. Lefebvre's goal was Salzburg and the destruction of Jellacic's force. He thus repaired the bridge at Wasserburg and sent his two divisions south-east to Altenmarkt on the 28th. The next day, Lefebvre's scouts brushed with Jellacic's outposts east of Salzburg as Wrede was preparing to break into the city. The Crown Prince with both cavalry brigades advanced on the left, while Deroy took his men to Teisendorf through Traunstein. Both divisions moved to Salzburg on 30 April, Stengel's brigade (three battalions) with half of Wagner's battery continuing on beyond the city to Hallein in pursuit of Jellacic.[100]

While Lannes, Lefebvre and Bessières were driving Hiller's Austrians out of Bavaria over the upper Inn, Massena pushed forward across the lower Inn at Passau and Schärding. On reaching the former city, he relieved the Bavarian depot battalion blockaded in the fortress of Oberhaus. This battalion, composed of depot companies from the 6th, 9th, 10th and 14th Infantry Regiments, had been formed in March to garrison the crucial fortress at the confluence of the Inn and Danube. Forced to retreat from the city into the fortress on 10 April when the Austrians invaded, the little garrison (about 800 Bavarian infantrymen, 100 Bavarian artillerists and some 50 French sappers) held out until Massena's arrival on 26 April. Greeting the hard-marching French at the city's gates, the Bavarians were quickly ordered to support Massena's efforts to cross the Inn. Three companies were transported over the river by boat to support the French commander's attack on the Innstadt. While the French and Italian (Tirailleurs of the Po) troops conducted the main assault, the Bavarian flanking crossings north and south of the Innstadt convinced the Austrians that resistance was futile. By 4 p.m. the suburb was in Allied hands and Massena's Corps was preparing to exploit its success. The Bavarians remained in Oberhaus, having suffered less than ten casualties in the course of the blockade and subsequent attack.[101]

MAY/JUNE - FLANK DUTY AT LINZ

With the end of April, the last Austrians were thus driven out of Bavaria. Napoleon dedicated himself to the offensive toward Vienna and the Bavarians were principally engaged in combating the lively insurgency in the Tyrol. The 1st and 3rd Divisions were employed against the Tyrolians as soon as Salzburg fell, but Wrede's Division covered the main army's advance down the Danube Valley for the first week of May. Departing Salzburg on 1 May, the division protected Napoleon's southern flank from Straßwalchen (1-2 May), Frankenmarkt (3 May) and finally Vöcklabruck (4-7 May). Ordered into the Tyrol on the 7th, Wrede was back in Salzburg by the 9th and soon found himself immersed in the difficult struggle against the rebellious mountaineers.[102]

Table 2-3: VII Corps at Linz in Early June
Corps staff cavalry from V/1st Dragoons

1st Division - GL Crown Prince Ludwig	2nd Division - GL von Wrede
staff company from 2nd Inf. depot	staff company from 3rd Inf. depot
staff cavalry from V/1st Chevauxlegers	staff cavalry from V/2nd Chevauxlegers
1st Leib Infantry	3rd Infantry *Prinz Karl*
2nd Infantry *Kronprinz*	6th Infantry *Herzog Wilhelm*
4th Infantry	7th Infantry *Löwenstein*
8th Infantry *Herzog Pius*	13th Infantry
1st Light *Habermann*	6th Light *La Roche*
3rd Light (two companies under Major Theobald)	2nd Chevauxlegers *König*
1st Dragoons (two squadrons)	3rd Chevauxlegers *Leiningen*
1st Chevauxlegers *Kronprinz*	Berchem's Line Battery
4th Chevauxlegers *Bubenhofen*	Dorn's Line Battery
Wagner's Line Battery	Caspers's Light Battery
Hofstetten's Line Battery	Dobl's Reserve Battery
Regnier's Light Battery	
Dietrich's Reserve Battery	
Leiningen's Reserve Battery	

Corps Artillery - Major Göschl
van Douwe's Light Battery

The Bavarians did not emerge from the mountains until late May, when the need to concentrate all his forces near Vienna led Napoleon to accept risks in the Tyrol. Initially instructed (28 May) to march to Vienna, VII Corps received new orders on the 30th directing it to relieve the Saxons of IX Corps in Linz so the latter could join the Emperor at the Austrian capital. Linz represented an important depot and bridgehead for the army and Napoleon was concerned that FZM Johann Graf Kolowrat-Krakowsky, commanding the Austrian III Corps, would attempt another assault against the city.[103] The Crown Prince, having departed St. Gilgen on the 28th, was at Lambach when the revised orders reached him; in the same period, Wrede had marched from Salzburg to Steyr. In accordance with these new instructions, Lefebvre united both divisions in Linz on 31 May, leaving

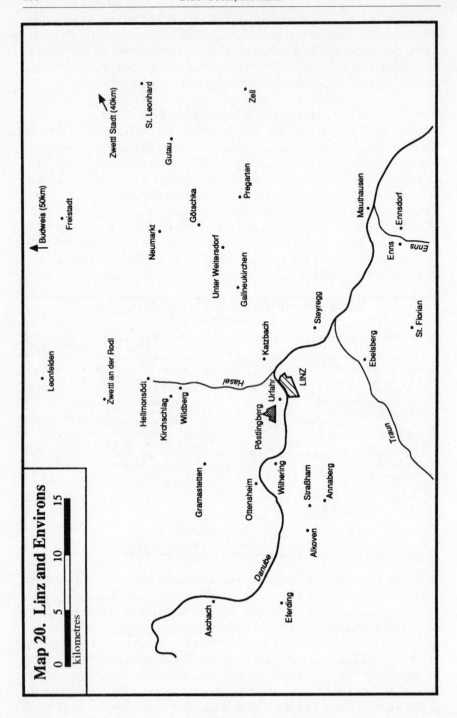

Map 20. Linz and Environs

only Deroy (6,800) to contain the Tyrolian insurgency. The 1st Division (7,500), bolstered by the addition of the 3rd Light, 4th Chevauxlegers and von Dietrich's Battery, was stationed on the north side of the Danube, while the 2nd (7,200) garrisoned Linz and watched the southern bank of the great river.[104] These dispositions were soon changed, however, and the divisions exchanged duties on 2 June. The Crown Prince's responsibilities on the southern shore included outposting the River Enns and establishing a mobile column to deal with Austrian incursions from across the Danube. The mobile column, composed of I/8, 4th Chevauxlegers and two of Wagner's guns, was formed on 6 June at Napoleon's order and operated between Ybbs, Amstetten and Wallsee.[105]

Duty at Linz was difficult and dull. Still not convinced of the Bavarians' ability to perform outpost tasks effectively, Lefebvre issued intricate instructions to his commanders, detailing precisely how they were to accomplish these duties.[106] Every day, a quarter of the troops were thus to be up and battle-ready from 11 p.m. to 3 a.m. and the entire garrison was to be under arms from 3 a.m. until reconnaissances showed no danger to exist. This sort of requirement came on top of the myriad other duties expected of VII Corps; the constant drilling, patrolling and construction work were particularly exhausting. The unpleasant situation was compounded by meagre rations. The area around Linz had been swept clean by previous corps and the Bavarians had to exist on bread and a half pound of meat per man per day from French magazines; even this ration was reduced in practice because the meat was measured 'in the French style' to include the weight of head and lungs much to the disgust of the Bavarians. Furthermore, the soldiers were not receiving regular pay, so they were unable to purchase supplements to their Army rations. Despite these irritations, there seems to have been general agreement that the prospect of engagement with the enemy's regular forces made the stay at Linz far preferable to continued combat with the vicious and elusive Tyrolians.[107]

To determine the strength and intentions of the Austrians north of Linz, on 3 June, Wrede sent patrols out along the four major roads leading to Linz north of the Danube; the only Austrians encountered were some Uhlans on the road to Gallneukirchen and these were quickly dispersed by the Schützen of the 6th Infantry. The next day, a larger endeavour was mounted toward Hellmonsödt. With three companies of the 7th Infantry, a cavalry platoon and a gun, GM Beckers advanced toward the town, but found an Austrian battalion holding the fortified manor at Wildberg. He withdrew after a 90-minute skirmish when a second enemy battalion made its appearance. Through these reconnaissances and reports from deserters, Lefebvre learned that the bulk of the Austrian III Corps had departed, leaving only FML Hannibal Graf Somariva with some 8-10,000 men north of Linz.[108] North of the river, a series of small skirmishes occurred along the fringes of the Bavarian perimeter on the 7th (Ottensheim), 8th (Steyregg) and 11th (Auhof and Gallneukirchen), but Somariva lacked the strength for any serious offensive operations. Partly to relieve the monotony and partly to chasten the enemy, Wrede conducted two brief forays on 19 and 23 June. In the first expedition, three battalions, four squadrons and Caspers' battery marched out to Ottensheim, drove off enemy patrols and destroyed some thirty boats the enemy had collected along the north bank. Having found no appreciable Austrian force on his left, Lefebvre next sent Wrede north to Hellmonsödt. With 6th Infantry, I/3, II/13, 2nd Chevauxlegers and the ubiquitous Caspers, Wrede headed north along side roads and encountered 2,000 Austrians with four guns in a fortified position at Kirchschlag. Personally leading II/13 and a squadron of chevauxlegers around the Austrian flank, he dislodged the enemy force and pursued them back through Hellmonsödt. Considering his task completed, the general marched back to Linz via the main road with 50 prisoners; GM Minucci simultaneously took a detachment to Gramastetten to divert Somariva's attention, but found no Austrians and returned to the bridgehead in the evening.[109] This was the 2nd Division's last action around Linz, several days later it was called to Vienna by new orders from the Emperor.

The 1st Division's encounters with the enemy in June were limited. The Austrians attempted raids across the Danube near Grein on the 16th and 19th; in the first instance, the Habsburg troops were driven off before they landed, in the second, about 120 men got on to the southern shore, but were quickly repulsed. Activity near Enns consisted of a cannonade on the 21st and two small raids on the 26th and 30th. In most cases, the Bavarians could not prevent the Austrians crossing, but reacted rapidly to drive off their attackers once they were ashore.[110]

JULY - WREDE TO WAGRAM AND ZNAIM

Events now moved rapidly for the 2nd Division. Alerted to move to Vienna on the 30th, Wrede's men transferred their responsibilities to the Crown Prince's

---

Table 2-4: Wrede's March to Vienna

Advance Guard
  Preysing's Cavalry Brigade
  Caspers's Battery

Main Body
  1st Brigade (GM Minucci)
  Artillery: Berchem, Dorn, Dobl, Hofstetten and Wagner
    [the latter two detached from 1st Division]
  2nd Brigade (GM Beckers)
  Baggage

Strength	
Infantry -	5,544
Cavalry -	1,103
Artillery -	768
Total --	7,415 men
	36 guns

troops at 10 p.m. that night and were en route for the Austrian capital by 2:30
a.m. on 1 July.[111] Reinforced by two batteries from the 1st Division, they
marched an average of thirteen hours and 40 kilometres per day to reach St.
Pölten on the evening of the 3rd. Here Wrede received a new message from
Berthier: 'My dear General, if you desire to participate in the affair before us,
you must arrive on the Isle of Lobau, near Ebersdorf at 5 a.m. on the 5th.'
Wrede thus set his weary soldiers on another long march on 4 July, bringing
them into Purkersdorf just outside of Vienna. Here again, new instructions
changed his plans: he was now to rest his division at Schönbrunn on the 5th after
marching another ten kilometres. In all, the division had covered more than 225
kilometres in slightly over four days, an impressive feat of marching by any
measure.

Approaching the great city, the men could hear the leaden roll of guns from
across the Danube. They seem to have presented a dreadful sight: 'The
Bavarian troops were so exhausted that they collapsed on the street corners and
their pathetic appearance awakened pity.' Hauptmann Berchem was so tired
that he twice dozed off and fell from his horse.[112] Despite his own exhaustion,
Wrede immediately betook himself to Napoleon's headquarters near Raasdorf
on the plain of the Marchfeld, leaving his men to recuperate and dry themselves
out (they had marched through a tremendous rainstorm the previous night). He
arrived at about 10 p.m. and was cordially greeted by Napoleon, but received no
orders until almost 1 a.m. Concerned that he and his men would lose their
chance for glory, the ambitious Bavarian was relieved when he finally learned
that the 2nd Division was to cross the Danube at dawn and await further instructions at Groß Enzersdorf.

The sun was already rising when Wrede returned to his men. Dressed in their
parade uniforms, the Bavarians crossed into the Marchfeld on the morning of the
6th to be met by the scuttling fugitives of the French left wing. 'In general',
wrote one cavalry officer, 'the initial appearance of the battlefield . . . was not
cheery'.[113] Expecting to be sent to the left to shore up the endangered flank,
Wrede reported to Napoleon. He found the Emperor of Battles completely composed and, to his not inconsiderable astonishment, was directed to join the
French Guard in reserve. The Guardsmen greeted the Bavarians with loud
cheers and Napoleon himself spoke a few words to them, praising their courage
and emphasizing the importance he attached to their arrival at this critical
moment in the battle. Before long, the entire Allied army seemed to be in
motion, taking the offensive across the field. While Davout steadily advanced
on the left, however, GD Etienne Macdonald's crucial attack against the
Austrian centre faltered and Napoleon sent for Wrede. His orders were brief:
'Now I unleash you; you see Macdonald's awkward position. March! Relieve
his corps, attack the enemy; in short, act as you think best!'

Wrede rapidly organized his men into three echelons: the four 6-pounder batteries in the first line, the infantry in the second and the cavalry brigade in the
third with Caspers' battery. At about 2 p.m., Wrede's column marched forward
past the bloody wreckage of Macdonald's Corps to come up on the Frenchman's
right between Aderklaa and Süßenbrunn. The appearance of the Bavarian guns

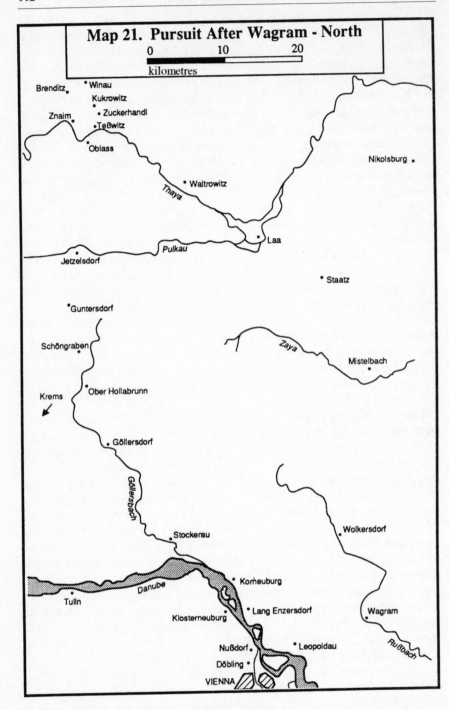

Map 21. Pursuit After Wagram - North

allowed Macdonald's enfeebled infantry to resume its own advance: 'I had no more artillery, but it was replaced by that of the Bavarians. Thirty pieces were placed in battery and suppressed the Austrian batteries. My troops resumed the offensive...'[114] Archduke Charles, however, had already decided on retreat, and Wrede cautiously followed the Austrian rear guards toward Gerasdorf, attempting to inflict as much damage as possible through artillery fire. Manhandling their guns forward, the Bavarians reached the base of the Bisamberg near Stammersdorf at about 5 p.m. and engaged in a lengthy duel with Austrian cannon on the slopes above.[115]

In the closing phases of the pursuit, between Gerasdorf and Stammersdorf, the cavalry took part in several attacks on Austrian infantry. Charges by lone squadrons of the 2nd and 3rd Chevauxlegers succeeded in scattering and capturing Austrian skirmishers but could make no impression on the masses of formed troops. Lieutenant Münch and a few troopers of *Leiningen* broke through the enemy's line of skirmishers, for example, aiming to attack the masses beyond. On hearing an Austrian officer shout 'Those few men can't hurt you! Prepare to fire!' however, the lieutenant and his handful of chevauxlegers wisely turned about and rode for safety. In one of the final mêlées of the day, the Polish Chevauxlegers of the Guard charged cavalry of the Austrian I Corps which was covering a battery of 12-pounders. Countercharged by the *Schwarzenberg* Uhlans, the Poles were forced to retire in haste and the whole great bundle of roiling lancers washed over Hauptmann Wagner's unfortunate battery. Ordered up to support the charge, the battery was caught in the process of unlimbering and was in great peril of being overrun. While most of the pieces quickly limbered and drove off, two of its cannon overturned and a number of the gunners and drivers were sabred or captured before the Austrian horsemen retired. Fortunately, the Uhlans were unable to carry off the guns and these were soon rescued by the Bavarians. While directing his guns against the Austrian cavalry, Wrede was wounded by an artillery shell and forced to leave the field. GM Minucci assumed command of the division and carried on the fight until almost 9 p.m., but no further progress was made.[116] The Bavarian division, having lost only 32 men during the course of this hot day, camped for the night between Gerasdorf and Massena's Corps at Leopoldau.[117]

There was to be no respite for the 2nd Division. At 5 a.m. on the 7th, the troops were up and moving, marching with the French Guard as Napoleon set out to determine the direction of Charles's retreat. The Emperor personally sent Oberst Lindenau with two squadrons of his regiment (*Leiningen*) on a reconnaissance toward Kornneuburg and Stockerau; the cavalry took a few prisoners on this little escapade while their comrades conducted a difficult if short march (twelve kilometres) to Wolkersdorf.[118] Attached to GD Auguste Marmont's XI Corps that night, Minucci's men were on the road again at 2 a.m. on the 8th. The *König* Chevauxlegers drove off Austrian pickets at Mistelbach and XI Corps bivouacked around this little town. The 9th brought a skirmish near Staatz where Preysing's Brigade distinguished itself in a charge against the Austrian rear guard's artillery and cavalry that cost the 3rd Chevauxlegers their commander, Oberst August von Floret; the division proceeded on to Laa, pushing its vanguard across the Thaya. The men of *Leiningen* buried their colonel, one of Wrede's oldest and closest friends, in a moving ceremony at 2 a.m. on the 10th before mounting up to continue the pursuit to Znaim.

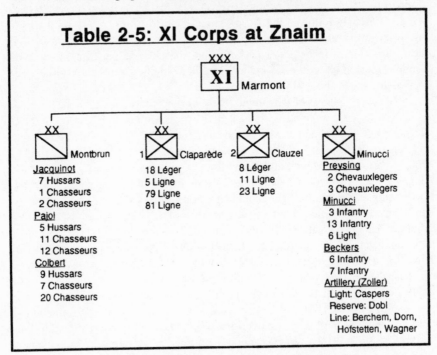

Table 2-5: XI Corps at Znaim

XXX
XI Marmont

XX Montbrun	1 XX Claparède	2 XX Clauzel	XX Minucci
<u>Jacquinot</u>	18 Léger	8 Léger	<u>Preysing</u>
7 Hussars	5 Ligne	11 Ligne	2 Chevauxlegers
1 Chasseurs	79 Ligne	23 Ligne	3 Chevauxlegers
2 Chasseurs	81 Ligne		<u>Minucci</u>
<u>Pajol</u>			3 Infantry
5 Hussars			13 Infantry
11 Chasseurs			6 Light
12 Chasseurs			<u>Beckers</u>
<u>Colbert</u>			6 Infantry
9 Hussars			7 Infantry
7 Chasseurs			<u>Artillery (Zoller)</u>
20 Chasseurs			Light: Caspers
			Reserve: Dobl
			Line: Berchem, Dorn,
			Hofstetten, Wagner

THE BATTLE OF ZNAIM (10-11 JULY)

The Bavarians had escaped the brutality of Wagram almost unscathed, but the clash at Znaim would cost them dearly. Although the corps started off at 3 a.m., the weather was cruelly hot and there were many watercourses to cross, so that Marmont did not come upon the Austrian positions around Znaim until almost noon. Austrian skirmishers had settled into the vineyards on the heights east of the little village of Tesswitz, and the Bavarian Schützen were sent forward to root them out. It was only when several guns and some formed companies of the 6th Infantry deployed, however, that the enemy could be compelled to retire. Having cleared the heights by about 2 p.m., Marmont ordered Minucci and GD Bertrand Clauzel forward to break through the Austrian defence and cut off what he supposed to be the Archduke's rear guard.[119]

Well supported by the Bavarian batteries (Marmont's only artillery) deployed on the heights and covered by the Schützen of the 13th Regiment, GM Beckers led the 6th Infantry into Tesswitz. He held the village for only a few minutes before Austrian reinforcements forced him to abandon it. Hardly deterred, Beckers gathered additional support (I/7, two companies of the 13th and two companies of French voltigeurs) and stormed the town again. With a constant stream of troops crossing the Thaya to the north, however, Charles had plenty of men to hurl into the fight for Tesswitz; a renewed effort thus pushed Beckers'

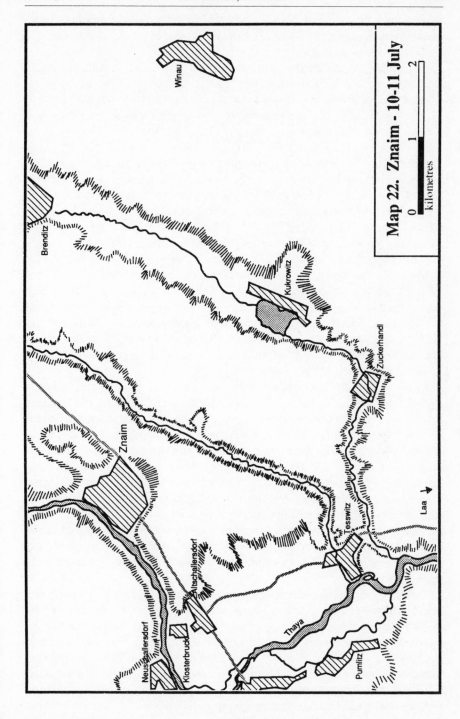

Map 22. Znaim - 10-11 July

men back to the very last houses of the village. Observing Beckers' plight, Marmont rode quickly to GM von Preysing:

> General, you see the desperate situation of your infantry and how they stand in need of support, but in this terrain I cannot order you to support them with your cavalry. If you wish to undertake it, however, and if you believe you can do it, you will certainly do me a great service, but I tell you again, I cannot order it.

The dangerous situation was clear enough and Preysing sprang to Beckers' assistance, sending Reibold's squadron of *König* to attack the Austrian infantry west of Tesswitz. Reibold was killed and his squadron was repulsed by heavy fire, but Preysing threw the rest of the regiment into the the fray and relieved the pressure on the infantry long enough for Beckers to reoccupy the town. The struggle raged back and forth through the streets with great ferocity. Steady Austrian reinforcements were met by additional Bavarian troops until almost all of Minucci's Division was involved in the vicious maelstrom. The only troops left were a few companies covering the artillery on the heights and II/7, which crossed to the south side of the Thaya to clear out Austrian skirmishers late in the afternoon. Finally, as darkness began to fall, the Austrians retired and left the burning village in Bavarian hands.[120] Relieved in the town by two of GD Michel Claparède's regiments (79th and 81st Ligne), Minucci took his exhausted division back behind the heights for the night.

The bitter fight for Tesswitz, in which the town seems to have changed hands at least four times, cost the 2nd Division 900 casualties, making it the bloodiest day for any Bavarian division in the 1809 campaign. Although the battle continued with renewed fury on the 11th, the Bavarians constituted the second echelon of Marmont's Corps and were not committed to any of the attacks on the heights of Znaim. The only exceptions were the Schützen of the 3rd and 13th Regiments and elements of the 6th Light, who advanced up the the vineyard-covered slopes several times, but took few losses. The artillery batteries provided supporting fire to Marmont's attacks from the bluff they had occupied the previous day, Lieutenant Dobl receiving a personal congratulation from the Emperor for his performance. The battle and the campaign ended at 6 p.m., when staff officers from both armies rode between the lines to announce the ceasefire.[121]

Marmont praised the Bavarian troops in his Order of the Day on 12 July: 'The Marshal, Duke of Ragusa, expresses his satisfaction with the valour shown by the Bavarian Division in its attacks on the village of Tesswitz and with the determination shown in the defence of the same.' He also visited both Minucci and Beckers at their camps to communicate his appreciation of the Bavarians' courage, promising to include this in his report to the Emperor. In later years, however, Marmont exhibited an almost petty bitterness, complaining of the 'softness' of the Bavarian troops and averring that whereas the entire Bavarian division was required to hold Tesswitz, the task was later accomplished by a single French regiment. The casualties suffered by the 2nd Division and their ability to launch repeated assaults on the village would seem clear argument against the Marshal's retrospective vitriol.[122]

In the uncertain period following the declaration of the armistice, the 2nd Division returned to Linz, departing Znaim on the 13th and marching by easy stages north of the Danube to join the 1st Division on the 20th. While Wrede's Division was enduring the strenuous marches and ferocious battles of July, the Crown Prince's men had coped with the wearing tedium of tense outpost duty and the constant annoyances of the enemy. There were minor disturbances along the Danube near Enns: a cannonade on the 5th and a raid on the 10th that cost the 8th Infantry some prisoners and almost resulted in the loss of two guns. The Austrians also attempted a bold probe against the bridgehead at Auhof and Katzbach on the 7th. This effort was broken up by a small column (composed of the 1st Light and half of van Douwe's battery) which threw the enemy back to Gallneukirchen. Finally, GM Joseph von Rechberg conducted a reconnaissance toward the same town on the 12th with I/1, a squadron of 1st Dragoons and a howitzer; pushing back the Austrian advanced posts and a small force he encountered at Götschka, he returned to Linz when faced with enemy reserves near Neumarkt. The armistice brought an end to these small combats and also made the presence of the 3rd Division superfluous. Over the 13th and 14th, the bulk of the 3rd Division had arrived in Linz. Ordered up from the Tyrol on 3 July, Deroy's troops took over duties on the southern bank of the Danube for a few days before returning to the mountains on the 17th. Relieved by the 2nd, the 1st Division marched for Salzburg on the 23rd and, by early October, Wrede's men would also be called to those parlous valleys and passes to combat the intractable Tyrolians.[123]

The Bavarians played a crucial role in the battles against the Austrian army in 1809. From the first nervous observations of cavalry pickets along the Inn to the final rounds of grape on the Thaya, the soldiers of King Max served their French Emperor well. If perhaps not as vigourous and durable as the Württembergers or as impetuous as the French themselves, they proved solid, courageous, reliable soldiers. And they were well led. Deroy was a competent veteran and Wrede, for all his ambition and obstreperous independence, was a valuable leader on the battlefield. Even the difficult Crown Prince, guided by the able Raglovich, performed satisfactorily. The cavalry brigadiers are also worthy of note; all three, particularly von Seydewitz and von Preysing, demonstrated a keen eye for the tactical situation and a sure ability to motivate their troopers. The infantry was steady, the cavalry determined in the attack (if not always wise in the defence) and the artillery both brave and capable. Moreover, all three arms displayed an excellent grasp of flexible tactical manoeuvre. Their weaknesses included outpost duty, marching (with several notable exceptions, they never matched the feats of the French and Württembergers), commanders' initiative (such as on 19 April) and command and control (Wrede on 20 April for example); they also acquired an unpleasant reputation for being hard on the local populations wherever they were quartered.[124] Many of these 'weaknesses', however, can be laid at the doors of their French superiors (e.g., Lefebvre and even Napoleon) and should not blind us to the value of the Bavarians as soldiers. Indeed, inspired by leaders such as Wrede at his best, the Bavarians performed marvellously under trying circumstances (e.g., his attack at Pfeffenhausen on 20/21 April or his pursuit of Jellacic). Napoleon and the French owed no little debt to the fidelity and valour of the Bavarian soldiers in 1809.[125]

NOTES

1: See Kurt Uebe, *Die Stimmungsumschwung in der Bayerischen Armee gegenüber den Franzosen 1806-1812*, München: Beck, 1939, pp. 45-7, 50-2.

2: Both quotes come from a 1799 report of the Bavarian Inspector General of Infantry, GM Franz Joseph von Gaza. Quoted in Ernst Aichner, 'Das bayerische Heer in den Napoleonischen Kriegen', in Hubert Glaser, ed., *Krone und Verfassung*, vol. III/1, München: Piper, 1980, pp. 241, 242. Benjamin Thompson Graf von Rumford was an American who fought for the English in the War of Independence; in Bavarian service after 1784, he enjoyed great favour from Kurfürst Karl Theodor, eventually reaching the post of Chief of Staff. He attempted to introduce a series of reforms in the Bavarian service including a new uniform of his own design.

3: Aichner, p. 242-8.

4: Oskar Bezzel, *Geschichte des Königlich Bayerischen Heeres unter König Max I. Joseph von 1806 (1804) bis 1825*, vol. 6/1 of *Geschichte des Bayerischen Heeres*, München: Schick, 1933, pp. 197-9. Wrede also made a major contribution to the new regulations; the section on skirmishing (4. Abschnitt) was almost entirely his work.

5: Ibid., pp. 66-73; Aichner, p. 243.

6: Aichner, p. 242-8.

7: An excellent account of the development of Bavaria and its relationship with France in the Napoleonic era is provided in Marcus Junkelmann, *Napoleon und Bayern*, Regensburg: Pustet, 1985.

8: Bezzel, *Heeres*, p. 19.

9: The battery was the tactical artillery unit and is used here as a measure of the army's strength. For administrative purposes, the artillery was organized into a single regiment of four battalions, each composed of three foot companies, one light company and one depot company (made up of personnel unfit for field service, they were intended to man the guns of Bavaria's fortresses). The lone train battalion (Artillerie- und Armee-Fuhrwesensbataillon) was also included in the artillery regiment.

10: The Garrison Regiment was composed of those officers and men no longer suited for field duty. It was divided into 8 'stations' throughout Bavaria: Rothenberg (headquarters), Nymphenburg, Oberhaus, Rosenberg, Eichstätt, Würzburg, Stadtamhof and Donauwörth. Its members wore a single-breasted dark-blue coat with white collar and cuffs, grey breeches, black gaiters and the ubiquitous Raupenhelm. It does not seem to have played any significant role in the 1809 campaign. Bezzel, *Heeres*, pp. 86-7 and Anlage 1. Sapherson gives its strength as 1,200 in 1809 (note, however, that the regiment's subordinates were not designated companies until 1811), C. A. Sapherson, *A Year at War: 1809*, Leeds: Raider, 1986, p. 33.

11: The mutiny resulted from the bewildering politics of the time: in 1803, Bavaria had acquired the Duchy of Würzburg, but in 1806, it was required to give up this territory (to compensate the former Grand Duke of Tuscany and Prince of Salzburg, Archduke Ferdinand of Austria; Bavaria was compensated for this loss by accessions elsewhere). The 12th Regiment contained a large number of native Würzburgers, who could not wait for all the details of this trade to be resolved. No longer considering Max Joseph their monarch, they became disorderly and about 450 eventually mutinied, marching safely back to Würzburg with much fanfare. The mutineers were soon followed by a French detachment, however, which apprehended most of them and turned them over to Bavarian military justice. The rebels were tried and most of the officers and NCOs punished; the remainder of the soldiers were marched back to Würzburg in dishonour. See Bezzel, *Heeres*, pp. 51-52.

12: Holding to an old tradition, each company was endowed with a title:

I. Bataillon	II. Bataillon
1st Grenadier company	2nd Grenadier company
1st Leib company	2nd Colonel's company
5th second Major's company	6th first Captain's company
7th second Captain's company	8th third Captain's company
3rd Lieutenant-Colonel's company	4th first Major's company

The Lieutenant-Colonel's and first Major's companies formed the depot. Strengths of line regiments and light battalions taken from Drouet d'Erlon's report of 12 April (Saski, vol. II, Situation Annex). The largest regiment was the 4th (1,655), while the 10th and 5th had the fewest men (each about 1,570); the other regiments ranged from 1,601 to 1,629. Note that these figures are not always in agreement with those in regimental histories.

13: Bezzel, *Heeres*, p. 199 and Friedrich Münich, *Geschichte der Entwicklung der bayerischen Armee seit zwei Jahrhunderten*, München: Lindau, 1864, pp. 211, 243. Although there was practically no time to acquaint these new Schützen with their duties as skirmishers, they performed well in the campaign. Note that two recent English language references incorrectly allot an additional company (Schützen company) to each battalion: George Nafziger, *The Armies of Kingdom of Bavaria and the Grand Duchy of Würzburg 1792-1815*, privately published, 1991; and Ray Johnson, *Napoleonic Armies*, London: Arms & Armour, 1984. A Schützen company was indeed formed in each battalion, but not until 29 April 1811 (other changes included reducing the number of men per company to 150 and adding a second depot company to each light battalion). The oganizational details used here are taken from Bezzel, Münich, and various regimental histories.

14: Notes on the light battalion commanders follow. The 2nd Light had been under OTL Ditfurth until 17 March 1809, when he was promoted and transferred to command the 11th Infantry; his place at the head of the battalion was taken by OTL Dominikus Wreden. Simultaneously, Major Freiherr von Donnersberg was promoted to Oberstlieutenant and assumed Wreden's previous post as commander of the 4th Light; 'Donnersberg' is often spelled 'Donnersperg'. The 5th Light's 'Butler' is spelled 'Buttler' in many accounts. The 6th Light was actually known as *Taxis* until 19 April when OTL Graf Thurn und Taxis turned over his battalion to OTL Freiherr von La Roche; Thurn und Taxis went to command the 7th Infantry (Friedrich Mändler, *Erinnerungen aus meinen Feldzügen*, Franz J. A. Schneidawind, ed., Nürnberg: Lotzbeck, 1854, p. 5). OTL Günther would be killed in the Tyrol in May and replaced by OTL von Treuberg.

15: The 7th Light Infantry was a relatively new unit, but, unlike its fellow light battalions, it could hardly be considered élite. Raised as the Tyrolian Jäger Battalion in 1807, it was originally uniformed in traditional Tyrolian colours (grey accented with dark-green and light-blue) in an effort to make service under the Bavarian flag more attractive to these recalcitrant mountaineers. The felt shako was also part of the recruiting scheme. The unit was thus provided with a certain degree of individuality. When the battalion was renamed as the 7th Light Infantry in 1808, the uniform was altered to resemble more closely that of its fellows; only the shako remained as a measure of distinctiveness. The battalion's performance reflected the attitude of most Tyrolians toward Bavarian rule: motivation was poor and desertion rife; its commander, OTL Günther, reported that it was composed of 'Tyrolians of the worst class' (25 April report). See Bezzel, *Heeres*, Anlage 1; and Johann von Heilmann, 'Der Feldzug von 1809 in Tirol, im salzburgischen und an der bayerischen Südgrenze,' *Jahrbücher für die deutsche Armee und Marine*, Bände 68 and 69 (1888), Band 88 (1893).

16: Each cavalry regiment was subdivided as follows:
   Field Units
   1st (Colonel's) Division: Leib Squadron and Colonel's Squadron
   3rd (Major's) Division: 2nd Major's Squadron and Rittmeister's Squadron
   Depot Units
   2nd (Lt. Colonel's) Division: Lt. Colonel's Squadron and 1st Major's Squadron.
   Bezzel, *Heeres*, p. 60. According to Drouet's report of 12 April, the cavalry regiments generally began the war with slightly more than 500 men in the saddle (Saski, vol. II, Situation Annex).

17: Quote from Rudolf Ritter von Xylander, *Geschichte des 1. Feldartillerie-Regiments Prinz-Regent Luitpold*, Berlin: Mittler und Sohn, 1909, p. 129. The comings and goings of the Bavarian artillery companies in 1809 are painfully complex. The personnel for the battery in the Tyrol, for example, were provided by two different companies (half of Binder's Company and half of Roppelt's Company). The six companies remaining in Bavaria were divided among the following locations: Forchheim (one company), Rosenberg and Rothenberg (one company), Rain and Landsberg (one company), Oberhaus (one-half Binder's Company and one-fourth Roppelt's Company), the depot in Munich (one-fourth of Roppelt's Company).

18: The three divisions were deployed to Augsburg, Straubing and Nürnberg. See G. Paulus, 'Bayerische Kriegsvorbereitungen, Mobilmachung und Einleitung zum Feldzuge 1809', *Darstellungen aus der Bayerischen Kriegs- und Heeresgeschichte*, Heft 2, München: Lindau, 1893. This monograph provides an excellent overview of the Bavarian preparations for the 1809 campaign (particularly the gathering of intelligence). After the conference, Napoleon, accepting Alexander's assurances of support, believed that the threat of Russian intervention would hold Austria in check, allowing him to clean up the untidy mess in Spain.

19: Junkelmann uses the phrase 'der glänzendste Feldzug' to describe 1809.

20: Paulus, pp. 117-23.

21: The procurement of draft animals for the Train Battalion provides a good example of the improvements, Bezzel, *Heeres*, p. 73.

22: Deployment to these locations was complete by 20 March.

23: Napoleon's letter to Max is from *Correspondence* 14901, 14 March 1809. Ludwig's comment is from a letter written to his father in 1807 while on his first campaign; it is typical of his sanctimonious attitude toward Napoleon and the French. Ludwig even engaged in a fevered correspondence with one of Vienna's leading ministers, Count Stadion, in the months before the war, writing such lines as: 'It is well known that I would rather fight against the French than for them.' Although his perfervid prose may have helped convince the Austrians that all of Germany was prepared to rise up against Napoleon, his sentiments were not representative of the feeling in the Bavarian Army and his youthful sound and fury came to naught. See Count Corti, *Ludwig I of Bavaria*, Evelyn B. Graham Stamper, trans., London: Thornton Butterworth, 1938, pp. 68-75.

24: F. von Fabrice, *Das Königlich Bayerische 6. Infanterie-Regiment Kaiser Wilhelm, König von Preußen*, II. Teil, 1805 bis 1835, München: Oldenburg, 1896, pp. 164-5.

25: Regimental histories frequently complain about the timing of this change and the confusion it caused for rapid, tactical deployment of the infantry. See, for example, Fabrice, pp. 160-1; Major Gerneth and Premierlieutenant Kießling, *Geschichte des königlich Bayerischen 5. Infanterie-Regiments*, Berlin: Mittler & Sohn, 1893, pp. 188-9; and Hauptmann Zoellner, *Geschichte des K. B. 11. Infanterie-Regiments 'von der Tann'*, *1805-1905*, München: Lindau, 1905, p. 54. The formation of squares was particularly troublesome (Franz Berg, *Geschichte des königl. Bayer. 4. Jäger-Bataillons*, Landshut: Rietsch, 1887, vol. I, p. 211).

26: In addition to its combat units, each division was allotted a company and a half-squadron to support the division commander and staff (e.g., perform escort, messenger, guard and reconaissance tasks). These units were drawn from regimental depots as shown. The companies numbered about 180 men and the cavalry half-squadrons about 60 troopers. In May, another half-squadron was detached for duty at Corps headquarters. See Anlage 10 to Oskar Bezzel, 'Die Maßnahmen Bayerns zum Grenzschutze im Feldzuge 1809', *Darstellungen aus der Bayerischen Kriegs- und Heeresgeschichte*, Heft 14, München: Lindau, 1905; and E. Heinze, *Geschichte des kgl. Bayer. 6. Chevauxlegers-Regiments 'Prinz Albrecht von Preußen' 1803 bis 1871*, Leipzig: Klinkhardt, 1898, p. 364. Drouet's 12 April situation report (Saski, vol. II, Annex) lists a slightly different distribution: 1st Division with one squadron (137 men), 2nd and 3rd Divisions each with a half-squadron of 60 men, a squadron of 126 men for the Corps headquarters.

27: As hostilities edged closer, Lefebvre desired greater concentration in his dispositions and thus pulled the 1st Division closer to the capital on 3 April (Eduard Freiherr von Völderndorff und Waradein, *Kriegsgeschichte von Bayern unter König Maximilian Joseph I.*, München, 1826, vol. II, p. 43). The shift of the 3rd Division (late March) was apparently made to conform with Napoleon's general concept of operations, which envisioned Deroy falling back through Freising to join the 1st Division and the majority of the French forces on the line of the Lech (as explicated in Berthier's orders of 21 March, *Krieg 1809*, vol. I, pp. 148-9). See also Heinze, pp. 326-7.

28: This detachment consisted of Seydewitz's cavalry brigade, the 5th Infantry, the 7th Light and three guns. It moved to Erding on the 10th.

29: Paulus, pp. 123-5; Zoellner, p. 56.

30: Deroy's directive quoted in Berg, vol. I, p. 212.

31: The King departed Munich for Dillingen on the 11th.

32: Lefebvre was not satisfied with the Bavarians' performance on scouting and outpost duty. Although he constantly reaffirmed his faith in their loyalty to King and Emperor, he repeatedly asked Berthier for French cavalry and light infantry to take up these tasks. *Krieg 1809*, vol. I, pp. 298-9; Binder von Kriegelstein, *1809*, p. 155.

33: The history of the 1st Chevauxlegers (redesignated 3rd Chevauxlegers in 1811) says the fight at Erding took place on the 15th, but the Austrian official relation (14th) seems more accurate and is used here (Emil Buxbaum, *Das königlich Bayerische 3. Chevauxlegers-Regiment 'Herzog Maximilian' 1724 bis 1884*, München: Oldenbourg, 1884, p. 122; *Krieg 1809*, vol. I, p. 244-245). Casualties at Erding were several wounded on each side (*Krieg 1809*, vol. I, p. 244; and Heinze, pp. 328-329). There was no real fighting at Moosburg as Scheibler's force (eight companies and two squadrons) greatly outnumbered the Bavarians (see *Krieg 1809*, vol. I, p. 250; M. Ruith, *Das k. bayerische 10. Infanterie-Regiment 'Prinz Ludwig'*, Ingolstadt: Ganghofer, 1882, p. 147).

34: This incident of the 15th is indicative of the curious state of hostilities during the first days of the campaign. The Austrians had repaired the bridge over the Isar here; Wrede's horsemen were to destroy it anew, but were chased off by the town's defenders (advance guard of IV Corps). On arriving at the bridge, the Bavarians had informed the Austrians of their mission and their intention to carry it out. Austrian reinforcements were brought up and the Bavarians were forced to depart without a shot being fired or a sabre raised. *Krieg 1809*, vol. I, pp. 247-8, 291, 297.

35: At about noon on the 15th, the end pieces of the bridges were taken apart and thrown into the river; the bridge supports, however, were not destroyed, and the Austrian pioneers found it a relatively easy task to repair. The authorities in Landshut had been taking precautions since 4 April: every night, the bridges were partially dismantled and the city gates barred (Alois Staudenraus, *Chronik der Stadt Landshut in Bayern*, Passau: Einhell, 1981, reprint of 1832 edition, pp. 29-30).

36: The small detachment at Bruckberg west of Gündlkofen was apparently from the 7th Light. Absent was the company of the 10th Infantry and its accompanying gun that had been detached at Moosburg; it retired toward Pfeffenhausen and rejoined its regiment late on the 17th at Siegenburg. These dispositions were developed by amalgamating information from the following sources: *Krieg 1809*, vol. I, pp. 309-10; Völderndorff, pp. 55-6; Franz Christoph, 'Die Isar-Uebergänge der Oesterreicher bei Landshut am 16. und

21. April 1809', *Verhandlungen des Historischen Vereins für Niederbayern*; Major Gerneth and Premierlieutenant Kießling, *Geschichte des Königlich Bayerischen 5. Infanterie-Regiments*, Berlin: Mittler & Sohn, 1893, pp. 194-201; Edmund Höfler, *Der Feldzug vom Jahre 1809 in Deutschland und Tirol*, Augsburg: Rieger, 1858, pp. 23-4; Josef Obpacher, *Das k. b. 2. Chevauxlegers-Regiment Taxis*, München: Bayerisches Kriegsarchiv, 1926, p. 180; Franz D. Reithofer, *Die Kriegsereignisse in Landshut am 16. und 21. April 1809 als die ersten in diesem Kriegsjahre*, Leipzig: Baumgartner, 1810 (some excellent eyewitness information); and Fritz Röder, *Geschichte des bisherigen k. B. 4. Jäger-Bataillons*, Landshut: Rietsch, 1890, pp. 10-11.

37: Small (e.g., three Uhlans) Austrian cavalry patrols had been appearing near the city since the 13th to distribute proclamations (Staudenraus, p. 29).

38: Quoted in *Krieg 1809*, vol. I, p. 310.

39: One of the *Taxis* squadrons had been detached to Pfettrach (later Furth) with two companies of the 7th Light and a 6-pounder to preclude the Austrians at Moosburg from interfering with the withdrawal. See Obpacher, p. 181; also Xylander, p. 140.

40: It is not clear exactly how many Austrian squadrons or regiments took part in this little engagement. *Krieg 1809* claims the only Austrian troopers to fight were Hardegg's 180 Uhlans and the two squadrons of hussars (vol. I, p. 314). Other sources claim much larger numbers of Austrians, to include the *Erzherzog Ferdinand* Hussars (for example, Heinze, pp. 330-1; Obpacher, p. 180; Stutterheim, pp. 111-2).

41: Obpacher, p. 181.

42: Losses taken from *Krieg 1809*, vol. I, p. 691; note that other sources, perhaps listing large numbers of lightly wounded, make the figures much higher for both sides (listing Austrian wounded in excess of 280 and counting Bavarian losses at 80 dead and 300 wounded. See, for example, Joseph Dauer, *Das königlich Bayerische 10. Infanterie-Regiment Prinz Ludwig*, Ingolstadt: Ganghofer, 1901, vol, IV, p. 224, and Reithofer, p. 19. Information on the 7th Light's desertion problem taken from Binder von Kriegelstein, vol. I, p. 166.

43: The Austrians lost about 25 men in this encounter; Bavarian losses were probably between 30 and 50. *Krieg 1809*, vol. I, pp. 333-5; M. H., *Kurze Darstellung der Geschichte des Königlich Bayerischen 4. Chevauxlegers-Regiment 'König'*, Berlin: Mittler & Sohn, 1895, p. 19.

44: Binder von Kriegelstein, vol. I, p. 184.

45: Binder von Kriegelstein (vol. I, p. 173) relates an interesting incident at the crucial Vohburg bridge. At the time of Wrede's approach, the bridge was guarded by II/3 of his division, but in the confusion created by Berthier's puzzling orders, the French gave serious consideration to destroying it. When some French appeared ready to implement the destruction contingency, the Bavarians intervened, fixing bayonets to chase their allies off the structure. A nearby battalion of the 13th Léger took up its muskets and an armed confrontation was barely avoided by the appearance of a senior French general who calmed both parties. Fortunately for the Allies, the bridge was left intact. See also Max Prielmayer, *Geschichte des k. b. I. Infanterie-Regiments König*, München: Huttler, 1881, p. 140; and Max Ruith and Emil Ball, *Kurze Geschichte des K. B. 3. Infanterie-Regiments Prinz Karl von Bayern*, Ingolstadt, 1890, p. 154.

46: It is interesting to note that there was no true infantry fighting in this little engagement, the Austrians were driven off by the artillery and cavalry. PLT Auvera, *Geschichte des kgl. Bayer. 7. Infanterie-Regiments Prinz Leopold von Bayern*, Bayreuth: Ellwanger, 1898, p. 415; Binder von Kriegelstein, p. 184; Höfler, pp. 57-9; *Krieg 1809*, vol. I, p. 364; Xylander, p. 141; Zoellner, p. 58.

47: This meant the division had to march along the north bank of the Danube, a longer route (11 kilometres) apparently chosen to avoid the possibility of an isolated division encountering a strong Austrian force (*Krieg 1809*, vol. I, pp. 412-13).

48: The bewildering movements of the Bavarian divisions on the 18th are not well addressed in any single source. The account here is compiled from several references including Oskar Bezzel, *Das K. B. 4. Infanterie-Regiment König Wilhelm von Württemberg vom Jahre 1806-1906*, München: Lindau, 1906, p. 49; Binder von Kriegelstein, vol. I, pp. 173-86; Gerneth/Kießling, p. 202; Prielmayer, p. 140; *Krieg 1809*, vol. I, pp. 341-3, 412-14.

49: Thierry's brigade consisted of infantry regiments *Kaiser* Nr. 1 (2,670 men in $2^2/3$ battalions) and *Lindenau* Nr. 29 (2,470 men in $2^2/3$ battalions). In the early morning of the 19th, he received, along with his new mission, the six squadrons of the *Levenehr* Dragoons (725 troopers), a half-battery each of cavalry and brigade guns. III/*Kaiser* (only four companies) and half a squadron of dragoons were left at Hörlbach, while all of *Lindenau*, $3^1/2$ squadrons and the brigade half-battery were deposited in Bruckhof. *Krieg 1809*, vol. I, p. 423-4.

50: That evening at Offenstetten, Thierry was able to collect about sixteen companies of infantry and $4^3/4$ squadrons of cavalry; the rest were casualties or had retreated to the south into V Corps' area. Thierry's casualties for the 19th cannot be determined with any accuracy, the Austrian reports combine the losses of 19 and 20 April; Lefebvre's report to Napoleon on the 19th claimed at least 400 prisoners. Both Regnier and Hofstetten were enrolled in the Legion of Honor. The details of the engagement at Arnhofen are derived from Fabrice, pp. 172-5; Prielmayer, p. 140; Höfler, pp. 70-4; *Krieg 1809*, vol. I, pp. 423-8, Anhang XXX;

Xylander, pp. 141-4 (Regnier's quote).

51: Bianchi's brigade consisted of the *Duka* (Nr. 39) and *Gyulai* (Nr. 60) Hungarian infantry regiments, each of three battalions, plus a brigade battery. Other guns may also have been available; Bavarian accounts speak of 18 Austrian artillery pieces.

52: The cannonades at Biburg and Siegenburg are described in Höfler, pp. 75-9; *Krieg 1809*, vol. I, pp. 429-32; Röder, p. 14; Xylander, pp. 144-5; Zoellner, pp. 58-9.

53: Mändler, pp. 6-7.

54: Allied command and control relationships on 20 April are far from clear. Von Hügel's Württemberg Light Brigade may have been attached to the Bavarian 1st Division at the outset of operations on the 20th, later to be transferred to Wrede's command. The entire VIII Corps initially marched between the two attacking Bavarian divisions; the bulk were held around Bruckhof, but von Hügel's men seem to have advanced as far as Sallingberg.

55: Quoted in Junkelmann, pp. 13-14.

56: Quoted from Ludwig's 22 April report to his father (Uebe, p. 51) and from his diary (Corti, p. 83). Napoleon's bedraggled appearance is described by the artist Albrecht Adam and the beer ration, 'drunk from pots and casseroles', is related by Private Deifl; both men were eye-witnesses to the event. Both quoted in Junkelmann, pp. 237-8 and p. 14. For another eye-witness's report on the enthusiasm of the Bavarian troops see: Franz Xaver Stoll, 'Kriegsberichte aus den Jahren 1800 und 1809, was sich in der Stadt und im Landgerichte Abensberg ereignet', J. Schuegraf, ed., *Verhandlungen des Historischen Vereins für Niederbayern*, Band 7, Landshut, 1860.

57: The comment on Napoleon's iron determination is from Rudolf von Xylander, 'Zum Gedächtnis des Feldzugs 1809 in Bayern', *Darstellungen aus der Bayerischen Kriegs- und Heeresgeschichte*, Heft 18, München: Lindauer, 1909, p. 19. Ludwig also noted the Emperor's 'will of iron' (Corti, p. 83).

58: This battalion had rejoined its regiment from Vohburg on the evening of the 19th.

59: Bezzel, *4. Infanterie*, pp. 51-3; Döderlein, pp. 121-6; Prielmayer, pp. 140-1; Höfler, pp. 81-8; *Krieg 1809*, vol. I, pp. 438-53; Xylander, pp. 146-7.

60: There is some confusion about the operations of the Bavarian northern attack forces after the engagement at Offenstetten. Most sources have the 1st Division bivouacking generally around Rohr and the 3rd at Bachl, but others state that some Bavarian troops took part in an evening action just north of Rottenburg. Here Hiller's columns, approaching from the south-west, collided with Morand's French Division. The Austrian 4th Infantry *Deutschmeister* crossed over the Laaber to the north and fought a bitter and bloody battle on a heavily wooded hillside. Stutterheim (p. 207), followed by the *Deutschmeister* regimental history (Amon von Treuenfest, *Geschichte des Kaiserlich Königlich Infanterie-Regiments Hoch und Deutschmeister*, Wien, 1879, p. 406), describes the capture of 'over 300 Bavarians'; the somewhat unreliable Gachot (pp. 81-2) says that the Bavarians (3rd Division) began to break and Lefebvre had to intervene to hold them to their duty. Both of these points are made by James Arnold in his recent study *Crisis on the Danube* (New York: Paragon House, 1990, pp. 113-14). However, the authors of *Krieg 1809* give *Deutschmeister's* opponents as the French 13th Léger and 17th Ligne (vol. I, text p. 462 and casualty list p. 700), and the official Bavarian history (*Der Feldzug von 1809 in Bayern*, prepared by the Bavarian General Staff, 1865, p. 69) notes that there were no Bavarian infantry units in the vicinity of the clash; neither the VII Corps after action report (Saski, vol. II, pp. 287-9), nor the relevant Bavarian unit histories make mention of any combat on the evening of the 20th. For Zandt's actions, see Herman Hutter, *Das Königlich Bayerische 1. Chevauxlegers-Regiment 'Kaiser Alexander von Rußland' 1682 bis 1882*, München: Oldenbourg, 1885, p. 192.

61: Berg, pp. 216-17; Gerneth/Kießling, pp. 204-5; Heinze. p. 335; Röder, pp. 14-15; Ruith, p. 149; Franz Schubert and Hans Vara, *Geschichte des K. B. 13. Infanterie-Regiments*, München: Lindau, 1906, vol. I, pp. 139-40. According to Ruith, three companies of the 10th Infantry under Major Büllingen were detailed to escort the large bag of prisoners back to Strasbourg.

62: Also from Ludwig's 22 April report (Uebe, p. 51).

63: See Aichner, p. 243; Hasso Dormann, *Feldmarschall Fürst Wrede*, München: Süddeutscher Verlag, 1982; J. Heilmann, *Feldmarschall Fürst Wrede*, Leipzig: Duncker & Humblot, 1881; Paulus, pp. 120-25; Zoellner, p. 56. Wrede turned against Napoleon in 1813 and attempted to intercept the retreating French army at Hanau in October but was soundly beaten by his intended prey; Napoleon's laconic comment became famous: 'I could make him a baron, but I could not make him a general.'

64: The order of crossing given here is the one most commonly stated. Höfler (pp. 88-9) puts II/3 across first, followed by 7th, 4th (*sic*) Chevauxlegers and half the light battery, then the 13th and the rest of the light battery; the 6th Infantry, 6th Light, 3rd Chevauxlegers and remaining artillery are not mentioned. Xylander (p. 147) gives the impression the cavalry crossed first; this is inconsistent with all other sources and seems tactically illogical.

65: Most sources mention this skillful combination of cavalry and artillery being employed near Aicha, but the regimental history of the *Leiningen* Chevauxlegers (Oskar von Sichlern, *Geschichte des königlich bayerischen 5. Chevauxlegers-Regiments 'Prinz Otto,'* München: regimental, 1876, p. 74) and Höfler (pp. 91-2) give the location as close to Pfeffenhausen. Based on the timing of both Bavarian and Austrian movements,

Aicha is almost certainly the correct location.

66: Wrede was incensed about Vandamme's theft of his battalions on the 20th and issued a strict Order of the Day on the 23rd threatening to initiate proceedings against any officer who obeyed unauthorized orders; unless otherwise directed, the only persons outside the Division who were authorized to direct its operations were Napoleon, Berthier and Lefebvre (Fabrice, p. 181; Heilmann, *Wrede*, pp. 127-33; Wrede's report is in Saski, vol. II, p. 289). General sources for the engagements along the 'southern axis' (Biburg and Siegenburg): Auvera, pp. 416-19; Fabrice, pp. 179-82; Höfler, pp. 88-93; *Krieg 1809*, vol. I, pp. 453-7; Ruith/Ball, pp. 156-9; Xylander, pp. 147-8; Zoellner, pp. 60-1.

67: Fabrice, p. 181 and *Krieg 1809*, vol. I, p. 456. It is not clear where the 6th Infantry went after seizing Hörlbach. *Krieg 1809* states the regiment followed some elements of Thierry's command through the woods to the east and south to arrive at Högetsing. Fabrice, on the other hand, relates an interesting story regarding Vandamme that conflicts with the Austrian commentary. Apparently, the French general came upon the regiment at about 4 p.m., asked for its colonel and ordered him to attack a wooded hill held by the enemy. Based on Vandamme's location at that hour (it seems he was with von Hügel's men near Perka), Fabrice assumes the 6th Infantry took part in the push against Radetzky's right flank and later, bereft of instructions, marched off on its own toward Rohr. Although the movements described in *Krieg 1809* seem the more logical (why and how would the 6th get back into the Abens valley?), the story about Vandamme rings true and apparently stems from an eye-witness. The story of the 6th cannot be determined with precision, but it highlights the confusing nature of the fighting on the 20th and the inadequacy of local command and control arrangements.

68: Auvera, p. 418; *4. Chevauxlegers*, p. 19; *Krieg 1809*, vol. I, pp. 473-5; Mändler, pp. 9-10.

69: The order to Wrede was written at 4 a.m., however, as he sent a message to the Emperor from Pfeffenhausen at that hour (Saski, vol. II, p. 301).

70: The 1st Chevauxlegers and 1st Dragoons were also soon across the bridge, indeed, *Kronprinz* claims to have been the 'first at the burning bridge'; the two regiments came under Wrede's leadership in the absence of their slain commander (Buxbaum, pp. 124-125; Hutter, pp. 192-193). See also Auvera, p. 420; Binder von Kriegelstein, pp. 256-268; *4. Chevauxlegers*, pp. 19-20; *Krieg 1809*, vol. I, pp. 478-490. The 13th Infantry took no part in the fighting on the 21st, its only casualties were caused by an exploding ammunition wagon (Zoellner, p. 61).

71: The 3rd and 4th squadrons, 3rd Chevauxlegers went with Preysing. See Fabrice, p. 183; *Krieg 1809*, vol. I, p. 493, vol. III, pp. 3, 9; Sichlern, p. 74; Völderndorff, pp. 88-89.

72: Lefebvre also had command of Demont's French Division, but this organization, composed of conscripts destined for Davout's Corps, was hardly combat-worthy and played only a small role in the Bavarian phase of the campaign. Lefebvre's command moved east along the Laaber with the infantry (Deroy and one of Demont's brigades) on the right closest to the brook (it hardly deserves the name river) and the cavalry, von Seydewitz's troopers and St. Germain's cuirassier brigade, on the left. Demont's other brigade crossed the Laaber at Leierndorf to follow the Austrian III Corps (*Krieg 1809*, vol. I, p. 523; Saski, vol. II, p. 302).

73: Late in the morning, Lefebvre dispatched a squadron of *Taxis* and a half-squadron of *Bubenhofen* to reconnoitre along the road to Landshut and establish liaison with Lannes (*Krieg 1809*, vol. I, p. 524).

74: The battalion lost about 150 men, at least half of whom were listed as missing. The 5th Light would lose even more in the course of the day (about 200), but its casualties were killed and wounded not deserters; it was thus considered a reliable outfit whereas the 7th was thought too flighty to withstand the rigours of village fighting. Desertion was such a problem in the 7th that of the 660 men it had had at the outset of hostilities, only 158 were still under arms by 25 April (Gerneth/Kießling, p. 207; Heilmann, 'Feldzug', p. 23; *Krieg 1809*, vol. I, p. 704).

75: The action at Schierling is described in Gerneth/Kießling, pp. 206-209; Heinze, pp. 335-337; *Krieg 1809*, vol. I, pp. 520-527; Obpacher, p. 185; Röder, pp. 15-17; Xylander, pp. 149-151. One of Demont's battalions was also sent into Schierling with the 5th Light (*Krieg 1809*, vol. I, p. 525; Saski, vol. II, p. 321).

76: Xylander, p. 151. Nor should the 4th Chevauxlegers be forgotten. This regiment spent four hours standing in formation as support for the batteries while shot ploughed up the earth all about; it was a matter of honour for cavalrymen to accept such tasks with equanimity, but it cost *Bubenhofen* its commander (badly wounded) and several troopers (Heinze, p. 336).

77: Davout recognized the enemy's numerical superiority (even if his master did not) and did not want to commit his Corps and Lefebvre's to a fight from which they could not extricate themselves.

78: Noted in Deroy's report as quoted in Schubert/Vara, p. 140.

79: *Krieg 1809*, vol. I, p. 491; Bezzel, *4. Infanterie*, p. 53.

80: *Krieg 1809*, vol. I, pp. 491-2.

81: One squadron of *Taxis* had been sent to establish liaison with Napoleon's approaching force. A squadron and a half from *Bubenhofen* were also detached to the south: the squadron occupied Langquaid, the half-squadron scouted toward the Landshut road. The *Taxis* squadron rejoined the brigade to participate in the attack on the Austrian battery, but the elements from *Bubenhofen* remained detached for the rest of the day (the squadron may have been posted as Napoleon's immediate escort to supplement the 1st Chevauxlegers).

Heinze, p. 337, and Obpacher, p. 184. Vieregg was promoted to General-Major in May (Hutter, pp. 186, 913).

82: From Deroy's report of 23 April, quoted in Gerneth/Kießling, pp. 210-11. The 3rd Division's two light battalions stood in front of Schierling in closed columns, temporarily brigaded with four of Demont's battalions.

83: Général Jean Jacques Germain Pelet, *Mémoires sur la guerre de 1809 en Allemagne*, Paris: Roret, 1824, vol. II, pp. 77-84.

84: Höfler, p. 111, and Obpacher, p. 185. Apparently, St. Sulpice was ordered to attack the battery simultaneously with Seydewitz; difficulties in crossing the narrow bridge at Eggmühl and an attack (repulsed) by the *Stipsicz* Hussars delayed the arrival of the French heavy cavalry (*Krieg 1809*, vol. I, p. 557; Obpacher, p. 185). Fabrice points out that Seydewitz's bold statement may well be apocryphal (F. von Fabrice, 'Nochmals die bayerische Reiter-Brigade Seydewitz bei Eggmühl', *Jahrbücher für die deutsche Armee und Marine*, Band 65, 1887). See also Ludwig von Madroux, 'Die bayerische Kavallerie-Brigade Seydewitz in der Schlacht von Eggmühl (22. April 1809)', *Archiv für Offiziere aller Waffen*, Jahrgang 3, Band 2, 1845.

85: The Crown Prince's Division observed the battle from the heights south of Schierling and was not actively involved in the fighting on the 22nd. Sources for the Bavarians' role at Eggmühl include: Berg, pp. 220-1; Binder von Kriegelstein, pp. 290-300; Fabrice, 'Reiter-Brigade'; Gerneth/Kießling, pp. 209-14; Heinze, pp. 337-44; Höfler, pp. 104-18; M. J., 'Die bayerische Reiter-Brigade bei Eggmühl', *Jahrbücher für die deutsche Armee und Marine*, Band 63, 1887; *Krieg 1809*, vol. I, pp. 542-61, 566-70; Obpacher, pp. 183-9; Röder, pp. 17-18; Ruith, pp. 149-50; Saski, vol. II, pp. 350-1; Schubert/Vara, p. 141; Xylander, pp. 151-4; see also Chapter 3.

86: From the diary of one of the battalion's officers, quoted in Berg, p. 222.

87: The actions of the two 1st Division mounted regiments on 23 April are unclear. The 1st Chevauxlegers apparently began the day as Imperial escorts, but both regimental histories indicate that the units also fought on the 23rd; they provide, however, few details (Buxbaum, p. 125; Hutter, pp. 195-196; *Krieg 1809*, vol. I, pp. 585, 589; Völderndorff, vol. II, p. 110).

88: Marulaz's correspondence from Saski, vol. II, p. 369. See also Mändler, pp. 12-14 and Georg Zechmayer, *Geschichte des Königlich bayerischen 14. Infanterie-Regiments und seiner Stammtruppen*, Nürnberg, 1885, pp. 13-14. When the chasseurs were attacked, the 6th Light had been disposed with two companies about Erharting and two in support to the rear.

89: Xylander, p. 155. Note that *Krieg 1809*, vol III, p. 39 divides Berchem's battery, putting half of it with the 3rd Regiment, the other half with the 13th. Dobl's 12-pounders remained north of the Rott and do not appear to have taken part in the battle.

90: As Graf Berchem was attempting to withdraw his last howitzer, the hail of Austrian shot killed the draft horses pulling the piece and overturned the limber. Rather than have their howitzer fall prey to the rapidly advancing Austrian infantry, Berchem's gunners threw themselves into the traces and dragged the piece back to Neumarkt. A lieutenant somehow acquired two farm horses in the town, hitched them to the howitzer and thus managed to get it back north of the bridge (Xylander, p. 156).

91: Bavarian accounts almost unanimously blame the French cavalry for introducing disorder and delay into their otherwise well-organized withdrawal. Mändler describes the Chasseurs as 'more hindrance than help' (p. 16).

92: The French lost at least 200 men, the Austrians some 1,400 (*Krieg 1809*, vol. III, pp. 59-60 and 655).

93: On the negative side, Zoellner points out (p. 62) that no thought had been given to defending on the south bank of the Rott; the Bavarian deployment across the stream was thus hasty and units were thrown into combat with no time to prepare or scout their positions. Both Wrede and Bessières might be held accountable for this lack of preparation. The engagement at Neumarkt is described in Auvera, pp. 421-4; Fabrice, pp. 183-8; *Krieg 1809*, vol. III, pp. 3-61, 655; Mändler, pp. 11-16; Ruith/Ball, pp. 161-5; Sichlern, p. 75; Xylander, pp. 154-6; Zoellner, pp. 62-5.

94: Bessières was unaware that Austrians had evacuated Neumarkt in the dawn hours of the 25th. (See *Krieg 1809*, vol. III).

95: Lannes was determined to strike Hiller before the Austrians crossed the Inn and asked Lefebvre for support. The latter could not commit the 1st and 3rd Divisions, but allowed Lannes the use of Wrede's men as long as they were directed toward Mühldorf, at which place Lefebvre intended to unite VII Corps on the 28th (*Krieg 1809*, vol. III, p. 120).

96: The Austrians also lost four guns. Somewhat less than half of these losses were probably captured Salzburg Landwehrmen; two of the four Salzburg Landwehr battalions (2nd and 3rd) apparently dissolved in a flurry of desertion during the battle around the city (*Krieg 1809*, vol. III, pp. 200-201).

97: Wrede's action's from 25-30 April are recounted in Auvera, pp. 424-5; Fabrice, pp. 189-91; Höfler, pp. *Krieg 1809*, vol. III, pp. 117-22, 180-2, 186-201; Mändler, pp. 17-20; Völderndorff, pp. 118-21; Xylander. pp. 157-8.

98: The 1st Light and II/8 were not with the division on the evening of the 25th or during its triumphal procession through the capital. II/8 had escorted some 3,000 Austrian prisoners to Landshut and handed their burden over to the 1st Light on the 24th. The transfer delayed the battalion's departure until the 25th and it did not rejoin its division until some days later. The 1st Light took the prisoners to Augsburg, turned them over to the French depot there and then joined the 3rd Division at Wasserburg on 6 May for the expedition into the Tyrol (Pfeffer, p. 94). The 1st Chevauxlegers rejoined the division on the 25th (Völderndorff, p. 110).

99: Parts of the 3rd Division were also busy with Austrian captives. The 5th Infantry took responsibility for 3-5,000 prisoners of war outside Regensburg on the 24th and did not rejoin its division until the 26th at Freising. The 1st Battalion marched with the rest of the division when it left for Wasserburg the next day, but II/5 shepherded its prisoners to Augsburg and did not return until 6 May.

100: Sources for the adventures of these two divisions in the latter days of April are: Bezzel, *4. Chevauxlegers*, p. 55; Döderlein, pp. 130-2; Gerneth/Kießling, pp. 215-20; Heinze, pp. 344-5; *Krieg 1809*, vol. III, pp. 129-33, 188-91, 197-201; Ruith, pp. 151-2; Völderndorff, pp. 121-3.

101: The Austrians never attempted to assault the fortress and their siege artillery only arrived in time to turn around and retreat to Linz. Sources: Fabrice, pp. 253-6; *Krieg 1809*, vol. III, pp. 85-97, 133-7; Ruith, p. 146.

102: Fabrice, p. 191.

103: Kolowrat had attacked VIII Corps here on 17 May, but the Württembergers and Saxons had handed him a severe repulse (see Chapter 3).

104: Figures include infantry, cavalry and artillery personnel and are taken from strength returns of 1 June; not included are some 1,870 on detached duty, 4,240 sick and 1,181 prisoners of war (Commandant Sauzey, *Nos Alliés les Bavarois*, Paris: Terana, 1988, pp. 147-8).

105: The outposts and garrisons along the Enns were taken over by the 3rd Light when I/8 was detailed to the mobile column (Döderlein, p. 150; Völderndorff, pp. 192-3; see also Feodor Grosch, Eduard Hagen and Albert Schenk, *Geschichte des K. B. 12. Infanterie-Regiments Prinz Arnulf und seiner Stammabteilungen*, München, 1914, p. 327).

106: Lefebvre is often criticized for this attitude, but there may have been considerable truth to his assertions: Wrede made similar complaints to the King during the stay in Linz (his reports of 17 and 23 June are cited in Fabrice, p. 206). Sauzey, pp. 147-58, includes the text of Lefebvre's orders. An Austrian source also confirms this, although the author goes on to point out that the Bavarians were at least superior to the Saxons (Franz Xaver Pritz, *Geschichte des Landes ob der Enns*, Linz: Haslinger, 1847, vol. II, p. 579).

107: Bezzel, *4. Infanterie*, p. 69; Fabrice, pp. 205-6; Gerneth/Kießling, p. 253; Völderndorff, pp. 188-93.

108: Kolowrat set out for the Marchfeld on 29 May with 13,800 men. Regular troops comprised only four battalions and four squadrons of Somariva's force, his remaining eleven battalions were Landwehr; his force of 8,550 also included half of a cavalry battery. Ludwig Freiherr von Welden, *Der Krieg von 1809 zwischen Oesterreich und Frankreich von Anfang Mai bis zum Friedensschluße*, Wien: Gerold, 1872, pp. 92-5.

109: Minucci's force consisted of two companies from II/3, 1½ from I/13, two from 6th Light, a squadron of *Leiningen* and one of Caspers' 6-pounders. The enemy force at Kirchschlag included four guns; they were supported in their retreat by an additional battalion and some 200 Uhlans at Hellmonsödt. The entire Austrian force engaged apparently comprised the *Peterwardeiner* Grenzer, a Landwehr battalion, two companies of Jägers and a division of *Meerveldt* Uhlans. Sources: Fabrice, pp. 206-7; *4. Chevauxlegers*, pp. 20-1; Heilmann, *Wrede*, pp. 154-5; Völderndorff, pp. 195-7; Xylander, pp. 178-9.

110: Döderlein, pp. 151-3. Additional sources for the actions of the Bavarians at Linz include: Bezzel, *4. Infanterie*, pp. 67-9; Fabrice, pp. 204-7; Max Leyh, *Die Feldzüge des Königlich Bayerischen Heeres unter Max I. Joseph von 1805 bis 1815*, vol. VI/2 of *Geschichte des Bayerischen Heeres*, München: Schick, 1935, p. 150; Mändler, pp. 31-2; Sichlern, p. 79; Völderndorff, pp. 188-201; Xylander, pp. 176-9.

111: Wrede's force when he departed Linz is given in a report of 1 July (quoted in Sauzey, p. 158); see also Heilmann, *Wrede*, pp. 155-6. Some sources (e.g., Bowden/Tarbox, p. 189) erroneously place the *Kronprinz* Chevauxlegers and two batteries with Massena's IV Corps at Wagram; the two foot batteries of 1st Division were the only units other than Wrede's to take part in the battle.

112: The impressions of an eye-witness quoted in Leyh, p. 151; and Berchem's report, cited in Xylander, p. 179. See also Gustav Wolf, *Der Eilmarsch Wrede's von Linz bis Wagram*, Innsbruck: Wagner, 1909; Wolf asserts that Wrede's march 'can be numbered among the fastest marches in military history'.

113: Ludwig von Madroux (then a junior officer in the *König* Chevauxlegers), 'August von Floret', *Archiv für Offiziere aller Waffen*, Jahrgang 3, Band 2, 1846, p. 189.

114: From Macdonald's after action report, quoted in E. Buat, *1809 De Ratisbonne à Znaïm*, Paris: Chapelot, 1909, vol. II, p. 268. Caspers had been brought forward early in the advance. The whereabouts of Dobl's Battery, however, are unclear. It had been attached to the Guard artillery when the Bavarians arrived on the field in mid-morning, but its subsequent actions are not known; it may have formed part of the Grand Battery. Dobl returned to the 2nd Division late in the evening. Xylander, pp. 180-3.

115: The artillerymen of most nations wore leather harnesses to which ropes could be attached enabling them to drag their pieces about the battlefield at need.

116: Napoleon is said to have commented on learning that Minucci had taken over the Bavarian division: 'Tell him to command his division as Wrede has and he will have my complete confidence.' Leyh, p. 153.

117: The Bavarian march to Wagram and participation in the battle are described in Buat, vol. II, pp. 260-75;

Fabrice, pp. 208-14; *4. Chevauxlegers*, pp. 21-2; Höfler, pp. 204-15; Leyh, pp. 150-3; Mändler, pp. 32-7; Sauzey, pp. 158-65; Sichlern, 79-82; Völderndorff, pp. 244-51; and Xylander, pp. 179-83.

118: Lindenau marched on Massena's right during the 8th, reaching Leitzersdorf (near Stockerau) where he was recalled (Buat, vol. II, pp. 326-7).

119: Marmont believed he faced only the enemy's rear guard. It was not until almost 5 p.m., when he was afforded a view into the area around Znaim itself, that he realized the bulk of the Austrian army 'at least 40,000 men' was here (his report of 10 July, quoted in Buat, vol. II, p. 350). It is not clear how much artillery Marmont had at his disposal at Znaim. The Corps' reserve guns had been left on Lobau and Xylander claims that only the Bavarian guns were present on 10 and 11 July, but Marmont mentions Montbrun's pieces (three horse batteries) and it is possible his two French divisions also had their divisional guns (two foot batteries each).

120: Minucci's initial opponents were the grenadiers of Steyrer's Brigade (5 battalions), these were later joined by Henneberg's Brigade (two regiments, I Corps); it is not unlikely that troops from other brigades of the Reserve and I Corps also took part in the fight as it grew in intensity (two other grenadier brigades were immediately available). Marmont's speech to Preysing is quoted in Josef Würdinger, 'Das Leben des königl. bayerischen Generallieutenants Maxim. Grafen v. Preysing-Moos', *Verhandlungen des Historischen Vereins für Niederbayern*, Band 9, 1863, p. 102; Madroux also cites it, claiming Preysing's recollections as his source (Madroux, 'Floret', p. 208).

121: Sources for the pursuit after Wagram and clash at Znaim: Karl Bornemann, *Napoleon bei Znaim*, Beiträge zur Geschichte und Landeskunde Südmährens, Heft 5/6, Geislingen/Steige: Südmährischen Landschaftsrat, 1975; Buat, vol. II, pp. 316-64; Fabrice, pp. 216-24; *4. Chevauxlegers*, p. 24; Mändler, pp. 37-41; F. R. von R., *Die Waffenthaten der Oesterreicher im Jahre 1809*, Wien: Hirschfeld, 1838, pp. 202-5; Völderndorff, pp. 251-63; Xylander, pp. 184-8.

122: Marmont was inducted into the marshalate on 12 July. See Marmont, *Mémoires du Maréchal Duc de Raguse de 1792 a 1832*, Paris: Perrotin, 1857, vol. III, pp. 251-252. Marmont's 12 July Order of the Day is reprinted in Sauzey, p. 169 and Völderndorff, pp. 258-259; Minucci's and Beckers' experiences are recorded in Fabrice, p. 220. Although Marmont's Order commends the 8th Ligne, other sources suggest the regiment was the 81st Ligne. Even Pelet praises Bavarian valour at Tesswitz (vol. IV, p. 272).

123: A detachment of the 2nd Division under Minucci garrisoned Passau in late July to replace Rouyer's Germans who had joined Lefebvre in Salzburg for the Second Offensive into the Tyrol. Wrede resumed command on 28 July. The Crown Prince, on the other hand, had been called to the French headquarters in Vienna and turned over command to the capable GM Clemens von Raglovich, his Chief of Staff. See Bezzel, *4. Infanterie*, p. 69; Döderlein, pp. 153-6; Fabrice, p. 225; M. J., 'Zur Erinnerung an den Königl. bayerischen General der Infanterie und General-Quartiermeister der Armee, Clemens von Raglovich', *Jahrbücher für die deutsche Armee und Marine*, Band 33, 1887; Völderndorff, pp. 263-7; Xylander, pp. 190-2.

124: See, for example, Henry Bonnal, *La Manœuvre de Landshut*, Paris: Chapelot, 1905, p. 353. The Bavarian propensity for looting and hard exactions is mentioned in John Elting, *Swords Around a Throne*, New York: Free Press, 1988, p. 399.

125: Not everyone was convinced of the Bavarians' loyalty. When he learned of Wrede's withdrawal on 17 April, the redoubtable Davout wrote to Berthier to express his fear that Wrede might commit 'some black treason' (Marshal Davout, *Correspondence du Maréchal Davout*, Charles de Mazade, ed., vol. II, Paris: Plon, Nouritt & Co., 1885, p. 473). Despite Crown Prince Ludwig's impassioned letters to Count Stadion before the war, I have found no evidence to indicate any high level Bavarian treason in 1809, although events during the Tyrolian campaign would lead to insubordination against Lefebvre and the Crown Prince's dislike for Napoleon became increasingly obvious. See Chapter 7.

CHAPTER 3:

All the King's Men

King Friedrich of Württemberg was a remarkable man. Reportedly so fat that a portion of his dining table had to be cut out to accommodate his girth, he was also sharply intelligent, autocratic, harsh and driven by a powerful ambition. Furthermore, his ponderous bulk belied an iron will and a surprisingly deep well of ruthless energy. Imbued with notions of enlightened despotism and a strong central state, he drew upon these personal qualities to increase the power of the throne and propel his little kingdom out of the 18th century and into the modern age. One of the tools he used in this endeavour was the army. Like the militaries of most small German states in the pre-revolutionary era, Württemberg's army had been a small, expensive, professional force, officered by minor nobles from throughout Europe and recruiting its soldiers from the lowest levels of society without regard for their nationality. It was an army of powdered wigs and cabinet wars, whose men fought for pay alone and whose officers might switch allegiances upon a whim or better offer. For Friedrich, however, the army was a potential vehicle of national integration, a weapon he could use domestically to undermine the entrenched power of the old, established estates and thereby expand his own control. Principally composed of leading burghers, these estates (Stände) were represented in a Diet which controlled the kingdom's pursestrings.[1] To Friedrich, they were an antiquated, inefficient impediment to the exercise of his personal will and the advancement of the realm in general. He intended to suppress them.

The army was also important in the international arena. Friedrich harboured a restless interest in territorial expansion, even at the expense of his fellow Rheinbund princes. A strong, competent military not only enabled Württemberg to pressure its smaller neighbours and fend off the larger ones, but also represented a valuable bargaining chip in Friedrich's relationship with Emperor Napoleon. Committed by the requirements of the Confederation Treaty to supply a relatively large contingent of soldiers, the king could reasonably hope that a sizable and effective army would distinguish him in the eyes of the Emperor of Battles and grant Württemberg a greater voice in European affairs. Thus, for reasons of state as well as a deep pride in himself and his nation, Friedrich embarked upon a modernization programme that would transform his stiff, 18th-century army into a compact force of the Napoleonic Age, flexible, aggressive and deadly.

The contingent that served Napoleon in 1809 was therefore the product of a comprehensive series of reforms implemented over the previous decade by the energetic king. Broad in scope, Friedrich's reforms touched most aspects of the military, from its composition to its place in society, and laid the foundation for the creation of a truly modern national army. One of the most significant steps in this direction was the enactment of an advanced conscription law in 1806. Among the principal weaknesses of the old conscription system was the practice of hiring substitutes, often criminals, ne'er-do-wells or other undesirables, to take the places of more wealthy and fortunate citizens. Some of France's other allies, particularly the smaller principalities (Hohenzollern and Isenburg, for example), maintained 18th-century recruiting practices such as this throughout the Napoleonic period and filled their ranks with foreigners if necessary, but Friedrich was determined to establish a national military rather than a force of hired mercenaries. Furthermore, his obligation to raise a contingent of 12,000 men for the Rheinbund placed unprecedented demands on the country's population and military structure. He thus expended considerable effort in promulgating fair (if strict) conscription laws that progressively reduced the number of citizens exempt from military duty and closely limited those cases where the purchase of substitutes or other evasions were authorized. Even a young man's ability to marry was subject to government approval if he was eligible for military service.[2] This is not to pretend that every citizen of the kingdom was eligible for the draft, far from it! Indeed, although all Friedrich's subjects were theoretically liable to be called up, the list of exemptions was quite long: nobles, the sons of civil officials to the 13th Rank, royal servants, larger landholders, lone sons of widows or infirm men, and the members of certain religious orders, to name only a few, all enjoyed some form of exemption from military service.[3] None the less, Württemberg's conscription regulations, further tightened by an edict issued in August 1809, represented a significant departure from the methods of the past and provided a broader base for the rapidly expanding army.

In addition to establishing a broader base for conscription, Friedrich sought to enhance the national character of his army by recruiting almost exclusively from within the kingdom. Not only were the foreign travels of Württembergers severely restricted, but those citizens who already resided abroad were enjoined to return to their fatherland or face the confiscation of all their lands and properties. Moreover, in another break with the past, the recruiting of foreigners was strongly discouraged and soldiers of non-Württemberg origin could only be accepted into the army as a last resort.[4] Likewise, foreign recruiters were banned from the kingdom and expelled by force if they dared defy Friedrich's decrees. The king was not ignorant of human psychology, however, and he provided for rewards as well as punishments in reforming his army. To compensate his subjects for their long tours of service (a minimum of eight years for an infantryman and ten for his counterparts in the cavalry or artillery) and their sacrifices on behalf of the nation, a number of measures were introduced to raise the social standing of the soldier, whether active or retired. Old veterans were thus guaranteed employment with the state and accorded small honours in their communities (special places in church, for example), while the widows and orphans of their fallen comrades could rely upon the king for financial support. Those who were wounded but managed to survive the crude and agonizing medical practices of the era might hope to pass their remaining days in relative comfort at an old soldiers' home (*Invalidenhaus*) founded by royal munificence. In recognition of battlefield bravery, medals and other awards were distributed generously to the deserving, and the particularly fortunate common soldier could even hope to become an officer. Conscription was never popular, but by these measures, Friedrich palliated some of its more negative aspects and helped his kingdom avoid some of the debilitating recruiting problems that plagued France and eroded the quality of its soldiery as the Napoleonic era dragged on.[5]

To lead the soldiers of his growing army out of the past and into the demanding future of Napoleonic warfare, Friedrich needed a corps of dedicated and imaginative officers. He thus took great interest in his officer corps, emphasizing professional competence, national origin, courage and loyalty. Consistent with his view of himself as an enlightened monarch, he drew his officers from most levels of society and promoted them on the basis of merit rather than birth.[6] His was not to be an army of ignorant aristocrats. True, the majority of the young men aspiring to be officers would still get their basic military education as cadets 'with the regiment', but Friedrich also established an academy in 1805 to provide a more formal foundation for officer training.[7] Moreover, he enhanced the social status of his officers, making military service more attractive, honourable and rewarding by expanding the nobility to include all officers of the guard and line officers of captain or higher rank. He also hoped to increase the percentage of native Württembergers in the officer corps by recalling men who had taken up the sword under other monarchs. Those who failed to heed the call could expect the severest treatment. One of the Austrian officers captured in the coming campaign, for example, proved to be a Württemberger who had failed to return to the fatherland; he was tried by court martial and punished as a traitor in 1810.[8] Still, like most German armies of the day, the number of foreign-born officers in Württemberg's army remained high, approaching 50 per cent in 1809, with the dominant foreign nationalities being Saxons, Bavarians and Mecklenburgers. The Mecklenburger Karl von Suckow, for instance, departing royal Prussian service, was commissioned as a lieutenant in Friedrich's Foot Guards in the summer of 1808. During his obligatory audience with the King, he mentioned his younger brother and was delighted when Friedrich promised a guard commission for the junior Suckow as well.[9] Despite the high percentage of foreigners, Friedrich, with his emphasis on loyalty, competence and honour, was able to create an officer corps of skilled professionals, justly proud of their army and well-suited to lead it.

Regardless of the national character of the military and the open opportunities for advancement, it was very much the *King's* army, owing its loyalty to its monarch alone and expected to follow his directives without qualm or question. Friedrich took great personal pride in the abilities and accomplishments of his military and regarded shortcomings or lack of professionalism as affronts to his royal prestige. From cadets at the military institute to proven officers of senior rank, therefore, the watchwords of the army's leadership were order, obedience and discipline. Those who strayed found their king utterly unforgiving of failure or perceived disloyalty. The unfortunate Oberst Eugen von Röder, for example, as commander of the infantry regiment *Franquemont*, was cashiered and imprisoned in August 1809 for obeying the orders of his French superior when those orders ran counter to Friedrich's instructions.[10] If stern, even harsh, in his punishments, Friedrich was also magnanimous in rewarding valour and competence. For Lieutenant Hayd, the King's gratitude meant elevation to the inherited nobility for his reported capture of more than 300 Austrians near Braunau on 30 April.[11]

The tactics of the Württemberg army also underwent reform just prior to the opening of hostilities. Previously based on Prussian drill, Württemberg infantry regulations were modernized through the introduction of several French concepts in a new regulation issued on 16 February 1809. Like their Bavarian allies, the Württembergers were required to adopt the hallmarks of the French army's tactical system: infantry columns and skirmishing tactics. Naturally, the line was retained as a basic battle formation, but the Württemberg army, unlike the Bavarians, did not shift from a two-rank to a three-rank line; the new regulations allowed the three-rank line to be formed if required, but this appears to have been the exception rather than the norm. Although only a few months were available to train the men in these new formations and modes of combat, Friedrich's soldiers learned well and soon proved themselves particularly adept at skirmishing. With war looming on the horizon, training was pursued with earnest intent and by April, the men had attained an unprecedented level of readiness.[12] From the soldier's point of view, this stress on training was not entirely positive. As one of Friedrich's men commented on 5 April: 'We Jägers would have it good in our quarters if it weren't for all the drilling, but not a day goes by where we don't drill, marching out with all our gear...'[13]

Through his juggernaut energy and intense personal attention, Friedrich thus increased the size of the little kingdom's military while improving its composition, training and status in Württemberg society. The Württemberg army of 1809 thus represents a microcosm of the changes sweeping through military structures across Europe in the early 19th-century as recruiters, logisticians and tacticians struggled to come to grips with the new and still developing modes of warfare. Friedrich, consistent with the image he held of himself as an enlightened despot, anticipated many of these changes and worked to institute them in his army. Its capable and faithful service in the 1809 campaign would show the value of his numerous reforms and give both Friedrich and Napoleon good cause for satisfaction.

On the eve of war in 1809, Friedrich's army was divided into two distinct elements. The first was the 12,000-man contingent required of Württemberg under the Rheinbund agreement. Beyond this contingent, however, and very much separate from it in Friedrich's mind, were several thousand additional troops nominally under the King's sole control. Jealously guarded as a symbol of his sovereign independence, this latter force was at Friedrich's disposal for the defence of his own territory and the maintenance of internal order. The distinction between these two sets of troops would cause considerable friction among French, Bavarian and Württemberg authorities as the war expanded beyond the Danube valley and Napoleon levied new military demands on his German allies.

The army's mounted arm consisted of four light cavalry regiments, three

squadrons of guard cavalry, a squadron of Leibjäger and a squadron of
Landdragoner. The light cavalry comprised two regiments each of Jäger zu
Pferd and Chevauxlegers. The Jäger regiments (*König* and *Herzog Louis*) were
brigaded together under GM Christian von Stettner, while GM Friedrich von
Röder commanded the brigade of Chevauxlegers (*Leib* and *Herzog Heinrich*).[14]
Although different in title and uniform, all four regiments were trained for stan-
dard light cavalry missions and all were organized with four squadrons (each

Table 3-1: The Württemberg Army in April 1809

Line Infantry Regiments

Organization: two battalions per regiment; one grenadier and three musketeer companies per battalion; company
strength 175 men; one depot company per regiment.

Uniform: dark-blue coat with distinctive colour on collar; cuffs, lapels, turnbacks; white breeches; helmet.

Regiment (start of 1809)	Colour	Regiment (end of 1809)
von Phull	yellow	*Prinz Paul*
Herzog Wilhelm	orange	*Herzog Wilhelm*
von Camrer	white	*von Phull*
von Franquemont	pink	*von Franquemont*
Prinz Friedrich	light-blue	*Prinz Friedrich*
Kronprinz	white	*Kronprinz*
von Neubronn	red	*von Koseritz*

Light Infantry Battalions

Organization: five companies per battalion (one served as depot).

Uniform: dark-green coat and breeches with distinctive colour on collar, cuffs, turnbacks; shako.

Foot Jäger Battalion *König* (commander: Major von Stockmayer)	black
Foot Jäger Battalion *von Neuffer*	black
1st Light Infantry Battalion *von Wolff*	light-blue
2nd Light Infantry Battalion *von Brüsselle*	light-blue

Light Cavalry Regiments

Organization: four squadrons each (plus depot).

Uniform: dark-blue coat with white leather gear and breeches for the chevauxlegers, dark-green coat with black
leather gear and green breeches for the Jägers; helmet for both.

Regiment	Jacket Colour	Distinctive Colour
Leib-Chevauxlegers-Regiment	dark-blue	brick-red
Chevauxlegers-Regiment *Herzog Heinrich*	dark-blue	yellow
Jäger-Regiment zu Pferd *König*	dark-green	pink
Jäger-Regiment zu Pferd *Herzog Louis*	dark-green	yellow

Guard Units

Garde zu Fuss Battalion

Organization: four companies.

Uniform: dark-blue coat with black facings piped white; white breeches; bearskin.

Garde zu Pferd Regiment

Organization: four squadrons.

Uniform: see note 15.

In addition, the following units were considered part of the king's 'household' (*maison du roi*):
Jäger Battalion *König, Leib-Chevauxlegers,* Jäger-Regiment *König,* 1st Horse Artillery Battery.

Garrison Battalion

Organization: approximately 500 men.

Uniform: dark-blue coat with scarlet facings; white breeches; helmet.

Artillery

Organization: two horse batteries, one foot battery, depot.

Artillery uniform: light-blue coat with black facings trimmed in yellow; light-blue breeches; Raupenhelm. Train
uniform: as artillery but a shako in place of the Raupenhelm.

about 125 sabres strong). In keeping with German military tradition, the First Squadron of each regiment stood on the right of the line and bore the honourary title 'Leib-Eskadron'. The guard cavalry included one Leib or Garde du Corps squadron (127 men) and two squadrons of Grenadiers (126 each); the Leibjäger squadron (130 men) and the small troop of Garde-Gendarmes (28 men) were incorporated into the Guard Regiment during the course of the campaign (June 1809), raising it to a strength of four squadrons.[15] The Landdragoner ('National Dragoons'), 150 strong, were essentially a national paramilitary force controlled by the Ministry of the Interior; intended for internal security duties, they were scattered about the realm in small detachments, but could augment the regular army in emergency situations. The four light regiments, 'the equal of any other light horse' in the estimation of one contemporary cavalry authority, would march with the mobile contingent, leaving the Guard cavalry and the Landdragoner to provide the mounted element of the home defence force under Friedrich's control.[16]

In infantry, Friedrich disposed of seven line infantry regiments, four light infantry battalions, a guard infantry battalion, a garrison battalion and a company of Landfüsiliere (a constabulary unit like the Landdragoner). The line infantry regiments consisted of two battalions, each of four companies (175 men) for a total of approximately 1,400 bayonets.[17] They wore black leather helmets with caterpillar crests and a short, dark-blue coat showing each regiment's distinctive colours on collars, cuffs and turnbacks. Like many armies of the era, regiments were named for their patrons (Inhaber) and names changed when these patrons expired or fell from grace. Two of the infantry regiment Inhaber died in 1809, resulting in a considerable shift in regimental names during the latter stages of the war. Furthermore, one regiment, *von Neubronn*, bore the special title of 'Füsilier-Regiment', but differed in no significant way from the rest of the line infantry.[18]

In addition to the line regiments, Württemberg also boasted four independent battalions of light infantry. Two of these were simply called light infantry battalions (leichte Infanterie-Bataillone) and were generally known by the names of their commanders: Obersts Adolf von Wolff and Felix von Brüsselle; the other two were designated as Foot Jäger Battalions (Fussjägerbataillone). Like the light battalions, the second Foot Jäger Battalion was named after its commander, Oberst Karl von Neuffer, but the first Jäger Battalion, led by Major Ludwig von Stockmayer, had been honoured with the title *König* in recognition of its distinguished performance in 1807. Suckow, encountering these men for the first time, was impressed by their appearance and handsome dark-green uniforms. Each battalion had 686 men in four companies, the front rank armed with rifled muskets (Buchsen) and the second with rifled carbines (Karabiner). Commanded by the thirty-six year old GM Ferdinand August Freiherr von Hügel, they would form the crack Light Brigade in the coming campaign.[19]

The Light Brigade and five of the line infantry regiments were allotted to the main army in the Danube valley, but Friedrich kept the remaining infantry units in Württemberg to provide for the defence of his realm: the Guards, line regiments *Prinz Friedrich* and *Franquemont,* the Garrison Battalion and the

Landfüsiliere. Moreover, he increased the size of his home army as the scope and intensity of the war grew throughout the spring and summer of 1809. The Guard Battalion, for example, with its four companies was similar in strength to the light formations at the start of hostilities, but grew to some 860 men with the addition of a Jäger company during the year. Other combat formations were created by drawing on the depot troops of the units in the field. Württemberg's Guard, line, light and Jäger units had depot companies which remained behind to train recruits and perform administrative functions while the field elements were away. As the war progressed, these depot troops were drawn into battle with insurgents on the kingdom's southern border, where they were organized into more or less permanent battalions to improve cohesion and simplify command (depot battalions *von Berndes* and *von Boxberg* and a Land-Scharfschützen Battalion).[20] The Garrison Battalion and the company of Landfüsiliere also represented potential sources of infantrymen, but neither played a major role in the war. The Garrison Battalion indeed supplied some officers for the new depot units, but only about half of its 500 men were normally fit for duty and its principal function was the security of the Hohenasperg fortress near Stuttgart. As the infantry counterpart of the Landdragoner, the fusiliers (150 men) continued to perform their regular internal security duties.[21]

The artillery of the Württemberg contingent amounted to twenty-two guns distributed among three batteries (two horse and one foot). Each horse battery had four 6-pounders and two 7-pounder howitzers, while the foot battery had eight 6-pounders and two howitzers.[22] The eighteen munitions wagons that belonged to the artillery were supplemented by an additional twelve in the Corps' reserve park; the reserve park also included sixteen wagons for small-calibre ammunition (a responsibility of the artillery) and various transport for other equipment.

The incorporation of all these men into the main army generated a degree of confusion. Intending to keep the Württemberg troops 'close at hand', Napoleon initially declined to attach them to an army corps but held them as 'a special reserve' with which he could weight other formations as required. He changed his mind in early April, however, and assigned the contingent to VIII Corps. This organization, to be commanded by the veteran Marshal Charles Augereau, was scheduled to include the Württembergers (minus one cavalry regiment), GD Dupas's small French infantry division from north Germany, and GD Rouyer's Division of miscellaneous Rheinbund troops. The detached Württemberg cavalry regiment was to be brigaded with the 7th French Hussars under GB La Grange et de Fourilles in GD Lasalle's Light Cavalry Division. As events unfolded, however, this organization was never implemented: Augereau never came to Germany, Dupas's infantry went to IX Corps, and Rouyer's men remained semi-independent. The Württemberg contingent of 12,676 men thus became the *de facto* VIII Corps.[23]

As with the Bavarians, the divisions of VIII Corps were led by Germans, but command of the Corps was entrusted to a Frenchman, GD Vandamme. In the complex command structure common to many Rheinbund contingents, the senior Württemberg officer, GL Franz Maximilian von Neubronn, was thus to have putative responsibility for the internal affairs of the entire contingent and serve as the intermediary between the men and their French commander;

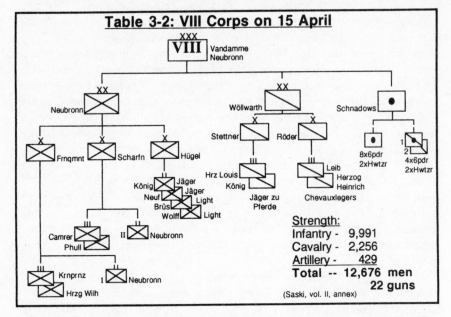

Table 3-2: VIII Corps on 15 April

Strength:
Infantry -   9,991
Cavalry -   2,256
Artillery -   429
Total -- 12,676 men
                      22 guns
(Saski, vol. II, annex)

Vandamme would transmit orders from above and exercise tactical command. Neubronn also headed the contingent's infantry division, consisting of two line brigades of five battalions each (led by GM Friedrich Graf von Franquemont and GM Georg von Scharffenstein) and the energetic GM von Hügel's Light Brigade of four. Oberst Wilhelm von Schnadows commanded the Württemberg artillery and GL Friedrich von Wöllwarth, an extraordinarily capable officer, rode at the head of the cavalry division.

Over and above the combat elements demanded by Napoleon, Friedrich took pains to ensure the logistical needs of his troops were met. Sceptical of the ability of the French logistical system to support his contingent, he ordered the establishment of a well-stocked magazine at Heidenheim and the creation of a wagon train capable of transporting provisions to the units in the field. These prudent measures would do much to ameliorate the soldiers' hardships in the opening weeks of the campaign.

APRIL - LIGHT BRIGADE'S GLORY

As with the other Rheinbund princes, Napoleon wrote to Friedrich from Valladolid on 15 January, discussing Austrian preparations for war and adding 'I suppose your troops are ready to march.'[24] By 20 March 1809, the Württembergers were gathered around Kirchheim (Cavalry Division), Ellwangen and Heidenheim, at which latter place General Vandamme arrived on 5 April to take command. Unfortunately for the two allies, Napoleon's choice angered the Württembergers. Général de Division Dominique-Joseph-René

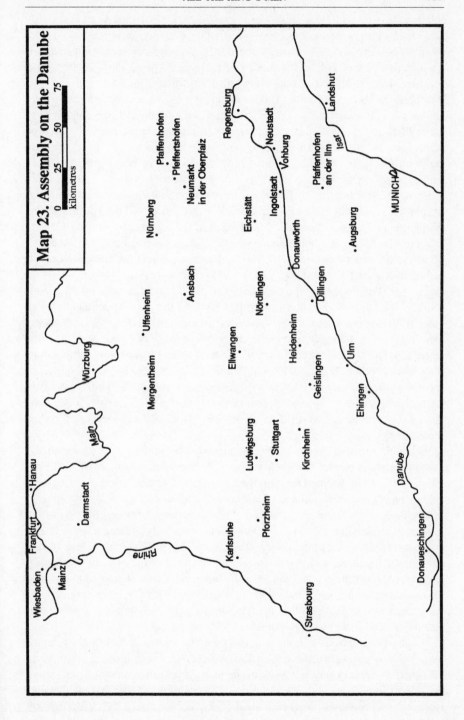

Map 23. Assembly on the Danube

Vandamme, Comte d'Unsebourg, was a competent tactician but a crude and difficult man. Proud and unco-operative with other generals, he was utterly devoted to Napoleon, but his bellicosity led the Emperor to comment 'if I had two Vandammes, I would have to shoot one of them!' None the less, he was a redoubtable fighter and Napoleon had selected him to command the Württemberg contingent in the 1806-7 campaign. Although the contingent performed well, Vandamme treated his Württemberg subordinates harshly, manipulating them for his own ends and constantly interfering in the internal affairs of the corps. By the conclusion of the campaign, his coarseness, arrogance and penchant for illicit profit had disgusted most of the senior Württemberg officers and come to the attention of their sovereign. Friedrich sought to resolve this problem at the Congress of Erfurt in September 1808, and obtained from the Emperor assurances that FZM Friedrich von Camrer would command the Württemberg contingent should it be needed in the foreseeable future. He was thus bitterly indignant when Vandamme was again appointed and protested vigorously to Napoleon in March of 1809. The French general, Friedrich stated, had treated his officers and commanders with 'callousness and rudeness beyond sufferance' during the campaign in Silesia, and his commander-in-chief, von Camrer, had already resigned rather than serve under Vandamme again. The other Württemberg generals had similar misgivings: 'All, starting with the commander-in-chief, are ready to serve under any French general your Majesty nominates for this purpose except General Vandamme, and I must join with them in requesting another choice.' The King's importunities were in vain. Napoleon, recalling the successes of the Württembergers in 1807 ('your majesty's [Friedrich's] troops know and esteem General Vandamme's bravery') and convinced that French officers had to be set over all allied contingents, refused to reconsider his decision.[25]

Although he finally relented, Friedrich was determined to put limits on the French general's power. Vandamme's charter as commander of an allied Corps did not permit him to interfere with the inner administration of the Württemberg armed forces, and Friedrich specifically prohibited his officers from engaging in any behaviour that might be viewed as obsequious or otherwise injurious to the honour of their King and service. Vandamme was to be treated professionally and obeyed in all appropriate matters, but GL von Neubronn, the senior Württemberg general and von Camrer's replacement at the head of the contingent, was authorized to arrest immediately any officer who attempted to advance his own interests through flattery of the French commander; offending officers were to be sent to Stuttgart that the King might personally remind them of who was the sovereign and who the subject.[26]

Despite these difficulties, the imminence of hostilities drove efforts to complete VIII Corps' organization. Vandamme held a thorough inspection from 5 to 10 April, expressing satisfaction with the state of his new command and taking the opportunity to increase the amount of ammunition carried by each soldier from 30 to 40 rounds with an additional 50 rounds per man to be transported by each battalion's ammunition wagon.[27] These measures proved timely, for the Austrians crossed the Inn as Vandamme completed his review and Berthier ordered VIII Corps south towards the Danube. Throughout the 11th and 12th, the men left their comfortable quarters and crossed the border into Bavaria, assembling around Dillingen (13 April) before moving farther east to Donauwörth and Rain. By the 15th, VIII Corps was tightly concentrated in the area between these latter two towns with one battalion and a cavalry regiment forward at Neuburg. The men noticed that the quality of quarters and provisions declined as proximity to the enemy increased.[28] The relative inactivity of the Corps (essentially limited to conducting small reconnaissances) was largely due to the conflicting and imprecise orders issuing from army headquarters as Berthier tried to act in accordance with his interpretation of Napoleon's directives.[29]

With the appearance of the Emperor at Donauwörth on the morning of the 17th, however, events began to move rapidly. Whereas Berthier had thought to follow his master's guidance by pulling most of the army back to the River Lech, Napoleon immediately began to orchestrate a general concentration forward to support Davout at Regensburg and seize the initiative from the sluggish Austrians. The Württembergers were thus ordered to Ingolstadt to form the centre of the army with the Bavarian VII Corps. Departing Rain before dawn on the 18th, Vandamme's men spent a wearing day on their feet. Allotted the same road as GD Nansouty's 6,000 heavy cavalry and the multitudinous vehicles of Imperial Headquarters, VIII Corps' progress was interrupted by frequent halts and the regiments did not reach their bivouacs until late in the evening. The Emperor also betook himself to Ingolstadt, escorted by *Herzog Louis* (from Donauwörth to Neuburg) and the *Leib-Chevauxlegers* (from Neuburg to Ingolstadt) in the absence of his guard (still en route from Spain).[30] Near Neuburg, where the Corps made a rest halt, Napoleon had GL von Neubronn brought to his carriage, complimented the general on the good appearance of the Württemberg soldiers and expressed the hope these men would bring honour to their monarch. He delivered similar praise to GM von Hügel that evening as the Light Brigade was assuming its picket duties near Ingolstadt. Leaving one battalion (II/*von Camrer*) behind to garrison the city, Vandamme and his men marched on the next morning to arrive behind the Bavarian positions along the River Abens late in the evening, exhausted after a long day's march in ceaseless rain. Cold and thoroughly soaked, the men passed a miserable night under the harsh April skies. Despite these lamentable conditions, the discipline and morale of the Württembergers were good, they were in the centre of a mighty army under the personal command of the Emperor and they looked forward to fighting a major battle within his sight. The stage was set for the Battle of Abensberg.

The Jägers of *Herzog Louis* spent the night of the 19th around Imperial Headquarters in Vohburg. Having escorted Napoleon throughout the rainy day, the men and their mounts did not reach the town until long after dark, wet, cold, tired and hungry. Although every structure in Vohburg was already crowded with troops, the Jägers announced that they were the Emperor's escort and space was made for them, more or less grudgingly, in several stalls and barns. They likewise managed to scavenge food for themselves. Fodder for their horses, however, proved a problem. Fortunately, a convoy of French forage wagons bearing fodder for Nansouty's Division was halted in the marketplace, providing the *Louis* Jäger with a perfect target. Each wagon was guarded by a cuirassier, so a Jäger with a rudimentary command of French was detailed to distract the French trooper with conversation while his compatriots slipped under the vehicle, slit open the heavy bags of imperial grain and allowed the contents to drain into royal Württemberg feed sacks. Repeated several times, this simple tactic provided sufficient fodder for the regiment's horses and gave the men another tale to tell the wide-eyed folks at home.[31]

THE BATTLES OF ABENSBERG AND LANDSHUT (20-21 APRIL)

The morning of 20 April found most of the soggy VIII Corps deployed around Neustadt, with von Hügel's Light Brigade near Mühlhausen in the woods west of Siegenburg (the Dürnbucher Forst).[32] Napoleon's plan called for the main weight of the attack to be borne by the Bavarians and Lannes's provisional French Corps; the Württembergers were simply to shield the right flank of VII Corps. Vandamme was thus initially ordered to take his entire corps to Siegenburg but, despite his best efforts, it proved impossible to execute these instructions. The congestion of troops, artillery parks and baggage trains on the narrow roads through the Dürnbucher Forst was such that VIII Corps could make little headway and its route of march was soon changed to bring it directly into Abensberg. Only von Hügel, with the Light Brigade, a horse artillery battery and the Leib-Eskadron of *Herzog Louis,* proceeded through the crowded forest toward Siegenburg to take up positions on the west bank of the Abens opposite the town. As the Emperor reconnoitreed the Austrian positions, however, he again modified the Württemberger's mission and, between 9 and 10 a.m., von Hügel received orders to march north to Abensberg and support the Bavarian attack toward Rohr. The initial plan seems to have been for the Light Brigade to be inserted into the battle between the 1st and 2nd Bavarian divisions (commanded by Kronprinz Ludwig and General Wrede respectively) to fill a gap in the attacking line. Leaving the battalions of von Neuffer and von Brüsselle (as well as the battery and the cavalry squadron) across from Siegenburg, von Hügel took his men along the left bank of the Abens to join the remainder of VIII Corps just east of Abensberg sometime before 2 p.m.[33] Napoleon chose this moment to address the Württembergers. Gathering the Corps around a small knoll later christened 'Napoleonshöhe' by the locals, the Emperor spoke to his men:

> Soldiers of Württemberg! You are about to go into battle against an enemy that has tyrannized Germany for many years. The Hungarians, Bohemians and Austrians have always viewed Germany as their own. As the protector of the Rhenish Confederation, I have placed myself at your head. Previously, your sovereign had but a handful of troops, they could only be viewed as a small contingent. I have increased his state and he now stands as a power in Europe. Show yourselves worthy of the honour to fight alongside the Grand Army, worthy of the trust I place in you. I am

alone in your midst with no Frenchmen about me. This is an unparalleled honour for you. Today I rely principally on you. I have never turned my back on the enemy and will certainly not do so today! In a month we will be in Vienna!

The effect of the Emperor's words and presence on his German allies was electric. The day was 'dreary, raw and rainy', but the Württembergers, just as the Bavarians earlier in the day, responded to this speech with enthusiasm: 'At last the mighty Prince of Battles was with the army, his eagle eye promising dramatic victories, the gripping impact of his very presence a spur to one and all.'[34]

Not long after the harangue, von Hügel's brigade (now consisting of *König, Wolff,* the two chevauxleger regiments, and a horse battery) began to advance east from Bruckhof up the valley of a small stream toward Sallingberg; in accordance with their original mission, they were to cover the widening split between the two attacking Bavarians divisions. Some of the Württembergers apparently reached the village itself before new orders sent them back to the Abens valley to assist Wrede.[35]

While the Bavarian Crown Prince had quickly defeated his opponent (General Thierry) near Offenstetten, Wrede's attack was only making slow progress. Skirmishing had begun at about 10 a.m., and by noon most of his infantry regiments were involved in the battle for the heights between Perka and the Hörlbachs. The attack had stalled, however, and shortly after 2 p.m., he requested and was granted support from von Hügel's brigade.[36] Pulled back from Sallingberg, the Light Brigade was sent into action on Wrede's right to reenergize the attack of the Bavarian II/3 Infantry near Perka. With the *König* Jäger on the left and *Wolff* on the right, von Hügel swept past Perka and up the slopes to the south to attack the right flank of Radetzky's Austrians near Langhaid. Meanwhile, the other battalion of the 3rd Bavarian Infantry had succeeded in clearing Siegenburg and was pressing east from the town. The elements of the Light Brigade which had been left west of the Abens opposite Siegenburg now advanced to join the Bavarian battalion in the village. The Württemberg horse battery assisted in the repulse of an Austrian cavalry attack, and the three battalions (*Brüsselle, Neuffer,* and I/3) then moved against Radetzky's left above the town.[37] Attacked by Württembergers and Bavarians from both Siegenburg and Perka, the Austrian general retired toward Kipfelsberg and von Hügel was able to reunite his brigade around Langhaid.

The allied attack continued, albeit in a rather confused fashion, throughout the afternoon. As soon as his men were reorganized, von Hügel pushed them across the valley that runs between Siegenburg and Irlach and towards the wooded heights south of the latter village. The *König* Jäger, leading the brigade, were in the process of crossing the valley, when their commander, Major von Stockmayer, was wounded in the ankle. Determined to stay with the fight, he had himself bound to his saddle and resumed his place at the head of the battalion. Driving into the woods south of Irlach, however, the battalion met a force of Austrian grenadiers (two battalions from II Reserve Corps) and were sent reeling back. As von Stockmayer tried to reorganize his troops, his horse was suddenly slain by an Austrian bullet, trapping the unfortunate major as it fell to the ground. Bound to the saddlery, Stockmayer was unable to extricate himself and was only rescued from imminent capture or death by the courage of his manservant, who rushed up with another steed, untied his master, and helped him to mount the second horse. The arrival of the other light battalions restored the situation, and the Württembergers soon advanced to seize the heights.[38] It was now near dusk and von Hügel, seeing little wisdom in a night action with exhausted men who were low on ammunition, called off the pursuit. His brigade bivouacked around Umelsdorf for the night.

Although the horse artillery provided excellent support to Hügel's battalions throughout the battle, the bulk of VIII Corps had spent the day in reserve, following the action at a distance. The cavalry followed the light infantry closely (only eleven squadrons as the *König* Jäger zu Pferd were escorting Napoleon and the *Herzog Louis* Leib Squadron was at Siegenburg), but the broken terrain afforded the troopers few opportunities to prove their mettle. They could only demonstrate their courage by retaining their composure under the galling fire of Austrian guns they could not reach. In the afternoon, Napoleon ordered GM von Röder to take the *Leib-Chevauxlegers* to the right toward Siegenburg with a horse battery. Here they found Marshal Bessières, newly arrived from Spain, who promptly took command of Röder's little force. At the Marshal's direction, Premierlieutenant von Blücher rode forward with a detachment to scout the strength of some Austrian cavalry. He manoeuvred his men with such skill and, one must presume, energy, that the Austrians withdrew and Blücher earned Bessières' honest praise.[39] The line infantry of the Corps spent most of the 20th near Bruckhof and camped that night near Siegenburg with the cavalry.

Early the next day (21 April) Napoleon pursued the broken Austrians to the bridges over the River Isar at Landshut. On his own initiative, Vandamme set VIII Corps in motion at 1 a.m. After several brief skirmishes with the Austrian rear guard (*Erzherzog Karl* Uhlans and *Gradiskaner* Grenzer) between Pfeffenhausen and Altdorf, the Württembergers arrived on the bluffs above Landshut. Here FML Hiller, commanding the Austrian left wing, was engaged in a desperate rear-guard action to allow his forces time to escape. To storm the suburbs protecting the crossings, Vandamme ordered the *von Neuffer* and *von Brüsselle* battalions to deploy. Before these two units could get into position, however, Allied cavalry had swept the Austrians from the field and cleared the way to the critical bridges. The two-battalion attack was therefore cancelled and only two companies were sent forward to follow the 3rd Battalion of the French 17th Ligne as it stormed across the flaming bridge and broke in the city's gate.[40]

The Württembergers had little opportunity to exploit the plunder available in Landshut: in the afternoon, the Light Brigade and the *Herzog Louis* Jäger were sent to support GD Saint Sulpice on the road to Regensburg. They arrived in Essenbach at 1:30 a.m. on the 22nd. While the *Herzog Louis* troopers unsaddled and rested their weary mounts, the Württemberg infantrymen were immediately sent on into the night toward Ergoldsbach with one squadron each of Bavarian Chevauxlegers and French cuirassiers under the command of French GB François Clément de la Roncière. After a fatiguing trudge over bottomless roads, the Light Brigade reached Ergoldsbach about 4 a.m., where the *König* Jäger surprised and captured an outpost of 42 Austrian hussars from the *Erzherzog Ferdinand* Regiment. The exhausted soldiers were finally granted a well-deserved chance to rest, having covered more than 60 kilometres and fought two major engagements in the preceding forty-eight hours.

THE BATTLE OF EGGMÜHL (22 APRIL)

In the meantime, Napoleon had gained a clearer appreciation of the tactical situation. New reports from Marshall Davout convinced him that he had only been pursuing part of the Austrian army and that the main enemy force under Archduke Charles still lay to the north about Regensburg. The Emperor immediately set his army in motion toward the enemy, declaring, 'I have decided to exterminate the army of Prince Charles today or at the latest tomorrow.' In the foggy dawn hours of the 22nd, Napoleon's couriers found VIII Corps camped around Altdorf north-west of Landshut and handed its commander his orders for the day. While reconnoitring toward Straubing, Vandamme was to take the bulk of the Corps north on the Landshut—Regensburg road to find the Austrian left flank. With the *Leib-Chevauxlegers* and some horse guns detached to conduct the reconnaissance, and the two battalions of the *von Neubronn* Füsiliers left behind to garrison Landshut, the rest of the Corps headed up the sloppy road toward Eggmühl, arriving at Ergoldsbach at about 7 a.m.[41]

At Ergoldsbach, after only three hours' rest, von Hügel's weary Jägers and light infantrymen were shaken from their sleep, formed up in the damp streets, and once again pushed north as the advanced guard of Napoleon's main army. Arriving at Buchhausen at about 2 p.m., they came into contact with FML Philipp von Vukassovich's Austrian Brigade and opened the Battle of Eggmühl. Vukassovich, with two weak battalions of *Peterwardeiner* Grenzer, four squadrons of *Erzherzog Ferdinand* Hussars and a cavalry battery, had occupied the village with a detachment of the Grenzer while holding the remainder of his little force on the heights to the north. The Württembergers attacked immediately, the *König* Jägers quickly clearing Buchhausen while the other light battalions swarmed through the fields and forests to both sides of the main road. Well coordinated with the advancing infantry, the cavalry and horse artillery deployed to seize the heights south of the Grosse Laaber in a fine display of energy and tactical prowess. Their pieces personally posted by the Emperor, the Württemberg horse batteries were soon engaged in a lively duel with Vukassovich's gunners as increasing numbers of French and German troops began to appear on the road from Landshut. The three cavalry regiments, echeloned behind their batteries, suffered considerably from Austrian shot and shell but displayed such fortitude that GL von Wöllwarth was moved to report: 'Despite this very heavy fire, which here and there tore away a man or horse, the cavalry's discipline and calm were never disturbed in the slightest, rather this fire was endured with a coolness that transcended all my expectations.'[42] It was not long before Vukassovich, discouraged by the heavy masses of allied cavalry approaching up the road from Landshut and the accurate fire of the Württembergers, recognized the futility of his position and wisely withdrew his

men across the Laaber to Eggmühl. In approximately half an hour, the
Württemberg advance guard was therefore master of the bluffs dominating the
Grosse Laaber's south bank and had opened the way for the deployment of the
main army.[43]

As more and more Allied troops arrived from the south, Napoleon began to
make preparations for a major attack against FML Franz Fürst von Rosenberg's
IV Corps on the heights north of the Laaber and ordered the Württembergers to
seize the Eggmühl bridge. Though only a small river, the Laaber and its marshy
valley represented a serious obstacle for formed cavalry and the bridge at
Eggmühl was of critical importance if Napoleon was to get his mass of heavy
cavalry on to the northern bank in an expeditious fashion. Recognizing its
importance, Vukassovich had left a battalion of his Grenzer to defend the bridge
while the regiment's second battalion occupied the actual hamlet and manor
house of Eggmühl. The remainder of his little brigade joined Rosenberg's IV
Corps on the heights north of the village.

The task of seizing the bridge fell to the Light Brigade. Advancing into the
heavy musket fire from the Croats and the crashing rain of iron from the
Austrian artillery on the heights to the north, the Württembergers were twice
repulsed by I/*Peterwardeiner*. Major von Stockmayer, however, rallied the
König Jägers and von Scheidemantel's company of *von Neuffer* to a third
attempt. The fire from the village and manor was terrible, Premier-Lieutenant
von Reinhardt's head was carried away by a cannon ball and the bridge was covered with dead and wounded, but von Stockmayer persisted. Finally, with
superb support from their horse artillery, the Württembergers stormed across the
little span scattering the Grenzer. Their impulse prevented the Austrians from
reorganizing and carried the Jägers to the gates of the walled manor house that
dominated the village. Undaunted by the heavy fire from this small fortress, the
König Jägers broke in the doors and set upon the garrison with bayonets and
musket butts. Charging from room to room, the Württembergers seemed
unstoppable and when Jäger Seitter wrenched a battalion's banner from one of
his opponents, the remainder of the manor's defenders surrendered. In the
meantime, the light infantry with the other three companies of *von Neuffer* had
cleared the village of Grenzer. Within minutes, the Light Brigade thus succeeded in capturing Eggmühl, its bridge, its manor and 300 Croats; the effort had
cost them 51 casualties. Jäger Seitter, personally presenting his trophy to the
Emperor, was rewarded with the Cross of the Legion of Honour and ten gold
napoleons. With this attack, however, the strength of the Light Brigade was
finally used up. Out of ammunition, muddy and exhausted, they collapsed in the
streets of little Eggmühl to watch the unfolding spectacle as thousands of Allied
horsemen trotted coolly into action.[44]

The capture of Eggmühl's tiny bridge by von Hügel's troops allowed the
Emperor to deploy his large force of cavalry (perhaps 7,000 men in $56^1/2$
squadrons) across the Grosse Laaber and open the next phase of the battle.[45]
The Allied squadrons trotted across the bridge and into the spongy meadowland
north of the Laaber, the ten Württemberg squadrons (*König, Herzog Heinrich*
and two squadrons of *Herzog Louis*) forming the centre, flanked on their

extreme left by Seydewitz's Bavarian brigade and on their right by the French heavy divisions of Saint Sulpice and Nansouty.[46] The goal of all this mounted might was the centre of the Austrian IV Corps (Rosenberg), and particularly the large battery of sixteen guns established on the heights north of Eggmühl. A great, confusing cavalry mêlée ensued as the Allies attempted to wrest these guns from their defenders. This phase of the action opened at 2.30 p.m. as von Seydewitz attacked the battery with his two regiments but was charged and hurled back by von Stutterheim.[47] The Württembergers overthrew the pursuing Austrian squadrons, but were themselves repulsed by heavy artillery and infantry fire. The Austrians now moved to attack the Allied cavalry in the valley. The Württembergers defeated the leading Austrian elements, but were pushed back by the enemy's reserves. By now, however, Seydewitz was advancing for his second attack and the French cuirassiers and carabiniers were beginning to move. Although Seydewitz was temporarily checked, the French heavies advanced in perfect order at a slow trot, heading straight for the Austrian guns. Reforming with 'amazing speed', the Württembergers launched their third charge of the afternoon, joining the French heavy regiments and Seydewitz's Bavarians, also in their third charge of the day, to finally overrun the battery.[48] The Austrians fought valiantly, but this awesome onslaught could not be stemmed. By 4 p.m., their centre was broken and twelve of their guns were in the hands of the jubilant Allied cavalry.

The capture of the grand battery finally broke the resistance of Rosenberg's Corps and he withdrew from the Eggmühl heights with Napoleon in close pursuit. The Württemberg light infantry collected numerous prisoners and the *König* Jäger zu Pferd overthrew an Austrian cavalry attack in the ensuing chase. The *Herzog Heinrich* Chevauxlegers also contributed to the pursuit. Detached on the Emperor's orders to support Davout, the GM Röder led the regiment to the army's left flank, where it helped hasten the enemy's withdrawal through the late afternoon and captured some 60 hapless Austrian infantrymen. Toward evening, the chevauxlegers combined with a squadron of French hussars to deliver a solid charge against some Austrian cuirassiers, but enemy reserves counter-attacked, capturing *Herzog Heinrich's* acting colonel and forcing the allies to retire under the cover of darkness.[49]

A night battle also awaited the troopers of *König* Jäger zu Pferd and *Herzog Louis* as the Allies pressed their pursuit of Rosenberg's broken corps. In an effort to delay the apparently tireless French, GM Andreas von Schneller's Austrian cuirassier brigade (regiments *Kaiser* and *Gottesheim*) joined von Stutterheim's decimated regiments and four squadrons of *Ferdinand* Hussars on a rise just south of Alteglofsheim. A dramatic cavalry battle erupted under the spring moonlight as these horsemen collided with some sixty Allied squadrons (more than 7,000 sabres). Deploying with serene professional confidence, Nansouty's cuirassier and carabinier regiments formed the Allied centre, followed by Saint Sulpice's division; with the Bavarians (ten and one half squadrons) held in reserve, the six Württemberg squadrons from Eggmühl (*König* and *Herzog Louis*) swung to their right into the open rolling fields east of the Regensburg road followed by the French 14th Chasseurs. They were soon trading blows with von Stutterheim's men in a wild twilight combat. The Austrians fought courageously, but they were outnumbered and poorly commanded. Charging bravely but separately against Nansouty's massed ranks, Schneller's regiments were swallowed up in a tide of steel-clad Frenchmen and routed. As the French heavies rode over their opponents, the Württembergers handily outflanked the exhausted Austrian light horsemen and sent them fleeing north into the darkness. Von Stutterheim himself barely escaped capture.[50]

One more victory was to be gained by Württemberg arms on 22 April. After reviewing the Württemberg troopers at 9 p.m. near Alteglofsheim, Napoleon sent the energetic GL von Wöllwarth to intercept Austrian baggage trains he expected to find along the Regensburg—Straubing road. Ordering the weary troopers of the *König* Jäger zu Pferd and the two squadrons of *Herzog Louis* back into the saddle, Wöllwarth immediately set out toward the Danube. It was now the second night the *Herzog Louis* Jäger had gone without rest, but they mounted with alacrity and rode off through the night to find the enemy. After questioning local villagers, Lieutenant von Adelsheim of *Herzog Louis* learned that Austrian cavalry were occupying some of the nearby towns and carefully guided the Jägers toward Geisling on the Straubing road. Alerted to the presence of the enemy by the lights in the houses and the barking of numerous dogs, Adelsheim approached the village quietly at about 11 p.m. and sent Sergeant Heinzmann forward to reconnoitre. Heinzmann crept close to one of the lighted homes and peered within to observe a group of Austrians dragoons, eating, drinking and relaxing with their pipes. The presence of the foe confirmed, the Württembergers surrounded the village and attacked with fearful shouts and trumpet blasts. Having neglected to post vedettes, the Austrians were taken utterly by surprise and tumbled out of their lodgings to find the dimly lit streets full of screaming Jägers and flashing swords. In a few minutes the unequal fight was over and an squadron of enemy dragoons was in the hands of the happy Württembergers. In the meantime, the *König* Jäger zu Pferd had found and captured a wagon train and its escort of 160 infantry at nearby Pfatter. Wöllwarth and his men returned to their bivouac near Alteglofsheim exhausted but satisfied with their accomplishments, particularly the seizure of several dozen Austrian horses, much needed to replace their own weary mounts.[51]

In recognition of their courage and stamina, Napoleon honoured the men of the *König* Jäger Battalion by assigning them as his body guard (Leibwache) at Alteglofsheim on the night of 22/23 April. The Jäger zu Pferd regiments, the *Leib* Chevauxlegers and the horse artillery were also encamped here, while the bulk of VIII Corps remained farther south along the Landshut-Regensburg road. The Württemberg line infantry played no part in the Battle of Eggmühl; allotted the end of the march column from Landshut (after the Württemberg Light Brigade and cavalry, the French heavy cavalry, Lannes' Corps, Massena's Corps and several other units), they spent 22 April in reserve.[52]

MAY - FROM THE INN TO THE DANUBE

After their exertions at Eggmühl, the Württembergers had a chance to rest. While Davout's men were storming Regensburg, VIII Corps spent 23 April recuperating near Alteglofsheim; only *Herzog Heinrich*, as part of Napoleon's escort, and *Leib* were present for the capture of the city.[53] Although grateful for a reprieve from the constant marching and fighting they had experienced since the 19th, the Württembergers suffered considerably from lack of provisions (despite the stocks captured at Landshut); the timely arrival of a resupply column from Heidenheim was thus more than welcome. Unfortunately, convoys from Heidenheim would only be able to follow VIII Corps while it remained in Bavaria, and lack of provisions would become a constant source of irritation for the Württembergers as the Allies drove for Vienna.[54]

A further irritation was Vandamme's meddling in the internal affairs of the contingent. Apparently convinced that the Corps' command structure was too clumsy, Vandamme suddenly and unilaterally removed the Light Brigade from the infantry division and placed it directly under his own orders on 24 April. Furthermore, he announced that the chief of staff and the commissary would henceforth report directly to him as corps commander. Although Vandamme may have been sincere when he said that these steps were necessary 'to comply with the intentions of the Emperor', his action abolished many of Neubronn's functions and outraged the Württembergers. They saw Vandamme returning to the evils of the 1807 campaign, interfering with their rightful prerogatives and inserting himself between them and their sovereign. Friedrich, who regarded this order as a violation of the agreement under which Vandamme had been placed in command in the first place, was furious and wrote a strong letter to the self-willed French general stating that 'the manner in which reports are forwarded to me and in which I transmit my orders and discipline neither can nor may change'. Royal ire from distant Stuttgart seems to have had little influence on its target, however, and the autocratic Vandamme continued to manage his German subordinates according to his own views of operational necessity.[55]

With the opening of the pursuit, another problem arose that would plague the Corps for the remainder of the campaign: detached duty. Despite the expressed desire of Friedrich and his officers (as well as Vandamme), Napoleon was accustomed to using his Confederation of the Rhine contingents in small detachments as line of communications troops. Thus, on 24 April, *Herzog Heinrich* was with Imperial headquarters, *von Neubronn* was guarding Landshut, and infantry regiment *von Phull* with two guns took up garrison duties in Regensburg. *Herzog Heinrich* returned to VIII Corps on the 26th, but the *Leib-Chevauxlegers* with GM von Röder were attached to Massena's IV Corps the same day (Röder assumed command of the German brigade in Marulaz's light cavalry division). As the pursuit into Austria continued, this dispersion of VIII Corps assets worsened: *von Neubronn*, *Leib* and *von Phull* remained detached (*von Phull* and its two pieces moved to Passau); *von Camrer* was ordered to garrison Braunau; and *Herzog Heinrich* was again assigned to duties at Imperial headquarters. Vandamme, pressured by the Württemberg generals, complained to Berthier, but to no avail.

The duties of these detached units were often strenuous. *Von Neubronn*, for example, spent much of its time transporting prisoners of war from its base at Landshut to the large French depot at Augsburg, escorting some 18,000 between

22 April and 9 May. Even when it finally marched to join the Corps at Linz, only about 900 men were actually with the regiment, the remaining 500 Fusiliers were still prodding captives back to Augsburg. The troopers of *Herzog Heinrich,* on the other hand, were attached to Imperial Headquarters to perform the demanding duties of 'staff dragoons' (Stabs-Dragoner): courier, relay, escort and other administrative functions which rapidly eroded the strength of the regiment. In addition to these tasks, *Herzog Heinrich* was required to deposit tiny detachments (four chevauxlegers each) at the post stations scattered along the road from Vienna to Ried. Constantly on the move and performing missions the men considered demeaning, the regiment was 'near total dissolution, as the number of combat effective horses is 205, while the number of disabled reaches the extraordinarily high figure of 167'. Despite this 'misuse', *Herzog Heinrich* maintained its battle spirit and fought with conspicuous bravery on the bloody fields of Aspern-Essling.[56]

With the fall of Regensburg, Napoleon reoriented his army, turning east toward the line of the Inn and the Salzach. Massena thus headed for Passau and Schärding while the Emperor himself gathered up his remaining forces to drive on Braunau and Burghausen. The Württemberg Corps was included in this latter column and Vandamme assembled his men at Neufahrn on 24 and 25 April, departing early (between 1 and 2 a.m.) on the 26th for Essenbach as the pursuit began in earnest. The march resumed the following morning, but there were few good routes available and the Württembergers had to share the one main road (*chaussée*) with French heavy cavalry and wagon trains as they laboriously made their way through Landshut to Vilsbiburg. This was a miserable experience for the foot soldiers. Slogging through the cold, pelting rain, the hunched blue columns spent seemingly endless hours on the road, constantly forced to the side and splattered with mud as hustling artillery batteries and haughty cuirassiers (notoriously disdainful of march regulations) splashed past.

The 28th brought more of the same. Characterized by confusion, delay, steady drizzle and increasing frustration, it was an enervating day of fruitless marching and countermarching. Initially slated to cross the Inn at Neu-Oetting, Vandamme was shunted west to Mühldorf when it was discovered the Neu-Oetting bridge had been destroyed. The Württembergers thus reached Neu- and Alt-Oetting south of the Inn via the bridge the Bavarians had repaired at Mühldorf. Here the Corps halted for the night. Unfortunately, it was late, all the local accommodation was already packed full, and the exhausted Germans were left to bivouac in the open under the incessant rain.[57] Napoleon ordered VIII Corps to Braunau early on the morning of 29 April, but bad weather, worse roads and the wound Vandamme had received at Eggmühl (it reopened, forcing the general to seek shelter) delayed the march and dusk found the bulk of the Corps spread along the road east and west of Winhöring.

A tiny part of VIII Corps did succeed in gaining Braunau on the night of the 29th. As a tactical security measure, Vandamme sent his two remaining cavalry regiments (*Herzog Louis* and *König*) ahead of the main body. The regiments halted in Marktl that evening, but an advanced detachment was pushed on toward Simbach under one of Vandamme's aides-de-camp, Adjutant-

Commandant Vincent. Vincent proceeded to send out his own advance guard, and this tiny force, twelve mounted Jägers under a Leutnant Hayd, trotted into Simbach across the river from Braunau at about midnight. Exhibiting the boldness that marked the operations of the French and their Allies, Hayd crossed the Inn with five Jägers early the next morning on a small raft. Finding the city surprisingly empty of enemy, he brought the rest of his little force over and accepted the city's keys from the mayor. He then left some of his men to hold the town and marched on foot with eight Jägers and a few French hussars to explore the area near Ranshofen. Here he found a monastery housing more than 300 sick and wounded Austrians as well as sufficient wine to entertain the Württemberg soldiers. After a brief conversation with the prior and several wounded enemy officers, the lieutenant loaded the Austrians' weapons and equipment into three requisitioned wagons and returned to Braunau with his miniature detachment. In all, it was an enterprising and audacious little reconnaissance, typical of the spirit that pervaded this army, but the tale of Hayd's adventure apparently grew with its telling, and by the time the story reached King Friedrich, Leutnant Hayd and his men had not only captured 300 armed and healthy Austrians but had also bagged a large provisions train. As a result, Friedrich elevated Hayd to the standing nobility and passed out decorations to each of the Jägers, an example of royal largess to inspire emulation in the rest of the contingent. Tragically, the lieutenant had only a few years to enjoy his reward; he died in some nameless Polish village in January 1813 during the retreat from Russia.[58]

By the time Hayd returned to Braunau on the afternoon of the 30th, the Light Brigade and both Jäger zu Pferd regiments were in Simbach, but the rest of the Corps, bogged in the dreadful roads, only reached Marktl. For the Emperor, impatiently pacing back and forth at Burghausen as the bridge was slowly repaired, Vandamme's progress was unacceptably slow and sharp reminders left no doubt that VIII Corps was to cross the Inn at Braunau without further delay.[59] The remaining Württemberg formations duly arrived opposite Braunau on the morning of 1 May and by 9 a.m. the Corps had begun its crossing of the Inn. With no bridge, however, the passage proceeded with painful slowness, the infantry ferried over on a few small and wretched boats, the artillery reaching the eastern bank via difficult fords. The lack of a bridge and the poor state of the boats caused the cavalry to march north to Schärding where they forded the river in columns of four on the 1st. The crossing at Braunau, on the other hand, could not be completed before the early hours of the 2nd. Leaving *von Camrer* behind to garrison Braunau, the weary Corps, drenched by the continuing rain, trudged several dozen kilometres further east before halting shortly after noon: Vandamme with the cavalry, light infantry and horse artillery at Riedau; the foot battery and the two remaining line infantry regiments (*Kronprinz* and *Herzog Wilhelm*) at Aurolzmunster.

Farther south, the rest of Napoleon's pursuit column had finally managed to rebuild the bridge at Burghausen and, with most of his forces now east of the Inn—Salzach obstacle, the Emperor drove for the next Austrian defensive line, the River Traun. Lannes reached the river at Wels on the 2nd and restored the bridge the following morning, while Massena grappled with Hiller for the possession of the span at Ebelsberg further north. The Württemberg Corps, its undetached elements finally reunited, spent the night in villages just west of Wels.

Vandamme was ordered towards Enns on 4 May and VIII Corps moved down the west bank of the Traun to use the bridge Massena had captured on the 3rd. The Corps thus had to traverse Ebelsberg, grisly with the wrack left by the previous day's ferocious battle. The columns were still moving through the smouldering village when a counter-order sent them back through its blackened streets to take up positions around Linz. Although some elements (apparently the cavalry and the Light Brigade) arrived in Linz in the late afternoon, the rest of the weary Corps would not close on the city until after midnight.[60]

RIDING WITH MASSENA: THE *LEIB-CHEVAUXLEGERS* (1-3 MAY)

Preceded in the pursuit by Lannes' command and the numerous French cavalry, most of VIII Corps thus experienced little contact with the enemy from 23 April to 4 May. The *Leib-Chevauxlegers,* however, attached to Massena's IV Corps since 26 April, added a bright little chapter to their history. Constantly employed with the advance guard ahead of the Corps' march columns, the Württemberg horsemen encountered Austrian hussar pickets from *Kienmayer* south-east of Riedau on 1 May. The foremost squadron (the Leib-Eskadron under Rittmeister Friedrich von Bismark) was leading the rest of the vanguard by about half an hour as it quickly pushed the Austrian vedettes back two or three kilometres into a small forest. Several companies of French voltigeurs hustled the enemy out of the trees, but the Württembergers emerged from the woodline to find themselves facing a dangerously large force of Austrian cavalry and infantry.[61] Directly ahead of Bismark's squadron was a skirmish line supported by an entire battalion of line infantry (III/*Jordis*), behind them two squadrons of *Kienmayer* Hussars and, further to the rear, the Rittmeister could clearly discern the formations of an entire enemy brigade. The only other allied troops in the immediate vicinity were the French voltigeurs, but these elected to remain in the relative safety of the woods. Deploying into the open beyond the sheltering trees, the Württembergers suffered the fire of the Austrian skirmishers while awaiting further orders, but the senior officer with the avant-garde, a French colonel from Massena's staff, appeared distinctly ill at ease and incapable of making a decision. Musket balls whistled past Bismark's head, picking off his men, and the Austrian hussars made ready to charge the outnumbered Württembergers, but still the colonel gave no orders. Finally, frustrated by the indecision of his French superior, von Bismark turned to his troopers, commanded 'Marsch! Marsch!' and spurred forward. Cheering, the men leaped forward behind him and overran the line of skirmishers in concert with the Baden Light Dragoons, who had fortunately appeared on the scene. The squadron was halted and disordered by the charge, however, and Bismark's horse was killed. Quickly extricating himself from his fallen mount, the determined Rittmeister hastily reformed his men and charged the approaching Austrian hussars. Fighting with desperate courage, Bismark and his men were able to contain the enemy until Majors Karl von Palm and Karl von Normann could bring their squadrons into the battle. Attacking from the flanks, these fresh Württemberger troopers combined with the Badeners and overthrew the hussars, chasing their defeated opponents for five kilometres before Austrian reserves brought the pursuit to a halt. For the loss of two dead and ten wounded, the Württembergers inflicted about 40 casualties on the *Kienmayer* hussars and captured some 90 *Jordis* infantrymen. At Massena's recommendation, Napoleon recognized Bismark's valour by awarding him the Legion of Honour on 5 May. Friedrich also decorated the squadron commander and distributed an additional twenty medals among the officers and men of the Leib-Eskadron. The French soldiers chose another way to demonstrate appreciation: they presented the *Leib-Chevauxlegers* with a cask of wine, saying 'pour la cavallerie allemande, qui est si excessivement brave'.[62]

As part of the Corps' vanguard, most of the *Leib* regiment was also present for the rear-guard battle at Eferding on 2 May. Although it took part in the pursuit of the Austrians, it saw no real action that day and lost only three horses. Von Palm's squadron, sent to scout the Corps' right flank and establish contact with Lannes later in the day, collected a few Austrian stragglers but found no formed enemy troops. The regiment was also on hand for the bloody struggle at Ebelsberg on the 3rd; standing in formation on the west bank of the Traun, it took losses from Austrian artillery fire, but this was an infantry fight and the chevauxlegers had no opportunity to engage the enemy.

VIII CORPS AT LINZ (4-16 MAY)

While the *Leib-Chevauxlegers* continued toward Vienna with Massena, the bulk of the exhausted VIII Corps, finally (4/5 May) closed on Linz.[63] Minus its many detachments, it now counted only eight battalions, eight squadrons and 20 guns (approximately 5,600 infantry and 980 cavalry). Its mission was to protect the army's line of communications along the Danube, rebuild the bridge linking Linz to Urfahr and secure a bridgehead across the river. Despite a severe lack of river-crossing materials, Vandamme decided to launch his men across the Danube on the 5th.[64] After displaying the entire Corps on the slopes south of the river at dawn to awe the Austrians, the French general ordered the Light Brigade to cross the Danube. An initial attempt by twenty men from von Scheidemantel's company of *von Neuffer* failed because of the Jägers' inability to handle their little boat. Seeing the plight of the frustrated Jägers, two civilian boatmasters from Ulm (in Linz on business) offered von Neuffer their services. With their help, Karl von Scheidemantel's and Karl von Seeger's companies of *von Neuffer* (200-300 men) were ferried across the Danube in two clumsy boats, covered by a heavy artillery barrage (about 8.30 a.m.).[65] The defenders consisted of ten companies of the 3rd and 4th Prachiner Landwehr battalions reinforced by some replacement detachments and a squadron of *Vincent* Chevauxlegers under GM Johann von Richter (total about 1500 infantry and 100 horsemen). Having no guns with which to respond to the steady fire from von Schnadows' cannon, Richter's Landwehr and recruits were rapidly demoralized. To their great surprise, therefore, von Neuffer and his men reached the north bank without casualties; they debarked and immediately assaulted Urfahr. The affair was over in less than thirty minutes. Attacked in the flank, the confused and ill-trained Landwehr took to their heels, leaving 180 prisoners, including General Richter, in the hands of the Württemberg light troops. The affair cost *von Neuffer* several wounded. By late morning, the rest of the Light Brigade and two squadrons of the *König* Jäger zu Pferd were also across, and the energetic Württembergers were already posting scouts in all directions. The bridgehead was established.[66]

VIII Corps remained in Linz for the next two weeks, resting, replenishing its supplies from the city's magazine, and rebuilding the bridge over the Danube (completed 8 May). Conscious of the threat posed to the bridgehead by the Austrians in Bohemia (FZM Kolowrat's III Corps), Vandamme sent the Württemberg light infantry and cavalry on periodic reconnaissances to the north. On 7 May, for example, Major Graf von Salm reconnoitred toward Freistadt with his squadron (Leib) of *König* and two companies of *von Neuffer* (von Starkloff and von Seeger). In a brief skirmish, he pushed an enemy detachment from Unter-Weitersdorf to Götschka, capturing some 20 Austrians for a loss of eight Württembergers, but he returned to Urfahr that evening without having reached his destination.[67] A second, stronger reconnaissance under Oberst von Breunig pushed through Freistadt on the 9th, but made no contact with the enemy.[68] The results of an extended reconnaissance conducted by GL Wöllwarth (11-13 May) were equally disappointing — only three Austrians were captured and a Württemberg cavalry post left in Freistadt was surprised and taken by *Merveldt* Uhlans on the 13th. Despite this setback, General Wöllwarth consistently proved himself a skillful and aggressive commander, providing Vandamme with good information and constantly seeking opportunities to attack the enemy.[69]

Although his attention remained focused on the threat to the north, Vandamme's area of responsibility expanded south of the Danube to the line of the River Enns as May progressed and French forces flooded east toward Vienna. One company from each of the Jäger battalions and a mixed detachment of cavalry from both regiments (about 100 horsemen) were thus sent to Steyr on the Enns on the 10th; they were reinforced by one company from each of the light battalions five days later. Fortunately for Vandamme, this increase in responsibility coincided with the return of many of VIII Corps' detached elements: *Neubronn* arrived in Linz on the 9th, I/*Camrer* on the 11th (II/*Camrer* was still at Ried near Braunau), and *Phull* with its two cannon on the 12th. The Corps thus counted thirteen battalions (7,388 men), eight squadrons (980 troopers) and all 22 guns by mid-May. Additionally, Bernadotte's Saxon IX Corps was now coming into supporting distance; its lead division reached the Eferding on the 16th.

THE BATTLE OF LINZ (17 MAY)

This support proved timely indeed, as FZM Johann Graf Kolowrat-Krakowsky's III Austrian Corps (18,000 infantry, 1,400 cavalry and 50 guns) was preparing to assault Urfahr in an effort to draw French forces away from Vienna and the

grand battle Archduke Charles was expecting there. Kolowrat began to move on
the 12th, but his slow advance and imperfect security procedures alerted the
Allies and reports of Austrian activity soon reached Vandamme. Concerned that

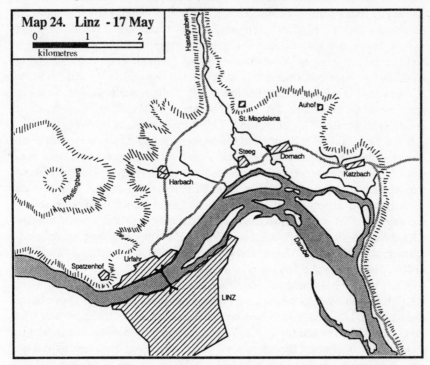

Map 24. Linz - 17 May

Linz might be in danger, Vandamme took the prudent course and ordered his
Corps in closer to Urfahr to provide better protection to the bridgehead. To
monitor enemy activities while the other outposts pulled back, a reconnaissance
detachment (72 Jägers of von Starkloff's company and 80 *Herzog Louis* troopers) was sent from Hellmonsödt toward Leonfelden on the morning of the 16th.
Coming upon an overwhelming enemy force (about 5,500 infantry, 200 cavalry
and six guns), the Württembergers were forced back to Zwettl an der Rodl.
Despite overwhelming odds, they conducted their withdrawal so skillfully that
their losses amounted to only three wounded and five prisoners, and the soldiers
marched into the bridgehead well satisfied with themselves. In addition to
returning with almost all of its men, the detachment brought back sufficient
information on Austrian strengths and dispositions to convince Vandamme an
attack was imminent.[70]

   Kolowrat was certainly moving, albeit torpidly, to assault the Urfahr position.
He had divided his forces into three columns: a right column (under FML
Somariva) was to advance on Urfahr from the north, a centre column (FML
Vukassovich) to attack through Gallneukirchen, and a left column (FML Saint
Julien) to support from the south-east along the Danube. Kolowrat himself
accompanied the centre column. The principal effort would be borne by the
centre and right columns, which were to be in position to attack simultaneously

on the afternoon of the 17th.

Vandamme arranged his defence by placing the cavalry and the light/Jäger battalions north and east of Urfahr on the main approaches to the bridgehead. To the east, one company of *Neuffer* was established in a picket line just beyond Katzbach with a detachment in Steyregg; west of Katzbach were three companies of *König* and seven squadrons from the Jäger zu Pferd regiments. The northern approach, where Vandamme expected the main attack, was covered by *Wolff* and *Brüsselle* at Ober Steeg with a small outpost on the heights at St. Magdalena.[71] Farther up the Haselbach valley, the remaining Jäger squadron (von Wagner's of *König*) and another company of *Neuffer* were at Wildberg under GM Stettner's command. The final company of *Neuffer* (von Scheidemantel's) was at Spatzenhof on the western flank. Von Scharffenstein's brigade (*Phull* and *Neubronn*) was held within the bridgehead ramparts, while von Franquemont's (*Herzog Wilhelm* and *Kronprinz*) was in Linz as reserve. One company each from the light/Jäger battalions and 100 cavalrymen were posted around Steyr, and I/*Camrer* was at Enns. In addition, elements of Bernadotte's IX Corps deployed across the river during the course of the day: the light cavalry of the advance guard under GM von Gutschmid arrived north of the bridgehead around 7 a.m. and GM von Hartitzsch's Infantry Brigade was in place behind it by the first hours of the afternoon.[72]

When Kolowrat's centre column debouched from the hills at about 2 p.m. on the 17th, it thus ran into the Jäger zu Fuss and zu Pferd. The fight opened in an almost languid fashion during the warm afternoon, the skirmishers of both sides slowly manoeuvring and firing, the Württemberg cavalry waiting dismounted by their steeds. Kolowrat, the success of whose plan hinged on timing, did not want to launch a serious attack until he knew Somariva was in position and was thus hesitant to commit his forces. In this tentative, restrained stage of the combat, the commander of *Herzog Louis*, Major von Waldburg, joked that, having missed breakfast, he would like a sip of wine before the battle. In true light cavalry manner, one of his subordinates, Lieutenant Finckh, rode the 100 or so metres forward to the village of Katzbach in search of an appropriate vintage for his chief. As he took delivery of a flask of Tyrolian wine, he noticed a group of Saxon hussars busily requisitioning quarters and food for the night, completely oblivious to the growing musket fire outside.

In fact, Kolowrat had finally received word that Somariva was en route and a spirited fight quickly developed around Katzbach as the Austrians began to attack in earnest. The Württembergers resisted stoutly, but were soon overpowered and evicted by pressure from Kolowrat's advance guard under FML Karl Graf Crenneville. The Saxons were mostly bundled up and captured in the ensuing confusion and Lieutenant Finckh barely escaped with his bottle.[73] The *König* Jäger did manage to go forward and regain the village temporarily, but the Austrian 6th Jäger Battalion, supported by II/*Peterwardeiner* Grenzer, were soon in control again. By 2.30 p.m., the 6th Jägers and three companies of Grenzer were attacking Dornach and threatening the bridgehead entrenchments. The other companies of the *Peterwardeiner* battalion were moving on through Auhof toward St. Magdalena, while additional infantry and Uhlans deployed beyond Katzbach.[74]

Before long, the 6th Jägers were lodged in the peripheral houses of Steeg and the rest of the advance guard was also gaining ground. Kolowrat judged the time ripe to bring up his main body. Another seven battalions thus emerged from the woods east of Katzbach, supported by two squadrons of *Hessen-Homburg* Hussars and a battery. The three companies of *Peterwardeiner* on the far right had just pushed the small Württemberg detachment out of the walled churchyard at St. Magdalena and all was proceeding fairly well for the Austrian commander when Kolowrat observed a great deal of dust and activity around the bridgehead.

Vandamme, overcoming his surprise that the Austrians would attack so late in the day, was taking swift countermeasures. The two line brigades, supported by the cavalry and the horse artillery, were ordered to attack the Austrian centre while the light battalions were sent against the enemy's right; from the south bank of the Danube, four guns of the foot battery were to direct their fire against the Austrian left (the other six were in the Urfahr redoubts). These aggressive moves were completely successful. Battalions *von Wolff* and *von Brüsselle* boldly clambered up the Magdalena-Berg, threw the Grenzer off, and turned south to take the Austrians north of Dornach in the flank. Meanwhile, *von Neubronn*, *von Phull* and the *König* Jägers stormed through the village and pressed Kolowrat's men back toward Katzbach.[75] Austrian Uhlans moved forward to relieve the pressure on their Jägers, but a wild charge by two squadrons of *Herzog Louis* overwhelmed them and sent them flying through Dornach, the Württembergers close on their heels.[76] By now (about 6 p.m.), the Austrians had been beaten back all along the battleline: von Scharffenstein's brigade was advancing out of Dornach toward Katzbach supported by the two cavalry regiments and the horse artillery, while *Wolff* was moving on Auhof with some elements of *Neuffer*; patrols from *Brüsselle* were scouring the woods north and east of St. Magdalena collecting up Austrian stragglers and posing a potential threat to Kolowrat's line of retreat. In addition, von Franquemont's brigade was about to deploy north of Dornach and some of Gutschmid's Saxon cavalry (three hussar squadrons and a half-squadron of *Herzog Albrecht* Chevauxlegers) was also approaching.[77]

An Austrian battery was situated on a height north of Katzbach, however, and its fire brought the Württemberg infantry to a halt. Determined to keep the attack rolling, General Wöllwarth sent the *Herzog Louis* troopers forward to deal with these guns. Riding hard, two squadrons of Jägers swung around the hill to the south and charged pell-mell up the steep slope, utterly surprising the Austrian gunners and temporarily silencing the battery. Austrian reserves rushed forward, but the lack of artillery fire had allowed other Württembergers to approach and another squadron of *Herzog Louis* rushed the hill from the north-west while the grenadiers of *von Phull* charged the battery frontally. The Saxon Hussars and Chevauxlegers sent by Bernadotte pounded up to seal the victory. The Austrians were thrown back to the east and all six guns fell into the hands of the Germans. With the capture of the battery, the fighting in this area slowly came to a close; the Austrians withdrew toward Gallneukirchen and the

Württembergers were too exhausted to send more than harassing patrols in pursuit.[78]

As the Austrian guns were being taken, a curious incident occurred near Auhof. Sergeant Weiss of *Herzog Louis* had served in the Austrian army up to 1805, during which time he had been cruelly punished by an officer for some minor infraction. When his district was ceded to Württemberg by the Habsburgs under the Treaty of Pressburg, he was taken into Friedrich's service as a *Louis* trooper. Now, on the field of battle, he recognized the man who had wronged him years before. Oberst Winzian, commander of infantry regiment *Manfredini* was attempting to regain his own lines when Weiss galloped forward and seized hold of him. The Oberst, nursing a wounded arm since Teugn (19 April), was unable to defend himself, and Weiss forced him to the Württemberg side of the field. As Weiss's comrades cheered, a final quaint touch was added to the scene: Winzian's servant, with his spare horse, rode up to join his master in captivity. Weiss was made an officer in reward for this audacious act of revenge.[79]

At about this time, Somariva put in a belated appearance on the Pöstlingberg above Urfahr (539 metres high). Although there were few Allied troops between him and the bridge, he could easily observe the retreat of Kolowrat's column from his vantage point and decided to withdraw his own force after a brief cannonade. Bernadotte twice sent his Saxons (elements of regiments *Prinz Friedrich August*, *Dyherrn* and *Prinz Maximilian*) up the difficult slopes against the Austrians, but their defensive position was very advantageous and both attacks were repulsed.

Vandamme, however, despite his friendship with Bernadotte, was not about to let the Saxons steal any of the day's glory. Somariva's troops had bivouacked for the night in their strong position and the French general was determined to dislodge them: he ordered General von Hügel to take the mountain. Although his men were out of ammunition and thoroughly exhausted, the energetic von Hügel gathered the *König* Jäger and Seeger's company of *von Neuffer* and advanced to the attack at about 10 p.m. With fixed bayonets, the weary Jägers struggled up the steep, wooded slopes in utter darkness, *von Brüsselle* following in support. They silently overwhelmed the first line of Habsburg pickets, but their approach was revealed when they came upon the second line and an alert Austrian raised the alarm. Trusting to surprise and audacity, the Württembergers gave a terrifying yell and threw themselves upon the enemy. The shocked Austrians, discovering the danger too late, initially put up a confused and desperate defence, but were soon fleeing through the dark woods in complete panic, chased by the screaming, whooping Jägers. In this bold night action, a few determined companies of Jägers hurled a numerically superior enemy out of an advantageous defensive position and captured close to 400 prisoners. It was a magnificent feat of arms. The threat to Urfahr was eliminated.

It remains to account for FML Franz Saint Julien's column. This general's forward scouts, about twelve horsemen, appeared near Mauthausen early in the morning and were fired upon from the south bank of the Danube by a company of I/*Camrer*. An adventurous *Camrer* lieutenant took nine men across the river in a small boat to cut off the Austrians, but soon found his own retreat route closed. Although the Württembergers attempted to defend themselves, their cause was hopeless and most of the bold little band were soon captured; only two of their number escaped to the south bank. Apparently thinking to fulfill his mission, Saint Julien unlimbered his artillery and opened a bombardment of the *Camrer* company, the only effect of which was to lighten to load of the Austrian ammunition wagons. The column, having contributed nothing to Kolowrat's plan, returned to Gallneukirchen at dusk.[80]

The action at Linz/Urfahr on 17 May was a signal victory for Vandamme and the Württembergers. At a cost of about 320 casualties (the Saxons lost an additional 88), they inflicted about 1,000 on their opponents and took six of his guns. The Württembergers had performed splendidly, and their monarch was generous in rewarding his army. Numerous promotions and awards were distributed to all ranks and the *Herzog Louis* Jäger zu Pferd were granted a special Standard of Honour (Ehrenstandarte) in recognition of their capture of the Austrian battery. Vandamme was very pleased and Bernadotte said of the Württembergers: 'Their deeds can only be compared with those we are accustomed to achieve with the most experienced French troops.'[81]

JUNE/JULY - RIVER RAIDS AND FLANK SECURITY

For VIII Corps, Linz/Urfahr was the last major engagement of the 1809 campaign. Their security mission remained, however, and in the days following the victory at Linz, the Corps found itself scattering large detachments both north and south of the Danube to keep the enemy off balance and shield the main army's line of communications from further disruptions. Indeed, Vandamme had received orders on the 17th to take 6,000 men south to guard the defiles leading out of the Alps into the Danubian Plain. Although the Battle of Urfahr delayed execution of these orders, the 18th saw GM von Hügel moving south toward Steyr with a small force. At the same time, GM von Stettner marched north from Linz through the Haselbach Valley toward Hellmonsödt. His detachment consisted of von Starkloff's company of *Neuffer*, fifty Jägers each from *Herzog Louis* and *König*, and fifty musketeers from *Herzog Wilhelm*. A brisk skirmish ensued when the detachment came upon a small Austrian rear guard near Hellmonsödt. The determined Württembergers pushed the Austrians out of the hamlet and began to pursue them, but called off the chase when additional Habsburg troops appeared on the road from Freistadt. By nightfall, Stettner and his men were back in the bridgehead.[82] Although they had inflicted but few losses on their foes in their expedition, the Württembergers again displayed a degree of initiative, aggressiveness and tactical competence that distinguished them from many of the other German contingents in Napoleon's army.

Over the next three days, VIII Corps turned over defence of the bridgehead to the Saxons and began moving out of Linz to assume new positions along the Enns from Steyr to the Danube. By 21 May, the Corps was therefore arrayed as follows:

Enns - Corps headquarters, GM von Franquemont, *Herzog Wilhelm*, *Neuffer* (three companies), 1st Horse Battery;

St. Florian - GL von Neubronn, *König* Jäger zu Pferd;

Kremsmünster - GL von Wöllwarth, *Herzog Louis, Brüsselle*, half of the 2nd Horse Battery;

Steyr (or en route) - GM von Hügel, *Kronprinz, König, Wolff*, one company of *Neuffer*, 100 detached cavalry, the other half of the 2nd Horse Battery;

Linz - GM von Scharffenstein, *Neubronn*, I/*Phull*, 200 Foot Jägers, 50 troopers from *König*, the foot battery and artillery park;

Wallsee and Ybbs - II/*Phull*;

Ried and Braunau - II/*Camrer*;

en route for Vienna - I/*Camrer*;

Vienna - *Leib-Chevauxlegers;*

Vienna and line of communications - *Herzog Heinrich*.[83]

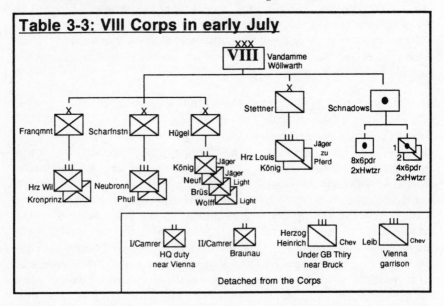

Table 3-3: VIII Corps in early July

From 22 to 24 May, GL von Wöllwarth led a reconnaissance south into the Alps, reaching Windischgarsten before being recalled. Other than this, the Corps' brief repose along the Enns was without incident and, on the 26th, it shifted east again, marching through Amstetten and Melk to arrive in St. Pölten on the 28th.

Given the mission of guarding Napoleon's line of communications from Vienna to Melk, Vandamme established his headquarters in St. Pölten and posted his brigades in Melk (von Scharffenstein), St. Pölten (von Franquemont), Herzogenburg (cavalry) and opposite Krems (von Hügel). They held this section of the Danube through the end of the campaign, keeping watch on the local populace and repulsing Austrian forays from across the river. The position was over-large for VIII Corps (Nübling claims each Jäger battalion had to observe almost ten kilometres of riverfront), and the Austrians were not slow to notice the thinness of the Württembergers' picket lines.[84] In the early morning hours of 31 May, they launched a raid (about 1,200 men) across the Danube near

Hollenburg and began to move up the Traisen Valley. Von Hügel, however, responded with aplomb. Using *Neuffer* to delay the Austrian advance, he gathered his brigade and the cavalry around Göttweig and launched a counter-attack towards the Austrian line of retreat at about 6.30 a.m. The Austrians discovered his plan too soon, however, and the little victory brought the Light Brigade only 50 prisoners.[85] Vandamme ordered the Württemberg artillery to set the city of Krems afire in an otiose effort to punish the Austrians and destroy their river boats; neither objective was achieved despite several hours of bombardment.[86]

At Napoleon's direction, the Württembergers launched a cross-river sortie of their own on 24 June: 360 men of *Wolff* under Major Küchler attacked an Austrian camp opposite Melk and seized about 90 prisoners.[87] As Napoleon prepared for his second attempt to cross the Danube, however, he drew VIII Corps closer to the Austrian capital to guard the river and monitor the behaviour of that city's population during the upcoming struggle. The Corps thus shifted east once more, establishing its right wing in Vienna and its left in Klosterneuburg (headquarters with Generals Vandamme and Wöllwarth at the latter).[88] Specifically, the Corps was disposed as follows: *Brüsselle* in Göttweig, *Wolff* at Melk, von Scharffenstein's brigade between Zwentendorf and Klosterneuburg, von Franquemont's two regiments from the latter to Vienna, GM von Stettner with *König* in Döbling and GM von Hügel commanding the two Jäger battalions along the river at Vienna.[89] The Württembergers were disturbed in their new positions on 3 July when about 800 Austrians sallied across the Danube at Greifenstein, but the enemy departed quickly when Vandamme sent reinforcements to the threatened locale (von Franquemont's brigade and the two Jäger regiments). A more serious attempt was made against the positions of *Brüsselle* on 6 July. At 1.30 a.m., the Austrians sent three columns of 800 men each over the river, striking at near Göttweig, Traismauer and Zwentendorf. The battle near Göttweig lasted until 6 p.m., with *Brüsselle* making such a stout defence (one village changed hands three times), that Austrian General Hardegg finally withdrew his force. The central group got as far as Herzogenburg, but was attacked and pursued with great élan by elements of Major von Salm's tiny cavalry detachment (part *Herzog Louis* and part *König*); likewise, the effort at Zwentendorf failed in the face of I/*Neubronn's* defence.[90]

Although these skirmishes along the banks of the Danube proved to be the last combat actions for most of the Württembergers before the armistice of Znaim, VIII Corps continued to figure prominently in Napoleon's calculations through the final days of the campaign. The night after Wagram (6 July), with the enemy situation far from clear, the Emperor was concerned for the safety of Vienna and the bridges at Lobau Island. Vandamme therefore received orders to extend his screen along the Danube by posting one of his brigades at Ebersdorf, while establishing contact with GD Reynier's Saxons across the river at Enzersdorf and GD Louis Comte Baraguey d'Hillier's Italians opposite Pressburg. Although he was to maintain his troops as far north as Melk, Vandamme's focus thus shifted to the south and he was soon placed under the command of Viceroy Eugène. Eugène, with the Saxons and Württembergers as well as his own Army of Italy, had the mission of protecting the main army's rear from threats out of Hungary as Napoleon pursued Charles north into Moravia. As Vandamme still retained responsibility for the area north of Vienna, Eugène was told to allow his new subordinate 'plenty of latitude' to act according to circumstances on the right bank of the river. Napoleon, moreover, considered Vandamme 'an officer of great zeal and talent' who could be relied upon to act appropriately within the bounds of the Emperor's intentions. These comprehensive instructions brought a large portion of the Württemberg Corps south of Vienna, and by 11 July, Vandamme's men were disposed to screen the river from Melk to Fischamend and react to threats from either Pressburg or Wiener Neustadt: Corps headquarters with four line battalions and six guns at Fischamend; one light battalion and a squadron at Ellend to reconnoitre toward Bruck an der Leitha; three line battalions and twelve pieces at Schwechat; *Herzog Louis* at Himberg to scout towards Wiener Neustadt and maintain liaison with Fischamend; the other three light battalions and four cannon just north of Vienna; and garrisons at the Göttweig and Melk monasteries provided by II/*Neubronn*. It was in these locations that the Württembergers learned that an armistice had been signed at Znaim on the 12th.[91]

With the conclusion of hostilities, the Württembergers lost the designation VIII Corps (the title was transferred to Junot's command in Saxony), but they remained in Austria until December, performing various security and garrison duties and acquiring a reputation as unpleasant guests.[92]

THE CHEVAUXLEGER REGIMENTS (MAY-JULY)

During its sojourn in Vienna, the Corps was finally reunited with the *Leib-Chevauxlegers*. This regiment had accompanied IV Corps on its march to Vienna and had temporarily left a small detachment at Wallsee, but it took no part in the small battles that occurred en route to the Austrian capital. The chevauxlegers probed to Fischamend with Marulaz on 14 May, but were assigned to the garrison of Vienna on the 15th, where they remained throughout June and July. Their losses during this period amounted to three troopers murdered by patriotic Austrian farmers and GM von Röder, somewhat ignominiously captured by local Landwehr while on a social outing.[93]

The other Chevauxlegers regiment, *Herzog Heinrich*, did not rejoin its comrades until after the conclusion of the armistice. Scattered in small detachments along the army's line of communications to mid-May, the bulk of the regiment was recalled to Imperial headquarters in time for the Battle of Aspern-Essling (21-2 May). Initially part of the Emperor's escort, the regiment was sent to replace the Baden Light Dragoons in Marulaz's division just before 6 p.m. on the 21st. Despite its weakness—innumerable detachments and demanding duties had reduced its strength to some 160 troopers—*Herzog Heinrich* distinguished itself in the heavy cavalry fighting that evening around Essling, launching more than eight '*chocs*' against the enemy before the order to retreat arrived. Seeing an isolated Austrian detachment, however, the regiment requested permission to charge again, and, their wish granted, the Württembergers attacked with vigour to overthrow their opponents. The quintessential light cavalryman of the age, GD Charles Lasalle, was thoroughly impressed and applauded the

valour and stamina of the Württembergers: 'After such a hard day and with
orders to withdraw, not even a French regiment would have done this!'[94] The
regiment was held behind Essling with the Hessian Chevauxlegers for most of
the 22nd, but apparently advanced through the village at about 4 p.m. to skirmish with Uhlans in the wake of the successful counter-attack by the French
guard.[95] The next several weeks brought the chevauxlegers some well-deserved
rest and the physical condition of man and horse rapidly improved. Finally
relieved of its onerous duties at headquarters in early July, it missed Wagram
when it was sent south with the French 1st Provisional Chasseurs and 25th
Chasseurs to guard the army's far right flank near Bruck an der Leitha.
Separated from its comrades, it remained in this area during the last phases of
the campaign to the armistice, fighting its final skirmish against some Austrian
hussars on the night of 14/15 July.[96]

TYROL AND VORARLBERG - THE CHALLENGE OF REBELLION

While VIII Corps was gathering laurels in the Danube valley, the remaining regular units of Württemberg's army and a collection of newly raised outfits were
engaged in defence of the homeland's soil against the incursions of rebels from
the Tyrol and the Vorarlberg. Inspired by the stunning successes of their
Tyrolian brothers, the inhabitants of the Vorarlberg had raised the flag of revolt
against Bavaria's King Max. Like the Tyrolians, the Vorarlbergers found
Bavarian rule oppressive. Although transferred from Austria to Bavaria in 1805
by the Treaty of Pressburg, they remained deeply loyal to the House of
Habsburg and were infuriated by the new regime that despised their religious
traditions, imposed unprecedented taxes and introduced conscription. This latter
measure was particularly hated and had encountered popular resistance as early
as 1807. Enforced with high-handed callousness by zealous officials, these
Bavarian laws embittered the local population and created a fertile field for the
seeds of rebellion. When insurgent emissaries from the Tyrol crossed into the
Vorarlberg in mid-April 1809, they thus found an avid audience for their appeals
and the entire region was soon in armed revolt. Before long, however, the insurgents discovered that enthusiasm alone would not sustain their rebellion.
Money, munitions and provisions were in short supply and in early May, the
rebels, supported by a small detachment of regular Austrian troops began to
launch raids into Bavarian, Württemberg and Baden territory to acquire these
necessities.[97]

With no garrisons in the Vorarlberg and all its troops committed in the
Danube valley or the Tyrol, Bavaria could do almost nothing to combat this new
insurgency. In desperation, Max Joseph wrote to Friedrich requesting troops to
protect the principal towns of the region, Bregenz and Lindau.[98] Württemberg's
king, however, was already being pressured by Napoleon to send men to the
Vorarlberg and was disinclined to succour his nominal ally further. None the
less, in response to Imperial demands, Friedrich sent GM Ludwig von Koseritz
with *Franquemont* and four guns to the kingdom's southern borders on 29 April,
where the general took up a position between Ravensburg and Wurzach on 4
May.

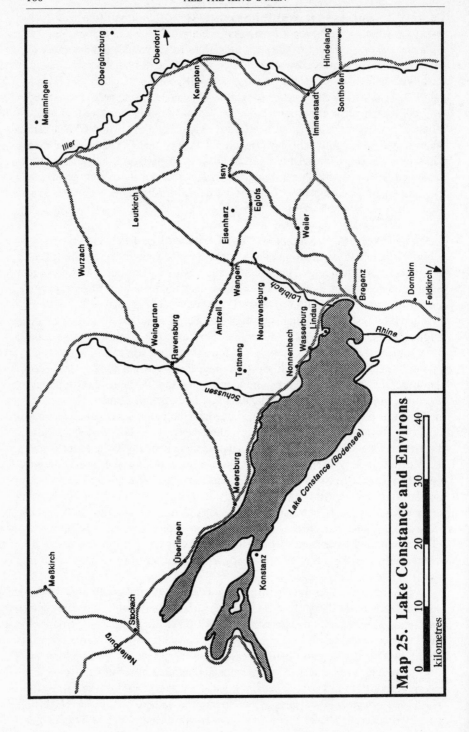

Map 25. Lake Constance and Environs

In the meantime, the strength and audacity of the Tyrolian and Vorarlberg rebels had prompted Napoleon to arrange for the security of his long line of communications through Germany. His instructions included the creation of a reserve division composed of a colourful hodgepodge of French and Allied units (Badeners, Bavarians, Bergers, Württembergers) under the command of GD Marc-Antoine Bonin de La Bininière, Comte de Beaumont. Headquartered at Augsburg, Beaumont's mission was daunting: in co-ordination with three sovereigns who barely co-operated with one another (the Kings of Bavaria and Württemberg and the Grand-Duke of Baden), he was to see to the defence of southern Germany from the Rhine to Bohemia and the security of Napoleon's link with France.[99] Württemberg's contribution to this division was one infantry regiment. Friedrich, though irritated at supplying soldiers beyond his obligation under the Rheinbund Treaty, could find no way to refuse the Emperor's request and *Franquemont* with its attached guns marched off on 15 May to join Beaumont's force near Kempten. It arrived on the 17th after a few brushes with insurgents and was immediately ordered south to join a French drive on Immenstadt and Füssen. The endeavour proved abortive, and the regiment was back in Kempten by the 19th, operating in this area until mid-August as part of GB Joseph Picard's Brigade.

The departure of *Franquemont* left Württemberg's southern border utterly exposed to partisan forays. Moreover, the inhabitants of southern Württemberg (Swabia) were relatively new citizens of the kingdom, having come under Friedrich's crown by the same Treaty of Pressburg that had deprived Austria of the Vorarlberg. Austrian influence and nostalgia for the old Holy Roman Empire still ran strong in the region and many of these subjects, not entirely satisfied with their new monarch, were thus sympathetic to the rebel cause. To shield his kingdom from external attack and forestall internal disruption, Friedrich had no choice but to commit more of his military to the area around Lake Constance. On 11 May, therefore, GM Johann Georg Graf von Scheler rode south leading I/*Prinz Friedrich* together with the depots of the light infantry and Jäger battalions (200 men), the two Guard Grenadier squadrons, some depot cavalry (about 50 troopers) and five guns. Scheler's little brigade arrived at the shores of the great lake on the 18th, and was joined shortly thereafter by II/*Prinz Friedrich*.[100] As the summer passed, King Friedrich ordered a variety of expedient measures to increase further the number of available formations: the depot companies of the infantry units in the field were deployed and later formed into two depot battalions (*von Berndes* and *von Boxberg*),[101] additional depot cavalry was likewise sent against the enemy, two companies of sharpshooters (Scharfschützen) were organized from volunteer foresters, and four Landbataillone (militia) were raised (*Stuttgart, Tübingen, Schorndorf, Heilbronn*).[102] The kingdom even established a small flotilla to patrol Lake Constance.[103] Over time, Württemberg's force thus grew to represent a major military commitment for the small kingdom. Combined with French and Baden troops, the Württembergers would prosecute 'la petite guerre' from May until the end of August.

The campaign against the Vorarlberg rebels can be divided into three phases.

The first, from April to late May, encompasses the start of the rebellion and the initial attacks into Bavaria, Württemberg and Baden, concluding with the gradual ebbing of the insurgent tide after Innsbruck falls to the Bavarians on 19 May. In the second phase (late May to July), the revolt is reignited and the insurgents return to the offensive with better organization and increased vigour; simultaneously, many of the Allied troops are called away to meet other dangers. The result is a general withdrawal by the Allies and a series of defensive battles around Lake Constance. Finally, in concert with the Second Offensive into the Tyrol, the Allies launch co-ordinated drives from east and north that strike into the heart of the Vorarlberg and put an end to the rebellion (early August).[104]

At the start of the war, the Allies had neither troops nor plans to cope with a serious threat in this region. The first phase therefore represented a period of organization and consolidation as France and its three German Allies gathered forces to counter the insurgents. In addition to Scheler's little brigade, Colonel François Grouvel, commander of the 4th Provisional Dragoon Regiment, arrived at Ravensburg on the 24th with a French detachment consisting of his regiment (500 men) and 100 infantry. At the same time, a small Baden contingent (two companies of Guard Grenadiers and a weak squadron of hussars) was taking up positions along the north-western shores of Lake Constance, from the city of Constance to Meersburg. Command and control of this multi-national army proved a complex problem. With the exception of *Franquemont*, none of the Württemberg units came under Beaumont's command; they co-operated with the French general but only acknowledged orders from their King. Grouvel, on the other hand, seems to have reported to Scheler (in French, of course) and Beaumont while accepting orders from both generals.[105] The Badeners, worried they would be swallowed up by the powerful and ambitious Friedrich, were chary of any relationship that threatened their fragile independence. Burdened by manifold competing interests, only the Emperor's overriding presence and the common threat faced by all parties allowed the Allies' intricate and delicate command structure to function at all.

While the Allies brought in reinforcements, the rebels were relatively inactive. A number of undefended towns were duly occupied and a few daring raids were launched into Allied territory (the ambush of a Bavarian depot convoy near Messkirch on the 13th was particularly embarrassing), but the Vorarlbergers, poorly organized and lacking centralized leadership, were incapable of initiating major operations. As a result, the only bloodshed the Württembergers saw in the first phase of the rebellion was a brief fight at Lindau on 20 May. Like many of the engagements in this part of the war, the combat at Lindau was little more than a skirmish, with casualties numbering less than five or so on each side. Although the firefight concluded with the withdrawal of the Württembergers, the insurgents, already demoralized by the increasing numbers of Allied troops and the negative turn of events in the Tyrol, essayed no further attacks and Colonel Grouvel was able to march safely into Bregenz on the 25th. Other than a few small brushes with the enemy, the first phase of the war against the rebels thus ended with almost no combat action for Friedrich's soldiers.

The second phase, on the other hand, opened with a distinct defeat for the

Allies. Having successfully occupied Bregenz, Colonel Grouvel decided his position was dangerously exposed when the inhabitants, their enthusiasm revived by word of new Tyrolian successes, began to stir again in the last days of May. To support his predominantly cavalry force (350 dragoons, 100 French infantrymen, 50 Württemberg Jägers), he requested infantry reinforcements from both Picard and Scheler. Picard responded on 28 May, sending first Major Pillement's Bavarian depot battalion with a gun and, several hours later, three companies of *Franquemont* under Oberstlieutenant Karl von Lalance to Grouvel's aid. From Scheler, Grouvel only received a half-company of *Prinz Friedrich*. Despite growing signs of popular hostility and warnings from Scheler, Grouvel led a mixed force of French, Bavarians and Württembergers (the 50 Jäger and the half-company of *Friedrich*) south towards Feldkirch on the 29th to gain intelligence on the insurgents' strength and intentions. Attempting to advance south of Dornbirn, however, the colonel found the valley blocked by rapidly increasing bands of rebels. As the alarm bells pealed and pealed through the early morning hours, the hills on Grouvel's left began to fill with crowds of insurgents, endangering his flank and his single escape route back to Bregenz. Grouvel recognized the threat and sent some of the German infantry forward to clear the slopes. The men of *Prinz Friedrich* advanced with boldness, but, unsupported by the Bavarians, who seem to have used much of the time since their arrival to imbibe courage, the Württemberg attack was repulsed and 24 men were captured.[106] Before long, the insurgents had seized the initiative and Grouvel's men, evacuating first Dornbirn and then Bregenz, were forced to retreat to the Loiblach, where Scheler had posted troops to cover their withdrawal. The Württemberg general apparently stood on one of the bridges over this small river and beat soldiers with the flat of his sword, but all efforts to stem the retreat failed and the Allies continued their retirement to Tettnang the next day. The three companies of *Franquemont* and two guns sent from Kempten under Oberstlieutenant Lalance had reached Bregenz on the morning of the 29th and were included in the withdrawal; ordered into Lindau as the rest of the little border army fell back toward the River Schussen, they would garrison the city until the conclusion of the campaign, leaving Picard with only five companies of Württembergers under his command in Kempten. Although the losses for the day were small (only the 24 prisoners and three wounded from *Prinz Friedrich*), King Friedrich was furious at this blow to his army's reputation and more troops were soon on their way toward Lake Constance.

Friedrich, however, must share some of the blame for the defeat at Dornbirn. From the outset of operations against the Tyrolians and Vorarlbergers, the corpulent monarch's policy had been to defend his own borders but to take no measures towards recovery of what he considered Bavarian territory in the Vorarlberg proper; other than the threat posed to his own realm, he regarded the insurgency as a Bavarian domestic issue which he was hardly obliged to acknowledge.[107] Von Scheler therefore felt himself unable to accede to Grouvel's request for infantry support as long as Grouvel was actually in the Vorarlberg. For his part, Grouvel undertook his reconnaissance on Beaumont's orders without notifying Scheler and by the time news of his expedition arrived in Württemberg headquarters, it was too late to support the advance.

In the wake of this miniature disaster, Friedrich issued an order on 6 June sending GL Friedrich von Phull to the Lake Constance theatre with reinforcements: five infantry depot companies, a depot squadron and two companies of volunteer Jägers raised from Württemberg foresters.[108] Von Phull was slated to lead the small border corps with GM von Scheler and GM von Koseritz, recalled from Kempten, as brigade commanders under his orders. In addition to these Württemberg units, a French infantry regiment (the 65th Ligne) and six companies of Badeners (three each of Jägers and Grenadiers) had also arrived north of the lake by mid-month.[109] Despite these reinforcements, however, further disappointment was in store for King Friedrich when an Allied reconnaissance in force along the Loiblach was thrown back by the insurgents on 13 June. Lindau was only saved by the bold intervention of the Badeners. A rebel probe against Lindau on the 20th was easily repulsed, but the Allied situation deteriorated in late June when an Austrian force from Bohemia (Kienmayer) advanced on Nürnberg and threatened northern Württemberg.

This new menace prompted the Württemberg king on 25 June to direct that a *corps d'observation* under his son and heir, Crown Prince Friedrich Wilhelm, be concentrated on the realm's eastern frontier.[110] Three days later, *Prinz Friedrich* and the depot companies were consequently withdrawn from the southern border to join the guard battalion, the *Heilbronn* militia battalion, the guard cavalry and eight guns around Ellwangen. Here they remained until the threat subsided in early July.[111] Although Phull was promised two militia battalions (*Stuttgart* and *Schorndorf*) as replacements for his departed infantry, the militia units were late in arriving (the first only reached him on 30 June) and proved poor substitutes for the regulars of *Prinz Friedrich*. The French infantry regiment was also reassigned in late June and Phull, his defences considerably weakened, felt compelled to pull back to the area around Ravensburg. Fortunately, the insurgents contented themselves with holding the line of the Loiblach and the Allies were able to pass the last days of the month in watchful peace.

As the first weeks of July passed, however, the Austrian threat to eastern Württemberg evaporated and Friedrich was free to turn his formidable attention to the problems and opportunities along the Bodensee. By the 13th, therefore, most of Württemberg's home defence corps was again facing the Vorarlberg, this time under the King's personal command.[112] Organized into three brigades under Scheler, Koseritz and Prince Paul, the Württemberg frontier corps included the Horse and Foot Guards, *Prinz Friedrich*, three companies of *Franquemont*, a depot squadron, the light and Jäger depots, four militia battalions, two depot battalions and the volunteer foresters for a total of 6-7,000 men and thirteen guns.[113]

The depot and militia formations merit further attention. Each of the line infantry regiments left behind a depot company when it deployed with the field forces and five of these were committed to Württemberg's southern border when the defeat at Dornbirn elevated concern for the kingdom's safety. Included in the observation corps at Ellwangen, they were joined by three additional companies and filled out with drafts from the Landbataillone to form two depot battal-

ions, *von Berndes* and *von Boxberg,* each of four companies (authorized strength
of 165 men per company). The men from the depots were often young recruits
with little training or experience, however, and the soldiers drawn from the mili-

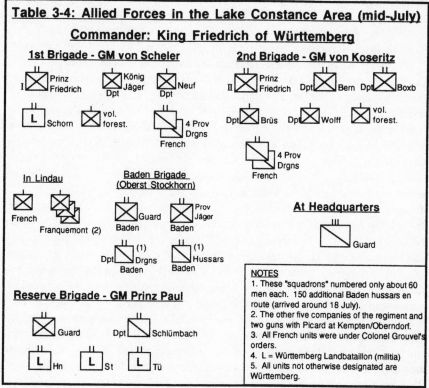

Table 3-4: Allied Forces in the Lake Constance Area (mid-July)
Commander: King Friedrich of Württemberg

1st Brigade - GM von Scheler

Prinz Friedrich | König Jäger Dpt | Neuf Dpt

L Schorn | vol. forest. | 4 Prov Drgns French

2nd Brigade - GM von Koseritz

Prinz Friedrich | Bern Dpt | Boxb Dpt

Brüs Dpt | Wolff Dpt | vol. forest.

4 Prov Drgns French

In Lindau

French | Franquemont (2)

Baden Brigade (Oberst Stockhorn)

Guard Baden | Prov Jäger Baden

Drgns Baden Dpt (1) | Hussars Baden (1)

At Headquarters

Guard

Reserve Brigade - GM Prinz Paul

Guard | Schlümbach Dpt

L Hn | L St | L Tü

NOTES
1. These "squadrons" numbered only about 60 men each. 150 additional Baden hussars en route (arrived around 18 July).
2. The other five companies of the regiment and two guns with Picard at Kempten/Oberndorf.
3. All French units were under Colonel Grouvel's orders.
4. L = Württemberg Landbataillon (militia)
5. All units not otherwise designated are Württemberg.

tia battalions were predominantly veterans who resumed their places in the ranks
with the greatest reluctance; it was not a promising mixture.[114] The militia battalions were likewise composed of four companies. Each company were supposed to count about 150 soldiers in its ranks, but that number was frequently
reduced by numerous desertions and the fillers donated to the depot formations
so that the militia battalion total of 600 men was seldom attained.[115] For uniforms, the depot soldiers retained the dress of their parent organizations, while
the militiamen seem to have worn simple, dark-blue frock coats, white breeches,
black gaiters and black shakos.

From 11 to 13 July, the Württemberg observation corps from Ellwangen
arrived in the Lake Constance area and deployed an outpost screen from
Wasserburg to Wangen (1st Brigade, Scheler) and from Eglofs to Isny (2nd
Brigade, Koseritz); supports were generally positioned three to five kilometres
behind these lines and the corps reserve (GM Prince Paul) was held near Royal
Headquarters at Weingarten. This reinforcement proved timely, as the insurgents launched a series of serious attacks from 14 to 17 July. Focused on Neu-
Ravensburg, Wangen, Eglofs and Isny, these attacks were carried out with con-
siderable courage, but there was no unity of effort and the Allies were able to

defeat the individual rebel columns in detail.

The two-day fight at Eglofs is typical of these tense little actions. The Allied outpost in this village consisted of the depot company from *Wolff*, 30 volunteer foresters and 20 French dragoons; its immediate support, depot battalion *Boxberg*, was located about four kilometres to the north-east in Eisenharz. At 4 a.m. on the 14th, the Allies in Eglofs were attacked by approximately 1,000 Vorarlberg partisans and forced back toward Eisenharz with a loss of 36 men, mostly from the light infantry. On learning the village had been lost, Friedrich ordered it retaken and GM Scheler sent couriers to II/*Prinz Friedrich* and the Baden Guards alerting them to march on Eglofs on the morning of the 15th. The rebels, however, had already returned to the offensive. Advancing with some 3,000 men in three columns, they overwhelmed *Boxberg* and drove it back on Wangen in such confusion that the battalion lost its baggage wagons, its war chest and a number of prisoners. Crying 'All is lost, all our people are captured!' the depot troops streamed into Wangen. Fortunately, Scheler arrived at about 6.30 p.m. to restore order and regain the initiative with II/*Friedrich*, a company of foresters, a French dragoon squadron, the Baden Guards and the two Baden 3-pounders. Throwing out a string of skirmishers and deploying his battalion of *Prinz Friedrich* in two long lines, he immediately advanced against the enemy around Eglofs, overthrew them and reoccupied the town. By his quick and decisive counter-attack, Scheler not only repulsed the insurgents but also managed to recapture the baggage, specie and prisoners the rebels had seized earlier in the day. A similar engagement took place the next day at Neu-Ravensburg, where the men of I/*Prinz Friedrich* distinguished themselves by their courage and celerity. Attacks against Neu-Ravensburg, Wangen and Isny on the 17th were also repelled and the insurgents retired behind the Loiblach that night to lick their wounds and consider the prospects for their rebellion.[116]

In the course of the fighting, the regulars and the light/Jäger depot companies displayed the determination and valour that characterized their actions elsewhere. The performance of the depot battalions, on the other hand, reflected their rather checkered composition: *Boxberg* did well enough at Eisenharz on the 14th, but broke and fled at Eglofs the next day; *Berndes* performed respectably at Isny on the 16th. The militia battalions, however, left much to be desired; the men, mostly married and long out of service, were dragged unwillingly back into the dangers and strictures of military duty and the battalions were generally considered unreliable. The Württemberg leadership was very glad to have the sturdy Badeners as allies, praising the soldiers and honouring the senior Baden officers with medals.[117]

Despite the compliments heaped upon their officers and men by Württemberg's King, however, the Badeners, as well as the Bavarians (whose troops were certainly not praised), remained suspicious of the autocratic and ambitious Friedrich; he was seen as casting a covetous eye on the lands of both of his allies. Relations between Württemberg and Baden were particularly difficult as Württemberg forces operating in Baden territory often abused the local populace (the militia battalions were especially notorious) and took unwarranted liberties with the Grand Duchy's sovereignty. The situation was further complicated by the presence of Baden troops under *de facto* Württemberg command (nominally they came under Beaumont). As the common threat from the rebels receded, these problems became more acute and it is not surprising that the Baden and Bavarian officials in Friedrich's headquarters co-operated in their attempts to restrain Württemberg's king.

Indeed, the mid-July offensive proved to be the last gasp of the Vorarlberg insurrection. While the Tyrolians continued the fight, the Vorarlbergers, discouraged by the defeat of the Austrian main army and the hopelessness of the Tyrolian insurgency, quietly went home. With the armistice declared, King Friedrich returned to Stuttgart on 17 July, turning over command to the Crown Prince. Allied troops now converged on the Vorarlberg from the east and north, but there was no more war to fight. Beaumont led a force of French and Bavarians over the Arlberg Pass to reach Dornbirn on 6 August and Friedrich Wilhelm occupied the capital of the Vorarlberg and centre of resistance, Bregenz, without bloodshed the same day. Obedient to the guidance he had received from his father, the Crown Prince rapidly withdrew his Württembergers and Badeners from the city, leaving only a detachment of 30 light infantrymen when he departed on the 7th. As far as Friedrich was concerned, the war was over and Württemberg troops would not be employed to quell Bavarian internal unrest.

Although the campaign of 1809 essentially ended for most of Württemberg's soldiers in mid-July, Oberst Eugen von Röder with his five companies of *Franquemont* and two guns remained attached to Beaumont's Division. From late May to early June, most of the regiment was quartered in Kempten, with Immenstadt and Füssen each occupied by one company (22 May). Occasional skirmishes took place between Württemberg and Tyrolian patrols and the rebels attempted several raids on *Franquemont's* forward companies in early June, but there were no serious engagements. Despite the lack of combat activity, this outpost duty was tiring. Being regular troops, Röder's men were far superior to Picard's raw French and Bavarian recruits in discipline and training and the French general relied on the Württembergers exclusively to perform his brigade's picket and patrol missions.

As part of the general Allied withdrawal in early June, Picard pulled the regiment, reduced to five companies by the departure of Lalance on 29 May, back to Kaufbeuren (600) and Oberdorf (200) on the 6th, leaving only a detachment of French infantry and cavalry to hold Kempten. The Württembergers were held in this reserve position until 13 July, when they returned to Kempten.[118] From here they attempted to establish liaison with King Friedrich's border corps at Isny (interrupted since the June withdrawal), sending out a detachment for this purpose on the 16th. Koseritz's men had their hands full fending off rebel attacks, however, and could not complete the link to Röder; after a day of incessant minor firefights, the detachment headed back to Kempten. Like the other Allied troops along the alpine borders, Picard's force at Kempten was subjected to an energetic, but ill-co-ordinated attack on the 17th which the Württembergers, French and Bavarians handily repulsed.

Röder and his soldiers were not so fortunate in early August. Although

Friedrich had specifically forbidden his commanders from participating in any offensive action after the conclusion of the armistice, Röder obeyed an order from Picard to send a company into the mountains as a link to Beaumont's force in the Tyrol. The company, led by Major von Obernitz, occupied Reutte on 8 August but was surrounded and forced to surrender in the early hours of the 9th. More than 100 Württembergers thereby fell into the insurgents' hands and King Friedrich was beside himself with fury. Without informing the French, he immediately ordered the return of *Franquemont* and its disgraced commander. The regiment's four remaining companies marched out of Hindelang on the night of 11/12 August and returned to Württemberg soil, where they were sent to join Lalance's companies on the shores of Lake Constance. Oberst Röder, exposed to the full wrath of his gargantuan sovereign, was tried by court martial for disobedience, sentenced to six months' imprisonment and dismissed from the service.[119]

By mid-August, therefore, with the exception of a small occupation force under GM von Koseritz (*von Franquemont, Prinz Friedrich*, Land-Scharfschützen), Württemberg's border defence forces had returned to their garrisons. These occupation troops were occasionally called upon to make demonstrations in support of Württemberg or even Bavarian sovereignty, but the insurgency had lost its sting and no further combat action was required.

While the war was thus winding down in late July and August, Friedrich increased the size of his army by creating several new units. The first of these was the Gardejägerkompanie. Formed near Stuttgart in late June with a small cadre from the Guard Battalion and a large collection of 'village boys', the company was sent to Lake Constance in mid-July and served as the headquarters guard for the Crown Prince. It took part in the march on Bregenz on 6 August but saw no action during its brief sojourn at the front. Also formed in July were a new dragoon regiment and a battalion of light infantry called the Land-Scharfschützen-Bataillon. The latter was assembled by combining the depots of the light and Jäger battalions with von Bülow's two companies of volunteer foresters. This battalion served briefly with the occupation corps in August and appears to have been mostly demobilized when the war ended, with a cadre retained on active duty while the majority of its members returned to forestry duties. Its members apparently wore a grey jacket with green facings at collars and cuffs, grey breeches and a cylindrical black hat like those of the Austrian Jäger.

The dragoon regiment was the result of a Royal Order dated 24 July. Formed from the depots of the four extant cavalry regiments, it was smaller than its sister units (only 102 men per squadron for a total of 409) and was initially only able to mount three of its four squadrons. Uniforms were requisitioned when the regiment was ordered into existence, but the troopers were not able to don their new dark-green coats until the end of August. The coats featured white collars and turnbacks and green lapels, all piped in scarlet; breeches and belting were white and the regiment's headgear was a dark-green shako with white metal trim. Sufficient horses were finally purchased to put every man in a saddle by the end of September and the regiment became the *Kronprinz* Dragoons when

Friedrich Wilhelm was declared its Inhaber on 11 October. Its only contribution to the campaign was to escort Napoleon when the Emperor passed through Stuttgart en route to Paris in late October.

Guard duty outside Napoleon's quarters was also performed by another new unit, II/*Scharffenstein*. Friedrich's intention to form another line infantry regiment from the eight depot companies in the Lake Constance area was declared on 24 July, but the demands of the border war kept the intended members of the unit on the realm's southern frontier until mid-August. Returned to Ludwigsburg on the 16th, they were reorganized and gradually provided with new uniforms, their distinctive colour being straw-yellow. The selection of General von Scharffenstein as their Inhaber was announced in September and the regiment received its standards in an imposing ceremony at Ludwigsburg in October. The end of 1809 thus saw the army of King Friedrich increased to a strength of one Guard infantry battalion, one Guard cavalry regiment, eight line infantry regiments, two Jäger battalions, two light battalions, a cadre light battalion, five line cavalry regiments and a garrison battalion.[120]

Whether in action against Austrian regulars or alpine insurgents, the soldiers of the strict King Friedrich proved themselves worthy allies to Napoleon in 1809. Under the able leadership of generals such as von Wöllwarth and von Hügel, they repeatedly displayed the highest soldierly qualities, impressing friend and foe alike with their skill, determination and loyalty to King and Emperor. Respected by their opponents and honoured by Napoleon, they even earned the admiration of the acerbic Vandamme. The Light Brigade, the cavalry and the horse artillery stand out as truly crack formations, but all demonstrated astonishing endurance and notable élan. One is forced to wonder what the outcome of Wagram might have been had VIII Corps stood in IX Corps' place on 5 and 6 July.

NOTES

1: The Stände, protected by the constitution of the Holy Roman Empire, may be likened to the estates (états) of pre-revolutionary France; in the Holy Roman Empire, only the monarchs of Württemberg and Mecklenburg had to contend with these trammels to their power. With the collapse of the old empire, Friedrich dissolved the Diet and gathered all power into his own hands (Volker Press, 'König Friedrich I. - Der Begründer des modernen Württemberg', *Baden und Württemberg im Napoleonischen Zeitalter*, vol. 2, Stuttgart: Cantz, 1987).

2: With matrimony an important exemption from service, the number of young stalwarts seeking wives grew after the enactment of the 1806 conscription laws. Friedrich issued a rescript in 1807 to restrict this dreadful practice. Paul Sauer, 'Die Neuorganisation des württembergischen Heerwesens unter Herzog, Kurfürst und König Friedrich', *Zeitschrift für Württembergischen Landesgeschichte*, Jahrgang XXVI, 1967, pp. 399-402.

3: Some Christian monastic orders were simply exempt while Jews were permitted to pay a fee in place of serving in the army.

4: Those who did not obey the order to return were considered outlaws, facing the confiscation of all property and the loss of their rights as citizens and subjects. Additionally, foreign recruiters were physically driven beyond the borders of the realm to curtail the loss of portential soldiers. Sauer, 'Neuorganisation'.

5: This trend toward a modern, national army continued in Württemberg throughout the Napoleonic era. The conscription law of August 1809 was similar to the French laws of 1798 and 'unprecedented in Germany' (Sauer, 'Neuorganisation', p. 406); it created a large reservoir of potential soldiers, allowing Friedrich to rebuild his army twice in 1812-13. It also created a great deal of resentment, not only due to aversion to military service, but also because the King used conscription to destroy the power of the ancien classes and meld the old and new elements of the kingdom together.

6: Sauer, 'Neuorganisation', 407 fn 34. Some were quite humble in background (sons of innkeepers or bookdealers), but almost none rose from the lower clases (e.g., farmers).

7: Few of its cadets would play a major role in 1809, but many of the graduates of its predecessor, the Hohen Carlsschule, would occupy high ranks in VIII Corps: for example, GM von Franquemont, commander of one of the line infantry brigades and Oberst von Kerner, VIII Corps Chief of Staff, Sauer, p. 407.

8: Sauer, 'Neuorganisation', p. 409. Friedrich was serious about pursuing nominal subjects and punishments could even be meted out to fathers if their sons refused to return to Württemberg (Günther Cordes, 'Das Württembergische Heerwesen zur Zeit Napoleons', in *Baden und Württenberg im Zeitalter Napoleons,* vol. 2, Stuttgart: Cantz, 1987, p. 278).

9: Karl von Suckow, *Aus meinem Soldatenleben,* Stuttgart: Krabbe, 1862, p. 111.

10: He spent six months in prison. Freiherr von der Wengen, *Der Feldzug der Grossherzoglich Badischen Truppen unter Oberst Karl von Stockhorn gegen die Vorarlberger und Tiroler 1809,* Freiherr O. von Stockhorn, ed., Heidelberg: Winter, 1910, p. 188.

11: Sauer, 'Neuorganisation', p. 413.

12: Hauptmann Fromm, *Geschichte des Infanterie-Regiments König Wilhelm I (6. Württ.) Nr. 124.,* Weingarten: regimental, 1901, pp. 35-6; and Albert Pfister, *Das Infanterieregiment Kaiser Wilhelm, König von Preussen (2. Württ.) No. 120.,* Stuttgart: Metzler, 1881, pp. 168-9.

13: From a letter written by Johann Georg Schäffer on 5 April 1809, quoted in *Baden und Württemberg im Napoleonischen Zeitalter,* Stuttgart: Cantz, 1987, vol. I.1, p. 430.

14: John Cook, 'The Württemberg Line Cavalry', *Empires, Eagles and Lions,* nos. 91, 92, 93; Otto von Pivka, *Armies of the Napoleonic Era,* New York: Taplinger, 1979, pp. 263-4; George Nafziger, *The Wurttemburg* (sic) *Army,* Leeds: Raider, 1987, p. 57. *Herzog Louis* was in the process of switching to plain dark-green breeches. They had previously worn 'Scharawaden', rather unusual hose which consisted of yellow breeches with dark-green leggings from the ankle to the upper thigh; *König* was never issued 'Scharawaden.'

15: The guard cavalry regiment was a new creation, established in March 1809 by taking one squadron each from the *Herzog Heinrich* and *Leib* regiments (at that time, each was five squadrons strong) and redesignating them as mounted grenadiers. When the Leibjäger joined the guard cavalry in June, they became the 1st Squadron, the Garde du Corps became the 2nd, and the two squadrons of grenadiers became the 3rd and 4th squadrons of the regiment. When formed as a regiment, the 1st squadron wore dark-green tunics, while the others wore dark-blue; collars, cuffs and turnbacks were yellow. All had tall bearskin caps, white breeches and steel cuirasses. Leo I. von Stadlinger, *Geschichte des Württembergischen Kriegswesens,* Stuttgart: Gutenberg, 1856, pp. 615-6.

16: General Graf von Bismark, *Ideen-Taktik der Reuterei,* Karlsruhe: Müller, 1829, p. 205. In 1809, Bismark was a Rittmeister in the *Leib-Chevauxlegers.*

17: The first company of the first battalion in each regiment was designated a grenadier company, the other seven were musketeers (Stadlinger, p. 617). The grenadiers were in no way distinguished from the rest of the regiment and cannot be considered true 'élite' companies like those in the French army.

18: Both Generals von Camrer and von Neubronn died during the 1809 campaign (of illnesses and age, not enemy action); their regiments were thus assigned new patrons. Not until 1811 would Friedrich order all the regiments to be numbered: *von Phull* - Nr. 1 (Inhaber had become Prince Paul), *Herzog Wilhelm* - Nr. 2, *von Camrer* - Nr. 3 (Inhaber became von Phull in August 1809), *von Franquemont* - Nr. 4, *Prinz Friedrich* - Nr. 5, *Kronprinz* - Nr. 6, *von Neubronn* - Nr. 7 (Inhaber became von Koseritz in 1809), *von Scharffenstein* - Nr. 8 (raised in autumn 1809).

19: Quote from Suckow, p. 109. The numeration of the light battalions is something of a mystery: some sources state they were not numbered until after this campaign, others list numerical designations for all four from the start of 1809. I have given the designations used in General von Camrer's report of 1 April (Württemberg Military Archives, file E271a50). The *König* Jägers would later receive the number 1, and von Neuffer's Battalion would become the 2nd Foot Jäger Battalion; it should also be noted that Jäger Battalion *König* was often referred to as the 'von Stockmayer Jägers'.

20: Unlike the regiments, the light, Jäger and depot battalions are named after their commanders.

21: The entire Landjäger Corps (Landdragoner and Landfüsiliere) was commanded by GM Franz von Etzdorf. The Garrison Battalion, commanded by GM Franz von Berndes, was often referred to as a 'regiment' (particularly in Berndes' own reports), but does not seem to have warranted such an exalted designation. Information on this battalion is from the Württemberg Military Archives, files E271a(12), E271a(27), E271a(50), and E271a(65).

22: *Krieg 1809,* vol. I, p. 648 and Heinz Kraft, *Die Württemberger in den Napoleonischen Kriegen,* Stuttgart: Kohlhammer, 1953, p. 145. Ammunition was apportioned to provide 110 rounds of ball and 20 of canister for each gun and 50 shells, 20 canister rounds for each howitzer (Gessler, Tognarelli and Ströbel, *Geschichte des 2. Württembergischen Feldartillerie-Regiments Nr. 29,* Stuttgart: regimental, 1892, p. 100). Other guns remained behind in Württemberg and would soon appear along the battle front around Lake Constance.

23: Quotes on the use of the Württemberg contingent and the formation VIII Corps are from *Correspondence,* 14920, 17 March 1809, *Correspondence,* 14975, 30 March 1809, and *Correspondence,* 15029, 8 April 1809. After the conclusion of the armistice, Junot's command in southern Germany would receive the designation

VIII Corps. Note that Lasalle's Division never received a Württemberg cavalry regiment as originally envisaged.

24   *Correspondence,* 14722, 15 January 1809.

25: Napoleon's attitude was that the superb performance of the Württemberger contingent in 1806/7 while under Vandamme proved the value of this command relationship. His replies only served to increase Friedrich's irritation. For the correspondence between the two monarchs from 17 March to 6 April see Schlossberger, pp. 129-30, 142-3, 148-9; Kraft, p. 144. Despite his insistence that Vandamme command the corps, the Emperor may have been prepared to accede to Friedrich's desires had the king pressured him further: in his 30 March 'Instructions for the Major General', Napoleon wrote 'If General Vandamme does not command the troops of Württemberg, we will give this command to General Demont, who speaks German, and General Vandamme will replace General Demont' (Demont commanded the reserve division in Davout's Corps); *Correspondence* 14975. For his own part, Vandamme learned of the King's displeasure from the French ambassador when he arrived in Stuttgart to pay a courtesy call on Friedrich prior to assuming his new command (Albert Du Casse, *Le Général Vandamme et sa Correspondance,* Paris: Didier, 1870, vol. II, p. 262).

26: See Kraft, pp. 145-6.

27: The additional ammunition was brought forward from the reserves maintained at Ludwigsburg. Kraft, p. 146. See also Du Casse, *Vandamme,* vol. II, p. 265.

28: Nübling, p. 86.

29: According to *Krieg 1809,* vol. I, p. 351, Rittmeister Bismark took his squadron of *Herzog Louis* to reconnoitre as far as Pfaffenhausen on the 16th (a scouting mission may have been conducted, but probably not by Bismark, he was assigned to *Leib-Chevauxlegers* during the entire campaign - Bismark, *Ideen,* p. 202). Responding to Berthier's exaggerated fears of the Austrian advance from Bohemia, Vandamme placed much of the Corps north of the Danube between Donauwörth and Monheim on the 16th: Chevauxlegers Brigade, *von Wolff, von Neuffer, Herzog Louis,* and Scharffenstein's Brigade. The other units of the Corps remained south of the river. Kraft, pp. 146-7; R. Starklof, *Geschichte des Königlich Württembergischen Zweiten Reiter-Regiments ehemaligen Jäger-Regiments zu Pferde Herzog Louis,* Darmstadt & Leipzig, 1862, p. 97.

30: *Krieg 1809,* vol. I, p. 411.

31: Starklof, *Zweiten Reiter,* pp. 99-100.

32: Von Hügel's men had set off at 3 a.m. on the 19th, far in advance of the bulk of the Corps, to support the Bavarians in their fight that day, but were halted at Neustadt early in the afternoon. Alerted at Neustadt at about 4 p.m., they were en route to Siegenburg when General Mouton, one of Napoleon's aides, rode up to tell Vandamme that the danger to the Bavarian right had passed and that the Württembergers were not needed. The Light Brigade camped where it was (near Mühlhausen) and thus took no part in the engagements of 19 April. Kraft, p. 149, *Krieg 1809,* vol. I, p. 438; Nübling, *Geschichte des Grenadier-Regiments König Karl (5. Württembergischen) Nr. 123,* Berlin: Eisenschmidt, 1911, p. 88.

33: Most accounts (e.g., Höfler, the Bavarian General Staff work, Binder von Kriegelstein and *Krieg 1809,* vol. I) state that Siegenburg was held by the Austrians on the morning of 20 April. Kraft (p. 150) disputes this based on his researches in the Württemberg archives, but the preponderance of evidence is against him.

34: Binder von Kriegelstein, p. 237. Kraft (pp. 190-1) and Nübling (p. 89) provide the text of Napoleon's speech which was translated into to German by the senior officers of the Corps (apparently von Theobald and von Franquemont).

35: It is not clear how far the Light Brigade advanced in execution of this first mission. Binder von Kriegelstein (p. 250), Höfler (p. 87) and Strack von Weissenbach (*Geschichte der Königlich Württembergischen Artillerie,* Stuttgart: Aue, 1867, p. 191) indicate that some elements reached Sallingberg itself and even engaged some of the Austrians fleeing the 1st Bavarian Division's attack. Kraft (p. 151) caustically denies this as a possibility but offers little evidence to support his contention. It seems most probable that some skirmishers probed into the village, but that the bulk of the brigade was somewhere between Sallingberg and Bruckhof when it was recalled to join Wrede. On the cavalry regiments, see units histories and the Bavarian General Staff history, p. 73.

36: Binder von Kriegelstein, p. 250. The command relationships on the 20th are far from clear. Von Hügel appears to have been assigned to Wrede's command for at least part of the afternoon; later, he seems to have come back under Vandamme. Likewise, Vandamme gave orders to Minucci's Bavarians (of Wrede's division) when the opportunity presented itself late in the day. Mayerhoffer von Vedropolje in the first volume of *Krieg 1809* (p. 456) points out that Vandamme and Wrede regarded each other as equals and did little to co-operate; Allied operations on 20 April were thus robbed of the coherence that might have increased the scale of the success against the equally disorganized Austrians.

37: Höfler, p. 92, Strack von Weissenbach, p. 192. The *Herzog Louis* Leib Squadron was also involved in this little action (Starklof, *Zweiten Reiter,* p. 102; Bavarian General Staff, p. 73).

38: Kraft, p. 151, Nübling, p. 91.

39: Oberleutnant von Neubronner, *Geschichte des Dragoner-Regiments König (2. Württ.) Nr. 26.,* Stuttgart: regimental, n.d., p. 14; Karl Spiess and Hans Ritter, *Geschichte des Dragoner-Regiments Königin Olga (1.*

Württ.) Nr. 25., Ludwigsburg: regimental, n.d., p. 38; Starklof, *Zweiten Reiter*, pp. 101-2; and Starklof, *Geschichte des Königlich Württembergischen vierten Reiter-Regiments Königin Olga 1805-1866*, Stuttgart: Aue, 1867, pp. 36-7. Oddly, Bismark (*Ideen-Taktik*, pp. 205-6) claims that *Leib* conducted an excellent charge against a superior number of Austrian hussars (Starklof says the enemy were Uhlans) on the 20th. Further, he states that the French Marshal Bessières participated in this attack and complimented the regiment on its courage and ability. As an officer of the regiment (Rittmeister) during the campaign, his words have great credibility, however, it seems unlikely that he is correct. Oberst Kerner's official report of the corps' operations remarks that Bessières complimented the *Leib* regiment but supplies no details (in Pelet, vol. II, p. 426); Spiess's history of the regiment makes no mention of Bessières, only noting that the regiment had no part in the Battle of Abensberg. Most probably, the detachment from *Leib* conducted an energetic reconnaissance which Bismark chose to call a charge; in the course of this action, they chased away some Austrian cavalry (Starklof, *Olga*).

40:   *Krieg 1809*, vol. I, pp. 479-80; Kraft, pp. 153-5; Pelet, vol. II, pp. 426-7.

41:   See footnote 46 below. Berthier's orders to Vandamme are in Du Casse, *Vandamme*, vol. II, pp. 273-4.

42:   Theodor Greisinger, *Geschichte des Ulanenregiments 'König Karl' (1. Württembergischen) Nr. 19 von seiner Gründung 1683 bis zur Gegenwart*, Stuttgart: Deutsche Verlags-Anstalt, 1883, p. 68.

43:   Kraft (pp. 158 and 160) describes the capture of 300 Grenzer and a flag in Buchhausen and the seizure of another 300 Grenzer with flag in Eggmühl. All sources agree on the Eggmühl episode, but no other source mentions the loss of an Austrian standard in Buchhausen (highly unusual given the value attached to unit banners): Kraft seems to have double-counted the 300 Grenzer and flag seized in Eggmühl (see below). Note on the artillery is in Gessler, Tognarelli and Ströbel, p. 104.

44:   *Krieg 1809* I, pp. 554-5; Nübling, 95-6; Kraft, pp. 159-61. In the capture of the manor house (Schloss) of Eggmühl, the Württembergers were supported on their right by the French III/12 Ligne from Gudin's division, who surrounded the structure from the rear. Some sources set Seitter's award at twenty napoleons, I have used the figure (ten) from Kerner's official report (Pelet, vol. II, p. 427). Finally, it is worthy of note that 20 to 23 April 1809 saw the practical extermination of the *Peterwardeiner Grenz* regiment: in the course of these four days, the regiment lost 36 dead, 64 wounded, 134 missing and 1,543 captured (*Kreig 1809*, vol. I, p. 705).

45:   The count of squadrons is as follows: French cuirassiers and carabiniers = 40 squadrons, Württembergers = 10, Seydewitz = $6^1/2$. An additional $11^1/2$ squadrons (Baden Light Dragoons = 4, other Bavarian = $7^1/2$) were also in the immediate area.

46:   Two squadrons of *Herzog Louis* (Münchingen's and the Leib-Eskadron) left the regiment and rode off towards Straubing sometime before the engagement at Eggmühl. It is not entirely clear when this occurred. Kraft, p. 158, says they marched with *Leibchevauxlegers* towards the Isar well before Buchhausen, whereas Starklof's detailed accounts (*Zweiten Reiter*, p. 106, and *Olga*, p. 38) has *Leib* and *Louis* scouting towards the Isar 'around evening' (possibly after the taking of Buchhausen, but just prior to the capture of Eggmühl?). Starklof's rendition is probably more accurate, and in any event, their actions do not appear to have been significant and they were not present for the Battle of Eggmühl.

47:   When Seydewitz's squadrons retreated after their first unsuccessful attack, they reformed between the Württemberg regiments and the French heavy divisions; the subsequent charges by the Württemberg cavalry were thus made on the Bavarians' left. The Austrian cavalry was composed of four squadrons each from the *Vincent Chevauxlegers* and the *Stipsicz Hussars*. All squadrons of both regiments (eight each) were also involved in the action at Eggmühl, and all performed with conspicuous bravery under GM Karl von Stutterheim. Binder von Kriegelstein, pp. 291-5; Bismark, *Ideen*, pp. 207-15; Fabrice, 'Reiter-Brigade', pp. 227-9; *Krieg 1809*, vol. I, pp. 555-9; Stutterheim, pp. 269-82.

48:   Binder von Kriegelstein, p. 295; Starklof, *Zweiten Reiter*, p. 107. *Herzog Heinrich* and *König* were heavily engaged, but the two squadrons of *Herzog Louis* in the Laaber valley remained in reserve and did not take part in the attacks described here.

49:   The commander, Oberst Karl von Jett, had been wounded at Abensberg and OTL Franz von Brockfeld was in temporary command (Greisinger, pp. 68-9). This engagement probably took place near Thalmassing. Note that St. Hilaire is probably in error when he mentions receiving support from *Bavarian* cavalry on the evening of 22 April (Saski, vol. II, p. 346); this German unit was almost certainly *Herzog Heinrich*. For the pursuit after the capture of the Austrian battery, see Kraft, p. 163; Nübling, p. 97.

50:   See accounts in Stutterheim, pp. 285-9; Bismark, *Ideen*, pp. 216-22; *Krieg 1809*, vol. I, pp. 566-70; Binder von Kriegelstein, pp. 299-301.

51:   Starklof, *Zweiten Reiter*, pp. 107-9; *Krieg 1809*, vol. I, pp. 578-9. The victim of the Württemberger's stealth and audacity was the 1st Major's Squadron of the *Riesch* Dragoons Nr. 6, who paid for their poor security procedures with about 100 prisoners; only one trooper of the squadron escaped to bring the tale to the regimental commander (*Krieg 1809*, vol. I, p. 708; and Ferdinand Strobl von Ravelsberg, *Geschichte des k. und k. 12. Dragoner-Regiments seit seiner Errichtung bis zur Gegenwart 1798-1890*, Wien: regimental, 1890, p. 118). The two *Herzog Louis* squadrons which had been sent east toward the Danube after the skirmish at Buchhausen rejoined the Corps late in the evening of 22 April; they did not take part in the expedition to

Geisling/Pfatter (Starklof, *Zweiten Reiter*, p. 106). *Leib* also returned to the fold during the night of the 22nd having had no apparent contact with the enemy (Spiess & Ritter, p. 39).

52: II/*Camrer's* part in the battle is not known. Left to garrison Ingolstadt during the march to the Abens, the battalion was apparently on the field during the Battle of Eggmühl (Stadlinger, p. 488). Kraft (p. 161) indicates it fought as part of Davout's Corps, but Felder locates it with the Light Brigade (R. M. Felder, *Der schwarze Jäger oder Württembergs Krieger in den Jahren 1805-1816*, Cannstatt: Ruckhäberle, 1839, vol. II, p. 16). Unfortunately, the regiment was dissolved in 1817 and left no unit history behind.

53: Kraft, p. 164; Spiess and Ritter, p. 39. The *Leib-Chevauxlegers* were accorded the honour of bearing ten captured standards into Regensburg on the 24th (Spiess and Ritter cannot explain why the honour fell to this unit - possibly another effort of Napoleon's to bind the Germans to him). *Leib* joined the rest of the Corps at Ober-Lindhart later that day.

54:   Kraft, p. 164. Kraft and others (such as Nübling) repeatedly mention the supply shortages experienced by the Württembergers in the campaign. Despite their value as combat soldiers, the Württembergers were still German auxiliaries and thus received less attention than actual Frenchmen when it came to quarters, victuals and new equipment. Still, it must be remembered that the French frequently took only minimal measures to care for their own soldiers; more often, the men were left to fend for themselves. Thus when GL von Neubronn and others complained to their sovereign about supply difficulties (Nübling, p. 98), their allegations against the French were based partly on fact; but their frustration must be blamed not only on French self-interest and neglect of the German troops, in large degree, these difficulties arose from the very manner in which Napoleon waged war.

55: Correspondence quoted in Du Casse, *Vandamme*, pp. 276-8.

56: The activities of the Fusiliers are described in Rudolf Köberle, *Geschichte des 4. Württemb. Infanterie-Regiments Nr. 122 von seiner Gründung 1806 bis 1874*, Ludwigsburg: regimental, 1881, pp. 7-8. Quotes regarding *Herzog Heinrich* are from Neubronn's, Wöllwarth's and Röder's reports in early May, cited in Greisinger, pp. 69-70. The two guns initially with *von Phull* were apparently at GD Rouyer's disposal for a brief time in late April and early May; they returned to VIII Corps around 12 May at Linz (see Saski, vol. III, p. 110).

57: Starklof provides details of the difficult and irritating events of these several days (*Zweiten Reiter*, pp. 110-13) as does Kraft (pp. 165-7). Trudging along muddy tracks under ceaseless rain or huddled on the damp ground about tenuous fires, the men of the Württemberg Corps gave ear to a rumour that Vandamme would allow his soldiers to bivouac in the open rather than take quarters in a designated town as long as the community in question met his price. Denied the option of writing their sovereign to complain, the troops expressed their feelings with a pithy bit of doggerel:

No bed tonight, no bed tonight!
Vandamme has got his purse all right.
If he'd not got his purse so tight,
we'd all have a bed tonight!

Whether the ditty was accurate or not, the soldiers would not come under roofs again until they completed the gruelling 56-hour crossing of the Inn at Braunau as April turned into May. Georg von Niethammer, *Geschichte des Grenadierregiments Königin Olga*, Stuttgart: Kohlhammer, 1886, p. 31; Fromm, p. 38. Vandamme, for his part, blamed his troops for molesting the local population and levying unauthorized 'contributions' in his name (Du Casse, vol. II, pp. 305-6).

58: This little episode illustrates the nature of patrols in the Napoleonic age. Conducted by junior officers with small detachments, such actions placed a significant burden on young officers, requiring independence, solid leadership skills and an ability to cope with the unexpected. Thus Hayd, apparently seeking horses for the Württemberg artillery as well as information about the enemy, was joined by French hussars from some unknown unit (probably in search of booty and adventure) as he headed for Ranshofen. Arriving at the monastery, he was introduced to the principal members of the order in residence and the Austrian military surgeons before being reluctantly shown to the stables. There followed a period of dickering as the lieutenant attempted to secure some of the horses or a monetary bounty for his men; the Frenchmen appeared particularly interested in the latter, demanding a *louis d'or* each. During this interlude, shots were heard without and Hayd, accompanied by the prior, rushed outside to find that the Württemberg troopers had located several barrels of wine and had attained a state of considerable inebriation as a result; they were amusing themselves by firing off the Austrian muskets they had discovered at the hospital. To keep from losing total control of his men, Hayd got everyone ready to leave, but, on the urgings of a sergeant, sent a few Jägers into the town to procure wagons for the Austrian gear they had confiscated. With this evidence of their adventure piled aboard three rickety vehicles, the Württembergers returned to Braunau, richer by several glasses of wine and 300 florins in silver and script. No horses were taken. See 'Berichtigung zweier in dem württembergischen Jahrbuche erzählten Anekdoten', *Oesterreichische militärische Zeitschrift*, Heft 7, Wien: Strauss, 1818, pp. 61-71; Kraft, p. 167; *Krieg 1809*, vol. III, pp. 231-2; and Sauer, 'Neuorganisation', p. 413, for the tale of LT Hayd's expedition.

59: Napoleon may have been unfair to Vandamme; the general claimed that while he had personally only reached Winhöring, his troops had pushed as far as Braunau itself (Vincent and Hayd). Still, the Emperor's intention had clearly been that VIII Corps should get the bulk of its troops to the river on the 29th or 30th and that Vandamme had been unable to accomplish. See *Krieg 1809*, vol. III, pp. 230-1; Saski, vol. III, p. 89.

60: *Krieg 1809*, vol. IV, pp. 176-7. They had marched 120 kilometres in $2^1/2$ days (Fromm, p. 38).

61: The Austrians were part of Shustekh's force and the detachment here included two squadrons of *Kienmayer* (250-300 hussars) and III/*Jordis* (800 men including the skirmishers). Bismark's squadron numbered about 130. The only other Allied troops in the immediate vicinity were the two or three companies of voltigeurs from the 4th Ligne who had cleansed the wood of Austrian skirmishers for the Württemberg cavalry.

62: 'For the German cavalry, which is extremely brave.' Bismark, *Reuter*, pp. viii-xii; *Krieg 1809*, vol. III, pp. 266-71, Spiess and Ritter, pp. 41-3; Starklof, *Olga*, pp. 39-45; Kraft, pp. 168-9. The whereabouts of the remaining squadron of the *Leib-Chevaulgers* (von Einsiedel's) is not clear.

63: The infantry had covered 125 kilometres in the last $2^1/2$ days (*Krieg 1809*, vol. IV, p. 181).

64: Vandamme hoped intimidation would persuade Austrian General Richter to relinquish the boats the Austrians had collected on the left bank. Late on the 4th, the French general imperiously demanded that Richter deliver up this shipping on pain of seeing Urfahr set aflame by cannon fire. He repeated the demand on the morning of the 5th after marching out the Corps with great fanfare. Naturally, Richter refused both times. The Württemberg artillery set some thirty buildings afire over the next several hours.

65: Muff and Wencher state that von Starkloff's company was also among the first ferried across.

66: Sources for this neat little action include Muff and Wenscher, pp. 20-1; Nübling, pp. 98-100; *Krieg 1809*, vol. IV, pp. 181-6 (includes a detailed description of Richter's detachment). The Württemberg General Staff rewarded the two ship-masters for their help. According to Austrian accounts, the Württembergers also happily plundered the entire region (Franz Kurz, *Geschichte der Landwehr in Oesterreich ob der Enns*, Linz: Haslinger, 1811, pp. 250-1).

67: The small Austrian force at Unter-Weitersdorf consisted of one squadron of *Erzherzog Ferdinand* Hussars and some 120 men from I/*Lindenau*. They were succoured by additional cavalry (probably another squadron of *Ferdinand*) near Götschka. The sources for the period 6-16 May are *Krieg 1809*, vol. IV, pp. 186-224; Starklof, *Zweiten Reiter*, pp. 118-23; Nübling, pp. 100-101.

68: Von Breunig (commander of *König* Jäger zu Pferd) had his own regiment, about 100 men from each of the light and Jäger battalions, the grenadier companies of *Herzog Wilhelm* and *Kronprinz* and two light guns. The same day, however, an Austrian detachment captured some Württembergers at Steyeregg and probed across the Danube to surprise a patrol of *Herzog Louis* and chase it into Linz.

69: Von Wöllwarth's force was composed of both Jäger zu Pferd regiments and *von Brüsselle*. The force's itinerary follows. 11 May: (cavalry) Gallneukirchen-Freistadt-St. Leonhard; (light infantry) Gallneukirchen-Neumarkt-Gutau. 12 May: cavalry to Gutau, entire force to Zell; patrols to west. 13 May: entire force from Zell to Gutau; one squadron *König* to Neumarkt; *von Brüsselle* and one squadron *Herzog Louis* to Mauthausen; remainder to Pregarten; patrols roamed west and north-west.

70: *Krieg 1809*, vol. IV, pp. 213-15; Starklof, *Zweiten Reiter*, pp. 124-7; Nübling, pp. 101-2.

71: *Krieg 1809*, vol. IV, p. 239. Starklof claims Vandamme expected the attack to come (as indeed it did) from the direction of Gallneukirchen (*Zweiten Reiter*, p. 129).

72: This disposition is derived primarily from *Krieg 1809*, vol. IV, pp. 238-9. According to Nübling, however, only 80 men from *Neuffer* were sent to Steyr (i.e., half of a company); he places all four of the battalion's subordinate companies at Urfahr for the battle (p. 100). See also Chapter 6.

73: Starklof, *Zweiten Reiter*, p. 130; *Krieg 1809*, vol. IV, p. 243.

74: The infantry was II/*Karl Schröder*, the Uhlans were *Merveldt*; Crenneville's cavalry battery was also unlimbering about this time. Basic sources are the official Austrian history (*Krieg 1809*, vol. IV, pp. 243-57); supplemented by Starklof, Kraft, Nübling and *Ges. des 3. württ. Inf-Regts*.

75: These three units attacked up the valley with the Jägers on the left, *Phull* in the centre and *Neubronn* on the right, aimed directly at the village; the three leftmost companies of *Neubronn* outflanked the village from the south while the other Württembergers rushed in from the west and north (*Krieg 1809*, vol. IV, p. 249; Müller, *Füsilier*, p. 7).

76: The attack was conducted by von Münchingen's and von Hartitsch's squadrons. Von Hartitsch (Leib-Eskadron) was already in position when the regimental commander, Major von Waldburg, ordered the charge. Von Münchingen's men, however, had to cross a small ditch just north of Steeg; the entire squadron negotiated this obstacle with one exception — Major von Münchingen: his horse balked and could not be brought to jump the bank and shoal. His men did not desire to leave their leader and he did not want to miss the fight. In this doubtless infuriating and embarrassing moment, the Major ordered his men back across the brook and took them south through Steeg at the gallop. They emerged and had barely linked with their fellows when the Leib-Eskadron charged. Hardly formed, von Münchingen's excited troopers leaped forward and joined in overthrowing the opposing $3^1/2$ squadrons of *Merveldt* Uhlans. Starklof, *Zweiten Reiter*, pp.

132-3.

77: Von Franquemont's brigade followed the attack, but was not engaged with the exception of von Köseritz's company of *Herzog Wilhelm* (*Geschichte des 3 württ. Inf-Regts.*, p. 227).

78: The attack on the battery was carried out by von Rassler's and von Seebach's squadrons. The Württemberg counter-attack and the dramatic seizure of the Austrian battery are well told in *Krieg 1809*, vol. IV, pp. 247-55; Starklof, *Zweiten Reiter*, pp. 133-42; Nübling, pp. 103-4. Because of the participation of the Saxon hussars in the attack, Bernadotte insisted they be given two of the cannon as trophies. See Chapter 6 for details of the Saxon participation and references.

79: Related in detail in Starklof, *Zweiten Reiter*, pp. 131-2, this wonderful story is retold in *Krieg 1809*, vol. IV, p. 255, with comments from Winzian's account added. See also 'Berichtigung zweier in dem württembergischen Jahrbuche erzählten Anekdoten', *Oesterreichische militärische Zeitschrift*, Heft 7, Wien: Strauss, 1818, pp. 71-77; and Erzherzog Johann, *Geschichte des K. K. Linien-Infanterie-Regiments Erzherzog Wilhelm No. 12*, Wien: Seidel & Sohn, 1877, vol. I, pp. 507-9. Weiss, like Lieutenant Hayd, died during the Russian campaign.

80: *Krieg 1809*, vol. IV, pp. 261-2. A tiny detachment of *Brüsselle* on the heights near Mauthausen does not appear to have been engaged.

81: Nübling, p. 106. Casualties from *Krieg 1809*, vol. IV, pp. 264-5. Neubronn's report of the battle is in Saski, vol. III, pp. 320-1.

82: The Austrian force was composed of the 5th Jägers, two companies of *Wenzel Colloredo*, and about 26 *Merveldt* Uhlans (*Krieg 1809*, vol. IV, pp. 266-71). See also Starklof, *Zweiten Reiter*, pp. 142-5.

83: *Krieg 1809*, vol. IV, p. 279; Starklof, *Zweiten Reiter*, pp. 145-7. The author of this portion of *Krieg 1809*, Maximillian Ritter von Hoen, freely admits that it is almost impossible to unravel the comings and goings of the Württembergers in the days immediately after the Urfahr engagement (p. 272). In the light of Nübling's account (p. 108), however, it seems possible that the '200 Jäger' in Linz were a company (most likely von Starkloff's since he had made the foray to Hellmonsödt) of *Neuffer*.

84: Nübling, p. 108.

85: GB Claude-Pierre Pajol, commanding one of Davout's cavalry brigades in the area, claimed that the Württembergers were not watchful and were thus surprised on the 31st: 'the Württembergers only exercised a mediocre surveillance' (Comte Pajol, *Pajol Général en Chef*, Paris: Didot, 1874, vol. II, p. 369). Kraft avers that von Hügel's men were not completely surprised, but that the Austrians made good use of the darkness and favourable winds to establish themselves on the southern shore (Kraft, pp. 179-80). See also Starklof, *Zweiten Reiter*, p. 150; Nübling, p. 108. This raid caused Napoleon considerable concern, and he ordered a variety of countermeasures in case Vandamme proved unable to repel the Austrians (Buat, II, pp. 9-10).

86: Von Weissenbach, p. 195; Kraft, p. 180.

87: The attack was supported by six Saxon and four Württemberg guns. The defenders were from the regiment *Josef Mittrowsky*, which lost about 100 dead and wounded in addition to the prisoners; Württemberg casualties were 25. Felder, vol. 2, pp. 37-8; Kraft, p. 184; von Weissenbach, p. 196. I have found no reference to this incident in Saxon sources (see Chapter 6 for Saxon actions in June).

88: GL von Wöllwarth replaced the severely ill GL von Neubronn at the end of June; von Neubronn died on 13 August. It should also be mentioned at this point that the situation between Vandamme and the Württemberg officers deteriorated in the end of May, culminating in a confrontation between Vandamme and von Hügel. When the latter appreared to disobey one of Vandamme's policies, he was summoned to Corps headquarters to account for his actions; Vandamme seems to have behaved with typical coarseness and arrogance. The two had never enjoyed good relations and when Vandamme referred to the Württemberger as a 'begger', von Hügel could tolerate no more. He attempted to resign his command of the Light Brigade, but was dissuaded by von Wöllwarth. As the senior Württemberg general, von Wöllwarth also helped to calm von Hügel when that determined and valiant officer, still angered by the maltreatment he had received at Vandamme's hands, asked for permission to engage the Frenchman in a duel (this occurred after the ceasefire). See Kraft, pp. 180-3.

89: Details for VIII Corps disposition on 4 July 1809. Von Scharffenstein had I/*Neubronn*, two guns in Tulln; II/*Neubronn* in Zwentendorf; *Herzog Louis* in St. Andrä; I/*Phull* in Greifenstein and II/*Phull* with two guns at Klosterneuburg. From von Franquemont's brigade, *Kronprinz* and *Herzog Wilhelm* were around Nussdorf with two guns. The horse artillery was with von Stettner and the Jägers were supported by four pieces. I/*Camrer* was at Kaiser Ebersdorf, the second battalion of the regiment still in Braunau. *Leib* was in Vienna, *Herzog Heinrich* at Bruck an der Leitha (see below). From Binder von Kriegelstein, II, p. 464. In addition, Bowden and Tarbox list two batteries of French artillery (12-pounders) and a sapper company attached to VIII Corps at the time of Wagram (*Armies on the Danube*, 2nd edition, p. 198).

90: Kraft, p. 185; Starklof, *Zweiten Reiter*, pp. 154-5. Von Salm's detachment included troopers from both Jäger zu Pferd regiments. Starklof describes the audacity of LT Vischer as he attacks a village occupied by over 80 Austrians. LT Vischer, with only eleven troopers each from the two Jäger regiments, overwhelmed the Austrians and even managed to take sixteen prisoners.

91: Dispositions from Buat, vol. II, pp. 318, 332; quotes from Napoleon to Eugène, *Correspondence*, 15506, 9 July 1809.

92: This reputation for harshness, even pillage, *vis-à-vis* the local population during the latter months of the campaign greatly angered Napoleon. See the comments of Vandamme's biographer and Imperial correspondence in Du Casse, *Vandamme*, vol. II, pp. 305-6, 311-12, 316-19.

93: Spiess and Ritter, pp. 45-6; Württemberg Offiziersstammrolle (Archives, D64, Bd. 3). After von Röder's capture, Oberst Ludwig von Walsleben, commander of the *Leib-Chevauxlegers*, was promoted to GM and given command of the Chevauxlegers Brigade (27 May); despite this advance, von Walsleben retained command of his regiment until August.

94: From GL Wöllwarth's report to Friedrich, quoted in *Geschichte des Ulanen-Regts. 'König Karl'*, pp. 10-11. Regimental strength and other details from Greisinger, p. 70. The regiment joined Lasalle as he rode forward with Piré's brigade to assist d'Espagne's cuirassiers; they arrived just in time to rescue Bessières who was beset by Austrian horsemen. The Württembergers distinguished themselves in combats with infantry, hussars and lancers, suffering a number of wounded from the lances of the *Schwarzenberg* Uhlans. *Krieg 1809*, vol. IV, pp. 491, 494. According to Felder (vol. 2, p. 34), the regiment lost nineteen men at Aspern including Oberst Jett, wounded for the second time in the campaign (the first time was at Abensberg).

95: The regiment's actions at Aspern are described in *Krieg 1809*, vol. IV, pp. 466, 617.

96: The three-regiment brigade was commanded by GB Nicolas Thiry (he was subordinate to GD Baraguey d'Hilliers). Austrian hussars attacked Württemberg vedettes on the night of 14/15 July in contravention to the recently signed armistice. Believing the Austrian behaviour to be the result of a misunderstanding, the local commander, Major von Palm, sent an officer and a trumpeter forward to inform the enemy of the ceasefire. The Austrians, however, fired on the Württemberg emissaries, killing the officer and mortally wounding the trumpeter. Von Palm instantly ordered his men to mount, charged the Austrians and overthrew them (Greisinger, p. 71).

97: Austrian troops that had reached the Vorarlberg by mid-May included: a company of *Lusignan*, 32 men of I/*Hohenlohe-Bartenstein*, a detachment of 9th Jäger Battalion, 63 Salzburger Jäger, Tyrolian partisans and 140 escaped prisoners of war for a total of about 750 infantry. Cavalry detachments amounted to 70 troopers (*Hohenzollern* Chevauxlegers and *Frimont* Hussars). Wengen, pp. 15-16.

98: Max's letter reached Friedrich on 5 May; he also wrote to Baden's Grand Duke to ask for assistance.

99: *Correspondence*, 14868, 8 March 1809, as well as 15136 and 15139 (29 April). Friedrich was informed of the formation of this division and Napoleon's desire for a Württemberg regiment in a letter from the Emperor dated 4 March (15157).

100: Von der Wengen (pp. 67, 69) and Nübling (p. 113). Interestingly, the infantry were transported in wagons, a relatively common practice in this theatre of war — wagons would also be used to move some of the troops to and from the position around Ellwangen (see below).

101: Some confusion exists between Depot Battalion *von Berndes* (commanded by Major von Berndes) and the garrison battalion, whose Inhaber was General-Major von Berndes. The confusion is exacerbated by the general's habit of referring to his unit as a 'regiment' although its strength (516 in September 1808) would not seem to support that designation (Württemberg Militärarchiv, file E271a(65)). A second garrison battalion was apparently raised during the war, but neither battalion took part in any combat operations during 1809 (Peter Wacker, 'Der württembergischen Feldzug gegen die Vorarlberger 1809', *Die Zinnfigur*, 8. Jahrgang, Heft 1 (15 Jan), 1959, p. 2).

102: The number of militia battalions actually formed is not clear. Stadlinger (p. 490) refers to the formation of five (the fifth being *Rottweil*), but other sources (e.g., Pfaff) only list four. To compound the mystery further, Wengen mentions a sixth name (*Ludwigsburg*) when describing the militia.

103: Although considerable effort went into the organization of this little inland navy, it saw practically no real action during the war. It may have exerted a certain deterrent influence on the energetic and imaginative Vorarlbergers, but its ability to fight on the waters of Constance was never truly put to the test. See Gerhard Wanner's entertaining little booklet (*Kriegsschauplatz Bodensee 1799/1800 und 1809*, Militairhistorische Schriftenreihe Heft 59, Vienna: Bundesverlag, 1987).

104: Adapted from Albert Pfister, *Denkwürdigkeiten aus der württembergischen Kriegsgeschichte des 18. und 19. Jahrhunderts im Anschluss an die Geschichte des 8. Infanterie-Regiments*, Stuttgart: Grüninger, 1868, p. 362.

105 Ibid., p. 367.

106: While the Bavarians seem to have been out of control in this instance, they were not the only army to fall prey to drink. Jakob Walter, a private in *Franquemont*, recalled the zeal with which Württemberg soldiers searched the wine cellars of Bregenz and the need for strict discipline to return men to their duties (Jakob Walter, *A German Conscript with Napoleon*, Otto Springer, ed. and trans., Lawrence: University of Kansas, 1938, pp. 177-9).

107: Friedrich did not hide his feelings from the Emperor, writing to Napoleon on 20 May that it was difficult for him to commit his troops to the reconquest of Bavarian land while his own territory was left exposed to the 'atrocious brigandage of these insurgents' (Schlossberger, p. 167).

108: The depot companies were from *Kronprinz, Phull, Herzog Wilhelm, Camrer* and (probably) *Franquemont*. Hauptmann von Bülow commanded the two small companies of volunteer foresters and Rittmeister Schlümbach led the depot squadron, apparently assembled from the depots of all four regular cavalry regiments (about 90 troopers, giving a total of some 150 depot cavalrymen along the lakeshore). With the arrival of the depot troopers, the two squadrons of Garde-Grenadiers returned to Stuttgart.

109: The depot troopers of the Baden Light Dragoon Regiment would follow several days later. Note that many sources describe the French unit as a regiment of Guard Grenadiers. As the Imperial Guard was with the Emperor in Vienna in June (having fought at Aspern), it seems far more likely this regiment was the 65th, which was assigned to Beaumont while it recovered from its ordeals during the opening phases of the campaign.

110: Friedrich had two sons and a daughter (two other daughters died in infancy). Crown Prince Friedrich Wilhelm (1781-1864) detested Napoleon and married Princess Charlotte of Bavaria in 1808 to avoid a Bonaparte spouse. In constant opposition to his domineering father, he ascended to the throne in 1816 and reigned under the name Wilhelm I until 1864. Friedrich's daughter Katharina (1783-1835) could not be spared a Bonaparte and became Queen of Westphalia as Jerome's wife. Son Paul (1785-1852) held the rank of General-Major and commanded a brigade in the campaign; Regiment *Prinz Friedrich* was named for his infant son (1808-1870).

111: Some sources (e.g., Wengen) give the number of Landbataillone as two. See Chapters 7 and 9 for discussions of Austrian operations against north-eastern Bavaria. An earlier Württemberg deployment to the north followed the adventurous breakout attempt of about 140 Austrian regulars from the Vorarlberg through Württemberg and Bavaria to Bohemia (!). When this little band was detected, GM von Scheler dispatched (22 May) 25 Chevauxlegers and 40 light infantry in wagons to give chase; they were followed by two companies under von Berndes. A squadron and 25 more light infantrymen were sent into the Danube valley on the 24th. Neither of these groups found the elusive Austrians and they were soon back with the rest of Scheler's troops. The Austrians were intercepted and destroyed by French dragoons and Hohenzollern infantry on the 27th near Neumarkt in der Oberpfalz (Bavaria). Wengen, p. 74. See Chapters 7 and 8 for more on this little episode.

112: Friedrich was forced to call on the military to quell two small uprisings within his own borders in late June and early July. A revolt against conscription in Mergentheim (now Bad Mergentheim) was quickly and harshly repressed (26-29 June), and a similar disturbance in the Nellenburg region (around Stockach) was put down with minimal bloodshed by GM Karl von Dillen with II/*Prinz Friedrich*, one squadron and one three-pounder (6-10 July). Dillen's detachment returned to the main corps on 16 July, leaving behind von Buhl's company of *Friedrich* with 62 local foresters and 24 Landdragoner to keep the peace. Wengen, pp. 133-42; Paul Sauer, *Napoleons Adler über Württemberg, Baden und Hohenzollern*, Stuttgart: Kohlhammer, 1987, pp. 128-31.

113: This figure only addresses the Württembergers and does not include the forces from Baden (a battalion each of Guard Grenadier and Jägers, a half-squadron each of hussars and light dragoons, 2 guns) or France (Grouvel's dragoon regiment and 90 infantry). In addition, a squadron of Baden hussars was en route for the Lake Constance area. The Württemberg artillery consisted of seven 6-pounders, four howitzers and two 4-pounders. Strack, p. 200; Wengen, pp. 144-6.

114: The depot battalions, named for their commanders (both majors), were composed of the following companies (Marx, pp. 3-5):
   I. *Boxberg - Kronprinz, Camrer, Prinz Friedrich, Neubronn;*
   II. *Berndes - Grenadiers-Garde, Phull, Herzog Wilhelm, Franquemont.*
   Major von Boxberg was replaced by Major von Kellenbach in the end of July, and Major von Pöllnitz assumed von Berndes' position in early August.

115: These militia battalions have been accurately called the first modern reserve units in Germany. For eight years after the completion of active duty, each Württemberg veteran was eligible to be recalled for service in the Landbataillone (four years in the '1st Accession' and four years in the '2nd Accession'). Unfortunately, these veterans, long out of service, did not meet Friedrich's expectations and Suckow even avers it was a mistake to form the battalions at all (p. 121).

116: Battle accounts are compiled from Felder, Marx, Nübling, Pfister (*Denkwürdigkeiten* and *Das Infanterie-Regiment Kaiser Wilhelm, König von Preussen (2. Württ.) No. 120.*, Stuttgart: Metzler, 1881) and Wengen.

117: Marx, pp. 5-9; Suckow, p. 121; and Wengen, pp. 114, 130, 155-63. Many of the men in the depot companies were drawn from the Landbataillone and shared the negative characteristics of these units.

118: Only the 600 men from Kaufbeuren went to Kempten, the other 200 remained at Oberdorf.

119: Pfister, *Denkwürdigkeiten*, pp. 378-9; Wengen, pp. 188, 190.

120: The Landbataillone were disbanded shortly after returning from Lake Constance.

CHAPTER 4:

You Have Saved My Honour and Life

Baden's ruler presented a strong contrast to Württemberg's proud monarch. Where King Friedrich was autocratic, aggressive and domineering, Karl Friedrich, Grand Duke of Baden, was aged (81 years old in 1809), withdrawn and ineffectual. He had not always been so incapable. A sovereign from the age of 18 (1746), Karl Friedrich had been 'one of the most outstanding representatives of enlightened absolutism', renowned for his intelligence and respected throughout the courts of Europe. Even Napoleon recognized the qualities of this 'honourable prince' who ruled over a small but variegated land with entrenched local interests and inherent incompatibilities.[1] Modest and pious, Karl Friedrich, in emulation of his hero, Frederick the Great, saw himself as the first servant of the state. Unlike Württemberg's Friedrich, who drew lessons of severity and power from his time in the Prussian king's court, Karl Friedrich established himself as a mild monarch who sought to rule 'with minimal force and coercion'. He thus modernized and humanized his realm's administrative, political and social structures to eliminate the remains of feudalism (outlawing serfdom, for example) without imposing a strong central state or eradicating local individuality.

By the time Napoleon's grace raised him from Kurfürst (Prince-Elector) to Grand Duke in 1806, however, Karl Friedrich was fading. Already 78 years old, he lacked the vigour and breadth of vision to encompass his new estate; the burdens of office weighed heavily on him, he tired quickly and became forgetful, easily distracted. An early death having deprived him of his eldest son and heir in 1801, he maintained the throne while his young grandson came of age, but the wearing passage of time sapped his strength and exacerbated his less positive characteristics. Never decisive or dictatorial, he became almost incapable of reaching a conclusion or even grasping the broad changes sweeping across the continent. The threads of the era slipped through his formerly agile fingers. He seems to have lost the lofty goals of his youth and focused on fatuous, almost petty desires: elevation to the rank of king (like his neighbour) and assurance that the children of his second marriage would be eligible for the throne.[2]

These circumstances had two principal results. First, the governance of the Grand Duchy devolved upon several energetic key officials. The introduction of a nascent professional bureaucracy had indeed modernized the Baden state and it was the chief ministers and officials of this new government who, in the absence of clear direction from their sovereign, increasingly ruled and decided in Karlsruhe. Second, the infirmity of the Baden state was not lost on Napoleon and he intervened with growing frequency to protect Baden's integrity and its value to him as an ally. Although its geographic propinquity to France made Baden naturally vulnerable to French influence, Napoleon may have allowed the Grand Duchy the same latitude he granted Bavaria and Württemberg had he not doubted its viability as a state. In addition to a monarch who was 'hardly still capable of rule', Baden was plagued by internal instability, chronic financial problems and, perhaps most glaringly, an army that seemed more a liability than an asset. Napoleon determined to rectify this situation and Baden soon found itself under considerable pressure to reform its state apparatus and military structure along French lines. The introduction of France's civil code (Code Napoleon) in Baden would not come until 1810 (it remained the basis of Baden's laws until 1896), but military matters moved more quickly.[3]

The Emperor had been disappointed with the performance of the Baden contingent in the 1805 and 1806-7 campaigns. Although Karl Friedrich's third son, Markgraf Ludwig, had directed a major reorganization of Baden's army in 1803, his efforts were guided by his experience in Prussian service and rapidly lost their relevance in the Napoleonic age. Moreover, Baden's military administration was still adjusting to the increased size of the state and its army (grown from 1,976 men in early 1803 to more than 8,000 by the summer of 1807).[4] As a result, mobilization in 1805 was painfully slow, training and equipment were inadequate and the contingent was tainted by discipline and desertion problems; the idea of fighting against their former Emperor, Franz of Austria, even caused many officers to resign rather than take service as Napoleon's allies. There was little improvement in the mobilization for the war with Prussia in the autumn of 1806. Although the Badeners had finally discarded their hair powder and queues,[5] they made few other concessions to the modern modes of warfare, maintaining their outdated Fredrickian tactics and outlook. The army's training was inadequate, its administration creaky, there were insufficient muskets for the infantry, no horses for the meagre cavalry and 'most of the staff officers were old and frangible'. The whole operation 'was almost a fiasco'. Napoleon told a Baden minister 'Your contingent is incomplete, it is poorly organized and the troops are not ready for battle'.[6] Marshal Lefebvre, whose X Corps included the Baden contingent at the siege of Danzig, wrote to his Emperor that, 'The Badeners are no good for work and no good under fire...I would gladly relieve myself of the whole lot.' Despite its numerous problems, the contingent was better than its reputation, always accomplishing its assigned missions and demonstrating considerable courage in combat. Napoleon may have recognized their qualities when he chided Lefebvre: 'Have patience, old soldier that you are, for these young soldiers who are just beginning and do not have your sangfroid in danger.'[7] The Badeners seemed to be made of the stuff of solid soldiers and, from Napoleon's perspective, they only lacked a guiding hand, a hand that he was most willing to provide.

In approaching the reform of his ally's military, Napoleon balked at nothing. On his insistence, Ludwig was relieved as Minister of War in January 1808 and sent into retirement at his country estate, removing what was perceived as the stifling grip of Prussian tradition from Baden's army administration. This impediment swept away, a comprehensive series of reforms was instituted, start-

ing with conscription laws. The regulations prescribed in three edicts on conscription promulgated in 1808 (followed by a fourth in early 1809) finally
declared military service to be the duty of all Baden citizens and progressively
reduced the number of exemptions to the draft. As in Bavaria and Württemberg,
military service still fell most heavily on the poorer classes of society, but the
recruiting base was broadened significantly and the state was able to meet its
Rheinbund commitments despite the heavy casualties of the coming campaigns.
Administrative controls were also centralized at the national level to improve
efficiency and spread the burden of the draft equitably across the country. The
army's remount service was likewise centralized to keep pace with the demands
for horseflesh as the military expanded.[8]

Coupled with these reforms in bringing the soldier into the army were several
aimed at caring for those he might leave behind if an Austrian bullet should
deprive the state of his services. With tours of duty that lasted from eight years
for the infantry and cavalry to twelve years for the artillery, soldiers were permitted to marry and carry on relatively normal lives in times of peace.[9] The
married trooper quartered in a barracks (many units were quartered on the population because of lack of barracks space), however, might find that 'normal'
meant he and his family had to share a room with several other soldiers, perhaps
allotted a corner to provide some illusory sense of privacy. Fortunately, beds
were intended to accommodate two sleeping soldiers, so there would presumably be room for both husband and wife under the same comforter. The man
who died wearing Baden's uniform could at least rest assured that his family
would receive a small stipend from foundations established by the government,
his widow being eligible until her own death or remarriage, his children to the
ages of 20 (boys) or 18 (girls). While the amounts doled out to widows and
orphans were often only sufficient to fend off starvation, conditions for the families of living soldiers on campaign were frequently even worse. In Napoleon's
day, it was not at all uncommon for a man's pay to be weeks or months in
arrears, but it would eventually reach him and the army had an interest in keeping him fed and healthy in the meantime. None of this was much comfort to his
wife and children back in Karlsruhe, who often lived in pathetic poverty in the
soldier's absence. To avoid these privations, some women preferred to accompany their spouses on campaign, performing domestic, nursing and other chores
on the march and even under fire. Many others, however, especially those with
children, could not march with the men and the state was forced to provide them
some minimal assistance. Despite their often benighted state, these women
could be a formidable bunch and woe betide the bureaucrat who was negligent
in his duties regarding the soldiers' wives. In 1805, 'hordes of the most vexed
termagants stormed the barracks administrator's office' when deliveries of fire-
wood were delayed. 'They occupied the steps and entrances and only by making the holiest of promises was he able to protect his grey head from their
fury.'[10]

Their wives and children more or less cared for, the soldiers themselves were
subjected to a barrage of 'stress and hectic' as major changes were introduced
throughout the army. First, Baden's infantry regiments were totally reorganized

along French lines. Since 1803, infantry organization had been based on companies of about 106 men, with four companies comprising a battalion and two battalions a regiment. In addition, a 'Garnisons-Regiment' of four companies was associated with each line regiment to serve as its depot and provide fortress garrisons. In 1808, however, the companies were enlarged to the French standard of 140 each and the number per battalion was increased to six, giving the regiment a total strength of more than 1,700 officers and men. In consonance with the French pattern, each battalion included one grenadier company, one voltigeur company and four companies of musketeers.[11] Moreover, for the first time, the regiments and companies, previously known by their Inhaber and commanders respectively, received numerical designations; the musketeer companies being numbered 1 to 8, with those of the first battalion bearing the odd numbers and those of the second the even. The manpower necessary to support these sweeping changes was provided by new recruits and the dissolution of the garrison 'regiments'. The latter were absorbed into their affiliated line units leaving only a small depot of two companies for each regiment.[12] Officers for these larger and more numerous companies, were obtained by accepting experienced foreigners, particularly expatriate Prussians and Kur-Hessians, into Baden service.[13]

Second, the officers, NCOs and men of Baden were required to abandon their Prussian methods and learn French tactics. The French drill regulations of 1791 were instituted and the Baden officers soon became adept at manoeuvring their units in column and deploying their élite companies as skirmishers.[14] Finally, as an outward sign of this dramatic injection of Napoleonic influence, the Badeners adopted French rank insignia (epaulets, etc.). The addition of expensive bullion epaulets and other accoutrements often proved a serious financial burden to poorly paid officers already saddled with enormous bills for their splendid and ever-changing uniforms, but this practical measure enhanced the uniformity and cohesion of the Grande Armée, permitting instant recognition of an officer's grade regardless of his nationality.[15] Less tangible was a gradual shift in attitude toward Napoleon and the French. Although often irritated by what they considered French arrogance and intervention, the Badeners had learned a great deal from their Gallic allies in 1805 and 1806-1807, adopting the aggressive, ruthless, mobile approach to warfare that characterized the campaigns of the Grande Armée. Moreover, they began to feel pride in fighting alongside the victorious eagles of France, under the eyes of the little man in the grey greatcoat, the victor of Austerlitz and Jena, the Corsican commoner who overthrew empires. The result of all these reforms and the experience of fighting two campaigns as allies of the French was thus a tough, compact force that fitted smoothly into the French organizational structure and was motivated by professional pride and more than a touch of Napoleonic glory.

By January 1809, the reorganized army of Baden consisted of four line infantry regiments, a light (Jäger) battalion, a battalion of Leib-Grenadier-Garde, two light cavalry regiments, a squadron of guard cavalry and three companies of artillery. The army's uniforms resembled those of their Bavarian allies in many respects, particularly in the Bavarian-style Raupenhelm worn by the infantry,

Table 4-1: The Baden Army in April 1809

Line Infantry Regiments

Organization: two battalions per regiment; one grenadier, one voltigeur and four fusilier companies per battalion; company strength 140 men; regimental depot.

Uniform: dark-blue coat; distinctive colour on collar, cuffs, lapels, shoulder-straps; white breeches; Raupenhelm.

Number	Title (Inhaber)	Distinctive Colour
1	Leib-Infanterie-Regiment *Grossherzog*	scarlet
2	Linien-Infanterie-Regiment *Erbgrossherzog*	deep yellow
3	Linien-Infanterie-Regiment *Graf Hochberg*	white
4	Linien-Infanterie-Regiment (no Inhaber)	deep red (in Spain)

Other Infantry

Jägerbataillon *von Lingg*

Organization: six companies (incomplete at start of campaign).

Uniform: dark-green coat with black facings; grey breeches; Raupenhelm.

Leib-Garde-Grenadier Battalion

Organization: five companies.

Uniform: dark-blue coat with red facings; white breeches; bearskin cap.

Cavalry

Light Dragoon Regiment

Organization: four squadrons plus depot.

Uniform: light-blue coat with scarlet facings; Raupenhelm

Hussar Regiment

Organization: four squadrons (incomplete at start of campaign).

Uniform: dark-green dolamn and pelisse with red facings; chamois or red breeches; black shako.

Garde du Corps

Organization: two companies.

Uniform: white coat with red facings; white breeches; Raupenhelm.

Artillery

Organization: Artillery Battalion of one horse and two foot batteries (one in Spain).

Artillery uniform: dark-blue coat with black facings trimmed in red; grey breeches; Raupenhelm. Train uniform: grey coat with black facings; white breeches; Raupenhelm.

artillery and light dragoons alike. Bavarian influence was also evident in the styling of the coat issued to the Baden line regiments; as opposed to the unique cornflower-blue of the Bavarian uniform, however, the Badeners purchased cloth dyed a conventional dark-blue.[16] The members of Jägerbataillon *von Lingg*, on the other hand, wore coats similar in cut to the line infantry but in the traditional dark-green of German light troops. Named for its commander, Oberst Johann von Lingg, the Jägerbataillon was intended to consist of six companies with the same establishment as those of the line battalions. The Leib-Grenadier-Garde Battalion numbered five companies (600 men) at the start of the year, but grew with the addition of another company during the course of the campaign. Unlike the other infantry units, their dark-blue coats were closed at the waist and decorated with eight horizontal lace battons across the breast. They were also distinguished by their headgear, a large black fur bonnet like that of the French guard.

Even in the earlier campaigns, Baden's artillery had been an exception to the generally poor state of readiness exhibited by the Grand Duchy's forces. Carefully instructed and supplied with good *matériel*, the artillery was already close to the French in quality and was 'highly prized' by its larger ally.[17] It was organized into an administrative battalion of one horse company (1st) and two foot companies (2nd and 3rd).

Baden's cavalry arm consisted of a light dragoon regiment, a hussar regiment (*von Geusau*) and a Garde du Corps squadron.[18] Commanded by Oberst Karl von Freystedt, the Light Dragoons were organized into four field squadrons (Rittmeister Julius Schimmelpfennig von der Oye, Oberstlieutenant Friedrich von Heimrodt, Major Georg Behagel, Oberstlieutenant Karl von Sponeck) and a depot squadron, each of the field squadrons containing 114 troopers. In addition to the ubiquitous Raupenhelm, the Light Dragoons had tunics like the infantry but in light-blue cloth with scarlet facings. The two weak companies (total strength of only 66 guardsmen) of Garde du Corps cavalry also wore the Raupenhelm, but were otherwise uniformed in a decidedly Prussian fashion: two rows of buttons paraded down the fronts of white tunics with red trim, the men's breeches were white and they wore tall black boots. The hussars maintained the traditional garb of their particular brand of light cavalry: a handsome and colourful Hungarian-style uniform of dark-green with red facings. This regiment was authorized four squadrons of 135 troopers each, but horses were still in short supply and most of the men were unmounted when the war began in April.

When Napoleon called on Karl Friedrich in January 1809 to prepare for war with Austria, however, the 4th Infantry[19] and a foot artillery battery (manned by the 3rd Company), nearly 2,000 men, had already been swallowed up by the grinding war in Spain. In his 15 January letter, the Emperor expressed his satisfaction with these troops and requested Baden prepare an additional contingent of 6,000 for a possible conflict with Austria 'because it is better to carry the war to the enemy than receive him in one's own land'.[20] By mid-February, the organization and training of Baden's contingent was fairly complete when fresh French demands threw the Grand Duchy's plans into disarray. Although the detachment in Spain had only been in that theatre of operations for about six months, its casualties already exceeded 600 men. Paris naturally looked to Baden to replace these losses and maintain the contingent's strength. A march battalion of 694 officers and men was thus hastily assembled and departed its homeland for the hopeless Iberian conflict on 4 March. Drawn from the line regiments, these replacements left a serious gap in the ranks of Baden's main army that could only be filled by inducting new recruits and reassigning some soldiers from the Guard Battalion. Even these measures were inadequate to bring the line units to their authorized strengths, however, and the Grand Duchy's battalions would head for Bavaria with less than their full complement of infantrymen. The Jäger Battalion was likewise incomplete, only four of its companies being fully manned and equipped as the contingent began to assemble.[21]

Despite the competing requirements of the guerrilla war in Spain, Baden's contingent for the Army of Germany was soon on a war footing. Initially slated to form the 1st Division of a special 'corps d'armée de la Confédération du Rhin', the field contingent under GM Valentin von Harrant comprised most of Baden's regular troops and was organized into two weak brigades (Oberst Karl von Neuenstein and GM August von Vincenti); only the Guard, the hussars,

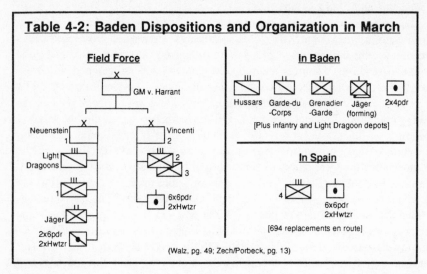

Table 4-2: Baden Dispositions and Organization in March

(Walz, pg. 49; Zech/Porbeck, pg. 13)

some depot infantry, the depot of the dragoon regiment and a few guns remained behind to protect the Duchy (Table 4-2). As many of the units intended for the Confederation Corps were already committed to Spain and Baden was both unwilling and unable to raise a full division, the Emperor abandoned the plans for the special corps and directed the incorporation of the Badeners into the 1st Division (Legrand's) of Marshal André Massena's IV Corps on 5 March. Between 14 and 17 March, the Badeners thus assembled around Pforzheim where they were reviewed by their new corps commander on the 19th.

Massena, the Duke of Rivoli, found the Baden troops 'very fine' but expressed concern to Berthier that they were 'composed entirely of conscripts'. Their appearance, bearing, uniforms and equipment had impressed him, however, and he seems to have been quite satisfied with this addition to his corps.[22] He was also impressed by one of the young officers he encountered at the Pforzheim review, Oberst Wilhelm Markgraf Hochberg, and invited the young nobleman to join his staff. The second son of Karl Friedrich's second marriage, Wilhelm was only 17 in 1809 and entered upon his new duties in Massena's headquarters with some trepidation: 'I was not comfortable with this new assignment: I left a position I understood for one that was completely unknown.' He was also worried about the mundane aspects of daily existence in his new environment: 'I also knew I would be better cared for among our own troops than in a headquarters where I knew no one.'[23] None the less, he accepted the post, served the gifted, but often difficult, Marshal well and proved himself an officer of considerable talent and leadership ability. Only three years later, he would display these abilities and an uncommon sense of honour as commander of the Baden contingents in the 1812 and 1813 campaigns.

While Markgraf Wilhelm rode off to prepare for his new duties, the Baden contingent remained in the Pforzheim area for the next two weeks. The officers made good use of this brief respite, conducting intensive drills and musketry exercises to accelerate the incorporation of the numerous new conscripts into their companies.[24] Although two weeks was far from adequate to turn village boys into true soldiers, the young recruits had at least learned the rudiments of their new profession by the time the contingent left its quarters for Ulm on 2 April. Guided by hard-eyed officers and the solid core of veterans from 1806-1807, their soldierly education continued as they marched through the cold rain and snow of early April to join the gathering army.

Arriving in Ulm on 6 April, the Baden infantry and artillery were reorganized into a single brigade and redesignated as the 2nd Brigade of GD Claude-Just Legrand's Division (Table 4-3).[25] Each of the infantry regiments numbered about 1,650 men, while the Jäger Battalion was some 560 men strong. The Light Dragoons, temporarily under Heimrodt's command (Freystedt was suffering from a lost altercation with a horse), were detached from the rest of their compatriots and assigned to the Corps' light cavalry division under GB Jacob-François Marulaz. This new organization, more practical in view of the size of Baden's contingent, made GM Vincenti superfluous and he was transferred to Imperial Headquarters to represent Baden's military interests to Napoleon and Berthier. GM von Harrant remained the senior Baden officer, but, as with the other allied contingents, the brigade was placed under the command of a French officer, Général de Brigade Baron Georges Kister. Like the Bavarians and Württembergers, the Badeners considered the imposition of a French commander an irritating affront; Harrant seems to have been particularly pained by the situation. Indeed, Massena, anticipating the Badeners' reaction, had refrained from mentioning Kister's impending appointment when he visited the court in Karlsruhe on 17 March, leaving that odious task for the French ambassador. He did, however, have the professional courtesy to inform Harrant of the change in command structure personally. Kister's qualities are hard to grasp. He is vari-

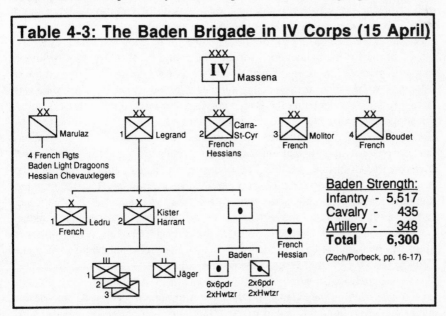

Table 4-3: The Baden Brigade in IV Corps (15 April)

IV Massena

Marulaz
4 French Rgts
Baden Light Dragoons
Hessian Chevauxlegers

1 Legrand

2 Carra-St-Cyr
French
Hessians

3 Molitor
French

4 Boudet
French

1 Ledru
French

2 Kister
Harrant

1 / 2 / 3

Jäger

Baden
6x6pdr
2xHwtzr

2x6pdr
2xHwtzr

French
Hessian

Baden Strength:
Infantry - 5,517
Cavalry - 435
Artillery - 348
Total 6,300

(Zech/Porbeck, pp. 16-17)

ously described as 'a very brave and worthy officer' and 'an old, declining man', but he had the good sense to arrive at a *modus vivendi* with Harrant which put the Frenchman in charge of the brigade's external activities and general direction while allowing the Badener complete authority for internal discipline and the execution of orders.[26]

In addition to problems with the command structure, the inclusion of the Badeners in a French corps illustrates another friction of coalition warfare: logistics. Baden's muskets were provided by an arms manufactory in Schmalkalden and were of slightly different calibre from the French weapons, so that the two allies could not share ammunition. According to Kapitän Karl von Freydorf of the Baden artillery:

> Général de Division Legrand as well as Kister and the others who had not known that our calibre was different from theirs were not a little horrified when they learned of this and saw themselves required to transport a double supply of ammunition. The Emperor had directed that no division's artillery park have more than 80 vehicles including the pieces, and ours already stood at 140, a number which could not be reduced.[27]

This irritation was compounded by problems with the rest of the Corps' ammunition supply. As a result of misunderstandings, staff negligence or over-confidence, IV Corps had departed France without filling its ammunition wagons and now found itself on the verge of a major campaign with hardly a round to fire. Urged on by caustic remonstrances from the Emperor, convoys were hastily dispatched to France, but the Corps was fortunate not to have been engaged in any major actions during the first week of the war. Apparently anxious not to repeat this error, the French artillery commander also sent three empty Baden wagons back to Karlsruhe to restock the contingent's supply of musket cartridges.

These empty wagons, splashing through the mushy snow to Baden, were evidence of the Corps' preparations for the impending conflict. As the likelihood of battle increased, Massena issued a flurry of orders to place IV Corps on a war footing. Among other measures, the number of rounds carried by each man was raised to 50 (thus depleting the Baden contingent's reserve stock of cartridges), bread rations for six days were requisitioned and three pairs of shoes were to be issued to each man. Units were also directed to conduct frequent inspections and exercises with particular emphasis on the younger troops, who were to drill twice daily. Unfortunately, the Corps was in constant motion throughout the beginning of April and some of these steps were never completed (the required bread ration, for example, was reduced to a four days' supply). Furthermore, these repeated and rapid movements allowed little time to co-ordinate quarters for the troops. Mistakes were common and difficult to rectify, leaving large numbers of tired soldiers, French and Baden alike, crammed into inadequate lodgings as they sought to escape the dismal weather.

Despite their logistical problems, their concern over the number of inexperienced conscripts in their ranks and their bitter disappointment at Kister's insertion into the command structure, the Badeners were in good spirits, well equipped, physically fit and ready for the coming campaign. They and their extra shoes would soon learn what it meant to campaign with the Emperor Napoleon.

April - By Forced Marches to the Inn

While the Baden brigade was joining the remainder of IV Corps in its rather dispersed assembly area, the Austrian army was trudging slowly toward the border to begin its offensive into southern Bavaria. When Archduke Charles crossed the River Inn into Bavaria on 10 April, Massena was given command of Oudinot's divisions in addition to his own corps and directed to assemble both about Augsburg, but Berthier's baffling orders and the extreme dispersal of the two corps made this a slow process. Attempting to comply with the plague of messages from headquarters, the infantry and artillery of the Baden Brigade, which had been moved to scattered quarters in the townships around Thannhausen on the 7th, were now (12th) shifted further south to the vicinity of Schwabmünchen, while the Light Dragoons were moved to the River Wertach just west of Augsburg. Miserable weather, conflicting orders, repeated changes in quarters, incessant drill and the final hectic preparations for combat filled the soldiers' days with turmoil, tension and confusion as the Badeners conducted 'some of the most strenuous movements of the campaign'.[28] Despite the exertions of staffs, commanders and men, however, IV Corps was still spread over some 4,000 square kilometres of southern Bavaria's rolling hills when Napoleon stepped down from his carriage in Donauwörth on the 17th.

The Emperor's arrival instantly accelerated the pace of operations and a flood of energetic new orders began to issue from army headquarters. Descrying a chance to crush the Austrian army, Napoleon directed Massena to leave a garrison on Augsburg while concentrating the majority of his forces between Aichach and Pfaffenhofen on the 18th ('the enemy is lost if Oudinot and your three divisions debouch before dawn'). At the bottom of the official order, he scrawled his famous injunction in his own hand: 'Activity, activity, speed! I rely on you!'[29] Unfortunately, IV Corps' dispositions precluded any hope of meeting Napoleon's ambitious timetable. Most units only received their orders long after daybreak on the 18th and it was well after noon before the men were formed and marching.

Thrust forward in the hasty advance, the Baden infantry and artillery passed through Augsburg on the evening of 18 April and continued on to Aichach, leaving the 3rd Infantry behind at Friedberg as part of the Augsburg garrison. Arriving at Aichach between 10 p.m. (18th) and 1:30 a.m. (19th), the Badeners were only granted two hours' rest before they were again up and on the road to the east. Another ten hours of marching under cold and steady rain brought the weary men to Pfaffenhofen at about noon on 19 April, having traversed 75 kilometres in less than 24 hours.

The Light Dragoons also arrived in Pfaffenhofen on the 19th. Not yet subordinate to Marulaz, the regiment departed its cantonments near Augsburg on the evening of the 17th and rode throughout the night and the next day to reach Aichach at 5 p.m. They had already been on the move for nearly twenty-four hours, but their reprieve was only temporary and at 7 p.m., the troopers were once more sloshing over the dark, muddy roads through Weilach (three hour break at about midnight) to Pfaffenhofen. Reaching this village at mid-morning on the 19th, the regiment was assigned to GD Michel Claparède's Division as its advanced guard and conducted tense reconnaissances across the enemy-filled countryside until early the next morning. Breaking camp to lead IV Corps' crucial drive toward the Austrian left flank, the dragoons rode east and finally linked with the rest of the corps cavalry just beyond Freising at about 10 p.m. on the 20th. Marulaz pushed his tired troopers ahead throughout the night and skirmished with Austrian cavalry at Moosburg early on the 21st, the Baden regiment taking a number of prisoners when it galloped to the assistance of the French 23rd Chasseurs-a-Cheval. Following this brief engagement, the Badeners were again separated from their French and Hessian allies, proceeding down the north bank of the Isar to Landshut with a brigade of French infantry (GB Florentin Ficatier's), while the bulk of the corps crossed the river and approached the city by the southern bank. Thoroughly exhausted after nearly four days in the saddle, the regiment rode into Landshut at about 9 p.m., long after the dramatic battle for the Isar crossings had flickered away into a vague pursuit.[30]

The Baden infantry and artillery was also too late to contribute to Napoleon's victory at Landshut. Departing Pfaffenhofen at 6 a.m. on the 20th after a well deserved rest, the Badeners marched for Unterbruck on the River Amper, but found the bridge destroyed and were forced to wait three hours before a frail and narrow span was thrown across the stream. In utter darkness, the infantry conducted an agonizingly slow crossing in single file, while the artillery and other vehicles trundled off to Haimhausen where an intact bridge had been located. The 21st of April was already an hour old before Legrand's men were finally assembled on the west bank of the Amper and ready to continue their advance.[31] Urged on by Massena, the Badeners slogged ahead through continual drizzle, crossed the Isar at Moosburg with the majority of the Corps and pushed on for Landshut. Despite their best efforts, however, they were still ten kilometres short of the city when they reached Kronwinkl at about 7 p.m. There was nothing more to be gained by further marching and, as darkness settled over the broad Isar valley, the weary brigade filed off the road and camped for the night.

When Napoleon discovered his misappreciation of the Austrian dispositions and turned his main army north, the Baden Light Dragoons were among the troops he sent hurtling up the road to Eggmühl on the morning of 22 April. As they attempted to negotiate the crowded streets of Landshut at about 6 a.m., they came to the Emperor's attention. Annoyed at the delays and traffic jams in the city, Napoleon ordered the Baden troopers to pass his vantage point at the gallop, adding that 'he did not care to see his cavalry move at any other pace'.[32] The Light Dragoons reached the heights south of the Laaber shortly after the Württemberg Light Brigade but were denied the honour of crossing swords with the Austrian horsemen. Initially ordered to join the massive cavalry attack on the Austrian battery north of Eggmühl, the regiment was almost instantly recalled by Berthier to protect the Emperor and his staff. In this capacity, it followed Napoleon to Alteglofsheim and spent the night near his headquarters.

The other Badeners also missed the battle. Near the end of the heavy column surging north from Landshut toward Regensburg, the footsore infantry battalions did not attain the Laaber until about 1 a.m. on the 23rd, many losing almost half their number in stragglers over the 50-kilometre route of march.[33]

As they sought their rest on the gruesome battlefield at Eggmühl, alive with the pitiful stirrings of the helpless wounded, the Badeners had good cause for weary pride. In $4^1/2$ days, they and the rest of IV Corps had covered some 200 kilometres of often bottomless tracks under dismal weather. Driven by Napoleon's iron will, they had displayed a prodigious capacity for marching, only rarely equalled by the French themselves, and earned the praise of friend and foe alike.[34] While they might wish for battle to relieve the grinding burden of incessant marches and offer opportunities for glory, the Badeners were beginning to experience what their French counterparts had discovered in 1805, that Napoleon made as much use of his soldiers' legs as he did of their bayonets.

The morning of 23 April saw the Badeners on the road to Straubing while Lannes and Davout stormed Regensburg in a vain attempt to catch Archduke Charles's retreating army. Massena's command now consisted of three infantry divisions (Claparède, Carra St.-Cyr, and Legrand with the Baden brigade), GD Jean Espagne's cuirassier division, the 14th French Chasseurs and the Baden Light Dragoons (the latter two detached from Marulaz's division). Marching via Plattling (24th) and Vilshofen (25th), he drove east to the Inn, arriving at Passau and Schärding on 26 April. That morning, the Baden Light Dragoons were the first to appear opposite Schärding, a small fortified town on the east bank of the Inn. The town's defenders, under FML Josef von Dedovich, opened fire on the Baden cavalrymen with artillery (two guns and a howitzer) and forced them to take cover. The dragoons, however, were only the advance guard of Legrand's Division, which was under orders to force a crossing at Schärding while the remainder of the corps seized the bridges at Passau. By early afternoon, the whole of the division had arrived and Dedovich's situation was hopeless. The half-battery of Baden horse artillery unlimbered and silenced the Austrian cannon, while French voltigeurs and the Baden Jägers opened up harassing fire from the river's western edge. When a summons to surrender was rejected by the Austrians, Legrand deployed the rest of his artillery (24 guns) and set the town afire, quickly convincing Dedovich to retire; by 6 p.m., French light infantry were in the city and the Austrian line along the Inn was unhinged.[35]

Although Massena had succeeded in overcoming the feeble Austrian resistance along the Inn, his corps was now exposed and unsupported. He thus concentrated his divisions at Schärding on the 27th but refrained from further advance until the Emperor could redeploy additional French forces from Regensburg. While most of the Corps was quartered on the right bank of the river, Legrand's men remained on the left from the 27th until the end of the month, repairing equipment and collecting stragglers in preparation for the next phase of the campaign. Of the Baden contingent, only the Light Dragoons crossed over to the eastern shore. Typically active, the regiment conducted numerous reconnaissances from its cantonments around Sigharting, skirmishing with Austrian hussars (*Kienmaier*) on the 29th and again on the 30th. That evening, as the Baden patrols were returning to Sigharting, the Light Dragoons were attached to IV Corps' advance guard under one of Massena's staff officers, Adjutant-Commandant Trenqualye. Combined with the French 4th Ligne and the Württemberg *Leib-Chevauxlegers*, the Baden cavalry would be in the lead when Massena renewed his advance into Austria.

MAY - BLOOD ALONG THE DANUBE: EBELSBERG AND ASPERN

May opened auspiciously for the arms of Baden. With Lannes and Vandamme finally across the Inn and Salzach, Massena's flank was covered and his vanguard was up and moving at dawn on the 1st. While the Württemberg chevauxlegers and French infantry probed along the Riedau-Neumarkt road, pushing Austrian skirmishers ahead of them, Trenqualye sent the Badeners north and south of the road to outflank the enemy's rear guard. There seems to have been little direct co-ordination between the various columns and the neat little victory that followed was mostly the result of good luck and individual initiative. As Rittmeister Bismark's Württembergers broke out of a wood and found an overwhelming Austrian force to their front, its commander was unaware that help was close by. Likewise, the temporary commander of the Baden regiment, Oberstlieutenant Heimrodt, was surprised when he attained the road and saw the Austrian skirmishers to his rear. While he watched, Bismark sent his lone squadron spurring into the Austrian skirmish line. Heimrodt quickly brought his two squadrons around and led them forward at the gallop. The hapless skirmishers, attacked by cavalry from front and rear in open terrain, were soon dead, captured or scattered to the four winds. Their comrades, however, four companies of III/*Jordis*, now opened fire on the light dragoons. Hidden by a swell of land, this formed infantry had previously escaped the Badeners' notice, but Heimrodt was equal to this new danger. Hastily reorganizing his men, he plunged ahead to charge the Austrian square. The infantry formation had loosened as the battalion attempted to retreat across country and the bold Baden horsemen were soon in among the panicked foot soldiers, whirling, slashing and cursing. Their commander wounded and their banner down, the Austrians lost all discipline and surrendered to Heimrodt's triumphant men as the other two Baden squadrons pelted up to encircle the bewildered infantry.[36] The men of the *Jordis* battalion had hardly fired a shot in their own defence. At the cost of one dead and two wounded, the Baden Light Dragoons had succeeding in breaking a square and capturing more than 700 Austrians.[37]

Heimrodt again distinguished himself by his initiative and courage on the 2nd. The French had pushed an Austrian delaying force through Eferding when the Light Dragoons arrived. Trenqualye immediately ordered Heimrodt to attack up a straight and slender, tree-lined road in the hopes of capturing the Austrians retiring east of the town. Skirmishers lined the road, nestling among the trees, but two guns were bouncing hurriedly away from the town and Heimrodt was determined to take them. Unmindful of the infantry's musket balls, he charged down the road at the head of a dozen Baden dragoons and a dozen French chasseurs. By some miracle, most of this little band reached the two guns and scattered the gunners. They were unsupported, however, and before the allies could take possession of their prizes, nearby Austrians counter-attacked. After a brief flurry of hand-to-hand combat, the remaining French and Baden troopers had to retreat, galloping back to the safety of their own infantry.

EBELSBERG (3 MAY)

The Light Dragoons remained with the vanguard under Trenqualye as IV Corps approached the Traun on 3 May.[38] Under orders to capture the bridge at Ebelsberg, the French and their German allies passed rapidly through Linz to

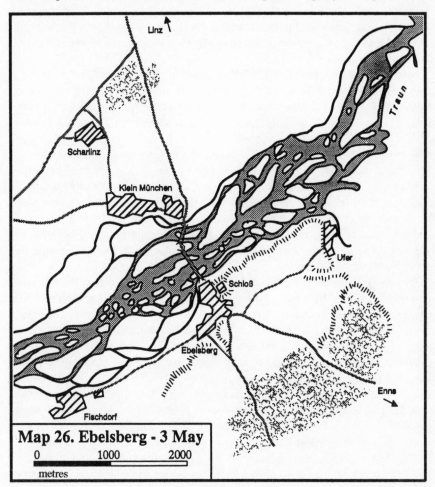

Map 26. Ebelsberg - 3 May

0   1000   2000
metres

encounter the Austrian rear guard just west of the river. Although pursued and disordered, the Austrians put up a stiff fight, attempting to hold their bridgehead west of the Traun until a tardy brigade (Schustekh's) could cross the river. Trenqualye took the Baden dragoons to intercept this brigade but found the Austrians too strong to attack and Schustekh was able to escape.

The ensuing Battle of Ebelsberg was a bloody affair. With Schustekh safely over the river, the Austrian rear guard began to withdraw. However, the river was spanned by only a single narrow bridge and, under increasing French pressure, the withdrawal soon degenerated into a pell-mell flight. The French followed literally on the heels of the fleeing Austrians, crossing the bridge with the panicked enemy columns and establishing themselves in Ebelsberg itself. First across was GB Louis Coëhorn's brigade (at about 11.30 a.m.), soon to be followed by the rest of Claparède's division (brigades Lesuire and Ficatier). Ferocious fighting surged back and forth across the little town as Austrian reserves attempted to evict the bold but outnumbered French. Casualties on both sides mounted rapidly, the dead and dying choking alleys, squares and homes.[39] Barely holding the western edge of the town, Claparède called for help and Massena sent messenger after sweating messenger to hurry the arrival of Legrand's Division.

Marching east on the Linz-Ebelsberg road, the men of the Baden Brigade responded to Massena's urgent adjutants by repeatedly accelerating their pace; by the time they reached the river, they were almost running, loading their muskets on the move.[40] Ebelsberg burned ahead of them. With Austrian cannon balls whistling overhead and a steady stream of wounded making their painful way to the rear, GB Kister initially ordered the brigade to approach the bridge by a route that would provide some cover from the enemy's guns. Markgraf Wilhelm of Baden would have none of this, however. Arguing that the Badeners must not be concealed from the Marshal in their first encounter with the enemy, he persuaded Kister to deploy the brigade in the open where friend and foe could observe its evolutions and discipline.[41] Fortunately, the Austrian gunners were more concerned with the bridge itself and the Baden infantry assuaged its pride at little cost.

By this time, about 3 p.m., Legrand had already led GB François Roch, Baron Ledru des Essarts' Brigade across the bridge and hurled it into the inferno. The situation remained desperate, however, and the Badeners were ordered across the long wooden span immediately. The press and confusion at the bridge was terrifying: fresh troops attempting to advance, the injured struggling to withdraw, harried adjutants rushing in both directions and corpses scattered underfoot. In the all-consuming urge to get across to the eastern bank, all impediments were cast aside and into the roaring Traun. Neither dead nor wounded, including French staff officers, were spared this dreadful treatment and a French grenadier who had lost a foot to a cannon ball was fortunate indeed when two Badeners took pity on him and bore him to a dressing station.[42]

The Baden Jägers, who had covered most of the seven kilometres from Linz at a trot, somehow managed to force their way across the bridge and through the gates of Ebelsberg, likewise blocked with broken guns, wagons, horses and men. Swinging to their left, the men deployed in the fields north of the town where the 26th Léger was under heavy Austrian pressure. Advancing with cool determination at about 4 p.m., the battalion was a timely reinforcement for the French light infantrymen. 'You have saved my honour and life,' called the commander of III/26 as he strode up to greet the Germans.[43] Together, the two units held the Austrians in check and secured the French left flank. As Hiller withdrew his corps in the late afternoon, the battalion joined the cautious pursuit, acquitting itself well and bringing in 50 prisoners.

The Baden line infantry did not play a major role in the battle. Despite the dreadful carnage and confusion around the bridge, the two regiments advanced enthusiastically in anticipation of their first real fight. The flames in the town ahead of them prevented their following the Jägers, however, and Legrand ordered them to retire to the west bank until the way could be cleared. This order, passed to the head of the column, could not be communicated to the rear ranks and a frightful scene ensued as the leading companies attempted to march back the way they had come while the trailing elements were still pressing toward Ebelsberg. The regiments finally managed to work their way off the bridge, wading through the shallows along the river's eastern marge to gain the heights north of the town. They remained in this area for the evening, bivouacking about two kilometres beyond the smouldering horror that was Ebelsberg. Unfortunately, it appears that someone unfriendly to the Badeners interpreted their retirement on the bridge as a retreat and reported their supposed unreliability to the Marshal. Legrand, while commending the Jägers, was thus forced to defend the behaviour of the line regiments in his reports to Massena.[44]

The Baden horse artillery deployed on one of the islands north of the Ebelsberg bridge and kept up a heavy fire throughout the battle. The foot guns did not arrive in time to contribute to the costly victory and the dragoons, utterly unsuited to village fighting, remained on the western shore as observers. The cavalry and both batteries crossed the Traun as the bridge was repaired, joining their respective divisions on the far shore during the course of the night.

Before continuing the advance on Vienna, IV Corps rested for several days between the Traun and the Enns, giving Napoleon the opportunity to recompense Massena's men for their courage and sacrifice. At a review of Carra Saint-Cyr's and Legrand's Divisions on the 5th, the Baden troops heartily echoed the cries of 'Vive l'Empereur' from their French comrades and proudly executed several tactical deployments under his stern eye. Making excellent use of the occasion to inspire his German allies, the Emperor praised their appearance and ability while distributing Crosses of the Legion of Honour, twelve to the dragoons and three to the Jägers. He also granted a boon as unexpected as it was welcome. In recognition of the Badener's performance, the entire brigade was henceforth entrusted solely to GM von Harrant's command and GB Kister was dispatched to assume the military governorship of Salzburg.[45] Two days later, through alternating spells of drenching rain and oppressive heat, the Badeners set out for Vienna, marching via St. Pölten and Schönbrunn to reach the Austrian capital on 12 May. The city capitulated the following day and the Badeners were delighted to receive quarters for the first time since their departure from Augsburg. Seated around 'a well-set table', the men 'forgot in an hour the discomfort of many weeks'.[46]

Several days later, the Baden 3rd Infantry Regiment *Hochberg* under Oberst Adam von Schöpf also arrived in Vienna. Its presence in Augsburg rendered unnecessary by the rapid advance of Napoleon's armies, the regiment departed its garrison on 24 April in the company of the Hessian Leib-Regiment.[47] Crossing into Austria at Braunau on 2 May, it reached Melk on the 10th where it came temporarily under the orders of Marshal Davout. The regiment remained with the Iron Marshal for three days until he was certain Archduke Charles would continue his march to Vienna and not attempt to force the Danube. After many long miles with poor provisions (the route had already been picked clean by Napoleon's experienced scavengers) and with no combat to lend purpose and excitement to their marches, the men of the 3rd Infantry reached Vienna on 16 May to take over the quarters recently vacated by their countrymen.

The bulk of the Baden Brigade departed Vienna at 2 a.m. on the 15th after only two days' rest. Napoleon, concerned about militia activity south-west of the city, dispatched GD Jacques Law, Comte de Lauriston with the 1st and 2nd Baden Infantry, the Jäger Battalion and the horse guns to disperse any potential military threat in the area and establish contact with Viceroy Eugene's Army of Italy approaching from the south. Marching via Altenmarkt, the brigade reached Wiener Neustadt on the 16th where Lauriston added GB Edouard Colbert's light cavalry brigade (7th and 20th Chasseurs, 9th Hussars) to his command. In the company of the French cavalry, the Badeners spent the remainder of the month conducting what was hardly more than a police action against scattered elements of poorly organized Landwehr and Landsturm. The brigade occupied the important Semmering Pass on the 18th, capturing 70 of its 1,000 defenders and scattering the rest with hardly a shot fired. Lauriston praised his German troops for 'advancing with the greatest ardour' against the enemy's 'fine position'.[48] Other than this incident and a brief, successful skirmish at Aspang on the 20th, however, late May was a time of fatiguing marches over steep mountain roads but little combat. Contact with Eugène's army was established on the 26th and by the 29th, the Badeners had returned to Wiener Neustadt to await new orders.

ASPERN (21-22 MAY)

Chasing Austrian militia over hill and dale in the spring heat, Lauriston's Badeners could hear the dull roll of guns echoing down from the bloody fields and alleys of Aspern and Essling 40 kilometres away to the north-east. Afraid that Archduke Charles would elude him, Napoleon boldly pushed his army across the Danube on 20 May with the aim of bringing Charles' army to battle and destroying it. The Baden 3rd Infantry Regiment and foot artillery battery marched with the rest of Legrand's Division as it traversed the long, shaky bridges on to Lobau island through the late afternoon. In the midst of crossing, however, the artillerymen experienced the first of a series of misfortunes that would plague the French throughout the coming battle: the bridge, strained by the melt-swollen waters of the great river, snapped, stranding the two separate parts of the battery. Almost ten hours passed before the sundered pieces of the battery were reassembled on the left bank. The broken bridges also interrupted the supply of provisions and the 1,445 men of *Hochberg* spent a hungry night on the islands in the Danube, waiting to cross to the left bank for their first struggle with the Austrian army.

In the early morning hours of the 21st, Legrand's men filed on to the broad plain of the Marchfeld, deploying south of Essling with GD Molitor's Division to their left at Aspern and GD Jean Boudet on their right toward Enzersdorf.

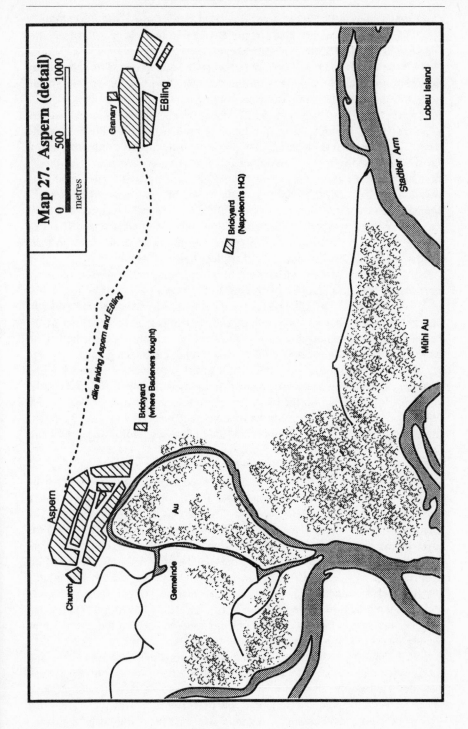

Map 27. Aspern (detail)

The Light Dragoon Regiment arrived several hours later about 260 strong.[49] The Baden cavalry, having guarded the Danube around Fischamend since the 15th, had been called north to Kaiser-Ebersdorf on the 20th to rejoin IV Corps in time for the coming battle. Oberst von Freystedt had recovered from his injury and was once again in command, but the damaged bridges kept the regiment, along with most of Marulaz's Division, waiting impatiently on the western bank until well after the sun had risen on 21 May. Between 9 and 10 a.m., Marulaz led his division on foot across the tenuous bridges, sending the Baden and Hessian light regiments off at the gallop to establish outposts north and west of Aspern once they set foot on the farther shore. As yet, there was no clear sign of the main Austrian army, no indication of Charles's intentions. Reconnoitring toward Hirschstetten at about 1 p.m., however, the German troopers broke through a screen of Austrian hussars to spot the heavy attack columns of Hiller's Corps marching on Aspern. Constantly skirmishing, the Badeners and Hessians fell back slowly before Hiller's avant-garde, retiring north of the town to form Marulaz's left as Austrian infantry and artillery began to deploy.

Hiller's initial attempt on Aspern was repulsed, but Austrian pressure increased as GdK Friedrich Heinrich Graf Bellegarde's I Corps came into action on VI Corps' left. To bolster Molitor's defence, Massena ordered some of Legrand's artillery into this key village and Hauptmann Holtz with four of the Baden guns was soon hurrying through its streets to unlimber near the hotly contested churchyard. Here, on relatively open ground, the Baden gunners engaged in a deadly duel with the more numerous Austrian batteries. When Markgraf Wilhelm brought the battery commander, Hauptmann Wilhelm Holtz, the order to move, Holtz apologized for his recent arrival on the field of battle. In jest, Wilhelm replied that the captain had arrived early enough to die. Moments later, just as the guns were unlimbering, the unfortunate Holtz's head was carried away by a cannon ball.[50]

The Light Dragoons, posted to support their sweating countrymen, also suffered considerably in the rain of iron west of Aspern. Fortunately, Marulaz, who had personally brought the regiment forward to this exposed position to shield the guns from Austrian cavalry, ordered the dragoons out of the murderous fire when the threat to the artillery passed. He intended the Badeners to utilize the cover of the village streets in their withdrawal, but only part of the regiment heard the command. As a result, Freystedt found that he had only about half his troopers when he reordered his ranks east of town; the remainder, Heimrodt's and Sponeck's squadrons, rode around the northern fringe of the village to resume their position on the left wing of Marulaz's Division. The Baden artillery was also ordered back at about this time and retired through the now blazing streets to rejoin Legrand.

It was about 5 p.m. Aspern had already changed hands several times and another Austrian column, II Corps under Hohenzollern, was approaching from the north. Outnumbered, with both flanks under heavy attack and cut off from reinforcements, Napoleon's situation was precarious. It was imperative that Aspern be held at all costs and Legrand, who had been shifted to a position south-east of the town between 2 and 3 p.m. to support Molitor, threw his two

French regiments into the fight in its battered and burning houses while the Baden 3rd Infantry was kept east of the village in reserve. To hold the Austrian II Corps in check while Legrand's attack progressed, the Emperor sent part of his cavalry forward across the open fields north of Aspern. Marulaz's troopers, including the two errant Baden squadrons, formed the leading echelon of this attack, Espagne's cuirassiers riding up slowly to the right and behind the light cavalrymen. Deploying on the extreme left of Marulaz's command, Leutnant Georg von Stern could see the neat lines of Austrian troops through the shifting battle smoke: artillery to the front, backed by tightly packed infantry in battalion mass formation and the Habsburg cavalry, orderly but useless, in a 'long white line' to the rear.[51] Heimrodt and Sponeck led their men into the charge with great élan but apparently insufficient order.[52] Pounding toward the bayonet-fringed masses of infantry, the Badeners were greeted by heavy volleys of mus-ketry that broke their impetus and forced them to recoil. Sponeck quickly rallied his troopers for another effort, however, and stormed forward shouting 'Follow me, boys!' Crashing into the enemy ranks, the dragoons fought bravely but could not break their opponents. Sponeck fell, Stern was wounded, Heimrodt's horse was killed under him and the squadrons were forced to retreat a second time.

Complaining bitterly that the French cuirassiers had failed to support them, the Badeners withdrew east of Aspern to reunite with Freystedt's detachment.[53] Napoleon, who had observed the Badeners' determined attacks, took a moment in the midst of the battle to review the dragoons, praising their daring and assigning them to his honour guard as a particular signal of Imperial satisfaction. Despite the dragoons' frustration, Napoleon's cavalry attacks in the late after-noon achieved their purpose: Hohenzollern's Corps was immobilized for the remaining daylight hours and the danger to Aspern and the weak French centre was averted. With the hope of bringing the rest of his army across the Danube during the night, Napoleon prepared to renew the struggle on the 22nd.

Sunset brought a brief respite for most of the combatants but not for the Baden infantry. Sometime after dark, the Badeners were ordered to evict a group of Austrian Jägers from a ditch they occupied just east of Aspern. Oberst von Schöpf entrusted this difficult mission to the voltigeurs of I/3. Creeping for-ward over a landscape littered with corpses and illuminated by the the burning village, the 1st Voltigeur Company surprised the weary Jägers and put them to flight, neatly seizing their objective for the loss of only six men. Although they expended all their ammunition,[54] the voltigeurs held their position throughout the night, beating off repeated Austrian attempts to dislodge them.

The second day's battle opened at about 3 a.m. To set the stage for his offen-sive against the Austrian centre, Napoleon ordered Massena to take and hold Aspern. The Marshal's initial attempt to wrest the village from the tenacious Austrians was repulsed and four Baden companies posted at the brickworks east of Aspern helped to check the Austrian pursuit. Meanwhile, the other eight companies of *Hochberg* were hurled into the dreadful streets alongside French regiments from Carra Saint-Cyr's and Legrand's Divisions. Temporarily halted by Austrian reserves, the regiment was quickly rallied and stormed through the

blazing ruins to capture more than 250 prisoners.[55] The Badeners remained in
the bitter fight for the rest of day, performing admirably in repeated charges into
the village and earning the praise of their French commanders and Austrian
foes.[56] As the battle died away in the early evening, the regiment was sent to
join Carra Saint-Cyr's men in the retreat back to Lobau while the rest of
Legrand's Division covered the evacuation. The 3rd Infantry followed the
French 24th Ligne across the bridge that linked the Marchfeld with the island at
about 11 p.m.,[57] running in columns of two on each edge of the span as cavalry
and artillery hastened over the middle. Many of the weak, weary and wounded
were ridden over or pushed off the bridge to perish in the dark waters below, but
the bulk of the regiment reached the island safely having proven itself in its first
test of fire at the cost of some 370 casualties. The foot artillery had also done
well. Legrand's artillery commander said that it had 'far exceeded his expectations' and Massena himself heaped it with praise.[58] If Oberst Schöpf aroused
Wilhelm's suspicions by hastening from Aspern with the 3rd Regiment's flag
'to bring it to safety', all three arms of the Baden army added considerable lustre
to their records on the bloody fields of 21-22 May.[59]

JUNE: HUNGARIAN ADVENTURE

In an effort to destroy the retreating Archduke Johann before he could unite with
his elder brother, Napoleon sent the Army of Italy into Hungary as May gave
way to June. Placed under Eugène's orders, Lauriston and his command led the
way, marching south to enter Oedenburg on the 29th[60] while the local inhabitants stared in astonishment. Over the next several days, Baden infantry and
French light cavalry conducted a series of reconnaissances to Steinamanger and
Güns, searching for news of Johann's strength and movements. Marching at
night to palliate the debilitating effects of the heat, the bulk of the brigade
arrived in Güns early on 5 June but decamped two days later to slip east towards
the River Raab. The Baden Jägers and horse artillery co-operated with Colbert's
cavalry to push aside a weak detachment of Hungarian Insurrection troops and
seize a crossing over the river at Sarvar on the 8th. This scene was repeated on
the 11th as the French and Badeners forced their way across the little Marczal.
Lauriston's men, now joined by GD Alexandre Montbrun's light cavalry brigade
(1st and 2nd Chasseurs, 7th Hussars), pressed ahead as the Viceroy's advance
guard.[61]

Johann's rear guard made a stand west of Papa on the 12th, but his
Insurrection troops were nearly worthless and the few line units were forced
back through the town by Eugène's superior numbers. The French cavalry bore
the brunt of the fight, but the Badeners, in the middle of the French line between
GD Michel Pacthod's Division and GD Emmanuel Grouchy's horsemen, played
an important role. Jogging forward alongside Montbrun's troopers, the Baden
infantry entered Papa on the heels of the fleeing Austrians. Although their ranks
were thinned by heat casualties, the perspiring companies hastened through the
town, maintaining their speed and order to deploy on the eastern side in an
'excellent manoeuvre'.[62] The skirmishers spreading out across the bright summer fields were quickly joined by the horse guns, rattling up and unlimbering at

Map 28. The Hungarian Theatre

speed to silence the enemy pieces. With the Austrian artillery beaten down, the foot soldiers resumed their advance and, after two hours of fighting, forced Johann's men to retire toward Raab and their main body. The Baden horse artillery and the panting men of the Jäger Battalion's Voltigeur Company pursued the enemy northward with their mounted French allies for several hours, bringing back considerable numbers of prisoners and large amounts of booty when they returned to Papa that evening. It had been a fine day for the French light cavalry and the Baden light infantry and artillery. Baden losses totalled only two dead and nine wounded, but their courage, competence and stamina impressed both Eugène and Lauriston. The horse artillery proved itself efficient and accurate, while the light infantry demonstrated tremendous endurance, keeping pace with the frequently trotting light cavalry for more than six hours.[63]

The horse artillery was in action again the next day, supporting the advance guard cavalry as Eugène pushed the Austrians north towards the Danube. Repeatedly silencing the enemy's rear-guard artillery (six pieces), the Badeners finally expended their ammunition and withdrew when relieved by several Italian batteries. These latter, however, were a poor match for the Austrian can-

non and several officers of the Chasseurs appealed to the Badeners to replenish
their ammunition as rapidly as possible and rejoin the vanguard.[64]

These skirmishes were the prelude to the Battle of Raab on the 14th. The
Badeners, supported by GD Louis Sahuc's cavalry division, formed the extreme
left of Eugène's line of battle with the mission of observing the enemy's right
wing, particularly an entrenched camp the Austrians had constructed on the west
bank of the Raab. The camp, occupied by GM Joseph Mesko von Felsö-
Kubiny's insurrection forces (approximately four battalions and four squadrons),
anchored the Austrian right and formed the base for a potential outflanking
move against the Viceroy's left. The Baden infantry manoeuvred well and took
part in the final advance late in the afternoon, but did not play a major role in the
battle. The horse guns, however, distinguished themselves once again, chasing
off Austrian batteries and holding the enemy's cavalry in check as the struggle
proceeded to its victorious conclusion.

Following the battle, the brigade was assigned the task of besieging the town
in co-operation with Lasalle's command (French cavalry and Hessian light
infantry).[65] Several times summoned to surrender, the garrison continually
refused until the town had been heavily bombarded and Lauriston had pushed
his saps close to the walls. His pride assuaged by at least a brief defence, the
fortress commandant signed a capitulation on the 22nd and the garrison marched
out with the honours of war two days later. The 24th of June also saw the
Badeners head north to rejoin the main army. En route, they halted for four days
(26-29 June) at the French entrenchments opposite Pressburg where they were
assigned to GD Jacques Puthod's Division of Davout's III Corps. Their sojourn
behind the breastworks was brief, however, for the Emperor's plans to attempt a
second crossing of the Danube were fast maturing and every man was needed on
Lobau Island. The brigade thus departed the Pressburg siege works at midnight
on the 29th and, marching north without pause, crossed over on to the bustling
island at 5 p.m. to resume their accustomed place in Legrand's division.[66]

The Light Dragoons were also involved in the campaign in Hungary. After
Aspern-Essling, Marulaz's division was ordered south as part of the cavalry
screen Napoleon was establishing to shield his strategic right flank. From 26
May until the end of the month, the Baden dragoons were quartered in Deutsch-
Altenburg, sending patrols out to scout for Austrians along the Danube.[67] As the
Army of Italy began to pursue Archduke Johann into Hungary, however,
Marulaz was sent farther east and south to protect Eugène's left. Assigned to
Lasalle's command, the division rode through Bruck an der Leitha (9 June) and
Halbturn (11 June) to reach the Raab on the 15th. Here Marulaz and his troop-
ers were assigned to Viceroy Eugène. Eugène directed the division (17 June) to
intercept General Mesko's insurrection forces, who had fled south after the
Battle of Raab while the bulk of Johann's army retreated north-east toward
Komorn. The Frenchmen and their German allies pushed deep into Hungary,
approaching Mesko's position at St. Groth on 19 June, but Mesko had been reinforced and Marulaz, grossly outnumbered, wisely decided to retire. Leaving
their campfires burning, the troopers silently departed their bivouac and rode for
Veszprim, arriving there early on the 22nd.

Although it failed to catch Mesko in time, the division had replenished its supply of horseflesh from Hungarian farms (despite strict Imperial injunctions to the contrary) and was well mounted when it headed back to the north-west on the 23rd. Reaching St. Johann on the 25th, it was returned to Lasalle's command with instructions to guard the region south and east of the Neusiedler See. With patrols probing as far as Güns and Oedenburg, Marulaz's men had a great distance to cover when they were finally ordered to join the rest of the army on Lobau Island. Leaving some eighty men behind to secure the area around Halbturn, the dragoons hurried north on 2 July and rode into the IV Corps' camps on Lobau Island late on the evening of the 4th.[68]

While their comrades were off on adventurous escapades through Hungary, the 3rd Infantry and the foot battery remained in Lobau. Although they were rewarded for their valour and competence at Aspern with Crosses of the Legion of Honour (four for the infantry and two for the artillery), many of the soldiers would doubtless have preferred the privilege of simply departing Lobau Island. Insufficiently provisioned, shorn of grass by hungry horses and eventually pestilential with typhus, the large island was an unenviable garrison much of the time. But chronic hunger, dreary guard mounts and seemingly ceaseless picket duty were occasionally relieved by surprises. The officers frequently dined with their young Markgraf, there were numerous deer to hunt for food and sport, and one day in late June a small man in a long grey greatcoat came up to the Baden infantry outposts along the arm of the Danube that separated the island from the Marchfeld. Tasting the soldiers' soup, he pronounced it 'bon, bon' and proceeded to take the place of the wide-eyed Baden privates. For the next half hour he stood their post, telescope at his eye, staring across the narrow band of muddy water at the Austrian activity on the opposite bank.[69]

JULY - WAGRAM AND ZNAIM

The Badeners were among the first of Napoleon's men to return to the Marchfeld as the final preparations for the coming battle were completed. To deceive Charles regarding the chosen crossing point for his coming assault, the Emperor had Legrand's Division establish a bridgehead south of Aspern on 30 June. Once the Austrian pickets had been driven off and a pontoon bridge constructed, Ledru's Brigade and the 3rd Infantry were brought across, followed at about 8 p.m. by the 1st and 2nd Regiments and the horse artillery, only just arrived from Pressburg. The brigade remained in the bridgehead throughout the 1st of July, constructing fortifications and performing outpost duty, but the three infantry regiments returned to Lobau early on the 2nd, leaving only the Jägers and the horse guns on the left bank. On the evening of the 4th, these too were recalled to their brigade as the contending thunders of Nature and Napoleon deafened the armies and gouts of rain poured out of the night sky.[70]

On this violent eve of the Battle of Wagram, the Light Dragoons arrived on Lobau and 3rd Infantry was once again detached from its brigade to assume special duties. In his intricately detailed instructions for the assault, Napoleon laid the responsibility for the defence of Lobau in the hands of GD Reynier and allocated him a force of seven battalions including one Baden regiment. The 3rd

Infantry was selected for this duty. While one battalion of *Hochberg* held the bridgehead south of Aspern, the other was broken up into small detachments to garrison the little islets lying between Lobau and the Marchfeld.[71] As the assault crossing began and the Badeners moved to assume their posts, Sergeant Zanwald and his detachment from 'Isle Lannes' managed to make prisoner some 300 Croats who had been cut off by the French advance.[72]

WAGRAM (5-6 JULY)

Meanwhile, the rest of the Baden brigade had crossed over the Stadtler Arm and taken post on the right of Legrand's Division, the infantry regiments in column, the Jägers and foot artillery deployed to the front, the horse guns following the infantry. In this fashion, the division advanced across the Marchfeld essentially unopposed, halting for the night just south-east of Süssenbrunn with its right resting on the village and the Baden Jägers in skirmish order on the far side. The infantry and artillery had neither fired a shot nor lost a man.

The Light Dragoons had a far more sanguinary day. Delayed by the incredible and almost uncontrollable press at the bridges emptying from Lobau toward Enzersdorf, the regiment could not cross on to the Marchfeld until about 7 a.m. At that hour, Marulaz moved his division into a position just south of Enzersdorf and, despite a drizzle of enemy shot, allowed most of the troopers to dismount and feed their horses since the animals had gone some eighteen hours without proper fodder. At about 9 a.m., however, the division was sent north-east of the town to cover the deployment of the infantry and hold the Austrian reserve cavalry in check. The Austrian horsemen indeed advanced but halted some 700 paces away from Marulaz's squadrons, brought forward their guns and proceeded to hurl a deluge of iron at the helpless Allied cavalry.   Maintaining this exposed position for several hours, the Badeners alone lost seventeen men and 45 horses before the general French advance forced the Austrians to retire and freed Marulaz (about 1 p.m.). Now reduced to 93 effectives, the dragoons were brigaded with the Hessian Chevauxlegers and the 14th Chasseurs under Chef d'Escadron Latour-Foissac and ordered to reconnoitre along the Danube in advance of Boudet's infantry division.[73] Bypassing resistance at Essling and Aspern, the French and Badeners executed a successful charge against an infantry battalion north of the latter village but were attacked in turn by Austrian hussars.[74] This bitter hand-to-hand cavalry struggle between the Badeners and their old foes of Riedau, the *Kienmaier* Hussars, cost the regiment another twenty men. Outnumbered and without support, Latour-Foissac soon disengaged his chasseurs and dragoons, retiring behind the Hessians to reform. For the remainder of the afternoon, the little *ad hoc* brigade followed Boudet's Division, linking with Marulaz again in the evening and assuming a covering position west of Leopoldau as darkness gathered.

The early morning hours of 6 July found IV Corps already in motion, advancing on Aderklaa with three divisions while Boudet protected the army's left flank. Finding the village occupied by the Austrians, Massena sent Carra Saint-Cyr's battalions forward, but the initially successful effort misfired and Legrand's men were called upon to cover the rout of their comrades. As Saint-

Cyr's men streamed past, the 1st Division, Baden brigade on the exposed left flank, advanced into a hailstorm of fire to fend off pursuit. Only when some semblance of order had been restored among the fugitives, could Massena allow Legrand to retire from his dangerous position, Ledru's Brigade withdrawing first, followed by the Baden Jägers and *Grossherzog*. Finally, the soldiers of *Erbgrossherzog* alone were left and an adjutant rode forward to bring them back in their turn. Unfortunately, he mistakenly ordered the regiment to form a square and the Austrian cannoneers delightedly poured shot and shell into the huge target presented as the Badeners faithfully carried out their instructions. Whole rows of men were cut down until the brigade Chief of Staff, Oberstlieutenant Karl von Francken, recognized the regiment's plight and spurred forward to correct the adjutant's error. As with the other Baden units, the withdrawal of the 2nd Infantry was executed in good order under the tension of growing Austrian pressure and the regiment succeeded in joining its fellows on a low rise between Breitenlee and Raasdorf at about 10 a.m.

On this slight elevation, the Baden infantry was surprised to see a tiny knot of weary horsemen in cornflower blue coats and high crested helmets. The Light Dragoons, starting the day only some 65 strong, had already suffered additional losses. As IV Corps headed for Aderklaa, the remains of the regiment had spurred forward with the rest of Marulaz's dwindling command to charge a line of Austrian guns. One of the pieces fell into the hands of the Badeners, but they were unable to drag it away before a heavy attack by GdK Johann Fürst Liechtenstein's reserve cavalry forced Marulaz to retreat. Having fallen back to the position east of Breitenlee with the rest of the Corps, the light cavalry now undertook to shield Massena's left flank as best it could while he led his men on their incredible flank march to Essling.

Leaving its horse artillery behind between Aderklaa and Süssenbrunn, IV Corps suffered heavily as it marched south across the front of Charles's army.[75] But the leading French regiments soon threw FML Johann Graf Klenau's advanced troops out of Essling and turned toward Aspern. In Essling, the Baden brigade, marching at the end of Legrand's column, was granted a brief but welcome rest.

> For two days, the sun had burned down on the broad, shadowless expanse with frightful intensity. Heat, thirst, lack of food and the exertions of the battle and the two-hour flank march had completely exhausted the troops. Many officers and men collapsed unconscious, others were seized by convulsions from the extraordinary strains and all were more or less drained and enervated.[76]

After only half an hour, however, the brigade was back on its feet, the Jägers probing toward Aspern in skirmish order while the foot artillery covered the advance of the infantry columns. As on the previous afternoon, Massena's Corps maintained this *ordre de bataille* as it pushed north-west across the rolling fields, following the retreating enemy into the darkness and finally halting for the night just west of Leopoldau. As usual, the Jägers enjoyed the rigours of outpost duty, placing their pickets toward the Brunn road at Gross Jedlersdorf.

Despite the losses suffered by his command, the energetic Marulaz boldly pressed the Austrian retreat. Attacking in concert with Lasalle's troopers, the light cavalry succeeded in breaking one square beyond Leopoldau but another held firm and several Habsburg regiments (an Uhlan regiment and, once again, the *Kienmaier* Hussars) pounded up to the rescue. The Austrians were eventually beaten off after a wild dusk mêlée, but the infantry had escaped in the meantime and the French cavalry was used up. The Light Dragoons, now diminished to some 40 or 50 effectives, and Marulaz's other exhausted regiments took up position at the foot of the Bisamberg to cover the front of their corps.

The men of *Hochberg*, thinking themselves relegated to nothing but spade work in the entrenchments, also had an opportunity to contribute to the costly victory at Wagram. While Massena's other three divisions were embroiled in the vicious fight for Aderklaa, Boudet had been pushed back toward Enzersdorf by the slow but steady drive of Klenau's Austrian VI Corps. His retreat exposed the French bridgehead south of Aspern to attack and the elements of the 3rd Infantry in the redoubt experienced some tense moments as an Austrian detachment advanced on their incomplete fortifications.

> Around noon, we were in complete uncertainty regarding the issue of the combat. For a moment, it was even rumoured that the battle was lost.

The defenders maintained their composure, however, and held off Klenau's men with well-directed musketry and artillery until Massena's progress encouraged a speedy Austrian withdrawal. In their haste, the Austrians abandoned a howitzer, pushing it into the Stadtler Arm in an effort to render it useless to the French. Oberst Schöpf instantly sent a party to recover this prize and GD Reynier made a present of it to the Badeners as an expression of his satisfaction with their performance under his command.[77]

Night thus slowly dropped a curtain over the glory and suffering of Wagram. The two days of battle had cost the Baden brigade's infantry and artillery 310 dead and wounded from a total initial strength of approximately 5,500.[78] The Light Dragoons had lost 48 of their original 147 sabres and about 90 horses, reducing the mounted combat strength of the regiment by more than 60 per cent. Oberstlieutenant von Heimrodt was wounded and had to turn over command of the small band of troopers to the senior remaining Rittmeister, Andreas Rottmann. The popular and respected commander of the contingent's artillery, Kapitän von Freydorf, was also badly wounded. His right foot smashed by an Austrian ball, he was borne back to a surgeon who amputated the limb. Supposed to have calmly smoked his pipe while the doctor sawed half his leg away, Freydorf quickly became a legend in the Baden military. Tough as nails, he equipped himself with a wooden leg which allowed him to mount a horse; he served his country for many more decades, eventually becoming Minister of War.

Von Freydorf's experience was characteristic of this great artillery battle: the number of severely wounded was unusually high as cannon balls were even less gentle to life and limb than musket rounds. Also indicative of the nature of the struggle was the expenditure of ammunition. Although the artillery was steadily engaged and the horse gunners even found it necessary to withdraw and reload, most of the infantrymen never fired their muskets; only the Jägers, as they advanced from Essling on Aspern, had an opportunity to engage on the enemy.[79]

PURSUIT (7-10 JULY)

As the sun rose on 7 July, the French army slowly took up the pursuit and, for the next several days, the Badeners were constantly in action against the Austrian rear guard on the road to Znaim. Leading the advance on Korneuburg, a small town surrounded by wall and moat, the few remaining Light Dragoons helped drive the Austrian outposts back into the village while Legrand brought his infantry to the front. As the afternoon melted toward evening, von Francken and the Jägers cleared a wood south-west of town and, reinforced by the voltigeur companies of the Baden regiments, moved on the Austrian defenders from the flank and rear. Bold Jägers were soon clambering over the barred Danube (west) gate into Korneuburg, while Hauptmann David Günther took part of his Jäger-Voltigeur Company around to the north and charged into town through the open gate on the Znaim road to capture more than 300 surprised and disconsolate Austrians. Although the barricaded gate was difficult to open, Legrand's cheering troops were soon marching through the town to take up positions beyond, the Baden Jägers and 1st Regiment left of the highway and the French to the right; the 2nd Infantry remained south-east of the town wall.[80] The enemy's solid formations and firm attitude foiled all attempts at pursuit.

The Jägers and Light Dragoons were involved in the skirmish at Stockerau the next day, the dragoons participating in an ill-fated attack on the Habsburg rear guard cavalry and the Jägers turning back the pursuing Austrian troopers with well-directed fire from the buildings skirting the northern edge of the village. That night, Massena sent Colonel Auguste Ameil toward Krems with his regiment (24th Chasseurs) and the Baden cavalry to make contact with the Württembergers and clarify the situation on the army's left; engaged in this operation, the Baden cavalrymen would not rejoin their Corps until after the Battle of Znaim.

There was another tough rear-guard fight on the 9th as Massena attempted to force his way into Hollabrunn. The Badeners, particularly the Jägers and the voltigeur companies (commanded on an *ad hoc* basis by the energetic von Francken), performed well, but the Austrian defensive position was strong and Legrand was unable to master the town. None the less, Charles continued his retirement, his rear guard evacuating the town early the following morning to establish a new delaying position at Schöngraben.

The 10th cost the Jägers ten men wounded as IV Corps pushed the Austrians off the hills around Schöngraben. In the vanguard as usual, the Jägers co-operated closely with the French light cavalry throughout the day, repeatedly sliding west to outflank the enemy's right wing and force them back to the next terrain feature. The Austrians conducted their withdrawal with skill, however, and Massena, unable to fight his way through their rear guard, had to call off his troops as darkness fell. The Corps camped in the open around Guntersdorf under endlessly streaming rain.

THE BATTLE OF ZNAIM (11 JULY)

While pushing the Austrian rear guard from hilltop to hilltop on the 10th, the sounds of the Bavarians' tough fight at Tesswitz were audible to Massena and his men. Although he might have known the enemy was present in strength to the north, the Marshal did not bring up his other divisions and Legrand's troops had to conduct most of the next day's battle on their own.

Massena's lead elements, the light cavalry and Legrand followed by St. Sulpice's cuirassiers, were up and marching early on 11 July, seeking to establish firm contact with the withdrawing enemy. Austrian outposts of Reuss's V Corps were encountered just south of the Thaya, but French and Baden skirmishers quickly threw these light troops over the river and gained control of the two bridges carrying the main road north to Znaim.[81] While the Jäger Battalion's Carabinier Company clambered over the barricades on the bridges, the other Allied skirmishers jumped into the water and splashed across, pushing the Austrians before them. Legrand's entire infantry was soon over the Thaya, Badeners on the left and French on the right, moving slowly toward Znaim. Deployed in long skirmish lines, the Jägers and II/2 advanced up the main road while the eight companies of *Grossherzog*, also *'en grande débande'*, cleared the vineyards from the road to the river. Only I/2 remained in close formation, held in reserve behind a low rise.

Thus far all had gone well for Massena, but at about 2 p.m., Reuss was reinforced by two brigades of grenadiers from the reserve and the Allied attack ground to a halt. The Austrians began to advance and, before long, the French brigade had to fall back, exposing the Baden right flank. As the Baden leaders moved to respond to this new situation, they and their men were struck by a series of simultaneous misfortunes. First, the reserve battalion of *Erbgrossherzog*, called forward to cover the withdrawal of its comrades, was taken under fire by the numerous French guns on the bluffs west of Klosterbruck. Their commander was slain instantly and the men began to waver as round after round plunged into their closely packed ranks. The support the skirmishers counted on to permit them to reform was thus shaken before it came into action. Second, the lowering grey clouds chose this moment to open and a thunderstorm of sudden and uncommon violence broke over the battlefield. In minutes, muskets became useless, visibility dropped to nothing and leaders' voices could hardly be heard over the pounding deluge. Units were momentarily bewildered and many men bolted for nearby houses to seek shelter. Into this nascent confusion charged the Austrian grenadiers.[82] The unformed French and Baden skirmishers were ill-prepared for this unexpected onslaught and fell back toward the bridges in considerable disorder, leaving many of their number in the hands of the Austrians.

Massena, however, was equal to this dangerous situation and Markgraf Wilhelm was immediately dispatched to bring the heavy cavalry forward at the charge. Slamming forward over the bridges, one of St. Sulpice's cuirassier regiments dramatically changed the tide of battle.[83] The grenadiers were ridden over or scattered in disorder and the Allied prisoners freed after mere minutes of captivity while the Baden foot battery, painfully dragged on to the heights south of Znaim, punished the fleeing Austrians with its well-aimed fire. As the cuirassiers trotted ahead toward Znaim, some particularly energetic officers and NCOs led small groups of infantrymen forward in the wake of the heavy cavalry and major elements of the Jäger Battalion and I/2 were soon pressing close to the walls of the town. Other leaders were reassembling their formations preparatory to resuming the attack when French and Austrian staff officers rode between the opposing lines of battle to announce the armistice. Having sustained 185 casualties during the engagement, the Baden Brigade bivouacked on the battlefield, gathered around campfires with their erstwhile enemies while their leaders wrangled over demarcation lines and future dispositions.

A small group of Baden Light Dragoons also fought at Znaim. While the tiny remnant of the regiment was reconnoitring toward Krems with Colonel Ameil, Leutnant von Stern reached the battlefield with his detachment. Relieved around Halbturn by the Württemberg *Herzog Heinrich* Chevauxlegers on 5 July, Stern took his men north across the Danube to find their regiment. Instead of taking the direct road from Vienna to Znaim, however, he followed Marmont's route and linked with the latter's corps on the 10th near Waltrowitz. His detachment, raised to a strength of 70 by the recovered and remounted men he had gathered along the way, Stern spent most of the 11th collecting intelligence for Marmont, but also found occasion to attack and 'throw into the Thaya' an Austrian infantry company. The charge cost his detachment one man killed and Stern was able to rejoin IV Corps on the following day.[84]

Although the battle at Znaim was not capped by a clear-cut victory, the Badeners had again displayed energy, initiative and tactical ability on a par with that of their French allies and received warm praise from both Massena and Legrand for their performance. Such recognition was welcome, but the attitude of the French rank and file was perhaps even more meaningful to the Germans: 'It filled the young soldiers with no little pride to be treated with open respect by the customarily victorious French army.'[85] This elevated status, however, was not cheaply purchased. *Erbgrossherzog*, for example, counted only about half its original number in its ranks and von Neuenstein had to report that 'no more than one quarter of the officers are still fit for duty'.[86] Even the 3rd Regiment, far from the guns of Znaim, had suffered terribly. Confined to Lobau Island, surrounded by marshland and thousands of hastily interred corpses, it was ravaged by typhus and mustered only about $1/3$ of its authorized effectives when it was finally transferred to garrison duty at Raab in late August.[87]

In all, the campaign cost Baden more than 1,000 of its sons dead (191) or seriously wounded (862); only 53 of the Grand Duchy's soldiers were captured by the enemy. Wounded men returned to duty and replacement detachments arriving from Baden through the summer and autumn filled many of the gaps in the ranks, but the contingent was still below strength when it marched home in January 1810.

INSURRECTIONARY ALARMS: TYROL AND VORARLBERG

As the men settled into a regular camp life of drill, manoeuvres and target practice, they were able to catch up on events in Baden. Through newspapers, correspondence and especially through contact with newly-arrived replacements, many of whom had now had some small experience in combat, the troops learned of the Vorarlberg insurrection and Baden's efforts to co-operate with its larger allies in suppressing the rebels.

Although the campaign of 1809 was over as far as the main armies were concerned, the insurrection in the Tyrol and Vorarlberg kept the French and their German allies occupied for some weeks to come. The guerrilla war prosecuted by the Tyrolians with their colourful folk heroes is relatively well known, less renowned is the activity of the Vorarlbergers in 1809. The Vorarlberg is the western-most tip of modern Austria, generally, the mountains south and east of Lake Constance. Incited by Austrian and Tyrolian agents, its inhabitants launched forays into neighbouring areas of Württemberg, Bavaria and Baden to foment unrest and harass French lines of communication. Unrest began shortly after the initiation of hostilities and, as the war progressed, all three states felt themselves increasingly threatened by the insurgents.

As the enthusiasm of the Tyrolians spilled over into Vorarlberg, Karl Friedrich found himself beset with new demands for military assistance. Not only had Max Joseph of Bavaria appealed to his Württemberg and Baden allies for support, Friedrich echoed and reinforced this request from Stuttgart and Napoleon pressed the Grand Duchy to find mounts for its Hussar Regiment and attach it to GD Beaumont's Reserve Division in Augsburg. In addition to these external demands, several internal considerations led Baden to commit troops to the theatre of war about Lake Constance. First, the King of Württemberg was heartily mistrusted and the leadership in Karlsruhe was convinced that he would make use of this opportunity to seize Baden lands along the great lake if no Baden military presence were available to limit Friedrich's vaulting avarice. Second, the southern portions of the Duchy were being overrun by Austrians prisoners of war who escaped from the huge convoys trudging toward Strasbourg and sought to make their way back home. These bands flaunted the power of the throne and represented a potential threat to the integrity of the state. Third, large elements of Baden's population were dissatisfied with their inclusion in the Grand Duchy and yearned nostalgically to renew their former attachment to the Habsburg Empire. If this disaffection were fanned by escaped Austrian prisoners heading south or energetic Vorarlberg rebels raiding north, the entire tenuous fabric of the new state could be torn apart. The government felt it had no choice but to respond to these incipient dangers militarily and on 7 May, Karl Friedrich instructed his Ministry of War to prepare a detachment for duty around Lake Constance.

Unfortunately, there were scanty forces available to counter these various threats. The Garde du Corps was tiny, the Leib-Grenadier-Garde Battalion and Hussar Regiment had been stripped of men and horses respectively to outfit the field force and the infantry regimental depots were still being organized.[88] None the less, Oberstlieutenant Ludwig von Cancrin of the hussars rode south on 9

May with a composite detachment consisting of a weak hussar squadron, two companies of Guard Grenadiers and two guns.[89] Sending Hauptmann von Reischach with 30 grenadiers and five hussars to show the flag in Constance, Cancrin reached Ueberlingen via Stockach on the 19th and made contact with GM von Scheler's Württembergers. Five days later, he took the bulk of his little force forward to Meersburg (rather than see the Württembergers occupy it) and remained there until the end of the month, taking no part in the embarrassing repulse at Dornbirn and maintaining a cool but proper relationship with Scheler.

Given the worrying turn of events in Vorarlberg in late May and the continued doubts about the loyalty of southern Baden, where attempts to carry out conscription were encountering surly resistance, the regime in Karlsruhe decided to send additional troops to the south. Marching through the regions of dubious loyalty, they would remind the inhabitants of the power of the central government before continuing on to reinforce Cancrin around Lake Constance. This mission fell to a new unit, the Provisional Jäger Battalion. Formed in April by combining the depot of the Jäger Battalion (330 men) with 107 men from the depots of the three infantry regiments, the battalion was organized into three companies under the command of Hauptmann Karl Pfnor. It was originally intended to join the brigade with IV Corps, thereby bringing the Jäger Battalion to its full strength of six companies, but the situation in the south required immediate action and the battalion departed Karlsruhe on 2 June for Lake Constance. Moving by short marches through the disaffected regions of the Grand Duchy, Pfnor reached the area around Meersburg on 15 June with a loss of only thirteen deserters.[90]

By the time the provisional Jägers arrived, however, the Baden forces in this theatre had been increased by the addition of the remaining companies of the Guard Grenadiers and command of the entire contingent had been invested in Oberst Karl von Stockhorn.[91] Under renewed pressure from Stuttgart and fearful of Friedrich's intentions, the grenadiers were sent south in wagons on 9 June and arrived in Meersburg on the 12th. The next morning, Württemberg infantry and the Baden hussars conducted a reconnaissance in force across the Loiblach but were chased back across by the insurgents and trapped in Lindau. Stockhorn, in a reserve position at Nonnenbach, improvised a tiny cavalry force by mounting gunners on artillery horses and sent these forward with the Schützen of the Guard Battalion to conduct a demonstration while he prepared the rest of his command to attack the following day. The demonstration appears to have had an unexpectedly decisive effect, however, for the rebels withdrew and Stockhorn's offensive became unnecessary. Von Cancrin was thoroughly pleased with the performance of his troopers and the excellent impression they made on the Württemberg leadership.[92]

On the 18th, a weak squadron (58 troopers) from the depot of the Light Dragoon Regiment reached Meersburg, bringing the Baden Brigade along Lake Constance to a strength of more than 1,200 infantry, 120 cavalry and two guns.[93]

Although most of the Badeners' days were passed in the relative boredom of drills and patrols, late June was highlighted by a bold insurgent operation against Constance. After considerable planning, a strong band of Vorarlbergers sailed across the lake from Bregenz and raided the city on the 29th while others feinted toward Lindau and Tettnang to divert the Allies' attention. The surprise of Constance was eminently successful and 37 Baden Jägers, almost the entire garrison of the city, fell into the hands of the rebels together with six small cannon. Oberst Stockhorn extemporized a marine force by loading 60 of his grenadiers and 40 Württembergers into local boats, but the flotilla failed to catch the enemy and returned to port empty-handed. On learning of the raid's satisfactory conclusion, the insurgents called off their diversionary attack and withdrew behind the Loiblach with six Allied prisoners; the only other casualty was Baden's pride.

In early July, reinforced by the Württemberg Observation Corps from Ellwangen, the Allies advanced to a new line running from Lindau through Wangen and Eglofs to Isny. The Badeners, assigned to GM von Scheler's 1st Brigade, reached their positions between Wangen and the lake on the 13th (see Table 3-4).[94] Their arrival was timely because next morning the rebels reacted, launching the first of a series of attacks that continued until the 17th. The Baden Brigade played a key role in repulsing these forays, the last serious eruptions of the Vorarlberg insurgency. From his central position at Amtzell, Stockhorn was able to respond quickly with the Guard Battalion and his tiny artillery, supporting the successful defensive actions at Wangen on the 15th and 17th. A few kilometres south-west, Cancrin's mixed force of Badeners and Württembergers at Neu-Ravensburg was attacked on the 16th and 17th, but the defenders held out until reinforcements could arrive to help repulse the insurgents. On both days, Cancrin counter-attacked in the afternoon with his infantry and cavalry accompanied by loud musical support from the combined Allied drummers. The Badeners performed well in these little skirmishes, moving with confidence, alacrity and evident offensive spirit; reporting on Pfnor's rapid advance on the 17th, Cancrin commented 'it was truly a joy to watch' and King Friedrich was moved to thank Stockhorn for 'his active support'.[95]

Throughout the remainder of July, the Baden Brigade, reinforced by 150 hussars on the 19th, held the area around Neu-Ravensburg, patrolling frequently and occasionally exchanging a few musket balls with insurgent bands.[96] For the rebels, however, the outlook was bleak. Added to the news of the armistice signed at Znaim, the disappointing results of this four-day effort discouraged the partisans and the rebellion in the Vorarlberg slowly began to flicker and die away. On 6 August, the Allies occupied Bregenz.

The Tyrol, however, still burned and Beaumont called on the Badeners to support his subordinate GB Picard. Stockhorn's Brigade, having participated in the march on the Vorarlberg's capital, had continued on to Weiler where it formed the link between the Württembergers around Lake Constance and Picard at Kempten. Beaumont's new request would take the Badeners even further from the borders of their homeland, but Stockhorn could find no way to refuse and moved his men to Immenstadt on the 15th.[97] The Baden Brigade remained in this area throughout November, forming combined detachments with the French to guard the exits from the mountains at Sonthofen and fighting a number of skirmishes with the restive Tyrolians. Cancrin, who was responsible for the

Allied post at Sonthofen, seems to have been a cool, competent commander and the troops exhibited calm determination in all these engagements. Despite the frequency of these frontier skirmishes and the numerical superiority of the rebels, the number of French and Baden casualties was minimal, normally no more than two or three were wounded in a day's fight and only one Baden Jäger died as a result of wounds during the entire three month period.[98]

As October drew to a close and the Third Allied Offensive into the Tyrol finally crushed the tenacious rebellion, von Stockhorn obtained permission from his French superiors to return home. Accompanied by honest praise from the French generals, the Baden Brigade departed Immenstadt on 11 November and crossed the Grand Duchy's borders three days later.[99]

Thus ended the campaign of 1809 for the soldiers of Baden. Despite financial strictures and the competing demands of the Spanish war, the Grand Duchy provided a sizable contingent to the Armée d'Allemagne and its men proved themselves worthy allies of the French. Reliable, courageous and disciplined, they earned praise wherever they fought, winning particular laurels for their performance at Aspern, Papa and Znaim. The Light Dragoons, the Jäger Battalion and the artillery seem to have been especially solid units. The Baden officers and NCOs were key to the contingent's admirable reputation. Consistently displaying exemplary valour, competence and initiative, they moulded their young soldiers into an effective fighting force and earned the respect of their French commanders. Thanks to these leaders, even the *ad hoc* brigade cobbled together along Lake Constance contributed to the ultimate Allied victory, serving as a dependable reserve in the skirmishes against the alpine rebels. The Baden troops ranked among the best of Napoleon's German allies in 1809, providing an apt prelude to their fortitude at the Berezina.

NOTES

1: Quotes from Sauer, *Adler*, p. 52.

2: Baden's representative at the negotiations for the Treaty of Pressburg and the construction of a new order in south-western Germany considered Karl Friedrich's desire for a royal crown utterly inappropriate and was too embarrassed even to mention his sovereign's desire to the French (Sauer, *Adler*, p. 100).

3: This recapitulation of Baden's situation in 1809 is drawn from Michael Hörrmann and Ulrich Hübinger, 'Auf dem Weg zum modernen Staat: Baden', in *Baden und Württemberg im Zeitalter Napoleons*, Stuttgart: Cantz, 1987, vol. I/1 and Sauer, *Adler.*

4: Siegfried Fiedler, 'Das Militärwesen Badens in der Zeit Napoleons', in *Baden und Württemberg im Zeitalter Napoleons*, Stuttgart: Cantz, 1987, vol. 2, pp. 258, 260.

5: The fact that Karl Friedrich's soldiers maintained their 18th-century hairstyles until 1806 is symbolic of Baden's outmoded military outlook in general. The queues and white powder, previously fundamental to a soldier's appearance, were eliminated for 'sanitary reasons' and each man was directed to rinse his head with cold water every morning (Sabina Hermes and Joachim Niemeyer, eds., *Unter dem Greifen*, Karlsruhe: Braun, 1984, p. 40).

6: Fiedler and Sauer. Quotes from Sauer, *Adler*, pp. 113-14.

7: Lefebvre and Napoleon quoted in Lt. Colonel Sauzey, *Le Contingent Badois*, Volume II of *Les Allemands sous les Aigles Françaises*, Paris: Terana, 1987, pp. 15-16.

8: Unlike Bavaria and Württemberg, Baden's conscription laws also applied to Jews (in the other two states, Jews could pay a fee rather than serve in the military). The Jewish population, however, refused to recognize this requirement until the Baden government granted them equal citizenship (*Greifen*, p. 54).

9: In Karlsruhe, for example, the garrison included 2,900 soldiers and 500 wives (*Greifen*, p. 33).

10: *Greifen*, pp. 32-3, 56. Despite these reforms, the situation for soldiers' families remained precarious. The lot of the soldiers themselves was little better; the rank and file were so poorly paid that they could not live from their earnings and the officers often lived a hand-to-mouth existence (Fr. von der Wengen, *Der Feldzug der Grossherzoglich Badischen Truppen unter Oberst Freiherrn Karl von Stockhorn gegen die Vorarlberger und Tiroler 1809,* Heidelberg: Winter, 1910, p. 38).

11   In May 1809, the designation changed from 'Musketeer' to 'Fusilier' for the centre companies of each battalion (*Greifen,* p. 55).

12:   The dissolution of the garrison regiments occurred in October 1808 and the new depots were located at Karlsruhe, Mannheim, Rastatt and Freiburg. The Garrison Regiments had been *von Lindheim* (associated with Regiment *Grossherzog*), *von Olzig* (*Erbgrossherzog*), *von Röder* (*Markgraf Ludwig*) and *von Biedenfeld* (*Harrant*). Fiedler, p. 262; *Greifen,* pp. 32, 55.

13:   That is, Hessians from Hesse-Kassel vice Hesse-Darmstadt. Napoleon had removed the Kurprinz (Prince-Elector) of Hesse-Kassel and incorporated his lands into newly created states such as the Kingdom of Westphalia.

14:   Fiedler, p. 262.

15:   See *Greifen,* pp. 81-3.

16:   The 4th Regiment received its commander as Inhaber on 1 July 1809 and thus took the name *von Porbeck*; it was renamed *von Neuenstein* on 24 October the same year after Oberst von Porbeck was killed. 'Uebersicht der Organisations-Geschichte des badischen Armeekorps seit d. J. 1604', *Badischer Militär-Almanach* 1 December 1854, p. 25.

17:   Karl von Zech and Friedrich von Porbeck, *Geschichte der Badischen Truppen 1809 im Feldzug der Französischen Hauptarmee gegen Oesterreich,* Rudolf von Freydorf, ed., Heidelberg: Winter, 1909, p. 2.

18:   In November 1809, Oberst von Freystedt would be named as Inhaber of the Light Dragoons, the regiment therefore receiving the designation Dragoner-Regiment *von Freystedt*. G. Bahls, *Das 3. badische Dragoner-Regiment Prinz Karl Nr. 22,* Bernard & Graefe, 1934, p. 17.

19:   The formation of the Baden contingent in Spain followed a rather unusual course. In addition to the artillery battery, two infantry battalions from different regiments (II/3 and I/4) departed for Spain in August 1808. In the beginning of 1809, these two battalions were combined and redesignated as the 4th Infantry Regiment (no Inhaber). Simultaneously, the two battalions back in Baden (I/3 and II/4) were combined as the 3rd Infantry Regiment *Graf Hochberg*. A side effect of these organizational changes was that the battalions of the new regiments continued to wear the distinctive colours of their former regiments until new uniforms were introduced in 1810 (thus the new 3rd Infantry's First Battalion had white facings while its Second Battalion, the former II/4, had deep red).

20:   *Correspondence* 14723. Both Sauzey (p. 20) and Zech/Porbeck (p. 10) provide slightly different renditions of the 15 January missive, indicating that Napoleon asked Baden to supply 8,000 men over and above the 2,000 already committed to Spain.

21:   The Baden brigade would lack 223 men from the line regiments and 300 from the Jäger battalion (the two companies still being formed did not march out with the battalion). It is also noteworthy that the 3rd Infantry seems to have had a high percentage of recent recruits: about 20% of the regiment's enlisted personnel apparently joined only 1809 and an additional 20% had been with the regiment for less than a year, that is, they had joined in 1808 and thus had no combat experience (based on analysis of the July 1809 casualty reports in Kriegs-Archiv des Grossen Generalstabes, Feldzug 1809 gegen Oesterreich, 48/4283).

22:   Massena's remarks quoted from a 19 March letter to Berthier (Saski, vol. I, p. 301). See also Général Koch, *Mémoires de Massena,* Paris: Paulin et Lechevalier, 1850, vol. 6, p. 51.

23:   Karl Obser, ed., *Denkwürdigkeiten des Markgrafen Wilhelm von Baden,* Heidelberg: Winter, 1906, vol. 1, p. 64.

24:   The infantry fired 14,000 musket balls and 3,000 rifle rounds during this two-week period (Zech/Porbeck, p. 15).

25:   Table 4-3 Note that the French situation report for 16 April cited in Saski (vol. II, annex) gives slightly different strengths: 5,494 infantry, 405 light dragoons, 369 artillery. Binder von Kriegelstein (vol. I, p. 353), apparently working from the same situation report, transposes the strengths of the Hessian Chevauxlegers (345) and the Baden Light Dragoons (405); he also inflates the number of Baden infantry officers by 100 (221 rather than 121). The artillery figure includes around 150 actual cannoneers and some 200 train personnel (A. Ferber, *Geschichte des 1. Badischen Feldartillerie-Regiments Nr. 14,* Karlsruhe: Müller, 1906, pp. 62-3).

26:   Obser, pp. 79-82. The positive comments on Kister's personality are from the Baden field journals while the negative appraisal is Wilhelm's own (describing Kister's indecisiveness at the Ebelsberg bridge). Massena's avoidance of unpleasantries in Karlsruhe is described in Koch, p. 50.

27:   Letter of 11 April, quoted in Zech/Porbeck, p. 19.

28:   Zech/Porbeck, p. 18.

29:   Saski, vol. II, p. 242.

30:   En route, the regimental surgeon, Dr. Cohaut, led ten dragoons into a woodline to capture more than 40 terrified Austrian stragglers (Ferdinand Rau, *Geschichte des 1. Badischen Leib-Dragoner Regiments Nr. 20 und dessen Stamm-Regiments von Freystedt von 1803 bis zur Gegenwart,* Berlin: Mittler & Sohn, 1878, p. 15).

31   As Legrand's Division assembled, the four musketeer companies of II/1 (*Grossherzog*) were detached under

Major Karl von Brandt to escort the division's reserve park. They were not relieved of this duty until well after the conclusion of the armistice (Zech/Porbeck, pp. 17, 37; Hauptmann Walz, *Geschichte des Linien-Infanterie-Regiments Grossherzog, Nro. 1*, 2 vols., written 1843-4, manuscript in the collection of the Wehrgeschichtliches Museum in Rastatt, vol. II, p. 60).

32: Zech/Porbeck, p. 41.

33: Most of these stragglers rejoined their companies during the night (Theophil von Barsewisch, *Geschichte des Grossherzoglich Badischen Leib-Grenadier-Regiments 1803-1870,* Karlsruhe: Müller, 1893, p. 67).

34: Almost every commentator, including the Austrian official historians, expresses astonishment at the feats of marching accomplished by Massena's men from 18 to 22 April.

35: The lovely little market town was reduced to ashes by the bombardment and Dedovich's attempts to destroy his provisions.

36: Heimrodt had taken the 1st and 2nd Squadrons south of the road while the 3rd and 4th rode to the north. These latter two helped the Württembergers dispatch two squadrons of *Kienmaier* before hurrying over to aid their countrymen.

37: Casualties are given in *Krieg,* vol. III, p. 268. The Austrian banner was recovered by a Baden trumpeter. When it was given to Lieutenant-Colonel Sainte Croix of Massena's staff for transport to the Marshal, however, it was somehow transformed into his trophy and earned him a promotion to Colonel. When the Marshal learned the true story, it was already too late and Sainte Croix was able to keep his new grade. Needless to say, his actions caused great resentment in the ranks of the Baden Light Dragoons.

38: The regiment was back under Marulaz, who had rejoined the corps on the night of 2 May. The Corps' Light Cavalry Division now consisted of a Rheinbund brigade (Baden Light Dragoons, Hessian Guard Chevauxlegers and Württemberg *Leibchevauxlegers*) and a French brigade (3, 14, 19 and 23 Chasseurs).

39: The horror of this violent battle was increased as buildings in the town caught fire, burning to death many of the wounded who had sought shelter in homes and shops.

40: To speed their arrival on the battlefield, the regiments ran and walked by turns, jogging for a time and then slowing to a standard marching pace until the men caught their breath. Zech/Porbeck, p. 84.

41: Obser, p. 79.

42: Barsewisch, p. 71.

43: Zech/Porbeck, p. 85 and J. D. Haffner, *Geschichtliche Darstellung des Grossherzoglich Badischen Armee-Corps,* Karlsruhe: Malsch und Vogel, 1840, p. 69.

44: At the end of his 3 May report, Legrand wrote: 'I am pained to learn that some persons have told your excellency the Baden regiments conducted a retrograde movement. This was conducted under my orders to allow several munitions caissons to leave Ebelsberg where they were on the point of exploding.' Freydorf (Zech/Porbeck, p. 86) suspects Pelet of this calumniating; Sainte Croix seems another possibility. Legrand expressed his satisfaction with the Jäger Battalion in his 4 May report to the Marshal (both reports are contained in Koch, pp. 388-9).

45: Obser, p. 81; Zech/Porbeck, pp. 94-5.

46: Barsewisch, p. 73.

47: This was actually the Badeners' second departure from Friedberg. The 3rd Regiment had marched out on the 23rd and been quartered for the night in Odelzhausen. Fears of Tyrolian irregular raiders caused the fortress commandant in Augsburg, GD Moulin, to recall it on the morning of the 24th. The regiment returned to Friedberg only to learn the Tyrolian threat was baseless and, united with its Hessian allies, said farewell to the fortress for the second time on the afternoon of 24 April. Zech/Porbeck, pp. 102-6.

48: Saski, vol. III, p. 316.

49: Lieutenant Franz von Hornig and 30 dragoons had been detached at Ybbs on 7 May, remaining there until the beginning of July (Rau, p. 21).

50: Obser, p. 86.

51: *Krieg,* vol. IV, p. 455. Their position made it almost impossible for the Habsburg horsemen to influence the coming fight.

52: *Krieg,* vol. IV, pp. 465-6.

53: Rau, pp. 23-4. During the 21st of May, the regiment's ranks were thinned by the loss of 24 men and more than 50 horses killed or wounded.

54: The Baden voltigeurs were the only infantry of that type to possess rifled muskets. Unable to utilize the cartridges of other Allied units and with their ammunition wagon stranded on the opposite bank of the Danube, the voltigeurs found themselves relying exclusively on the bayonet as the night progressed. Zech/Porbeck, p. 116.

55: Zech/Porbeck, p. 118.

56: Zech/Porbeck, p. 119; Heller von Hellwald describes the French, Badeners and Hessians as 'extraordinarily brave' (Friedrich Heller von Hellwald, *Der Feldzug des Jahres 1809 in Süddeutschland,* Wien: Carl Gerold's Sohn, 1864, vol. II, p. 48). Unfortunately, the regiment seems to have been involved in an incident of fratricide, firing on some withdrawing Hessians in the wild, smoky confusion of the street fighting in Aspern (see Chapter 5).

57:    The Light Dragoons crossed at about 8 p.m.

58:    Zech/Porbeck, p. 121.

59:    Obser, p. 87. Markgraf Wilhelm also disparaged the Hessian Brigade commander, GM von Nagel, claiming he had to coax the general out of hiding in a declivity.

60:    The Jäger Battalion remained at Neuenkirchen until the 30th, when it marched south through Oedenburg to reach Neckenmarkt on the 31st.

61:    Lauriston's men had linked with the Army of Italy on the 9th east of Sarvar.

62:    The Austrian General Ettingshausen, watching the battle from the high ground north of Papa, used these words to describe the Baden and French deployment out of the village. He also mentions being 'heavily pursued' by enemy cannon during the withdrawal. Hans von Zwiedineck-Südenhorst, *Erzherzog Johann von Oesterreich im Feldzuge von 1809,* Gratz: Styria, 1892, p. 85.

63:    Barsewisch, pp. 74-5; Zech/Porbeck, pp. 133-6.

64:    The Frenchmen apparently felt that their cavalry accompanied by the Baden guns formed an invincible team. Ferber, p. 71, Zech/Porbeck, p. 136.

65:    Lasalle's men arrived on the western side of the River Raab on 17 June; Lauriston established communication with them the next day (see Chapter 5).

66:    GM von Harrant had taken ill on the 26th and turned command of the brigade over to Oberst von Neuenstein. Only the two Baden howitzers participated in the bombardment of Raab. The two 6-pounders had been fired so often that they had to be sent to Vienna on the 15th to have their touchholes rebored; they rejoined their comrades on the 29th on the road to Lobau (Ferber, pp. 71-2).

67:    The Baden and Hessian light cavalry regiments were brigaded together under Oberst Freystedt's leadership; Oberstlieutenant Heimrodt assumed command of the Light Dragoons in his place.

68:    These men were divided into two detachments of 50 (Leutnant Stern) and 30 (Leutnant Behagel) men; they would only rejoin their regiment at Znaim. During this period, GD Baraguey d'Hilliers commanded the French forces protecting Napoleon's southern flank, including these detachments of Baden dragoons. It was a tense time for LT Stern. He had been escorting a convoy of fodder back from Hungary in late June when he chanced upon elements of the Army of Italy under d'Hilliers' command. Although the French immediately considered his supplies their property and ordered him to remain, Stern managed to escape their grasp with his precious cargo. D'Hilliers put a price of 50 ducats on the head of the supposed marauder and Stern was not at all happy to come under the Frenchman's orders. By disguising his signature, he managed to pass undetected but he greatly welcomed the orders that returned him to his regiment on 5 July (Zech/Porbeck, p. 147).

69:    Zech/Porbeck, pp. 121-2. Curiously, Zech and Porbeck state that the 3rd Regiment conducted almost no training during its stay on Lobau after Aspern. Contrasting the inactivity of the Badeners with the busy training programme of the French units, they aver that 'poor provisions prohibited any exertion for the troops'.

70:    The four companies of *Grossherzog* (under Major Brandt) which had been guarding the division's parks throughout the campaign were detailed to serve as assistant gunners during the preparatory bombardment on the night of 4/5 July (Obser, pp. 91-2).

71:    According to Napoleon's orders, this battalion was to be disposed as follows: 335 of its men amongst the small islets around Lobau (25 each on isles St. Hilaire, Massena, Lannes and Espagne, 35 on isle Alexandre, 200 on isle Moulin), 400 to be kept in reserve. Orders quoted in full in Buat, vol. II, pp. 166-72.

72:    These Grenzer from the *Wallisch-Illyrien* Regiment were on what the French titled 'Isle Pouzet' (Zech/Porbeck, pp. 152-3).

73:    Zech/Porbeck, p. 156. The figure of 193 in Rau (p. 27) would appear to be a misprint. The Hessians were reduced to about 250 men (perhaps a bit high - see Chapter 5) and the 14th Chasseurs are said to have numbered only 50! It appears that the detachment of 30 men and one officer left in Ybbs had not yet returned to the regimental fold.

74:    The battalion seems to have been in line although subsequent authors (e.g., Bahls) often describe its formation as a square; although the foot soldiers held their fire with commendable skill until the cavalry was only thirty paces away, they fired high and the horsemen thus burst upon them almost untouched. Freydorf (Zech/Porbeck, p. 157) speculates the infantry may have been a battalion of the *Warasdeiner-St. Georger* Grenzer.

75:    The horse artillery remained in this vicinity throughout the remainder of the struggle, departing only once to replenish its ammunition supply.

76:    Zech/Porbeck, p. 164.

77:    A lieutenant and 25 men from the regiment were captured when Austrian cavalry surprised them in the open fields; they had been sent out to make contact with the approaching IV Corps troops (Zech/Porbeck, p. 163). This quote is from a Baden surgeon named Meier who was tending wounded in the rear, cited in Captaine Veling *Nos Alliés Allemands,* Paris: Frères, 1909, pp. 265.

78:    This number does not include the four companies attached to the artillery park.

79:    For casualties, see Kriegs-Archiv des Grossen Generalstabes, Feldzug 1809 gegen Oesterreich, 48/4283 and

Zech/Porbeck, Beilage 4. Buat (Vol. II, p. 308) gives a slightly higher total of 370 dead and wounded. Von Freydorf's story appears in almost every account of the battle (e.g., Ferber, p. 75; Zech/Porbeck, pp. 165-6) and even made a deep impression on young Karl Obermüller, who heard the tale from a returning soldier at the age of 5 (Karl F. Obermüller, *Aus der Zeit der Fremdherrschaft und der Befreiungskriege*, Karlsruhe: Müller, 1912, pp. 5-6).

80:    The Badeners accomplished this audacious feat at the cost of only 14 wounded. Pelet (vol. IV, p. 254) mistakenly credits the French 26th Léger with storming the town (Zech/Porbeck, p. 171).

81:    The tireless Jäger Battalion and the four voltigeur companies of the line regiments made up the Baden portion of this force. Gachot credits them with saving the first bridge from destruction by their prompt approach but claims they exasperated Massena by wavering when sent against the convent (Gachot, vol. 6, pp. 310-11). Note that one company of the 2nd Infantry (Etzdorff's) was absent escorting prisoners and thus missed the battle (2nd Regiment's report of 15 July in Kriegs-Archiv des Grossen Generalstabes, Feldzug 1809 gegen Oesterreich, 48/4283).

82:    The Austrian attack was led by the Leiningen Grenadier Battalion supported by the rest of its brigade (Murray's) and the battered battalions of Reuss's V Corps; the second grenadier brigade remained in reserve. See Ludwig Freiherr von Welden, *Der Krieg von 1809 zwischen Oesterreich und Frankreich von Anfang Mai bis zum Friedensschlusse,* Wien: Gerold, 1872, p. 208; and Binder von Kriegelstein, vol. II, p. 412.

83:    This was the 10th Cuirassiers, who captured 2 guns and some 800 prisoners as they broke and rode through the advancing grenadiers (Buat, vol. II, p. 363; Pelet, vol. IV, p. 271; and Koch vol. VI, p. 350). Baden accounts tend to give credit for this decisive charge to the 1st Cuirassiers (Zech/Porbeck, p. 195); indeed, Massena apparently sent Markgraf Wilhelm to the 1st Regiment to order it to attack (Obser, p. 97), but the regiment was mired in poor ground and could not disentangle itself from the mud in time to charge. Gachot (vol. 6, p. 314) errs in claiming the 12th Cuirassiers made the counter-attack. See also Hellwald (p. 273) and French regimental histories.

84:    Leutnant von Hornig and the 30 dragoons detached at Ybbs also returned to the regiment after Znaim. The actions of Leutnant Behagel and his 30 troopers (also left in the Halbturn area) are not clear. Zech/Porbeck, pp. 200-201.

85:    Barsewisch, pp. 88-9. This author also points out that a healthy competition developed between the French and Baden regiments of Legrand's Division during the period of the armistice; in one of his Orders of the Day, Massena complimented the division on the state of its training and emphasized that the other divisions of the corps were 'far behind' Legrand's.

86:    *Erbgrossherzog's* 1st Grenadier Company, for example, had been reduced from 140 to 62 men. Barsewisch, p. 88.

87:    The First Battalion, assigned to escort prisoners to Linz after Wagram, was spared some of this misery. The strength of the regiment at the conclusion of hostilities is difficult to determine. With its colonel, adjutant and scribe ill, the 'normal reports' ceased to arrive at the War Ministry in Karlsruhe, leading to a series of indignant remonstrances from the army's bureaucrats. Schöpf's casualty report of 24 July lists over 300 wounded, not including the multitudes of sick (Kriegs-Archiv des Grossen Generalstabes, Feldzug 1809 gegen Oesterreich, 48/4283.) Barsewisch and Zech/Porbeck list a mere '5 officers and 300 soldiers in the ranks' at the end of August, while Haffner gives 100 men detached to the artillery and 571 with the regiment (Barsewisch, p. 89; Haffner, p. 98; see also Zech/Porbeck, p. 201).

88:    The Garde du Corps saw no action during the campaign, its only contribution being to station 24 troopers across the Rhine from Strasbourg to stanch the flow of escaping prisoners of war. Wengen, pp. 74-5.

89:    All of these units were well below authorized strength, the hussar 'squadron' counting 63 troopers in the saddle and the two grenadier companies totalling 209 men; the detachment's two cannon were 4-pounders served by sixteen artillery and six train personnel. Adding two surgeons and Cancrin himself, the strength of the force came to 297 men. Ibid., p. 50.

90:    The strength of Pfnor's battalion on departing Karlsruhe seems to have been about 375; the other men apparently remained behind in the depot. The battalion made part of its journey in wagons. *Badischer Militär-Almanach*, 1854, p., 46; Wengen, pp. 5-6, 89-93.

91:    This reinforcement consisted of the three old companies of the Guard battalion and the cadre of the new sixth company, which only attained operational strength in the course of the campaign. Total strength of the detachment was 644 men (Ibid., p. 97). Stockhorn was the commander of the Guard Grenadiers; von Cancrin resumed his place at the head of the hussars.

92:    As a sign of the Württemberg's respect, two companies of Baden grenadiers and some hussars were detached to guard GL von Phull's headquarters. Wengen, p. 108.

93:    This estimate assumes approximately 400 Jägers and over 800 grenadiers. While the Baden cavalry in this theatre can be counted with relative accuracy, the exact strengths of the infantry formations are difficult to determine.

94:    Specifically, the hussars and two Jäger companies at Neu-Ravensburg, one Jäger company at Wangen, the grenadiers and the two guns at Amtzell. Württemberg troops were disposed with a Jäger depot company each in Wasserburg and Wangen, 60 volunteer foresters in Neu-Ravensburg and I/*Prinz Friedrich* in

Tettnang. There was a squadron of French dragoons each in Wasserburg and Wangen. The Baden dragoons remained near Meersburg to patrol the lakeshore and a detachment of Jägers occupied the peninsula north of Constance.

95:     Quoted in Wengen, pp. 160, 164.

96:     At the insistence of the government in Karlsruhe, all Baden troops were united under Stockhorn in Neu-Ravensburg on the 25th.

97:     Some Baden troops remained behind to protect Baden territory and support civil officials around Lake Constance: approximately 100 grenadiers, 50 hussars and 30 dragoons. The depot dragoons were all united at Immenstadt in the end of August and departed on 1 September for Bohemia via Kempten and Augsburg as replacements for their regiment's losses.

98:     Skirmishes took place on 3, 17 and 22 September and 20, 21, 22 and 26 October. As portrayed in the Baden accounts, these Tyrolian attempts were tentative and disorganized.

99:     Beaumont and Picard had by this time been replaced by Generals Lagrange and Vaufreland respectively. Wengen, pp. 205, 209.

CHAPTER 5:

The Indefatigable Hessians

Unlike the Badeners, the troops of Hesse-Darmstadt entered into the 1809 campaign with an established reputation for courage and competence. They had achieved this repute through their exertions and sacrifices in the struggles of 1806-7. Their monarch, Landgraf Ludwig X, relying on Prussian support, had managed to hold a neutral course in 1805, but the crushing of Austria in that campaign, the net of alliances France was weaving across southern Germany, and increased pressure from Paris convinced Ludwig that his throne's survival depended on Napoleon. With French territory beyond the Rhine just visible from the windows of his residence, Ludwig had little choice: in July 1806, he became one of the founding members of the Rheinbund with the exalted title of Grand Duke Ludwig I. Barely two months later, his military obligations under the new Confederation Treaty pulled his little army into the lightning campaign against his erstwhile guarantor, Prussia.

Mobilization for the war proceeded at a frustratingly torpid pace and the German units that were fielded found themselves hard put to keep up with the fast-marching French. None the less, two Hessian fusilier battalions arrived in time to stand the test of fire on Jena's fields as part of Augereau's VII Corps.[1] As the rest of the Hessian contingent was slowly organized in October and November, it was assigned line of communications duties, eventually reaching a strength of nine battalions, one cavalry squadron and a half-battery of artillery (around 4,000 men); almost every soldier in the Grand Duchy was thus committed to the campaign. The men distinguished themselves at the sieges of Graudenz and Stralsund in early 1807 and returned to Darmstadt with French plaudits ringing in their ears. Even Marshal Lefebvre, who expressed such peevish exasperation at the abilities of the Badeners, praised his Hessian units. After witnessing a brilliant little combat where the Hessian light horse played a notable part, he greeted the German troops enthusiastically: 'From now on we shall no longer say 'as brave as a Frenchman' but rather 'as brave as a Hessian!''[2]

When war erupted between France and Spain in 1808, three of Ludwig's battalions and four guns marched off to join the French on the Iberian Peninsula. Once more under Lefebvre's command (he now led IV Corps), the Hessians participated in a number of engagements but Napoleon branded them 'detestable', complaining that they 'did not maintain the reputation of their country's troops and did not come up to the opinion held of them in the Polish campaign'.[3] Their disappointing performance was regarded as an aberration, however, and the French welcomed Ludwig's men into their ranks as war with Austria

approached. Indeed, the Imperial summons issued from Valladolid on 15
January honoured the Hessian soldiery:

> My brother, I have received your Royal Highness' letter of 30 December
> 1808. It pains me to see that your troops, who acquired such praise during
> the campaign in Poland, have not supported their reputation in this one; the
> fault lies with the generals who command them. The Hessian is a brave
> and good soldier. If your Highness will give them leaders of merit, such as
> those who commanded in the past campaign, they will reclaim the reputa-
> tion they have deserved for many centuries.
>
> The conduct of Austria leads one to fear that that power is about to carry
> out follies that will entrain its ruin. It is necessary that your Highness'
> troops be prepared and your contingent complete, taking into the account
> the troops with the Army of Spain. I would be pleased if your Highness
> would tell me how many days it will take to assemble your troops and how
> many men I may rely on.[4]

Thus did the long arm of the Emperor stretch out to command his allies.

Ludwig responded willingly. Although his Rheinbund commitment would
have been met by a contingent of 2,400 soldiers, the Grand Duke offered twice
the required amount. It was an offer the French were only too glad to accept. 'It
is His Majesty's intention', Berthier wrote to Massena on 23 March, 'that you
request of his Royal Highness the Grand Duke of Hesse-Darmstadt a contingent
of 4,736 men and 564 horses as he has proposed in place of the 2,400 men previously requested.'[5]

Table 5-1: The Hessian Army in April 1809

Infantry

Organization: three battalions per *brigade*, two in the musketeer regiment plus one fusilier battalion; four companies
per battalion; company strength 170 men; depot.
Uniform: dark-blue coat; distinctive colour on collar, cuffs, turnbacks; white breeches; bicorne hat.

Unit	Jacket Colour	Distinctive Colour
Leib-Garde *Brigade*		
Leib-Garde-Regiment	dark-blue	red
Leib-Garde Fusiliers Battalion	dark-green	red
Leib *Brigade*		
Leib Regiment	dark-blue	light-blue
1st Leib Fusiliers Battalion	dark-green	light-blue
Gross- und Erbprinz *Brigade* (before departing for Spain)		
Gross- und Erbprinz Regiment	dark-blue	yellow
2nd Leib Fusiliers Battalion	dark-green	yellow

Cavalry

Garde-Chevauxlegers Regiment

Organization: three squadrons.
Uniform: dark-green coat with black facings trimmed red; white breeches; black helmet.

Garde-du-Corps

Uniform: buff coat with red facings and white trim; buff breeches; bicorne hat.

Artillery

Organization: Three companies manning two foot batteries (one battery in Spain).
Artillery uniform: dark-blue coat with black facings trimmed in red; dark-blue breeches; shako. Train uniform:
dark-blue coat with red facings.

The 'brave and good' Hessians available to answer the Emperor's call thus numbered more than 4,800 officers and men comprising two infantry *'brigades'*, a light cavalry regiment and an artillery battery with supporting train troops.[6] The infantry *brigades* were unique to Hesse-Darmstadt. The functional equivalent of regiments in other armies, each included three battalions in its formal structure: a regiment of two musketeer battalions and a semi-independent fusilier battalion to perform light infantry functions.[7] Both types of battalion had the same basic organization, each containing four similar companies numbered 1—4 in the 1st musketeer battalion and 5—8 in the 2nd; although the 1st Company in the musketeer regiments and fusilier battalions was honoured with the title 'Leib-Kompanie', it differed in no wise from its sister companies. There were no 'élite' units *per se*, but the fusilier battalions, like French voltigeurs, enjoyed a somewhat special status and were frequently detached from their *brigades* to undertake demanding missions with the light cavalry.

The two *brigades* in Hesse at the start of 1809 were the Leib-Garde-Brigade, consisting of the Leib-Garde-Regiment and the Leib-Garde-Füsilier-Bataillon, and the Leib-Brigade, comprising the Leib-Regiment and the 1st Leib-Füsilier-Bataillon; the Gross- und Erbprinz-Regiment and the 2nd Leib Fusiliers made up the Gross- und Erbprinz-Brigade in Spain.[8] All infantrymen wore the same basic coat, dark-blue for the musketeers and dark-green for the fusiliers, with each *brigade's* distinctive colour shown on collars, cuffs and turnbacks. The ensemble was topped with a black bicorne hat, creating, on the whole, a rather antique picture. Toward the end of the war, shakos were introduced for the infantry, but issue was still incomplete when the contingent returned to Darmstadt in January 1810.

The Hessian artillery, on the other hand, with their black felt shakos, presented a modern aspect. Their dark-blue uniform was similar in cut to that worn by their infantry compatriots but faced with black trimmed in red. The 140 officers

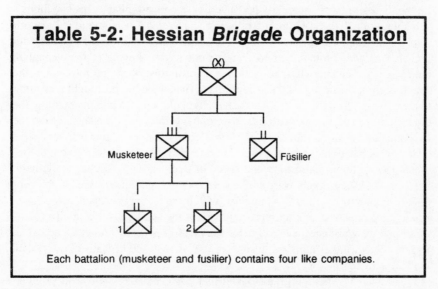

Table 5-2: Hessian *Brigade* Organization

Each battalion (musketeer and fusilier) contains four like companies.

and men assembled for the campaign manned a battery of five 6-pounders and one 7-pounder howitzer. An additional 108 soldiers were provided by the artillery train to drive the artillery pieces and manage the contingent's thirty-five other vehicles. This train organization was relatively new, having been militarized in March the previous year to correct the unsatisfactory support formerly provided by civilian contractors. A year after its formation, however, the artillery train still lacked some of the basic equipment and skills required by its tasks. According to the Adjutant-General's Report of 9 March 1809, the train had no trumpeter, its harnesses and saddlery were inadequate, and 'many of the train personnel ride very poorly or not at all'. Train-Lieutenant Müller, newly raised in rank from sergeant, was sternly adjured to repair these deficiencies in the few weeks remaining before the contingent headed into combat.[9]

Ludwig's cavalry regiment, the Garde-Chevauxlegers, was small by the standards of the day. Its three squadrons contained only 340 men, of whom a mere 312 were actual combatants. Commanded by Oberst Chamot, the regiment was handsomely uniformed in dark-green tunics and breeches with black facings and red trim. In common with many of their fellow Rheinbund troopers, the Hessian light horsemen wore a black leather helmet topped by a black caterpillar crest not unlike the Bavarian Raupenhelm. In addition to the chevauxlegers regiment, Ludwig's mounted troops included a small Garde du Corps to decorate the palace and a force of Landdragoner for internal security duties; neither of these units, however, took an active part in the 1809 campaign.[10]

A comparison of the Hessian and Baden contingents in 1809 illustrates Napoleon's judicious treatment of his German allies. On the one hand, Baden was regarded as something of a liability, its government plagued by weakness and indecision, its army of indifferent quality and unprepared for Napoleonic warfare. The solution, in the Emperor's eyes, was massive French intrusion into the inner workings of both the state and the military. On the other hand, Ludwig's regime was apparently perceived as stable and reliable, his battalions a valuable adjunct to La Grande Armée. The Hessians were required to adopt some of the trappings of commonality and they conducted limited practise with French drill and commands immediately prior to the opening of the campaign, but their peculiar internal organization was left undisturbed and throughout the active portion of the war, they seem to have manoeuvred and fought according to their own version of the old Austrian drill regulations. While maintaining the old drill, however, the standard infantry combat formation was changed from the two-rank to the three-rank line in 1808. That same year, four sappers were added to each battalion after the French model and other steps were taken to promote organizational uniformity and speed of deployment. Old habits die hard, however, and the soldiers were still expected to execute manoeuvres in the two-rank formation if required.[11] Combined with these tactical changes were administrative reforms designed to improve the lot of the soldier and his family or survivors. Pay was increased, administrative abuses were reduced and, as in Baden, funds were established to care for the widows and orphans of men killed in the line of duty.

If Bavaria, Württemberg and Baden had already made significant progress toward the creation of truly modern, national armies, Hesse-Darmstadt was on the cusp between the military norms of the eighteenth and nineteenth centuries in 1809: the uniforms, tactics and outlook of its soldiers simultaneously reflecting the stiff, mercenary past and the more flexible, national future. Despite numerous reminders of bygone years, however, the contingent Ludwig sent to Napoleon in 1809 was tough, well-trained and commanded by a fine body of experienced officers; its traditions and history giving it solidity without laying a dead hand on its battlefield performance. In the coming campaign, the men would meet the Emperor's highest expectations.

On 31 January, Ludwig issued the order mobilizing his army, directing it to assemble in the Grand Duchy's capital by mid-March. This was an involved process. To reduce the financial burden a large standing army placed on the state's exchequer, it was a standard practice of the era to release most soldiers from duty for the greater part of the year in times of peace. While the furloughed ('*beurlaubt*') men returned to their civilian occupations or sought temporary employ, the number of men actually in the ranks performing daily duties might be 50 per cent or less of a unit's wartime complement. This system not only benefited the treasury but bolstered the country's work force and provided individual soldiers with an opportunity to supplement their meagre pay.[12] The obvious disadvantages were the long mobilization period required to bring an army up to full strength and the potentially debilitating effect on unit training and cohesion caused by the soldiers' long separation from their combat organizations. The French and Hessians mitigated the first in 1809 by Napoleon's early call to the Rheinbund and Ludwig's immediate response; the irritating delays of 1806 were avoided and the Hessian army took the field at full strength.[13] The training problem was addressed by periodic manoeuvres and the maintenance of an experienced cadre in each unit. The Hessian army had been recalled and manoeuvred just prior to the Congress of Erfurt in the autumn of 1808 so that mobilization procedures and tactical drill were still relatively fresh in the soldiers' minds when they were summoned back to the colours three months later. It was the cadre, however, that preserved each unit's skills and spirit while the majority of its members were absent. Experienced NCOs were particularly prized. The artillery, for example, relied on one Sergeant Ling, who had been shaping recruits and reminding veterans of their duties for thirteen years.[14]

When Napoleon permitted his allies to demobilize their armies after the alarms of 1808, Hesse's forces were drastically reduced. The number of men in the ranks fell to 50 or 60 per company in the Leib-Garde, while the Leib *Brigade* retained even fewer, only 25—35 on active service in each company.[15] The mobilization process required to bring these skeleton formations back to full strength was time-consuming, but, thanks to Ludwig's expeditious response to Napoleon's demands, his entire contingent was assembled in the capital by 16 March.

The companies gathering in Darmstadt in 1809, however, were significantly different from those that had marched off to Jena three years earlier. Where other German monarchies had enlarged their armies through the creation of new units, Hesse chose simply to increase the size of its existing companies. It was a dramatic increase. The companies that fought beside the French in 1806—7 had had an average strength of approximately 100, but the companies of 1809 numbered about 170 officers and men: generally three officers, twelve NCOs, three musicians and 152 soldiers (including ten Schützen). The two *brigades* that marched against Austria thus contained more than 4,200 infantrymen compared to the 3,600 foot soldiers in all three *brigades* during the war with Prussia.[16]

Under the command of GM Karl Friedrich von Nagel, the Hessian contingent departed Darmstadt in three columns on 20, 21 and 22 March to arrive in Mergentheim several days later. Destined to join Massena's IV Corps, the Hessians remained in Mergentheim for more than a week as the corps slowly took form east of the Rhine. Finally, on 2 April, von Nagel took his men south, reaching Dillingen on the 6th, where the contingent was reviewed by its new division commander, GD Claude Carra Saint-Cyr. Here the Hessians were also introduced to their new French brigade commander, GB Baron Joseph Schiner. Schiner, forty-eight years old and a Swiss by birth, established a command relationship with Nagel similar to that between Baden's General Harrant and his French overseer GB Kister. Schiner thus provided the interface between the Hessian Brigade and the French division and corps command structure while Nagel saw to the actual execution of the orders he received and handled the internal affairs of the contingent. Fortunately, although Ludwig was opposed to Napoleon's command arrangements, the friction and resentment that encumbered the Badeners' interaction with their superior does not seem to have been a major problem in the Hessian case.[17]

On 10 April, the day the Austrians crossed the Inn, the Hessians passed over the Danube, marching south to Zusmarshausen where they were integrated into

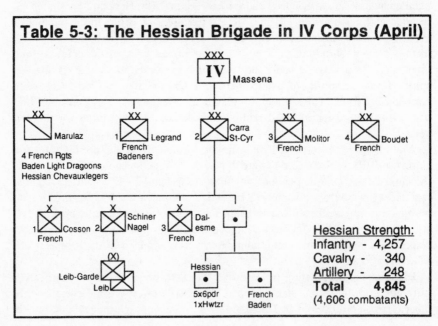

Table 5-3: The Hessian Brigade in IV Corps (April)

Hessian Strength:

Infantry -	4,257
Cavalry -	340
Artillery -	248
Total	**4,845**

(4,606 combatants)

IV Corps. The six infantry battalions under Schiner and Nagel became the 2nd Brigade of Carra Saint-Cyr's 2nd Division, while the Hessian battery was incorporated into the divisional artillery under Lieutenant-Colonel Verrier; Chamot's horsemen were assigned to GB Jacob Marulaz's Cavalry Division, but that general's troopers were scattered all over south-western Bavaria and the chevauxlegers did not actually link with their division until the 19th. The opening of the war thus found the Hessians assembled about 23 kilometres west of Augsburg, well-trained, well-led and as prepared as they could be for the bloody trials on the horizon.

APRIL - HARD MARCHES, HARD WEATHER

Unfortunately, IV Corps was not concentrated when the campaign began and the initial days of the war were marked by frenetic attempts to do everything at once. The Hessians were thus subjected to the same confusion, haste, error and frustration that plagued the Baden Brigade: constant drill, repeated adjustments in quartering assignments, and an incessant flurry of activity as staff officers, commanders and train personnel struggled to comply with headquarters' directives on shoes, ammunition, fodder, food and flints. In this bewildering environment, the Hessians were shifted south-west to Burtenbach on the 12th and then north-east to Ried three days later. It was here that cogent, emphatic orders finally reached them on the 18th. Napoleon had at last arrived and taken the reigns of the army firmly in his grip.

The Hessian contingent rendezvoused with the rest of Carra Saint-Cyr's Division at Scheppach that same day (18 April) and, the Garde Chevauxlegers leading, marched east for Augsburg. Entering the city at about 6 p.m., the division halted long enough for the men to draw a three-day ration of *zwieback* before pushing on across the Lech; the Leib Regiment was left behind to join the Baden 3rd Infantry as part of the fortress' garrison. The remainder of the contingent continued ahead through the night, drenched and shivering in the cold April rain as they stumbled along dreadful back roads in utter darkness. Reaching Aichach at about 3.30 a.m., the column made a rest halt, but after only two hours the troops were once again on their feet, trudging through the dank, grey dawn and the length of the day to arrive in Pfaffenhofen as the sun was setting on the 19th. They had been on the road for more than thirty-four hours, covering 60 gruelling kilometres in the final twenty-four hours. Little knots of weary stragglers were left huddled all along the route of march—the Leib *Brigade* alone lacked 130 men when it reached Pfaffenhofen—but cohesion was maintained and most of the laggards soon rejoined their companies.[18]

The Hessians enjoyed a few hours of well-deserved rest, but Napoleon's need for soldiers was immediate and his messages correspondingly urgent; the following morning, the men were marshalled on the muddy roads again, slogging through the wretched weather to stop near Freising at 1.30 a.m. on the 21st. At 6 a.m., they were moving once more, driving for Landshut and the vulnerable left flank of the Archduke's army. But Landshut had already fallen and there was no combat to relieve the numbness and tension, the dull agony of ceaseless straining in the rain: halting near the city at about 6 p.m., the men simply collapsed in their bivouacs.

The Hessian battalions joined the endless column of muddy blue figures headed north for Eggmühl in the early hours of 22 April. Their 50-kilometre march, however, did not bring them to the eerie, moonlit battlefield until 9 p.m., long after the sharp struggle had concluded. Moving slowly past the corpses and near-corpses in the tricky blue-grey light, the men continued across the Laaber to camp around the Sanding villages where Davout's men had spent their blood in the victorious afternoon. It was well after midnight before they halted; there was no food to be had and the exhausted men threw themselves to the ground to steal whatever sleep they could before the drums called them to their feet again.

On the morning of 23 April, as Napoleon pressed Archduke Charles across the Danube at Regensburg, IV Corps was sent east to the Isar and Carra Saint-Cyr's Division joined Claparède's, Legrand's and d'Espagne's men on the road to Straubing. That evening the troops received a welcome issue of bread, meat and brandy. These were the first regular rations they had enjoyed since departing their cantonments west of Augsburg five days earlier, and they drove for the Inn the next day in somewhat better spirits despite the return of wretchedly cold and rainy weather. The corps arrived before Passau on the 26th and Claparède's Division forced a crossing of the Inn while the combined Schützen of the four Hessian battalions (about 160 men) scoured the south bank of the Danube for signs of the enemy. At the same time, Legrand and the Badeners were busy driving the Austrian garrison out of Schärding. Exploiting his subordinates' successes, Massena brought the rest of his divisions across the river the following day, sending Carra Saint-Cyr's men south via Schärding to a position just east of the devastated little town. The Hessian infantry remained in bivouac here through the end of April as IV Corps waited for the remainder of the army to cross the Inn and the Salzach.[19]

While their footsore comrades were wearing out their shoes, the Hessian cavalrymen were winning praise for their performance in a number of hot little actions with Marshal Bessières' extemporized corps. The regiment suffered its first casualty when illness forced Oberst Chamot to remain behind at Aichach on the 18th; he returned to Hesse for the duration of the campaign. Now under Major von Münchingen's command, the chevauxlegers proceeded to Pfaffenhofen the next day where they were physically united with General Marulaz and the rest of the corps cavalry division. Moving out on the morning of the 20th, Marulaz's men passed through Freising in the afternoon to reach the banks of the Inn at Moosburg late in the evening. A sharp cavalry fight swirled around the Moosburg bridge the next morning as the French forced their way over the river, but the Hessians were not called into the fray.[20] The crossing won, Marulaz led his division on to Landshut, participated in the evening's pursuit of Hiller's battered corps, and finally halted just west of Geisenhausen having covered almost 40 kilometres in the course of the long day. The Hessian troopers had ridden hard, pushing their horses at the trot or gallop much of the day, but, once again, they had had no opportunity to close with the enemy and dismounted late in the night without having drawn their sabres.

Their first brush with the enemy came on the morning of the 22nd. While most of the French and German forces were driving north toward Eggmühl, Napoleon detached Marshal Bessières with about 19,000 men to pursue Hiller's 31,000.[21] As Bessières' advanced guard, Marulaz had his men mounted and moving by 3 a.m., and, leading the way, the Hessians bumped into the Austrian rear guard at Egglkofen at about 10 a.m. With support from I/19th Chasseurs, the chevauxlegers boldly forced their way into the village, but were disrupted by musketry from Austrian infantry in the buildings, charged by two squadrons of *Erzherzog Karl* Uhlans and pressed back toward the north. Two squadrons of the 3rd Chasseurs that galloped to their assistance were balanced by two further squadrons of Habsburg Uhlans and the skirmish ended in a draw with only minor losses on either side. Among the casualties was Major von Münchingen, wounded in the shoulder by a lance thrust and only saved from capture by the courage and quick thinking of his men. An old hussar like Marulaz was not to be deterred by such minor setbacks, however, and he immediately sent the Hessians ahead to seize the bridge over the Inn at Mühldorf. Skirting around the Austrian rear guard, the chevauxlegers, now led by Rittmeister von Dalwigk, the able commander of the Leib-Eskadron, approached the river at about dusk but were met with musket fire and driven off. It being considered too late in the day to attempt any further action, the regiment called in its patrols and bivouacked where it was. Given the uncertain situation, Marulaz issued strict orders for his squadrons to remain on full alert during the night and few of the Hessian troopers got any real rest as the 22nd became the 23rd. The Austrians indeed disturbed the regiment several times during the night, but the vigilant Hessian pickets under Premierlieutenant von Breidenbach repulsed each of these repeated probes.[22]

With dawn the next day, the regiment was joined by Marulaz's Chief of Staff, Adjutant-Commandant Ransonnet, and moved on Mühldorf again. Despite considerable enemy fire, the 2nd Squadron, Lieutenant von Breidenbach in the lead, charged into the town and neatly captured about 90 Austrian infantrymen. Unfortunately, the bridge at Mühldorf as well as another further upstream had already been destroyed and the chevauxlegers retired about two kilometres north of the town to await further orders. Instead of new instructions, however, the night brought an Austrian attack; Hiller had turned on the overconfident Bessières. In the first hours of 24 April, the Hessians were surprised and hustled out of their position, falling back on the Bavarian 13th Infantry with the rest of Marulaz's squadrons. As the morning revealed a major Austrian advance against Wrede's Division at Neumarkt, the French and Hessian cavalry, useless in the hilly and forested terrain south of the town, was withdrawn to the north over the Rott. The Garde Chevauxlegers remained in reserve during the day's battle and pulled back to Vilsbiburg that night with the rest of Bessières' Corps.[23]

Bessières, stunned by the Austrian aggressiveness at Neumarkt, was slow to return to the pursuit, and the Hessians did not resume their march to the east until the 27th. Major von Münchingen, hardly recovered from his lance wound, was once more in the saddle at the head of his troopers as they arrived in Alt-Oetting across the Inn that evening. He led them on to Tittmoning the following

day where he received a communication from GB Marulaz promising him the
Legion of Honour for his 'outstanding conduct' on the 22nd: 'I have personally
spoken to the Emperor and informed him of my complete satisfaction with the
Hessian Garde-Chevauxlegers.' Although the Hessian cavalry had yet to fight a
serious battle, they had impressed the French leaders and Napoleon made good
on Marulaz's promise when the regiment rode to Burghausen on the 24th;
reviewing the Hessian squadrons along with elements of Lannes' Corps and the
Guard, the Emperor expressed his pleasure with their performance and awarded
the coveted cross to von Münchingen and two other deserving chevauxlegers.
That afternoon, the Hessians headed north to Braunau, crossed the Inn and
assumed outpost duty east of Altheim.[24]

MAY - TO VIENNA AND ASPERN

With his main body finally across the Salzach, Napoleon lost no time in reviving
a vigorous pursuit of Hiller. While Bessières and Lannes continued the advance
toward Wels, Marulaz's Division was ordered north to rejoin IV Corps which
was desperately short of light cavalry. The division departed Altheim at mid-
morning on 1 May and, late that night, rode into Riedau where Baden and
Württemberg cavalry had battered an Austrian rear guard earlier in the day.[25] A
steady downpour soaking him and his troopers, Marulaz learned of this tough
engagement and, in view of the proximity of an apparently significant Austrian
force, kept most of his men on alert in the saddle throughout the night. He
swung east toward Neumarkt on the morning of the 2nd but encountered resistance just beyond the village and sent the Hessians forward to clear the way.
Unaware that the Austrians had destroyed the bridge over the stream ahead, the
Chevauxlegers found it impossible to cross the watercourse and took a few casualties as they attempted to turn back to the safety of the town; the promising
Rittmeister Dalwigk was among the dead, his loss much lamented by his regiment. His route blocked, Marulaz headed north to the Schärding-Eferding road,
arriving in the latter town as evening fell.[26]

The Hessian infantry had reached Eferding much earlier that day. After several days' rest near Schärding, the Hessian battalions had been pushed forward
at 1 a.m. on 1 May to support the Baden and Württemberg cavalry regiments
forming Massena's advanced guard; in this role, they proceeded slowly along
the main Schärding-Linz road, reaching Waizenkirchen at about 1 a.m. on 2nd.
The vanguard ran into considerable resistance around Eferding that morning and
Carra Saint-Cyr was called up to throw his division's weight into the sharp little
action that developed around this town. In a series of small, hectic engagements, the French steadily pushed the men of Bianchi's Brigade back, but, in the
late afternoon, the Austrian rear guard attempted to hold a position across the
road near Strassham. Carra Saint-Cyr now committed the Hessians, sending
them south of the road to climb a long, low ridge and outflank the Austrian left.
The combined Schützen of all four battalions leading the way, followed at a
600-metre interval by the Garde Füsiliers, the Hessians advanced aggressively
but were almost unopposed and soon found themselves in possession of the

ridge and a small collection of prisoners. The Hessian battery unlimbered on the ridge to send a few rounds after the retreating Austrians, but Massena had received reports of a large enemy force near Linz and suspended further offensive action to consolidate and rest his corps. The Hessians suffered no losses in this brief skirmish.[27]

With the arrival of Marulaz's men in Eferding, the Hessian contingent, minus the Leib Regiment, was once again united under Massena's immediate command. The Chevauxlegers thus rode east the next morning in the company of six other French and Rheinbund cavalry regiments: 3rd, 14th, 19th, and 23rd Chasseurs, Baden Light Dragoons, Württemberg *Leib-Chevauxlegers*. The division helped drive the Austrians back on the Traun, but most of the fighting seems to have fallen to the French squadrons and the Hessians did not play a significant role; the ensuing combat in Ebelsberg was strictly an infantry and artillery fight from house to house, and the cavalry did not cross the river until after 5 p.m.. Likewise, Carra Saint-Cyr's Division was too far back in IV Corps' march column to play an active role in the brutal struggle at Ebelsberg. The men passed over the long wooden bridge, gruesomely littered with broken bodies, in the late afternoon, but recrossed after only a few hours on the eastern bank.

Crushed and blackened corpses of the previous day's battle still clogged the doorways and alleys of Ebelsberg when the Hessians returned at 1 a.m. on the morning of 4 May. Passing through the smouldering village, they marched to the town of Enns and bivouacked there for the next two days while the entire corps waited for the bridge over the River Enns to be repaired. This waiting period was highlighted by hectic activity to prepare for an Imperial review on the 5th. That morning, Napoleon had Carra Saint-Cyr's Division mustered in the pleasant spring fields rolling down to the Danube and strode slowly across the front of the formation, asking the men if they had stood in the trenches at Graudenz and taking the opportunity to decorate two Hessians for their performance in 1807. Concluding the review by putting the Hessians through a series of drills, he made a point of complimenting Nagel on the appearance and bearing of the men and the renown of their valour.[28] Thus, even though the Hessian infantry had yet to fight a serious engagement in the present campaign, Napoleon was able to demonstrate tangibly the rewards of loyal service and bind his German soldiers more closely to his person.

The Hessians crossed the Enns at 4 p.m. on 6 May and bivouacked near Ennsdorf on the eastern bank of the river, but the advance on Vienna did not truly resume until the 7th. Carra Saint-Cyr took his men to Blindenmarkt that day, detaching at Napoleon's order two companies of the 1st Leib Fusiliers to patrol the banks of the Danube between Melk and Wallsee.[29] Marching via Melk (8th), St. Pölten (9th) and Sieghartskirchen (10th), the Hessian soldiers reached the outskirts of the Austrian capital on the 11th, swinging south to take up positions near Simmering. The Chevauxlegers, although reduced to a mere 140 effectives by the exertions of the campaign, were allowed little opportunity to recover;[30] posted at Fischamend, they were to join the cavalry screen south of the city, patrolling the Danube and securing the army's rear from annoyances out of Hungary. The rest of the Hessians were billeted in the city once it capitulated, enjoying their dry, if somewhat tight, quarters and regular, if rather skimpy, rations after a month of punishing marches and bivouacs in the rain. The campaign had also taken its toll on their shoes and clothing and Carra Saint-Cyr made arrangements to supply his German troops with new garments and footwear.[31]

In Vienna, the Hessian Brigade was brought back to full strength by the arrival of the Leib Regiment from Augsburg. Departing that crucial depot city on 24 April, the Hessian regiment, in the company of the Baden 3rd Infantry, had marched a long, hard route via Braunau and Melk to rejoin its comrades on 15 May. At 2 a.m. next day, however, both fusilier battalions and the Schützen of the Leib-Garde musketeer battalions headed south to Bruck an der Leitha. Reinforced by two French horse guns and placed under Major Gall (commander of the 1st Leib Fusiliers), this detachment was to provide infantry support to the cavalry screen Montbrun was establishing below Vienna. It arrived the same day after a march of about 45 kilometres and remained on the Hungarian border for the next two weeks, ending the month in a position near Wolfsthal.[32] Like their Baden cousins farther to the south-west, the Hessian light infantry could clearly hear the ominous rumble of artillery that signalled the deadly struggle at Aspern-Essling.

ASPERN-ESSLING (21-22 MAY)

Having occupied the enemy's capital, the Emperor's eye turned to stare intently across the Danube toward the broad, flat Marchfeld and the Austrian *Hauptarmee*, the Habsburg prop he had failed to crush at Regensburg. He must now seek out that army and eradicate it. To maintain the momentum of victory that had carried the French juggernaut to Vienna, Napoleon thrust Molitor's Division over the river to seize Lobau Island on 18 May while he gathered his army south-east of the city. A series of bridges was hastily thrown across the turbulent branches of the Danube over the next two days and on the morning of the 21st, IV Corps led the way across to the Marchfeld.

Carra Saint-Cyr's men were marshalled near Kaiser Ebersdorf just after midnight on the 21st, waiting with varying degrees of patience, zeal and terror to step on to the slender spans bobbing and swaying in the swells of the great river. Before they could cross, however, the tenuous connection snapped, splitting IV Corps in two and leaving the 2nd Division helpless onlookers as their outnumbered comrades fought for their lives on the fringes of the Marchfeld throughout the day. It was 6 p.m. before Carra Saint-Cyr's brigades made their way over the repaired bridges, sometimes wading up to their ankles on the uncertain span, and took up positions about 600 metres south of Aspern. Even as they were in the process of crossing, the bridge broke again, leaving one of the Hessian guns and three of the ammunition wagons stranded on the Vienna side of the treacherous river.

While the Hessian infantry and artillery were anxiously peering toward the gunfire over the swift, turbid waters, the Garde-Chevauxlegers had already been plunged into action. Urged to the utmost haste, Marulaz had brought his

Cavalry Division to the bridges on the afternoon of the 20th and begun to cross, but breakage almost immediately isolated the general and a lone squadron (II/3rd Chasseurs) on one of the intermediary islands. Here the impatient hussar waited for more than sixteen hours before the bridges were sufficiently repaired for his troopers to join him. Between 9 and 10 a.m. next day, the division finally crossed the fragile constructions, the German regiments at the head of the column, leading their horses at the walk. Marulaz had been led to believe that a battle was already in progress, however, and, on reaching solid ground, he sent his men galloping pell-mell for the next bridge with no regard for order or precedence. By this combination of measured caution and hell-for-leather urgency, Massena's cavalry reached the Marchfeld in the late morning of the 21st.[33]

In conjunction with the Badeners, the Hessian cavalry was vectored off at speed to relieve the French vedettes west and south-west of Aspern (16th Chasseurs). It was about 1 p.m. and there was almost no sign of the enemy, but a detachment composed of a half-squadron from each regiment under the command of Baden Lieutenant Gailing was pushed out towards Hirschstetten as a

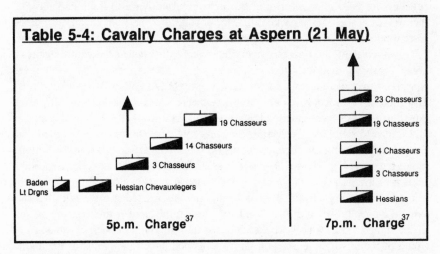

Table 5-4: Cavalry Charges at Aspern (21 May)

19 Chasseurs
14 Chasseurs
3 Chasseurs
Baden Lt Drgns   Hessian Chevauxlegers

5p.m. Charge[37]

23 Chasseurs
19 Chasseurs
14 Chasseurs
3 Chasseurs
Hessians

7p.m. Charge[37]

precaution. Brushing away some Austrian hussars, Gailing's little command came upon the advanced guard of Hiller's VI Corps and withdrew, slowly and in good order, on Aspern. Austrian hussars in cautious pursuit of the retiring German horsemen recoiled in the face of heavy fire from French infantry outposts along the edges of the village and were put to flight by the Baden and Hessian reserves.[34] It was 2 p.m.; the Battle of Aspern had begun.

Through the remainder of the long, hot afternoon the Hessian Garde-Chevauxlegers fought alongside the rest of Marulaz's regiments in the furious struggle to hold off the numerically superior Austrians. Initially posted north of Aspern, the division had been moved to a more sheltered position just east of the village at about 4 p.m. when new orders arrived sending it into a cauldron of fire. The French situation was desperate: Massena had succeeded in reclaiming Aspern but his position was enclosed in an arc of Austrian batteries, damage to the bridges interrupted and delayed the arrival of reinforcements, and

Hohenzollern's fresh II Corps was slowly deploying opposite the vulnerable centre of the French line between Aspern and Essling. At about 5 p.m., Napoleon turned to Bessières and ordered him to charge Hohenzollern's lines with the available cavalry. Marulaz's Division, supported by a half dozen cuirassier regiments, led the way, deploying in the middle of the battlefield at the trot and charging headlong through the gun-smoke into the Austrian batteries:

> General Marulaz, at the head of the 3rd, 14th and 19th Chasseurs, the Baden Dragoons and the Hessian Chevauxlegers, executed repeated charges against the battalion squares. The close formations of the enemy, his large numbers, and the cross fire of his batteries did not permit [Marulaz] to push home all his charges; he had to content himself with holding the terrain he had won...[35]

At the left rear of Marulaz's echeloned formation, the Hessian sabres played a full part in these charges, riding through the Austrian gun lines and hurling themselves at the tightly packed infantry beyond, but the light cavalry's attacks were repulsed, as were the subsequent efforts of the heavy regiments. The same fate awaited the Allied cavalrymen when danger threatened the centre again at about 7 p.m.. Pulled back to a position west of Essling after their first charges, Marulaz's men were thrown forward as evening fell to hold off an Austrian cavalry attack. Formed in a deep column, the regiments crashed into the first Austrian line and penetrated it but were struck in the flanks by heavy cavalry and forced to retire hastily; Marulaz's Chief of Staff, Ransonnet, was killed and the general himself almost captured, his horse slain and his hat lost in the tumult. None the less, Napoleon's objective was attained in both cases: the imperiled French centre was protected and a major Austrian attack averted.[36]

Over on the French left, the Austrians had succeeded in regaining half of Aspern by 7 p.m. when the vicious battle amidst the smoke, flames and corpses of the ruined village finally flickered down into intermittent bursts of musketry. South of the town, the Hessian infantry remained under arms most of the night, awaiting the dangerous dawn.

When they finally crossed over from Lobau to the left bank on the evening of the 21st, the two Hessian musketeer regiments were posted in the Gemeinde Au behind Massena's left flank. With the Leib-Garde on the right (north) and the Leib Regiment on the left, the brigade was held in reserve for the remainder of the day as the fighting tapered off, but the early hours of the 22nd saw them thrown into Aspern's dreadful maelstrom. Napoleon intended to break the Austrian centre with Lannes' Corps and exploit his anticipated advantage with Davout's veterans. As a precondition, however, he had to regain possession of Aspern and Massena was exhorted to seize the village at first light. The night was hardly restful, but Massena's French and Baden infantry attacked with vigour at about 3 a.m. and, after four hours of brutal house-to-house combat, the village was firmly in French hands. During these initial assaults (about 5.30 a.m.), the Hessians were moved forward to the eastern fringe of the blazing town, a position which would allow them either to support the battle in Aspern or to advance into the open fields north-east of the village as a link to Lannes' II Corps.[38] Massena detached Hauptmann Weller's company (the 4th) of the Leib-Garde Regiment and placed it on the southern edge of Aspern, probably to guard two improvised footbridges leading to Molitor's position in the Gemeinde-Au.[39]

With all his French and Baden infantry committed to the desperate struggle around Aspern, the four Hessian battalions now represented Massena's last reserve. The Austrians could not afford to leave IV Corps in possession of the town, however, and renewed enemy pressure soon forced Massena to bring some of the Hessians into the fight. Weller's Company, Major Scharnhorst's II/Leib, and the Schützen of I/Leib were thus called forward sometime after 7 a.m.[40] Drums rolling, the Hessian companies charged through the smoke-filled streets, adding new impetus to the French attack and carrying Massena's battle-line forward until Austrian reinforcements checked the assault's momentum near the centre of town. By now, Austrian guns had set most of Aspern afire and the flames, combined with dust, smoke and collapsing buildings, made it impossible to maintain large bodies of troops in the hellish town. Massena thus temporarily withdrew most of his men from Aspern, leaving only skirmishers who were relieved at thirty-minute intervals; the Hessians, for example, kept two companies in the town while the others retired to its eastern fringes. The Austrians too were forced to evacuate many of their troops from the village so that a revived attack by IV Corps at 10 a.m. met only disorganized resistance. Led by II/Leib, this new assault succeeded in bringing almost the entire town, including the walled church, under French control. The Hessians of Captain Koeniger's Company broke the determined Austrian defence of this key redoubt and stormed over the wall into the churchyard, taking more than 80 prisoners. In its enthusiasm, this bold company advanced west beyond the village, but was caught in the open fields by a cruel infantry and artillery crossfire and quickly withdrew under heavy losses.[41]

Retreating to the church, the Hessians had only a short while to enjoy their victory under its battered steeple, as they were overwhelmed by a powerful Austrian counter-attack and thrown back toward the middle of town at about 11 a.m. Koeniger himself was badly wounded and taken prisoner as he tried to limp back to an aid station. In the turmoil of their withdrawal, the Hessians were apparently fired upon by the Baden 3rd Infantry and fell back in consider-able haste and confusion carrying many of the French and Baden troops with them in their flight. The Badeners almost lost a flag in the general disorder and Hiller's men were soon masters of most of the village.[42]

Napoleon could not tolerate the threat posed to his left by Hiller's advance and immediately ordered GD Philibert Curial to assist Massena at Aspern with three battalions of Young Guard Tirailleurs. The Marshal lost no time in hurling these fresh forces into the corpse- and debris-choked streets supported by I/Leib; simultaneously, the remaining three companies of I/Leib-Garde pushed into the open ground north-east of Aspern to outflank the village's defenders and main-tain contact with Lannes' troops on the right. Most of the Leib Regiment's 2nd Battalion, rallied by its commander, Major Scharnhorst, on the village's south-eastern outskirts, also stormed back into the smoke and flames where parts of the unfortunate Koeniger's Company and the regiment's Schützen still contested Austrian possession of the town. Although the assault columns were briefly halted, the tireless Massena led the 4th and 46th Ligne into the fray and the French once again conquered the bloody ground of the churchyard.[43]

This attack came just in time to rescue a desperate little knot of Hessians. Characteristic of the confused house-to-house fighting in Aspern, small groups of men on both sides were repeatedly isolated as the impassioned armies swept back and forth through the town. In this instance, a handful of Leib Regiment Schützen had been cut off near the central square as the retreating Allies and pursuing Austrians swarmed past. Hastily barricading themselves in a large, stone building, these men, led by a simple hornist named Walz, defended their little fortress with fierce courage against overwhelming odds. When the enemy penetrated the ground floor, Walz, now wounded, led his impromptu command up to the second floor and continued to resist until relieved by his returning comrades.[44]

But the Allied success was short-lived. The Austrians launched yet another counter-attack at 1 p.m., capturing most of the town as the French and Germans recoiled in confusion. Contributing to the disorder was another tragic instance of mistaken identity. According to Major Scharnhorst's after action report:

> The repeated attacks of the enemy, fighting desperately for the village, drove the ever-present Marshal Massena to order up a French battalion as reinforcement. It was past noon when this battalion approached at the charge... I joined the head of this column with my flank company and we must have advanced some 100 paces at the charge when the French battalion opened a heavy fire to its left flank. To our sorrow, we instantly discovered that its target was elements of Koeniger's retreating company which the French had mistaken for Austrians. Efforts by my adjutant and me to rectify the error were fruitless. Still about this business, we received heavy musket fire from a strong column which had entered the village from the right under the protection of the numerous [enemy] artillery; the French battalion was so disconcerted that it fled, taking a portion of our people with it.[45]

Massena was now forced to reach for his final reserve, II/Leib-Garde. Hurling forward this last fresh battalion and inspiring his battle-weary troops by his personal example, the Marshal was able to regain part of Aspern, but the attack lost all momentum in a boil of bitter, confused street fighting in the centre of the village: 'The combatants fell upon one another with bayonets and musket butts, stones and shingles were not disdained as weapons, while sharpshooters sought their targets in the intervals, and, in the open areas, canister balls rattled about as individual guns that had been dragged forward to support the infantry joined the struggle.' Finally, at about 2 p.m., additional Austrian forces pushed the French and their German allies back to Aspern's southern and eastern edges. As their comrades retired through the rubble of the village and Lannes' Corps fell back to the ravine between Aspern and Essling, the three Hessian companies north-east of Aspern had no choice but to retreat as well.[46]

The mid-afternoon thus found IV Corps clinging to the south-eastern fringes of the ruined town. Units were continually rotated in and out of the terrible streets as ammunition supplies were exhausted and disordered battalions reformed, but despite the ferocity of the combat in the gutted homes and blasted gardens, the French no longer represented a serious threat to the Austrian hold on the village. The Leib-Garde Regiment was sent into Aspern again in the latter half of the afternoon and two companies of II/Leib were deployed as skirmishers and pushed up to the ditch north-east of the town when the Austrian centre temporarily withdrew, but, as Massena began to pull his troops out of the village at about 5 p.m., the entire Hessian brigade retired to the small copse it had occupied on the night of 21/22 May.

To hold the Austrians in check, Massena established a chain of skirmishers along the fringes of Aspern and the Hessians were called upon to contribute six companies. Although the command was now very low on ammunition, cartridges were consolidated and Hauptmann Weber led forward a detachment of 400 men from all four battalions.[47] These men remained in position, keeping up a lively fire until about 8 p.m., when their ammunition was practically gone and the general retreat to Lobau was under way. The order to withdraw came as a surprise to most of the Hessians. As one survivor wrote, 'We had never considered the possibility that we would have to call off an attack while under Napoleon's command.' None the less, they returned to the little wood, reformed and marched across the bridge to the island with the rest of their division at about 11 p.m.[48]

Hauptmann Kuhlmann of the Hessian artillery had brought his howitzer, two of his cannon and three ammunition wagons across the Danube before the bridge snapped on the evening of the 21st; stranded on the Vienna side of the river, Premier-Lieutenant Müller was to lead the lone remaining gun and all other vehicles over at the earliest opportunity. The continual interruptions of traffic across the river made this impossible, however, and Müller was finally ordered to unpack the contingent's ammunition and load it on to boats for transport to Lobau Island. In the meantime, Kuhlmann and his gunners had become involved in the battle. Ordered forward at about 6 a.m., the Hessian pieces deployed in the open ground east of Aspern with the rest of Carra Saint-Cyr's artillery and opened fire. Progressively withdrawn, first to the road connecting Aspern with Essling and then some metres farther south, the Hessians gradually expended most of their ammunition and, at about 10 a.m., received the order to pull out of the firing line. The little battery remained in the rear, out of range of the Austrian guns, until the onset of evening when it again advanced and unlimbered. The battle was slowly fading, however, and the Hessians retreated to Lobau during the night without firing another shot.[49]

The Garde Chevauxlegers were detached from Marulaz's Division on the morning of the 22nd and posted behind Essling with the Württemberg light horsemen of *Herzog Heinrich* at about 7 a.m., thereby freeing a French cavalry brigade for the crucial action in the centre. Although the Württembergers participated in the defence of the village in the late afternoon, the Hessians apparently remained in reserve, taking no active part in the battle after the first day. The regiment withdrew in the evening and was reunited with its division on Lobau Island.[50]

The cavalry and artillery had their parts to play in the bloody fighting on 21 and 22 May, and they played them with honour and courage, but the Hessian casualty figures show which formations bore the brunt of the combat. The Chevauxlegers lost a total of sixteen men (seven dead and nine wounded), while the small artillery battery was fortunate enough to suffer no human casualties whatsoever, despite the fact that it stood in open ground under Austrian artillery fire for several hours.[51] The infantry, on the other hand, paid a considerable blood tax in this its first major engagement of the war. The Leib Regiment alone took 399 casualties (64 dead, 155 wounded and 180 captured) from an initial strength of approximately 1,200. Committed later in the action and spared the brutal contests at the church, the Leib-Garde's casualty figures were less than those of its sister regiment but still significant: 50 dead, 124 wounded and 107 missing for a total of 281. Included in the wounded was General Schiner. Taken in sum, the Hessian infantry suffered more than 25 per cent casualties [52] in Aspern's gory streets on 22 May. These losses, combined with the skill and undeniable valour demonstrated by the brigade, gave full proof to the trust Napoleon had placed in his Hessian allies and earned Ludwig's men sincere praise from their French commanders. In recognition of their loyal service, Napoleon visited the Hessian battalions on Lobau on 29 May, questioning the individual soldiers about the struggle at Aspern and expressing his open satisfaction with their performance in the battle. He departed with the words 'ce sont de beaux hommes'.[53] Further acknowledgement came at a review on 25 June, where twenty-two crosses of the Legion of Honour were distributed to officers and men in the Hessian musketeer battalions (thirteen to the Leib Regiment, nine to the Leib-Garde); the redoubtable hornist Walz and several fellow Schützen were among the recipients.[54]

Unfortunately, conditions on Lobau were hardly amenable to recovery from the injuries of combat. The history of the Leib Regiment paints a vivid picture:

> The troops, exhausted by the two-day battle, enervated by hunger and thirst, found nothing on Lobau Island but a drink of unclean river water and a bivouac site on a marshy meadow. A painful lack of victuals was soon evident. Horse meat and stinging nettles flavoured with gunpowder qualified as delicacies. Only after the 25th, when the main bridge was repaired, could food supplies be delivered.[55]

These sorts of privations eventually abated somewhat, but new plagues soon arose to make the soldiers' lives miserable. The first and most debilitating was rampant disease, particularly dysentery which, despite stringent efforts to maintain hygiene, spread and decimated the ranks. Its ravages claimed dozens of men, including GM von Nagel, who had to turn over command of the contingent to Oberst von Lehrbach of the Leib-Garde *Brigade* on 2 June. The second was manual labour. Napoleon intended to fortify Lobau to resist any attack and support his planned offensive against Archduke Charles. This required days of dreary, often backbreaking, construction work, most of which fell to the infantry. The men detested this duty despite the additional pay they received as compensation and most seem to have yearned for a return to honest soldier's tasks like marching and fighting. 'Completely cut off from the rest of the world', the Hessian musketeers remained on Lobau under these conditions until the end of June, passing their time between the latrines and the fortifications as the great army and its energetic captain prepared for the next contest with Archduke Charles and his white-coated battalions.[56]

JUNE - PRESSBURG AND HUNGARY

While the Emperor was praising their musketeer comrades, the Hessian fusiliers were earning laurels of their own in distant Hungary. Following the repulse at Aspern-Essling, Napoleon sought to unite his main army with Prince Eugène's Army of Italy while preventing Archduke Johann from joining his elder brother, Charles. Key to these aims was Pressburg on the left bank of the Danube and a bridgehead the Austrians were constructing across the river from the city. The task of eliminating the bridgehead was entrusted to Davout, whose forces for this mission included one division of his own corps (GD Charles Gudin's), GD Charles Lasalle's cavalry and Major Gall's fusilier detachment with its two French guns.[57] Arriving in Hainburg on 31 May, the Marshal made preparations to test the bridgehead's defences the next day.

The bridgehead was an island separated from the mainland of the right bank

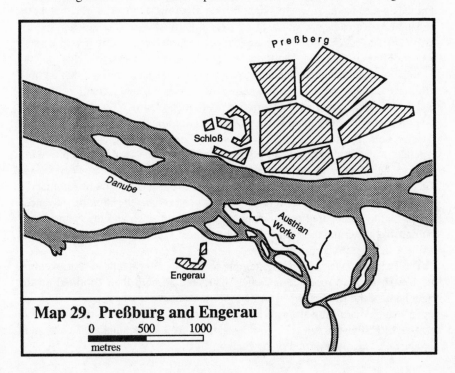

Map 29. Preßburg and Engerau

0   500   1000
metres

by a shallow arm of the Danube and largely covered by the village of Engerau. After a thorough reconnaissance, Davout ordered the Hessians and their pair of guns forward with the 16th Chasseurs to probe the Austrian position. Schützen in the lead, the Hessians attacked with 'speed and determination' at 7 p.m. and forced their way into the village, but Austrian resistance proved too strong and Davout withdrew the detachment after two hours of battle. This reconnaissance in force cost the Hessians eight dead and 65 wounded but revealed the strength of the Austrian position and gained them the praise of the Iron Marshal: 'The troops of Hesse-Darmstadt conducted themselves very well,' he wrote to Napoleon on the 2nd.[58] One of the casualties was an officer candidate of the fusiliers, Korporal Heger. Heger's hat was knocked from his head by an Austrian bullet in the course of the fight, but the corporal, renowned for his humour, instantly scooped it from the ground and swung it in the air, shouting 'a badge of honour, Captain!' Moments later, he fell to the ground, struck by a better-aimed ball which soon brought his death.[59]

As Heger lay dying, his comrades were once more in action. Bringing up additional French troops and guns, Davout undertook a second assault at 5 p.m. on 3 June. The Hessian Schützen again formed the vanguard, followed by the two fusilier battalions and the 12th Ligne. Under Major von Gall's cool, professional eye, the Hessians advanced with veteran steadiness, the Garde Fusiliers manoeuvring as if on the drill field despite heavy enemy fire.[60] Joined by a company of voltigeurs, they stormed into the village, cleared it in a brief flurry of house-to-house fighting[61] and pressed towards the bridgehead, urged on by GB Claude Petit, sword in hand, shouting 'Let's go, brave Hessians, forward!' The bridgehead island was protected by a shallow stand of water, but Petit, undaunted, overcame the obstacle by having it filled with fascines and led his men across to break into the incomplete Austrian defences. Occupying a small sector of the bridgehead, Petit's advanced troops, the Hessian Schützen, the French voltigeur company and a Hessian fusilier company, endured half an hour of intense canister and musket fire before their casualties and a counter-attack by two Austrian battalions threw them out. Although the main body, enfiladed by several enemy batteries, had also suffered heavily, morale was unshaken and an Austrian attempt to exploit the success of their counter-attack was handily repelled. The highly respected Petit had just ordered the entire column to withdraw to the village and was praising the men for their performance when he was hit in the head by a canister ball and killed. The death of their commander notwithstanding, the men retired to Engerau in an orderly fashion, the advanced troops taking up covered positions along the edge of town and the formed units pulling back behind the village to reduce their vulnerability to the Austrian artillery firing from across the river.

The French made two more attempts to storm the bridgehead that evening. Each was bloodily repulsed and the Austrians still held their foothold on the right bank of the Danube when firing tapered off at about 10 p.m..

This sanguinary little struggle cost the Hessian detachment 25 dead and from 100 to 150 wounded but added immeasurably to their reputation.[62] The stern and laconic Davout reported to the Emperor:

I must make particular mention of the Hessian troops, who rival Your Majesty's in courage, and of Graf von Gall, the major commanding these troops. This commander displayed the greatest valour; officers and soldiers alike, there is no one who will not acknowledge him as well as his troops.[63]

The 16th *Bulletin de la Grande Armée* announced that 'the Hessian fusiliers fought very well' and Lasalle wrote to Ludwig to laud 'the brave Hessians, who behaved so courageously in the recent battles'.[64] Based on the recommendations of these two generals, Napoleon authorized the award of twelve Crosses of the Legion of Honour to von Gall's detachment.

If the Pressburg bridgehead had not been eliminated, it had at least been contained and Davout was now ordered to extend his operations south to co-operate with Viceroy Eugène's Army marching up out of Italy. Cavalry being fairly useless at the bridgehead but ideal for the open plains of Hungary, Lasalle's command was sent downstream along the Danube toward Raab. The Hessians and their two guns remained with the quintessential hussar general to provide infantry and artillery support, marching to Kittsee on 5 June and reaching Ragendorf four days later. Here the eight Hessian sappers, working 'practically unaided', established a bridge 'in record time' over the Kleine Donau on to the Kleine Schütt island.[65] GB Hippolyte de Rosnyvinen, Comte de Piré's Brigade and the Hessians used this bridge to occupy the island, moving to Frauendorf on the 12th and Hedervar the following day. On the 14th, as the Battle of Raab was being fought, the Hessians marched for Halaszi, where the two companies of 1st Leib Fusiliers were left to guard the bridge while Lasalle himself took the Schützen and Garde Fusiliers to Raab with GB Pierre Bruyères' Brigade. When the Hessians arrived before Raab's walls on the 16th, the siege of the little fortress was already in progress. Gall's men were assigned the western sector of the siege lines between the Raab and Rabnitz Rivers, remaining in place through the successful conclusion of the operation on 22 June.[66]

With the fall of Raab, the Emperor called every available man to Vienna. The Hessians thus set out for Halaszi early the next day, united with the Leib Fusiliers there and continued north, attaining Lobau Island on 4 July and rejoining their respective *brigades* in Carra Saint-Cyr's Division. On the road north, they encountered the two fusilier companies that had been detached to Ybbs, Wallsee and Melk back in May.[67] Although their sojourn in these towns had been uneventful, the Hessians took part in a small skirmish at Wolfsthal on the night of 20/21 June as they were marching to find their battalions. The Austrians at Pressburg had sent a raiding party across the Danube that evening to harass the French on the right bank. Hearing the firing, the Hessian commander, Hauptmann Merk, rousted his men out of bed on his own initiative and marched toward the crackling musketry. Attacking with the bayonet in the darkness, the Hessians took 150 prisoners and helped drive off the Austrian raiders, earning the respect of the French officers for their timely intervention and display of initiative.[68]

As they parted from Davout and Lasalle in late June, von Gall's men received warm praise for their performance between Pressburg and Raab. The Marshal had been impressed by the 'zeal and exactitude' displayed by the Hessians in their 'daily service' and the gallant Lasalle had come to regard the fusiliers as his 'children'. He was sorry indeed to lose his 'indefatigable Hessians'.[69]

The Chevauxlegers also spent the month of June in Hungary. Departing Lobau on 25 May with the rest of Marulaz's troopers, the regiment was brigaded with the Baden Light Dragoons and spent several days at Deutsch-Altenburg, patrolling the Danube upstream to Fischamend. With the advance of the Army of Italy, however, the cavalry was shifted progressively farther south, moving to Guntramsdorf on 3 June, through Bruck (9th) to the Raab River (15th) and finally pushing deep into Hungary in pursuit of the retreating GM Mesko. Unable to snare the elusive Austrian general, Marulaz took his men to Veszprim on the 22nd but headed back north the next day as the army began to gather on Lobau. The Hessian cavalrymen returned to that crowded island on 4 July, bivouacking under the terrifying thunderstorm that preceded the Battle of Wagram.[70]

JULY - WAGRAM AND ZNAIM

By the late afternoon of 4 July, the entire Hessian contingent was thus united under Massena's control for the coming struggle. Before their combat with the Austrians, however, the Hessians had to endure an assault from the elements as a savage thunderstorm and more than 100 French guns combined to rend the darkness. Throughout the dreadful night of 4/5 July, the men, some knee-deep in water, waited for the order to cross on to the Marchfeld, their ears battered by the rolling thunder and the incessant pounding of the French bombardment, their vision seared by muzzle blasts and lightning bolts.[71] Except for the flashes of gun and nature, the night was utterly black and the rain came down in buckets.

Under the cover of this cataclysmic storm, Napoleon launched his army on to the Marchfeld and, by 6 a.m., Carra Saint-Cyr's soldiers were across the Stadtler Arm of the Danube, forming south of Gross-Enzersdorf with the rest of IV Corps. Some hours passed before the Emperor felt he had enough force to advance, but slowly his great armament began to roll forward, pushing Austrian advanced troops out of the way as it made room for the thousands of men still pouring over from Lobau. It was an unparalleled military spectacle, battalion after battalion marching over the bright green fields in close column, guns and brilliantly plumed light cavalry in the van, the clear dawn light glinting on 150,000 bayonets and sabres. 'It was an extraordinarily beautiful sight,' wrote General von Nagel.[72]

Massena, on the army's left, had his first objective in Gross-Enzersdorf and sent the 46th Ligne to storm the village at about 10 a.m. while the Hessian Brigade took position between the town and the Stadtler Arm. A pause of about two hours now ensued as more French units were pushed into line, but the grand advance resumed about noon, IV Corps heading in the general direction of Leopoldau, clearing the army's flank along the Danube as it progressed. After the violent overture to the passage, the tense excitement of the crossing at dawn and the martial splendour of the army in motion, the remainder of 5 July was something of an anticlimax for Massena's men. Led by the artillery and some light horse, the corps moved west at a stately pace, the guns occasionally unlimbering to encourage the Austrian covering force's withdrawal.[73] Most of Carra Saint-Cyr's Division (his three French regiments, the Hessian Garde Fusiliers and combined Schützen) pushed on toward Leopoldau where they spent the night behind the cavalry screen; the other five Hessian battalions, minus their Schützen, slid slightly to the right and bivouacked just west of Breitenlee in advance of Molitor's men. The Hessian gunners suffered a few casualties from Austrian skirmishers early in the day, but the infantry saw no action and took no losses. The soldiers' principal complaints were the oppressive heat and resultant thirst. The artillerymen even resorted to drinking the rainwater that had gathered in the hollows of their gun carriages.[75]

The Hessian Chevauxlegers had also crossed on to the Marchfeld in the early morning hours of 5 July. Initially posted north-east of Gross-Enzersdorf, the regiment was sent towards the Danube with the Baden Light Dragoons and the 14th Chasseurs in the early afternoon. Under the orders of the latter's commander, Chef d'Escadron Antoine Latour-Foissac, the little brigade got itself into a scrap north of Aspern, but the French and Badeners conducted the swordplay and the Hessians remained slightly to the rear in support, providing a firm rallying point for their allies. Retired behind the infantry after this engagement, the troopers saw no more action on the first day of Wagram, rejoining their division near Leopoldau in the evening and camping there for night. Where his Baden comrade had experienced a hard day indeed, von Münchingen, now an Oberstlieutenant, had no casualties to report.[76]

WAGRAM, THE SECOND DAY (6 JULY)

If the first day of Wagram cost the Hessians only a few wounded, the second was a much more expensive proposition. During the night, Massena had received orders to leave Boudet along the Danube and close up on the army's centre at daybreak, assuming a position south-east of Aderklaa behind Bernadotte's Saxon Corps. When IV Corps reached its assigned place in the line of battle, however, Massena found that the Saxons had evacuated Aderklaa around dawn and that the Austrians were now in happy possession of the village. It was about 7:30 a.m.. Napoleon rode up, learned to his astonishment and disgust that Bernadotte had abandoned this crucial strongpoint to the enemy without a fight, and immediately ordered Massena to retake it, supported on the right by IX Corps. The Marshal had arrayed his three divisions in echelon formation with Molitor on the right, Legrand on the left and Carra Saint-Cyr in the centre directly opposite Aderklaa. The execution of the attack thus fell to the 2nd Division and its commander began looking for ways to take the strong Austrian position in the flank. In Massena's eyes, however, there was no time to lose and his subordinate's considerations smacked of delay. Once more the fiery Massena of Rivoli, he had his carriage driven forward amidst Carra Saint-Cyr's battalions and told the general, 'Enter the village, my friend, and slaughter those vermin!' Within moments, the 24th Léger and 4th Ligne were plunging toward the village with great shouts of 'Vive l'Empereur' issuing from every throat.[77]

The Hessians stood on the right of the division in closed battalion columns with artillery and skirmishers deployed in front: the Garde Fusiliers were placed on the extreme right of the line, the Leib Fusiliers to their left, then the Leib-Garde Regiment, and finally the Leib Regiment on the brigade's left flank.[78] Directed to support the two French regiments, they set off with parade ground precision, artillery in the lead, banners glowing in the sharp morning light. About half-way to the village, the guns unlimbered adjacent to the Saxon batteries and resumed a steady bombardment. Firing poorly manufactured Austrian ammunition, the gunners, sweating and cursing, had to use a tool called a 'worm' to clear the gun barrels of cartridge remnants after every third shot or so.[79]

It was now the infantry's turn to surge forward and the insistent rumble of drums sent the Hessian foot soldiers ahead into a storm of canister and musket balls. The disciplined battalions appeared irresistible, advancing in perfect order with great élan, accompanied by repeated cries of 'Vorwärts! Avancez!' Uneven terrain disordered the ranks, but spirits were high and the left-most battalion of the Hessian Brigade (II/Leib) was soon pushing its way into the eastern portion of Aderklaa with the Schützen. The remaining battalions, continuing their advance beyond the town, again found the ground cut up by ditches, dams and bogs, delaying their progress, skewing their alignment and cohesion. Order was soon lost and the attack proceeded by clumps and bunches in the face of a formed enemy. Casualties had not yet been too heavy, but the Austrians were recovering from their initial shock, their fire increased and the advance halted. Flanks exposed and lacking artillery and cavalry support, the Hessians stood their ground and attempted to reply to the Austrian fire, engaging in a brutal firefight with the superior Habsburg force at 80 to 100 paces. Losses mounted. Within minutes, seven officers and rows of men from the Leib Fusiliers were down. Individual cannon balls tore through five or six men in the tight masses; a lone shell killed or wounded thirteen in II/Leib. The troops wavered. Remaining officers strove to retain control, but the Austrians now moved to counter-attack and the disordered Hessian battalions broke, streaming back across the difficult ground to join the ruins of the 24th Léger and 4th Ligne in a confused mass of fugitives south-east of Aderklaa.

The Austrian attack threw II/Leib back into the eastern houses of the village where it was caught in a terrible crossfire between friend and foe. In vicious hand-to-hand fighting reminiscent of Aspern, the battalion suffered cruelly: Major von Scharnhorst fell mortally wounded protecting a flag, two other officers were killed and five wounded, leaving only one officer in the battalion untouched. Among the wounded was Hauptmann Raabe, who escaped the death trap with bayonet wounds in the chest and arm and two blows to the head from musket butts. As the Austrians overwhelmed the desperate Hessian defence, the battalion's two standard bearers, Kempf and Bornemann, struggled to rescue their precious flags. Kempf was captured but managed to free himself and hid in a dovecote until he could make his way back to his comrades. Bornemann courageously defended his charge, refusing to surrender and finally falling with his head crushed by a butt stroke. The Austrians cut off his hand to seize the flag he still tightly gripped.[80]

In the short time between about 7.30 and 9 a.m., Carra Saint-Cyr's Division had been mangled. As he rallied his men on the low heights east of Raasdorf, a mere 1,000 Frenchmen and 500 Hessians were still with their colours.[81] Saint-Cyr personally ordered von Nagel to move still farther to the rear and gather every member of the division he could find; during the afternoon and evening, the Hessian general collected some 400 of his countrymen and about an equal number of French which he led back into the ranks the following morning.[82] These losses notwithstanding, in the late morning of 6 July, with the sun basting man and beast, there still remained a battle to win. Napoleon was hardly non-plussed by the discomfiture of one division and he now sent Massena on his famous flank march, telling the Marshal's astounded aide to 'Ride and tell Massena that he will attack and that the battle is won'[83] The remaining Hessians accomplished this movement from Raasdorf through Essling to Aspern and west with the other units of IV Corps, suffering some casualties from Austrian artillery but engaging in no further combat that day. As the sun sank and Archduke Charles's army slipped away into the night, the men of Hesse collapsed to the earth near Leopoldau in utter exhaustion. Most were asleep as soon as they hit the ground and at least two fusiliers died in their instant slumber when Austrian cannon balls crashed amongst the thinned and weary ranks.[84]

The brief combat at Aderklaa had cost the Hessian Brigade dear, the infantry units losing a total of 739 dead, wounded and prisoners from an overall strength that was well below ideal when they entered the battle.[85] As at Aspern, the Leib *Brigade* was hit hardest. Its losses alone accounted for approximately 68 per cent of the Hessian infantrymen killed, maimed or missing in the fearful fight. Indeed, the toll exacted from II/Leib was so heavy that Oberst Beck, the *brigade* commander, ordered its companies amalgamated into the 1st Battalion. GB Schiner, however, would not hear of this and countermanded the directive, stating that the battalion could be proud of 'its small number of remaining heroes'.[86] The artillery mourned the loss of six men dead and nineteen wounded; five of its six pieces had been put out of action by Austrian fire in the course of the day.[87]

The Hessian horsemen were also in action on the 6th. During the IV Corps' morning march toward Aderklaa, the regiment took part in Marulaz's attack on an Austrian battery west of the town, losing 20 men captured and several wounded when Habsburg cavalry countercharged. One Hessian cavalryman was lucky to escape with his life. Seized by Austrian dragoons, the appropriately named trooper Georg Hufnagel ('horseshoe nail') thought he saw an opportunity and attempted to escape. Instantly surrounded by foemen, he fought desperately until his sabre was broken and both he and his horse were wounded. His opponents, embittered by his violent resistance, were about to put an end to his obstreperous existence when he was recognized by an Austrian officer. The officer had previously served in the Garde Chevauxlegers and promptly announced that he would personally deal with anyone who touched the overjoyed Hessian.[88] Most of Hufnagel's compatriots evaded the Austrian cavalry, however, and spent the greater part of the day with their division on Massena's left flank. As the afternoon became evening, the Chevauxlegers probably charged the enemy's withdrawing right wing about Leopoldau with Lasalle and

Marulaz, but apparently came through these final attacks unscathed. They bivouacked near Leopoldau having lost one officer and 24 men in the day's fighting.

PURSUIT TO ZNAIM (7-11 JULY)

The Garde Chevauxlegers rode toward Korneuburg with the corps' other light cavalry regiments on 7 July, but were relegated to covering an artillery battery and took no part in the combat. The following morning, the weak regiment formed the corps' advance guard with the Baden Light Dragoons and the 24th Chasseurs. Reaching Stockerau, these three regiments were sent to attack some Austrian hussars on the heights above the town, but the enemy was reinforced and the charge repulsed. The Allied cavalry pelted back down the slopes and was only saved from further injury by the cool intervention of the Baden Jägers. It was the Chevauxlegers' last fight. When von Münchingen rallied the remains of his 'regiment', he counted only 40 mounted men and was granted permission to remain in Stockerau to collect his scattered troopers and locate remounts. The Hessian troopers spent several days in the town, but the armistice was signed before von Münchingen and his men could rejoin their corps and they entered their bivouac near Znaim without drawing their sabres in anger again.[89]

The cavalry and Legrand's Division led Massena's columns in the pursuit toward Znaim, Carra Saint-Cyr's men following slowly behind as Napoleon attempted to determine the exact directions of Charles's retreat. The Hessians thus only marched to Lang Enzersdorf on the 7th and Korneuburg on the 8th, as the Emperor was still unsure of Austrian movements. In the face of skillfully conducted Austrian rearguard actions and concerns about a possible threat out of Bohemia, IV Corps pressed north, Carra Saint-Cyr's Division camping just beyond Göllersdorf on 9 July and reaching Schöngraben the following noon. Here the Hessian gunners threw a few shells at the withdrawing white-coats, but the division was not otherwise engaged and merely marched ahead in the wake of Legrand's men as night came on. The Hessians slept in the open north of Guntersdorf under a drenching rain.

That night, Massena received a letter from Berthier urging him to move on Znaim and assist Marmont who was engaged with what appeared to be the Austrian rear guard (but was in fact Charles's main army).[90] The Marshal put his men on the road early the next morning but Carra Saint-Cyr, third in the line of march after Legrand and the cavalry, did not reach the heights above the Thaya until about 2 p.m.. As they moved into position near Oblass on the right bank of the river, the battle was raging and the Hessians had an excellent view of the bitter struggle; from Legrand's advancing skirmishers on the left to Marmont's divisions on the right, the scene presented an awesome spectacle of blood and gunfire under the lowering clouds. The division remained south of the Thaya until late afternoon when Legrand's thunderstorm débâcle caused Massena to commit his reserve. Carra Saint-Cyr's three French regiments were sent across the stream at about 4 p.m. on Legrand's right and three Hessians battalions followed about one hour later. Directed to occupy Tesswitz and establish contact with Marmont's Corps, the two fusilier battalions, I/Garde and the combined Schützen made their way over the Thaya on ladders and planks. Quickly moving through the village, they launched a sudden, 'well-conducted attack'[91] against the Austrians in the vineyards to the north-west, 'earning themselves the universal admiration of the French generals' according to Nagel's report. Although their attempt to continue on towards Znaim itself was checked, they were preparing to try again when the surprising news of the ceasefire put an end to the day's fighting. Their brief intervention in the combat had cost only eight men wounded.[92]

The Hessians remained on Austrian soil for five more months, periodically changing the site of their encampment according to the dictates of the political—strategic situation. They received good rations, constructed comfortable huts for themselves and were well regarded by the French: 'Ludwig's birthday on 25 August was also celebrated festively. General Desaix, who had replaced Carra Saint-Cyr on 2 August, invited all the commanders to a banquet and offered a toast to the Grand Duke, the good ally.'[93] Napoleon was generous with decorations and his officers followed his example, 'expressing their satisfaction with the performance and attitude of the Hessian troops freely and frequently'.[94] Despite the praise and provender, the men yearned to return to their hearths and there was great rejoicing when the earnestly desired order to march came in late December. The entire brigade made a grand entry into gaily decorated Darmstadt on 21 January 1810 and passed in review before their sovereign and an excited throng of citizens.[95] It was a well-deserved homecoming for a contingent that had suffered 344 dead, 983 wounded and 137 missing, approximately one-third of its original strength, in the course of a gruelling campaign.[96] Rated by some as the best of the Rheinbund infantry, the Hessians had been praised by French commanders from Napoleon down, but perhaps no accolades were worth more than those of the Iron Marshal, who told his Emperor that France 'could not be better served than by these troops'.[97]

NOTES

1: The 3rd Nassau Battalion was also present.

2: Lt. Colonel Sauzey, *Les Soldats de Hesse et de Nassau*, volume VI of *Les Allemands sous les Aigles Françaises*, Paris: Terana, 1988, pg. 42. At this time, the Hessians were assigned to GD Rouyer's Division of Lefebvre's X Corps; in 1809, Rouyer would command a combined division consisting of the contingents from numerous Rheinbund principalities (see Chapter 8).

3: Quotes from *Correspondence*, 14544, 10 December 1808 ('detestable') and the 17th *Bulletin of the Army of Spain* quoted in Sauzey, *Hesse*, pg. 162.

4: *Correspondence*, 14719, 15 January 1809.

5: Sauzey, vol. VI, pp. 61-62 and Koch, vol. VI, pp. 48-9.

6: W. von Bigge, *Geschichte des Infanterie-Regiments Kaiser Wilhelm (2. Grossherzoglich Hessisches) Nr. 116*, Berlin: Mittler & Sohn, 1903, pg. 102. Other authors, forgetting the train troops, list only 4,700 men. See Carl Röder von Diersburg, *Geschichte des 1. Grossherzoglich Hessischen Infanterie- (Leibgarde-) Regiments Nr. 115*, Fritz Beck, ed., Berlin: Mittler & Sohn, 1899, pp. 145; and Ludwig Kattrein, *Ein Jahrhundert deutscher Truppengeschichte dargestellt durch derjenigen des Grossh. Hessischen Kontingents*, Darmstadt: Schlapp, 1907, pg. 20. Above and beyond the line infantry, Johnson (pg. 74) and Sapherson (pg. 39) mention four garrison battalions which remained behind in Hesse during the war.

7: The French viewed the Hessian *brigades* as regiments composed of two line battalions and a light battalion (Bigge, pg. 102). For the purposes of this book, the term *'brigade'* is italicized to indicate the Hessian usage.

8: Given the peculiar Hessian organization, their use of the term *'brigade'* and their convoluted unit names, it is easy to see how contemporaneous French staff officers and subsequent historians could lose their way in the

Hessian 'ordre de bataille'. The picture is further muddled by the fate of the Gross- und Erbprinz-Brigade. En route to Spain, this unit was completely reorganized along French lines into a regiment of two battalions, each of six companies. This was accomplished by distributing the fusiliers amongst the two musketeer battalions, but had the negative result of hopelessly intermingling green and blue uniforms when the Hessians were formed for inspection.

9: Fritz Beck, Karl von Hahn and Heinrich von Hahn, *Geschichte des Grossherzoglichen Artilleriekorps 1. Grossherzoglich Hessischen Feldartillerie-Regiments Nr. 25 und seiner Stämme*, Berlin: Mittler & Sohn, 1912, pg. 161.

10: The Garde du Corps wore a decidedly Fredrickian heavy cavalry uniform of buff and red. The Landdragoner, all 96 of them, had dark-green uniforms like the chevauxlegers but with red distinctions. See Fritz Beck, *Geschichte des Grossherzoglich Hessischen Gendarmeriekorps 1762-1905*, Darmstadt: Hohmann, 1905, pp. 31-40, 145-6.

11: These comments on tactical reforms, of course, do not apply to the Gross- und Erbprinz Brigade which, as mentioned above, had undergone a major reorganization prior to its deployment to Spain. See Bigge, pp. 100, 102; Diersburg/Beck, pp. 140-1; and A. Keim, *Geschichte des Infanterie- Leibregiments Grossherzogin (3. Grossherzoglich Hessisches) Nr. 117*, Berlin: Bath, 1903, pg. 186. For Hessian competency with French drill, see Note 27 below.

12: This is not to say that every trooper could or did find satisfactory work; many lived in absolute penury when not actually in uniform.

13: In contrast, the exigencies of the war in Spain forced the Baden contingent to detach more than 600 veterans and incorporate a host of raw conscripts just before the initiation of hostilities.

14: Beck, *Artilleriekorps*, pg. 161. Selected soldiers were also recalled as needed to perform important tasks such as the fabrication of ammunition (Bigge, pg. 100).

15: Diersburg/Beck, pg. 141; E. Caspary, *Geschichte des dritten Grossherzoglich Hessischen Infanterie-Regiments (Leib-Regiment) Nr. 117*, Darmstadt: Lange, 1877, pg. 36.

16: Caspary, pg. 37. The Leib-Garde numbered 2,141 (2,046 combatants) and the Leib *Brigade* 2,095 (2,003 combatants) when they set out for the campaign (communication from Dr. Diether Degrief of the Hessisches Staatsarchiv and Diersburg/Beck, pg. 145).

17: Ludwig complained 'with bitterness' in a mid-March letter to Massena; the Marshal promised to raise the matter to the Emperor but advised the Grand Duke that Napoleon was unlikely to change the arrangement (Koch, vol. VI, pp. 49-50).

18: Diersburg/Beck, pp. 146-147; Bigge, pp. 103-4.

19: Massena has been subjected to considerable condemnation for not pressing Hiller's detachment in the final days of April, however, he was well in advance of the rest of the army, in the dark regarding much of the general situation, and communications from Berthier led him to believe he would not be supported before several days had elapsed. See, for example, Binder von Kriegelstein, vol. II, pp. 50-3; *Krieg 1809*, vol. III, pp. 157-61; Petre, pg. 222.

20: See Chapter 4.

21: Wrede's Bavarian and Molitor's French infantry divisions, Jacquinot's Brigade of light cavalry, and Marulaz's cavalry minus the Baden Light Dragoons and the 14th Chasseurs. See also Chapter 2.

22: Karl von Zimmermann, *Geschichte des 1. Grossherzoglich Hessischen Dragoner-Regiments (Garde-Dragoner-Regiments) Nr. 23*, I. Theil, Darmstadt: Bergsträsser, 1878, pg. 138. The Austrian official history, however, does not mention any attacks on the Hessians during the night of 22/23 April.

23: See Chapter 2 for details of the Battle of Neumarkt.

24: The actions of the Chevauxlegers Regiment from 22 to 30 April are drawn from *Krieg 1809*, vol. III, pp. 8-13, 35, 120, 247-8; *Journal historique des opérations militaires de la division de cavalerie légère du général Marulaz*, Saski, vol. II, pp. 358-9, 368-9; and Zimmermann, pp. 138-40.

25: See Chapters 3 and 4.

26: *Krieg 1809*, vol. III, pp. 265, 271, 316; Saski, vol. III, pp. 108, 113; Zimmermann, pp. 140-1.

27: Hessian accounts generally refer to this action as Annaberg, the name of a tiny hamlet about 700 metres south-west of Strassham on the ridge. See Bigge, pg. 104; Diersburg/Beck, pg. 148; *Krieg 1809*, vol. III, pp. 307-15; as well as Chapters 4 and 5 of this work. The preceeding histories only mention 'a few prisoners'; a contemporary account, however, lists the number of captives as 150 (*Theilnahme der Grossherz. Hess. Truppen an dem Kriege zwischen Oestreich und Frankreich im Jahre 1809*, (written in October 1809), Darmstadt: Auw, 1850, pg. 7). Kattrein (pg. 21) claims the Hessian artillery pursued the enemy with fire, but the artillery unit history (pg. 163) states that the rapid retreat of the Austrians gave the Hessians no chance to shoot.

28: These exercises were carried out using the French drill instructions and orders given in French by one of Napoleon's adjutants, Mouton, had to be translated by Nagel and the battalion commanders. The troops were only vaguely familiar with French drill, however, and the required movements and manoeuvres were carried out in a rather clumsy fashion. See Bigge, pg. 105; Diersburg/Beck, pg. 149.

29: The towns of Ybbs and Wallsee each received a Hessian garrison of one company and one gun. In addition, as noted in Chapters 3 and 4, the force at Wallsee included a detachment of Württemberg *Leib-Chevauxlegers* and a detachment of Baden Light Dragoons accompanied the Hessians to Ybbs. Above and beyond these detachments, Bigge states that 50 Hessians were sent to garrison Melk. See Beck, *Artilleriekorps*, pg. 163; Bigge, pg. 105; Hauptmann Klingelhöffer, *Geschichte des 2. Grossherzoglich Hessischen Infanterie-Regiments (Grossherzog) Nr. 116*, Berlin: Mittler & Sohn, 1888, pg. 21; *Krieg 1809*, vol. III, pg. 485.

30: During the campaign in southern Bavaria and the subsequent advance on Vienna, the cavalry had often been called upon to travel 6-8 hours at the trot. Small wonder the regiment was so reduced! In addition, the Hessian chevauxlegers, like the Baden and Württemberg regiments, were valued for their ability to speak German and were thus the preferred source of manpower for scouting, detached missions and courier duty. *Krieg 1809*, vol. IV, pg. 684; *Theilnahme*, pg. 6; Zimmermann, pg. 142.

31: Gachot, vol. VI, pg. 226. The quarters appear to have been very tight indeed: one account claims as many as 70-80 soldiers were housed in some of the buildings (Diersburg/Beck, pg. 150).

32: Gall's detachment thus included all four companies of the Leib-Garde Fusiliers, two companies of the 1st Leib Fusiliers (the other two plus a detachment of 50 men had not yet returned to their battalion from Ybbs and Wallsee), and the Schützen of the two Leib-Garde musketeer battalions. The Schützen were provided to make up for the companies absent at Wallsee and Ybbs. According to Keim (pg. 188), Klingelhöffer (pg. 21) and *Krieg 1809* (vol. III, pg. 634), only the Schützen of the Lieb-Garde took part in this expedition — about 80 men; Bigge, however, claims (pg. 106) that the Schützen of all four musketeer battalions joined Montbrun at Bruck. See Saski, vol. III, for Napoleon's order directing the detachment of the Hessian fusiliers (pp. 283) and Montbrun's report of their arrival (pg, 290).

33: *Krieg 1809*, vol. IV, pp. 377-8, 416-17.

34: *Krieg 1809*, vol. IV, pp. 417-18, 424-6. Casualties in this mounted skirmishing were slight, but the Hessians lost a fine junior officer when Oberlieutenant Breidenbach, who had so ably commanded the outposts in April, was mortally wounded.

35: *Journal Marulaz*, Saski, vol. III, pg. 346.

36: *Krieg 1809*, vol. IV, pp. 462-70, 485-9.

37: In the 5 p.m. charge, the 23rd Chasseurs were apparently off to the right rear of the division providing flank security. Only about half of the Baden regiment took part in the 5 p.m. attack and the regiment had been retired to Napoleon's guard by the time the second charge occurred (see Chapter 4).

38: Forced to consider threats from two directions, Schiner made the even numbered platoons orient left towards Aspern while the odd numbered platoons continued to face forward (north).

39: *Krieg 1809*, vol. IV, pg. 525.

40: This attack occurred between 7 a.m. and 10 a.m., probably close to 9; the exact time cannot be determined.

41: Keim, pg. 188; *Krieg 1809*, vol. IV, pp. 562-9. Drawn primarily from Nagel's and Scharnhorst's reports; Keim's account of the Hessians in the Battle of Aspern is particularly valuable (although it must be balanced with other reportage). The incredibly detailed description of the battle in the fourth volume of *Krieg 1809* was compiled from close study of all available French and Austrian sources as well as participants' reports and letters in the Baden and Hessian state archives.

42: *Krieg 1809*, vol. IV, pg. 568.

43: Keim, pp. 188-189.

44: Walz's rescuers, Leutnant von Lesch and a band of sturdy Schützen, captured 45 Austrians as they cleared the stone building (Keim, pp. 188-9).

45: Quoted in Keim, pp. 189-90. Scharnhorst also maintained that his battalion was the only unit defending Aspern around noon on the 22nd; this is not confirmed by French or Austrian sources and is most likely an honest mistake arising from his preoccupation with his battalion's intense fight and the impossibility of a single participant gaining an overall impression of the tangled struggle.

46: *Krieg 1809*, vol. IV, pp. 574-81 (quote on pp. 579-80).

47: Indicative of Massena's aggressive spirit, the initial orders to Weber's detachment were to *attack* Aspern, but before the Hauptmann could set off on, Carra Saint-Cyr appeared and informed him the mission had been changed; Napoleon had learned that the bridges over the Danube had been broken yet again and, as no reinforcements would be forthcoming, he directed that all offensive activity be curtailed. Weber thus deployed 200 of his men in a skirmish line (the remaining 200 were probably kept formed to support the skirmishers) and held the Austrians in check by a vigorous musketry until ordered to retire. *Krieg 1809*, vol. IV, pg. 640.

48: Struggling through the mass of confusion at the bridge to the island, the Hessians finally reached their assigned bivouac area on Lobau sometime after midnight. Diersburg/Beck, pg. 154; Caspary, pg. 39; Keim, pp. 190-192; *Krieg 1809*, vol. IV, pp. 630-640, 645. Quote from the anonymous author of 'Feldzug der 2ten Division 4ten Armeecorps der Armee von Teutschland im Jahr 1809', *Pallas*, Jahrgang 2, Stück 6, 1810, pg. 626.

49: *Artilleriekorps*, pg. 164. When Carra Saint-Cyr's guns were moved back for the second time during the morning, the howitzers were placed even further to the rear and took no further part in the battle.

50:    *Krieg 1809*, vol. IV, pp. 535, 617, and Beilagen 8-12; Zimmermann, pp. 143-5.

51:    It should be noted, however, that the Garde Chevauxlegers had 52 horses killed, resulting in a $1/3$ reduction of the regiment's mounted combat power. The artillery's losses totalled only two horses dead.

52:    These figures, taken from *Krieg 1809*, vol. IV, pg. 697, represent the initial assessment of the brigade's losses and do not include the lightly wounded who might be expected to return to duty in a week or two. None the less, the regiments would fight the rest of the campaign without most of these men. When the war was over and prisoners had been exchanged, the number of actual 'blood casualties' proved to be considerably less: Leib-Garde had thirteen dead, 150 wounded, four still missing; Leib had suffered eighteen dead, 107 wounded and 38 still missing. See also Diersburg/Beck, pg. 153; Caspary, pg. 39; Keim, pp. 191-2.

53:    'These are good men'; quoted in Diersburg/Beck, pg. 155.

54:    *Theilnahme*, pp. 13-14. Walz's health broke during the retreat from Russia; unable to continue, he explained to his lieutenant that 'the Russians should not take an old soldier like me alive' and shot himself (Keim, pg. 189).

55:    Keim, pg. 192. See also eyewitness comments in 'Feldzug der 2ten Division 4ten Armeecorps der Armee von Teutschland im Jahr 1809', pg. 627.

56:    See, for example, Diersburg/Beck, pp. 154-5. Quote from 'Feldzug der 2ten Division 4ten Armeecorps der Armee von Teutschland im Jahr 1809', pg. 628.

57:    Buat, vol. II, pp. 36-37. Gudin only had three of his five regiments (12th, 21st and 85th Ligne); the other two (7th Léger and 25th Ligne) were left at Fischamend.

58:    Louis Nicolas Davout, *Correspondence du Maréchal Davout*, Charles de Mazade, ed., Paris: Plon, 1885, No. 750. Casualty figures from Diersburg/Beck, pg. 156. From the Austrian commander, GM Friedrich Freiherr von Bianchi, comes the praise for the Hessians' 'speed and determination', see his *Vertheidigung des Brückenkopfes vor Pressburg, im Jahre 1809*, Pressburg 1811, pg. 10.

59:    Bigge, pg. 107.

60:    *Theilnahme*, pg. 16.

61:    The French captured more than 400 prisoners in this attack.

62:    Description of the Combat at Engerau assembled from the following sources: Bianchi, Bigge, pp. 107-9; Buat, vol. II, pg. 37; Diersburg/Beck, pp. 156-7; Hellwald, vol. II, pp. 87-90; Keim, pg. 194; Klingelhöffer, pg. 22; *Theilnahme*, pp. 16-19, Welden, pp. 60-1. Casualty figures from Bigge and Diersburg/Beck.

63:    Davout, No. 751, 3 June 1809.

64:    16th Bulletin quoted in Sauzey, vol. VI, pg. 70; Lasalle's letter quoted in Bigge, pg. 109.

65:    F. G. Hourtoulle, *Le Général Comte Charles Lasalle 1775-1809*, Paris: Copernic, 1979, pg. 241.

66:    The Hessians thus held the so-called 'Vienna Suburb' of Raab, covering the main gate into the fortress town; GB Bruyères' men (13th and 24th Chasseurs) apparently occupied the 'Szighet Suburb' between the Rabnitz and the Kleine Donau. GB Piré's Brigade (8th Hussars and 16th Chasseurs) remained on the Kleine Schütt and does not seem to have included any Hessians during the actual siege. See Bigge, pp. 109-11; Diersburg/Beck, pp. 157-1; Vaudoncourt, vol. I, pp. 373-4, 383-5.

67:    Two companies (Dupuis and Merk) of the 1st Leib Fusiliers and 50 men from Gödecke's Company of that battalion.

68:    Bigge, pg. 111; Klingelhöffer, pg. 23; *Theilnahme*, pp. 19-20.

69:    Davout, No. 797, 23 June 1809. For Lasalle's paternal regard for the Hessian battalions see Hourtoulle, pg. 240; his comment about his 'infatigables Hessois' is from a report to Davout, 18 June 1809, quoted in Buat, vol. II, pg. 51.

70:    Marulaz cited in Buat, vol. II, pg. 6; Zimmermann, pp. 145-6. See also Chapter 4.

71:    *Artilleriekorps*, pg. 165.

72:    From Nagel's report to Ludwig, quoted in Diersburg/Beck, pg. 159.

73:    The artillery fired slowly in the main, at ranges of from 1,200 to 1,600 paces using ricochet fire 'because the enemy did not stand firm and evacuated almost every village without a fight' (*Artilleriekorps*, pg. 166).

74:    The Schützen of all six battalions had again been formed into a combined unit (Bigge, pg. 111).

75:    *Artilleriekorps*, pg. 166.

76:    This résumé of the chevauxlegers' peregrinations on 5 July is assembled from Binder von Kriegelstein, vol. II, pg. 322; Rau, pp. 26-8; *Theilnahme*, pg. 21; Zimmermann, pg. 146; and Marulaz's report cited in Koch, vol. VI, pp. 433-4. Curiously, Zimmermann claims the Hessians twice crossed blades with the Austrian *Hessen-Homburg* Hussars; that regiment, however, was busily engaged with Davout's troopers on the Austrian left (Heller, vol. II). Rau's description of the enemy as *Kienmaier* Hussars seems more reasonable. Rau gives the Hessian regiment's strength as 250 on 5 July; Hessian writings do not give a figure, but Rau's seems rather high. Bowden and Tarbox are clearly mistaken when they list the regiment with four squadrons (sic) and 348 men, in other words, at full strength (pg. 189). See also Chapter 4.

77:    Gachot, vol. VI, pg. 265. The Marshal had been thrown from his horse several days earlier; the resultant injuries prevented him from mounting and at Wagram he commanded his troops from a calèche drawn by a team of white horses.

78:    Bigge cites this order of battle, where the fusiliers went into battle apart from their *brigades*, as an indication of the relative independence enjoyed by the fusilier battalions (pg. 113).

79: *Artilleriekorps*, pg. 167.

80: The Hessian role in the fight for Aderklaa assembled from the following sources: *Abriss der Grossherzoglich Hessischen Kriegs- und Truppen-Geschichte 1567-1871*, Darmstadt: Zernin, 1886, pg. 50; *Artilleriekorps*, pg. 166; Bigge, pp. 112-14; Binder von Kriegelstein, vol. II, pp. 345-6; Buat, vol. II, pp. 245-50; Caspary, pp. 39-40; Diersburg/Beck, pp. 159-60; Keim, pp. 194-6; *Theilnahme*, pp. 22-3. Kattrein is mistaken when he places the Hessian attack <u>south</u> of Aderklaa (pp. 28-9).

81: Bigge, pg. 114; Diersburg/Beck, pg. 160; Keim, pg. 196.

82: Diersburg/Beck, pg. 161.

83: Binder von Kriegelstein, vol. II, pg. 352.

84: Bigge, pg. 114.

85: Infantry casualty figures are from the official Hessian account of the action, kindly provided by Dr. Diether Degrief of the Hessisches Staatsarchiv; they are in general agreement with those in Buat (vol. II, pg. 308), Diersburg/Beck, Caspary and Keim. Information on the strength of the Hessian Brigade at Wagram is very sketchy, there being no pre-battle strength report in the Hessian archives. According to Keim (pg. 197), the Leib *Brigade's* two musketeer battalions together numbered between 650 and 700 men while the 1st Leib Fusiliers counted only some 400 in its ranks before the battle, for a total *brigade* strength of no more than 1,100. If Keim is correct, the assumption of analogous figures for the Leib-Garde *Brigade* would put the latter's strength at a mere 1,300-1,400, yielding a 5 July total of only 2,400-2,500 infantrymen for the entire contingent.

86: Quote from Keim, pg. 197. The dead also included Oberstlieutenant Bechtold, the brigade's chief of staff.

87: *Artilleriekorps*, pg. 167.

88: Hufnagel recovered from his wound and served in his regiment until 1830 (Zimmermann, pg. 147).

89: Rau, pp. 172-4; and Zimmermann, pg. 148 (Zimmermann mistakenly gives 9 July as the date for this skirmish). Binder von Kriegelstein (vol. II, pg. 387) indicates that the Hessian cavalry was intended to accompany Colonel Ameil and the Badeners toward Krems but their grave weakness made participation in the expedition impossible. Note that the regiment seems to have suffered most from a lack of suitable horseflesh as its human casualties for the campaign were not that high. Losses totalled about 70 men and 180 horses for the entire war.

90: Quoted in Buat, vol. II, pg. 343.

91: Binder von Kriegelstein, vol. II, pg. 413.

92: Bigge, pp. 115-16; Bornemann, pp. 39-41; Diersburg/Beck, pp. 162-3 (quote from Nagel's report on the latter page); Julius Wisnar, 'Die Schlacht bei Znaim im Jahre 1809', in the *Jahresbericht des k. k. Gymnasiums in Znaim für das Schuljahr 1909 1910*, Znaim: Lenk, 1910. The Hessian artillery was just crossing the Thaya when the battle ended and thus took no active part in the fight (*Artilleriekorps*, pg. 167).

93: Diersburg/Beck, pg. 164. Napoleon's birthday (15 August) had also been an occasion of great festivity, with officers' banquets, soldiers' buffets, parades, awards, fireworks and music.

94: Bigge, pg. 116.

95: When they marched into the captital, the Leib-Garde battalions were each formed into five companies, the new companies being composed of men sporting the new shakos that had finally begun to appear in the last months of 1809. Diersburg/Beck, pg. 165 and communication from Herr Alfred Umhey of Germany.

96: Casualty figures from Keim, pg. 199. It is worth noting that Napoleon also considered adding Hessians to his forces in central Germany, demanding two additional battalions and four guns from the Grand Duchy in late July (*Correspondence*, 15597, 30 July 1809). These forces were to join Junot's Corps in Saxony, but there is no evidence that they were ever formed.

97: Davout, No. 797, 23 June 1809. Bowden and Tarbox describe the Hessians as 'the finest of all the infantry fielded by the Confederation of the Rhine' (*Armies on the Danube*, 2nd edition, pg. 52).

CHAPTER 6:

Old Army, New War

O f all the Rheinbund contingents, the Saxon IX Corps is the most controversial. Commanded by the ambitious, contentious Prince of Ponte
Corvo, Marshal Bernadotte, and severely battered at Wagram, the army
fell under a cloud of disgrace that tainted its reputation for the remainder of the
Napoleonic epoch.

In 1809, Saxony was a relic, a creaky, somnolent leftover from the age of
Frederick the Great and Maria Theresa. It was an antique, absolutist construction, cobbled together from a congeries of hereditary and acquired lands and
hardly touched by the waves of revolutionary change washing over Europe.
Twenty different 'constitutions', thirty-six judicial systems, seven financial
administrations and thirteen separate customs regimes tangled the land in a
mare's nest of bureaucratic complication and hindered the development of
national sentiment. Serfdom still existed and the court considered the population childlike, ill-fit for involvement in the processes of governance.[1] Despite a
prosperous middle class and a growing stratum of industrial workers, the Saxon
state and society were dominated by a dull, tradition-bound aristocracy and a
pertinacious bureaucracy. Although loyal to its sovereign, this government
bureaucracy found its first interest in self-preservation and clung tenaciously to
the routine and etiquette of the past, actively opposing all proposals for reform.
The atmosphere at court was consequently rigid and stifling, hollow form was
valued over practical substance and information that arrived via non-standard
channels was blandly disregarded.[2] Initiative and innovation were unwelcome
in Dresden; indeed, they had no place in a bureaucracy characterized by a degree
of back-biting, petty intrigue and convolution that would have awed Byzantium.

The putative head of this government and the product of its Byzantine ways
was King Friedrich August. A modest, simple, unassuming man, 'more notable
for his moral qualities than his abilities as a statesman', he was trusting of others
and 'distinguished himself by the generosity of his sentiments' in the face of an
'egoistic Europe'.[3] Napoleon called him 'the most honest man to ever hold a
royal sceptre'[4] and he impressed all who knew him with his humility, intelligence and quiet consideration. Perhaps his most remarkable quality was his loyalty. He regarded obligations as 'something sacred'[5] and his loyalty once given
to a superior or subordinate was never retracted. Having signed a treaty with the
victorious Napoleon in late 1806, he became the Emperor's most devoted vassal,
committing himself and his kingdom to Napoleon's star on the strength of his
perception of duty and obligation: 'twice he [Napoleon] had it in his power to
destroy me,' the King wrote, 'he did not do it and I owe him eternal gratitude'.[6]

Unfortunately, Friedrich August utterly lacked the vision, determination and drive demanded by the age. Repressed in his youth by two domineering regents, he was thrust into a career consonant with neither his temperament nor his upbringing and would clearly have preferred to pass through the entire Revolutionary/Napoleonic epoch without involving himself in its conflagrations. Hesitant and irresolute, he made decisions with the greatest reluctance and found it impossible to step outside the obsolete strictures of 18th-century court life. His positive qualities were thus diluted by crippling indecision and naïveté. The senior ministers and generals in Dresden routinely took advantage of their monarch's weaknesses, cleverly manipulating him for their own ends, overburdening him with mountains of meaningless trivia to divert his attention from other matters. Their focus, however, was almost exclusively internal and they hid their eyes and minds from the climactic events beyond their borders. Even when he became aware of incompetence or malfeasance, Friedrich August could seldom bring himself to dismiss an appointed official; mediocrity was tolerated, even sheltered, and rank abuses proliferated. In the words of one frustrated general, Saxony 'waddled along in potbellied equanimity', its ruler ineffectual, its government lax, grossly inefficient and willfully ignorant.[7] It is hardly surprising that Friedrich August and his advisers found the radical changes wrought by the French Revolution and the awful dynamism of Napoleon completely incomprehensible.

If the Saxons lacked the mental tools to grasp the change swirling around them, they were keenly aware that their kingdom's survival depended on the good will of the French Emperor. From the time of the Seven Years War, Saxony, then an Electorate, had been dominated by its powerful neighbour to the north, Prussia. Dragooned into Prussian service when Berlin declared war on Napoleon in 1806, Friedrich August's army fought in the opening battles of the conflict and shared in the humiliation of the stunning defeat at Jena. But the Emperor was generous in victory. Gathering the conquered Saxon officers in the grand hall of Jena's university, he adroitly played upon Saxony's resentment of the overweening, parvenu Hohenzollern kingdom, portraying himself as a liberator and paroling the 7,000 Saxon prisoners in his power.[8] Two months later, Elector Friedrich August felt himself compelled to join the Confederation of the Rhine, accepting the rank of king along with a commitment to provide 6,000 troops to Napoleon's army in Silesia. The treaty with Napoleon brought a gust of fresh air into dusty, porcelain Dresden, occasioning a certain degree of anti-French sentiment, but the Saxons soon became almost slavishly deferential to their new allies. Ministers truckled to French colonels and cringed if the Emperor's name were mentioned. Davout was feted like a royal prince while travelling through Dresden and Talleyrand drolly averred that the Saxons had made the French ambassador, Jean-François Bourgoing, into a 'viceroy'.[9] Despite this anxious dread of French displeasure, its entry into the Rheinbund changed little in Saxony; state, society and military stirred in their torpor but remained fearfully ensconced in their familiar web of obsolete 18th-century routines.

Prussian dominance was nowhere stronger than in the Saxon army. Formal, rigid and unimaginative, it employed outdated linear tactics of the Prussian variety and was unprepared for the speed, flexibility and violence of Napoleonic warfare. The Bavarians, Württembergers and even the Prussians themselves were developing modern, national armies as a result of their encounters with the French war machine, but Saxony had apparently learned almost nothing from recent military history. Instead of adapting to the evolving nature of combat, it remained locked in the past, its army composed of 'mere bondsmen',[10] its officers promoted on the basis of birth rather than merit. Regulations were obeyed simply because they were regulations; their validity under altered circumstances was left unquestioned. The King himself seems to have been ensnared in the comfortable trammels of precedence and routine, unable to introduce reforms that might upset the traditional order of military affairs and dismay his plodding, officious generals.

Many of the ills of the Saxon army can be laid at the feet of its senior leadership. From regimental colonels to the Minister of War, the Saxon military establishment was burdened with a collection of superannuated senior officers distinguished only by their incompetence. General Ferdinand von Funck characterized the prevailing regime as one of 'atrophied pedantry' and believed the civilian ministers sought to preclude the development of a rival power base within the military by intentionally appointing ineffectual officers to key positions. Senior officers often seemed to be blithely ignorant of military fundamentals and realities. In 1807, for example, ponderous staff generals in Dresden believed they were satisfying the requirements of their positions by giving detailed instructions for the posting of vedettes on the River Bobr ninety miles away. These men naturally gave preference to subordinates who were stamped from the same mould as themselves. Junior officers were thus considered adequately schooled if they dressed precisely according to the meticulous uniform regulations and 'knew enough to swear, thrash and count 96 paces to the minute'.[11]

An incident from Funck's experiences illustrates the impact of these debilities. During the 1809 war, a renegade Prussian hussar officer named Schill led a raid into Saxony attempting to rouse the populace against Napoleon. Appearing before the walls of Wittenberg, he threatened the tiny Saxon garrison and caused great consternation at Friedrich August's court. Funck, the Inspector General of Cavalry, immediately dispatched orders for elements of the *Zastrow* Cuirassiers near Leipzig to march on Wittenberg. The regiment acknowledged receipt of the orders, but hours passed with no further word and Funck, assuming the unit had become lost, rode out personally to locate the presumedly errant troopers. His orders had read, 'Move out immediately upon receipt, before midnight without fail', but when he reached the village at 5 a.m., he was appalled to find the regiment still abed. Hauling out a bugler, he had 'boots and saddles' sounded and set out for the colonel's quarters.

> At last the colonel appeared. I went for him. He made the excuse that they had only just taken in fodder and he had to distribute it before they could move out. I had to exercise a good deal of self-control to keep my

hands off him. I dispatched orderlies to the villages of the sections and sent on an advanced guard of 80 troopers under Major von Schönfeld. The colonel remained apathetic - then he asked what he was to do about the fodder.

The regiment, it seems, did have the requisite fodder, but instructions from the Minister of Defence through GL Kaspar von Zastrow stated that it was not to be distributed until that very day. Surely the colonel had to defer to orders from the minister? With five hours already lost, Funck was beside himself with fury.

'And don't you know that I am your Inspector whom you have to obey on the spot or be placed under arrest? And did I not head my order: 'On the express command of His Majesty the King'?'

'It is very awkward when one never knows whose orders one ought to follow. Every one issues orders and it is impossible to please everyone.'

'I'll give you a word of advice. Take the orders of the man you are most afraid of, and I give you my word that is who I mean to be. By seven o'clock the regiment has either fallen in and is on the move or you are under arrest. You will find your instructions in my orders.'

Funck returned to court and 'poured out his heart to the King' who kindly forgave him for losing his temper. The cavalry eventually got under way, 'but neither the minister nor Zastrow was reprimanded'.[12]

One further archaic evil deserves mention. In the 18th century, the administrative affairs, particularly pay and ration funds, of regiments and companies were in the hands of unit commanders and *Inhaber* (patrons); judicious manipulation of a unit's active strength could yield tidy sums to supplement an officer's regular salary. The Napoleonic era brought a change. As truly national armies began to develop, the military was no longer the exclusive preserve of the nobility and in states like Baden, Bavaria and Württemberg, the old system was swept away. The Saxons, however, proved remarkably resistant to reform and the old system persisted with a peculiarly pernicious twist. By a complex tangle of rules and norms, subsistence allowances intended to provide for regimental commanders and their staffs on campaign were paid instead to the various regimental *Inhaber*. A colonel whose regiment deployed to the field therefore faced the prospect of incurring extensive debt because he would have to bear these subsistence expenses personally, while the old generals who were regimental *Inhaber* drew substantial allowances for active service without ever leaving the comfort of their estates. Company commanders also had reason to shun active duty. Their income increased for every man on furlough and the prospect of active service meant trying to cover the generally higher expenses of campaigning with a reduced allowance from the treasury. Even when their companies were placed on an active footing, some unscrupulous commanders tried to keep their men in barracks, thereby reducing expenditures in the hopes of pocketing the difference. Another holdover from an earlier age, this convoluted system remained in place until 1810, fostering a general reluctance to leave garrison and sapping the army's ardour for active campaigning.[13]

In their general outlines, these problems were not unknown to the French and, combined with the Saxon combat record, they gave Friedrich August's army a dubious military reputation. The Saxon contingent forced into Prussian service in 1806 was of indifferent quality, no better prepared than their Prussian masters to meet *La Grande Armée* in combat. Despite their antiquated tactics, some units performed with conspicuous bravery, but most were merely bewildered by the pace of action and found themselves bundled up in the general defeat.[14]

Pressured to join the Rheinbund, Friedrich August signed the Treaty of Posen with Napoleon on 11 December, committing his country to provide a contingent of 20,000 in case of future war and agreeing to supply 6,000 men for the ongoing struggle. The army harboured considerable anti-French sentiment, however, and these troops, marching toward Silesia in early 1807, initially proved more bane than benefit: a mutiny by several battalions in February was only quelled when cuirassiers arrived to restore order, and the regiment assigned to Jerome for the siege of Breslau took to its heels at the first opportunity. These incidents seem to have been cathartic. A combination of shame at their insubordinate outburst and surprised gratitude for the decent treatment received from the French (as compared to the haughty 'comradeship' of the Prussians) brought improved morale and ability.[15] Desertion remained a problem, but the infantry served well at Danzig, the cavalry distinguished itself at Friedland and, by the close of the campaign, Napoleon could say that his newest allies were 'good soldiers'.[16] This positive comment was much qualified however. While the French held the Saxon cavalry in high esteem, the infantry was less well regarded; it was the common opinion that the Saxons could be useful if closely associated with French troops but that they required much more experience in the new style of war.[17] Saxony's soldiers had thus been both reprehensible and valiant in their first campaign under Napoleon's eagles and they entered the war of 1809 with a correspondingly checkered reputation.

The Saxon army counted twelve line infantry regiments (Feld-Regimenter), a Guard Grenadier Regiment, a Swiss Guard Company, a Garrison Company and three 'half-invalid' (Halb-Invaliden) companies on its rolls in 1809. The line regiments were organized into two battalions with four musketeer companies and one grenadier company each for a total of ten companies per regiment (the 1st Musketeer Company in each regiment was the Leib Company). The grenadier companies, however, were almost always detached from their parent regiments and combined into special grenadier battalions named for their commanders; such a battalion normally contained the grenadier companies of two regiments (four companies total). The authorized strength of a company was about 170 officers and men, including a corporal and ten Schützen. A line regiment with its two musketeer battalions should thus have counted some 1,370 in its ranks and the strength of a combined grenadier battalion should have been approximately 700. Infantrymen of all types were in short supply in 1809, however, and the average field strength of Saxon line regiments and grenadier battalions at the start of the campaign was 1,100 and 560 respectively. Even these numbers were only attained by the incorporation of large drafts of inexperienced recruits into the infantry battalions; there was little time to train these men before the Army marched out of Dresden in mid-April.[18]

Known by the names of their Inhaber, the line regiments were dressed in uncomfortable uniforms of stiff, clumsy and obsolete appearance, little changed since the end of the Seven Years War: a white coat, white breeches and a black bicorne hat; grenadiers were distinguished by their moustaches and an Austrian-pattern bearskin bonnet. Strict adherence to the details of the uniform regulations was monitored with fanatical zeal by the officious senior generals and even

Table 6-1: The Saxon Army in April 1809

Line Infantry Regiments

Organization: two battalions per regiment; one grenadier company, four musketeer companies per battalion; company strength 180 men; regimental depot. Grenadiers habitually served in separate battalions.
Uniform: white coat; distinctive colour on collar, lapels, cuffs; white breeches; bicorne hat, bearskin for grenadiers.

Regiment (Inhaber)	Distinctive Colour
König	red
von Cerrini	red
Prinz Anton	dark-blue
Prinz Clemens	dark-blue
Prinz Maximilian	yellow
von Burgsdorff	yellow
Prinz Friedrich August	light-green
von Low	light-green
von Oebschelwitz	light-blue
von Dyherrn	light-blue
von Niesemeuschel	crimson
von Rechten	crimson

Other Infantry

Leib-Grenadier-Garde Regiment
Organization: two battalions, each of five companies, company strength 90 men (below strength in 1809).
Uniform: red coat with yellow facings; white breeches; bearskin.

Schweizer Leibgarde
Organization: 120 men.
Uniform: yellow coat with light-blue facings, bicorne hat.

Garrison and Half-Invalid Companies
Organization: 205 men (Garrison Company); 176 men (1st Half-Invalid Company), 121 men (2nd), 118 men (3rd).
Uniform: white coat with black facings; white breeches; bicorne.

Heavy Cavalry Regiments

Organization: four squadrons per regiment (plus depot).
Uniform: buff coat with distinctive colour on collar, cuffs, turnbacks; black half-cuirass; bicorne hat.

Garde du Corps	dark-blue
Karabinier-Regiment	red
Leib-Kürassier-Garde	red
von Zastrow **Cuirassiers**	yellow

Light Cavalry Regiments

Organization: four squadrons per regiment (plus depot) for chevauxlegers; eight squadrons for Hussar Regiment.
Chevauxlegers uniform: red coat with distinctive colour on collar, cuffs, turnbacks, lapels; bicorne hat. Hussar uniform: white dolman with light-blue trim, light-blue pelisse, white breeches, mirliton hat with light-blue 'wing'.

Prinz Clemens **Chevauxlegers**	light-green
Prinz Johann **Chevauxlegers**	black
Herzog Albrecht **Chevauxlegers**	dark-green
von Polenz **Chevauxlegers**	light-blue
Hussar Regiment	(light-blue and white)

Artillery

Organization: two light and two heavy batteries; one pontoon company.
Artillery uniform: dark-green coat with red facings; buff breeches; bicorne. Train uniform: light-blue coat with black facings trimmed in red; bicorne. Pontooneer uniform: as artillery but with red breeches and waistcoats.

the otherwise reasonable King. Reforms in the name of comfort or utility were considered transgressions against a sacrosanct tradition, while officers emptied their pockets to keep pace with frequent incidental elaborations.[19] The Saxon uniforms had one additional disadvantage: they had the same base colour as the coats of the Habsburg infantry, a circumstance that would cost many Saxons their lives on the field of Wagram.

The Leib-Grenadier-Garde Regiment was organized as the line regiments with ten companies in two battalions. The Guard Grenadier companies were smaller than their line counterparts, however, numbering about 90 men each, so that the paper strength of the entire regiment stood at slightly over 900. Its members wore a striking uniform of bright red with yellow facings topped by a bearskin bonnet, but the regiment was well below establishment when the 1809 campaign began and only some 584 officers and men actually marched out with IX Corps. The 120 men of the Schweizer Leibgarde (Swiss Life Guards), a ceremonial unit performing duties at the royal palaces, were rather garishly turned out in bicornes and yellow coats with light-blue distinctions. The Garrison Company and the Half-Invalid Companies were also more or less sedentary outfits. The garrison soldiers were assigned to the fortress of Königstein south of Dresden, while the prisons at Waldheim (1st), Torgau (2nd) and Eisleben (3rd) were each occupied by a Half-Invalid Company.

If the reputation of the Saxon foot soldiers was ambiguous, that of its cavalry was excellent. Ranked among the finest in Europe and highly prized by Napoleon,[20] the Saxon mounted arm included four heavy and five light regiments but was extremely short of qualified mounts in 1809. The uniform of the heavy regiments was a large black bicorne, a buff coat and a black cuirass; after the Austrian fashion, however, only the breast plate of the cuirass was worn. On paper, the carabinier and cuirassier regiments each had 724 men organized into four squadrons; much smaller, the Garde du Corps had the same number of squadrons but a strength of only 428. In strength and organization, Saxony's four chevauxlegers regiments were similar to the cuirassiers, but the men wore vivid red coats with contrasting facing colours. As with the heavies, their big bicorne hats gave the light horsemen a somewhat antique appearance. The troopers of the Hussar Regiment also wore a hat left over from the previous century: the mirliton, or winged cap. This black cap with its light-blue cloth 'wing' topped a traditional Hungarian-style hussar uniform of white and light-blue. In addition to its unique uniform, the regiment was distinguished from its fellows by its large size: 1,065 horsemen organized into eight squadrons like the Austrian light cavalry.

According to its tables of organization, therefore, the army should have been able to field an impressive total of forty squadrons of superb cavalry. In reality, however, many of Saxony's fine horses had been grudgingly turned over to the French after the Jena débâcle and, at the start of the 1809 campaign, the kingdom could mount no more than about half of its troopers. Even the twenty squadrons that took the field with IX Corps could only be put into the saddle by rushing young, partially trained horses into service, a tremendous injustice in the eyes of the proud Saxon cavalrymen. Despite these lamentable deficiencies in the quality of its horseflesh, Friedrich August's cavalry was extraordinarily well trained and still possessed of the 'old knightly spirit' which had sustained it through a long and honourable history.[21]

The artillery was Saxony's weakest arm. Scattered about the country in small garrisons and suffering from years of general neglect, its training emphasized theoretical instruction and its sub-elements were only brought together once a year for a short period to manoeuvre and fire with actual guns. This tenuous familiarity with gun drill was exacerbated by second-rate pieces and a dearth of experience in battlefield operations at the battery level. Field batteries were formed on mobilization by equipping peacetime artillery companies with guns and combining them with newly activated personnel and horses of the train. Two 'light' and two 'heavy' foot batteries, each consisting of four 8-pounder guns and two 8-pounder howitzers, were assembled in this fashion to accompany IX Corps to the field in 1809. The 'light' and 'heavy' designations were derived from the weight of the pieces and did not indicate horse versus foot artillery as in most other armies. Indeed, the Saxon army had no horse artillery at the start of the war and even the officers of these foot batteries went unmounted.[22]

The artillery train was another weak point of the Saxon Army. Assembled immediately prior to the conflict from levies provided by the counties of the realm, the train personnel generally came from the worst elements of society, including vagabonds and released felons, men who often had no conception of horses or harness. The lone peacetime team was so undermanned that it could only deploy one gun at a time during the artillery's annual firings and there was no time to prepare it or the newly mobilized teams to meet the demands of modern warfare. The fundamentals of their duties and familiarity with their batteries had to be acquired on the march, resulting in artillery that showed itself slow and inept on the battlefield.

The Saxon artillery also supervised a Pontooneer Company of 73 men. Although it managed a small bridge train of six pontoons and a reconnaissance punt, there is no record of this unit being used in action during the campaign.[23]

Consistent with its uniforms and outlook, the tactics of Saxony's army in 1809 had hardly changed from the time of the Seven Years War. The infantry manoeuvred and fought in line, placing the greatest emphasis on precise alignment and the mechanical execution of tactical evolutions. The bayonet attack, delivered after a salvo at short range, was still considered irresistible, but manoeuvre in column was not practised, square formation was a cumbersome process and skirmishing was the exclusive province of the forty-four Schützen in each battalion. The mounted regiments employed the standard tactics of the day, although the Saxon squadrons were unusual in forming their troopers in three lines instead of the normal two; this third rank contained the most skilled riders and provided scouts, skirmishers and couriers as required. Tactically, the artillery had remained in the previous century: the gunners and train personnel of the field batteries had almost no opportunity to exercise together as battery teams, vigorous integration with the other arms seems to have received little attention and the massing of guns on the battlefield was a foreign concept. The battery drill regulations, according to one observer, 'resembled a book of instruction for a complex dance' which 'lacked all simplicity and which no one had ever actually implemented'. Inexperienced and poorly trained, the batteries were unwieldy and had the greatest difficulty executing such basic drills as limbering, shifting position and unlimbering.[24]

Napoleon called Friedrich August's rather antiquated army into Imperial service on 15 January 1809,[25] but the King did not issue his own mobilization order until 25 February, more than a month later. None the less, soldiers on leave were recalled to the colours and a 'mobile division' of about 14,000 men under the command of GL Joachim Friedrich Gotthelf von Zezschwitz was gathered around Dresden by mid-March. Increased by the addition of two infantry regiments, a grenadier battalion and three cavalry squadrons on the 24th, the contingent was designated the IX Corps of the Army of Germany and reorganized into two divisions, each consisting of two infantry brigades and one cavalry brigade.[26] The Corps totalled slightly more than 19,000 men, but shortages of soldiers and horses left many battalions and squadrons understrength and forced the Saxons to alter the internal organization of both the Leib Grenadiers and the Garde du Corps: for the duration of the campaign, the two weak battalions of grenadiers were combined into one, while troopers of the latter regiment were consolidated into only two squadrons. Artillery support was provided by twenty-four pieces in four batteries; two additional guns were held in reserve in the Corps' artillery park. The tiny pontoon detachment also marched with the park. Von Zezschwitz remained the senior Saxon general, but, consistent with Napoleon's policy, a Frenchman, Marshal Jean-Baptiste Bernadotte, the Prince of Ponte Corvo, was placed in overall command of the Corps.

Bernadotte was an interesting and complex character. Destined to become the King of Sweden, he had been born a lawyer's son in Gascony in 1763 and entered the army as a private in 1780. The Revolution gave him an opportunity to rise and he was soon a Général de Division fighting with republican fervour (he reportedly had 'Death to Tyrants' tattooed on his arm) in Germany and Italy. His early military career showed him to be possessed of not inconsiderable tactical talent, a notable ability to motivate troops and a vaulting ambition. Success brought him prominence, but he ran foul of Napoleon in the Consulate years, his political aspirations, touchy pride and high self-esteem coming between the two men and laying a foundation of suspicion and rancour, especially on Bernadotte's part, that would not dissipate.[27] His perplexing behaviour at the double battle of Jena and Auerstädt, where he failed to arrive on either battlefield, cast a shadow over his reliability and by 1809, he had managed to make enemies of a number of the army's senior leaders, including Berthier.[28] As a military governor in the Hanseatic cities from 1807 to 1809, he had gained extensive experience in dealing with Germans and was renowned for his courtesy, charm and adroit handling of difficult civil-military problems. He was equally famous, however, for an inflated opinion of his own importance, a similar view of his own military genius and a propensity to let temper overcome wisdom in violent verbal outbursts.[29] The man who arrived in Dresden on 22 March was thus a competent officer who cared for his troops and received their

Top left: King Maximilian I. Joseph of Bavaria (1756–1825). One of Napoleon's staunchest allies, King Max struggled to conceal his son's intemperate pronouncements. (Author) **Top right:** Crown Prince Ludwig of Bavaria (1786–1868). Young, proud and self-willed, Ludwig loathed Napoleon and was full of romantic notions of freeing 'Teutschland' from the French 'yoke'. Despite these sentiments, he enthusiastically reported the battlefield successes of his 1st Division to his royal father. (Author) **Above left:** General Lieutenant Karl Phillip Freiherr von Wrede (1767–1838). Commanding the Bavarian 2nd Division, the ambitious Wrede was one of Napoleon's favourites, but his independence brought repeated conflict with his Corps commander, Lefebvre. (Author) **Above right:** General Lieutenant Bernhard Erasmus von Deroy (1743–1812). The solidly competent Deroy commanded the 3rd Bavarian Division; he died during the Russian campaign of wounds received at the battle of Pultusk. (ASKB)

Top: King Friedrich of Württemberg (1754–1816). Friedrich, Jerome and the Emperor himself were the only allied monarchs to command their troops in the field during the campaign. This depiction shows the corpulent king at his headquarters near Lake Constance in July 1809. (ASKB) **Above left:** Friedrich Wilhelm, Crown Prince of Württemberg, (1781–1864). Friedrich Wilhelm detested Napoleon and chafed under the supervision of his domineering father; he commanded Württemberg's home defence forces at Ellwangen and later around Lake Constance. (Author) **Above right:** Général de Division Dominique Vandamme (1770–1830). Tough and capable on the battlefield, Vandamme proved maladroit when dealing with his Württemberg subordinates and their strong-willed king. (PH)

Top left: Karl Friedrich, Grand Duke of Baden (1728–1811). By 1809, Karl Friedrich was aged and indecisive; effective rule of the Grand Duchy was exercised by several key ministers under continuous French pressure. (AU) **Top right:** Ludwig I, Grand Duke of Hesse-Darmstadt (1753–1830). Ludwig's duchy willingly provided Napoleon with some of the best Rhinebund troops. (ASKB) **Above left:** Marshal André Massena (1758–1817). The veteran marshal, one of Napoleon's ablest subordinates, commanded IV Corps, which included the Baden and Hessian brigades. (PH) **Above right:** Général de Division Claude-Just Legrand (1763–1815). 'One of the bravest and most humane generals in the French army' (Bellange), Legrand had entered the Royal Army as a private in 1778, rose rapidly and served with great distinction until severely wounded at the Beresina. In 1809, he commanded the 1st Division of Massena's IV Corps. (ASKB)

Top left: Marshal François Lefebvre (1755–1820). An Alsation by birth and a tried veteran, Lefebvre seemed a perfect choice to lead VII Corps, his high-handed treatment of his Bavarian subordinates and his inability to quell the Tyrolean revolt led to his relief in October. (ASKB) **Top right:** Marshal Jean Bernadotte (1763–1844). Bernadotte was very popular with his Saxon troops, but his haughty pride and mediocre battlefield performance brought his relief after Wagram. (PH) **Above left:** Général de Division Jean-Baptiste Drouet, Comte d'Erlon (1756–1844). Initially assigned to be Lefebvre's chief of staff, the reliable Drouet took command of VII Corps in October. (Author) **Above right:** Général de Division Jean-Louis-Ebénézer Reynier (1771–1814). This taciturn but capable Swiss led the Saxon contingent after Bernadotte's dismissal. He would command the corps again in the dreadful struggle of 1812–13. (PH)

Top left: King Friedrich August of Saxony (1750–1827). Though personally loyal to Napoleon, Friedrich August presided over a realm that was utterly unprepared for modern warfare. (Author) **Top right:** Jerome Bonaparte, King of Westphalia (1784–1860). Jerome's record as king and commander is a curious mixture of earnest effort and feckless luxury. (AU) **Above left:** General-Major Christoph Freiherr von Gutschmid (1762–1812). Promoted to general officer rank on 4 April, this wily hussar led the IX Corps advance guard with skill and courage throughout the campaign. Like many of his fellow Saxons, he fell in Russia in 1812. (Author) **Above right:** Oberst Johann Adolf von Thielmann (1765–1824). Ambitious, energetic and aggressive, Thielmann exhibited considerable drive and boldness as commander of Saxony's home defence forces. With Karl von Clausewitz as his chief of staff, he would command the Prussian III Corps in the Waterloo campaign. (Author)

The Battle of Abensberg (20 April). Mid-morning on 20 April: Napoleon gives orders to his staff as Crown Prince Ludwig's 1st Bavarian Division advances against the Austrians in the Seeholz (centre distance). The roofs and church spires of Offenstetten, where the Austrian general Thierry has his main position, can be seen beyond the woods in the distance. Württemberg skirmishers and cavalry under Hügel's command deploy to the Crown Prince's right beyond the farmstead. In the foreground a Bavarian light artillery battery marches out through the gates of the Abensberg (left), the gunners mounted on the distinctive *wurst* wagons; two Württemberg Jägers can be seen on the far right. (ASKB)

The Battle of Znaim (11 July). Napoleon observes the fire of Lieutenant Dobl's Bavarian Battery and some French horse artillery, as Marmont's Corps advances on the second day of the battle. (ASKB)

The Battle of Eggmühl (22 April). It is mid-afternoon and St-Hilaire's men, having gained Unter Laichling (left centre), are engaged in a desperate struggle for the copse beyond the village. In the foreground, General Deroy gives orders to his staff on the heights overlooking the battlefield. His division (centre) provides infantry and artillery support to St Hilaire while French and German cavalry storm the smoke-wreathed Austrian Grand Battery (far right). (ASKB)

The Battle of Linz (17 May). In their bold and celebrated charge, the troopers of the *Herzog Louis* Jäger zu Pferd Regiment (colloquially known as the 'Louis Jäger') capture an Austrian battery in the closing hours of the afternoon. A proud King Friedrich presented the regiment with a special standard of honour to commemorate this feat (ASKB)

Above: The church at Aspern. Some of the campaign's heaviest fighting took place around this little, walled churchyard on 21 and 22 May. (Author) **Below:** The Battle of Aspern (21 May). Baden light dragoons engage Austrian hussars in the tumult outside Aspern on the first day of the battle. (AU)

The Battle of Wagram (6 July). While Aderklaa burns (far right), Wrede's infantry (left) advances behind its line of guns to support the attack on the Austrian centre. Allied cavalry clashes with Austrian Uhlans in the distance. (ASKB)

Above: The fall of Innsbruck (12 April). From his litter, the wounded Oberst Karl von Ditfurth attempts to rally his desperate 11th Infantry Regiment moments before his death and the final collapse of resistance. (AU) **Below:** Bombardment of Kufstein. In this contemporary Bavarian depiction of the first blockade, enthusiastic Tyrolean rebels cheerfully bombard the little fortress with a variety of often unreliable artillery. The garrison's stout defence represented the only Bavarian success on the Tyrolean front during the dark days of April. (ASKB)

Above: Bavarian infantry, in their distinctive Raupenhelms, pause for a rest on the march. (AU)
Below: *König* Jägers of General von Hügel's élite Light Brigade. His elevated rank notwithstanding, Hügel retained nominal command of the *König* Jägers in 1809; Major von Stockmayer, however, actually led the battalion in the campaign. (AU)

Top left: The heroes of Landshut and Eggmühl; Bavarian chevauxlegers (left) and dragoons (right) in camp. (AU) **Top right:** A Württemberg trooper of the *Herzog Louis* Jäger Regiment, which executed the brilliant charge at Linz on 17 May. (AU) **Above left:** Baden infantrymen stop for a pipe. Note the linen trousers often worn on campaign in place of the cumbersome breeches and gaiters. (AU) **Above right:** Hessian troops in the antique, Frederickian uniforms they wore at the start of the campaign. By the end of the year they were in transition to a more modern appearance. (AU)

Above: Baden Guard Grenadiers in their bivouac during the Vorarlberg campaign. The figure at right is an officer's servant. (AU) **Below:** Saxon infantry; officers, musketeers and a grenadier in their antiquated and uncomfortable white uniforms. (AU)

Top left: Saxon-Gotha musketeer and officer. Saxon-Gotha provided six musketeer and two grenadier companies for the 4th Rheinbund. (AU) **Top right:** The simple white uniform of this Westphalian fusilier reveals the strong French influence that pervaded Jerome's army. This soldier belongs to the 5th Regiment, which was destroyed at Halberstadt. (AU) **Above left:** Like his Westphalian counterpart's, this Berg grenadier's uniform closely resembles the French model. (AU) **Above right:** The styling of the uniforms worn by these Mecklenberg-Schwerin infantrymen reflects the Duchy's close political and military ties to Prussia. (AU)

warm loyalty in return, but also an eristic, ambitious and untrustworthy subordinate and comrade, too fond of intrigue and principally concerned with promoting his own interests.[30]

The Marshal immediately objected to his new appointment. Napoleon ignored him, but Bernadotte, seeing no prospect for glory or advancement in commanding allied troops and fearing an 'unseen hand' operating against him at Imperial headquarters,[31] continued to protest vigorously, vehemently and often.

> I have already had the honour of entreating Your Majesty to relieve me of command of the Saxons. I have already explained to Your Majesty that I feel unequal to the task of leading foreigners. (11 April) [32]

Table 6-2: IX Corps on 8 April 1809
Marshal Bernadotte, Prince of Ponte Corvo, commanding

1st Division - GL von Zezschwitz
    1st Infantry Brigade - GM von Hartitzsch
        combined Leib Grenadier Garde Battalion
        2nd Grenadier Battalion (Major von Bose)
        3rd Grenadier Battalion (Major von Hake)
        König Infantry Regiment
        I/*von Dyherrn* Infantry Regiment

    2nd Infantry Brigade - GM von Boxberg
        Prinz Maximilian Infantry Regiment
        Prinz Friedrich August Infantry Regiment
        Prinz Anton Infantry Regiment

    Cavalry Brigade - GM Freiherr von Gutschmid
        Garde du Corps Regiment (in 2 sqdns)
        2 sqdns of the Karabinier Regiment
        Prinz Clemens Chevauxlegers (4 sqdns)
        3 sqdns of the Hussar Regiment
        1 sqdn of *Herzog Albrecht* Chevauxlegers

2nd Division - GL von Polenz
    1st Infantry Brigade - GM von Lecoq
        Prinz Clemens Infantry Regiment
        von Low Infantry Regiment
        von Cerrini Infantry Regiment

    2nd Infantry Brigade - GM von Zeschau
        von Niesemeuschel Infantry Regiment
        II/*von Oebschelwitz* Infantry Regiment
        1st Grenadier Battalion (Major von Radeloff)
        4th Grenadier Battalion (Major von Winkelmann)

    Cavalry Brigade - GM von Feilitzsch
        Leib-Garde Kürassier Regiment (4 sqdns)
        Prinz Johann Chevauxlegers (4 sqdns)

    Corps Artillery - Major von Birnbaum
        1st Heavy Battery: Hoyer
        1st Light Battery: Bonniot
        2nd Heavy Battery: Coudray
        2nd Light Battery: Huthsteiner
        Artillery Park with 2 reserve guns
        Pontoon Detachment

Saxon Strength:

Infantry	-	12,613
Cavalry	-	2,803
Artillery	-	821
TOTAL	-	**16,237** combatants
others	-	2,859 staff, pontooneers, train, etc.
Grand Total	-	19,096

Note: Grenadier Battalion Composition

Battalion:	Grenadier Companies of:
von Bose	*Prinz Friedrich August & von Burgsdorff*
von Hake	*Prinz Clemens & von Oebschelwitz*
von Radeloff	*Prinz Anton & von Niesemeuschel*
von Winkelmann	*von Low & von Cerrini*

Source: Exner, pp. 16-21.

He also badgered the Emperor and Chief of Staff with complaints about the quality of the Saxon soldiers. The day after his arrival in Dresden, he wrote to Napoleon that 'The Saxon troops will not be able to render Your Majesty any service if they are not combined with a French force superior to their own; I believe the only way to take advantage of them is to incorporate them by brigade into some French divisions.'[33] Three days later, he reviewed the Corps and provided this assessment to the Emperor:

> I have the honour to inform Your Majesty that I have reviewed the Saxon troops. I have sent the Major General [Berthier] the strength of their force and their location. I had them brought together and had them execute the principal combat manoeuvres. I was very satisfied with their instruction which I had not expected. The cavalry above all is well trained and has as much cohesion as the young horses of which it is almost entirely composed will permit. There is a large number of recruits in the infantry, but the commanders and officers evidence much good will. None the less, I continue to think that this body of troops, acting alone, will not be as useful to Your Majesty as they would if distributed by division within the French *corps d'armée*, because [military] affairs here are characterized by great dilatoriness. The artillery is poorly organized; the train above all is very defective.[34]

A report of the 28th expressed further frustrations, suspecting the Saxons of exaggerating the number of combat effective soldiers.[35]

Despite his misgivings and injured pride, Bernadotte set about the task of preparing IX Corps for war with professional thoroughness, eliciting a strong positive response from his new charges. Not only did the troops soon come to recognize his renowned concern for the common soldier but Bernadotte, unlike his friend Vandamme, made especial efforts to establish and maintain good relations with the allied generals. By these measures, he won the 'attachment and complete trust of the officers and soldiers', instilling a sense of enthusiasm and awakening a martial spirit in the men.[36]

Positive spirit, individual courage and excellent cavalry were the best features of the Saxon Corps in April 1809. On the negative side, however, the contingent suffered from several potentially debilitating frailties. First, the Saxon Army clung to the tactical concepts from the age of Frederick. Stiff and formal, these archaic tactics impeded battlefield manoeuvrability and made the Saxons slow and cumbersome when compared to their agile and inspired French allies.[37] Second, the Saxons had little experience in combat and were unfamiliar with the organization and employment of large military formations. The army was slow to recognize the imperatives of Napoleonic warfare and had not taken advantage of the lessons it might have learned from its brief brushes with combat in 1806 and 1807. This relative inexperience with the new style of war was compounded by the manner in which the army was organized for the 1809 campaign. Previously distributed through allied armies in small detachments, the Saxons were uncomfortable with the command, control and support of large divisions and corps. Although a combined division had marched with Lannes in 1807 and two divisions had been temporarily formed in response to the alarms of autumn 1808, Saxon generals and their staffs were hardly prepared to take large tactical formations into combat.[38]

The third major weakness was perhaps the most serious. Many of Saxony's military deficiencies could have been overcome, or indeed might never have developed, had the Army been endowed with capable senior leaders. Unfortunately, most of the men occupying positions of high responsibility in 1809 had attained their ranks by connections, birth and plodding, precise adherence to the details of regulation. Overaged and outmoded, they lacked the fundamental technical skills required of a commander: 'The staff officers and captains were too old to devote themselves to His Majesty's service with mental and physical vigour and freshness; the average age of the colonels stood at 65, that of the staff officers and captains at 60 and 50 respectively.' An extreme example was General of Infantry Heinrich von Boblick, who, at 90 years of age, was still retained as the commandant of the Königstein fortress. Even the Saxon military hierarchy recognized the fatuity of this situation, so Boblick was given a deputy, GM Friedrich von Burgsdorff, who was a mere 72 years old. A contemporary observer, coming upon some of these antiques as he departed Dresden in mid-April, wryly described 'Six white, old-fashioned coaches, each with a six-horse-team and just as many drivers, allocated to transport a half-dozen seventy-year-old wheezers in generals' uniforms into the countryside, because inside the fortress, in sight of which they were taking their first rest stop, they would be too exposed to the insults of the enemy.' Ancient, inexperienced and incompetent, leadership of this sort was a burden to the army.[39] The men deserved better.

Finally, the choice of Bernadotte as commander of the Saxon field force was a potential problem. Despite his abilities, Bernadotte's reputation in the French army and the enmity that poisoned relations between him and the Emperor placed IX Corps under a shadow from its inception. Moreover, the Marshal constantly and vociferously complained about his command, lamenting his plight and begging for better troops. These factors combined with the Corps' inherent debilities to stain the reputation of Friedrich August's men as the campaign of 1809 progressed.

April-May - First Encounters: Bohemia and Poland

On 14 April, an Imperial missive reached Bernadotte in Dresden, ordering him to take IX Corps south through Thuringia to Bavaria. Although the departure of the Corps and Saxony's far-flung garrison requirements would leave the Kingdom itself almost denuded of troops, Napoleon correctly identified Bavaria as the crux of the campaign and sought to concentrate all his forces for the decisive struggle. Public sentiment in Saxony, however, 'was not completely favourable toward France' and news of the Army's departure created foreboding and dark concern rather than enthusiasm.[40] Otto August Rühle von Lilienstern, an soldier of fortune who accompanied the Army on the campaign, depicted the scene in Dresden.

It is decided. — Anticipating imminent separation, the dilettantes of society, who normally host a public concert in the Clothmakers' Hall every two weeks during the winter, had decided to gather today (14 April) for the last time this year. As always, the benches were occupied by hundreds of young women and girls, and the rest of the hall was packed full, mostly by officers. Suddenly there arose a tumult; the officers were hastily called away; a soft lament arose from the whitening women, the music stopped and the entire assembly streamed outside. No one could provide definite information. I hurry to my friend, the Hauptmann. The order to march is here, he tells me. Tomorrow at daybreak, the Second Division marches, the day after, the First will follow.[41]

The population, some in fear, some in 'secret joy', expected an Austrian army to appear before the capital city's gates at any moment, but IX Corps marched away regardless, heading north along the Elbe to Meissen, GL Georg von Polenz's 2nd Division on the 15th, GL von Zezschwitz's 1st Division the following day. Just as Max Joseph of Bavaria was forced to abandon the Tyrol temporarily, the Emperor's strategic vision left Friedrich August no choice but to send his Army to the Danube valley, leaving his capital and realm practically defenceless. In a sombre cavalcade, the King and his court departed Dresden for Leipzig on the 16th.[42]

Although his ultimate destination was the theatre of combat in southern Bavaria, Bernadotte initially took his command via a circuitous route through Thuringia and the Upper Palatinate (Oberpfalz). Napoleon was concerned about insurrection in Westphalia and IX Corps' curious path apparently resulted from his desire to have a large ready reserve at hand in case of further disturbances in his brother Jerome's kingdom.[43] Simultaneously, the Saxons served a second purpose, providing a convenient threat to Bohemia to worry the Austrian high command and mask Napoleon's intentions. By the time the Corps reached Weimar by relatively easy marches on the 23rd, however, the threat of serious rebellion had subsided and Bernadotte received new orders to head south, prepared to continue on to the Danube or into Bohemia as circumstances dictated.[44] After a day of rest, the Marshal took his Saxons via Rudolstadt to Schleiz (28 April) where the men were allowed another rest day. The march resumed on the 30th, the main body proceeding to the area south of Plauen while the advance guard was pushed forward to Adorf.

The last day of April saw the Saxons in their first combat, the honour falling to the advance guard. This force included 200 infantry (the Schützen and other individual soldiers from *König*) and an improvised cavalry 'regiment' composed of the three hussar squadrons and the lone squadron of *Herzog Albrecht* Chevauxlegers. Its commander was 47 year-old GM Christoph Freiherr von Gutschmid, described by a contemporary as 'the very image of a true hussar; brave to the point of audacity; firmly decisive, circumspect and sly; in the saddle day and night regardless of the weather.' At about 2 p.m., two of Bernadotte's staff officers appeared at Gutschmid's command post in Adorf with instructions to conduct a reconnaissance toward Eger on the Bohemian border. Fifty hussars

and chevauxlegers rode off with the officers, but basic march security was
neglected and the detachment was surprised by a small patrol (17 troopers) from
the *Schwarzenberg* Uhlans a few kilometres north of the town. Taken in the
flank, the Saxon cavalrymen were scattered after a curt skirmish.[45] Their officers, dashing forward to restore order, blundered into a marsh, where they were
cut down and captured by the enemy lancers. Fortunately, a pair of veteran hussar corporals named Böhme and Gelbert recognized the weakness of the Austrian
force, quickly rallied their comrades and led them back at the gallop to free their
officers from the fleeing Uhlans. The skirmish thus ended honourably for the
Saxons as did another brief clash between patrols near Asch.[46] Although each
side lost only about a dozen men in these minor encounters, they brought home to
officers and men alike the reality of combat and had two important results for IX
Corps. First, its subsequent marches were conducted with columns ready for
action and patrols placed to the front and flanks for security. Second, the attitude
of the men began to change, the Army's relatively friendly perception of their old
Austrian comrades in arms gradually losing place to a more combative spirit.[47]

As the Saxons tramped through continual snow from Dresden toward the
Danube, von Zezschwitz sent glowing reports back to his sovereign: the troops
were in good spirits, very well provisioned and eagerly conducting rapid, disciplined marches despite the inclement weather. Bernadotte's appreciation of the
situation was not as rosy. Although satisfied with the 'good will' of the troops,
the disgruntled Marshal repeatedly voiced his concerns in a spate of reports
through late April and early May, focusing particularly on the slowness of the
Saxons, the inadequacies of their artillery and the urgent need for experienced
French troops to bolster the fighting power of the Corps.

> 20 April to Napoleon: 'Your Majesty knows that the Germans do not
> march like French troops...'
> 26 April to Napoleon: 'I am quite content with the Saxon Army; the
> troops march, it is true, far slower than ours, but they demonstrate much
> good will; none the less, I cannot repeat enough that a French division is
> very necessary to provide them [the Saxons] an example and encourage-
> ment; if I had one, I would not hesitate to march directly on Prague. The
> Saxon generals themselves recognize the necessity of such support.' [48]

Notified on 28 April that GD Pierre-Louis Dupas's small French Division (5th
Léger, 19th Ligne and twelve guns) was to be included in IX Corps, Bernadotte
sent a pleased reply to Berthier ('this division, weak as it is, will be very useful
next to the Saxons') but continued to bombard headquarters with other complaints.[49]

> 30 April to Berthier: 'The Saxon Army has no light artillery whatsoever
> and its foot artillery is extremely poor. I may point out to Your Highness
> that the Dutch Division in Hamburg has two perfectly organized light
> artillery companies; one of these could be put at the disposition of the
> Army of Germany.'[50]

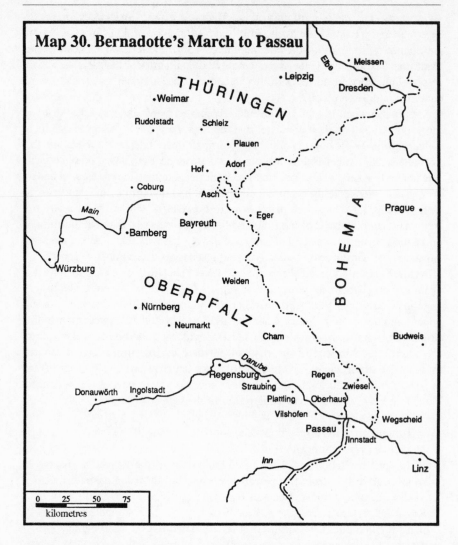

Map 30. Bernadotte's March to Passau

The march south continued, the main body passing through Hof (1 May) and Weiden (4 May) to reach Cham on the 8th, where it was reunited with Gutschmid's advance guard. Gutschmid and his small force had skirted the Bohemian border as they pushed to the south-east, protecting the main body from enemy observation and launching little forays into Austrian territory to gather intelligence. His troopers rode into Eger unopposed on the 2nd and skirmished briefly with Austrian cavalry on the 5th and 6th, collecting sufficient information for Bernadotte to conclude that western Bohemia was occupied by only scattered enemy forces.[51] The Marshal consequently decided to attempt a small raid into Bohemia on 7 or 8 May to give his troops some experience and build their confidence. New orders from Berthier forced him to abort this plan, however, and IX Corps turned toward the Danube, heading for Passau in two columns, one via Straubing and the other via Regensburg.[52]

As his Corps moved slowly toward the great river, Bernadotte anxiously awaited the appearance of Dupas's Frenchmen, but his staff officers, scouring the countryside of eastern Bavaria, had thus far failed to locate the division (lost to the limited abilities of 19th-century command and control techniques), and he felt compelled to address the Emperor again.

6 May to Napoleon: 'I have the honour of renewing to Your Majesty the request to add some French troops to the Saxon Army, which is in large part composed of recruits who are weakened every day by the fatigues of the marches. This Corps, placed on the flank of Your Majesty's Army, absolutely must be stimulated by the example of troops accustomed to war. Without such, Your Majesty can expect nothing but the most feeble results. Every day, I am obliged to place the pickets myself.'

10 May to Napoleon: 'Unaccustomed to continual marches without rest, the troops are extremely fatigued...Your Majesty will allow me to repeat once more that to operate with success the Saxon Army absolutely must be supported by a body of French troops.'[53]

Finally, riding into Passau with the advance guard on the 11th, the Marshal found the long-awaited French regiments and could report to Napoleon that 'The union of Dupas's Division with the Saxon troops produced the best effect upon the morale of these troops; the generals themselves and all of the commanders are very pleased that their soldiers are under the eyes...of the French.' This weak division barely comforted Bernadotte, however, and he added, 'I ask Your Majesty to order the reinforcement of Dupas's Division by at least one regiment of infantry and one of cavalry.'[54] Rouyer's German Division was also in the city and the Saxon main body arrived the following day.

May 12 thus saw the entire IX Corps gathered in Passau. Although slow by French standards, the march from Dresden, broken by only two rest days, had been a major achievement and a sudden introduction to Napoleonic warfare for the Saxons. 'Thus does the current style of warfare change our perceptions,' wrote Zezschwitz to his King. 'Only a short time ago, one would have considered it impossible to march from Weimar to Passau over a far from direct route without rest.'[55]

POLISH INTERLUDE

Under the Treaty of Tilsit in 1807, Napoleon's newest royal ally, Friedrich August, acquired the title of Grand Duke of Warsaw. This political expedient on Napoleon's part brought a great expanse of land and thousands of additional subjects under Saxon suzerainty but also imposed an increased garrison requirement, straining the Kingdom's defence resources. When the war started in April 1809, eight battalions, six squadrons and numerous artillery detachments, about 5,000 men, were sprinkled throughout Poland and Silesia, too distant to reinforce IX Corps or provide direct protection to the realm itself. The largest of these forces was GM Ludwig von Dyherrn's combined arms detachment with the Polish main army under Général de Division Prince Joseph Poniatowski near

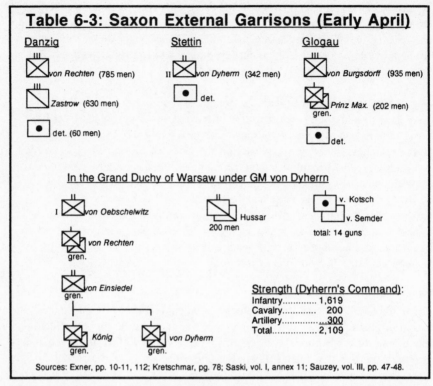

Table 6-3: Saxon External Garrisons (Early April)

Danzig

von Rechten (785 men)

Zastrow (630 men)

det. (60 men)

Stettin

II von Dyherrn (342 men)

det.

Glogau

von Burgsdorff (935 men)

Prinz Max. (202 men)
gren.

det.

In the Grand Duchy of Warsaw under GM von Dyherrn

I von Oebschelwitz

von Rechten
gren.

von Einsiedel
gren.

König   von Dyherrn
gren.   gren.

Hussar
200 men

v. Kotsch

v. Semder

total: 14 guns

Strength (Dyherrn's Command):
Infantry............ 1,619
Cavalry............ 200
Artillery..............300
Total................ 2,109

Sources: Exner, pp. 10-11, 112; Kretschmar, pg. 78; Saski, vol. I, annex 11; Sauzey, vol. III, pp. 47-48.

Warsaw (Table 6-3). When the conflict opened, orders were sent recalling this detachment to Saxony, but by the time the messenger reached Dyherrn other events had intervened to preclude his immediate departure.

Included in Austria's strategic design for 1809 was an operation against the Grand Duchy of Warsaw. Intended to knock Poland out of the war, shield the Habsburg monarchy from Russian intervention and draw Prussia into the conflict as an ally, this task was entrusted to Archduke Ferdinand d'Este, commanding VII Corps, approximately 30,200 men in twenty-five battalions, forty-four squadrons and fourteen batteries. If he was successful against the Poles and the Russians remained quiescent, Ferdinand was hopefully given the rather grandiose mission of turning west and crossing the Elbe to rendezvous with the Main Army in south—central Germany. Attempting to follow his orders but delayed by bad weather and worse roads, the Archduke crossed into Poland on 15 April and headed for Warsaw. In response, Poniatowski assembled the 14,000 men and 41 guns of his small Polish-Saxon army in the excellent position along the Mrowa Stream at Raszyn about ten kilometres south of the capital and waited for the enemy.[56]

The army's position was well chosen, offering the best chances for the Polish general's inexperienced and outnumbered force. The Mrowa was a small watercourse, but its banks were exceedingly marshy and recent rains had rendered the low ground almost impassable to formed bodies of troops. In the area of the battlefield, bridges afforded unhindered crossing at only three points: the villages of

Michalowice, Raszyn and Jaworow. The roads leading to these bridges, however, were carried over the marshes on narrow dikes and thus easily covered by the fire of infantry and guns posted on the heights north of the stream. The villages themselves formed excellent strongpoints and essentially defined the major elements of the Polish Army: GB Lukasz Bieganski on the right at Michalowice (two battalions, four guns); GB Ludwik Kamieniecki on the left at Jaworow (two battalions, six guns); two more Polish battalions with the Saxon infantry and artillery occupied the centre around Raszyn. Poniatowski had also placed an advanced force under GB Michal Sokolnicki (three battalions, six guns) at Falenty across the Mrowa and kept a Polish cavalry regiment, a squadron of Saxon hussars and five horse guns in reserve two kilometres north of Raszyn. The other Saxon hussar squadron and half of a Polish squadron were stationed to guard the extreme right flank near Blonie and a battalion and two guns were kept at Wola. Finally, GB Aleksander Rozniecki commanded a screening force of four cavalry regiments and four horse guns located several kilometres to the south to cover the main position.[57]

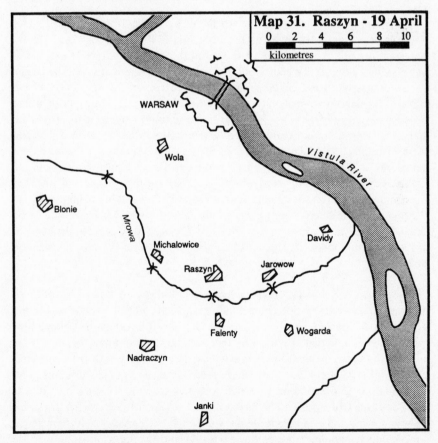

Archduke Ferdinand approached the Raszyn position in the late morning of 19 April, driving in Rozniecki's cavalry screen by about noon and slowly

deploying his own advance guard.[58] Surprised at finding the entire enemy army
before him, he decided to attack immediately with his main effort at Jaworow on
the shortest route to Warsaw. Confounded by difficult terrain and Polish bullets,
however, the main attack soon dissolved into a time-consuming search for bridg-
ing materials and the battle came to focus on the action in the centre.[59] Here
Sokolnicki's men and the *Vukassovich* Infantry Regiment contested possession
of Falenty from 3 to 5 p.m., when the Austrians finally succeeded in evicting the
tenacious Poles. Pursuing their advantage, the Habsburg foot soldiers pressed
into Raszyn itself, but fire from the Saxon guns brought their advance to a halt
and a sudden counter-attack by Dyherrn's infantry hit them in the left flank and
threw the white-coats back across the brook. Ferdinand reinforced *Vukassovich*
with a battalion each of *Weidenfeld* and *Davidovitch*, however, and renewed the
assault at about 7 p.m. The Poles again lost Raszyn and the *Weidenfeld* battalion
apparently advanced in the twilight to push the Saxons out of a wood north of
the village. The engagement came to a close as full darkness fell, the Austrians
withdrawing into and behind Raszyn, the Poles and Saxons maintaining their
positions to the north.[60]

The struggle had been expensive for the green Polish troops, costing about
1,400 in dead, wounded and missing including 300 Saxons and, at 10 p.m.,
Poniatowski held a counsel of war to determine whether his force could undertake another battle. In the course of the discussion, Dyherrn informed the Prince
that his command, bound by the orders he had received on 15 April, would have
to depart for Saxony immediately. Considering the loss of Dyherrn's troops and
his own casualties from the day's fight, Poniatowski decided to retreat on
Warsaw during the night and accepted a temporary ceasefire offered the next
day by Ferdinand.[61] Under the terms of the ceasefire, the Poles evacuated their
capital on the 21st and withdrew to the north, allowing the Austrians to enter the
city but sparing it the ravages of a siege. Dyherrn took this opportunity to lead
his men home, praised for having 'fought valiantly' but leaving behind a degree
of resentment for abandoning an ally in his darkest hour. Marching via Thorn
(attained on 2 May) and stopping briefly at Torgau (14 May), the detachment
was united with Oberst Thielmann's command at Wilsdruff west of Dresden on
20 May.

THE BATTLE OF LINZ (17 MAY)

As Dyherrn and his men approached their homeland and Napoleon was entering
Vienna, IX Corps was moving east up the Danube. Bernadotte had granted his
weary troops a rest day at Passau on the 13th, putting the time to good use by
inspecting the city's defences and reviewing Dupas's and Rouyer's Divisions.
The uniforms of the latter, particularly the well accoutred Nassau contingent,
made a strong impression on Friedrich August's soldiers. In the words of one
member of the Corps staff, 'The Saxon officers could not find enough praise for
the fine bearing and elegant appearance [of Rouyer's Germans]...which created a
not completely comfortable contrast with the old-fashioned costumes of the
Saxon Army.' One of Rouyer's Koburg officers echoed the Saxon assessment:
'These troops ... with their old-fashioned uniforms, created a general sensation;

looking at them, one felt oneself removed to a different century.' [62]

The Saxons would have little rest in Passau. Concerned about Austrian forces operating on his long left flank as he moved on Vienna with the main army, Napoleon ordered Bernadotte to move IX Corps to Linz 'as soon as possible'.[63] The courier bearing these instructions (dated 9 May) reached Corps headquarters on the 13th and the 1st Division departed the pleasant environs of Passau the following day, covering the 57 kilometres to Waizenkirchen before halting for the night. The 2nd Division marched for the same destination on the 15th, while the 1st was ordered to head on to Linz. En route, however, another courier arrived with tidings of the fall of Vienna and new orders: given the unclear situation in the Tyrol, the Corps was to wait for further information from Marshal Lefebvre before proceeding to Linz; if VII Corps' position was grave or if the army's line of communications was threatened, Bernadotte was to move south and assist the Bavarians. Bernadotte therefore stopped the Saxon 1st Division at Eferding and set the 16th aside as a rest day to await further news from his fellow Marshal in the mountains.[64]

At Eferding, three messages arrived that changed his plans for the 17th. From the Emperor and Berthier came orders to join with Vandamme at Linz and move into Bohemia in co-ordination with the main army's crossing of the Danube; and that evening, a note arrived from Vandamme reporting his conviction that an Austrian attack on the Linz bridgehead was imminent and requesting Bernadotte's immediate support. Preparations were accordingly made to march on the morning of the 17th and at least some Saxon quartering parties even reached Linz on the 16th. During the day, word also came in that Austrian patrols had been spotted near Ottensheim and the Marshal posted the Corps' avant-garde to watch the river at Aschach and Wilhering.[65]

The advance elements of IX Corps were on the road by 4 a.m. on the 17th, the 1st Division's Cavalry Brigade leading, followed in echelon by GM Friedrich von Hartitzsch's 1st Brigade and GM Adolf von Boxberg's 2nd. Gutschmid and his troopers were thus the first to reach Linz, at about 7 a.m., and it was not until about 1 p.m. that the dusty foot soldiers of the 1st Brigade began to pull into town. They were granted little time to recover from their 25-kilometre march. As Rühle von Lilienstern relates, he was calmly sitting himself down to pen a letter when 'a tumult arose outside our windows' and he and his Hauptmann friend rushed outside:

> In the market place, the infantry stood ready to march, and, as we reached the bridge, the rattle of musketry could be distinctly heard and smoke was beginning to gather in the distant valley. The Marshal and his staff had halted near the village of Urfar (sic) on the far side of the river, in the act of giving the necessary orders for the disposition of the troops. General Vandamme commanded up ahead; some Württemberg battalions and a pair of guns filed out at speed; a dead officer and a few badly wounded privates were brought in on carts. Now I knew things were in earnest.[66]

It was about 2 p.m. and Kolowrat's main column was in the process of debouching from the woods east of Dornach along the road to Gallneukirchen. The Württembergers were completely capable of containing this poorly managed attack, however, and the two Saxon brigades merely deployed across the river and took up supporting positions on the slopes 1,500 metres due north of the Linz-Urfahr bridge. Waiting in the warm afternoon sun, the neatly ordered ranks were joined by the cavalry quartermasters, pelting up out of the valley on lathered mounts, their business in the villages below rudely interrupted by the appearance of the enemy.[67]

As Vandamme's Württembergers beat back the Austrian attack and began to take the offensive on their own, the Saxon light cavalry, three squadrons of hussars and one half of the *Herzog Albrecht* Chevauxleger squadron, was sent forward to support the advance. Arriving in the centre of the battlefield, they trotted ahead with the Württemberg *Herzog Louis* Jäger zu Pferd to neutralize a battery in the centre of the Austrian line, the keystone of Kolowrat's defence. Looking east, Rittmeister Karl von Czetteritz und Neuhaus, commander of the 2nd Hussar Squadron, saw '...a steep hill, perhaps fifty or sixty feet in elevation, which was occupied by between four and six cannon; back behind it to the left stood the infantry, below the hill were posted Uhlans.' The hussars, dust dulling their blue and white uniforms, began to move forward, the battery firing a poorly aimed volley of canister that flew harmlessly over their heads. A second, better directed blast left several empty saddles, but the men pressed on and the Austrian Uhlans wheeled away granting free access to the slope. As the Saxons were trotting forward, two Württemberger squadrons, swinging up from the south, had surprised the battery and were happily sabring gunners but found themselves threatened by Austrian infantry supports. Pounding down from the north, the hussars and a third squadron of *Herzog Louis* fell upon the Austrian infantrymen with a vengeance and sent them flying in panicked retreat. 'Our 3rd Squadron', wrote von Czetteritz, 'got in amongst some infantry and cut them down.' The battery was securely in Allied hands and Kolowrat had no choice but to withdraw. For their part in this bold feat the Saxon horsemen were awarded two of the six captured guns.[68]

The troopers were jubilantly celebrating their success when a new threat to the Allied bridgehead developed. Kolowrat's right-hand column, about 3,100 men under FML Somariva was supposed to co-ordinate its arrival on the battlefield with the main force, but lethargy and poor roads had delayed it and the white-coated infantry did not appear on the Pöstlingberg until about 7 p.m. This steep hill dominated the Urfahr bridgehead and the entire valley around Dornach, providing the Austrian commander with a tremendous terrain advantage. He also enjoyed the advantage of surprise: there was only one Württemberg Jäger company and a few guns in the works protecting the bridge and the Saxon division was facing west toward the valley where the day's fight had been decided. From the heights of the Pöstlingberg, however, Somariva could clearly witness the withdrawal of Kolowrat's main body and decided nothing serious could be undertaken that day; he would satisfy his mission and his honour by lobbing a few shells at the bridgehead and retiring. He therefore opened fire from the heights and advanced Oberst Leuthner with three battalions and some Jägers down the hill toward Harbach to secure a route of retreat to Hellmonsödt.

GL Zezschwitz's Division was ill-disposed to meet this new threat: Gutschmid's hussars and chevauxlegers were still off beyond Dornach, the rest of the cavalry was east of Harbach, while Hartitzsch's and Boxberg's Brigades (arrived about 6 p.m.) were posted between the latter village and the bridgehead fortifications oriented to the west; two Saxon batteries (Coudray's and Bonniot's) stood on the incline behind the infantry. The two Saxon batteries were the first units into action, firing at Leuthner's men as they descended the hill. The white-coats continued their advance despite this fire, however, brushing aside some small Saxon and Württemberg outpost detachments and slipping north-east along the edge of the valley to make good their escape to Hellmonsödt. The Saxon guns, greatly disadvantaged by the terrain, were also ineffective against the Austrian artillery atop the Pöstlingberg and Bernadotte quickly turned some of his infantry about to drive off Somariva's force. Under the Marshal's personal leadership, I/*Dyherrn*, I/*Prinz Friedrich August*, and a company of II/*Prinz Maximilian* advanced up the heavily wooded slopes in the gathering darkness; the other three companies of II/*Prinz Max* followed in reserve and I/*Prinz Max* shifted to guard the left flank of the attackers. The Saxon infantry drove forward through the trees twice but was repelled each time by the strong Austrian defence. Nightfall appeared to make further offensive efforts futile and Bernadotte broke off the engagement at about 10 p.m. with the Habsburg infantry still firmly entrenched on the hilltop.[69]

This first serious combat for the Saxon infantry illustrated the limitations of its training and organization. Unprepared for modern war:

> [T]he officers of the regiment [*Prinz Friedrich August*] were not a little embarrassed when Marshal Bernadotte rode up during the fight and ordered: 'Forward in skirmish order!' As the trained skirmishers, the Schützen, had been given up to the newly formed Schützen battalions and the other men were not trained in this form of combat, there was nothing to do but give the troops instructions to fan out, remain in their files and press ever forward, 'whereby many a shot was loosed into the blue. Since all continued to go forward, however, the soldiers soon learned what to do and had good success.'[70]

Two or three hours on a dusky hillside do not make true skirmishers, however, and the Saxons would suffer from their antiquated tactical forms through the remainder of the campaign, particularly when they were faced with the frightening speed and violence of a major Napoleonic battle at Wagram. If 'it was not easy for the officers and men to adapt to skirmishing tactics', the Saxon foot soldiers had shown courage and an honest desire to please their Marshal in the evening attacks on 17 May. They bivouacked for the night satisfied with their accomplishments in the day's battle and fully expecting the struggle to be renewed the next morning.[71]

Saxon casualties for the 17th were relatively low: seven dead, 74 wounded and seven captured with an unknown but probably small number of missing.[72] In return, the contingent had had its first taste of serious combat and gained some self-confidence. The light cavalry had performed with courage and dash and the infantry had evinced good morale despite its outmoded tactics, so that GL von Zezschwitz could report to his King: 'I must praise the performance of the Hussars and the detachment of *Albrecht* and, among the infantry, that of the *Friedrich* Regiment, which distinguished itself.' Bernadotte also lauded the performance of his men: the light cavalry's charge had been 'as fortunate as it was fearless' and the Saxon infantry had 'advanced on the enemy with impetuosity, chasing him from all his positions'.[73]

RECONNAISSANCES AND REORGANIZATIONS

The day after the battle, Bernadotte expanded an organizational modification he had initiated while IX Corps was in Passau. It had long been a common practice in the Saxon Army to unite the Schützen of each battalion into separate detachments under the command of a specially selected officer; Bernadotte, however, frustrated at the Corps' lack of light troops, took this traditional practice one step further and consolidated the Schützen of each brigade into an independent Schützen-Abteilung (section or detachment) on 8 May. The battalions committed to the assault on the Pöstlingberg thus had no trained skirmishers to respond to Bernadotte's command 'Allons, tiraillez!' On the 18th, the four Abteilungen, each augmented by 40 additional soldiers, were formed into two provisional Schützen battalions under tough but popular commanders: the serious Hauptmann Albrecht von Metzsch commanding the 1st and Major Christoph von Egidy, "a rugged warrior", taking the 2nd. Internally, each battalion was composed of four companies for a total of about 540-560 officers and men, the 2nd Battalion being slightly smaller than the 1st. Still carried on the rolls of their parent regiments as 'detached', the men of these two battalions were united by their green plumes but otherwise lacked a common uniform, leading Napoleon to ask if they were a unit of recruits or stragglers when he reviewed them for the first time.[74] In fact, assembled from the better soldiers and carefully selected officers, the Schützen Battalions were élite organizations, and, as with all élite formations, the value of combining the superior soldiers into special units has been questioned. Certainly they performed well in 1809 and again in 1812, but their creation was a 'heavy loss' for the line battalions, depriving them of trained skirmishers and hampering the adoption of modern, Napoleonic tactics throughout the Saxon infantry.[75]

Major von Egidy's Schützen were engaging the enemy the day after their battalion was organized. The anticipated renewal of the Austrian attack had not occurred after the Battle of Linz, rather Kolowrat had disappeared into the hills and Allied detachments had to be sent probing north and east to locate his forces. A Württemberg reconnaissance column confirmed the Austrians' withdrawal toward Hellmonsödt on the 18th, but the situation in the east was unclear and, on the 19th, a Saxon patrol was sent up the Gallneukirchen road to collect information. This first patrol, consisting of 60 hussars under Rittmeister von Czetteritz und Neuhaus, rode into Unter Weitersdorf at about 9 a.m. and picked up excellent intelligence on Kolowrat's dispositions from several local inhabitants, one of whom happened to be a transplanted Saxon. Continuing north-east, von Czetteritz encountered a mixed picket line of Austrian infantry (*Peterwardeiner* Grenzer) and cavalry (*Hessen-Homburg* Hussars) just beyond the village and, considering his reconnaissance mission accomplished, withdrew after exchanging a few shots with the enemy.

General Vandamme was not satisfied with the results of this little operation, however, and von Gutschmid was ordered to push his scouts all the way to Neumarkt. He consequently reinforced the somewhat astonished and miffed von Czetteritz with 26 chevauxlegers and 26 Schützen and sent him up the road again. This time, the Saxons skillfully overwhelmed the thin Austrian line, pushing the Grenzer and hussars back on their supports (at about 4 p.m.). These supports, three squadrons of *Hessen-Homburg* , were led by an energetic Major named Medvey, who immediately advanced and charged with 70 of his men, hurling back the Saxon cavalry. The steady fire of the Schützen halted the Austrians and allowed the Saxon horse to escape, but the withdrawal of their cavalry left the light infantrymen exposed and they were overrun in their turn, seventeen falling into the hands of Medvey's troopers. In all, 36 of Czetteritz's men were taken prisoner, including the lieutenant commanding the Schützen detachment. Gathering up their wounded, the Saxons hastened back to Katzbach.[76]

General von Gutschmid was not the sort of man to let such a reverse go unavenged and he set off toward Neumarkt at about 6 p.m. at the head of a strong detachment composed of all three squadrons of hussars, the *Prinz Clemens* Chevauxlegers and the *von Egidy* Schützen; the two Karabinier squadrons were left in Katzbach. Dropping three of the Chevauxleger squadrons and a Schützen company at Gallneukirchen as a reserve, von Gutschmid's force came upon the Austrian vedettes beyond Unter Weitersdorf between midnight and 1 a.m. The old Saxon hussar general slipped his Schützen Battalion off to the left to outflank the enemy position while his lead unit, Rittmeister von Gecka's 2nd Squadron of *Prinz Clemens*, advanced straight up the road. As von Gecka's horsemen galloped forward through the darkness to scatter the brown-clad Grenzer, however, they were countercharged and overthrown by a half-squadron of enemy hussars.[77] One chevauxleger was killed and twelve wounded, including the Rittmeister, but, north of the road, von Egidy's men had already pressed the Croat pickets back and now pivoted to open fire on the Austrian hussars from the flank and rear. Their position turned, the Austrians retired into the night. Von Gutschmid pursued, attacked GM Crenneville in a strong position just south of Neumarkt at 3 a.m. on the 20th with von Egidy's bold Schützen and again forced the Austrians to retreat. He occupied the town without opposition an hour and a half later, remaining there until recalled shortly after dark.[78]

Despite several setbacks, these small actions of 19 and 20 May had a positive effect on the morale of IX Corps in general and the Schützen in particular. 'I am incapable of depicting to Your Majesty the excellent spirit prevalent in the two Schützen Battalions, one witnesses how a body of troops, so chosen and com-

manded by competent and select officers, can rise above the norm,' wrote
General von Zezschwitz. Von Gutschmid proved himself a determined and
aggressive advance guard commander and the Schützen seem to have responded
to his leadership. Moreover, the co-operation between light infantry and light
cavalry in these skirmishes laid the foundation for the strong fraternal relationship that would develop between Schützen and the hussars through the remainder of this campaign and grow to enthusiasm in 1812.[79]

To remedy further the lack of mobile troops in his Corps, Bernadotte directed
the establishment of a horse artillery battery on 20 May. Entrusted to Premier-
Lieutenant Karl von Hiller, it was rather a hodgepodge arrangement. The personnel for the battery, Hiller, a second lieutenant and ninety-four men, were
drawn from the foot batteries and added to the general ills of the Saxon artillery
a complete unfamiliarity with equitation. The fifty-seven train personnel transferred from the commissariat were doubtless little better. The mounts themselves were scraped together by utilizing some of the horses captured on the
17th and requisitioning the remainder, but most of these were poor beasts mar-
ginally suited to their new duties. Finally, the two 'light' 8-pounders from the
reserve park were combined with two similar pieces from Huthsteiner's Battery
to provide Hiller's men with guns. The result was a small battery whose performance 'remained far behind expectations' and which, encumbered by horses the
men hardly knew how to handle, 'could not be employed other than as a foot
battery'.[80]

The Saxons remained in and around the Linz bridgehead until the end of May,
initially deployed with Lecoq and Boxberg on and below the Pöstlingberg,
Gutschmid east of Katzbach on the Neumarkt road, Zeschau, Hartitzsch and
most of the cavalry south of the river.[81] On the 24th, however, as Vandamme's
men prepared to depart, the entire Corps was brought to the north bank of the
Danube to shield the crucial crossing point. Two days later, IX Corps' area of
responsibility was extended to the east. Bernadotte's dispositions were consequently altered again, the Karabiniers being pushed south to Steyr and Major
August von Hake's grenadiers moving to Enns to cover this expanded area while
minor detachments took post as far east as Wallsee and Ybbs to maintain tenuous communications with Melk.

Despite the integration of Dupas's men into his command and the minor but
heartening Saxon successes of 17 and 19 May, the Prince of Ponte Corvo was
still dissatisfied with IX Corps. The Emperor wanted Bernadotte to push north
into Bohemia, manoeuvring 'on Budweis or on Zwettl according to circumstances and the movements of the enemy',[82] but the Marshal believed his Corps
completely incapable of independent operations on this scale and continued to
pester Napoleon with complaints about his troops. A principal subject of his 21
May report, for example, was the Saxon artillery:

> The Saxon Army has no light artillery whatsoever; I ask Your Majesty to
> authorize me to take with me six pieces of Württemberg light artillery; I
> could leave ten Saxon guns in their place ... in the bridgehead. In sum,
> Sire, I would prefer to enter Bohemia with no artillery at all rather than

have a species that is of no use to me.[83]

A letter written to Berthier seven days later was even more blunt:

> ...Your Highness has already received my last letter in which I exposed the impossibility of my attacking the enemy...To debouch from here with any hope of success, a force much more numerous than mine is required and, above all, more experienced troops and generals familiar with the command of independent columns.
>
> The Saxons, I repeat, are incapable of acting independently and there is not one of their generals whom I could trust with a detached operation. I ask Your Grace to bring my situation to the Emperor's attention...
>
> If I had 8,000 or 10,000 French troops, I could attempt something; without guaranty of any great success, I could at least count on the energy and experience of such troops; but, I repeat, with the Saxons I can do nothing.
>
> If the enemy attacks me with the forces at his disposal, far superior to mine, I will regard myself very fortunate to maintain my position. In any case, His Majesty may be certain that I will do my duty...[84]

While Bernadotte industriously corresponded with the Emperor, he kept his troops occupied with numerous small reconnaissance patrols and apparently interminable labour details working on the bridgehead fortifications, duty the Saxons disliked as much as any other line soldiers. 'Our position is marked by the most exhausting fatigues,' reported Zezschwitz, 'barely 20,000 men must perform the duties of 40,000.'[85] The men were generally glad when they were relieved by Lefebvre's Bavarians and called farther east toward the main army.

A curious and unpleasant incident occurred while IX Corps was ensconced about Linz. Late on the night of 28 May, a punitive detachment consisting of the *Egidy* Schützen Battalion and two squadrons of hussars led by GM von Gutschmid occupied Mauthausen, a small town on the Danube about 23 kilometres east of Katzbach. A patrol of thirteen Schützen had been captured here on the 27th and Mauthausen's citizens were suspected of having betrayed the Saxons to nearby Austrian forces; Gutschmid was ordered to extract revenge by 'plundering' the town. Arriving with the dawn, the Saxon soldiers were formed in the market-place, informed of their mission and sent forth to awaken the inhabitants 'with musket butts on doors and window panes'. The officers were ordered to prevent violence against the townspeople and 'after a time, "assembly" was blown and [the Saxons] marched back' to Katzbach. This incident, insignificant in itself, was not isolated and illustrates the frictions between the Austrian civilian population and IX Corps which soon gave the Saxons a nasty reputation as occupation troops.[86]

JUNE - DANUBIAN DOLDRUMS

June began inauspiciously for IX Corps. Relieved at Linz by VII Corps on 31 May, Bernadotte put his men on the road to Vienna, sending the Karabiniers and von Hake's grenadiers ahead along the route of march to Amstetten. Setting out

at 8 a.m., the two detachments arrived in the town late in the day to find wel-
come rest in an untroubled locale after a tiring ten-hour march. The local
French commandant assigned billets for the weary Saxons and apparently told
Major von Hake that the area was safe and untenanted by Austrian troops. The
major consequently neglected normal security precautions (e.g., outposting nearby villages) and contented himself with posting a few guards at the entrances to
Amstetten itself and placing fifty men in the market square as a reserve. Von
Hake's decision proved costly, for at about midnight, Austrian infantry, probably alerted and assisted by the townspeople, overwhelmed the watchposts and
attacked the sleepy detachments. Surprised grenadiers and carabiniers tumbled
out of their quarters, but all was confusion in the blackness and the Saxon officers had great difficulty assembling their partially-clad men. Many of the cavalrymen, separated from their mounts by the Austrian raiders, stamped about in
impotent fury as muskets flashed in the dark streets. Fortunately for the Saxons,
some fifty carabiniers had been left behind in Steyr when the bulk of the two
squadrons departed. Commanded by Premier-Lieutenant von Seydlitz, the big
horsemen suddenly appeared on the outskirts of town and roared through the
streets at the gallop, catching the Austrians in the rear and forcing them to
retire.[87]

This sanguinary little affair cost the Saxons 62 casualties and no small amount
of pride. On learning of the raid, Friedrich August was even moved to admonish
his commanding general:

> As this incident, which has to my regret cost the lives of many brave sol-
> diers, could have been avoided had, as is evident in the reports, our soldiers
> not considered themselves safe and had the appropriate security measures,
> which should never be absent, been observed, thus must I recommend, dear
> general, that you take the most earnest precautions with the troops I have
> placed under your command, so that they will no longer be exposed to 'sur-
> prises' of this sort.[88]

Additionally, the skirmish at Amstetten spurred the Saxon soldiers to distrust
and suspect the civilian population. Citizens of Amstetten were widely supposed to have abetted the Austrian military, action clearly against the norms of
war as the Saxons understood them. They came to fear, even hate, the local villagers and, as the rest of IX Corps marched for Amstetten, it was 'filled up with
malicious disgust toward the poor market town'.[89] Brutality was the result. For
one ordinary Saxon cannoneer, this was hardly surprising:

> That the traitorous inhabitants had much to suffer upon the return of the
> Saxons was not to be wondered at and we thus saw many villages go up in
> flames. Only the fact that Marshal Bernadotte, whom the Saxons highly
> honoured, had his headquarters in Amstetten prevented the town from
> being plundered and fired.

None the less, Rühle von Lilienstern found that 'the small, dark homes were mostly plundered, the wretched household possessions demolished' when he rode into Amstetten on 1 June.[90]

Major elements of IX Corps reached the little city on the afternoon of 1 June, exacting their revenge in the surrounding area. They had started departing Linz on 31 May, moving in small columns as they were replaced by the Bavarians, the last Saxon positions (those on the Pöstlingberg) being turned over to VII Corps troops at 2 a.m. on the 1st. The columns, now reordered, marched on for St. Pölten the next night at 11 p.m. and reached their destination on the 4th. Dupas preceded the main body with an advance guard composed of his division, the two Schützen battalions, two grenadier battalions (*Radeloff* and *Winkelmann*), *Prinz Clemens*, and one squadron each of hussars and carabiniers; GM von Gutschmid commanded the Saxon troops of this force. Dupas and Gutschmid were temporarily posted on the Danube at Mautern to link the outposts of III Corps in the east with VIII Corps in the west, but moved to St. Pölten when relieved by the latter on the 7th.[91] The IX Corps rear guard also shifted to the St. Pölten camp on the 7th. This command, comprising GM Heinrich von Zeschau's Brigade and the two Garde du Corps squadrons, had halted at Oed on 1 June and moved to Melk the next day to await the arrival of the Württembergers. By 10 June, therefore, the entire Corps was concentrated in a large camp around St. Pölten, anticipating further orders and lamenting the paucity of food: 'The approach to the great French army at Vienna caused tremendous difficulties with regard to provisions...subsistence has become very scarce, forage is particularly short.' [92]

While settled in its huts at St. Pölten, IX Corps underwent a major reorganization. Bernadotte, travelling to Imperial headquarters in Vienna, had laid the Saxon manpower problem before Napoleon and obtained permission to combine the two understrength battalions of each regiment into one large battalion of 24 officers, four or five surgeons and 950 to 970 NCOs and men.[93] Bernadotte's order directing these changes reached GL von Zezschwitz on 9 June and was put into effect the following day by incorporating the soldiers of each 2nd battalion company into the like-numbered company of each 1st battalion.[94] Similarly, the two separate line infantry battalions, I/*Dyherrn* and II/*Oebschelwitz*, were amalgamated into a single combined battalion commanded by Oberstlieutenant Heinrich von Klengel. The excess personnel generated by this measure, chiefly officers and NCOs, were sent back to Saxony to serve as cadre for the formation and training of new units. This column of senior leaders, much of it burdened by age and heavy epaulets, departed St. Pölten on 12 June under GM von Boxberg and arrived in its homeland six weeks later: five colonels, two lieutenant-colonels, seven majors, seventy-eight junior officers, four auditors and 207 NCOs. It is perhaps indicative of the antiquity and utility of some of these officers that their number included five regimental commanders and two battalion commanders; Boxberg himself was sixty-one years old and retired in 1810.[95]

The Schützen battalions were also reorganized. With additional drafts from the infantry battalions, each Schützen battalion was now authorized more than 700 men in four 173-man companies. Not all the new men were as select as the original Schützen, but they helped to fill the ranks and the battalions lost nothing of their élite character. The infantry battalions, evidently feeling the loss of their light troops, created new 40-man Schützen detachments and trained them to obey drum signals.

Along with this amalgamation, the internal order of battle of the Saxon divisions was modified, the grenadiers being consolidated into the 1st Brigade of the 1st Division and the Schützen battalions placed under the 1st Brigade of each division for administrative matters (Table 6-4). At Napoleon's order, three of these élite battalions (*Metzsch, Radeloff* and *Winkelmann*) were attached to Dupas's Division in the middle of the month. Additionally, a 'staff battalion' (Stabs-Bataillon) of 400 men under Hauptmann Karl von Oehlschlägel was created from the 'less able-bodied' soldiers; not intended as a combat unit, this bat-

Table 6-4: Reorganized IX Corps (10 June 1809)
Marshal Bernadotte, Prince of Ponte Corvo, commanding
Staff Battalion

1st Division - GL von Zezschwitz
   1st Infantry Brigade - GM von Hartitzsch
      combined Leib Grenadier Garde Battalion
      1st Grenadier Battalion (Major von Radeloff)†
      2nd Grenadier Battalion (Major von Bose)
      3rd Grenadier Battalion (Major von Hake)
      4th Grenadier Battalion (Major von Winkelmann)†
      1st Schützen Battalion (Major von Metzsch)*†

   2nd Infantry Brigade - GM von Zeschau
      König Infantry Battalion
      von Niesemeuschel Infantry Battalion
      combined infantry battalion (OTL von Klengel)
        (I/*von Dyherrn* & II/*von Oebschelwitz*)

   Cavalry Brigade - GM Freiherr von Gutschmid
      Garde du Corps Regiment (in 2 sqdns)
      2 sqdns of the Karabinier Regiment
      Prinz Clemens Chevauxlegers (4 sqdns)
      3 sqdns of the Hussar Regiment
      1 sqdn of *Herzog Albrecht* Chevauxlegers

   Saxon Artillery - Major von Birnbaum
      1st Heavy Battery: Hoyer (to 1st Division)
      1st Light Battery: Bonniot (to 1st Division)
      2nd Heavy Battery: Coudray (to 2nd Division)
      2nd Light Battery: Huthsteiner (to 2nd Division)
      Horse Battery: von Hiller
      Artillery Park
      Pontoon Detachment

2nd Division - GL von Polenz
   1st Infantry Brigade - GM von Lecoq
      Prinz Clemens Infantry Battalion
      von Low Infantry Battalion
      von Cerrini Infantry Battalion
      2nd Schützen Battalion (Major von Egidy)*

   2nd Infantry Brigade - Oberst von Steindel§
      Prinz Anton Infantry Battalion
      Prinz Maximilian Infantry Battalion
      Prinz Friedrich August Infantry Battalion

   Cavalry Brigade - GM von Feilitzsch
      Leib-Garde Kürassier Regiment (4 sqdns)
      Prinz Johann Chevauxlegers (4 sqdns)

French Division - GD Dupas
   Brigade GB Gency
      5th Léger (2 battalions)
   Brigade GB Vaux
      19th Ligne (3 battalions)
   Artillery - Colonel Bardenet
      two foot batteries (12 guns)
   French infantry strength: 3,433 (as of 4 July)

Saxon Strength (approximately 1 July):
   Infantry   - 12,200
   Cavalry   - <u>2,450</u>
   TOTAL   - **14,650** (plus artillery, staff, pontooneers, etc.)
   French Infantry 3,433 (plus gunners and small staff)
   Total   - 18,083

* Assigned to these Saxon brigades for administrative purposes only, detached out for operations.
† Attached to GB Vaux's Brigade of Dupas's Division as of mid-June.
§ Promoted to General-Major on 20 June.
Grenadier Battalion Composition as in Table 6-1.
Sources: Bowden/Tarbox, pg. 192 (French troop strength); Exner, pg. 29, 48; Kretschmar, pg. 74. Saxon troop strength estimated by comparing figures from Exner, Binder-Kriegelstein (vol. II, pp. 360-361), Bleibtreu (pg. 218), Buat (vol. II, pg. 159), Sauzey (vol. III, pp. 47, 55-56), Treitschke (pg. 44), Welden (pg. 151).

talion relieved first line formations of a number of onerous tasks, including guard duties and all ancillary details 'behind the front lines'.   One foot artillery battery was permanently attached to each of the infantry brigades (the putative horse battery seems to have remained under Corps control), but the administrative chain of command for the cavalry was left basically unchanged.[96]

The day following the reorganization, Zeschau's Division moved to Perschling and Gutschmid's detachment rode to Sieghartskirchen, but IX Corps generally remained in and around St. Pölten until the end of the month, training and waiting for orders while tense expectation mounted on both sides of the Danube.[97]   The scent of battle was in the air and, as June bled into July, the Saxons and Dupas's Frenchmen were gradually shifted east toward Vienna, Lobau Island and the broad Marchfeld, taking advantage of whatever rest and revictualling they could find in preparation for the proximate struggle.[98]

July - Blood and Confusion at Wagram

By 3 July, Bernadotte's divisions, French and Saxon, were concentrated around Kaiser Ebersdorf on the right bank of the Danube and, shortly after midnight, the Corps began to cross over the great pontoon bridges on to Lobau Island. Camped on the western side of the island opposite the Mühlau, the Saxons received a visit from the Emperor on the following afternoon.   Their bivouac was barely organized when Napoleon, accompanied by only one aide, appeared and had the closest regiments gathered together.   Speaking through General von Gutschmid, he addressed his Saxon allies:

> Tomorrow there will be a battle - I count on you - Within four weeks, I will return you to your homeland - Colonel Thielmann has chased the enemy out of Saxony!

Loud cries of 'Vive l'Empereur!' crowded the summer air as Napoleon rode on.[99]

As night fell, the Saxons, like the other temporary denizens of the overpopulated island, were assaulted by contending blasts of guns and thunder.   French batteries had opened a tremendous cannonade to cover the army's crossing on to the Marchfeld, provoking, in reply, an Austrian barrage which dropped dozens of shells into the Saxon bivouac.   The *Radeloff* grenadiers were forced to abandon their camp, but the Saxons were fortunate enough to lose only twenty casualties to this ineffectual shelling.   None the less, it was an eerie and frightful night, 'a night out of MacBeth' as one participant described it.[100]   Their campfires quenched by the downpour or doused to eliminate targets for the Austrian gunners, the men were left in utter darkness, subjected to the violence of man and nature: cannon balls crashing through the trees overhead, rain and hail drumming down, thunder, lightning and artillery shattering the night and causing the earth to tremble.   Despite the imminent danger of slaughter with the coming of dawn, therefore, the troops were glad to see the sun rise on a clear and brilliant day.

Table 6-5: Organization of IX Corps at Wagram (5 July)
Marshal Bernadotte, Prince of Ponte Corvo, commanding
Staff Battalion

Advance Guard (GM von Gutschmid)
  Prinz Clemens Chevauxlegers (4 sqdns)
  3 sqdns of the Hussar Regiment
  1 sqdn of *Herzog Albrecht* Chevauxlegers

1st Division - GL von Zezschwitz
  1st Infantry Brigade - GM von Hartitzsch
    combined Leib Grenadier Garde Battalion
    2nd Grenadier Battalion (Major von Bose)
    2nd Schützen Battalion (Major von Egidy)

  2nd Infantry Brigade - GM von Zeschau
    König Infantry Battalion
    von Niesemeuschel Infantry Battalion
    combined infantry battalion (OTL von Klengel)
      (I/*von Dyherrn* & II/*von Oebschelwitz)*

2nd Division - GL von Polenz
  1st Infantry Brigade - GM von Lecoq
    Prinz Clemens Infantry Battalion
    von Low Infantry Battalion
    von Cerrini Infantry Battalion

  2nd Infantry Brigade - GM von Steindel
    Prinz Anton Infantry Battalion
    Prinz Maximilian Infantry Battalion
    Prinz Friedrich August Infantry Battalion

  Cavalry Brigade - GM von Feilitzsch
    Leib-Garde Kürassier Regiment (4 sqdns)
    Garde du Corps Regiment (in 2 sqdns)
    2 sqdns of the Karabinier Regiment

Saxon Artillery - Major von Birnbaum*
  1st Heavy Battery: Hoyer (to 1st Division)
  1st Light Battery: Bonniot (to 1st Division)
  2nd Heavy Battery: Coudray (to 2nd Division)
  2nd Light Battery: Huthsteiner (to 2nd Division)
  Horse Battery: von Hiller

Detached (for all or part of 5 July):
  To Lobau Garrison (GD Reynier)
    3rd Grenadier Battalion (Major von Hake)
    4th Grenadier Battalion (Major von Winkelmann)

  Operating Independently
  Dupas's French Division with
    1st Grenadier Battalion (Major von Radeloff)
    1st Schützen Battalion (Major von Metzsch)

  To Oudinot's II Corps
  Prinz Johann Chevauxlegers (4 sqdns)

* Coudray's and Hiller's batteries with two of Huthsteiner's guns were left behind on Lobau due to congestion at the bridges and did not rejoin the Corps until early on the morning of the 6th.

Grenadier Battalion composition as in Table 6-1.
Source: Exner, pp. 48-50.

THE BATTLE OF WAGRAM: FIRST DAY (5 JULY)

Allotted a position to the right rear of Massena's IV Corps in the French Army's second line, IX Corps did not begin to pass over the Stadtler Arm of the Danube on to the Marchfeld until about 10.30 a.m. and was not fully across until the early afternoon. It was already weakened by detachments. In the orders for the attack, grenadier battalions *Winkelmann* and *Hake* had been assigned to the Lobau garrison under GD Reynier's orders and sometime after noon, *Prinz Johann* was attached to Oudinot to cover his artillery, apparently without Bernadotte's knowledge. Subtracting the two additional battalions with Dupas's Division (*Metzsch* and *Radeloff*), the Saxon Corps crossed onto the Marchfeld with only twelve battalions and sixteen squadrons. Moreover, Hiller's and Coudray's batteries with two of Huthsteiner's guns, half of the Corps' artillery, were delayed by the congestion and confusion at the bridges and remained on Lobau until early on the 6th, leaving Bernadotte with only fourteen Saxon pieces on 5 July. This situation was further aggravated when the 1st Division and Kapitän Johann von Hoyer's Battery were ordered to remain near Gross Enzersdorf to guard the bridges from Lobau until Marmont's Corps arrived; IX Corps was thus reduced to Gutschmid's advance guard plus Dupas's and Polenz's Divisions as it entered into the Battle of Wagram.[101]

Bernadotte began to advance across the broad fields at about 2 p.m., forming the left of the army's second echelon. As the Emperor's mighty armament advanced, its lead elements diverged, Oudinot heading for Baumersdorf and Massena for Breitenlee. Dupas, considerably forward and slightly to the right of the Saxon troops, was thrust forward to fill the gap between these two corps: French regiments and artillery in the front followed by the two Saxon battalions. His march thus initially took him toward Raasdorf, which he easily captured with the 5th Léger at about 3.30 p.m.; from this village, however, he was direct-ed to the north to shield Oudinot's left wing. His own left unsupported, he had to place first one, then two battalions in square on that flank to ward off an Austrian cuirassier division retreating from Raasdorf toward Aderklaa. It was after 5 p.m. before Bernadotte's Saxon Division was close enough for Dupas to recall his squares and focus his attention solely on the enemy forces across the Russbach. By this time he had reached a position less than a kilometre south of the stream and three of the squadrons from *Prinz Johann,* relieved in the mid-afternoon by Colbert's regiments, had ridden over from II Corps to operate on his left flank.[102]

Not far from Raasdorf, as they marched north, Dupas's men encountered a familiar figure on horseback. Addressing the grenadiers of Major Heinrich von Radeloff's Battalion through an adjutant, the Emperor called out 'Saxons, are you brave?' In response, the Saxons waved their caps and muskets in the air, shouting 'Vive l'Empereur' at the top of their lungs. Smiling, Napoleon rode on. The grenadiers would soon have need of all their courage.[103]

Meanwhile, the Saxons had swung around Gross Enzersdorf and turned north-west toward Raasdorf, von Gutschmid leading with the hussars, *Prinz Clemens,* and *Herzog Albrecht* followed by Polenz's infantry; the artillery and GM Wilhelm von Feilitzsch with the rest of the cavalry were farther to the rear. Arriving before Raasdorf, GM Friedrich von Steindel sent the *Prinz Anton* Battalion forward to assist the 5th Léger in driving the Austrians out. The bat-talion stormed toward the village without firing, seized its southern fringe and rejoined its comrades after a few moments of brief, almost bloodless fighting.

Moving beyond Raasdorf, the Saxons encountered more determined resis-tance from Liechtenstein's Cavalry Reserve. Gutschmid, pushing the advance guard toward Aderklaa at about 5 p.m., thus found himself opposed by GM Roussel d'Hurbel's Brigade of cuirassiers (*Herzog Albrecht* and *Erzherzog Franz*) as he reached approximately the level of the Neu Wirtshaus.[104] The Austrians were in a position to threaten the left flank of the infantry and

Bernadotte sent his chief of staff (GB Maurice-Etienne Gérard) to Gutschmid with instructions to remove this threat to the Corps. Equally alert to this danger, GL von Zezschwitz simultaneously sent *his* chief of staff (Oberst Karl von Gersdorff) to Gutschmid and ordered Feilitzsch to reinforce the advance guard for a combined attack against the Austrian brigade.

Gutschmid's two regiments were arrayed in echelon about 900 paces east of the Austrians, Hussars on the right and somewhat forward, *Prinz Clemens* to their left rear.[105] For some reason, this latter regiment, only about 250 strong, boldly but foolishly advanced to the attack before the rest of the Saxon cavalry was up and duly suffered a severe repulse at the hands of the numerically superior Austrian heavies. The white-coated squadrons choose to receive this charge from the halt rather than countercharging as was standard practice, a tactic which was to cost them dearly several minutes later.

As the Leib Kürassier Garde rode past Raasdorf, therefore, they were greeted by the fleeing fugitives of *Prinz Clemens*. Speeding through the intervals between the Leib Kürassier squadrons, the light horsemen almost tore away the outermost cuirassiers, but the fresh riders held their formation, dressed their ranks and deployed for the attack under Gutschmid's and Feilitzsch's experienced eyes.[106] The Saxon commanders arranged their troopers in echelon opposite Roussel's ranks, with the three Hussar squadrons at the right front followed in sequence to the left rear by the Leib Kürassiers, the Garde du Corps, the Karabiniers and finally the lone squadron of *Herzog Albrecht*, reduced to only about 60 men. At Gutschmid's signal, this impressive mounted force began to trot forward in disciplined order toward the waiting Austrians, breaking into a pounding gallop as they closed on the enemy. Roussel again chose to receive the Saxon charge from the halt, his front rank waiting with bared sabres across their thighs, while the men of the second rank prepared to fire their carbines. The discharge of these weapons at 20 to 30 metres distance, however, caused the hard-riding Saxons almost no casualties and did nothing to dispel the fury of their charge. The Leib Kürassiers and part of the Garde du Corps slammed into *Herzog Albrecht* Cuirassiers (Austrian) while the 2nd and 3rd Squadrons of the Hussar Regiment overlapped the Habsburgers' left flank; the other half of the Garde du Corps, the Karabiniers and the *Herzog Albrecht* Chevauxlegers (Saxon) plunged into the lines of the *Erzherzog Franz* Cuirassiers. A frenzied, slashing mêlée ensued, but within minutes, the outnumbered white-coats were fleeing for their lives, leaving behind 85 prisoners and numerous dead. The Austrian troopers retreated behind Aderklaa to rally, Lederer's Cavalry Brigade holding off Saxon pursuit.[107]

As they were trotting forward toward the enemy heavy cavalry, the Saxon hussars on the extreme right of the line were taken under fire by previously unnoticed Austrian infantry. Major von Lobkowitz and Rittmeister von Lindenau coolly pivoted the 1st Squadron to the right and charged the offending foot soldiers. In a short fight, the infantrymen were ridden down, losing their guidon and many prisoners to the exultant hussars. Presenting the banner to Napoleon the following day, the four troopers who had wrenched it from its escort were rewarded with gold and Imperial praise: the Emperor is reputed to have told them that 'he cherished this outstanding regiment as one of the bravest in his army'.[108]

As the sweating but triumphant troopers rode back to reform north of Raasdorf, they were met by a happy Bernadotte, who called out to the officers of the Leib Kürassiers: 'I have always counted on you, but today you have exceeded my expectations!' He had good cause to be satisfied. The Saxon cavalry charges had effectively cleared the entire field between Raasdorf and Aderklaa and allowed the infantry of IX Corps to advance towards the latter village.[109]

Indeed, at about 6 p.m., the lead elements of von Polenz's Division had reached the level of Aderklaa and by 7 p.m., the division was arrayed north and east of the village, about 1,500 paces south of Wagram; the cavalry deployed on

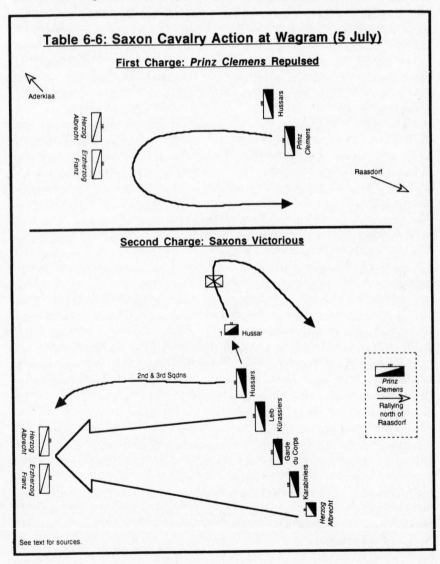

Table 6-6: Saxon Cavalry Action at Wagram (5 July)

First Charge: *Prinz Clemens* Repulsed

Aderklaa

Herzog Albrecht

Erzherzog Franz

Hussars

Prinz Clemens

Raasdorf

Second Charge: Saxons Victorious

1 Hussar

2nd & 3rd Sqdns

Hussars

Leib Kürassiers

Garde du Corps

Karabiniers

Herzog Albrecht

Herzog Albrecht

Erzherzog Franz

Prinz Clemens

Rallying north of Raasdorf

See text for sources.

Polenz's left. At about this hour, GD Savary, the Duke of Rovigo, rode up to Bernadotte with orders from the Emperor to attack Wagram. Despite the lateness of the hour, Davout, Oudinot and Eugène were soon in receipt of similar orders. Consequently, as evening fell towards night, much of the army was advancing on the Russbach Heights to undertake what amounted to a vast reconnaissance in force.[110]

Posted in front of the Army of Italy, Dupas's battalions were included in the attack. While a battalion of the 19th Ligne and the 1st Company of *Metzsch* joined Oudinot's assault on Baumersdorf, the rest of the division slowly advanced toward the heights, artillery leading, infantry behind with *Radeloff* on the left flank, 5th Léger and *Metzsch* in the centre and 19th Ligne on the right.[111] As the division approached the Russbach, the artillery was rapidly withdrawn and the infantry rushed forward under heavy canister fire, waded the hip-deep stream, reformed and stormed up the low rise. Smoke from their firing and the blaze that was now Baumersdorf blinded the Austrian gunners and they fled when French and Saxon infantrymen loomed out of the murk and westering sun to charge through their batteries. Striking the seam between Bellegarde's I Corps and Hohenzollern's II Corps, the French offensive was surprisingly successful. Dupas's hastily reordered infantry surged ahead, scattering the first line of Austrian foot soldiers and pressing Bellegarde's left while MacDonald led another force against Hohenzollern's right. The Saxon Schützen particularly distinguished themselves. Unfortunately, as they came up on Dupas's right rear in the gathering darkness, MacDonald's men mistook Metzsch's white-coated Saxons for Austrians and opened fire, shocking and confusing the Germans. This misfortune coincided with a strong Austrian counter-attack under Charles's personal leadership and before long the entire mass of French and Saxons was flooding back across the Russbach to safety.

Casualties in Dupas's Division were heavy and confusion was worse. Battalion *von Metzsch*, for example, was broken into three pieces. Metzsch himself and about 300 Schützen became separated from the division and spent the night alone somewhere between Dupas and IX Corps; in the morning they were placed under Zeschau's command. The 1st Company, retiring from Baumersdorf, was likewise unable to locate its division commander and bivouacked north of Raasdorf. Only Premierlieutenant Schneider and 43 men found their way to the division. On reporting to Dupas, that 'rather coarse warrior' clasped the lieutenant's hand and heaped the Schützen with praise: 'I will tell the Emperor and the Prince of the Saxons' endurance. Captain von Metzsch is a brave and courageous man.' True to his word, his official report stated that the *Metzsch* Battalion 'had conducted itself very well' during the battle on the 5th. The same report also stated that the *Radeloff* Grenadiers had 'disappeared in the last attack'. This unlucky battalion suffered heavily for its part in the night's struggle. Premierlieutenant von Buchner, the lone officer still fit for duty, and a mere twenty grenadiers finally made their way into the IX Corps camp that night. Their number having increased to about 170 by morning, they were incorporated into Major Karl von Bose's Battalion for the remainder of the battle.[112]

While the army's centre was engaged in this confused and bitter struggle on the Russbach Heights, IX Corps was quiescent, awaiting the belated arrival of the 1st Division from Enzersdorf. With only Polenz's infantry and eight guns (Bonniot's Battery and two of Huthsteiner's pieces) available and with all his requests for reinforcements refused, Bernadotte can perhaps be excused for delaying his attack, but an opportunity was probably lost as he slowly jockeyed for position in front of Wagram. The Saxon cavalry came up from Raasdorf at about 8 p.m. to assume a protective position on the Corps flank, but the two brigades of the 1st Division did not come into sight until almost an hour later, by which time the other French attacks had been repulsed. Despite the lack of support and the rapidly dwindling daylight, Bernadotte sent GM Karl von Lecoq's Brigade toward Wagram at about 9 p.m. after a feeble preparation by the out-numbered Saxon guns. Schützen in front, the Saxon soldiers went forward with vigour, but lost their tactical formation as they splashed through the muddy Russbach and encountered the walls and gardens on the edge of the village. The Saxon artillery had managed to set the village ablaze and bright tongues of flame reached up into the night sky, casting a ghastly illumination on the con-tending battalions and filling the streets with smoke. Lecoq led his men into the market square several times, only to be driven off by heavy musketry from the numerically superior Austrians. Uncomfortable outside their regular formations, the Saxons kept their grip on the south-western portion of the town but could

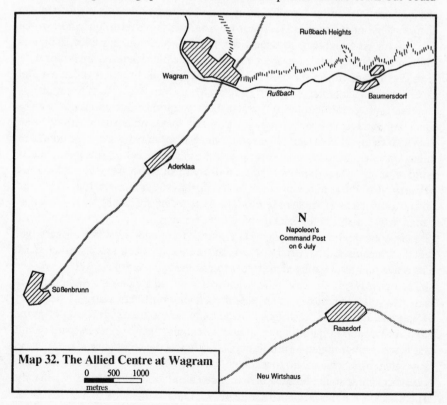

Map 32. The Allied Centre at Wagram

0   500   1000

metres

make no further progress and Bernadotte ordered Zeschau's newly arrived brigade into the inferno to relieve Lecoq. Joined by *Prinz Maximilian* of Steindel's command, this attack also became disordered as it crossed the turbid brook and soon came to a halt in Wagram's fiery, smoke-choked alleys.

In the flickering light of the fires, white-coated forms, some advancing, some withdrawing, cluttered the area between IX Corps' neatly ordered, uncommitted ranks and the flaming houses of Wagram. There seemed little hope of success, but the Saxons still clung to their small gains and Bernadotte was determined to make another attempt. At that moment, the last Saxon infantry brigade, von Hartitzsch's three battalions of grenadiers and Schützen, hove into sight out of the gathering dusk. Galloping over to the grenadiers, one of the Marshal's adjutants brought Hartitzsch the order to storm 'the burning village', but neglected to tell the Saxon general that his countrymen were already fighting in the blazing streets ahead. The consequences of this order, the darkness and the general confusion were tragic. Their general in the lead, the Leibgarde, the *Bose* Grenadiers and Egidy's Schützen advanced to the attack in line, muskets lowered, bayonets fixed and hammers cocked. Their neat formations disordered as they waded across the Russbach, the battalions hastily reformed and pressed ahead through the blackness into increasingly deadly enemy fire. General Hartitzsch had just been struck down, mortally wounded, when clusters of white-coated forms appeared to advance on the grenadiers from Wagram. Discharging their first volley from the hip, the grenadiers reloaded and continued firing toward the shapes ahead of them. The Saxon officers soon discovered to their horror that they were shooting at their own men, but it took several minutes to cease the firing and by then the damage had been done. Receiving musket fire from their rear, the Saxons in the streets and houses believed themselves outflanked and fled from the village, crashing into Hartitzsch's men in their efforts to escape. A simultaneous counter-attack by two Habsburg battalions cleared out the remaining Saxons and, by 11 p.m., Wagram was firmly in Austrian hands.

Withdrawing in considerable disorder, the Saxon infantry assembled north of Aderklaa, their retreat covered by the two remaining battalions of Steindel's Brigade (*Prinz Friedrich* and *Prinz Anton*), drawn up to the west of the road between that village and Wagram. The confusing struggle in the town had been costly: almost half of the men in *König* and *Low* were casualties, while the other battalions each suffered losses in excess of 30 per cent. In addition, two of the brigade commanders, Lecoq and Hartitzsch, and numerous other officers had fallen at the head of their troops during the action. It was a much weakened IX Corps that painfully gathered itself together in the last hour of 5 July.

The first day of the Battle of Wagram was over and the ensuing night was surprisingly still. The Saxon camp roused itself in momentary alarm at the sound of approaching cavalry, but this turned out to be the three squadrons of *Prinz Johann* returning to the fold and all was soon quiet again. Hoyer's Battery and odd batches of stragglers dribbled into the camp as the night progressed, but the only other action was a brief reconnaissance by 50 volunteers from the Leib Kürassiers and a squadron each of Garde du Corps and *Prinz Johann* which only served to confirm that the Austrians held Wagram in strength.[113]

The failure of IX Corps' attack on Wagram on 5 July can be ascribed to several factors. First, Napoleon's conduct of the general battle was less than exemplary. The entire reconnaissance in force was hastily conceived and executed; it has the appearance of a last-minute gamble. Although it came close to achieving notable success, the day was too far gone to expect decisive results and Napoleon appears to have made little effort to co-ordinate the various attacking forces. Compounding the lack of direction from Imperial Headquarters was Bernadotte's lacklustre conduct of the tactical fight. While Dupas, Eugène and Oudinot were straining the Austrian centre, Bernadotte was waiting for his other division and badgering Napoleon for more troops; by this delay of almost two hours, he missed the chance to attack Bellegarde's right at Wagram at the same time that Dupas was pressing the Austrian's left. Furthermore, he demonstrated little tactical finesse when his attack was finally launched. There was no synchronized assault, no attempt to outflank the village, the Saxon brigades were thrown against Wagram piecemeal and defeated in detail.

In Bernadotte's defence, IX Corps was very weak in infantry (no more than about 9,500 considering the multiple detachments) and artillery (fourteen pieces) when it moved against Wagram and Napoleon did nothing to reinforce it despite two requests from the Marshal; additionally, the growing darkness combined with the obstacle posed by the Russbach created almost insurmountable command and control problems for the Saxons. These considerations argued for Bernadotte calling off the attack after testing the enemy position. In very similar circumstances on the army's right flank, Davout wisely halted for the night, preserving his Corps' strength for the 6th, but several Saxon historians indicate Bernadotte did not wish to end the day without attaining some glory and the seizure of Wagram was his sole opportunity.

A final aspect of the failure is found in the fundamental frailties of the Saxon Army itself. Although the Saxon soldiers and officers were courageous enough, their scanty and outmoded training made them uncomfortable in the sort of unordered combat (skirmishing and street fighting for example) at which the French excelled. Lacking the tactical flexibility and initiative of the French, they did their best but were unable to overcome the deficiencies in their training and experience. The combined result of all these factors was a bloody repulse that lowered IX Corps' morale and caused soldiers on the eve of a renewed struggle to lose some faith in their leaders.

There was yet another dimension to the difficulties faced by IX Corps on the night of 5/6 July. In Bernadotte's eyes, the failure of the attack at Wagram had been caused by Napoleon's refusal to support him with reserves and the machinations of the 'hidden hand' at headquarters against him. The following day, he complained bitterly to the Emperor, aiming a shot at Berthier when he claimed that 'an act of treachery or disloyalty' had gone near to depriving him 'of the fruits of thirty years of faithful service' by removing Dupas from his command on the day of battle. In his high dudgeon, he also indulged his temper by expressing rather jejune criticisms of Napoleon's competence, expostulating to GD Mathieu Dumas that the youngest sub-lieutenant in the army would have seen the importance of Wagram and sent him [Bernadotte] 20,000 men; he concluded his tirade with his most famous utterance: that he would have been able to 'compel the Archduke Charles to lay down his arms almost without a blow' by executing 'a scientific manoeuvre'. These remarks when reported to Napoleon placed further strain on the tense relationship between the Emperor and the Marshal.

Bivouacking on the field of battle that night in the face of an external enemy, IX Corps was also besieged by internal problems that would sap its strength and efficiency when the battle reopened: the Saxons' morale had received a severe shaking, their commander, justly or unjustly, felt deeply 'indignant and aggrieved', and Napoleon 'was in no mood to make allowance for any shortcomings on his part or that of his Corps'.[114]

THE BATTLE OF WAGRAM: SECOND DAY (6 JULY)

In the earliest hours of 6 July, both wings of the Austrian Army lurched forward to attack Napoleon's flanks. As the base of the Austrian right's move, Bellegarde pivoted his I Corps on Wagram and advanced in the dissipating darkness toward Aderklaa at about 3.30 a.m. To his great astonishment and delight, a patrol of *Klenau* Chevauxlegers reported that, except for dozens of helpless Saxon wounded, the village was empty. Bellegarde reacted rapidly and shortly after 4 a.m. Austrian infantry was in comfortable possession of this key strongpoint without a shot being fired.

Having received orders to close up with the Army of Italy and feeling himself exposed at Aderklaa, Bernadotte had irresponsibly abandoned the village to the Austrians and withdrawn his Saxons to a new position. The Corps' strength (there were probably something over 6,000 Saxon infantry still in the ranks) and the state of its morale after the previous night's fiasco were other contributing factors. Whatever the cause, dawn found the Saxon troops drawn up in two lines some 1,000 metres south-east of Aderklaa, cavalry on the left. Anticipating the imminent arrival of Massena on his left, the Marshal slid to the north-west, closer to the Army of Italy, between 6 and 6.30 a.m.; the cavalry was now placed on the right and Dupas's tiny force (arrived from around Raasdorf) to the rear. Initially refusing his right to mitigate the ceaseless artillery fire from the heights above Wagram, Bernadotte had to pull back his left as Bellegarde's Corps swung up in line with Aderklaa. To counter the Austrian move, he arrayed all twenty-six Saxon guns in front of the Corps and a deadly duel was soon in progress between these pieces and Bellegarde's batteries. Solid shot screamed through the warm summer air, digging up great furrows and ripping ghastly holes in the ranks on both sides. The Saxons, enfiladed by the Austrian guns above Wagram, were at a particular disadvantage and suffered terribly: the Leib Kürassiers lost fourteen horses to one shot as they attempted to shift position and, over the next three hours, fifteen of the Saxon guns would be rendered useless by Austrian fire.

It was now about 7.30 a.m. Massena was up and Carra Saint-Cyr was slowly preparing to storm Aderklaa. Bernadotte, ordered to co-operate in the attack, sent Dupas's 'Division' (with about 100 Saxon Schützen) and three Saxon battalions (Leib-Garde Grenadiers, *Prinz Max* and *Prinz Friedrich*) forward to support Saint-Cyr. As the French and Hessians stormed through Aderklaa and beyond, the Saxon battalions and Dupas succeeded in forcing their way between Aderklaa and Wagram. They did not stay there long. At about the same time that the Saxons and Dupas were reaching the area between the two villages, a strong Austrian counter-attack threw back Saint-Cyr's left and pressed into Aderklaa; the fleeing soldiers of the 24th Léger were saved from Habsburg sabres by the timely intervention of several Saxon squadrons. The same Austrian counter-attack also struck Bernadotte's troops and they were soon retreating in great disorder, threatened by pursuing squadrons of *Klenau* Chevauxlegers. Fortunately, Bernadotte was on hand with the Saxon cavalry to drive off the Austrian horsemen and cover the panicked infantry. Although the Saxon troopers were quickly brought to a halt by murderous artillery fire from their right flank, their appearance at the right moment caused the Austrians to break off and withdraw.

The French centre was now (about 9 a.m.) in dire danger and Napoleon arrived in the nick of time to bring some order to the wild confusion. Riding among the Saxon troops, he urged them to stand fast, telling them that all would soon change and even speaking to them in his crude German: 'Saxons! Don't run! Manoeuvre!' He sat briefly in Massena's coach to direct that Marshal towards Aspern and had a brusque encounter with Bernadotte in which harsh words seem to have been exchanged. Before long, however, Massena was off on his famous flank march, the even more renowned 'Grand Battery of Wagram' had been formed to take IV Corps' place and the Army of Italy had swung to the left to cover the gap left in the line by Bernadotte's withdrawal.

What had happened to IX Corps? The prevailing confusion makes it difficult to determine what actually transpired in Bernadotte's command between 9 a.m. and noon. It is clear that the Saxons supported the attack on Aderklaa in the early morning and that they were back near Raasdorf, rallying and reforming, by midday. The question revolves around the hours between these two villages, specifically, whether or not the Saxon infantry were routed after the repulse at Aderklaa. French authors almost uniformly state that IX Corps fled the field in complete panic on the morning of the 6th, giving rise to a legend that has become an assumed fact in Napoleonic studies. Saxon writers, on the other hand, either gloss over the withdrawal (e.g., Exner) or go to great lengths to defend their countrymen, quoting Zezschwitz ('Our retreat was completely controlled') and Bernadotte ('If it were possible to exceed your [Saxon] cavalry in excellence, your infantry would have done so today') to prove the steadiness and valour of the Saxon foot soldiers. As with most controversies, there is probably some truth on each side. The Saxon artillery clearly held its ground (no guns were lost despite the fury of the battle) and the cavalry performed with its wonted skill and courage. The same, however, cannot be said of the infantry. If some Saxon units, or parts of Saxon units, retreated in good order and only when commanded to do so, hundreds of individual soldiers, like their French allies in Carra Saint-Cyr's Division, almost certainly ran for the rear in terror. The French participants in the battle (e.g., Massena, Pelet, Marbot, Savary, Dumas) did not create their tales of Saxon rout out of whole cloth and the very fact that

IX Corps was combat ineffective for the remainder of the day argues against those writers who would have the entire Corps retreating 'as if on the drill field'. Running pell-mell across the plains and jostling Massena's carriage as they streamed past, the Saxon fugitives left their Corps a useless, empty husk and created an image in Napoleon's mind that endured until his death.[115]

In any event, except for the artillery, the Saxon Corps was out of action by noon and took no further part in the Battle of Wagram. The remaining eleven guns under Birnbaum's command were ordered into the front line again at about 3 p.m. and took up firing positions on the left of some French batteries near Gerasdorf until night brought an end to the fighting. The remainder of the Corps collected itself around Raasdorf until evening, when it marched west to bivouac for the night near Leopoldau.

Casualties from the two days of battle devastated the ranks of IX Corps. The Saxons alone lost 603 dead, 2,277 wounded and 1,358 missing for a total of 4,238 men, or approximately 30 per cent of their strength (as of 1 July); Dupas reported an equally dreadful cost in blood: 534 dead and 1,985 wounded. Foot soldiers accounted for most of the Saxon losses (3,761 = 89 per cent), the most battered battalions being *Prinz Max* (lost 470), *Low* (409), *Metzsch* (332) and *Radeloff* (251). Cavalry losses were 446, which is to say a little over 10 per cent of the total casualties but nearly 20 per cent of the Corps' mounted strength. Although engaged in a brutal three-hour duel with the Austrian artillery in which fifteen of its pieces were dismounted, the casualty rate among Saxon gunners was very low: only twelve men killed, sixteen wounded and three missing.[116]

The Relief of Bernadotte and the End of the Campaign (7-14 July)

The IX Corps suffered one additional casualty several days after the Battle of Wagram: its commander. Infuriated by an Order of the Day issued to the Saxons by Bernadotte, Napoleon relieved the fiery Gascon and sent him away to 'take the waters' back in France. On 9 July, therefore, IX Corps was dissolved and GD Jean-Louis-Ebénézer Reynier, a tough, taciturn Swiss known for his honesty and tactical ability, assumed command of the Saxon contingent. Bernadotte's order, issued on 7 July at Leopoldau, was even more bombastic than most documents of its ilk and seemed almost calculated to offend the French Army and confirm the Prince of Ponte Corvo's reputation as an untrustworthy braggart.

Saxons, on 5 July, between 7,000 and 8,000 of you pierced the centre of the enemy's army and fought your way to Wagram despite the efforts of 40,000 of the enemy supported by fifty guns; you fought until midnight and you bivouacked in the middle of the Austrian lines. On the 6th at daybreak, you renewed the combat with the same perseverance. Amidst the ravages of the enemy's artillery, your living columns remained as motionless as bronze. The great Napoleon witnessed your devotion; he numbers you among his brave warriors. Saxons, a soldier's fortune consists in doing his duty, you have nobly done yours.

Inflammatory and 'inexact' as this order was to the French, the entire event might have passed quietly had a German newspaper in Frankfurt not picked it up and published it. Convinced Bernadotte had intentionally distributed 'this inconceivable Order of the Day' to the German press, the French officer corps was outraged. Savary recorded Napoleon's reaction: 'The Emperor was put out by this conduct; he could not tolerate that someone would simultaneously commit such an impropriety and fallacy, but he did not want to injure the men who had risked their lives in his service. None the less, the outburst was extreme and he did not believe he could let it pass.' On 5 August, the Emperor issued a confidential rescript on the matter. It was distributed to the marshalate alone; the public, the Saxons, even Reynier were kept ignorant of its contents:

His Majesty expresses his displeasure with the Marshal Prince of Ponte Corvo for his Order of the Day dated Leopoldau, 7 July, which was inserted in almost every newspaper in the following terms: [there followed a reprint of Bernadotte's order].

Independent of the fact that His Majesty commands his army in person, it is he alone who distributes the degree of glory which each merits.

His Majesty owes the success of his arms to French troops and not to any foreigners. The Prince of Ponte Corvo's Order of the Day, tending to give false pretensions to troops at least mediocre, is contrary to the truth, to politics and to national honour. The success of the 5th is due to the corps of the Marshals the Duke of Rivoli and Oudinot who pierced the enemy's centre at the same time that the corps of the Duke of Auerstadt was turning his left.

The village of Deutsch-Wagram was not in our possession on the 5th; that village was taken, but not until the 6th at noon by the corps of Marshal Oudinot.

The corps of the Prince of Ponte Corvo did not remain *as immobile as bronze*: it was the first to retreat...His Majesty wishes that this expression of his discontent serve as an example so that no other marshal will attribute to himself the glory that appertains to others.

His Majesty orders, however, that this present Order of the Day, which could grieve the Saxon Army in spite of the fact that the soldiers know well they do not deserve the praise given to them, remain secret and be sent only to the marshals commanding army corps.[117]

Bernadotte's relief, however, was the result of a combination of factors and his Order of the Day was only the proximate cause, the straw that broke the Emperor's patience. His patience had been tried severely in 1806 when many of Napoleon's subordinates urged the most draconian penalties for Bernadotte's failure to contribute to the dual victory of Jena-Auerstädt. That incident planted seeds of distrust that sprouted three years later. In 1809, Napoleon and Berthier must certainly have wearied of Bernadotte's jeremiad; his continual complaints, even if based in fact, often resembled excuses for inaction and were inconsistent with the hyperbolic plaudits he handed the Saxons immediately after Linz and Wagram. Furthermore, his performance in the campaign had been uninspiring. While encamped about Linz, he inflated Austrian strength and evinced little interest in pressuring the enemy in Bohemia as Napoleon had repeatedly directed. At Wagram, he showed himself sluggish and testy. He demonstrated tremendous personal courage and made every effort to conserve the lives of his troops, but his tactical performance was poor and soldiers were needlessly sacrificed in unco-ordinated, unsupported attacks on both the 5th and the 6th; the abandonment of Aderklaa was a particularly egregious error. Having failed to accomplish his missions, he haughtily attempted to blame his mysterious enemies in Imperial Headquarters and even Napoleon himself. His martyred vainglory reached its height when he spoke to the Saxons after the battle on the 5th:

I wanted to lead you to the field of honour but you had nothing but death before you. You have done all I had a right to expect of you, but you will receive no justice because you were under my command.' [118]

Bernadotte's angry analysis proved prescient. The reputation of the Saxon infantry became inextricably bound to that of its commander in 1809, reinforcing the already unflattering image most French had of the Saxon foot soldiers. Many later writers, mindful of Bernadotte's treachery and Saxon defection in 1813, have tended to link the man with his men, even to the point of spuriously asserting that Wagram might have foreshadowed Leipzig.[119] The obvious fallacy of such claims does not automatically render the Saxon contingent into an éite band of heroes, but even if the Saxons were not the most reliable troops in the Grande Armée in 1809, their association with the proud and peevish Prince of Ponte Corvo has probably added an unfair additional taint to their history for the past 180 years.[120]

The Saxons were stunned when Bernadotte announced his imminent departure. GL von Zezschwitz wrote to his king: 'The Prince of Ponte Corvo just summoned me and explained to me that he is turning over command of his troops, including the Royal Saxon contingent, to General Reynier ... I hasten to report this unexpected and extremely unpleasant news.' According to the Saxon Chief of Staff, Oberst von Gersdorff, the soldiers were 'inconsolable' and our faithful commentator, Rühle von Lilienstern, wrote to his sister:

The grief and consternation over this completely unexpected development is great and widespread. Officers and soldiers had been very attached to the Prince because he cared for them and demonstrated such a concern for them at every opportunity that it seemed he himself was a Saxon and knew no higher interest than their welfare.

It was thus a shocked and dispirited contingent that reported for duty with the Army of Italy on 10 July.[121]

The exigencies of war, however, allowed the Saxons no time to ponder Bernadotte's sudden relief. The Corps had moved from Leopoldau to Gross Enzersdorf on the 7th as the main army took up its hesitant pursuit of Archduke Charles. Here the combat troops of the Corps were reunited with the Staff

Battalion and parks which had remained in the latter village during the battle. While most of the units rested, collected stragglers and repaired their equipment, the light cavalry took up positions to the east, with a detachment of 60 hussars posted as far as Orth and patrols scouting even farther; Austrian hussars spotted in the distance quickly retired in the direction of the River March. Saxon patrols exchanged a few shots with Austrian troopers on the 8th as well, but Gutschmid's hussars were withdrawn toward Wittau later in the day to prepare for more serious operations.

To shield his army's rear from Archduke Johann's rather half-baked schemes, Napoleon had assigned the Saxons and Württembergers to the Army of Italy and directed the Viceroy to drive the Austrian outposts back across the March and seize crossings over that river. To this end, Eugène ordered a strong reconnaissance for 9 July. While French patrols scouted other parts of the river, GM von Gutschmid led the Saxon advance guard north-east to Marchegg. Composed of the Hussars, *Prinz Clemens*, *Egidy*, and two guns, Gutschmid's command sparred indecisively with an enemy detachment just west of the town and took a few casualties before returning to Leopoldsdorf with information on the enemy's strength and dispositions. Armed with this intelligence, Eugène cautiously moved his army east on the 10th; the Saxon Corps halted around Lassee and its cavalry, screening towards the river, skirmished with Austrian horsemen. The Saxons shifted a few kilometres to the north-east on the 11th, bivouacking around Baumgarten, where Reynier reinforced Gutschmid's advance guard with von Metzsch's Schützen and three squadrons of *Prinz Johann*. The 12th saw the Corps ten kilometres further north between Angern and Zwerndorf.

The following day, the Saxon advance guard crossed quickly over the March, many of the horses swimming, and advanced on Pressburg. En route, word arrived that the armistice had been signed at Znaim and Gutschmid, having occupied Stampfen (now Stupava), opened a parley with his Austrian counterpart, the 'hot-headed but brave' Landwehr Oberst Leopold von Trautenberg. Trautenberg was not disposed to believe the armistice story and sent a combined arms force forward to attack the Saxons. Gutschmid, spying the moving columns, turned his horse about and bolted from the parley rendezvous at the gallop to rejoin his command. Before he could arrive, however, three squadrons of *Stipsicz* Hussars had attacked and captured a squadron of *Prinz Johann* which, trusting in the truce, had incautiously dismounted. Acting on his own initiative, the commander of *Prinz Johann* countercharged and overthrew the Austrian hussars moments later, freeing the Saxon prisoners and sending the enemy pelting south in confusion. The chevauxlegers reformed while Major von Egidy, also taking matters into his own hands, advanced out of Stampfen at the run with three companies of his Schützen. His objective was a battalion of *Beaulieu* and two guns which were moving on the village and after softening the tightly packed enemy mass with skirmish fire, he led his men into the attack with the bayonet. Almost simultaneously with the infantry charge, the rallied squadrons of *Prinz Johann* (all three) broke into the Austrian formation from the rear. Resistance soon came to an end and the Saxons could jubilantly report the capture of 352 men, two guns and a standard. Austrian casualties also included

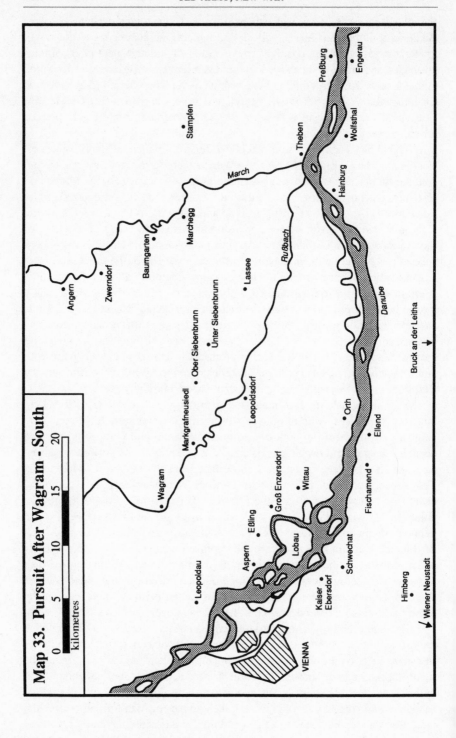

Map 33. Pursuit After Wagram - South

some 84 dead, not a few of whom were victims of Saxon wrath, hapless infantry cut down by chevauxlegers angry over the perceived violation of the truce. Saxon losses totalled one dead, one missing and 28 wounded. Reynier was naturally pleased with the results of the action and von Zezschwitz informed his monarch that 'the enemy officers themselves say that they have never seen such an attack'.

His brigade thus roughly handled and under considerable personal danger (Gutschmid had the Austrian Oberst escorted and loudly directed the guards to split the colonel's head if any Austrian opened fire), Trautenberg and his superior in Pressburg, GM Bianchi, resumed negotiations and concluded an agreement with the French and Saxons. Accordingly, on 14 July, the Austrians retired into Hungary, the remainder of the Saxon contingent crossed over the March and Reynier established his headquarters in Pressburg.[122]

Thus ended the Saxon contingent's participation in the Danube valley campaign of 1809. Despite Napoleon's promise on the eve of Wagram, Friedrich August's men did not return home until mid-January 1810, passing over the Bohemian mountains in miserable winter weather. Although greeted with joy by the home population, the men of the former IX Corps departed Austria under a cloud. The experiences of 1809 seemed to confirm French impressions of the Saxons as epitomized by the Emperor himself: 'They were the worst troops in the army,' he said, while exiled on St. Helena. This low opinion, doubtless linked to the friction between Napoleon and Bernadotte, has echoed down through the years, defining the reputation of Saxon arms. Sauzey, ninety-eight years later, reflected the prevailing view: 'For seven years they [the Saxons] fought courageously whenever French troops were at their side in numbers; but their valour was always relative: left to themselves, in independent formations, they exhibited numerous frailties.' Saxons have contested this perception ever since. Indeed, the rout of the entire IX Corps at Wagram is probably an exaggeration, but Bernadotte's and Zezschwitz's accounts are likewise hyperbole; those were not men of 'bronze' on the Marchfeld, but men of flesh, and many fled.[123]

None the less, in assessing the Saxon Army of 1809, several glaring weaknesses are apparent. The cavalry proved professional, brave and tactically competent, but the infantry and artillery, while sharing the quality of courage with their mounted brothers, were poorly trained and burdened with obsolete tactical precepts that severely limited their usefulness on the battlefield. The Schützen, being a well-trained élite, were a notable exception to this general rule. Fighting with skill and determination at both Wagram and Stampfen, they earned the praise of French and Austrians alike and showed themselves far superior to their line comrades. Under good leadership, such as that provided by the aggressive von Gutschmid, the Saxons could perform adequately, but exposed on the Marchfeld under Bernadotte's hesitant command, they suffered cruelly and faltered. The blood spilled by IX Corps along the Danube did, however, have at least one positive result for the Saxon Army: Friedrich August's eyes were opened to the problems of his military and a thorough series of tactical and administrative reforms was instituted which helped prepare Saxony's soldiers for the dreadful rigours of the 1812 and 1813 campaigns.[124]

NOTES

1: Oakley Williams, ed., *In the Wake of Napoleon, Being the Memoirs (1807-1809) of Ferdinand von Funck, Lieutenant-General in the Saxon Army and Adjutant-General to the King of Saxony*, London: Lane, 1931, pp. 61-3.

2: Williams, pp. 94-5.

3: André Bonnefons, *Un Allié de Napoléon, Frédéric-Auguste Premier Roi de Saxe et Grand-Duc de Varsovie*, Paris: Perrin, 1902, pp. XVI, XX, XXII.

4: Bonnefons, p. 264.

5: Bonnefons, p. 504.

6: Alfred Rambaud, *L'Allemagne sous Napoleon Ier (1804-1811)*, Paris: Perrin, 1897, p. 85. The unfortunate King suffered accordingly when Napoleon's star failed in 1813. See also Bonnefons, pp. 292-3.

7: Bonnefons, p. 502; Williams, pp. 11-12, 58 (von Funck's quote from this work).

8: Bonnefons, pp. 180-1; Rambaud, p. 75; Lt. Colonel Sauzey, *Les Saxons dans nos Rangs*, volume III of *Les Allemands sous les Aigles Françaises*, Paris: Terana, 1987, pp. 18-30. Napoleon's proclamation to the Saxon officers was carried to Dresden by von Funck, initiating an association between the Emperor and the Saxon staff officer that would continue throughout the period. The Emperor was not entirely beneficent: Saxony was required to pay an indemnity of more than 25 million francs, approximately one million for each one thousand of Friedrich August's soldiers who had served with the Prussians.

9: Bonnefons, p. 267, 503; Williams, pp. 61-3, 139, 156-9 (Talleyrand's statement).

10: Williams, pp. 128-31.

11: This paragraph is based primarily on Funck's memoirs (Williams, pp. 61-3, 81, 164-5) and Bonnefons excellent summary (p. 283). Davout's impression was similar, see John G. Gallaher, *The Iron Marshal*, Carbondale & Evansville: Southern Illinois University Press, 1976, p. 176.

12: Condensed from Funck's account in Williams, pp. 267-70; see pp. 249-54 for other examples of the incompetence, duplicity and blithering indecision that characterized the highest levels of Saxony's military. Details of Schill's raid and the Saxon/Westphalian reaction are in Chapter 9.

13: O. Schuster and F. A. Francke, *Geschichte der Sächsischen Armee von deren Errichtung bis auf die neueste Zeit*, vol. II, Leipzig: Duncker & Humboldt, 1885, p. 299; Williams, pp. 138-9, 270-1.

14: The *Aus dem Winkel* Grenadier Battalion, the *Kurfürst* Regiment and the chevauxlegers earned especial notice for their courage (Artur Brabant, 'Die Sachsen in früheren Kriegen von 1740 bis 1871', in *Sachsen in grosser Zeit*, Edmund Hottenroth, ed., vol. I, Leipzig, 1923, p. 52).

15: Elting, pp. 401-2; Williams, pp. 139-40, 150-1.

16: Quoted in Sauzey, vol. III, p. 41.

17: Sauzey, vol. III, pp. 30-44.

18: Strengths compiled from regimental histories (citations below), Moritz Exner, *Die Antheilnahme der Königlich Sächsischen Armee am Feldzuge gegen Oesterreich und die kriegerische Ereignisse in Sachsen im Jahre 1809*, Dresden: Baensch, 1894, pp. 4-6, 17-19; Thomas E. Devoe, 'Saxon Garrison and Invalid Companies', *Empires, Eagles and Lions*, Issue 88 (1 June 1985); and Otto von Pivka, *Napoleon's German Allies (3): Saxony*, London: Osprey, 1979, p. 5. See also *Krieg 1809*, vol. IV, p. 225. It is worth noting that the musket issued to the Saxon infantry was crudely made, earning it the nickname 'cow's foot' (Kuhfuss).

19: Funck was absolutely infuriated by the disutility of the Saxon uniforms, the pointless fervour with which the prevailing pattern was defended and the draconian punishments meted out to offenders. He does, however, record a small victory: preventing the introduction of silver foil sabretaches for the hussars (Williams, pp. 131-7).

20: See, for example, Elting, p. 402; Sauzey, vol. III, pp. 42-3; Funck alludes to Napoleon's praise (Williams, pp. 89, 113-14).

21: Strength figures from Exner (p. 7); quote also from Exner (p. 9).

22: The artillery park also included two reserve pieces which would later be used to form a small horse battery (Exner, p. 20; A. von Kretschmar, *Geschichte der kurfürstlich und königlich Sächsischen Feld-Artillerie von 1620-1820*, Berlin: Mittler & Sohn, 1876, p. 71-4; and Generalmajor von Werlhof, 'Bernadotte und die Sachsen bei Wagram 5. und 6. Juli 1809', *Beiheft zum Militär-Wochenblatt*, Heft 1, 1911, p. 15). The older, heavier Saxon guns weighed 3,323 pounds, the newer only 2,663 (Otto von Pivka, *Armies of the Napoleonic Era*, New York: Taplinger, 1979, p. 23). In the past, Saxon infantry regiments had each been allotted regimental artillery pieces and orders seem to have been issued for each regiment and grenadier battalion to take these 3- and 4-pound guns into the 1809 campaign: four per infantry regiment, two per grenadier battalion (E. G. M. Freiherr von Friesen, 'Dresden im Kriegsjahre 1809', *Mittheilungen des Vereins für Geschichte Dredens*, Heft 11, 1893, p. 6). Some sources thus claim that the Saxons had 46 regimental guns on the campaign, but no account makes any specific mention of these guns in action, so that even if they were present for the campaign, it is unlikely that they made any significant contribution. See Schuster/Francke, p. 271; and H. Bucher, 'Die Theilnahme der sächsischen Truppen an den Kriegsereignissen vor hundert Jahren', *Dresdener Anzeiger,* 179 Jahrgang, Nos. 185 and 186 (6-7 July 1909).

23: Exner, p. 20; Schuster/Francke, p. 273.

24: Description of Saxon tactics taken from Exner, p. 9; Kretschmar, pp. 71-4; Werlhof, pp. 15-16. Quote about the weaknesses of the artillery is from an Oberst named Heinrich Aster who apparently witnessed the Saxon artillery's disasterous début before Bernadotte on 24 March 1809 (cited in Friesen, p. 14).

25: *Correspondence* No. 14721.

26: Note that the 2nd Division was initially entrusted to GM von Barner; he was replaced by GL von Polenz when the latter returned from Warsaw (Exner, pp. 15-16).

27: Bernadotte declined to support Napoleon during the coup of 18 Brumaire and was vaguely implicated in some anti-Consular intrigues in 1802. Still, Napoleon apparently continued to trust him and considered him for high positions, even thrones. See Sir Dunbar Plunket Barton, *Bernadotte and Napoleon 1763-1810,* London: Murray, 1921, p. 209.

28: Davout was another foe. The prickly Vandamme, on the other hand, was a staunch friend. Barton, *Bernadotte,* pp. 200-3, 210-11.

29: These were known as 'gasconades'.

30: In addition to Barton's detailed biographies, see Elting (pp. 126-8) for a good thumbnail sketch of Bernadotte and T. A. Heathcote's chapter in David Chandler (ed.), *Napoleon's Marshals,* New York: Macmillan, 1987. The Marshal's care of his troops and their response to him is noted in J. A. U., *Der Feldzug Frankreichs und seiner Verbündeten gegen Oesterreich im Jahre 1809,* Meissen: Goedsche, 1810, p. 120.

31: There may have been some justification for this fear. Napoleon's Chief of Staff had little love for the thorny Gascon and was apparently not above conspiring to sully Bernadotte's reputation. Barton, *Bernadotte,* pp. 204-8; Sir Dunbar Plunket Barton, *The Amazing Career of Bernadotte,* London: Murray, 1929, pp. 215-16; Léonce Pingaud, *Bernadotte et Napoléon 1797-1814,* Paris: Plon, 1933, p. 96.

32: Quoted in Barton, *Bernadotte,* p. 207.

33: 23 March 1809. Saski, vol. I, p. 368.

34: 26 March 1809. Saski, vol. I, p. 397.

35: 28 March 1809. Saski, vol. I, p. 412. This problem apparently continued and, on reaching the Danube, the Marshal ordered strict reviews to determine the true strength of each company (Bernadotte to Napoleon, 9 May 1809, Saski, vol. III, pp. 217-18).

36: Quote from Exner (p. 15). Funck says the Saxons 'idolized' their commander (Williams, p. 247) and Bonnefons (p. 297) claims they were enthusiastic about the Marshal who led them into fire.

37: The cavalry must be considered an exception here. Cavalry tactics, at least at the regimental level and below, had changed little from the Seven Years War and the Saxon troopers were able to give a good account of themselves where their infantry and artillery counterparts appeared clumsy and anachronistic.

38: Exner, pp. 9-10; Werlhof, p. 14. The crippling weaknesses generated by the old promotion system had not gone unrecognized, and a Royal Order announced new promotion criteria on 26 February 1809: future officer promotions were to be based 'primarily on competence, outstanding merit and proven zeal, secondly on physical fitness'. This order came too late to effect the character of the officer corps in the war with Austria, but it did facilitate the rapid elevation of several competent senior officers in 1809 (such as Funck, Thielmann and Gersdorff) and laid the groundwork for subsequent improvements (Georg von Schönberg, *Geschichte des Königl. Sächsischen 7. Infanterie-Regiments 'Prinz Georg' Nr. 106,* Leipzig: Brockhaus, 1809, vol. II, p. 4). See also *Geschichte des Königlich Sächsischen 3. Infanterie-Regiments Nr. 102 'Prinz Regent Luitpold von Bayern' 1709-1909,* Berlin: Mittler & Sohn, 1909, p. 150.

39: Exner, pp. 4 (first quote), 16-21. Contemporary's insight from Otto August Rühle von Lilienstern, *Reise mit der Armee im Jahre 1809,* Rudolstadt: Hof- Buch- und Kunsthandlung, 1810, vol. I, pp. 130-1. The problem was not limited to the officer ranks: there were NCOs in their 60s and common soldiers who had seen 40 or 50 birthdays. The problem was particularly acute in the artillery where most of the officers and many of the NCOs were over age (Friesen, pp. 6-9; Werlhof, p. 15).

40: Quote from Bonnefons, p. 287; see also *Krieg 1809,* vol. IV, pp. 226-7.

41: Rühle, vol. I, pp. 120-9. Rühle later became a General-Lieutenant in Prussian service.

42: Rühle, vol. I, pp. 121, 128-9.

43: The abortive efforts of Katte and Dornberg had aroused the Emperor's concern. See Chapter 9.

44: Exner, p. 23; *Krieg 1809,* vol. IV, pp. 226-8. The instructions for Bernadotte were dated 19 April (Saski, vol. II, pp. 274-5).

45: Many of the Saxon troopers and their mounts were new to army service and unaccustomed to the sight of the long, deadly lances and flashing pennons (Rühle, vol. I, pp. 185-7). The description of Gutschmid is from an officer in Egidy's battalion cited in Albrecht von Holtzendorff, *Geschichte der Königlich Sächsischen Leichten Infanterie von Ihrer Errichtung bis zum 1. October 1859,* Leipzig: Geisecke & Devrient, 1860, p. 10. Note that the general's name is often spelled 'Gutschmidt' but I have used the version in Heinrich A.

Verlohren, *Stammregister und Chronik der Kur- und Königlich Sächsischen Armee von 1670 bis zum Beginn des zwanzigsten Jahrhunderts,* Leipzig: Beck, 1910.

46: While their fellows clashed with Austrians on the road to Eger, a detachment of twenty hussars and chevauxlegers chased off a patrol of seven Uhlans at Asch, capturing one of the enemy horsemen. For details of both skirmishes, see *Krieg 1809,* vol. IV, pp. 229-31; and M. von Süssmilch gen. Hörnig, *Geschichte des 2. Königl. Sächs. Husaren-Regiments 'Kronprinz Friedrich Wilhelm des Deutschen Reichs und von Preussen' Nr. 19,* Leipzig: Brockhaus, 1882, pp. 61-3.

47: *Krieg 1809,* vol. IV, p. 231; Rühle, vol. I, pp. 187-8.

48: Saski, vol. II, pp. 298-9; vol. III, pp. 42-3. See also Rühle, vol. I, p. 185.

49: Saski, vol. III, p. 65.

50: Saski, vol. III, pp. 89-90.

51: Exner (p. 25) and Süssmilch (pp. 63-4) give 3 May as the date of the bold ride into Eger, but the Austrian official history, using archival materials and contemporary reports, argues it actually occurred on the 2nd (*Krieg 1809,* vol. IV, pp. 230-1).

52: *Krieg 1809,* vol. IV, p. 232; Johannes A. Larrass, *Geschichte des Königlich Sächsischen 6. Infanterie-Regiments Nr. 105 und seine Vorgeschichte 1701 bis 1887,* Strassburg: Kayser, 1887, p. 511. The first column, apparently consisting of the vanguard and the 1st Division, reached Straubing on the 9th; the 2nd Division and at least some of the artillery (probably two batteries) marched through Regensburg. See August Kummer, *Erinnerungen aus dem Leben eines Veteranen der Königlich Sächsischen Armee,* Dresden: Meinhold & Söhne, n.d., p. 4; Larrass, p. 135; Georg von Schimpff, *Geschichte des Kgl. Sächs. Garde-Reiter-Regiments,* Dresden: Baensch, 1880, p. 301; Schuster/Francke, vol. II, p. 273; Süssmilch, p. 64.

53: Saski, vol. III, pp. 177-8 and 231.

54: Bernadotte to Napoleon, 12 May 1809, Saski, vol. III, pp. 253-4.

55: Schönberg, vol. II, p. 6. See also Larrass, p. 135.

56: French, Austrian and Saxon versions of Polish place names generate tremendous confusion about spellings. For the sake of simplicity, I have used the spellings from one of the best accounts of the Battle of Raszyn: Alois Veltzé, *Kriegsbilder aus Polen, Steiermark und Ungarn,* volume XI of *Das Kriegsjahr 1809 in Einzeldarstellungen,* Emil von Woinovich, ed., Wien: Stern, 1910.

57: In addition to Dyherrn's detachment, Poniatowski's command included the following Polish forces: 1st, 2nd, 3rd, 6th and 8th Infantry Regiments (two battalions each); 1st and 5th Chasseurs a Cheval; 2nd, 3rd and 6th Lancers (all cavalry regiments of three squadrons); three foot batteries (eighteen guns) and one horse battery (nine guns). Note that many sources (e.g., Exner, p. 10) list a detachment of 90 cuirassiers from the *Zastrow* Regiment with Dyherrn's command. They appear in none of the accounts of Raszyn, however, and it is unlikely they were anywhere near the battlefield. They had probably been assigned to Dyherrn in late 1808 or early 1809 but had returned to join the remainder of their regiment in Danzig sometime in March 1809.

58: Order of Battle for the Austrian VII Corps at Raszyn (minus detachments). Numbers in parentheses indicate the number of battalions or squadrons:

Advance Guard (GM von Mohr)
    Kaiser Hussars, Nr. 1 (6) - one squadron on east bank of Vistula
    1st *Siebenbürger Wallachen* Grenzer, Nr. 16 (1)
    2nd *Siebenbürger Wallachen* Grenzer, Nr. 17 (1)
    Vukassovich Infantry, Nr. 48 (3)
    1 light and 1 brigade battery
FML Mondet

GM Civilart	GM Trauttenberg
de Ligne Infantry, Nr. 30 (3)	*Baillet* Infantry, Nr. 63 (3)
Kottulinsky Infantry, Nr. 41 (3)	*Strauch* Infantry, Nr. 24 (3)
1 brigade battery	1 brigade battery

GM Pflacher
    Weidenfeld Infantry Nr. 37 (3)
    Davidovitch Infantry, Nr. 34 (3)
    1 brigade battery
FML Schauroth
    GM Gehringer
        Palatinal Hussars, Nr. 12 (8)
        Szekler Hussars, Nr. 11 (8)
    GM Speth
        Somariva Cuirassiers, Nr. 5 (6)
        Lothringen Cuirassiers, Nr. 7 (6)
        1 cavalry battery

59: FML von Schauroth covered Ferdinand's left with four squadrons of hussars (three of *Palatinal,* one of *Kaiser*), a light battery and (initially) four companies of *Vukassovich* (Veltzé, pp. 17-18).

60: Unfortunately, there are no extant Saxon accounts of the Battle of Raszyn; either Dyherrn never filed a report or it has been lost over the years. This summary has been assembled from the following sources: 'Das k. k. Husaren-Regiment Palatinal im Feldzuge 1809', *Oesterreichische militärische Zeitschrift*, Heft 6, 1847, pp. 232-6; Exner, pp. 112-14; Jaromir Formanek, *Geschichte des k. k. Infanterie-Regiments Nr. 41*, Czernowitz: Czopp, 1887, vol. II, pp. 28-30; Mayerhoffer, pp. 191-2; Johann B. Schels, 'Der Feldzug 1809 in Polen', *Oesterreichische militärische Zeitschrift*, Heft 3, 1844, pp. 289-304; Franz J. A. Schneidawind, *Der Krieg Oesterreich's gegen Frankreich, dessen Alliirte und den Rheinbund im Jahre 1809*, Schaffhausen: Hurter, 1842, vol. I, pp. 199-200; Roman Soltyk, *Relation des Opérations de l'Armée aux Ordres du Prince Joseph Poniatowski pendant la Campagne de 1809 en Pologne contre les Autriciens*, Paris: Gauthier-Laguione, 1841, pp. 147-55; Veltzé, pp. 12-24; Welden, pp. 316-19. See also reports by Poniatowski and Colonel Saunier in Wladyslaw de Fedorowicz, *1809 Campagne de Pologne*, Paris: Plon, 1911, vol. I, pp. 335-7, 348-50 and 399-400. Maps very kindly provided by the Austrian Kriegsarchiv. Regimental histories mentioning the Polish interlude include Kretschmar, p. 78; H. von Schimpff, *Geschichte der beiden Königlich Sächsischen Grenadier-Regimenter: Erstes (Leib-) Grenadier-Regiment Nr. 100 und Zweites Grenadier-Regiment Nr. 101, Kaiser Wilhelm, König von Preussen*, Dresden: Höckner, 1877, pp. 138-9; Süssmilch, p. 82.

61: Austrian losses for the battle were 400-500. Polish casualties are much more difficult to determine, but based on the number of dead, wounded and captured (about 1,400) and the estimated strength of Poniatowski's army (some 9,000-9,500 after subtracting these losses and the Saxons), there may have been 1,000 or more stragglers still absent from the army on the night of 19/20 April. Given the newness of the Polish Army, this is not an unreasonable amount and would give a loss figure of 2,300 or so as listed in Mayerhoffer (p. 192) and Welden (p. 319).

62: Rühle, vol. I, p. 238. The Koburg officer was Lieutenant Schauroth of the 4th Rheinbund (Wilhelm Freiherr von Schauroth, *Im Rheinbund-Regiment der Herzoglich Sächsischen Kontingente Koburg-Hildburghausen-Gotha-Weimar während der Feldzüge in Tirol, Spanien und Russland 1809-1813*, Alexander Freiherr von Schauroth, ed., Berlin: Mittler & Sohn, 1905, p. 12).

63: Orders in Saski, vol. III, pp. 216-17.

64: *Krieg 1809*, vol. IV, p. 234; Rühle, vol. I, p. 242; Saski, vol. III, p. 286.

65: *Krieg 1809*, vol. IV, p. 234; Saski, vol. III, pp. 285-6.

66: Rühle, vol. I, p. 258.

67: Süssmilch, p. 65. Some of the Hussar Regiment's quartermasters were surprised and captured in the initial Austrian onslaught (Rühle, vol. II, p. 11; see also Chapter 3).

68: According to the version of this episode in the Hussar Regiment's history, the Saxon horsemen 'practically chased the enemy guns into the hands of the Württemberg Jägers'. The award of these guns was made at Bernadotte's insistence, rather to the disgust of the Württembergers. For more on this incident and the battle in general, see Chapter 3 of this work; *Krieg 1809*, vol. IV, pp. 238, 253-4, and Beilagen 3a and 3b; and Süssmilch, pp. 64-6. Quotes from Hauptmann von Czetteritz und Neuhaus extracted from Neil Litten, 'The Role of the Saxon IX Army Corps in the Combat around Linz on 17th May 1809', *Empires, Eagles and Lions*, Issue 99 (March-April 1987), pp. 40-1.

69: The account of the infantry attacks on the Pöstlingberg is drawn from: Exner, pp. 31-2; 'Aus der Geschichte des k. k. Linien-Infanterie-Regiments Baron Fürstenwerther Nr. 56', *Oesterreichische militärische Zeitschrift*, Heft 11, 1846; *Krieg 1809*, vol. IV, pp. 258-9; Larrass, p. 135; Schönberg, vol. II, pp. 7-8. Some Saxon sources credit their infantry with driving off the Austrians, but this seems to be an error. The confusion may have its source in the retreat of Oberst Leuthner's detachment which apparently occurred about the same time that the Saxons were beginning their advance. The Saxons certainly contributed to driving off Leuthner and holding Somariva's remaining (albeit small) forces in check, but it was the Württemberg Jägers who cleared the Austrians off the mountain in their daring night attack (see H. v. Schimpff, p. 139; Schuster/Francke, vol. II, p. 274; and Chapter 3). See also the eyewitness account of Sous-Lieutenant Ferdinand von Larisch, an officer in the 3rd Company of I/*Prinz Friedrich August*: 'Meine zweite Campagne', *Bautzener Nachrichten*, Nos. 21-5, 1883.

70: Schönberg, vol. II, pp. 7-8; Larisch also recounts this episode.

71: Quote from Hauptmann Friedel, *Geschichte des 7. Infanterie-Regiments 'König Georg' Nr. 106*, Leipzig: Jacobsen, n.d., pp. 38-39. Exner (p. 31) describes the Saxons' enthusiastic reception of Bernadotte.

72 Casualties from Enxer, p. 32 and *Krieg 1809*, vol. IV, p. 265.

73: First quote from Schönberg, p. 8; second from Bernadotte's battle report to Napoleon, 18 May 1809 (Saski, vol. III, pp. 318-20). The Marshal's motives have been questioned by several historians (e.g., Hugo Kerchenawe and Maximilian Ritter von Hoen in *Krieg 1809*, vol. IV, p. 232). Saluting Saxon 'impetuosity' in this 18 May message hardly seems consistent with his previous descriptions of the Saxon infantry as lack-lustre and slow. Likewise, he lionized the Saxons in letters to Friedrich August while heaping them with obloquy in his reports to the Emperor. It may even be surmised that he sought to explain any personal inactivity or failure in advance by denigrating the soldiers under his command. Nor was this pattern to cease with the victory at Linz.

74: Company strength was only about 138 men in the 1st Battalion when it was formed in May. The 2nd Battalion was somewhat weaker as it drew Schützen from the eleven infantry battalions of the 2nd Division where the 1st Battalion drew its members from the twelve battalions of the 1st. Both Schützen battalions were considerably strengthened during the June reorganization (Holtzendorff, pp. 9-10). See also Exner, p. 26; *3. Infanterie-Regiments Nr. 102*, pp. 151-2; *Geschichte des Königl. Sächs. Schützen-Regiments 'Prinz Georg' No. 108*, Leipzig: Jacobsen, n.d., p. 9; Larrass, pp. 135-6; Carl Lommatzsch, *Geschichte des 4. Infanterie-Regiments Nr. 103*, Dresden: Heinrich, 1909, p. 155; Schönberg, vol. II, p. 8; Schuster/Francke, p. 277.

75: Werlhof, pp. 16-17.

76: Schuster & Francke mistakenly meld these two small recon actions into one (pp. 274-5).

77: The exact progress of this little affair is unclear. The text here represents an amalgamation of the Austrian account (*Krieg 1809*, vol. IV, p. 275) and that in the *Prinz Clemens* regimental history (*Geschichte des Königl. Sächs. Königs-Husaren-Regiments No. 18*, Leipzig: Baumert & Ronge, 1901, pp. 166-7). Süssmilch's detailed version (pp. 68-9) is quite different: a hussar detachment of 40 under Leutnant Hagke led Gutschmid's column and overthrew the Austrian cavalry pickets east of Unter Weitersdorf; Gecka's squadron followed Hagke's party but no mention is made of the discomfiture of the chevauxlegers. Given the frequent parochialism of regimental histories, it is quite possible that both accounts are correct, in other words, that Hagke's 40 hussars succeeded initially but Gecka's troopers were beaten when they tried to advance.

78: This record of events on the 19th and 20th is assembled from: Exner, pp. 32-3; *Königs-Husaren*, pp. 166-7; *Krieg 1809*, vol. IV, pp. 273-6; Schuster/Francke, pp. 274-5; *Schützen-Regiment*, p. 10; Süssmilch, pp. 66-9. Note that my assessment is based primarily on Saxon sources and differs markedly from the Austrian official relation in *Krieg 1809* with regard to actions at Neumarkt in the early hours of the 20th: as portrayed in *Krieg 1809*, the Austrian forces retreated from the skirmish at Unter Weitersdorf undisturbed, abandoning Neumarkt to the Saxons; Saxon sources (particularly Exner, Süssmilch, Schuster/Francke and *Schützen-Regiment*) very clearly relate a short fight south of the town that the Austrian official historians overlooked.

79: Holtzendorff, pp. 11-16; Schuster/Francke, p. 275; *Schützen-Regiment*, p. 10 (quote from this book).

80: Exner, pp. 26-7 (first quote); Kretschmar, p. 74 (second quote); *Krieg 1809*, vol. IV. p. 280.

81: GM von Gutschmid's force included the *Egidy* Schützen, the hussars, the *Prinz Clemens* Chevauxlegers and, after the 21st, the horse battery; though not specifically stated in published sources, it is reasonable to assume the *Herzog Albrecht* squadron was also present with Gutschmid.

82: Berthier to Bernadotte, 19 May 1809, Saski, vol. III, p. 330. The Zwettl referred to here is Zwettl Stadt.

83: Bernadotte to Napoleon, 21 May 1809, Saski, vol. III, p. 348.

84: Bernadotte to Berthier, 28 May 1809, Sauzey, vol. III, p. 53.

85: Quoted in Exner, p. 34.

86: This story is related by Franz Kurz, *Geschichte der Landwehr in Oesterreich ob der Enns*, Linz: Haslinger, 1811, (vol. II, pp. 291-4) and by Süssmilch (p. 70), who further states that it was Bernadotte who directed the punishment of Mauthausen.

87: Exner, p. 35, Rühle, vol. II, pp. 75-81. The Amstetten raid coincided with an attack on a Württemberg detachment farther downstream, much to the annoyance of Napoleon who demanded explanations from his generals (Buat, vol. II, p. 10). Kurz (pp. 294-7) claims that the Austrian raiding force numbered only slightly over 100 'heroes' and that it suffered less than 10 casualties.

88: Exner, p. 36.

89: Rühle, p. 75.

90: First quote from Kummer, pp. 6-7; second from Rühle, vol. II, p. 82. Excesses committed against the civilian population apparently continued through June; Du Casse states that the Württembergers and Saxons took turns blaming one another when complaints of abuse were raised by local Austrian authorities (Du Casse, *Vandamme*, vol. II, p. 311).

91: Shortly after arriving in Mautern, the advance guard was joined by Hiller's horse battery (Süssmilch, p. 70). Dupas was apparently an abrasive fellow, irritating the Saxons with condescension and insensitivity (Exner, p. 37). According to Schuster/Francke (p. 275), the grenadier battalions with Dupas at Mautern were *Radeloff* and *Hake* rather than *Radeloff* and *Winkelmann*; *Hake* having previously served as the Corps advance guard, this arrangement would not have been unreasonable, but given the subsequent attachment of *Winkelmann* to Dupas's Division, this latter unit seems the more likely choice.

92: From one of Zezschwitz's reports quoted in Exner (p. 36).

93: This figure, given by Exner (p. 28), is exclusive of musicians.

94: For example, the men of the 1st Company, II/*König* were used to bring the 1st Company, I/*König* up to the new strength; the 2nd Company, II/*König* fell in on the 2nd Company, I/*König*, etc. Bernadotte's instructions to the Saxon commander are in Exner (p. 27).

95: The senior officers were selected from those who were either excess or whose age made them incapable of bearing the fatigues of the campaign or assuming command (Exner, p. 28). The history of the *König* Infantry states that 'there were not a few officers and NCOs who were hardly fit to meet the physical and mental demands of a campaign' (H. von Schimpff, p. 140).

96: Exner, pp. 28-30; Larisch, Nr. 23. Von Hoyer's and Bonniot's batteries were assigned to the brigades of the 1st Division, Coudray's and Huthsteiner's (only four pieces) to those of the 2nd (Kretschmar, p. 74). In practice, the cavalry tended to be organized for the mission of the moment without regard for formal arrangements. The grenadiers numbered between 540 and 560 men per battalion. Evidently neither of the Schützen battalions ever reached full strength; Egidy counted only 688 men under his command on 17 June. Details on the reorganization of the Schützen are from Holtzendorff, p. 18.

97: Werlhof (p. 17) castigates Bernadotte for not training his men while they passed the weeks in and around St. Pölten. Rühle (vol. II, p. 166) and Larrass (p. 136), however, state that training was conducted, particularly for the new infantry battalion Schützen, who engaged in target practice and skirmishing according to drum signals (unlike the original Schützen in Metzsch's and Egidy's battalions who used horn notes to guide their actions). See Larrass's work; Holtzendorff; and Eduard von Treitschke's monograph 'Die königl. sächsischen Truppen in der Schlacht bei Wagram, am 5. und 6. Juli 1809', *Zeitschrift für Kunst, Wissenschaft und Geschichte des Krieges*, Band 43, 1838.

98: The 1st Division occupied Sieghartskirchen on the 25th, while Bernadotte took his headquarters and Dupas's Division with its three Saxon battalions into the Austrian capital. Zeschau proceeded to camp six kilometres east of Purkersdorf on the first day of July when Lecoq's Brigade replaced it at Sieghartskirchen; Steindel apparently remained in St. Pölten until 2 or 3 July. Württemberg sources (see Chapter 3) mention participation by six Saxon guns in VIII Corps' successful raid across the Danube at Melk on 24 June; I have found no reference for this in Saxon sources, but it is certainly possible that a battery from the 2nd Division supported the Württembergers in their assault.

99: Quoted in Süssmilch, p. 71.

100: Rühle, vol. II, p. 277.

101: The movements of the 1st Saxon Division on the afternoon of 5 July are unclear. Some sources (e.g., Exner and Buat who follows him) place the division immediately behind Polenz in the advance across the Marchfeld. Other equally authoritative commentators (e.g., Hoen, *Wagram*) state that the 1st Division was left behind to guard the crossing points and did not rejoin the rest of the Corps until the evening. A third possibility is that only one brigade of the division was assigned to guard the crossings. The latter option is suggested by Rühle's eyewitness statement that a 'brigade of Saxon infantry had remained behind to cover the crossing point...until the Army of Dalmatia arrived to relieve it' (quoted in Friedrich M. Kircheisen, ed., *Feldzugserinnerungen aus dem Kriegsjahre 1809*, Hamburg: Gutenberg, 1909, p. 124), as well as the author of 'Gedanken über die beiden Schlachten auf dem Marchfelde bei Wien', *Pallas*, Band 2, 1809.

102: Dupas's actions taken from Buat, vol. II, pp. 213-14. The other squadron of the *Prinz Johann* Chevauxlegers was left with Oudinot (G. Schimpff, p. 305). Some sources have this regiment supporting Davout, but that Marshal was distant and well supplied with cavalry; it seems more likely that the Saxons were temporarily attached to II Corps, which was close by and short of horse.

103: Recounted in *3. Infanterie*, p. 157.

104: The rest of Hessen-Homburg's Cavalry Division, three other cuirassier regiments (*Kaiser, Kronprinz Erzherzog Ferdinand, Moritz Liechtenstein*), was also in the area; one regiment from the division (*Hohenzollern*) had earlier retired behind Markgrafneusiedel and was therefore in no position to influence the fight with the Saxons.

105: The location of the lone *Herzog Albrecht* squadron at this juncture is not clear.

106: Although Pelet says Gérard led the Saxon charge on the 5th, Saxon sources (e.g., Exner, p. 52) specifically state that the French general only brought Bernadotte's order to attack, the actual charge was carried out by Gutschmid.

107: The peculiarities of European aristocratic and military relations left over from the Frederickian era are illustrated by this engagement: on each side there was a regiment which had Herzog Albrecht of Sachsen-Teschen as its Inhaber, the Austrian *Herzog Albrecht* Cuirassiers (No. 3) and the Saxon *Herzog Albrecht* Chevauxlegers. This curious fact has attracted much attention from subsequent commentators, with many claiming that the two regiments directly opposed one another and that the Saxon light horse overthrew the Austrian heavies. From Schimpff's and Exner's detailed accounts, however, it seems the two *Albrecht* regiments did not fight each other directly but were rather involved in the same general mêlée and it is certainly clear that the lone Saxon squadron did not single-handedly attack and rout the Austrian regiment of six squadrons. A further curiosity is the orthography of the duke's name: Saxon sources uniformly refer to him as Albrecht, while the Austrians report Albert; for simplicity, the Saxon version is used here. Several Saxon authors mistakenly identify the other Austrian cuirassier regiment as *Lothringen* (No. 7); that regiment was with VII Corps in Poland.

108: The Saxon report of this attack spoke highly of Lindenau, saying that 'his courage knew no bounds' (Exner, p. 50). The identity of the Austrian infantry is something of a question. Exner describes the unit as a battalion of *Clerfayt* Infantry, but there was no regiment with this name in the Austrian army in 1809; the *Czartoriski* Infantry Regiment (No. 9) had borne the name *Clerfayt* until 1802 and would take it again in 1888, but that regiment was on the Bisamberg as part of V Corps and did not participate in the Battle of

Wagram. Another possibility is the *Chastler* Infantry (No. 46) which was part of Nordmann's Advance Guard and *could* have been on the scene between Raasdorf and Aderklaa; that unit's history, however, clearly places it near Markgrafneusiedel and makes no mention of an encounter with Saxon cavalry. Hoen is probably correct when he suggests it was three companies of *Beaulieu* Infantry (No. 58). See Friedrich von Hermannsthal, *Geschichte des Tyroler Feld- und Land-, später 46. Linien-Infanterie-Regiments*, Krakau: Czas, 1859; Maximilian Ritter von Hoen, *Wagram*, volume 8 of *Das Kriegsjahr 1809 in Einzeldarstellungen*, Wein: Stern, 1909, p. 43; Manfried Rauchensteiner, *Die Schlacht bei Deutsch Wagram am 5. und 6. Juli 1809*, Militärhistorische Schriftenreihe Heft 36, Wien: Bundesverlag, 1977, p. 19; Werlhof, pp. 18-19.

109: Saxon casualties in this engagement were 174; other than the 85 captured cuirassiers, Austrian casualties are not known, but Bernadotte's report credited the Saxons with taking 500 prisoners. In addition, *Prinz Clemens* in its rallying point north of Raasdorf was able to collect numerous riderless horses to serve as remounts for Saxon troopers. This account assembled from the following sources: Binder von Kriegelstein, vol. II, p. 321; Buat, vol. II, pp. 214-15; Exner, pp. 49-52; Hoen, pp. 43-4; *Königs-Husaren*, pp. 168-9; 'Das Kürassier-Regiment Kronprinz Ferdinand in der Schlacht bei Wagram am 5. und 6. Juli 1809', *Oesterreichische militärische Zeitschrift*, Heft 6, 1844; M. S. von Lichterfeld, *Regiments-Geschichte des Königlich Sächsischen Garde-Reiter-Regiments*, Berlin: Vobach, 1904, pp. 14-15; Pelet, vol. IV, p. 182; G. Schimpff, pp. 303-4; Süssmilch, pp. 72-3.

110: Buat, vol. II, p. 219.

111: Treitschke's fine study, p. 52 and Holtzendorff, p. 20. Other sources give Dupas's array as follows from left to right: *Radeloff*, 5th Léger, 19th Ligne, *Metzsch*.

112: By comparing their remaining effectives on the morning of the 6th to their strengths on 1 July (583 and 572 respectively) *Radeloff* had losses of more than 65 per cent and *Metzsch* lost more than 30 per cent on the 5th. Figures taken from Exner, pp. 56-8; Hoen, *Wagram*, p. 55; Neil Litten, 'Saxon Strength and Losses at Wagram', *Empires, Eagles and Lions*, Issue 84 (Dec 1984); and *Schützen*, pp. 11-12 (quotes). Litten gives casualty figures for each battalion after both days of the battle: *Radeloff* - 251 and *Metzsch* 332. French losses were equally debilitating: on the morning of the 6th, Dupas could only form two battalions from his two regiments. Metzsch, whom Dupas had placed under arrest during the march to Vienna for committing 'some small excess', died in the Russian campaign.

113: One of these patrols apparently penetrated into the main square of Wagram before being driven off by Austrian infantry and artillery fire. Sources for Dupas's actions and the Saxon attacks at Wagram on 5 July include Buat, vol. II, pp. 218-20; Exner, pp. 52-8; Hoen, *Wagram*, pp. 46-55; Kretschmar, pp. 75-6; Larisch, Nr. 23; Larrass, pp. 137-9; H. v. Schimpff, pp. 141-3; Schuster/Francke, pp. 278-81; *Schützen*, pp. 11-13; Werlhof, pp. 19-21. *Prinz Johann* apparently helped Bessières and the French cavalry to stem the retreat of Eugène's men after their repulse from the Russbach Heights (Buat, vol. II, pp. 224-5); on returning to IX Corps, however, the regimental commander, Oberst von Trützschler, was given a severe dressing down by Bernadotte for leaving the Corps without orders; the Oberst defended himself by pointing out that his orders had come directly from the Emperor (Exner, p. 55). There is some confusion about the subordination of Egidy's Battalion on 5 July; I have followed Holtzendorff (Egidy with Hartitzsch's Brigade), but other sources imply the battalion was under Le Coq's command.

114: Quotes and paraphrasings in this and the previous paragraph from Barton, *Bernadotte*, pp. 217-221.

115: Savary says, for example: 'I had seen the feebleness with which his [Bernadotte's] troops fought' (Anne-Jean-Marie-René Savary, *Mémoires du Duc de Rovigo*, Paris: Bossange, 1828, vol. IV, p. 189). It is from Marbot that we have the story of Napoleon's verbal revenge against Bernadotte: supposedly coming upon the IX Corps commander as he was trying desperately to reform his men, Napoleon is said to have asked cuttingly if 'this was the sort of scientific manoeuvre by which you would compel the Archduke to lay down his arms?' Principal sources for the second day's fighting include: Binder von Kriegelstein, vol. II, pp. 344-7; Buat, vol. II, pp. 245-51; Mathieu Dumas, *Memoirs of His Own Time*, Philadelphia: Lea & Blanchard, 1839, vol. II, pp. 202-5; Exner, pp. 58-62; Hoen, *Wagram*, pp. 70-81 (Napoleon's appeal to the Saxons on p. 81); Kretschmar, pp. 76-7; Larisch, Nr. 24; Larrass, pp. 139-40; H. v. Schimpff, p. 143; *Schützen*, p. 13; Werlhof, pp. 21-4.

116: Saxon casualties taken from Exner (p. 104) and Litten (*Empires, Eagles and Lions*, Issue 84). French casualties from Buat, vol. II, p. 308.

117: Bernadotte's and Napoleon's Orders of the Day to the marshals and Savary's quotes from Savary, *Mémoires*, pp. 192-194; the Marshal and the Emperor are also quoted in a host of other sources (e.g., Exner and Barton).

118: These comments may never have come to Napoleon's attention and may even have been accurate, but they were practically insubordinate and clearly inappropriate for a corps commander addressing his men. Quoted from a letter by GL von Gersdorff, the former Saxon contingent Chief of Staff, in *Militair-Wochenblatt*, No. 353 (29 March 1823), p. 2615. The publication of some of Napoleon's dictation in the 1820's led to an earnest exchange of letters between Gersdorff and General Gourgaud, one of the Emperor's final comrades.

119: At Leipzig in October 1813, several thousand Saxon troops defected to Napoleon's enemies during the battle; Pelet erroneously thinks to see the first inklings of this 'betrayal' in 1809: 'Did defection on the field of battle begin here?' (Pelet, vol. IV, p. 191).

120: For an impassioned defence of the Saxons, see articles by Tom Devoe and Jean A. Lochet in *Empires, Eagles and Lions*, Issues 74 (1 Sep 1983), 76 (1 Dec 1983) and 77 (15 Jan 1984). In another article in this little journal, Chevalier Delbert A. Starr argues in favour of Saxon courage, pointing out that Saxon soldiers at Wagram accounted for 20 per cent of the recipients of Saxony's highest military award, the St.-Heinrichs-Orden, during the entire 179-year history of that order (Issue 79, 15 Apr 1984).

121: Zezschwitz and Gersdorff quoted in Werlhof, pp. 24-5; Werlhof also gives a concise history of the relief of Bernadotte and its relation to Napoleon's view of the Saxons. Rühle's quote is from his letters in Kircheisen, *Feldzugserinnerungen*, pp. 142-3. The order relieving Bernadotte of command was dated 9 July (*Correspondence* 15507) and the Marshal apparently departed the next day; however, when the Army's 30th Bulletin *publically* announced the dissolution of IX Corps, it stated that the Corps had been dissolved on the 8th (30 July 1809, *Correspondence* 15599).

122: An outpost of *Prinz Clemens* was also surprised by the Austrian attack on the 13th and fell back with a loss of three men; the regiment rode to join the main battle but arrived after the enemy battalion had surrendered. Egidy had only three companies at hand because one had been left behind at Baumgarten (Holtzendorff, p. 34). Trautenberg's force also included two Landwehr battalions and two squadrons of *Trentschiner* Insurrection Hussars (who fled). Sources for the movements and skirmishes from 7 to 14 July are: *3. Infanterie*, pp. 161-2; Exner, pp. 64-6; Heller, vol. II, pp. 283-4; *Königs-Husaren*, pp. 170-2; Larrass, p. 142; *Schützen*, p. 14; Süssmilch, pp. 76-80; Welden, pp. 224-30.

123: Napoleon quoted in Werlhof, p. 27; Sauzey, vol. III, p. 44. Additionally, it must be mentioned that the Saxons earned for themselves an unenviable reputation for harshness and excess in dealing with local populations.

124: Sadly, many of the Saxons, like thousands of their Rheinbund brothers, would never return from the Russian campaign. Of the officers featured in this chapter, General Gutschmid, Major Egidy, Hauptmann Metzsch, Hauptmann Hoyer, Premierlieutenant Hiller and Premierlieutenant von Seydlitz would find their deaths in French service in 1812.

Part II
THE WAR IN THE
TYROL AND OTHER THEATRES

CHAPTER 7:
The Alps Aflame

Riding through the Tyrol in July 1809, Colonel Louis-François Lejeune described the countryside with an artist's eye:

> The valley was bathed in light, and, warmed by the flood of rays, was converted for the nonce into a celestial land from which ethereal vapours rose on every side. The scene filled me with a kind of ecstasy, and my soul seemed to take to itself wings and float away into space with the clouds of mist....When I think of the lovely valleys of the Tyrol, and recall the effect they had upon me, I feel sure that the gate of heaven is at the brink of the waterfalls...

Regarding the population of the region, however, Lejeune the soldier commented:

> The sturdy inhabitants of the Tyrol, whose passionate indignation at their separation from Austria and incorporation with Württemberg and Bavaria in 1805 was ever on the increase, waged war upon us from their mountain fastnesses with indomitable courage and skill, harassing us the more as they attacked us in the rear; and the insurrection even seemed likely to spread to the route by which our reinforcements were expected from France....Many able men, such as Andreas Hofer, Hartel, Arco, Speckbacher, Schmidt, Adel and others, with the Capuchin monk Haspinger, placed themselves at the head of the insurgent peasants, giving their orders in the name of God and the Holy Virgin and fighting with extraordinary courage.[1]

These dedicated mountaineers would prove a constant annoyance to Napoleon's plans, conducting a bitter insurgent campaign that eventually opened a great rift between the Emperor and his Bavarian allies.

Bavaria had acquired the Tyrol from a shocked and humbled Austria via the Treaty of Pressburg in December 1805. Stretching from the Bavarian border to the northern shores of Lake Garda, the region represented a tremendous increase in land (250,000 square kilometres) and population (600,000) for Max Joseph's realm, and its incorporation into Bavaria helped to justify Max's elevation to king in 1806. The tradition-conscious inhabitants of the Tyrol, however, had been associated with the Habsburg family since 1363 and immediately resented the transferal of their beloved peaks and vales to Bavarian sovereignty. This

powerful undercurrent of dissatisfaction was exacerbated by the Munich government's attempts to impose its modern, enlightened rule on a land almost
unchanged since the Middle Ages. Austria's rulers had generally refrained from
interfering in the internal social, political and military structures of the Tyrol,
preferring to leave the land to lie peacefully different but loyal. King Max initially appeared to acknowledge an equally unique position for the Tyrolians
within his realm, promising that the traditional rights and privileges of the people would be left unchanged. Unfortunately, Bavaria's ardent bureaucrats were
a persistent lot. Filled with the grim zeal and righteous conviction of the
Enlightenment, they were intent on establishing a centralized state where all the
constituent parts were equal and alike under the benevolent hand of the absolute
monarch.

Manifold changes were introduced as the Bavarian government expanded its
control over the region; relatively slow at first, the pace of change increased dramatically when Max granted his people a new constitution in May 1808. One of
the first measures to rouse the anger of the populace was the imposition of a poll
tax to support the stationing of Bavarian troops on Tyrolian soil. Previously
almost unknown in the Tyrol, this and other taxes were extremely unpopular.
The taxes also served to compound other economic difficulties. Under Vienna's
poor monetary policies, the Tyrol, like the rest of the Austrian Empire, suffered
from rampant inflation. The measures introduced by the Bavarians to arrest this
evil inflicted considerable financial hardship on the Tyrolians, especially the
farmers, while the prohibitions of Napoleon's Continental System stifled trade
and resulted in a loss of revenue for the cotton, artisan and transportation indus-
tries. A number of political and administrative changes were also undertaken by
the Bavarian regime with a peculiar reckless determination. Heedless of the
strong regional traditions, the Bavarians eliminated the ancient Tyrolian constitution which supposedly guaranteed representational rights to the peasants as
well as other elements of society.[2] Moreover, as the urge grew for faster change
and more complete integration into the Bavarian state, officials from the older
parts of Bavaria began to replace native Tyrolians, and official references to the
old names or symbols of the Tyrol vanished. Thus the red Tyrolian eagle was
removed from governmental heraldry and even the administrative regions of the
Tyrol were allocated new, bland designations with little relation to their ancient
titles. To the proud Tyrolians, strongly rooted in local lore, this was a cruel
blow.

All the friction occasioned by these changes might have been managed had
the Bavarians not offended the Tyrolians in three other areas. First, the simple
farmers of the Tyrol were deeply religious and closely tied to local priests and
mendicant monastic orders. This attachment to religion was an obstruction to
the Bavarian administration which considered strong religious belief to be
vaguely superstitious and saw the church as another subordinate element of the
larger state. The dissolution of various monasteries and other religious institutions and petty interference with local religious practices and festivals generated
bitter anger among the population and created an image of the predominantly
Catholic Bavarians as veritable Protestants if not outright heathens. The second

problem was conscription. An Imperial decree of 1511 had placed a military
service obligation on every male Tyrolian, but had simultaneously exempted
them from taking part in combat beyond the frontiers of their land. This edict
had been carefully observed by the Habsburgs, and even the Bavarian government dared not tamper with this most sacred tradition until 1808. In that year,
the promulgation of the new constitution, increasing demands from Napoleon
and the approaching war with Austria drove the administration to look to the
Tyrol; in February 1809, local magistrates were informed that 1,000 conscripts
would be required from the region. Fear of the draft had caused young Tyrolian
men to take evasive action as early as 1807 and the announcement of the official
demand met with immediate popular outrage. Feeling that King Max had
betrayed his promise to them, the Tyrolians successfully resisted Bavarian
attempts to impose conscription and Munich was forced to abandon its effort in
March. The failure of this administrative action weakened the standing of the
Bavarian officials and instilled considerable confidence in the restive Tyrolians.

Finally, the Bavarian bureaucrats charged with administering the Tyrol seem
to have executed their duties with a remarkable degree of *naïveté* and insensitivity. Instead of approaching this proud, simple and isolated people in a circumspect manner, introducing reforms gradually and judiciously to ease the impact,
the majority of officials behaved with reckless arrogance. The Tyrolians were
regarded as superstitious bumpkins whose obduracy would be overcome by
strict application of the government's regulations. The satisfaction exhibited by
many Bavarian bureaucrats as they interfered in the region's most cherished traditions and expunged the last vestiges of its independent identity left deep
wounds. These wounds might have healed had the rules been applied with a
milder, more understanding hand, but the harshness with which the Bavarian
administrative structure was imposed upon the Tyrol embittered the population,
engendering distrust and hatred for the Bavarians and their king. Thus, despite
the apparent similarity of these two peoples, it is hardly surprising that the campaign in the Tyrol was marked by deadly cruelty and enduring passion.[3]

The campaign in the Tyrol is generally divided into three phases. The first
phase, from April until mid-May, encompasses the initial expulsion of the
Bavarians from the region and their first offensive to regain it. In the second
phase, from late May to July, Bavarian forces available to control the Tyrolians
were reduced as a consequence of Napoleon's determination to gather the
greater part of his army at Vienna in preparation for the decisive battle with
Archduke Charles. The insurgents were thus able to push the Bavarians
(Deroy's Division) out of Innsbruck and launch numerous raids into Bavaria
proper. With the armistice signed, Napoleon could turn more of his military
might against the stubborn Tyrolians, but a second offensive by Bavarian and
other German troops was repulsed at Bergisel on 13 August and the Allies were
again forced to withdraw. A number of skirmishes occurred in the ensuing
weeks as negotiations for a final peace with Vienna dragged on. The conclusion
of the war with Austria on 14 October, however, gave the Emperor a free hand
in the Tyrol. In this third phase, French units joined Bavarian and other German
troops in the last offensive into the mountains, capturing Innsbruck on 1

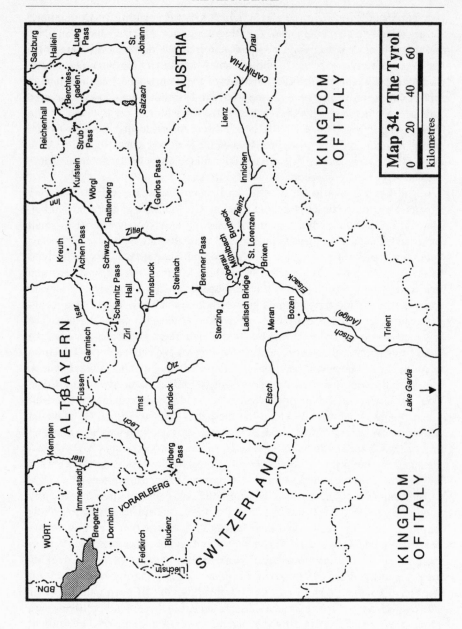

Map 34. The Tyrol

November and quelling the final spasms of the uprising in December.[4] Geographically and operationally, the struggle against the insurgents took place in three different zones. While principal actions of the regular army were in the Inn valley, the *ad hoc* formations of Oberst Maximilian Graf Arco and Oberst Graf Oberndorff fought mainly in the area of 'Altbayern' due south of Munich; finally, Major Joseph von Pillement's battalion of depot troops operated between Ulm and Lake Constance against the Vorarlberg rebels.[5] The Bavarians also had to cope with Jellacic's Division and local insurgents around Salzburg, and contribute troops to repel Austrian forays from Bohemia. With such responsibilities, it is not surprising that Bavaria resembled an armed camp in the spring and summer of 1809.

At the beginning of hostilities in April, there were some 4,560 Bavarian troops in the Tyrol under the command of GL Georg Freiherr von Kinkel. Concentrated at the key points on the route from Italy to Bavaria, this small force was intended to protect Napoleon's communications with Viceroy Eugène and to facilitate the passage of reinforcements from the latter's Army of Italy to the Army of Germany in the Danube valley. The small size of the occupation force was dictated by the Emperor's clear strategic vision. Napoleon was aware of the potential danger represented by rebellion in the Tyrol, but he also recognized that victory or defeat would be found along the banks of the Danube. The Austrian main army under Archduke Charles was the principal instrument of the Habsburg war effort; in destroying it, Napoleon hoped to bring Vienna to its knees and likewise ensure the ultimate collapse of any Tyrolian unpleasantness. The French Emperor and the Bavarian General Staff thus accepted a risk in the Tyrol to concentrate the majority of their forces along the Danube for the decisive battle; although this proved to be the correct strategic decision, it would lead to the virtual annihilation of von Kinkel's force and grant the insurgents an easy victory early in the war.

All subsequent myths to the contrary, neither the Bavarians nor their French allies were surprised by the Tyrolian uprising. The Bavarians were fully aware of the widespread dissatisfaction in the region and were informed of the early contacts between Tyrolian activists and the Austrian government. Kinkel was thus provided with cogent instructions to keep his forces concentrated around Innsbruck and Brixen, launching expeditions only when necessary and always in strength sufficient to assure success.[6] When the war began, his forces were disposed as follows: Kinkel himself with 11th Infantry, one squadron of 1st Dragoons and three guns in Innsbruck; 2nd Light, half of 4th Light, the other squadron of 1st Dragoons and two guns at Brixen under Oberstlieutenant Dominikus Wreden; half of 4th Light and one gun at Sterzing; and the 3rd Light spread along the Inn valley from Hall to Rattenberg.[7] The Bavarians were thus positioned to carry out their primary missions, but were noticeably isolated and far from assistance. To make matters worse, Bavarian military efforts in the Tyrol lacked an energetic guiding hand. The local commander, the 68-year-old GL von Kinkel, was officious, pedantic and indecisive, wanting in the drive and imagination necessary to cope with the challenges of a popular rebellion in difficult, unfamiliar terrain. The Bavarian government found neither the time nor the firmness to replace the old general before hostilities opened.[8]

Rebellion in the Tyrol was an integral part of the Austrian war plan. A popular insurgency supported by regular troops would not only tie down French forces and threaten Napoleon's line of communications but would also help preserve the alpine link between Charles's army on the Danube and Johann's two corps in Italy. To realize its plan, the government in Vienna had invested considerable effort in fomenting unrest and laying the foundation for a reconquest of the Tyrol. The appearance of Austrian troops was thus to be the signal for the inhabitants to rise against the Bavarians and French. This signal was given on 9 April when elements of the Austrian VIII Corps under FML Johann Gabriel Marquis Chasteler de Courcelles crossed the border from Carinthia (Kärnten) into East Tyrol and advanced on Lienz.[9]

Table 7-1: Initial Dispositions in the Tyrol (April)

Innsbruck and South

Innsbruck (GL von Kinkel)
  11th Infantry Regiment (Oberst Ditfurth)
  one squadron of 1st Dragoons (Major Erbach)
  three guns

Sterzing (Major Speicher)
  two companies of 4th Light Battalion
  one gun

Brixen (Oberstlieutenant Wreden)
  2nd Light Battalion
  two companies of 4th Light Battalion
  Leib Squadron of 1st Dragoons
  two guns

En route from Italy via Brixen (French replacement troops)
  GD Bisson: 2,500-3,000
  GD Lemoine: 2,500-3,000

Down the Inn Valley

Hall and Vicinity (Oberstlieutenant Bernclau)
two companies of 3rd Light Battalion

Schwaz to Rattenberg (Major Theobald)
Schwaz: half company of 3rd Light
Strass: half company of 3rd Light
Rattenberg: one company of 3rd Light

Kufstein (Major Aicher)
Provisional Light Battalion
  (depot troops of 1st, 2nd, 5th, 6th Light)
fortress artillerymen
60 guns

APRIL - SURPRISE, RETREAT, SURRENDER

At the news of the Austrian invasion, the Tyrolians rapidly mobilized into small, local companies. The first Bavarians to suffer casualties at the hands of these local bands were Oberleutnant Weller's light infantrymen, part of Wreden's command. On outpost duty at Innischen, six of these men were captured by some particularly zealous Tyrolians on the first day of the war. The next day, the lieutenant, prudently withdrawing toward Mühlbach, attempted to destroy the bridge at St. Lorenzen but failed in the face of a swiftly gathered group of villagers; with the loss of thirteen more men captured, he continued his withdrawal under constant harassing fire from the enthusiastic Tyrolians. Wreden could offer his subordinate little succour. Isolated in Brixen, he had decided to join Kinkel at Innsbruck and marched north on the 10th, intending to demolish the bridge at Ladritsch (over the Eisack above Oberau) en route. As at St. Lorenzen, however, spontaneously assembled peasants defended the bridge with vigour and Wreden was unable to carry out its destruction. He tried again early on the 11th with no better success, but seemed to receive significant reinforcement when a large column of French troops arrived from the south later in the day. This column of 2,500 men was en route from Italy to join the French main army in Bavaria and its commander, GD Baptiste Bisson, had no intention of getting into a fight with his collection of new conscripts.[10] Finding the road clear, he proceeded north, leaving a disappointed Wreden in his wake. Almost simultaneously, a few regular troops of Chasteler's advanced guard appeared and Wreden, convinced the Austrian corps was approaching, decided to follow Bisson. Unfortunately, the Tyrolians were greatly encouraged by the arrival of the Austrians and managed to cut off and capture some 200 Bavarians composing Wreden's rear guard.

The situation was even more dismal to the north. At Sterzing, Major Speicher with two companies of the 4th Light was forced to surrender when the town was attacked by some 5,000 insurgents under Andreas Hofer. The Bavarians were evicted from the town but formed a square in a nearby meadow and held off the Tyrolians with musket and cannon fire for most of the day. The Tyrolians, including several women, eventually advanced behind hay wains, shot down the Bavarian gunners and forced Speicher to capitulate; 400 Bavarians laid down their arms, unaware that Bisson and Wreden were only a few hours away.[11] Innsbruck, the capital of Tyrol, was also beset by rebels on the 11th. Oberst Karl von Ditfurth, commander of the 11th Infantry, took four companies and marched out against the rapidly growing insurgent force south of the city, but was unable to break through and retired as night fell. A Major Zoller was sent towards Zirl with two companies in an effort to outflank the rebels south-west of Innsbruck, but a band of courageous Tyrolians stopped him and forced him to retreat with a loss of 70 prisoners.[12] Despite the dangerous position of his own command, Kinkel found time to express his annoyance with Wreden and issue a set of impossible orders.[13]

Disasters continued to mount for the Bavarians on the 12th. During the night, the 3rd Light had been attacked in its isolated posts in the Inn valley. After a tenacious defence, Oberstlieutenant Friedrich Ritter von Bernclau and two of his companies were taken prisoner when their ammunition was exhausted; thanks to the alertness and determination of Major von Theobald, however, the other two companies were able to elude the Tyrolians and eventually find their way to Kreuth, the only formed Bavarian troops to escape the débâcle.[14] The dawn saw an energetic assault on Innsbruck itself. Although Ditfurth conducted a desperate defence, the situation was hopeless, the outskirts of the city were soon in the hands of the Tyrolians and Kinkel decided to attempt a negotiated retreat to Bavaria. Before talks could begin, however, the Tyrolians had forced their way across the Inn and were storming through the streets. Forming his shaken men into a square, Ditfurth temporarily held the enemy at bay, but the defence collapsed when he was mortally wounded and, by 10 a.m., the Bavarians had to yield.[15] Some infantry and dragoons led by Major Friedrich Graf von Erbach managed to evade immediate capture by breaking out to the north-east, but they too were forced to surrender when they were trapped at Hall.[16] Bisson and Wreden thus found the gates of the city closed against them when they arrived on the morning of the 13th from Steinach. Initially incredulous, Bisson was convinced of the situation by a brief conversation with the captive Kinkel and gave the order for his column to stack arms. In the space of five days, therefore, with almost no help from the Austrian regulars, the Tyrolians had succeeded in driving the Bavarians from their land and capturing the astounding total of two generals, 130 senior and staff officers, 3,860 Bavarians, 2,050 Frenchmen and seven guns.[17] Most of the Bavarians, particularly the artillerymen and light infantry, fought bravely, but they were foredoomed by their isolated deployment and the impassioned determination of the Tyrolian peasants.[18]

The sudden expulsion of its occupation forces from the Tyrol shocked the Bavarian government, but no action could be taken until the Austrian main army had been defeated and thrown back into Bohemia. Bavarian dismay increased as small groups of Austrian regulars and Tyrolian insurgents penetrated into Bavaria proper, plundering and burning with impunity. While the Austrians apparently behaved well, many of the Tyrolians were nothing more than marauders and their depredations only served to inflame Bavarian passions.[19] Furthermore, while Austro-Tyrolian bands were occupying Immenstadt and Füssen (22 April), emissaries from Innsbruck were igniting the fires of rebellion in the neighbouring Vorarlberg. About 100 cavalrymen from the depots of the 1st, 2nd and 3rd Chevauxlegers and the 1st Dragoons were sent to establish a line of outposts against the Tyrolians south of Munich on 29 April, but they could do little more than observe the enemy and listen helplessly to the urgent pleas of the populace.[20]

The only bright spot in this landscape of defeat and defencelessness was the little fortress of Kufstein on the Inn. Armed with 60 guns of various calibres, garrisoned by 573 infantrymen and artillerists, and provisioned to withstand a three-month siege, Kufstein proved too tough for the small force of Tyrolians and Austrians under Oberstlieutenant Samuel von Reissenfels that surrounded it on 17 April.[21] When the first summons to surrender was delivered by two insurgents, the fortress's resolute commandant, Major Maximilian von Aicher, had one of the farmers dragged off to the dungeons and evicted the second with the promise that any other Tyrolians who appeared before the fort's gates would be promptly hanged.[22] He likewise scorned Reissenfels' pompous demands for capitulation and used his plentiful artillery to overpower the meagre batteries of the encircling troops. With few guns, little ammunition and only 900 regulars, Reissenfels could neither bombard nor assault the fortress with any hope of success.[23] None the less, he continued the blockade until 12 May when the approach of Deroy's Division forced him to withdraw. Kufstein was never seriously threatened once the Bavarians were inside the fort's walls, but Aicher's determination and aggressiveness provided a boost to Bavarian morale in the gloomy days of early April.

MAY - THE FIRST BAVARIAN OFFENSIVE

The reunification of Lefebvre's Corps on 30 April presaged the end of the Tyrol's first liberation. From its position at Salzburg, VII Corps was to secure Napoleon's right and rear as the Emperor advanced on Vienna. Wrede was thus dispatched from Salzburg for Vöcklabruck on 1 May to maintain contact with the main army, while Lefebvre remained in Salzburg with the 1st and 3rd Divisions to continue operations against Jellacic and reoccupy the Tyrol.[24]

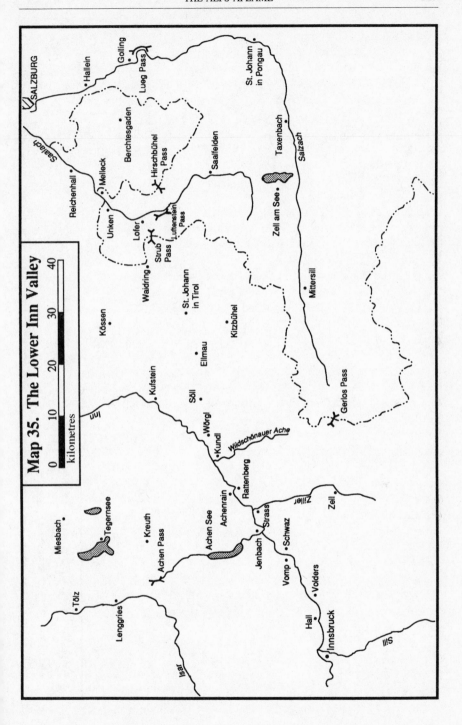

Map 35. The Lower Inn Valley

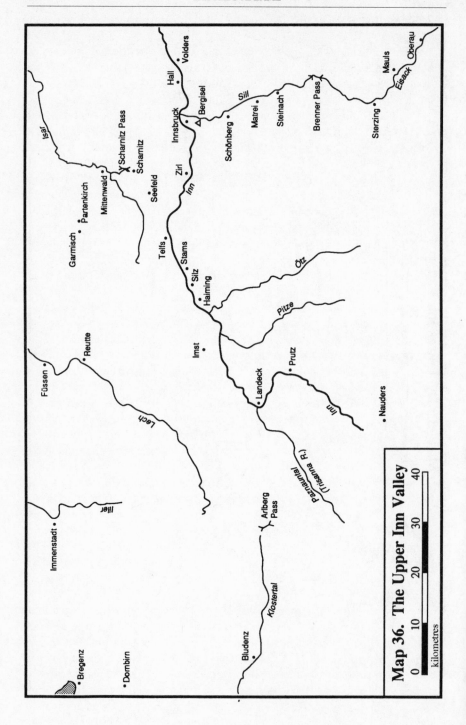

Map 36. The Upper Inn Valley

Included in Napoleon's orders to Lefebvre (29 and 30 April) were instructions to open and hold the Lueg Pass, currently occupied by Jellacic's Division.[25] On the evening of the 30th, Lefebvre therefore sent GM von Stengel with the 8th Infantry, I/4, a squadron of the 1st Dragoons and two guns (from Wagner's battery) to seize the pass and follow Jellacic's Austrians.

Stengel surprised the Austrians at Golling on the morning of 1 May, drove two companies of *Warasdiner-Kreutzer* Grenzer out of the town, and pressed on for the pass itself. The Austrian position, however, reinforced by fortifications and well defended by three companies of Grenzer, was naturally strong and repeated efforts by the 8th Infantry failed to gain them possession of the pass. In the face of this tough resistance, Stengel called off his assaults at 2 p.m. and withdrew his exhausted troops to Golling during the night. Determined to open the pass, Lefebvre reinforced Stengel with a battalion (II/2) on the 2nd and sent GM Rechberg with the 1st Infantry and the remainder of Wagner's battery to Golling on the 3rd. By noon on 3 May, therefore, the Bavarians had six battalions, a squadron and a battery around Golling and the 1st Division's Chief of Staff, GM Clemens von Raglovich, arrived to assume overall command of the operations to seize Lueg Pass. Keeping Rechberg's force and I/8 in front of the pass, Raglovich instructed Stengel to outflank the Austrians by marching up the Lammer valley. Struggling up the narrow, snow-filled gorge on the 4th, Stengel's Bavarians were able to take the village of Abtenau and push the Austrians (two companies of *Esterhazy*) back to the south-east, but were themselves thrown back beyond Abtenau by a Habsburg counter-attack the following day.[26] This Austrian success at Abtenau saved the pass. In a bold operation the preceding night (4/5 May), the Bavarians had sent two companies forward to seize the heights overlooking the pass on the east and west. The western column under Major Rummel was completely successful, surprising the enemy and capturing the heights together with 70 prisoners. The eastern force ran into trouble, but by the morning of the 5th the Bavarians were in a good position to drive home their attack on the pass. News of the reverse at Abtenau, however, caused Lefebvre to recall his men and most of the troops returned to Golling on the evening of 5 May, leaving the strategic pass in Jellacic's hands. A Bavarian outpost was maintained on the western heights above the pass until 10 May when the entire force retired to Hallein. That day saw the beginning of the First Offensive and two days later Lefebvre brought the Crown Prince's men back to Salzburg to provide a secure link to the Danube valley and support Wrede's advance up the Inn.[27]

Meanwhile, west of Salzburg, some of Deroy's men had been engaged in an attempt to relieve the Kufstein garrison. GM Karl von Vincenti departed Salzburg on 2 May with a small force composed of the 14th Infantry, I/5, 7th Light, two squadrons of 4th Chevauxlegers and two guns. Depositing II/14 at Melleck to secure his communications with Lefebvre, Vincenti endeavoured to approach Kufstein from the north-east via the narrow defile through Sachrang while Chef d'Escadron Montélégier's command (II/4, one squadron of 1st Dragoons, one gun), detached from the 1st Division on 27 April, advanced up the Inn from Rosenheim. Vincenti was repulsed at Sachrang on the 4th, however, and both officers retired on Rosenheim the following day to await reinforcements. Deroy hoped to renew the relief effort on 9 May, but Lefebvre was planning a concerted offensive into the mountains and directed Deroy to hold off until the 12th.

THE FIRST BRUTAL MARCH ON INNSBRUCK

The plan for what was to be the first of three offensives into the Tyrol was fairly simple. Wrede, returned from the Danube valley to participate in the operation, would march from Salzburg toward the Inn valley via the Strub Pass while Deroy pushed south from Rosenheim to relieve Kufstein; the two forces would converge near Wörgl and proceed up the Inn to occupy the Tyrolian capital. The Crown Prince would remain at Salzburg with his Division and part of Deroy's to maintain communications with the main army, now rapidly approaching Vienna. On the eve of the offensive, Lefebvre's Corps was disposed in a long arc from Rosenheim to Salzburg and Hallein. Deroy had Vincenti's and Montélégier's commands at Rosenheim, where he had been reinforced by II/5 and 1st Light, returning from escorting prisoners to Augsburg. Ludwig and Wrede were in and around Salzburg (Wrede had arrived on the 9th) with five of Deroy's battalions and most of his cavalry.[28] Between these two points were the two surviving companies of the 3rd Light (Berchtesgaden), II/14 (Melleck), and a squadron of the 4th Chevauxlegers (from Salzburg to Reichenhall). Farther west, Oberst Graf von Arco was assembling a small 'corps' of depot and volunteer formations around Benediktbeuren.

Wrede opened the First Offensive into the Tyrol on 10 May. Reinforced by six companies of the 9th Infantry from Deroy's Division and accompanied by Lefebvre, he bivouacked his division at Unken on the 10th and broke camp early the next morning, picking up II/14 as he advanced on the Strub Pass. The defenders were few (about 300 Tyrolians and 100 Austrian regulars with two small guns) but determined; three attacks by Minucci's men (6th Light plus a battalion each from the 3rd and 13th Regiments) were thrown back with loss while the difficult terrain defeated Wrede's personal attempt to outflank the position with II/14.[29] Finally, after a thorough artillery preparation, an attack by the 3rd Infantry drove off the tenacious defenders and the 2nd Division continued its march to Waidring. The nine-hour battle had cost the Bavarians 66 and the Tyrolian/Austrian force about 70 casualties. The following morning (12 May) brought a 4 a.m. surprise rebel attack, but the Bavarians, using their artillery to good effect, repulsed their assailants and pressed on to Ellmau under constant harassment from the insurgents. The six companies of the 9th Infantry were left behind to secure the area around Lofer.[30]

The bitter nature of this insurgent war is grotesquely illuminated by Wrede's march from Strub Pass to Innsbruck. The Bavarian soldiers, frustrated by an enemy they often could not see and excited by tales of the abominations committed upon their comrades in April, seem to have cast aside all semblance of humanity: 'if all of the Tyrol had had a neck, I would have cut it off with my sword'. They were frightened and angered by a foe that fought them with uncommon ferocity, an entire population that viewed them with hate: 'I saw

---

Table 7-2: The First Offensive Into the Tyrol (12 May)

Advancing on Strub Pass	Advancing on Kufstein
2nd Division (Wrede)	**3rd Division (Deroy)**
3rd Infantry	GM Vincenti
6th Infantry	5th Infantry
7th Infantry	I/14
13th Infantry	1st Light
six companies of 9th Infantry	7th Light
6th Light	two squadrons of 4th Chevauxlegers
3rd Chevauxlegers	Roy's Battery
two squadrons of 4th Chevauxlegers	
	Montélégier's Command
	II/4
At Melleck (3rd Division)	one squadron of 1st Dragoons
II/14 (joins Wrede on 11 May)	one gun

In and Around Salzburg	**Kufstein (Major Aicher)**
1st Division (Ludwig)	Provisional Light Battalion
- Includes surviving two companies of 3rd Lt	(depot troops of 1st, 2nd, 5th, 6th Light)
- Plus 2nd Chevauxlegers	fortress artillerymen
- Minus elements with Deroy	60 guns
GM Siebein (3rd Division)	**Oberst Arco's Command**
10th Infantry	
5th Light	Provisional Infantry Battalion (Hammel)
2nd Dragoons (ordered to join Deroy)	(depot troops: 1st, 2nd, 5th, 7th Inf., 1st, 2nd Lt.)
two companies of 9th Infantry	Provisional Cavalry Squadron (Lerchenberg)
remaining division artillery	(depot troopers: 1st Drgns, 1st, 2nd, 3rd Chev.)
	1st, 2nd, 3rd Gebirgsschützen Divisions
	Munich volunteer Schützen

---

boys 12 to 14 years old fire pistols at us, I watched men and women on the roofs hurling shingles and stones at us.'[31]   In the soldiers' minds, their mission was thus one of vengeance and punishment, undertaken against rebels who had risen against their rightful monarch. The result was bloody, ashen and dreadful: villages were burned, churches desecrated, homes plundered and hundreds of people coldbloodedly murdered as the advance into the Tyrol progressed. Many of the Bavarians themselves were appalled at the behaviour of their fellows: 'Sadly, I must be witness to horrors I can only curse,' GM Heinrich von Siebein told a local official; another Bavarian wrote home that 'the cruelty of our people is said to exceed that of the French in Spain'.[32] Word of these brutalities spread quickly through the mountains but only served to arouse the wrath of the Tyrolians and add more fighters to their ranks. Thus hatred generated hatred and atrocities committed by one side brought forth bloody reprisals in an accelerating spiral of vicious passion. Wrede felt compelled to issue a stern and pained Order of the Day from Ellmau on the 12th:

Yesterday and today, days when I have had cause to be pleased with many a brave deed performed by our division, I have seen cruelties, murders, plundering and arson that offend my innermost soul and make bitter every happy moment I have previously had in thinking of the accomplishments of the division. Soldiers! it is true we have fought yesterday and today against rebellious subjects of our gracious king who have been misled by the House of Austria and its powerless promises; but who gave you the right to murder the unarmed, to plunder houses and hovels, to burn

homes and villages? Soldiers! I ask you, how low have your feelings of
humanity sunken in the last two days?[33]

The Bavarian advance continued toward Innsbruck on the 13th. Completely
misapprehending the situation, Chasteler had rushed up the Inn valley to deal
with what he assumed to be a small Bavarian reconnaissance probe.
Encountering Wrede at Söll, he was quickly disabused of this notion, but was
unable to extricate himself from the unequal fight (approximately 10,000
Bavarians against 4-5,000 Austro-Tyrolians). Despite the desperate efforts of
the insurgents and Chasteler's small force, the Bavarians pushed them steadily
back toward the Inn, where the river's broad valley allowed Wrede to use his
cavalry to good advantage. The 3rd Chevauxlegers were particularly active,
launching several charges and capturing a number of Austrian cannon. At
Wörgl, the staunch Austrian resistance finally broke and Wrede's horsemen
chased the remaining enemy all the way to Rattenberg, some even fighting on
foot in the town while they waited for the infantry to catch up. The division had
had a remarkably successful day, capturing 3,000 soldiers and insurgents, nine
guns and three standards for a cost of some 200 Bavarians wounded and killed;
Chasteler's corps was crushed and he himself almost made prisoner.[34]
Expansively lauded by Lefebvre, Wrede's men spent the night at Rattenberg.[35]

The Bavarians pressed forward the next day (14 May). Under incessant
harassment from the insurgents, Wrede led his men forward with firmness and
energy. A serious skirmish broke out around Strass as the Tyrolians attempted
to defend the bridge over the Ziller, but some well-placed howitzer shells and
the appearance of Deroy's Division on the far bank of the Inn convinced the
Tyrolians that their situation was hopeless. They retired toward Schwaz and
Wrede camped for the night immediately south of Strass.

In accordance with Lefebvre's plan, Deroy had advanced toward Kufstein on
the morning of 12 May. Pushing south along the Inn, his columns encountered
some rebel defences, but the 1st Light quickly overcame all resistance and by 3
p.m. the men of the 3rd Division were exchanging cheers with the fortress garrison.[36] Linking with Wrede at Wörgl on the 15th, Deroy regained II/14 and proceeded upstream along the north bank of the Inn.

Wrede also resumed his advance on the 15th. Moving on the south bank of
the river, his division had to overcome one enemy position after another as the
Tyrolians fought desperately to delay the Bavarian march. Fighting was particularly brutal in the town of Schwaz. The insurgents had determined to stop the
Bavarians here and Wrede had to lead his men into the town four times before
they were able to drive out the last of the defenders. The Bavarians were able to
save the burning Inn bridge, but Schwaz itself and several neighboring villages
fell victim to the fires started by the vicious street fighting.[37] Pushing through
the smoke and flames, the 2nd Division crossed to the north side of the Inn and
spent the night in the open ground opposite Schwaz. The tough resistance
offered by what seemed to be the entire population of the Inn valley infuriated
the Bavarian troops and the cruel scenes of the past several days were repeated
in Schwaz: robbery, arson and the mutilation of prisoners were almost common-

place; as one officer had feared, the behaviour of the troops had become frightening, beyond the remedy of orders.[38] For their part, the Tyrolians eagerly set
upon Bavarian stragglers at every opportunity (the Bavarians regarded this as
base murder rather than warfare) and seem to have thrown captured soldiers into
the blazing buildings of Schwaz.[39] The war was barely a month old, but both
sides had already drunk deeply from the bitter cup of vengeance.

The battles at Wörgl and Schwaz had opened the way to Innsbruck, but
Lefebvre was concerned about his communications with Salzburg and decided
against an immediate advance. Wrede's troops were involved in heavy skirmishing south of Schwaz on the 16 May, while Deroy, who had spent the 15th
guarding the Ziller valley near Strass, marched down the southern bank of the
river to just short of Schwaz.[40] Both sides now needed to gain time, Lefebvre to
secure his rear and the Tyrolians to recover from the recent battles. An agreement for a 36-hour ceasefire was reached after confused negotiations and
announced on the afternoon of the 17th, Lefebvre promising to renew his offensive if the Tyrolians did not decide to conclude their rebellion and accept
Bavarian suzerainty peacefully. But the Tyrolian camp was anything but unified. While the defeats of the past five days and the departure of the Austrian
regular troops had cast a pall of depression and hopelessness over the insurgency, the fires of resistance still burned strongly and the Tyrolians could not
agree to lay down their arms. On the morning of the 19th, trammelled by conflicting desires, the Tyrolians sent a deputation to request more time to consider
Lefebvre's offer. Regarding their proposal as a poor ploy, however, the Marshal
rebuffed them and promptly ordered Wrede to advance. Caught off guard, the
Tyrolians were confused and a peculiar scene presented itself when Wrede
resumed his march toward Innsbruck at 9 a.m.: without clear direction, neither
submissive nor aggressive, dozens of Tyrolians, weapons in hand, stood along
the sides of the Bavarian march columns at a respectful remove, observing their
enemies with great curiosity but offering no resistance as the soldiers continued
toward the capital.[41] Innsbruck was occupied peacefully on the afternoon of 19
May and Lefebvre was satisfied the rebellion was over. He thus offered no
objection when Napoleon ordered him to take two of his divisions north into the
Danube valley to support the main army, leaving Deroy alone to enforce
Bavarian rule in the Tyrol.

A NATIONAL EFFORT I: BAVARIAN RESERVE AND IRREGULAR FORCES

The reoccupation of Innsbruck also put an end to the Tyrolian incursions into
Bavaria proper and allowed Oberst Graf Arco to march into Tyrol through the
Scharnitz Pass with several newly raised formations. These new military units
were the product of great efforts on the part of Munich's administration to meet
Napoleon's demands and provide an adequate defence for the Bavarian home-
land. As far back as March, Napoleon had ordered the formation of twelve
'bataillons de milice' to protect his lines of communications and secure
Bavaria's borders.[42] Financial restrictions and lack of qualified officers and
NCOs precluded full compliance with this directive, but a royal order of 6 April
initiated the formation of six reserve battalions, each battalion composed of four

companies of 135 men and a battalion staff of eight. Under the provisions of the 1808 constitution, these battalions were designated 'Nationalgarde I. Klasse', but received the same pay, equipment and discipline as the regular military; they were likewise expected to perform the same missions as the line units and were not restricted to home defence.[43] The depots of the active regiments and battalions represented another source of emergency manpower. These, however, had already been combed to bring the field units up to strength, to man fortresses and to provide staff troops for the three divisions. The remaining soldiers were often unfit for strenuous field duty. In a report to the king on 24 April, GL Georg Graf von Ysenburg warned 'After yesterday's dispatch of all the mounted troopers, the cavalry depots can only be regarded as a clumsy and ungainly mass, there is likewise little to hope for from the infantry depots in the complete absence of artillery as they are generally composed of young and untrained recruits.'[44] Moreover, the battles in southern Bavaria, the loss of the Tyrol and general indecision generated an irregular stream of orders concerning the depots and reserve battalions, so that these troops were constantly on the move, shifting from one garrison to the next and only absorbing recruits with difficulty. Thus the formation of the reserve battalions proceeded slowly and the situation remained unstable until late May and early June when the six nascent battalions and most of the depots were collected around Munich, Ulm and Augsburg.[45]

While these steps were being taken to increase the regular military, a number of royal decrees established temporary, irregular formations to defend the homeland. The first of these was the militarization of the Kordonisten in late April. In the absence of regular military forces, the Kordonisten, a civil organization normally responsible for policing the kingdom's highways, were formed into a Landes-Defensionsbataillon ('national defence battalion') under state Highway Inspector von Xylander to assist in border security. Resurrecting an emergency contingency from 1805, two special volunteer organizations were then called into existence in early May. Royal orders of the 7th and 8th respectively established the Gebirgsschützenkorps (literally 'mountain rifle corps') and the freiwilliges Jägerkorps ('corps of volunteer hunters').

The Gebirgsschützen were recruited from the alpine regions of southern Bavaria and the War Ministry seems to have regarded them as a hearty bunch of mountain-crafty folk, ideally suited to supplementing the line units, reserve battalions and Jäger in the kingdom's rugged border areas. With their detailed local knowledge and general alpine expertise, they were to help the other troops overcome their unfamiliarity with mountain warfare while contributing to the defence of their own 'peaceful hearths'. Under the overall command of Oberst Graf von Arco, the Gebirgsschützen were to be formed into three 'divisions' under the senior forestry inspector of each locale: 1st Division Traunstein District (500 men), 2nd Division Rosenheim District (1,000 men) and 3rd Division Garmisch District (also 1,000 men). The individual Schützen were supposed to be organized into Rotte (squads) of 50 men each, with four such squads being led by a local captain. The volunteers received daily pay, but, as a cost savings measure, were required to provide their own weapons and clothing; their 'uniform' thus consisted of their civilian clothing decorated with a blue-

and-white cockade. Discipline was to be administered outside of the military system and the men were not subject to the strict codes of military discipline and justice. From the outset, therefore, the Gebirgsschützen were a half-military and half-civil organization, a curious admixture that eventually failed to meet the government's high expectations.

If the Gebirgsschützen was a rather catch-as-catch-can operation, the freiwilliges Jägerkorps had something of an élite character about it. Divided into foot and mounted Jäger, the corps was to be composed of hunters and foresters as well as the sons of minor nobles and other well-to-do classes. A degree of financial security was a prerequisite because the men were not only expected to provide their own weapons, but also their own horses in the case of the mounted Jäger. As a mark of their special status, the ordinary Jägers were addressed with the formal 'Sie' (as opposed to the familiar 'Du') and received the same treatment as line NCOs. They were also granted uniforms: a green coat with yellow collar and long green trousers with yellow stripes topped by a round hat for the foot Jägers; for the mounted troopers, a black tricorne hat and long green coat with yellow collar and epaulets; black leather equipment was common to both foot and horse Jägers. The size of a Jäger company was fixed at 135 men and four to six companies were to comprise a battalion, but the number of battalions and squadrons to be formed was left undetermined, pending the response to the king's call to arms. Ordered to assemble in Munich, the Jägers received as their colonel that city's forestry inspector, Graf von Oberndorff, who had commanded a similar contingent in 1805. Oberndorff was subordinate to von Arco, and both Bavarians fell under the operational control of French GD Beaumont, commanding the 'division de réserve' in Augsburg.[46]

Two other types of combatants were called to arms in defence of the Fatherland in 1809: the Nationalgarde II. Klasse (National Guard Second Class) and local militias. Intended to 'maintain security and order within the country against domestic and foreign enemies', the Nationalgarde II. Klasse was supposed to be organized into 'Mobile Legionen' (mobile legions). Each of Bavaria's fifteen Kreise (counties) was responsible for the raising of one legion which would bear the name of the Kreis and consist of from four to eight battalions depending on the Kreis's population.[47] Commanded by a major, who was either appointed by the King or elected by the unit, each battalion was numbered and was to consist of four numbered companies of 176 men including 30 Schützen. For a uniform, the men of the legions wore a grey coat with lightblue collar over their civilian clothes, the ensemble completed by white pantaloons and a black felt shako. Formation of the mobile legions was ordered on 6 July and immediately encountered stiff resistance throughout the country, particularly in the northern Kreise. One battalion (II/Isarkreis) was eventually formed, but performed so poorly that it was disbanded after only a month.

The local militias (Nationalgarde III. Klasse) generally proved more reliable. Although the Nationalgarde III. Klasse was not formally called out in 1809, a number of districts and municipalities raised contingents of citizens' militia (Bürgermilitär) to protect hearth and home.[48] The militias performed a variety of useful duties, such as escorting prisoners of war and guarding towns, thereby relieving the regular military of these responsibilities.[49] But they also took the field against the Tyrolian and Vorarlberg insurgents on multiple occasions, demonstrating dedication and earning Defense Minister GL Johann Graf von Triva's praise: '...the citizen's militia performed its garrison duties in 1809 with professionalism and sacrifice, there is little improvement required...the Nationalgarde II. Klasse, however, despite all cost and effort, never managed to achieve any significant degree of utility.'[50]

THE LONG SOUTHERN BORDER I: TYROLIAN RAIDS INTO BAVARIA

Bavaria's energetic efforts to provide for the defence of its home soil were prompted by the increasing audacity and scope of the Tyrolian incursions into Altbayern. From their footholds in Immenstadt and Füssen, the Tyrolians launched forays up the river valleys into Bavaria, while the Vorarlbergers harassed the Bavarian, Württemberg and Baden districts around Lake Constance. Although there was little direct co-ordination between the two basic groups of insurgents, their activities naturally tended to ebb and flow with the fortunes of war in the Inn valley. In the early days of May, therefore, as optimism was prevalent amongst the rebels, a number of bold strokes into the lowlands were prepared. The Vorarlbergers thus attacked Lindau on 2 May while the Tyrolians were raiding Oberdorf and Obergünzburg. Kempten was entered and burned on the 4th and Memmingen hit by 1,500 Tyrolians on the 11th. In most of these instances, the insurgents captured the town, disarmed any local militia, and removed treasuries, food stocks and other items of value before setting parts of the town to the torch. The Vorarlbergers also managed to surprise and loot a Bavarian convoy of 222 wagons attempting to remove the matériel of several depots to the safety of Ulm. Attacked in Messkirch, the 150-man escort was scattered by the rebels (about 270), who promptly gathered anything valuable from the loaded wagons and returned to Bregenz by boat.[51]

The French and Bavarians, with almost no trained troops at hand, were driven to desperate measures to contain these incursions and GD Beaumont was detailed to shield the long border with the Tyrol. Arriving in Augsburg on the 12th, Beaumont sent GB Joseph Picard (500 cavalry, 250 infantry and two guns plus the Kordonisten of the Lechkreis) toward Memmingen the next day and attached to his command a Franco-Bavarian force from Ulm under Major Pillement. The latter detachment had been assembled by the active Oberst Lessel, fortress commandant in Ulm, and possessed a rather calico complexion with some 439 Bavarian infantry, two French infantry companies, 40 municipal Schützen, 24 municipal horsemen, a gun and even about 50 French cuirassiers.[52] Pillement's troops reached Illertissen on the evening of the 13th and waited there for orders from Picard, who had marched to Krumbach. The two columns entered Kempten the next day to find it empty of enemy, and occupied Memmingen peacefully on the 15th. The next night, some volunteer foresters from Ulm were able to surprise and disperse two detachments of Tyrolians on the roads from Kempten to Füssen and Immenstadt. Pillement's attempt to enter the latter town on the 19th was unsuccessful: ambushed by superior numbers of insurgents, he was obliged to withdraw after an hour's fight. The same day a battalion of citizen volunteers under Police Director Andrian-Werburg arrived in Kempten to reinforce Pillement's little force. Lefebvre's seizure of Innsbruck, however, had demoralized the Vorarlbergers and, presenting their submission to Picard on the 21st, they retired into the mountains.[53] With his headquarters and reserve in Kempten, Picard thus occupied Füssen, Immenstadt and Weiler without resistance.[54]

The Tyrolians had also continued their raids and marauding in the region south of Munich. The thin line of cavalry posts was reinforced on the 1st of May and again on the 7th, but the Bavarians could initiate no effective offensive action until the middle of the month when Arco's corps began to take form.[55] Arriving in Tölz on the 14th, Arco found the 2nd Division of the Gebirgsschützenkorps had already reached 663 men in Miesbach and Lenggries, while the 3rd counted some 314 in Diessen. Three days later, on the 17th, he received more regular troops from the depots in Munich and, with 773 regular infantry plus 180 cavalry, he felt himself strong enough to move against the Tyrolians.[56] On the night of the 18th, he marched on Mittenwald with about 270 men, hoping to reach the town before daybreak and surprise its defenders.[57] Delayed by poor roads, his detachment arrived outside the town as dawn was breaking on the 19th, but was turned back by superior strength (the Tyrolians numbered about 3,000) and forced to retire via an exhausting march over extraordinarily difficult mountain paths. None the less, when Lefebvre's drive up the Inn valley got under way, Arco returned to the offensive. Advancing to Partenkirchen, the 2nd Gebirgsschützen Division reported Mittenwald free of insurgents and the 1st Gebirgsschützen Division occupied both the town and the Scharnitz Pass on 22 May. Arco quickly established liaison with Deroy in Innsbruck and sought to solidify his control over the area. Although he watched the inhabitants carefully and received submissive delegations from many of the surrounding districts, he was unable to maintain his position when the ferocity of the Tyrolians was rekindled toward the end of the month.

THE SECOND BATTLE OF BERGISEL (29 MAY)[58]

In Innsbruck, Deroy was busy re-establishing Bavarian rule in the Tyrol, monitoring Austrian and Tyrolian movements and securing his communications with Salzburg. With Wrede's departure for the Danube (23 May), Deroy had only ten battalions, four squadrons and three batteries to keep the entire region subdued: 10th Infantry, 5th Light and two batteries in Salzburg; two companies of II/9 in Lofer; the other six companies of the 9th in Rattenberg; 7th Light and one battery in Hall; 5th and 14th Infantry, 2nd Dragoons in Innsbruck.[59] The Tyrolians had marked the departure of 'the principal mass of the enemy army under the Angel of Death Frede [Wrede]' and had convinced the vacillating Chasteler to return to Innsbruck and risk another battle with the Bavarians.[60] Deroy's scouts thus began to report signs of increasing enemy strength and aggressiveness in the Sill valley towards the Brenner Pass in the last week of May.[61] To determine the enemy's strength and intentions, Deroy organized a reconnaissance in force for the 25th, sending two companies (I/5), a dragoon platoon and a gun up the west side of the Sill and a grenadier company (I/14) up the east; the columns were to unite at Matrei and establish an observation post. Shortly after leaving their positions at about noon, however, the Bavarians ran into superior Austro-Tyrolian forces and had to withdraw toward Innsbruck. Hofer and the Austrian commander, GM Ignaz Freiherr von Buol-Bärenburg, had also chosen 25 May for their next move and had begun assembling early in the morning to advance on the capital. With some 6,400 Tyrolian rebels and 1,200 Austrians, they slowly overpowered the Bavarians and pushed them out of the hills into the low ground south of the city. Deroy reinforced his line and was able to contain the Austro-Tyrolian advance, but his own attempts to storm Bergisel were repulsed despite the bravery of his men. A heavy rainstorm ended the fight at about 7 p.m. and the Tyrolians, deeply disappointed with the meagre results of the day, retired up the Sill during the night. The Bavarians were thus able to reoccupy their previous outposts the next morning, having lost some 114 men in the course of the day.

As the Tyrolians withdrew, Deroy was cautiously confident: his communications to Mittenwald and Salzburg were fairly sound and the 10th Infantry was en route from Salzburg to reinforce the Innsbruck garrison. None the less, he knew that his position was exposed and he was not about to let himself be trapped in the city as Kinkel had been. Based on the reports of his active reconnaissance patrols, Deroy believed an attack to be imminent and accordingly alerted his men on the 28th. The 10th Infantry, the remainder of the 9th (two companies) and Peters' battery thus found much of the Bavarian camp under arms when they arrived that evening to bring Deroy's strength up to about 5,240 infantrymen, 408 cavalry and eighteen guns. The troops were kept on alert throughout the night of 28/29 May and there was little surprise in the 3rd Division headquarters when a detachment of the 7th Light returned from Zirl at 8 a.m. to report the town in Tyrolian hands and the link with Arco broken.[62]

Heartened by the news of Aspern and Hofer's impassioned patriotism, the Tyrolians and Buol's Austrians renewed the struggle for Innsbruck, and thus for all of Tyrol, on the morning of 29 May. With 12,000 Tyrolians, 1,270 Austrian infantry, 87 Austrian chevauxlegers and six guns at his disposal, Hofer planned to attack the Bavarian positions at dawn from the east, south and west, while simultaneously seizing the Inn bridges at Hall and Volders and applying pressure north of the river from Zirl.[63] The Tyrolians scored their first successes of the day at these two crossings over the Inn. The platoon (14th Infantry) guarding the bridge at Volders was attacked at 6.30 by overwhelming numbers of partisans and forced to retreat across the river despite the rapid arrival of another platoon from Hall. The Bavarians defended themselves with desperate courage, but even with additional reinforcements (two companies of I/5 and a cannon), they could not prevent the Tyrolians from destroying the bridge. Nor could the Bavarians maintain the security of the Hall bridge. Two companies of II/14, a half-squadron of dragoons and two guns contested the crossing with the rebels, but after the bridge had changed hands three times, the Bavarians had to withdraw to the north bank and content themselves with the destruction of the span. The best route to Salzburg, along the south bank of the Inn, was now denied to Deroy.

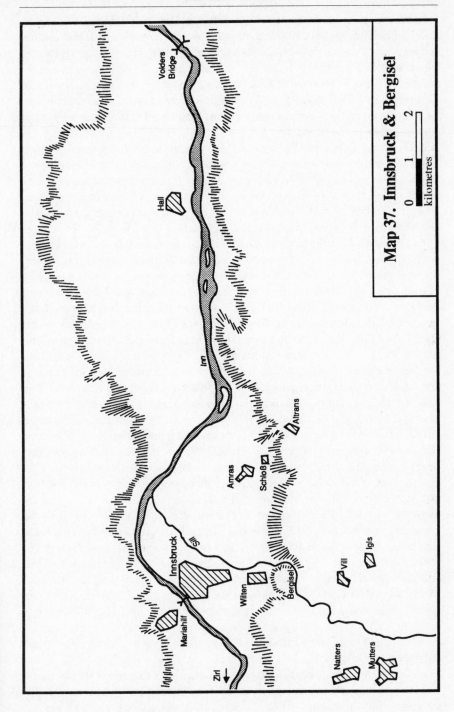

Map 37. Innsbruck & Bergisel

In the meantime, a hot combat had developed south of Innsbruck. Starting on the right near the Inn at about 7 a.m., the Austro-Tyrolian assault had quickly spread west to engulf the entire Bavarian line. The enemy could not break the Bavarians' stout resistance, but by noon, their courageous and energetic attacks compelled Deroy's troops to fall back into the meadows and farmsteads beneath Bergisel. Shortly thereafter (about 1 p.m.), Deroy received a report of the Tyrolian advance from Zirl toward Innsbruck. He decided to launch a powerful counter-attack against the forces on Bergisel to defeat them before the column from Zirl could deploy. Formed in three columns, the Bavarians launched repeated assaults against the hills, only to be repulsed with loss.[64] The centre column briefly managed to gain a foothold along the main road before two companies of Austrian regulars, supported by a few chevauxlegers and four guns, counter-attacked to push the Bavarians back down the slopes. By 2.30, the Austrians and Tyrolians had resumed their attack, advancing to the foot of Bergisel and evicting the hard-fighting Bavarians from the last of the farmsteads there. The Bavarians retired in good order to the Wilten monastery and a number of other previously fortified structures in the valley and opened a heavy fire against those who ventured forth from the cover of the trees along the base of the hill. As on the 25th, the Bavarians could not drive the Tyrolians from the forested heights, but neither could the insurgents essay a serious attack in the open valley floor where the Bavarians, with their formed infantry, cavalry and artillery, held a distinct tactical advantage.

Hofer and the Austrians decided to wait until the flanking column from Zirl had its demoralizing effect upon Deroy's Division. They waited in vain. The flanking column, led by the normally energetic Major Teimer, advanced in a slow and hesitant fashion and never truly threatened Deroy's rear; the Bavarian commander did not even find it necessary to send reinforcements to his detachment north of the river (two companies of II/14, a half-squadron and two guns).[65] Weakened by the large detachments he had sent to help in the fight against Arco at the Scharnitz Pass, Teimer could not press his attacks and was driven off by the disciplined fire of the Bavarian infantry and guns. In the meantime, a brief ceasefire had been declared (4 p.m.), ostensibly to allow the Austrians to demand Deroy's surrender. In reality, the Austro-Tyrolian force was running out of ammunition and hoped to mask their weakness through the ruse of negotiations. By the time Deroy had rejected the summons and the attackers had resupplied themselves with cartridges, it was 6 p.m. and darkness was falling. Although the firefight was resumed for a brief time, no significant actions were undertaken by either side and night brought an end to the day's bloodshed. The Second Bergisel Battle was over. Bavarian casualties for the 29th amounted to about 130 dead and 500 wounded, with the 10th Infantry bearing the greatest cost (some 277).[66]

While the Austrians and Tyrolians planned the next morning's attack, Deroy was busy implementing a deception of his own. Utilizing one of warfare's oldest tricks, he had his outposts light a large number of watchfires and conduct obvious, active patrols to keep enemy scouts at bay; his pickets fraternized with their opponents to lull suspicions and distract attention from any sound of departure. Then, with wagon wheels and horses' hooves muffled, the 3rd Division marched silently away into the darkness. By 6 a.m. on the 30th, Deroy's men had reached Vomp, where the main body halted to allow the slower trains to catch up. The disorganization of the Austro-Tyrolian force at Innsbruck precluded any serious pursuit, but the 3rd Division's retreat, resumed at noon on the 30th and conducted over the difficult byways north of the Inn, was constantly harassed by groups of local insurgents, who blocked the way to the south bank of the river and inflicted numerous casualties on the Bavarian column.[67] Several times the Bavarians had to clear their path with the bayonet; the 9th Regiment distinguished itself in one such attack, just as *Preysing* consistently demonstrated its firmness in the demanding role of rear guard. The night of the 30th was spent at Achenrain and the next day's march, made under continued skirmishing, brought the tired men under the protective guns of Kufstein.[68]

Arco's positions around Scharnitz had also been attacked on the 29th. Although most of his outposts were captured (e.g., the infantry and eleven chevauxlegers at Zirl) and the pass lost, Arco counter-attacked vigorously. His light infantrymen boldly clambered up the steep slopes south of Mittenwald and chased the Tyrolians into the open terrain beyond the pass, where they were set upon and decimated by the small Bavarian cavalry force; some of the troopers even dismounted to pursue fugitives into the wooded hills with pistols and carbines.[69] Arco thus regained the pass but found all of his southern outposts taken. A small detachment sent against the Tyrolian positions in the Leutasch valley on the 30th, however, was unsuccessful and Arco had to content himself with the possession of Mittenwald under constant harassment from Tyrolian skirmishers. The end of the month therefore saw the Bavarians evicted from the Tyrol for the second time, with no immediate prospect of regaining the lost province and facing the imminent threat of renewed incursions into Altbayern.[70]

INSURGENT SUCCESS IN THE VORARLBERG

The Vorarlbergers also revived their rebellion in late May, sallying forth from the mountains and harassing the French and Württembergers (under Colonel Grouvel) in Bregenz. To discover the extent of the insurgents' preparations, GD Beaumont ordered Grouvel to undertake a reconnaissance toward Feldkirch, reinforcing him for this undertaking with two companies of Pillement's battalion from Weiler (about 350 men and one gun).[71] The Bavarians departed Weiler on the 28th and arrived at Bregenz the next morning. Forming Grouvel's left, they were to clear the heights that loomed east of the road from Bregenz to Feldkirch. The mixed column of French, Bavarian and Württemberg troops reached Dornbirn with little difficulty but encountered stiff resistance from the swiftly gathered rebels when Grouvel tried to advance further. Attacked from the front and the left, Pillement's men were bundled up and driven back in confusion, while the rest of the Allied force retreated in growing disorder. The Bavarian gunners proved inept and, much to Grouvel's disgust, only managed to fire their piece spasmodically. Unable to stem the insurgents' advance, Grouvel retreated back to Dornbirn, then Bregenz and finally to the Loiblach where he received support from Scheler's Württembergers. The Bavarians, barely trained and largely incapacitated by drink, seem to have been more a hindrance than a help during the withdrawal; Grouvel referred to them as a 'herd of sheep' who had to be protected to prevent their falling into the enemy's hands.[72] While the French and Württembergers pulled back toward Lindau, Pillement returned to Weiler. The next day, he was ordered back to Kempten with his entire force as General Picard sought to concentrate his command in the face of new raids on Füssen (31 May). With few reliable troops (the unseasoned French and Bavarian infantry proved almost useless on outpost duty), the French general prepared to call in his isolated detachments and retire to a more secure position deeper in Bavaria. The Vorarlbergers, like their Tyrolian brothers, thus managed to free their land of foreign troops by the end of May.

JUNE - DEFENCE OF THE REALM

Encouraged by their recent successes, the Tyrolians and Vorarlbergers carried the war into southern Bavaria in June, once again threatening the safety of the kingdom and Napoleon's line of communications. The loss of Lindau and Bregenz prompted Beaumont to pull Picard's force back from its exposed positions on Bavaria's southern border in early June. With his headquarters and reserve (including Pillement's detachment) in Kaufbeuren, Picard garrisoned Schongau, Oberdorf and Kempten (the latter including some Bavarian infantry) and sent patrols south to observe the insurgents. At the same time, most of the Bavarian volunteer foresters were sent home with royal thanks for their service. On the 14th, Andrian's battalion was also dissolved, its place taken by Kordonisten and one company of volunteer citizens who wanted to stay by the flag; Andrian retained command until early July. Although the Vorarlbergers were quite active farther west against the Baden and Württemberg troops, the only combat involving the Bavarians was a weak raid on Kempten which the garrison easily repelled (19 June).

Arco also began June with a retreat. Attacked at Mittenwald on the 2nd by an overwhelming number of rebels, he conducted a valiant defence but was forced to withdraw to Benediktbeuren with a loss of 52 men. Two days later, he was ordered to retire further and marched for Wolfratshausen, leaving a detachment of 100 infantry (4th Company) and 75 cavalry at Starnberg under Hauptmann Storchenau to watch the road from Weilheim to the capital. The Gebirgsschützen in Partenkirchen also evacuated their positions and moved back to Murnau on the 2nd, continuing their retreat to Weilheim when a large body of Tyrolians advanced from Partenkirchen on the 6th. These insurgents, under Teimer's leadership, marched into Partenkirchen on 5 June and reached Weilheim on the 6th, but were thrown into a panic by the threat of Storchenau's cavalry and returned to Murnau the same day; by the 7th, they were back in the Tyrol around Scharnitz.

Despite the impotence of this latest incursion, the defeat at Mittenwald and the anticipated threat to Munich had led the government to recall Deroy from Rosenheim on 4 June. That general, having rested his men at Kufstein, had withdrawn to Rosenheim on the 2nd to improve his supply situation. Leaving GM Siebein with the 9th Infantry, a half-squadron and three guns to guard the opening of the Inn valley, he immediately headed for Munich with the rest of his division. Riding in advance of his men, he reached the capital on the morning of the 6th and ordered the following dispositions upon learning the apparent gravity of the situation: GM Vincenti (three battalions, a half-squadron, one and a half batteries) was to proceed from Höhenkirchen to Benediktbeuren and Tölz; two companies of the 5th Infantry were to relieve Storchenau at Starnberg; and GM von Seydewitz would support Arco at Wolfratshausen with the rest of the troops (three and a half battalions, three squadrons, the light battery).[73] Deroy accompanied Seydewitz to Habach on the 7th in an attempt to cut off the rebels at Weilheim, only to discover that the enemy had already retreated; Arco advanced to Kochel and Storchenau to Weilheim. Deroy remained around Weilheim until the 13th, but the threat to Munich had receded and he returned to Rosenheim with three battalions, two and a half squadrons and one and a half batteries to relieve Kufstein from the Tyrolians' second blockade. Vincenti was left with four battalions, a squadron and a battery to support Arco between Murnau and Tegernsee.[74] Reaching Rosenheim on the 16th, Deroy collected replacements and a large wagon train of supplies and was able to reprovision the fortress on the 18th without opposition, returning to his encampment at Rosenheim that evening.

The last weeks of the month passed in relative quiet for Deroy's and Arco's commands despite continual small encounters with Tyrolian patrols. Deroy responded to urgent pleas for help from the French commandant in Salzburg, GB Kister, sending II/5 to the city on 21 June, followed by the bulk of the division on the 24th.[75] The Bavarian general arrived in Salzburg on the 25th to find that Kister's fears were greatly exaggerated and that the Frenchman believed his defensive needs were completely satisfied by the addition of II/5 to the city's garrison (the 5th Light had been in Salzburg since 30 April). Leaving II/5 in the city with Kister, Deroy marched back to Rosenheim on the 27th, arriving two days later with the intent of launching another foray to relieve Kufstein. The close of June thus found the 3rd Division and Arco's command spread from Salzburg to Murnau and Pillement's provisional battalion in Kaufbeuren, all warily observing the activities of the restive Tyrolians and Vorarlbergers.[76]

A National Effort II: Reorganizing the Reserves

The Bavarian military also introduced two organizational changes in June. First, an Army Order of 25 June decreed the establishment of six more reserve battalions, bringing the total to twelve. Each infantry regiment, except the 11th,[77] was thus to receive a reserve battalion which would wear that regiment's uniform and bear its name (e.g., 'Reservebataillon 1. Linien-Infanterie-Leibregiments', 'Reservebataillon 2. Linien-Infanterieregiments', etc.).[78] As with the first set of six reserve battalions, the new units would consist of four fusilier companies with the same strength, organization, discipline and responsibilities as the regular line troops. To help overcome the severe shortage of trained leaders, the new battalions were to be formed by combining new recruits with the depots of existing regiments. Additionally, it was hoped that these measures would speed the formation of the first six battalions, which had not reached their assembly points until the end of May and were not yet fit for combat. These orders increased the bustle of activity in the Bavarian interior as more than 3,000 new soldiers were called up and existing depots and half-formed reserve battalions were sent marching to their newly appointed destinations.[79] With so many depot troops already committed against the enemy, however, several months would pass before the last of the depot companies and provisional units were amalgamated into the new reserve battalions.

The second organizational change was the dissolution of the Gebirgs-schützenkorps. A curious combination of military and civilian institutions from its inception, the Gebirgsschützenkorps had proved an unwieldy weapon, a great disappointment to the authorities in Munich and more bane than benefit to Arco. Discipline, obedience and reliability were the most glaring problems. While regular soldiers were unwilling to take orders from the leaders of the corps, the Schützen resisted the authority of the line officers, and neither officer had the disciplinary tools to enforce obedience on members of the other organization. 'There were conflicts and quarrels daily,' said Hauptmann Baur, Arco's Chief of Staff, and Arco, calling them 'extraordinarily troublesome men', repeatedly requested the disbanding of the corps. Perhaps the greatest source of friction was the reluctance of the Schützen to serve outside their home districts. Believing they had been called to arms to defend hearth and home, the Schützen initially followed Arco's orders out of patriotism, but grew increasingly stubborn as the war continued; on 20 May, therefore, the government restricted Arco to employing the Schützen within their original districts. This measure did nothing to ameliorate the fundamental inconsistencies in the organization of the corps, however, and the situation continued to deteriorate. By early June, elements of the 2nd Division were openly refusing to move outside their own districts and the commander of the 3rd Division found it necessary to ask for military assistance in rounding up the Schützen who were leaving his ranks in growing numbers: 'Nothing could impede the desertion of the Gebirgsschützen, which reduced that unreliable corps to a very few.' Finally, in response to Arco's pleas, the government issued a new rescript on 10 June. Although the mission of the corps was unchanged, the previous command structure of three divisions united under Arco was eliminated and replaced with a system which emphasized the responsibilities of the local civil authorities. The revised status of the corps satisfied all parties. As a purely civil institution which co-operated with the military in defence of the border districts, the Gebirgsschützenkorps continued to perform valuable service throughout the war, and Baur could honestly comment that 'even in the most dangerous periods, one could rely on these bold mountaineers almost more than on the line soldiers'.[80]

THE LONG EASTERN BORDER:
AUSTRIAN INCURSIONS FROM BOHEMIA AND THÜRINGEN

While the inhabitants of southern Bavaria struggled to repel assorted bands of insurgents and marauders, the eastern regions of the kingdom were plagued by plundering groups of Austrian Landwehr raiding over the border from Bohemia. The towns of Zwiesel and Regen were particularly afflicted and the pleas of local authorities reached military ears in Munich and Passau during the first week of June. On the 12th, the War Ministry ordered the provisional battalion at Oberhaus to assist the local militias, but the order was already obsolete when it was issued; a company of Bavarians (combined from the depot troops of the 6th and 9th Infantry) and a company of Weimar Jägers had already departed the fortress for Zwiesel on 9 June. This tiny force scored a minor success when it captured the leader of an Austrian raiding party and fourteen of his men on the 19th. The Bavarian and Weimar soldiers skirmished with the enemy again on the 26th, but their presence along the border seems to have deterred the Landwehr and there were no further significant raids.[81]

Austrian sorties into northern Bavaria were more serious. In an effort to disrupt Napoleon's line of communications and encourage central Germany to revolt against French rule, the Austrians launched an expedition into Bayreuth and north-eastern Bavaria in June.[82] A force commanded by FML Radivojevich (4,200 infantry, 200 cavalry and four guns) departed Eger on 9 June, crossed the Bohemian border and marched into the city of Bayreuth four days later.[83] Austrian patrols were soon probing toward Bamberg, Nuremberg and Regensburg: Bamberg was raided and partially burned on the 14th and a small force entered Nuremberg on the 26th.[84] These incursions caused great concern in Munich but the only available forces were a variety of Bavarian depot formations and French provisional units.[85] The Austrian presence in Nuremberg excited particular attention and French GD Jean Delaroche moved on the city by forced marches with the French 1st Provisional Dragoon Regiment and a Bavarian 6-pounder from Regensburg. Hearing of his approach, the Austrians evacuated the city on the night of 27/28 June and headed for Bayreuth. Entering Nuremberg, Delaroche decided to pursue and called on the fortresses of Forchheim and Rothenberg to send assistance. A detachment of 227 men and a gun under Hauptmann Hannet joined the French commander near Hilpoltstein at midnight on the 28th and the Franco-Bavarian force established an ambush for the Austrians north of Betzenstein early the following morning.[86] The Austrians were caught by surprise when the Allies opened fire at 4 a.m., but they recovered quickly, recognized Delaroche's weakness, and attacked. Their assault broke the Allied line, forcing the French and Bavarians to retreat (by separate routes) to Forchheim. Despite the disappointing result of this little action, the French and Bavarians had generally performed well, managing to capture and keep two Austrian guns.[87]

Meanwhile, GD Jean-Andoche Junot, the Duc d'Abrantes, had received instructions to move on Bayreuth with elements of the French Reserve Corps from Hanau and drive off the Austrian intruders. Marching via Würzburg at the head of 4,750 men, Junot reached Bamberg on 5 July. Here he found GD Delaroche with two French provisional dragoon regiments, about 510 Bavarian depot infantrymen and two guns. Delaroche and the 1st Provisional Dragoons had departed Forchheim for Bamberg on 3 July with a detachment of about 200 Bavarians from the fort's garrison. The 5th Provisional Dragoons, coming by forced marches from the Regensburg—Passau area, had acquired an additional detachment of Bavarian infantry (309 men) as well as two guns at Forchheim

Table 7-3: Allied Forces in North-east Bavaria (8 July)

Under GD Junot, Commander of the Reserve Corps

1st Division of Reserve Corps (GD Rivaud)

1st Brigade (GB Lameth)
(IV/19, IV/25, IV/28 Ligne)
2nd Brigade (GB Taupin)
(IV/36, IV/50, IV/75 Ligne)

Dragoons (GD Delaroche)

1st Provisional Dragoons
5th Provisional Dragoons

Junot's Strength (approx.)	
French Infantry -	4,500
Bavarian Infantry -	510
Cavalry -	1,200
Artillery -	273
Total --	6,483 men
	14 guns

Bavarian Infantry

(drawn from depots of 4th & 8th Infantry, 5th Light)

Artillery

12 French guns (2 x 12-pdrs, 8 x 6-pdrs, 2 x howitzers)
2 Bavarian guns (3-pdrs)

Fortress Garrisons

Rosenberg	**Forchheim**	**Rothenberg**
depot of 10th Infantry (one company) half company of artillery	depots of 4th & 8th Infantry (two companies each) depot of 5th Light artillery company	depots of 5th & 6th Infantry (one company each) depot of 3rd Light half company of artillery

before proceeding to Bamberg. Although the Bavarians were only supposed to escort the French cavalry to Bamberg, Delaroche kept them in the town and Junot ordered them to accompany his corps as he marched east to attack Radivojevich on the 6th.[88] Over the next two days, the Habsburg commander retired before the Allies, pulling out of Bayreuth on the 7th to establish a position at Gefrees and await reinforcements. A lively engagement developed in and around this little town on 8 July. Under the hot summer sun, the French and Bavarians tried to dislodge their opponents from the hills, but Radivojevich held and the Allies had to fall back when FML Kienmayer arrived with fresh Austrian and Braunschweig troops. Pursued by the Braunschweigers, Junot retreated via Kirchenthumbach (9 July) to Amberg (10 July), his 500 Bavarians taking position at nearby Sulzbach. The enemy broke off the chase on the 10th and the pursuit force retired to Hof where it joined the main body of Kienmayer's command on the 11th to turn against Jerome's Westphalians.[89]

Junot, still at Amberg, was joined by additional Bavarian troops under Oberst Preysing on the 14th. Although called a 'brigade', this force actually consisted of the combined battalion (depot companies of 6th, 9th, 10th and 14th Infantry) that had held the Oberhaus fortress at Passau plus a battery of four guns. Departing Passau on the 3rd, the combined battalion reached Neustadt an der Donau on the 8th, was joined by its little battery, and continued on to arrive in Nuremberg on the 12th. The Provisional Light Battalion from Kufstein had been destined for Preysing's brigade, but the exigencies of the overall situation demanded its presence on the kingdom's southern border. Marching to Amberg on the 14th, Preysing incorporated Junot's other Bavarian depot troops into his

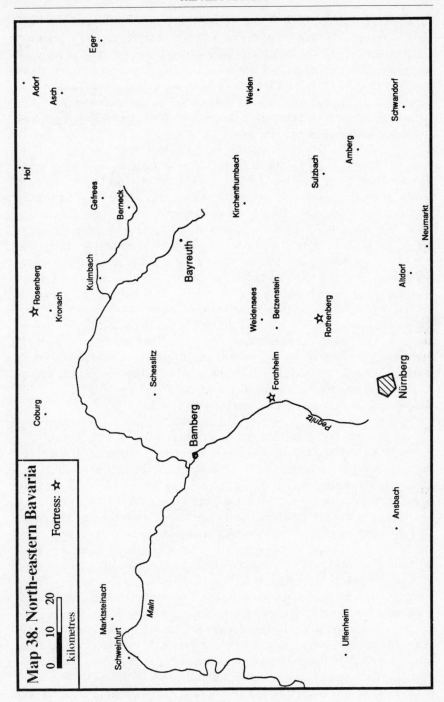

Map 38. North-eastern Bavaria

Fortress: ☆

0 10 20
kilometres

band (these had since been organized into two companies), released to their depots a number of soldiers unsuited for field duty, and thus created a single battalion of 720 men in six companies. By 17 July, Junot and the Bavarians had returned to Bayreuth, where they learned of the armistice that had been declared six days earlier. Although French and Bavarian forces remained around Bayreuth until the Treaty of Schönbrunn was signed in October, there was no further combat action and none of the reserve battalions eventually formed in the Nuremberg area ever engaged the foe.[90]

July - The Second Offensive Opens

In early July the 3rd Division was unexpectedly called to the Danube valley as Napoleon prepared for his second attempt to cross the Danube. The 1st and 2nd Divisions had been occupied in protecting the army's strategic left from Linz to Ybbs since the end of May, but the Emperor now (1 July) called his favourite, Wrede, to Vienna to share in the glory of the climactic grand battle. Deroy was therefore ordered to Linz to take his place but decided to reprovision Kufstein and gather his scattered forces before complying with these new instructions. With the 5th Reserve Battalion, recently arrived from Munich, he marched up the Inn on the 5th and arrived at the fortress almost without incident.[91] The fort's stores having been replenished, the Provisional Light Battalion exchanged places with the 5th Reserve and returned to Rosenheim on 6 July with Deroy.[92] Temporarily leaving behind I/9 (Audorf) and 7th Light (Reichenhall), Deroy's much reduced force headed for Linz on the 7th, followed the next day by Vincenti's troops from south of Munich.[93] Their sudden departure thus left Arco alone to defend southern Bavaria from the Lech to the Inn.

The Long Southern Border II: Renewed Raids into Bavaria

Although Arco's corps remained an expedient creation, during July it assumed a rather more regular complexion. The dissolution of the Gebirgsschützenkorps removed an irritating source of friction and the arrival of the 1st Reserve Battalion, the Provisional Light Battalion, two provisional companies (from 3rd and 4th Light) and two guns made up for the loss of some line depot troops as well as the numerous officers and cadre drafted from Arco's force to create new formations.[94] Fortunately, the insurgents remained relatively quiescent during this period, allowing Deroy's troops to depart unmolested and granting Arco time to incorporate his new units and organize his defence. The only disturbance in the first half of the month was a brief and successful skirmish at Walchensee on the 3rd. Otherwise, the men were occupied with patrols, drills and the construction of field fortifications. By the 10th, Arco's little corps had achieved the basic composition it would maintain through the next offensive into the Tyrol: 1st Reserve Battalion (four companies), Provisional Light Battalion (now reorganized with one company each of 3rd, 4th, 5th and 6th Light), one company each of the 1st and 2nd Light Battalions, Rittmeister August Graf von Lerchenfeld's combined squadron (depot troopers from 1st Dragoons, 1st, 2nd and 3rd Chevauxlegers), three guns and a howitzer. With a strength of approximately 1,540 cavalry and infantry, the corps was posted in a long screen from Murnau to Tegernsee with Arco holding his small general reserve in a central position at Benediktbeuren. Local Gebirgsschützen supplemented the regular troops in their daily patrols and were available at short notice in emergencies.[95]

Oberst von Oberndorff's freiwilliges Jägerkorps also saw its first combat in July. Almost disbanded when the rebellion in the Tyrol seemed suppressed, the corps' organization was hastened after the second retreat from Innsbruck. It was late June, however, before a battalion and a squadron were ready to deploy to the endangered southern border, and the first contingent, consisting of three companies, the staff and twelve mounted Jäger, did not leave Munich until 6 July. Arriving at Audorf on the evening of the 8th, this force relieved I/9 and assumed its patrols and outposts the next day with the help of 83 Gebirgsschützen from Rosenheim. The 4th and 5th Companies left Munich two days later with two guns to take over the positions of the 7th Light near Reichenhall on the 15th.[96] Finally, the 6th Company (140 men) marched from the capital on the 17th to watch over the border near Fischbach with 28 mounted Jäger.[97] The Jägerkorps saw its first action on the 16th when a company at Audorf repulsed an Austro—Tyrolian foray.

The Austrians and their insurgent allies launched their last major effort into southern Bavaria on 17 July. Intended to be a co-ordinated push by Tyrolians and Vorarlbergers, six columns of insurgents supported by small detachments of Austrian regulars advanced against the Bavarians' principal defensive positions in the early morning hours. The alert Arco, however, had received intelligence concerning the rebels' intentions and his men were well prepared when patrols found the enemy around Walchensee at 5 a.m. Arco's outposts were pushed back to Kochel but the colonel himself rapidly appeared with reinforcements and the partisans were unable to make an impression on the main Bavarian position despite eight hours of desultory battle.[98] Several kilometres to the east, another band of rebels floated down the Isar on rafts, attacked Lenggries and drove the Bavarian outposts back toward Tölz. Fortunately, Arco had foreseen such an eventuality and had sent Hauptmann Gräf with a company of the 1st Reserve to Tölz on the morning of the 17th. Reinforcing the men of the 1st Light and calling the local Gebirgsschützen to arms, Gräf assembled a colourful and determined little force, led it against the rebels and put them to flight. Checked on the 17th, the Austrians and Tyrolians attempted to renew their offensive the next day at Murnau. With about 300 men, Hauptmann Baur held off an enemy force of 2,000 for almost two hours before retreating to the east in the hopes of encountering reinforcements. As on the previous day, Arco was soon at hand. Learning of Baur's plight, he had bundled an infantry company into wagons and set off for the battle with this mobile infantry, twenty horsemen and a gun. Linking with Baur, he quickly formed his men, fired a few artillery rounds in preparation and attacked. He was completely successful. While Lerchenfeld overthrew the Austrian cavalry and personally captured a gun, the inspired Bavarian infantry energetically pressed the Austro-Tyrolian force, whose flagging morale was indicated by the loss of more than 100 prisoners and two banners in addition to the cannon and an unknown number of dead and wounded; Bavarian losses totalled 46. Arco's performance in his difficult command fully justified his sovereign's trust. Displaying intelligence, decision and celerity, he repeatedly defeated superior numbers of Austrians and Tyrolians with a ragtag force of untrained recruits, junior leaders and recalcitrant local militia.

The following week passed in relative quiet for the men of Arco's and Oberndorff's corps. The Jägers fought a small skirmish on the 20th and a company of the 2nd Reserve was rushed from Munich to Miesbach by wagon to help local Schützen repel border marauders, but for most of the troops the days were filled with the routine of patrol and outpost duty.[99] On the evening of the 26th, however, both Bavarian corps were placed under the command of French GB Louis Pelletier, Comte de Montmarie and ordered to concentrate at Kreuth in preparation for a second effort to crush the Tyrolian insurrection. By the night of 27 July, the two corps were assembled in the town, watching the urgent signal fires of the Tyrolians flicker on the distant peaks.[100] This time, the Allies planned a concentric attack on the region, with the Bavarians entering from the north and French troops driving in from the east and south.[101] As part of this larger concept, GB Montmarie was to support VII Corps' advance up the Inn valley by crossing the Achen Pass with Arco's and Oberndorff's men. After sending his heavy 6-pounders back to Munich, Montmarie departed Kreuth at noon on the 28th and crossed over into the Tyrol with 2,860 soldiers and three guns.[102] Continuing south the next day, the column encountered resistance at the Achensee but quickly overcame the insurgents, repaired a damaged bridge and resumed its progress to Jenbach on the Inn. Marching into the valley by the latter town, Montmarie was pleased to see VII Corps on the opposite bank of the river. The next day, his small force marched upstream to Hall, clearing the northern bank of the river while Lefebvre's command proceeded along the southern shore to enter Innsbruck that evening. The month ended with Arco's men occupying Hall and the Jägers returning downstream to Rattenberg with a gun and 50 of Arco's cavalry to guard the line of communications back to Bavaria.

THE SECOND MARCH ON INNSBRUCK

With the signing of the armistice at Znaim, Napoleon's attention again turned to the Tyrol. Determined to expunge the insurrection, the Emperor immediately dictated new orders for Lefebvre and sent glittering young staff officers riding hard for Linz, their perspiring mounts gasping in the July heat. Deroy's men, the first of whom had only reached Linz on the 13th, were thus turned about and sent back to the dreaded mountains after only four days along the Danube. They reached Salzburg three days later. For his part in the Second Offensive, Deroy was to seize the Lueg Pass and advance on Innsbruck indirectly via the long and difficult Salzach and Ziller valleys. On 24 July, after probing the defences of the pass with II/9 for two days, he attacked. Some heated skirmishing ensued, but Deroy, through the intervention of a local clergyman, eventually persuaded the insurgents in the gorge to surrender and the 3rd Division marched through the pass the next morning without incident. Moving via St. Johann (26),

Table 7-4: Lefebvre's Forces in the Second Offensive (25 July)

Corps staff cavalry from V/1st Dragoons

1st Division - GM von Raglovich
staff company from 2nd Inf. depot
staff cavalry from V/1st Chevauxlegers
1st Leib Infantry
2nd Infantry *Kronprinz*
4th Infantry
8th Infantry *Herzog Pius*
1st Light *Habermann*
3rd Light (two companies under Major Theobald)
1st Dragoons (two squadrons)
1st Chevauxlegers *Kronprinz*
Hofstetten's Line Battery
Pamler's Line Battery (5 pieces)
1/2 Roy's Line Battery (1 x 6-pdr, 2 x hwtzr)
Regnier's Light Battery
French sapper company

German Division - GD Rouyer
4th Rheinbund
5th Rheinbund
II/6 Rheinbund
attached Bavarian units:
4th Chevauxlegers *Bubenhofen*
van Douwe's Light Battery

3rd Division - GL von Deroy
staff company from 5th Inf. depot
staff cavalry from V/4th Chevauxlegers
5th Infantry *Preysing*
9th Infantry *Ysenburg*
10th Infantry *Junker*
14th Infantry (six companies)
5th Light *Butler*
2nd Dragoons *Thurn und Taxis*
Gotthardt's Line Battery
1/2 Roy's Line Battery (3 x 3-pdrs)

Other Units
Salzburg:
  I/6 Rheinbund Regiment
  8th Reserve Battalion (forming)
  Wagner's Line Battery
Kufstein:
  5th Reserve Battalion
Reichenhall:
  two companies of 14th Infantry
  one gun (from Pamler)
Lueg Pass:
  7th Light *Treuberg* (two companies)
Munich:
  2nd Reserve Battalion (two companies)
  7th Reserve Battalion (forming)

GB Montmarie's Command
Under Oberst Arco:
1st Reserve Battalion
Provisional Light Battalion
  (depot troops: 3rd, 4th, 5th, 6th Light)
Provisional Cavalry Squadron (Lerchenberg)
  (depot troopers: 1st Drgns, 1st, 2nd, 3rd Chev.)
provisional company of 1st Light
provisional company of 2nd Light
Vögler's Company of 2nd Reserve Battalion
volunteer Gebirgsschützen
2 x 3-pdr, 1 x hwtzr
Under Oberst von Oberndroff:
Jäger Battalion
Jäger Squadron

GD Beaumont's Reserve Division
Tyrol Front (not all took part in offensive):
elements of French 65th Ligne
miscellaneous French infantry detachments
2nd Provisional Dragoons
3rd Provisional Dragoons
Bavarian Provisional Battalion (Pillement)
  (depot troops: 1st, 2nd, 5th, 7th Inf. Rgts.)
Bavarian Landesdefensionsbataillon
Württ. *Franquemont* Infantry (five companies)
8 x 6-pdr, 4 x hwtzr
Vorarlberg Front (see Chapter 3):
French infantry company
4th Provisional Dragoons
Baden Brigade
[Württemberg corps - not under Beaumont]

Taxenbach (27) and Mittersill (28), the bulk of the division reached Zell in the Zillertal on 30 July after two prolonged skirmishes and a tough climb over the Gerlos Pass.[103] The next day, better roads and a lack of opposition allowed Deroy to bivouac at Volders in the Inn valley and the 1st of August saw his division in the Tyrolian capital.[104]

While Deroy swung off on his torturous route to the south and Montmarie entered the Inn valley from the north, Lefebvre led the rest of his command up the middle. Departing Salzburg on 27 July with the 1st Division (commanded by Raglovich in the Crown Prince's absence) and GD Rouyer's little division of Germans, the Marshal moved directly on Innsbruck.[105] There was almost no opposition. The garrison at the Strub Pass capitulated at Lefebvre's approach and most of the march was conducted through desolate valleys and strangely silent towns 'like a funeral procession': the inhabitants had fled fearing Bavarian reprisals.[106] Under these somewhat eerie conditions, the column continued its advance, occasionally sighting groups of insurgents in the distance, but seldom exchanging shots with them. Lefebvre camped at Söll on the night of the 28th, linked with Montmarie on the 29th and entered Innsbruck the following evening.

The last element of Lefebvre's expanded command in the northern Tyrol was Beaumont's Division de Réserve with Pillement's Bavarian battalion. On 17 July, as part of their general offensive into southern Bavaria, the Tyrolians had attacked Kempten with a force of approximately 3,600 partisans, 300 Austrian regulars and two cannon. Approaching from the south and south-west, the attackers drove in the Bavarian outposts, but were thrown back when Pillement himself arrived with reinforcements.[107] Pillement seems to have developed his counter-attack with considerable speed and energy, while the Austro-Tyrolian withdrawal was slow and confused. Catching up with their foes, Pillement's infantrymen were in the process of outflanking them on the left and right when about 60 French dragoons executed a fine charge and captured both of the Austrian guns. With their flanks in danger and their artillery taken, the rebels lost heart and fled, leaving behind some 200 dead and numerous wounded. Pillement and his men had performed with skill and courage, erasing the taint their reputation had borne since the unhappy fight at Dornbirn in May.[108] Pillement could also praise the behaviour of a company of the Landes-Defensionsbataillon and a number of volunteer foresters who valiantly aided the regular soldiers in the battle.[109]

Unfortunately, the Bavarians placed a different sort of blot on their record when they entered the Tyrol in late July. Called south to participate in the Second Offensive with the greater part of Beaumont's Division, Pillement's men formed the rear guard as the division marched over the Scharnitz Pass on the 30th. When they arrived in Seefeld that evening, the Bavarians, some of whom had experienced the defeats and humiliations of April, put the little town to the torch out of vengeance. Beaumont complained to the Bavarian government and this sort of pointless arson was not repeated, but the march of Pillement's battalion through the Tyrol and the Vorarlberg would be sullied by the same lamentable plunder and bitterness that characterized the entire campaign.

AUGUST - THE SECOND OFFENSIVE REPULSED

Napoleon wanted to take advantage of the armistice to extinguish the Tyrolian uprising quickly and finally. The continued resistance of the mountaineers not only cost him troops that might be crucial should the Austrians resume the war, but also damaged the prestige of French arms and served as an inspiration to incipient opposition across the continent. He therefore issued stern orders, writing to Lefebvre on 30 July: 'You have the power in your hands, you must be dreadful and act in such a manner that some of the troops may be withdrawn from the region without fear of a renewed uprising. I await word that you have not fallen into a trap and that my armistice is not for nought.'[110] To comply with his master's desires, Lefebvre decided to move on Brixen with a strong force and link up with GD Jean Rusca's column approaching from Lienz and GB Luigi Peyri's Italian troops from Verona. In addition, he intended to send several smaller columns into the further reaches of the Tyrol to quell disturbances and preclude a recrudescence of rebellion. Throughout the region, the

Bavarian forces were to re-establish order and security, collect weapons and eliminate any remaining bands of partisans, using whatever means might be necessary to achieve these ends.

To establish the link to Peyri's and Rusca's forces and extend Bavarian control into the southern Tyrol, Lefebvre sent Rouyer's Division over the Brenner Pass toward Brixen on 1 August. Accompanied by the Bavarian 4th Chevauxlegers and van Douwe's battery, the division met disaster at Oberau on the 4th and 5th and was only saved from destruction by the energetic intervention of Oberstlieutenant Wittgenstein with 1st Light and a squadron of the 1st Dragoons.[111] Disbelieving reports of Tyrolian strength and determination, Lefebvre himself rode south to the Brenner on the 5th at the head of the 1st Division. He found the road to Rouyer cut and only after his advance guard had broken through surprisingly firm Tyrolian resistance was he able to march into Sterzing (6 August). Attempting to drive south on the 7th, Lefebvre finally experienced for himself the difficulties his soldiers had come to loathe: narrow valleys with swift, unfordable streams, a fierce and durable foe who rolled boulders and trees down the slopes upon Allied columns jammed on the roads, bullets that whistled in from all directions, every inhabitant's hand turned against the invader with passionate intensity. Although the Bavarians were learning the art of mountain warfare, progress was slow, and the nagging fear of encirclement and surrender began to tug at Lefebvre's mind.[112] When the lead Schützen stormed into Mauls, he halted the advance and pulled back to Sterzing to await the salutary influence of the other Allied columns.

While Rouyer's and Raglovich's Divisions were grappling with the insurgents south of the Brenner, Beaumont's troops with Pillement's Battalion marched from Zirl over the Arlberg Pass into the Vorarlberg, arriving at Bludenz on 5 August. To maintain contact with this force, Lefebvre directed Deroy to send a detachment into the upper Inn valley toward Landeck. The Marshal hoped, however, that Deroy's men would soon be in a position to push up the Etsch valley, gain access to Meran and outflank the Tyrolian defences south of Innsbruck. Deroy sent his first troops out of Innsbruck on the 3rd and garrisoned the upper Inn valley from Landeck (reached on the 5th) back to Zirl before proceeding with the more dangerous expedition toward Meran.[113] By the 8th, the valley seemed sufficiently secure to risk further advance and Oberst Ludwig von Burcheidt with 10th Infantry, two squadrons of his 2nd Dragoons and two guns headed upstream from Landeck. Near the town of Prutz, however, his column encountered determined resistance from hastily gathered rebels and was forced to halt.[114] Recognizing their parlous situation, the Bavarians tried to return to Landeck during the night, but the insurgents, alerted by the sound of the horses and vehicles, unleashed a frightening storm of boulders, logs and bullets; I/10 managed to escape, but II/10, the cannon and most of the dragoons were halted and surrounded. The entire force, some 800 Bavarians with two guns, surrendered the next morning. Under constant harassment from ever-growing clouds of rebels, I/10 conducted an exhausting 70-kilometre retreat down the Inn, gathered up the 5th Infantry and reached Zirl at 9 p.m. on the 9th. The 9th Infantry also made a foray on 9 August, but its attempt to reach the Oetz valley was repulsed at Haiming and all its skill and courage was required to bring the regiment back to Zirl by about 10 p.m. The day had been disastrous. In addition to the physical cost (more than 1,000 men and two guns), the catastrophe at Prutz and the harried retreat down the Inn demoralized the Bavarians and gave renewed impetus to the Tyrolian insurgency, already buoyed by the successes against Rouyer. Deroy retired on Innsbruck the next day, leaving I/5 and a company of the 5th Light north of the river.[115]

Lefebvre also sought safety in retreat. Although joined by Arco's corps late on the 7th, the Allied force could not remain at Sterzing. Suffering from a shortage of supplies and continual, enervating skirmishes, Lefebvre hoped to gain some relief by calling for a temporary ceasefire on the 9th. When his emissaries rode forward under a white flag to parley, however, the Tyrolians dragged them from their horses, robbed them and held them captive, meanwhile launching a sudden attack on the Bavarian picket line; GM Raglovich would have been taken except for the courage and strength of one of his escorts. Raglovich restored the situation with an improvised counter-attack and the Bavarian captives were returned the next day when Lefebvre threatened to hang his collection of Tyrolian prisoners. But the French Marshal had had enough: late on the 10th, under steady pressure from the insurgents, the corps withdrew through Arco's rearguard to Innsbruck.[116] Arco's last men returned to the city at about 5 p.m. and the countryside was left to swarms of excited rebels. The evening of 11 August thus found the Bavarian 1st and 3rd Division and Arco's corps in Innsbruck and Rouyer's battered Rheinbund Division in Hall. The stage was set for the next Bergisel Battle.

THE THIRD BERGISEL BATTLE (13 AUGUST)

In Innsbruck morale was low. Deroy, observing the entrance of the 1st Division into the city, commented, 'The First Division looked dreadful today and we are not much better off.'[117] Lefebvre's personal outlook was equally bleak; the solid military reputation that had led the Emperor to select him for this command was rapidly slipping through his fingers. His troops were shaken, their leaders discouraged, provisions were short and the line of communications increasingly threatened by the revived insurgency. Moreover, these negative factors crowded into Lefebvre's considerations against the background of Kinkel's calamity and Deroy's prudent withdrawal. The result was a grim, pessimistic assessment of the situation. When Hofer struck, therefore, the commander of VII Corps was already half convinced that retreat was inevitable.

On 13 August, with some 17,000 men, Hofer launched three columns against the Bavarian positions around Innsbruck: one toward Volders, one west of Bergisel and one up the main road from the Brenner Pass. A subsidiary force threatened the Bavarians north of the Inn. The battle was fierce, but the events of the previous struggles repeated themselves: the Tyrolians made initial gains against the surprised defenders but were unable to push their attacks into the open ground between the hills and the city; likewise, the Bavarian counter-attacks could not dislodge the mountaineers from their strong positions in the hills. The battle raged with great bitterness until 8 p.m., when exhaustion of men and ammunition brought a halt to the bloodshed. The leaders on both sides faced significant decisions that night. Hofer's peasant partisans were short of everything, including the will to continue the struggle on the 14th, and only the innkeeper's personal reputation and the energy of his subordinate leaders kept the rebels at their posts. The Bavarian situation, on the other hand, though certainly not ideal, was by no means hopeless. The battle on the 13th had been tough but only the 3rd Division had been engaged and its casualties were not unbearable (about 350).[118] Lefebvre, however, could not know of the Tyrolians' plight. He too was running out of ammunition and food, moreover, a supply train had been captured by the Tyrolians in the Achen valley and his trusted adviser Arco had been killed as he rode to reconnoitre an insurgent position between Hall and Rattenberg.[119] Concerned about the discontent in his ranks and convinced his position was ultimately untenable, the Marshal decided on retreat.

Fortunately for the Bavarians, the 14th passed peacefully and the 1st Division, herding a collection of hostages, was able to march out of the Tyrolian capital that evening. Gathering up Rouyer's troops at Hall, Raglovich continued on to Schwaz, where he was joined by 3rd Division the following day. The withdrawal was almost undisturbed, although Deroy's rearguard engaged in steady skirmishing as it proceeded downstream on the morning of the 15th. As Hofer and the Tyrolians joyously entered into Innsbruck for the third time, Lefebvre was uniting his forces at Schwaz. With all his units (1st and 3rd Bavarian Divisions, Rouyer's Division and Montmarie with Arco's and Oberndorff's corps) collected around this town, he granted his weary and dispirited men a day of rest.[120] He also decided to reorganize his corps, hoping by these actions to demonstrate to the insurgents (and Napoleon) that he was not being forced from the Tyrol by enemy pressure but rather by logistical exigencies.[121] The 16th of August thus saw the dissolution of Arco's brave corps as its reserve units, provisional companies and depot detachments were reduced or disbanded to provide replacements to their parent regiments or battalions. The reorganization provided the 1st Division with a significant number of experienced troops, while the 3rd was able to fill some of the gaps in the 5th Light's ranks. Those units whose parent organizations were assigned to Wrede's Division (6th Light, 2nd and 3rd Chevauxlegers) were ordered to proceed to Linz and Passau to join the 2nd Division. The lonely reserve companies of the 2nd and 4th Light Battalions were attached to the 1st Division until their units could be rebuilt.[122] Finally, a temporary volunteer battalion was created within the 1st Division to guard the flanks and rear of the column when the retreat resumed. To prepare for the next stage of the withdrawal, 1st Light was sent to Rattenberg on the morning of the 16th and Deroy moved his division to Wörgl the same night. The rest of Lefebvre's troops, protected from the rebels' incessant harassments by the volunteer battalion, joined Deroy on the 17th.[123]

From Wörgl, the Bavarians continued their retreat by two routes. Deroy and Oberndorff headed down the Inn to the familiar landscape around Kufstein on the night of 17/18 August, while Lefebvre with Raglovich's and Rouyer's Divisions turned east and crossed the Strub Pass to arrive in Salzburg on the

20th.[124] Once again, as in April, the Tyrolians, with no assistance from the regular Austrian military, had evicted the Bavarian invaders from their mountain home. Despite the Bavarians' courage and ability, the Second Offensive had been a failure.

THE PRICE OF FAILURE: FRANCO-BAVARIAN RECRIMINATIONS

The dramatic disasters of early August seriously exacerbated the tensions between the French Marshal and his Bavarian subordinates. Napoleon, whose principal interest was the expedient pacification of the Tyrol, was furious that this second attempt to subdue the stubborn mountaineers had been so miserably defeated. That the undertaking had been commanded by one of his marshals only served to heighten his anger. Lefebvre sought to defend himself by blaming the Bavarians. In a 16 August report to Max Joseph, he implied that Bavarian demoralization had been the principal cause of the retreat and in his letters to Napoleon he not only complained about poor morale but practically branded his officers and men as traitors: 'When I sit at table and close my eyes, the remarks that reach my ears lead me to think I am in the Austrian camp and not the French.' The Bavarian king was naturally incensed at the accusations made against his troops. Demanding reports from his commanders, he wrote to his friend Berthier in Vienna:

It is not without great astonishment that I hear the Duke of Danzig throws the entire blame for the unfortunate undertaking in the Tyrol upon my troops.....It is a great misfortune, my good friend, that the poor planning of its commander is costing my army the good reputation it earned for itself at Thann, at Abensberg under the eyes of the Emperor, at Wagram and at Znaim. The number of dead and wounded also speaks for my army, not even counting a good twenty officers wounded and killed. Be the advocate of my army to the Emperor.[125]

Both sides also condemned each other for the brutalities of the second occupation: while Lefebvre denounced the soldiers for committing excesses that only increased the Tyrolians' will to resist, Wrede informed his king that: 'If this Marshal had never stepped into the Tyrol, the soldiers of the 2nd and 3rd Divisions would never have ceased to be humans and the Tyrolians might have listened to the voice of reason after the engagement at Wörgl.'[126] The Emperor, unable to find the truth through these contradictory representations, attempted to calm his Bavarian allies through his correspondence with the king and Wrede but took no immediate action against Lefebvre. As a result, the atmosphere in VII Corps continued to deteriorate, aggravated by the Marshal's treatment of his men. Behaving erratically under the pressure of frustration and humiliation, Lefebvre lauded the Bavarians to their monarch one moment and publicly berated entire battalions the next. The effect was toxic. Command was hampered by ill will and morale plummeted as the Bavarians developed a hardened hatred for their commander and a lasting aversion to all things French. The army 'grumbled from drummer to general'.[127]

ON THE DEFENSIVE AGAIN

As friction around the harried Duke of Danzig increased, his soldiers went about the quotidian business of protecting their country's borders. As in June, the defence of the region from the Lech to Salzburg was entrusted to the 3rd Division while the 1st Division held the area around the latter city. GM Siebein with three battalions, a squadron and a battery was to combine with Oberndorff's corps (three battalions, a squadron, five guns) to form a cordon

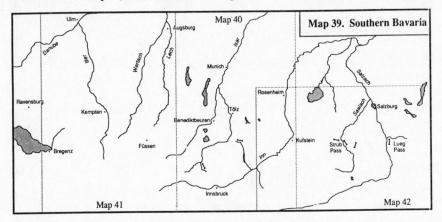

Map 39. Southern Bavaria

south of the Bavarian capital.[128] Siebein and Oberndorff departed Kufstein on the 19th and assumed their positions two days later, Oberndorff's Jägers covering the front from around Murnau to Habach and Siebein's troops continuing the line from Benediktbeuren to Miesbach.[129] Apparently, Oberndorff's march from Kufstein presented a rather discouraging picture to the military eye. GM Siebein recorded that 'I found the battalion led by Major von Freudenberg as stragglers, all the inns were full of members of the battalion and in all the villages, vehicles had to be requisitioned to bring up the lazy and the tired. A large number lay here and there next to the road and in the woods. Waible's battalion was more orderly.'[130] Deroy, after ensuring Kufstein was adequately supplied, retired to Rosenheim on the 23rd and likewise distributed his five battalions and three squadrons from that town to Traunstein where he was tied to the 1st Division's patrols.[131] The Bavarians retained these positions until the end of the month, undisturbed by the insurgents except for a brief skirmish fought by 1st Light at the Strub Pass on the 31st.[132] Of the Tyrol, only this area around Strub and the fortress of Kufstein remained in Bavarian hands.

Pillement's provisional battalion had crossed over the Arlberg Pass into the Vorarlberg with the rest of Beaumont's Division by 7 August. During the ensuing weeks, the battalion was scattered throughout the Vorarlberg, the 1st and 4th Companies going to Lindau and the 2nd providing part of the garrison of Bludenz; the 3rd Company was sent to Weissbach near Füssen to rejoin Picard's command. The Tyrolians, inspired by their recent successes, attempted to reignite the fires of insurrection in the Vorarlberg in late August, pushing over the pass on the 21st to threaten Bludenz. The region was too heavily occupied by the Allies, however, and the message of renewed rebellion attracted little

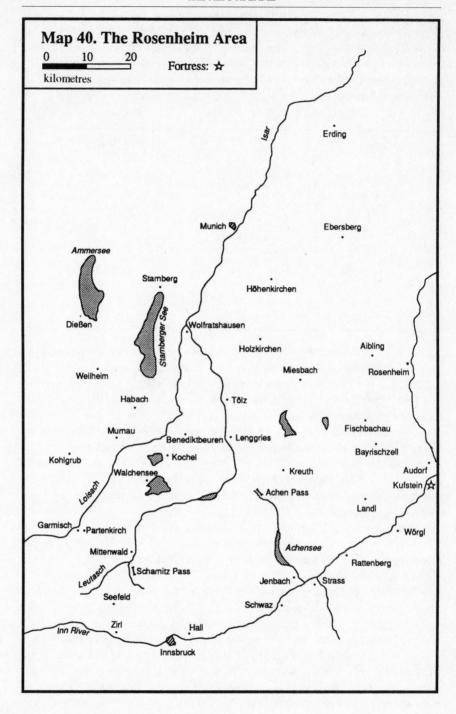

Map 40. The Rosenheim Area

0   10   20

kilometres

Fortress: ☆

Isar

Erding

Munich

Ebersberg

Ammersee

Stamberg

Höhenkirchen

Dießen

Starnberger See

Wolfratshausen

Weilheim

Holzkirchen

Aibling

Habach

Tölz

Miesbach

Rosenheim

Murnau

Benediktbeuren

Lenggries

Fischbachau

Kohlgrub

Kochel

Bayrischzell

Walchensee

Kreuth

Audorf

Loisach

Achen Pass

Kufstein ☆

Landl

Garmisch

Partenkirch

Achensee

Wörgl

Mittenwald

Rattenberg

Leutasch

Scharnitz Pass

Jenbach

Strass

Seefeld

Schwaz

Zirl

Hall

Inn River

Innsbruck

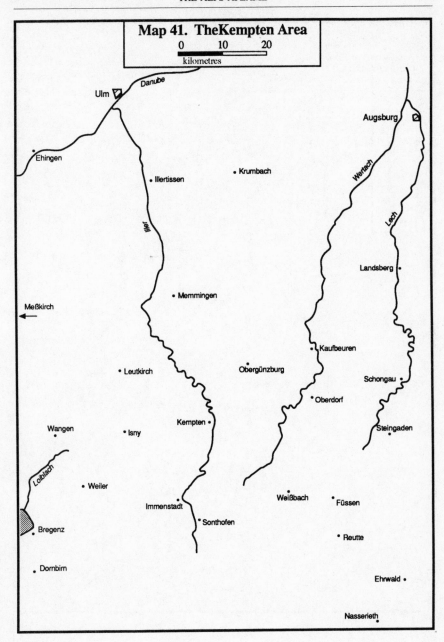

Map 41. TheKempten Area

0 10 20

kilometres

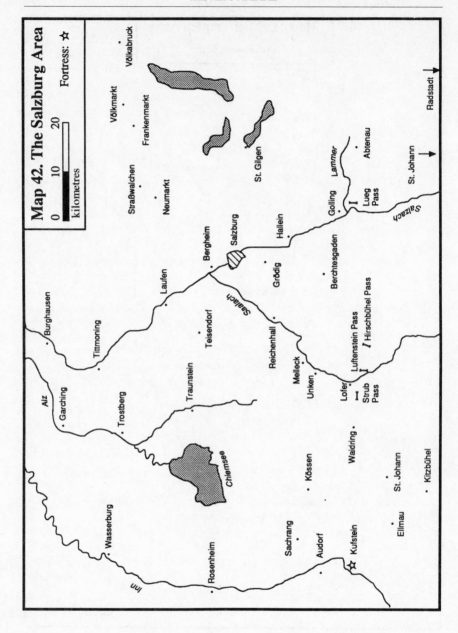

Map 42. The Salzburg Area

Fortress: ☆

0   10   20
kilometres

response. Although the Tyrolians launched a few abortive sorties against the
Allies, they could neither alter the basic military situation nor rouse their
Vorarlberg brothers to another effort. Pillement's 2nd Company was primarily
responsible for repelling a weak thrust at Bludenz on the 30th, and the 3rd
Company helped defeat a similar attack on Füssen the same day.[133]

SEPTEMBER - TYROL TRIUMPHANT

The Bavarian defences from the Vorarlberg to the Inn remained untroubled
through September and the month passed quietly for Deroy's and Pillement's
men. The only combat experienced by either command in those cool autumnal
weeks was a brief skirmish at Weissbach on the 19th, where Pillement's 3rd
Company chased off some Tyrolians with the loss of one man. If the enemy was
dormant, the Bavarians were in constant motion, using the time to complete the
organizational modifications begun with the creation of the reserve battalions in
April and June. On the same day as the 3rd Company's little scuffle, the 7th
Reserve Battalion arrived in Lindau from Landsberg to relieve Pillement's
troops in that city and Bludenz (4th Company). Toward the end of the month,
two companies from the 11th Infantry's depot in Munich also joined the troops
already on border duty, incorporating the depot troops of the regiment that had
served with Pillement since May. With the arrival of these reinforcements,
Pillement's battalion was dissolved and most of its constituent troops returned to
their parent units.[134] As September closed, the Bavarian units under French GD
Joseph Lagrange thus included the 7th Reserve Battalion in Lindau (three companies) and Bludenz (one company), two companies of the 11th Infantry (one
each in Bludenz and Weissbach) and three companies of the Landes-
Defensionsbataillon in and around Füssen.[135] The latter unit, however, had performed poorly, the Kordonisten vanishing *en masse* when the insurgents threatened to attack their pickets; it was therefore transferred to less dangerous duty in
Wolfratshausen at the end of the month.

The men of Siebein's and Oberndorff's commands also occupied themselves
with organizational matters in September. Reinforced by the 1st Reserve and
Vögler's company of the 2nd Reserve on the first of the month, Oberndorff was
able to extend his positions to the west as far as Steingaden and shift his forces
to more satisfactory locations.[136] The Bavarians also found considerable reas-
surance in the arrival of General Beaumont with 5,500 French and Bavarian
troops on the 1st. Beaumont's force, headquartered in Munich, established itself
in a semicircle south of the capital with a dragoon regiment each at Ebersberg
and Diessen and infantry detachments at Weilheim and Holzkirchen. Von
Xylander's company of the Landes-Defensionsbataillon was in Wolfratshausen
and the corps reserve, including one Bavarian light company, was retained in
Munich.[137] The support afforded by these units, raw as they were, permitted the
departure of the 7th Reserve from Wolfratshausen for Landsberg on the 3rd,
from which fortress it marched off to the Vorarlberg on the 12th. Deroy's positions remained essentially unchanged from August, until the 14th Infantry was
called away to help Lefebvre around Salzburg on the 27th. The 9th Regiment
was brought east to take the 14th's place and Beaumont provided 800 infantry

and 200 cavalry under Lieutenant-Colonel Boinsot to fill the hole in Siebein's line. Although the French cavalry detachment and the two provisional dragoon regiments were pulled away only three days later, Siebein received a squadron of the 2nd Dragoons to assume at least some of their tasks; the veteran Bavarian troopers represented a welcome relief from the untrained and ill-disciplined French dragoons. Deroy also called out some of the local Gebirgsschützen to assist in the wearing patrol and outpost duties. The month concluded with the disbanding of the Landes-Defensionsbataillon, which was broken up to be absorbed into the Mobile Legions.[138]

While their comrades were engrossed in the details of daily duty and organizational changes, the men of the 1st Division fought a series of small but desperate battles south and west of Salzburg. Unfortunately, the positions Lefebvre had selected to shield the city were dangerously exposed, particularly those held by the *Leib-Regiment* around Lofer and the Strub Pass. Isolated, undermanned and easily surrounded, they offered an active enemy the opportunity to fall upon the Bavarian outposts and destroy them one by one. Sporadic Tyrolian raids highlighted the regiment's peril and Crown Prince Ludwig, supported by some of the French staff officers, made several attempts to persuade Lefebvre to reinforce or withdraw the corps' outposts. The Marshal, however, remained adamant, refusing to modify his orders. On 25 September disaster struck.[139] In the early morning hours, overwhelming numbers (7—8,000) of rebels stormed against the Bavarian outposts with sudden ferocity. The men of the 1st Infantry fought courageously and held for a time, but were forced to withdraw toward Melleck as the Tyrolian pressure increased. Approaching the hamlet, they found their retreat route cut off by the enemy and the River Saalach. Many saved themselves by leaping into the cold waters, but organized resistance ceased and more than 300 men were captured by the jubilant insurgents; several dozen more, including many wounded, found they could not maintain their strength against the pull of the algid stream and floated into Reichenhall as corpses during the next several days. Advancing over the passes into Bavaria, the Tyrolians forced the remnant of the *Leib-Regiment* back into Reichenhall and probed south to threaten Berchtesgaden.[140]

The same day also witnessed an attack on Stengel's defences in and around Lueg Pass. The 8th Infantry fought valiantly and well but could not hold the pass against the large force of Tyrolians and Salzburgers commanded by the Capuchin monk Peter Haspinger. Retreating in an orderly fashion to the valley around Golling, I/8 was reinforced by II/4 and easily defeated all efforts of the rebels to press their attack into the low ground beyond the pass. Bavarian losses totalled only 37 and the men had performed well, but Stengel believed his position to be too exposed and, leaving vedettes towards Golling, he pulled back to Hallein in the late afternoon. This threat in the Salzach valley and the near encirclement of Reichenhall moved Lefebvre to abandon Berchtesgaden on the 26th and pull an infantry regiment (the 14th) from Deroy's unengaged command the next day. On the 28th, however, contrary to all orders, Stengel gave up his position at Hallein and retired some 5—7 kilometres back towards Salzburg. Haspinger's partisans were delighted to occupy the town the next day. Lefebvre was furious at Stengel's unnecessary withdrawal and demanded that the general explain his conduct to a military tribunal. In view of the insurgent threat across his front, however, the Marshal could take no immediate action to regain Hallein.[141] The end of the month thus found the 1st Division and associated troops concentrated at Reichenhall (GM von Rechberg), just south of Salzburg (GM von Stengel) and in the city itself (Rouyer and others).[142] Another humiliating defeat had been inflicted upon the Bavarian Corps by the Tyrolian insurgents, contributing further bitterness to relations between the Corps and its commander.

OCTOBER - THE THIRD OFFENSIVE

Fearing for the safety of Salzburg, Lefebvre's first goal in October was the reconquest of Hallein. His plan called for two columns to assault the town on the morning of 3 October: on the west bank of the Salzach, GM Stengel would feint with II/4 while GB Montmarie conducted the main attack on the east bank with 14th Infantry and supporting troops.[143] In the pre-dawn hours, Montmarie's column advanced under cover of a thick fog. Their approach unnoticed, they fell upon the Tyrolians with sudden violence, rapidly broke their resistance and chased them back to Hallein. The barred gates of the town were smashed in with axes and the Tyrolians fled after a brief street fight. The Bavarians pursued the insurgents almost to Golling before halting for the night, having suffered only some 27 casualties as opposed to Tyrolian losses of about 90. Two days later, four companies marched over the mountains from Reichenhall to retake Berchtesgaden.

THE RELIEF OF LEFEBVRE

The Bavarians had once again evicted their opponents from Altbayern and were slowly returning to the offensive, but an internal disaster was brewing as the tension between Lefebvre and his subordinates had reached crisis proportions. Angered by the arrogance of the French and their intrusions into the internal affairs of the Bavarian Army, some Bavarians became almost openly insubordinate. Not the least of these was the Crown Prince himself, whose hatred for Napoleon had only increased over the course of the campaign. Although the tribunal that reviewed Stengel's behaviour at Hallein exonerated the general, his conduct was certainly suspicious and there is some indication that Ludwig at least tacitly approved of his disobedience.[144] Lefebvre, for his part, insulted the Bavarians from the Crown Prince to the lowest private, inspiring disgust and indignant fury among his subordinates. Although the Marshal's tendentious reports portrayed recent events to the Emperor in a very biased fashion, word of the increasing friction in VII Corps could not fail to reach Napoleon's ears. Clearly recognizing the danger of the situation but frustrated by his inability distinctly to apportion guilt, Napoleon sought to display firmness and understanding simultaneously, emphasizing the paramount military importance of discipline and obedience. His initial reaction to the newest reports of Bavarian recalcitrance in the face of Lefebvre's orders was violent and probably intended to shock his allies: 'What prevents me from having a Crown Prince shot?' At the same time, however, he wrote to Wrede in an attempt to placate the Bavarians and restore vigour and obedience in VII Corps. Expressing his respect for Ludwig ('I know you love the Crown Prince and I love him as you do') and candidly describing his irritation, he asked for Wrede's assistance: 'speak to your comrades and see to it that they do not dishonour themselves'.[145] As these words were being carried to Wrede, however, another message was making its way to Lefebvre, and on 11 October the obstreperous Marshal departed for Vienna.

Lefebvre was replaced by his former Chief of Staff, GD Jean-Baptiste Drouet, Comte d'Erlon. Although he assumed his first corps command under the most trying circumstances, Drouet was equal to the challenge. Forty-four years old, he was honest and intrepid, a pure soldier whose combat experience included the wars of the revolution and the campaigns of 1805, 1806 and 1807. In the latter year, he served as chief of staff to Lefebvre at Danzig and Lannes at Friedland. He had ably seconded the Duke of Danzig throughout the present campaign, but where his commander had displayed indecision and a limited capacity to learn from experience, Drouet had carefully observed the Corps' operations in the mountains and was prepared to apply the lessons he drew from the two failed offensives. In addition to the tactical problems of mountain warfare, he also had to overcome the tensions emanating from strained Franco-Bavarian relations. The atmosphere in the command was too sour to permit an immediate improvement with Drouet's appointment, but with a co-operative attitude and demonstrated military competence, he was at least able to arrest its further deterioration. He also benefited from the support of Max Joseph. In a letter to his son, the king wrote: 'You will find a good difference between Drouet and le Fevre. The first has intelligence and the Duke is an old ass.' [146]

ONCE MORE TO INNSBRUCK

It was fortunate that the new commander was already familiar with his corps: the same day the Treaty of Schönbrunn was signed officially ending the war with Austria (14 October), the Emperor dispatched orders to VII Corps directing an immediate resumption of operations against 'ces miserables Tyroliens'.[147] These new instructions arrived in Salzburg on the 16th and Drouet set his Corps in motion that very night. As in July, the Bavarians were to be the northern component of a concentric attack on the Tyrol from Carinthia, Italy and Salzburg/Bavaria; the operation would be under the overall direction of Viceroy Eugène. The three Bavarian divisions would attack on a relatively narrow front along three axes: Reichenhall to Lofer (1st Division), Traunstein to Kössen (2nd Division, brought south from the Danube valley) and Rosenheim to Kufstein (3rd Division). Oberst Zoller of the 4th Infantry would be left behind at Hallein to observe Lueg Pass.[148]

One of the ways in which Drouet gained the respect and confidence of the Bavarians was by involving them in the planning process, and the concept for the 1st Division's attack on the 16th and 17th was the result of a combined effort. Principally the work of GM Rechberg in close co-operation with local Bavarian officials, the plan called for a bold and risky night attack to secure the passes from Reichenhall to Lofer. With the invaluable assistance of local guides, the Bavarian troops set forth on the night of the 16th.[149] The weather was miserable, cold rain mixed with snow, and the mountain paths were difficult and confusing in the dark; without the aid of their guides, the attack columns would never have reached their appointed objectives. The inclement weather served to mask the Bavarian movement, however, and kept the complacent Tyrolian pickets indoors near a warm fire. At dawn on the 17th, therefore, Rechberg's sudden attack surprised and overwhelmed the insurgents at Melleck and Unken; offering only brief and disorganized resistance, they soon fled in wild confusion, leaving behind 300 dead and 400 prisoners, including the son of the rebel commander. Rechberg's column suffered a total of nine wounded. By nightfall, the Bavarians were in Lofer and the Crown Prince could write to his father that he had experienced one of the happiest days of his military career.[150] The defeat of 25 September was efficiently and effectively avenged.

Table 7-5: Bavarian Forces in the Third Offensive (17 October)

VII Corps staff cavalry from V/1st Dragoons

1st Division - GL Crown Prince Ludwig
staff company from 2nd Inf. depot
staff cavalry from V/1st Chevauxlegers
1st Leib Infantry
2nd Infantry *Kronprinz*
4th Infantry
8th Infantry *Herzog Pius*
1st Light *Habermann*
3rd Light (two companies under Major Theobald)
1st Dragoons (three squadrons)
1st Chevauxlegers *Kronprinz*
French sapper company
Regnier, Hoffstetten, Wagner, van Douwe

2nd Division - GL von Wrede
staff company from 3rd Inf. depot
staff cavalry from V/2nd Chevauxlegers
6th Infantry *Herzog Wilhelm*
7th Infantry *Löwenstein*
13th Infantry
14th Infantry
6th Light *La Roche*
Reserve Company of 2nd Light
2nd Chevauxlegers *König*
two squadrons of 4th Chevauxlegers
Caspers, Berchem, Ulmer
howitzers of Dietrich and Leiningen

3rd Division - GL von Deroy
staff company from 5th Inf. depot
staff cavalry from V/4th Chevauxlegers
5th Infantry *Preysing*
9th Infantry *Ysenburg*
10th Infantry *Junker* (reduced)
5th Light *Butler*
2nd Dragoons *Thurn und Taxis*
4th Chevauxlegers *Bubenhofen* (two sqdns)
Gotthardt, Pamler, Roys

Oberst von Oberndorff's Command
1st Reserve Battalion
2nd Reserve Battalion
1st and 2nd Jäger Battalions
Jäger Squadron
2 x 6-pdr, 2 x 3-pdr, 1 x hwtzr

Other Units
Salzburg: 8th Reserve Battalion
Kufstein: 5th Reserve Battalion
In Bavaria (not under Drouet):
  Baden Brigade
  Württ. *Franquemont* Inf. (five companies)
  misc. French units

GM Minucci's Brigade (at Linz)
3rd Infantry *Prinz Karl*
4th Light *Donnersberg*
3rd Chevauxlegers *Leiningen*
Dorn, Dietrich (12-pdrs), Leiningen (12-pdrs)

In the Vorarlberg
11th Infantry (two companies)
7th Reserve Battalion
[Württ. corps north of Lake Constance]

To protect his right flank as he pushed west, Ludwig sent two columns to seize Weissbach on the 18th: the first (II/8) crossing over the Hirschbühel from Berchtesgaden and the second (1st Infantry, I/8) advancing from Lofer. The next day, some of the Tyrolian districts offered to submit to Bavarian rule and GM Rechberg took the 1st Infantry, 2nd Infantry and 1st Dragoons south to Saalfelden and Zell am See to accept the capitulation. The 8th Infantry returned to their division. His left secure, the Crown Prince continued on toward the Inn

valley, reaching St. Johann on the 20th to link with Wrede's Division. The 2nd
Division, departing Traunstein late on 16 October, had reached Kössen on the
17th, St. Johann on the 18th and Kundl two days later after an extraordinarily
difficult march in dreadful weather over wretched paths that had not seen an
army 'in human memory'.[151] Other than the painfully poor byways it traversed,
the division encountered no resistance. The progress of Deroy's troops was
equally unhindered. Arriving at Kufstein on the 17th, the 3rd Division relieved
the final, weak blockade of the fortress and proceeded up the valley to Wörgl the
next day.[152] With these advances, particularly GM Rechberg's, the insurgent
positions around Pass Lueg were outflanked and Oberst Zoller at Hallein
received orders to push through the pass and establish liaison with Rechberg.
Although he had skirmished with the insurgents over the previous several days,
Zoller crossed the pass unopposed and reached St. Johann on the 21 October.
Linking with a detachment from 2nd Infantry (six companies and a howitzer) the
following day, Zoller continued his march toward the Inn while Rechberg
moved up the Salzach valley toward the Gerlos Pass.[153]

    In the meantime, the bulk of VII Corps advanced up the Inn. By the 24th, the
Crown Prince was in Hall and Wrede had brushed aside Tyrolian skirmishers to
occupy the low ground between that town and Innsbruck; Deroy was posted
with a brigade each at Schwaz and Rattenberg to secure the Corps' line of communications and pacify the countryside. While the 3rd Division was occupied
with innumerable patrols to remote valleys and villages, the 1st and 2nd
Divisions were engaged in incessant skirmishes with the insurgents. GM
Beckers conducted a reconnaissance in force into Innsbruck on the 25th, bringing back several Tyrolian officials, stacks of incriminating documents and nearly 100 liberated Bavarian prisoners when he returned north of the river in the
evening. Oberst Dallwig of the 13th Infantry was not as fortunate as the general.
Heavily engaged with the insurgents near Hall on the 27th, he proposed a truce
to distribute a proclamation from Viceroy Eugène to the Tyrolian people. As his
soldiers were mingling with their erstwhile foes, however, they were suddenly
betrayed and attacked by the rebels. The duplicitous Tyrolians captured more
than 300 Bavarians with their ruse; Dallwig himself was only freed by the decisive action and sharp bayonets of several fearless grenadiers.[154]

    Bitter skirmishes were a daily occurrence until the end of the month. The
Bavarians held their positions and hoped that Hofer and the other Tyrolian commanders would agree to submit to Max and Napoleon peacefully. The Tyrolian
leadership was badly divided, however, and Hofer vacillated between capitulation and fanatical resistance as contending parties sought to sway him.
Meanwhile, partisans gathered at Bergisel and the scattered Bavarian detachments concentrated in the Inn valley. Rechberg came into Hall on the 27th from
the Gerlos Pass, and Zoller rejoined the 1st Division the next day, having
marched via St. Johann (26th) and Wörgl (27th). Their arrival was timely. The
stubborn resistance of the rebel bands had convinced Drouet that the Tyrolians
would not give in without further combat, and he ordered his commanders to
prepare for a renewed advance.

    Oberndorff's corps also took part in the October invasion. On the 23rd, he received orders to advance through the Scharnitz Pass and establish liaison with Drouet near Innsbruck. Arriving in Mittenwald late on the night of 24 October, he attacked the next morning and seized the pass despite determined resistance.[155] An attempt to push a detachment forward to Zirl was repulsed, however, and Oberndorff's little force had to content itself with holding the pass and Mittenwald until VII Corps cleared the enemy from the area around Zirl.

Oberndorff's command included the only members of the Nationalgarde II. Klasse called to arms for the 1809 campaign. On 7 October, the formation of the 2nd Battalion of the 10th Mobile Legion (Isarkreis) was ordered. The creation of the battalion was to occur in Munich on the 12th, after which the unit would take up defensive duties near Miesbach, replacing the departed 10th Infantry. Two companies actually left Munich on the 25th for Miesbach under Hauptmann Jehle, but recruiting had encountered severe problems and these companies were sadly understrength (total 184 men). The other two companies were even worse, totalling only eighteen men, including five officers. The intended recruits for the battalion, former members of the Landes-Defensionsbataillon and new conscripts, proved surprisingly reluctant to serve in the new unit and on 2 November, depot troops from Munich (40 men from the depot of 2nd Light) had to be sent to some districts to enforce the necessary conscription. Although the numbers increased, reaching about 350 in November, dissatisfaction, indiscipline and insubordination also grew. With inadequate provisions, clothing and equipment, the battalion had become more trouble than it was worth; it was disbanded on 19 November when the threat from the Tyrol was finally eliminated by the success of the Third Offensive.[156]

NOVEMBER/DECEMBER - THE REBELLION CRUSHED

At 3 a.m. on 1 November, VII Corps advanced to the final Bergisel battle. The Bavarians had occupied the Tyrolian capital with a detachment since 28 October but Drouet now brought the full power of the 1st and 2nd Divisions south of the Inn to engage the insurgents in the hills. Hofer, with about 8,000 men, had vague plans to attack Innsbruck on the 1st, but the Tyrolian efforts were slow, lacking cohesion, purpose and energy. The Bavarians, on the other hand, moved with alacrity and cool professionalism. The 1st Division led the way across the river, deploying to the south-east to protect the Bavarian left. Covered by a thick morning fog, the 2nd Division followed, crossed the bridge and continued straight on through the city to deploy in the cold meadows between the city and the hills. As at Wagram, Wrede placed his 24 guns in the first line with the infantry in attack columns to their rear. As the sun rose and the fog lifted at about 9 a.m., the combined batteries opened fire with devastating effect, levelling the insurgents' crude breastworks and instantly silencing their few cannon. When his artillery had shaken the rebels, Wrede sent in his foot soldiers. Charged by I/6, II/7, I/13 and two companies of 6th Light, the Tyrolians could not hold. Their left broke almost immediately, and the Bavarian infantry pushed up on to the heights, outflanking the rebel centre. Here there was no desperate fight as there had been on 13 August, but only a brief exchange of lead before Hofer's men scattered to the four winds in panicked flight. By noon, the insurgent left and centre had evaporated. Fighting on the Tyrolian right lasted for another hour or two but the 1st Infantry, II/2 and the 1st Dragoons had also gained the heights by mid-afternoon. A clumsy and belated rebel attack north of the Inn was easily repelled by the 1st Light.[157] Reinforced by GM Rechberg with I/2, two squadrons of the 1st Chevauxlegers and a half-battery, the Bavarians took the offensive toward Zirl, drove off their attackers and fired across the river to speed the rout of the enemy south of the Inn.[158]

After the victory at Bergisel, the Bavarians south of Innsbruck held their positions for several days, observing the enemy for renewed activity while GM Rechberg established contact with Oberndorff's command at Seefeld (3 November). Rechberg pushed on into the Upper Inn valley with 1st Light, I/2, I/4 and two squadrons of 1st Chevauxlegers. By the 9th, he had garrisoned the major points in the valley as far as Imst. An attack against the latter town was repulsed on the 11th after a tough fight that cost the Bavarians 47 casualties. Raglovich and Wrede, meanwhile, had begun to advance up the Sill valley toward the Brenner Pass; Schönberg was occupied on the 6th and Beckers forced his way into Steinach on the 7th against heavy resistance.[159] The 7th also saw the arrival of GM Minucci in Innsbruck. Minucci had departed Linz on 30 October and marched via Salzburg for the Inn valley with the 3rd Infantry, the resurrected 4th Light, the 3rd Chevauxlegers and his artillery. Most of the guns were deposited in Salzburg and *Leiningen* took up liaison duties around St. Johann and Lofer, so Minucci only had his infantry, two guns and a squadron of 2nd Dragoons (relieved by the 3rd Chevauxlegers) when he reached the mouth of the Ziller on the 6th. Learning that rebellion had been re-ignited in the Ziller valley, he immediately marched on Zell and stormed the town with the 3rd Infantry. The enemy fled and Minucci was able to continue his interrupted journey to Innsbruck the next day. With these reinforcements and the general collapse of the insurrection, Wrede was able to send a battalion and a half-squadron over the Brenner to Brixen on the 11th to establish a link with General Baraguey d'Hilliers' French troops (who had arrived on the 8th). The same day, the 2nd and 3rd Divisions went into cantonments to protect their troops against the increasingly harsh weather.[160]

While the insurgency had lost most of its energy in the northern part of the Tyrol, the south-western portions of the province were still unwilling to lay down their arms. Uneasy about the weakness and scattered nature of his dispositions, Rechberg at Imst requested reinforcements, and Drouet responded by sending Raglovich with the entire 1st Division to quell the Upper Inn and its tributary valleys. Over the next several days, the 1st Division clamped a tight hold on the Upper Inn region, extending its grip to Landeck and Prutz and pushing detachments up the Oetz and Pitze valleys. Key towns in the Inn valley were strongly garrisoned to maintain the connection to Innsbruck and Oberndorff's corps, now under Raglovich's command, was posted from Reutte to Seefeld to secure the passes back into Bavaria itself. The operation was well conceived and carried out with careful thoroughness.[161] Tyrolian attempts to surprise the Bavarians and break their grasp on the valleys thus failed in the face of alert patrols and well-placed reserves (19, 20, 21 November). This continued insurgent activity seemed to emanate from the Paznauntal and Raglovich decided to launch a foray up the valley to strike at the heart of the resistance. He marched west out of Landeck on the 24th but, after initial success, his detachment was forced to retreat to escape encirclement, losing 36 prisoners in the process.[162] Considering this setback, the general expected a revived outbreak of insurgent activity, but the 24th proved to be the 1st Division's last combat action for 1809. The following day, rather to Raglovich's surprise, a Tyrolian delegation returned the Bavarian prisoners and announced the complete submission of the valley to King Max's authority. As the month closed, Raglovich sent the 1st Light up the Inn valley to Nauders, establishing unhindered contact with the French forces around Meran on 1 December.

While the pacification of the Tyrol proceeded peacefully in the areas occupied by the 1st and 2nd Divisions, the 3rd Division had to contend with the last sporadic outbursts of rebellion along the Lower Inn. Much of the region still defied the Bavarians, refusing to surrender weapons and menacing Deroy's smaller detachments. A patrol of the 14th Infantry was captured near Schwaz on 27 November and on the 30th a small outpost of 50 men (5th Infantry) was almost overwhelmed by 200 Tyrolians before reinforcements arrived to drive off the rebels. Like Raglovich, Deroy was able to identify the source of these continued attacks and sent Oberst Metzen (commander of the 5th Infantry) up the Wildschönau valley on 2 December with eight companies to quash resistance once and for all.[163] Metzen's force met no opposition, however, and the colonel disarmed the area with relative ease, returning to the Inn valley a week later. With this small sortie, disturbances in the 3rd Division's area of responsibility also came to an end and the Bavarian army settled into the demanding but peaceful task of occupying the Tyrol.

November also brought an end to fighting in the Vorarlberg. The Bavarian garrison of Bludenz (one company each of 7th Reserve and 11th Infantry), attempting to probe toward the Arlberg Pass, skirmished with Tyrolian insurgents in the Klostertal on 20 October and again on 14 November, but the inhabitants of the Vorarlberg did not revive their rebellion. As Raglovich's advance into the Upper Inn valley progressed, even the die-hard Tyrolian rebels in the Klostertal quietly gave up the struggle and vanished over the mountains to their homes. The other Allied troops gradually left the Vorarlberg during November and by the 20th, only the Bavarians remained to watch over the now peaceful land. Oberstleutnant Wreden brought a special 'corps' into the region in the latter part of the month to replace the departed allies, but the insurrection was over and his only function was to disarm the region completely and observe the quiet and orderly re-establishment of Bavarian rule.[164]

With the successful conclusion of the Third Offensive, the tragic Tyrolian campaign came to a close. Although a number of factors contributed to the final Allied victory, the improved tactics of the Bavarian Corps warrant particular consideration. By October, the commanders and troops of VII Corps had learned hard lessons about mountain warfare and, under Drouet's leadership, they applied those lessons with energy and professional efficiency. Although they could never match the native cunning and local knowledge of the

Tyrolians, the Bavarians adapted many of the insurgents' techniques to their own use. They thus learned to attack at night, to outflank or bypass difficult resistance and to control the heights with swarms of light troops. The attack on the Melleck-Lofer area on 16/17 October is the best example of these tactical improvements. As always, the Bavarian regulars remained the masters of the low and level ground and the Bavarian cavalry and artillery continued to be a terror to the rebels. Furthermore, the commanders approached the Third Offensive with less arrogance and far greater thoroughness than previously. Employing their new tactics to good effect, they proceeded slowly and methodically, pushing reconnaissance forces into the remote valleys and only advancing into Innsbruck when the line of communications to Bavaria and Salzburg was secure. Deroy's grip on the lower Inn valley and the constant vigilance of his patrols was thus crucial to the Corps' success. This thoroughness and the cautious, steady expansion of control precluded disasters like the surrender at Prutz on 8-9 August and gradually brought the countryside under firm Bavarian control.

Another aspect of the Bavarian tactics in the Third Offensive was the reduced level of brutality when compared to the preceding operations. In part, this was the result of a conscious policy to pacify rather than exterminate the Tyrolians and in part, it was generated by the increased confidence of the Bavarian soldiers and the hopeless nature of the insurgents' situation, but much of the credit must go to Drouet. By his steady, competent leadership, the French general overcame the prevailing tension in VII Corps and won the respect of his Bavarian subordinates. Well suited to independent command, his circumspection and decision contrasted strongly with Lefebvre's vacillation. Where the latter, unrestrained in expression and uncertain in behaviour, intruded into strictly Bavarian command matters and disrupted the internal structures of the Corps, Drouet called the Bavarian leaders into his counsels, including them in the decision-making process and accepting their advice. Unfortunately for the French, the friction that had developed in the first offensives into the Tyrol left ineradicable scars. Lefebvre's transgressions were compounded by Napoleon's failure to treat the Bavarians with the consideration they felt they had earned on the battlefield. The bitter relationship between the Emperor and the Crown Prince made these difficulties more acute and less susceptible to amelioration. The Bavarians thus came to see first Lefebvre, then Napoleon and all things French as symbols of oppression and France's willing friend slowly began to regard itself as an ally in chains. A debilitating poison entered into the relations between Paris and Munich after 1809; the cruel war in the vales of the Tyrol is largely to blame.

Despite the friction with the French, the war with the Tyrolian and Vorarlberg insurgents was a major patriotic effort for Bavaria. Both government and population responded with energy and enthusiasm to the urgent demands of home defence in the grim days of April and May. Regular units, reserve battalions, provisional units, volunteer Jäger, Gebirgsschützen and Mobile Legions all placed heavy requirements on the nation's manpower pool and the entire kingdom came to resemble a vast armed camp full of movement, colour and activity. If some of these organizations did not meet expectations, most displayed a degree of patriotism that gratified their monarch, performing strenuous duties for months with little beyond Max's thanks as a reward. The depot units and reserve battalions deserve particular mention. Cobbled together in haste from the rawest materials, they gradually proved their mettle in repeated encounters with the insurgents. Bavaria's wide-ranging exertions in 1809 represented a significant contribution to the Allied war effort, not only shielding her own population from the depredations of the rebels, but ensuring the security of the Napoleon's line of communications and freeing regular troops for the critical battles with the Austrian army.

NOTES

1: Louis-François Lejeune, *Memoirs of Baron Lejeune*, Nancy Bell, trans., Felling: Worley, 1987, vol. I, pp. 332-3.

2: In practice, the peasants seldom had any say in the ruling of the land, but the replacement of the Tyrolian constitution with the Bavarian had a direct and negative impact on some of the wealthier, more prominent classes. Josef Hirn, *Tirols Erhebung im Jahre 1809*, Innsbruck: Haymon, 1983, pp. 65-70.

3: One Bavarian official sadly commented that 'Where the Austrians ruled too little, perhaps the Bavarians fell into the error of ruling too much' (Hirn, p. 95). Good summaries of the Bavarian regime in the Tyrol are contained in Junkelmann, pp. 258-65 and Meinrad Pizzinini, 'Die bayerische Herrschaft in Tirol', *Krone und Verfassung*, Hubert Glaser, ed., München: Hirmer, 1980, pp. 254-9.

4: Tyrolian accounts generally refer to the three 'Liberations' of the Tyrol, whereas the Bavarians speak of the three 'Offensives' into the region. The phases here are adapted from Leyh.

5: The term 'Altbayern' (old Bavaria) is used to distinguish between the older traditional parts of the country and its newer acquisitions, particularly the Tyrol.

6: It is unlikely, however, that anyone anticipated the subsequent bitterness of the campaign; see Leyh, pp. 142-3; Werner Köfler, *Die Kämpfe am Bergisel 1809*, Militärhistorische Schriftenreihe Heft 20, Wien: Bundesverlag, 1983; Paulus, pp. 125-30.

7: The elements detached from the Bavarian Corps were sent to the Tyrol in mid-February when attempts to enforce conscription encountered active resistance: 3rd Light, 4th Light, the two squadrons of Dragoons; a battery of mixed guns under Hauptmann Binder was also assembled and ordered into the mountains (Pizzinini, p. 258). The 11th Infantry, 2nd Light and 7th Light were garrisoned in the Tyrol.

8: See Johann von Heilmann'Der Feldzug von 1809 in Tirol, im salzburgischen und an der bayerischen Südgrenze', *Jahrbücher für die deutsche Armee und Marine*, Bände 68 and 69 (1888), Band 88 (1893).

9: Chasteler's force consisted of seven battalions of regulars (the 9th Jäger Battalion plus three battalions each of *Hohenlohe-Bartenstein* and *Lusignan*), two battalions of Villach Landwehr, three squadrons of *Hohenzollern* Chevauxlegers and 17 guns. Three more Landwehr battalions (Klagenfurt) were to join the force over the coming days; an additional four (two each from Bruck and Judenburg) were alloted to Chasteler's undertaking but had not yet completed formation. The total force numbered some 10,000, almost equally divided between Landwehr and line troops. This order of battle is based on Viktor Schemfil, 'Das k. k. Tiroler Korps im Kriege 1809', *Tiroler Heimat*, XXIII Band, 1959. See also Max Gruber, *Bruneck und das westliche Pustertal im Jahre 1809*, Schlern-Schriften No. 86, Innsbruck: Wagner, 1952, p. 20; Joseph Freiherr von Hormayr, *Das Heer von Innerösterreich unter den Befehlen des Erzherzogs Johann im Kriege 1809 in Italien, Tyrol und Ungarn*, Leipzig und Altenburg: Brockhaus, 1817, pp. 229-30, 391; and Eberhard Mayerhoffer von Vedropolje, *Oesterreichs Krieg mit Napoleon I.*, Wien: Seidel & Sohn, 1904, p. 91.

10: Bisson's column consisted of replacements and several 4th battalions for regiments in Germany; the men had little ammunition, minimal training and were ill-prepared to fight. The column was in Bozen on the 9th and Brixen on the 10th. A second convoy of 2,500-3,000 French replacements under GD Louis Lemoine (two 4th battalions, two march battalions, three march squadrons, three guns) reached Brixen on the 12th, but returned to Bozen the same day when the roads north were found to be occupied by rebels; under constant threat of attack, his force departed Bozen the next day and marched to Trient (15 April). See Mayerhoffer, pp. 97-99. Bisson appears to have been a rather remarkable fellow, an old soldier known for his gargantuan appetite and skills as a toper, he was supposedly capable of consuming eight bottles of wine at dinner without evincing any ill effect (Elting, p. 164).

11: On arriving in Sterzing, Wreden's Bavarians apparently wanted to avenge themselves on the town; Bisson, whose Frenchmen were regarded as more well-behaved than the Bavarians, is credited with saving the town from the torch. Speicher and his men were incarcerated in a castle about an hour from Sterzing, but none of the locals revealed the location to Bisson or Wreden (Hirn, p. 296).

12: Hirn's generally reliable account claims the Bavarians were amazingly lazy and poorly led at Zirl. They are said to have spent much of their time in the local taverns rather than driving off the 40 Tyrolians who initially opposed their attempt to cross the Inn (Hirn, pp. 302-304).

13: Kinkel ordered Wreden to protect the bridges the sensible lieutenant-colonel had been trying to destroy. Moreover, he was to scatter his men about in small detachments and not to allow them to be overawed by superior numbers of insurgents. These orders, intercepted by the Tyrolians, indicate Kinkel's unrealistic appraisal of the situation and perhaps explain why he chose to await the Tyrolian attack in Innsbruck rather than withdrawing to a better position. The orders, issued on the 11th at 10:15 p.m., are quoted in Gruber, pp. 24-5.

14: Oberstlieutenant Bernclau had deployed his 3rd Light with two companies in and around Hall (Bernclau himself was here), a company in Rattenberg and a half-company each in Schwaz and Strass. Major Theobald in Schwaz wisely pulled in his outposts as the alarm bells began to ring; he was thus able to escape with the bulk of the two companies scattered from Schwaz to Rattenberg. Even so, his detachment lost 98 men (from about 400) and would have lost more had the Tyrolians not released a lieutenant and his 24 men after disarming them. Around 80 of Bernclau's soldiers were taken in the convent at Volders, the others fell into Tyrolian hands when the insurgents overran Hall. See C. Baur, *Der Krieg in Tirol während des Feldzugs von 1809*, München: Baur, 1812, pp. 9-10; Mayerhoffer, Map 11; Völderndorff, pp. 36-8.

15: Monteglas bitterly blamed Kinkel and Ditfurth for remaining in the city to be attacked by overwhelming numbers rather than attempting to withdraw downstream toward Rattenberg (quoted in Hirn, pp. 307-8).

16: It is not clear how many men Graf Erbach led out of the city. Estimates of the number of dragoons, for example, range from 120 to 'a few'; Völderndorff gives the strength of the entire column as 470. Encircled and forced to dismount outside of Hall, Erbach and his troopers had to watch as the joyous Tyrolians assayed equitation on their captured Bavarian mounts. See Baur, pp. 8-9; Hirn, pp. 312, 321; Köfler, *Bergisel*, p.20; Sauzey, p. 108; Völderndorff, p. 39.

17: Mayerhoffer, p. 98.

18: The Austrian accounts uniformly praise the courage of the Bavarians at Sterzing and during their much-harassed marches through the narrow wooded valleys towards Innsbruck. Descriptions of the engagements generally indicate the high quality of the Bavarian gunners and light infantry. The 11th Infantry, on the other hand, did not cover itself with glory; in addition to inept handling, the unit seems to have lacked spirit, to have been psychologically overwhelmed by the sudden, vigorous onslaught of the Tyrolians.

19: Hirn, p. 350. By mid-April, Austrian forces in the Tyrol included Chasteler's 'corps', and two detachments from Jellacic's Division under OTL Taxis (some 800 men in two companies of *de Vaux* Infantry, four companies of Salzburg Jäger, one company of the 2nd Salzburg Landwehr and $1/4$ squadron of *O'Reilly*) and OTL Reissenfels (about 900 men in four companies of *de Vaux*). Austrian Order of Battle amalgamated from Hirn, Hormayr, pp. 235, 255; *Krieg 1809*, vol. III, p. 81; Mayerhoffer, p. 99; and Anton H. Wagner, *Das Gefecht bei St. Michael-Loeben am 25. Mai 1809*, Militärhistorische Schriftenreihe Heft 51, Wien: Bundesverlag, 1984, p. 19.

20: Each regiment contributed a detachment of about 25 men under a lieutenant. They established pickets towards the following towns: Landsberg (1st Chevauxlegers), Weilheim (2nd), Tölz (3rd), and Rosenheim (1st Dragoons). See Bezzel, 'Grenz', pp. 117-118, 188, and Völderndorff, p. 136.

21: Aicher had held the post of garrison commandant in Kufstein since 1806 and thus knew the fortress and surrounding terrain perfectly. In April 1809, he commanded 471 infantrymen provided by the depot troops (variously called provisional, 5th, and reserve companies) of the 1st (127), 2nd (127), 5th (149) and 6th (68) Light Battalions in addition to 98 gunners; the light infantry companies were organized as the 'provisorisches leichtes Bataillon' (Provisional Light Battalion) under Hauptmann von Chario. His artillery included some rather large weapons: four 60-pound mortars and thirteen 18-pounder cannon. With one of these monster mortars, Corporal Amont managed to hit an Austrian powder magazine with his third lob, thereby neutralizing a battery of three guns for 24 hours. From Maximilian Schlagintweit, 'Kufsteins Kriegsjahre (1504, 1703, 1809)', *Darstellungen aus der Bayerischen Kriegs- und Heeresgeschichte* Heft 12, München: Lindau, 1903, pp. 27-8, 33.

22: Hirn, p. 352.

23: Reissenfels had only about nine field pieces (five cannon and four howitzers); these had been captured in the preceding week but were provided with very little ammunition. Brief bombardments (several hours in duration) began on the 25th and continued in a desultory fashion until the 28th when news of the defeats atround Regensburg apparently arrived in the Austrian camp; the batteries were dismantled on the 29th although the blockade was maintained for several more weeks. Sauzey, *Bavarois*, p. 134, estimates the number of insurgents around Kufstein to have been between 7,000 and 8,000.

24: Although Salzburg (an independent entity until 1805) was not part of the Tyrol, combat within the old principality is addressed here because of similarities in the nature of the terrain and the style of warfare. Moreover, the operations of the Bavarian Corps around Salzburg were closely linked to its attempts to subdue the Tyrolians.

25: Jellacic's Division comprised (1 May): *Esterházy* Infantry Regiment Nr. 32 (three battalions), *De Vaux* Infantry Regiment Nr. 45 (two battalions), *Warasdiner-Kreutzer* Grenz Infantry Regiment Nr. 5 (two battalions), three weak battalions of Salzburg Landwehr (1st, 3rd, and 4th), three platoons of *O'Reilly* Chevauxlegers, and a battery of 3-pounders (Wilhelm Wachtel, 'Die Division Jellacic im Mai 1809', *Mitteilungen des K. und K. Kriegsarchivs,* dritte Folge, Band VIII, 1911, Anlage 1). See also Werner Köfler, *Die Kämpfe am Pass Lueg im Jahre 1809*, Militärhistorische Schriftenreihe Heft 41, Wien: Bundesverlag, 1980, p. 7; Gedeon Freiherr Maretich von Riv-Alpon, 'Die Gefechte in der Umgebung von Salzburg in den Jahren 1800, 1805 und 1809', *Streffleur's Oesterreichische Militärische Zeitschrift,* XXXIV Jahrgang, Band I, Heft II (February), 1893; and Wagner, p. 20.

26: Stengel actually sent a portion of his brigade (I/4 and II/8 under Oberst Zoller, commander of the 4th Infantry) into the vale on the afternoon of the 3rd. Zoller took Abtenau on the afternoon of the 4th and was joined by Stengel with a half-squadron of the 1st Dragoons and II/2 that evening. See Döderlein, Hutter, Köfler, Maretich, Wachtel and Moritz Ritter von Reichert, *Das Königlich Bayerische 2. Infanterie-Regiment 'Kronprinz'*, München: Oldenbourg, 1913.

27: Köfler, *Lueg*, pp. 8-9, Leyh, pp. 144-5. To reinforce the Crown Prince for this mission, the 10th Infantry and 5th Light were attached to the 1st Division. The division not only occupied Salzburg and watched Jellacic, but placed cavalry posts at St. Gilgen (one squadron of 1st Dragoons) and along the road from Neumarkt to Vöcklabruck (three squadrons of 1st Chevauxlegers). The two companies of the 3rd Light that Major Theobald had managed to bring out of the Tyrol occupied Berchtesgaden (Völderndorff).

28: It is not clear when the 2nd Dragoons rejoined Deroy's Division. The regimental history (Obpacher, p. 192) claims the dragoons were with the division for the advance on Kufstein on the 12th, but this is not confirmed by other sources.

29: The battalion remained with Wrede until 15 May when it rejoined Deroy at Rattenberg. Deroy had also left a gun from Roy's Battery with II/14. Furthermore, Wrede, who took all four of his batteries into the Tyrol, had also been reinforced with four howitzers from Van Douwe's and Gotthardt's Batteries; these were found to be particularly useful in the mountains.

30: While Wrede stormed the Strub Pass, the attached companies of the 9th Infantry under their commander, Oberst Peter de la Motte, conducted a feint toward the Luftenstein Pass south of Lofer (Adolf Pergler, *Selbst- und Landesverteidigung der vereinten Pinzgauer und Tiroler in den Jahren 1800, 1805 und 1809 an den Pässen Botenbühel, Strub und Luftenstein,* Lofer, 1906, pp. 40-1).

31: If Napoleon hoped to eliminate a threat to his flank and his prestige by subduing the Tyrolians, many of the Bavarians viewed it as an opportunity to 'dreadfully avenge the the blood of our brave comrades' (from a Bavarian pamphlet printed in May, cited in Hirn, p. 399). The other two quotes are both from common soldiers (Deifl and Mändler respectively), cited in Junkelmann, p. 266.

32: Quoted in Hirn, p. 400.

33: The order is reprinted in Völderndorff, pp. 141-3.

34: Hirn, pp. 400-3; Leyh, p. 146; F. R. von R., *Die Waffentaten der Oesterreicher im Jahre 1809*, Wien: Hirschfeld, 1838, pp. 106-8; Sichlern, pp. 77-8.

35: The 9th Infantry Regiment bravely attempted to force the Luftenstein Pass south of Lofer on the 12th and 13th, but was thrown back with loss as the Tyrolians, reinforced by a few line troops, hurled bullets, boulders and logs down on the unfortunate Bavarians. Hormayr (pp. 275-6) and Pergler (pp. 42-5) give the Bavarian losses as over 400 men (and several barrels of beer!). Simultaneously on the 13th, the 3rd Light was turned back from an expedition to force the Hirschbühel from Berchtesgaden.

36: Deroy had also dispatched Oberst von Metzen with six companies of the 5th Infantry to outflank the Austrians in the Inn valley. Reaching Bayerischzell on the 11th, Metzen attacked the pass near Landl but was unable to overcome its defenders; he withdrew to the Inn and joined Deroy that evening at Kufstein (Völderndorff, p. 143). The 13th was spent clearing out pockets of rebel resistance and disarming the local populace; the 3rd Division apparently came in sight of the 2nd on the afternoon of the 14th but their junction was not really effected until the following day.

37: Both sides have traditionally blamed each other for starting the fires that destroyed this little town, but it seems most likely the buildings were ignited as a side effect of the heated combat in the streets. The violent struggle would also have precluded effective measures to contain the flames once they began to spread.

38: Quoted in Hirn, p. 405.

39: Franz J. A. Schneidawind, *Der Krieg Oestereichs gegen Frankreich, dessen Alliirte und den Rheinbund im Jahre 1809*, Schaffhausen: Hurter, 1842, vol. 2, p. 105.

40: The 9th Infantry, with two companies around Lofer and six companies under GM Siebein at Rattenberg and Strass, was entrusted with holding open Lefebvre's communications with the 1st Division in Salzburg. Major Theobald's two companies were still in Berchtesgaden. Völderndorff, pp. 153-4.

41: Hirn, p. 437.

42: In typical Napoleonic fashion, these instructions were remarkably specific, detailing not only the organization of each battalion (four companies) but also their desired deployment (Bezzel, 'Grenzschutz', p. 79).

43: Each reserve battalion wore the uniform of an existing line infantry regiment although it had no other specific affiliation with that regiment: 1st Reserve (uniform of the 1st Infantry), 2nd Reserve (4th), 3rd Reserve (3rd), 4th Reserve (5th), 5th Reserve (13th), 6th Reserve (9th).

44: Ysenburg was the commander of Generalkommando Nuremberg and thus responsible for a number of depots. Quoted in Bezzel, 'Grenzschutz', p. 78. Note that unit depots were ruthlessly stripped to provide troops to the field. During the war, most of the line regiments sent out depot detachments of varying sizes (depending upon the number of fit recruits available in the depot), while some of the light battalion depots were the source of 'provisional companies' as well as depot detachments: for example, the 5th Light had a provisional company in the Kufstein garrison (about 150 men) and a depot detachment

45: In Munich: 1st and 2nd Reserve Battalions, depots of 1st Dragoons, 1st Chevauxlegers, 1st, 2nd, 5th and 7th Infantry Regiments, 1st Light and 4th Light. In Ulm: 5th and 6th Reserve Battalions, depot of 13th Infantry. In and around Augsburg (all of the depots and reserve battalions had been ordered to this city on 5 May, but were later dispersed when the French garrison commander, GD Jean Moulin, objected that the city could not support such a mass of soldiery): 3rd and 4th Reserve Battalions, depots of 3rd, 9th, 11th and 14th Infantry Regiments, 6th Light and 7th Light, all four remaining cavalry depots and a provisional company of the 3rd Light (departed for Munich on 30 May). In Forchheim: depots of 4th and 8th Infantry Regiments, 5th Light. In Rothenberg: depots of 6th Infantry and 3rd Light. In Rosenberg: depot of 10th Infantry. The beginning of hostilities found the depot of the 2nd Light in Trient; unable to make its way to Bavaria, the depot remained in Italy until 1810, while a provisional company from the battalion took part in the first blockade of Kufstein and the later offensives into the Tyrol . Bezzel, 'Grenzschutz', pp. 78-82, 180-9. Note that other depot units were either with the field forces as staff troops or occupying imperiled border fortresses (Passau and Kufstein), see Chapter 2.

46: To protect his lines of communication and the territories of the Rheinbund rulers, Napoleon had established a 'corps d'observation' at Hanau under Marshal Kellermann. As one of Kellermann's subordinates, Beaumont was responsible for border defence and internal security from Lake Constance to the Bohemian border.

47: The Kreise in 1809 were all named for their principal rivers: Main, Pegnitz, Naab, Rezat, Altmühl, Oberdonau, Lech, Regen, Unterdonau, Isar, Salzach, Iller, Inn, Eisack, Etsch. Note that the last three were all in the Tyrol and could thus hardly be expected to supply enthusiastic legions.

48: When the royal decree announcing the formation of the national guard was promulgated (6 July), the Gebirgsschützen and Jäger had already been in existance for some weeks; they were retroactively declared to be part of the Nationalgarde III. Klasse (Bezzel, *Heeres*, pg, 109). The members of the Bürgermilitär organizations were to perform police and guard duties within their home cities; they were not designed to be field combat troops (Bezzel, 'Grenz', p. 92 and *Heeres*, p. 109).

49: A series of complex regulations governed the organization of the Bürgermilitär, but basically, the size of the force depended upon the wealth and population of its district. By regulation, a company had to have a minimum of 60 men; the basic building block was the fusilier company, but if four such companies were raised, they could constitute a battalion and one could be designated a grenadier company. If there were at least two fusilier companies, a company of Schützen could be established. Cavalry could be recruited if a city could afford to mount at least 60 troopers (minimum required for a squadron) and artillery companies could be formed if guns were available. The basic uniform of the fusiliers, grenadiers and cavalry were simple, dark-blue coats with light-blue distinctions, dark-blue breeches and bicorne hats (the grenadiers, however, were authorized bearskins). Schützen had the same knee-length coats, but in dark-green with grey breeches. Artillerymen were to wear pike grey coats with red trim and grey breeches (Lipowsky, *Bürger-Militär-Almanach für das Köingreich Bayern 1809*, München: Fleischmann, 1809, pp. 89-150).

50: Triva to Monteglas, 13 April 1812, quoted in Bezzel, *Heeres*, pg,. 109. However, it should also be noted that they were only effective when well supported by regular military forces. Left to themselves, they were invariably disarmed by insurgent raiders, their weapons serving to improve the armament of the rebels (see Ferdinand Hirn, *Vorarlberg Erhebung im Jahre 1809*, Bregenz: Teutsch, 1909, pp. 117-18). Principal sources for the organization, uniforming and performance of these paramilitary organizations are Bezzel, 'Grenzschutz' and *Heeres* as well as Julius Schmelzing, *Darstellung der mobilen Legionen oder der Nationalgarde IIter Klasse im Königreich Bayern aus den Gesetzes-Quellen*, Nuremberg: Zeh, 1818.

51: The materiel was from the depots of the 11th Infantry, 1st Light, 4th Light, 6th Light, 7th Light, 1st Dragoons and 1st Chevauxlegers; most of the escorting troops were not considered fit for field service. See Freiherr von der Wengen, *Der Feldzug der Grossherzoglich Badischen Truppen unter Oberst Karl v. Stockhorn gegen die Vorarlberger und Tiroler 1809*, Heidelberg: Winter, 1910, pp. 55-9.

52: Beaumont found about 1,200 Bavarian depot cavalry and 1,500 depot infantry available to him in mid-May as well as three French provisional dragoon regiments which Picard had brought with him from Strasbourg on 29 April. Two further provisional dragoon regiments soon joined him from Hanau. Major Pillement's detachment was composed of men from the depots of the 9th, 11th, 13th and 14th Infantry Regiments and the 3rd, 6th and 7th Light Battalions.

53: The adventurous attempt of the small Austrian regular detachment in the Vorarlberg to escape to Bohemia (see Chapters 3 and 8) also caused some alarm in the Bavarian rear area. Learning of the Austrians' appearance in Ehingen, Oberst Lessel in Ulm sent 100 French dragoons, 100 men from the 13th Infantry depot and a gun to intercept them on 22 May, but the Austrians moved on and Lessel recalled his little column. A small Bavarian detachment (70 men under Hauptmann Grafenstein) from the depot of the 1st Infantry, however, returning from escorting prisoners to Strasbourg, received word of the Austrian presence and laid an ambush for them near Geislingen an der Steige. On the morning of the 23rd, the Austrians approached Grafenstein's position. Unfortunately, his men were discovered by an enemy patrol and the bold Grafenstein, not trusting his raw recruits in a fire fight, saw no choice but to charge. The Austrian cavalry fled, but the infantry opened fire, wounding Grafenstein and one of his men. The Austrians sought safety in avoiding combat and quickly withdrew, leaving behind twelve prisoners; Grafenstein's wound precluded any thought of pursuit. Bezzel, 'Grenz', pp. 100-1.

54: One of Pillement's companies and one company from the Württemberg *Franquemont* Regiment, plus a few cavalry in Immenstadt; some 200 troops of all arms in Füssen; Pillement himself in Weiler with 500 men of his battalion, 40 chevauxlegers, two French dragoon squadrons and 25 Bavarian foresters; the remainder of Picard's men, including Andrian-Werburg's volunteers, remained in Kempten. Bezzel, 'Grenz', pp. 98-9.

55: On 1 May, the posts in Landsberg and Weilheim were each reinforced by 25 men from the depot of the 7th Infantry and a similar detachment from the 1st Infantry's depot was sent to Tölz. On 7 May, OTL Max Graf von Seyssel d'Aix marched out of Munich with 250 infantry and 60 horsemen from the depots in the city. Seyssel took 50 infantry and 20 cavalry with him to Tölz, and send 100 foot soldiers and 20 troopers each to Diessen and Miesbach, the assembly points for Arco's Gebirgsschützen. Bezzel, 'Grenz', p. 118.

56: Arco's line infantry was comprised of depots from the 1st Infantry (192), 2nd Infantry (164), 5th (144) and 7th Infantry (67), 1st Light (64) and 2nd Light (142); these troops made up a provisional battalion under Major Hammel with four companies: 1st from 1st Infantry, 2nd from 2nd Infantry, 3rd from 5th and 7th, 4th from the two light battalions. A provisional cavalry squadron under Rittmeister Graf Lerchenberg was formed with elements from the 1st Dragoons (96), 1st (40), 2nd (24) and 3rd (16) Chevauxlegers. Some volunteer Schützen from Munich under Hauptmann Jehle also marched with these depot troops. Note that the light troops were in addition to those in the Provisional Light Battalion.

57: About 120 depot soldiers from the 1st Infantry, 100 Gebirsschützen, 20 Munich volunteers and 80 cavalrymen. The infantry were transported in wagons.

58: Different authors provide different numbers for the various fights at Bergisel; I use the following:
First 'Battle' - April surrender of Bisson and Wreden
Second Battle - 29 May (prelude engagement on 25 May)
Third Battle - 13 August
Fourth Battle - 1 November

59: With Wrede had gone those elements of the 1st Division that had accompanied Deroy from Rosenheim; he also took those squadrons of the 4th Chevauxlegers that had made the march to Innsbruck (the remainder were between Melleck and Salzburg). Deroy's strength was 3,853 infantry, 408 cavalry and twelve guns: part of 9th Infantry (982), 7th Light (446), 5th Infantry (1,249), 14th Infantry (1,176), 2nd Dragoons (408). Gedeon Freiherr Maretich von Riv-Alpon, *Die zweite und dritte Berg Isel-Schlacht,* Innsbruck: Wagner, 1895, p. 30.

60: The comment on Wrede's withdrawal was made by the insurgent leader Speckbacher, quoted in Leyh, pp. 156-157. Much to the Tyrolians' disgust, the Austrian commander had pulled most of his troops back into the valley of the Rienz and Drau (the Pustertal); only after extended negotiations, expressions of indignation and even threats, was Chasteler brought to turn his tired columns about and repair to the Sill valley.

61: A cavalry patrol reported Austrian entrenchments at the Brenner Pass on the 21st, a squadron skirmished with Austrian Jägers near Steinach on the 22nd and Deroy himself observed rebels at Schönberg on the 23rd. Köfler, *Bergisel,* p. 29, and Riv-Alpon, pp. 31-3.

62: The 7th Light, only 446 strong, had been reorganized into two companies; the excess officers and NCO's were ordered to Augsburg to unite with the battalion's depot and establish two new companies, thereby bringing the unit up to full strength. These excess personnel departed Innsbruck early on the 29th under Major Hermann, intending to cross the mountains at Scharnitz and continue on for Augsburg; they were accompanied by one of Peters' howitzers which Deroy had promised to loan to Arco. Reaching Zirl at 6.30 a.m., they were fired upon, but were fortunate enough to escape with the loss of only two officers captured. Riv-Alpon, pp. 104-5.

63: About 10,000 of the rebels could be considered good quality irregular forces. The remainder were new, partly organized partisan companies.

64: The Bavarian troops available for these attacks were 5th Infantry (one and a half battalions), 9th Infantry (one battalion), 10th Infantry (one and a half battalions) and I/14.

65: Teimer instigated and led many of the raids into Bavaria proper.

66: Combined from Köfler, *Bergisel,* p. 35, and Riv-Alpon, p. 191; Völderndorff gives a total of 256 dead and wounded (p. 202).

67: In a skirmish at Rattenberg, OTL Günther, commander of the 7th Light was killed (Völderndorff, p. 203).

His place would be taken by OTL Treuberg, thus giving the battalion a new name.

68: Deroy's losses during the two-day retreat were 165, including a substantial number of missing (113).

69: Arco's two guns (6-pounders), finally arrived from Munich on the 28th, also contributed to his little victory, throwing the enemy into panic and disrupting his attempts to organize.

70: Sources for the events in late May (Inn valley and Mittenwald area) include Baur, pp. 20-33, Bezzel, 'Grenz', pp. 117-22; Köfler, *Bergisel*, pp. 24-36; Heinz Kuckenburg, *Soldat in Ulm*, Biberach an der Riss: Höhn, 1985, p. 134; Leyh, pp. 156-8; Riv-Alpon; Völderndorff, pp. 175-9, 202-4.

71: Three companies of *Franquemont* and two guns were also sent to Grouvel from Kempten (see Chapter 3).

72: Grouvel's battle report and Württemberg accounts of the engagement at Dornbirn are scathing in their comments on the Bavarians, although Grouvel (perhaps not the most able officer himself) praised Pillement's personal competence. Unfortunately, the report Pillement prepared to defend his men has been lost. See Bezzel, 'Grenz', pp. 102-4; Johann Gunz, 'Der Krieg der Vorarlberger im Jahr 1809,' *Militair-Wochenblatt*, Nos. 206, 210, 211, 212 (3 June-15 July 1820), pp. 1467-8; Hirn, *Vorarlbergs*, pp. 167-82; Pfister, *Denkwürdigkeiten*, pp. 367-8; Wengen, pp. 79-83.

73: Vincenti: 10th Infantry and 7th Light. Seydewitz: 5th and 14th Infantry.

74: Deroy: II/5, 10th Infantry. Vincenti: I/5, a cavalry platoon and two guns at Murnau; 14th, four guns and the rest of the chevauxlegers at Habach; one company of 7th Light each at Tölz and Tegernsee; the force at Murnau, under OTL Schmöger, was given the additional mission of maintaining contact with the French dragoons at Schongau, although the French Colonel Prevost 'only rarely sent patrols' to keep in touch with the Bavarians (Baur, p. 49). Arco remained at Kochel with a detachment (82 infantry and 26 cavalry) at Benediktbeuren.

75: I/9 was left at Rosenheim with a gun and two companies of II/9 were dropped off at Reichenhall to watch the pass at Hirschbühel, still held by the Tyrolians. Deroy thus entered Salzburg with two companies of II/9, 10th Infantry, three squadrons and a battery. En route back to Rosenheim, the 7th Light replaced the two companies of the 9th at Reichenhall, so that all of *Ysenburg* was reunited when the division returned to Rosenheim on the 29th. GB Kister had been the French commander of the Hessian brigade prior to assuming duties as the military governor of Salzburg (see Chapter 5).

76: Arco achieved good results by providing his patrols with dogs to help locate and track the Tyrolians. Sources for the combat actions in June: Baur, pp. 33-53; Bezzel, 'Grenz', pp. 104-7, 122-9, Gerneth & Kiessling, pp. 150-1; Leyh, pp. 158-60; Völderndorff, 205-10.

77: The entire 11th Infantry had been captured at Innsbruck in April and its only active element was the depot detachment with Pillement. A new 1st Battalion was formed for the regiment in late November near Lake Constance.

78: As a consequence of this order, all of the initial reserve battalions were renamed according to the uniforms they wore and many were assigned new garrisons:

April-June (initial name)	after June (new name)	New Garrison/Assembly Point
1st Reserve in Munich	1st Reserve	Munich
2nd Reserve in Munich	4th Reserve	Passau
3rd Reserve in Augsburg	3rd Reserve	Augsburg
4th Reserve in Augsburg	5th Reserve	Kufstein
5th Reserve in Ulm	13th Reserve	Ulm
6th Reserve in Ulm	9th Reserve	Forchheim
	2nd Reserve	Munich
	6th Reserve	Augsburg
	7th Reserve	Munich
	8th Reserve	Salzburg
	10th Reserve	Bamberg & Rosenberg
	14th Reserve	Nuremberg & Rothenberg

79: To ease the burden on Augsburg and its environs, some of the depots previously stationed there were moved to new locations: 11th Infantry and 7th Light to Neuburg, 2nd Dragoons to Ansbach, 3rd Chevauxlegers to Dillingen, 4th Chevauxlegers to Bamberg.

80: The information on the Gebirgsschützenkorps is derived from Bezzel, 'Grenz', pp. 127-8 and Baur, pp. 43-50. The full quote from Baur (p. 44) is: 'The mixture of civil authority and military rigour would not thrive. Only in the mountain regions themselves, such as Tölz and Miesbach, was patriotism able to overcome all difficulties; and up to the last moment, even in the most dangerous times, one could rely on these bold mountaineers almost more than on the line soldiers.'

81: A surprise attack on a work party from the 9th and 14th Regiments did succeed in capturing a few men of the *Ysenburg* depot on the night of the 27th outside of Passau. See Chapter 8 for a detailed account of the 19 June fracas.

82: Formerly part of Prussia, Bayreuth was now under French administration.

83: Radivojevich's command consisted of two battalions of *Deutsch-Banater* Grenzer, four battalions of Landwehr (1st and 2nd Tabor, 2nd Chrudim, 4th Königgrätz), $1\frac{3}{4}$ squadrons of Uhlans and four 3-

pounders. Gustav von Kortzfleisch, *Geschichte des Herzoglich Braunschweigischen Infanterie-Regiments und seiner Stammtruppen 1809-1867,* Braunschweig: Limbach, 1896, p. 66; Welden, p. 98.

84: A depot detachment of 105 Bavarians, sent from the fortress at Forchheim to enforce conscription along the Main, barely escaped from Bamberg to return to its safe walls.

85: A detachment of 200 Bavarian infantry with two guns deployed from Forchheim after the raid on Bamberg to support a tiny French cavalry force near Schesslitz. The Bavarians reached Schesslitz on the 19th where they found about 50 French infantry and 60 chasseurs à cheval, but returned to their fortress on the 21st without encountering the enemy. Schneidawind, *Krieg 1809,* vol. II, p. 174.

86: Delaroche was the French commandant in Regensburg. Hannet's detachment was formed from men in the depots of 3rd Light, 5th and 6th Infantry.

87: This engagement is usually known by the name of the nearest village: Weidensees. A Bavarian force of 300 men from the depot of the 8th Infantry and two 6-pounders had been dispatched from Forchheim to unite with Delaroche, but arrived too late for the little skirmish and returned to its starting point on the 30th.

88: Only one of Junot's three divisions, GD Olivier Rivaud de la Raffinière's 1st Division, was available for the operation against Radivojevich; the 2nd (GD Eloi-Laurent Despeaux) was still forming at Hanau and the 3rd (GD Joseph Lagrange) was under Beaumont's orders around Augsburg (Mayerhoffer, pp. 186-187). Rivaud's weak division was composed of six 4th battalions: those of the 19th, 25th and 28th Regiments in GB Charles Lameth's brigade, and those of the 36th, 50th and 75th Regiments in GB Eloi-Charlemagne Taupin's for a total of about 4,500 men. It is unlikely Delaroche's two provisional dragoon regiments (1st and 5th) amounted to more than about 1,200 men (approximately 600 each) despite Napoleon's desire for each regiment to count 1,000 troopers in its ranks (von Kortzfleisch's estimate of 2,500 French cavalry is inaccurate). Junot also had the twelve cannon of his corps 'artillery reserve' manned by about 250 gunners and a tiny detachment of Würzburg train troops (22 men). The Bavarians Junot dragooned into accompanying him numbered 510 infantry from the depots of 4th Infantry, 8th Infantry and 5th Light, as well as 23 artillerists with the two guns captured at Betzenstein. See Buat, vol. I, pp. 308-309; Hermann Helmes, 'Die Würzburger Truppen vor hundert Jahren', *Archiv des historischen Vereins von Unterfranken und Aschaffenburg,* Nr. 55, 1913, p. 127; Kortzfleisch, p. 65; Saski, vol. I, pp. 545-6; Schneidawind, *Krieg,* vol. II, p. 186; Bavarian regimental histories.

89: Kienmayer brought up an additional Austrian force of $1^1/3$ line battalions, three Landwehr battalions, a Jäger company, two squadrons of Uhlans and six guns (four 3-pounders and two howitzers); he also commanded a contingent of Braunschweigers (two battalions, a Schützen company, a hussar regiment, two guns, two howitzers) and Hessians (four infantry companies and two small squadrons). Kortzfleisch, p. 66. See also Chapter 9.

90: The following Reserve Battalions were in the process of forming in north-east Bavaria: 9th, 10th and 14th. Three companies of the 3rd Reserve and one company of the 13th Reserve were sent to Preysing on 26 July; they departed to join their battalions with Oberndorff's corps on the Tyrolian border on 25 October (Preysing's Brigade was disbanded on the 21st of that month). Bezzel, 'Grenz', pp. 164-8.

91: The 5th Reserve, three companies strong, departed Munich for Kufstein on the 2nd. The battalion's fourth company (Hauptmann Kreith) comprised the depot troops of the 5th Infantry assigned to Arco's force; these men marched for the capital on the 2nd but did not join their comrades in Kufstein, rather left Munich to assume staff support duties in the 3rd Division headquarters on the 23rd, replacing the depot company of the 13th Regiment.

92: Hearing that Deroy was planning to come to his aid against the rather weakly prosecuted second blockade, Aicher had ordered two forays on the 2nd, each of about 60 men and a 3-pounder; with no sign of Deroy, the detachments returned to the fort in the evening. Another sally was made on the 5th by approximately 60 men with a 3-pounder to clear the way for Deroy. Schlagintweit, pp. 35-6.

93: Additionally, II/5 and 5th Light remained in Salzburg. Deroy thus marched for Linz with II/9, 10th Infantry, three squadrons and two batteries; arriving on the 13th, he was joined the next day by I/5, 14th Regiment, a squadron and a battery. I/9 was relieved on 9 July and caught up with Deroy's column on the 11th at Schwanenstadt, while 7th Light was only reunited with its division on the 19th at Frankenmarkt, having been relieved on the 15th. Bezzel, 'Grenz', pp. 133-4; Gerneth & Kiessling, pp. 252-3.

94: Hammel's Provisional Battalion was disbanded. Departures: Kreith's 5th Infantry depot company (2 July); depot troops of 2nd and 7th infantry (10 July). Arrivals: Provisional Light Battalion (6 July); 1st Reserve and provisional company of 3rd Light (8 July); reserve company of the 4th Light, one gun and one howitzer (10 July). In addition, the corps lost some cadres and gained some replacement personnel. Hauptmann Vögler's Company of the 2nd Reserve would join on 20 July.

95: Detailed dispositions: companies of 3rd, 5th, 6th Light, 40 chevauxlegers, one gun in Murnau; a company of 1st Reserve and sixteen dragoons at Habach; 4th Light company, a company of 1st Reserve, 40 Gebirgsschützen, 20 dragoons, one gun at Kochel; 1st Light company and Gebirgsschützen (70) at Tölz with outposts to Lenggries; 2nd Light company and Gebirgsschützen at Tegernsee with outposts to Kreuth; the reserve at Benediktbeuren consisted of two companies of 1st Reserve and 104 cavalry with the howitzer and the lone 6-pounder (the other two guns were 3-pounders, the 6-pounders having been found too unwieldy to be of much utility in the difficult terrain).

96: The first detachment was commanded by Major von Freudenberg and had a total of 517 men. The second detachment was about 300 strong under Major Waible.

97: Hauptmann Kreith's depot company of the 5th Infantry, withdrawn from Arco to Munich on the 2nd, was ordered to reinforce the Jäger at Fischbachau on the 18th but was halted in Tölz by Arco. The company remained with the latter commander until the 23rd when it marched off to the 3rd Division in Salzburg and replaced the provisional company of the 13th Infantry on staff support.

98: A rather curious incident occurred during the engagement at Kochel. Hoping to limit the bloodshed, Arco decided to call on the rebels to accept a ceasefire. Previous experience, however, had shown that military emissaries were invariably held captive by the Tyrolians. The colonel thus asked for volunteers from the inhabitants of Kochel. The village baker, a fellow whose name is sadly lost to history, offered to undertake the mission in return for some small remuneration. His offer was accepted, and, clad only in his nightshirt and long underwear, the plucky baker rode toward the enemy on an old white nag, waving a white kerchief and shouting at the top of his lungs, 'don't shoot, I am the baker of Kochel!' His appearance seems to have excited more amusement than hope amongst the Bavarians and the Austrians took no notice of him whatsoever. Baur, p. 68; Bezzel, 'Grenz', p. 135.

99: The company of the 2nd Reserve (Hauptmann Vögler with 150 men) came under Arco's command. On the 20th, Arco was also given temporary command of a weak squadron of French dragoons (70 men), who operated west of Murnau for 'a few days' before returning to Beaumont's Division.

100: Most of Arco's troops arrived in Kreuth around 4 a.m. on the 27th; Oberndorff's command marched in that night at about 9 p.m.

101: Overall responsibility for the northern attack groups was given to Marshal Lefebvre; he thus commanded his own 1st and 3rd Divisions, Montmarie's force and Beaumont's Division.

102: Arco with 1,880 men and Oberndorff with 980. In addition, Arco had several hundred Schützen from Miesbach under his control during this little engagement. Although they voluntarily accompanied Arco out of their home districts and actually into the Tyrol, their presence outside Altbayern aroused considerable irritation in the government. Stern messages reached Arco and the Schützen returned home on 9 August.

103: Deroy fought with rebels for seven hours at Taxenbach on the 27th and encountered further resistance on the 29th on the eastern side of the Gerlos Pass.

104: At Volders, Deroy was rejoined by GM Siebein with most of the division's artillery and trains under the protection of 9th Infantry and three squadrons of the 2nd Dragoons. Siebein had diverged from the main column at Mittersill the take advantage of the superior roads through Kitzbühel and Wörgl to the Inn valley.

105: See Chapter 8 for details of Rouyer's force. The 1st Division marched out of the Linz bridgehead on 24 July and arrived in Salzburg two days later. Both the Bavarian 1st Division at Linz and Rouyer's Division at Passau were relieved of their defensive responsibilities by Wrede's troops.

106: Baur, p. 93.

107: A number of Vorarlbergers also took part in the combat. The initial attack was made by some 600 insurgents against Bavarian pickets on the main road one half hour south of Kempten. This force was deflected to the west when 150 Bavarian reinforcements arrived under Hauptmann Khuen. In the meantime, another column (3,000 rebels and 300 Austrians with two guns) was advancing against the city from the west. The Allied force here (150 Bavarians of the 13th Infantry, 80 French infantry and 60 French dragoons) was outflanked and forced to retire. They were withdrawing in good order when Pillement appeared at the head of 200 men and turned the column around. Aided by Khuen's company, Pillement took the offensive and soon put the entire enemy band to flight.

108: The rebels appeared before Kempten on the 22nd, but did not attack; another attack on the 25th was repulsed by the Württembergers of *Franquemont*.

109 This was the last action of the Ulm foresters. They were released from military service in early August with the thanks of their king, who said of them: 'By their courage in the battles of May, June and especially that of 17 July, they proved themselves the equals of the regular troops.'

110: Quoted in Köfler, *Bergisel*, p. 40.

111: Rouyer reached the Brenner on the 1st and Sterzing on the 2nd, then rested his men for a day before proceeding south on the 4th. Wittgenstein marched out of Innsbruck on the 2nd with 1st Light and the 1st Dragoons (still only two squadrons strong) to hold the Brenner while Rouyer advanced. Relieved at the pass by II/1, he reached Sterzing on the 3rd, leaving one squadron to perform liaison and security duties on the road back to Innsbruck. See Chapter 8 for details of Rouyer's action.

112: The Tyrolians, with their intimate knowledge of the terrain, a strong tradition of home defence and enthusiastic support from the local inhabitants, enjoyed a tremendous tactical advantage over the Bavarians in the mountains. Adept at ambushes and dispersed skirmishing from cover, one of their favorite tactics was to block a narrow valley with an abattis, dismantled bridge or similar barrier and surprise the Bavarians when their march column was delayed in clearing the obstacle. In addition to bullets, the partisans inflicted physical and psychological damage by rolling huge boulders and logs down the steep slopes. These natural weapons would be prepared in advance at key points along the enemy's route of march in great 'stone batter-

ies' (Steinbatterien), causing terror and destruction when they were set loose ('stone avalanches' -
Steinlawinen). This tactic was used with devastating effect at the Pontlatz Bridge on 8 and 9 August, where
gigantic rocks bounded down the slopes in the darkness to crush men, horses and vehicles, making escape
impossible. The Bavarians slowly learned to counter these techniques by deploying light infantry into the
mountains along their routes of march to clear the heights of rebels. The 1st Light did this effectively at
Mauls on 7 August, surprising the Tyrolian defenders in the town when they charged down from the commanding slopes. The process was slow and exhausting, however, and the Bavarians were never able to
match the Tyrolians' familiarity with the rugged terrain.

113: The 9th Infantry occupied Silz and Stams, while the 5th held Landeck (I/5) and Imst (II/5); Deroy remained
in Innsbruck with the rest of the division.

114: This fight is generally known as the Battle of the Pontlatz Bridge (Pontlatzer Brücke).

115: Two newly formed companies of the 7th Light arrived on the 9th from that battalion's depot in Munich
(departed Munich on 5 August). The other two companies were still at Lueg Pass, where they had been
deposited as garrison on 24 July.

116: Arco's corps had been called forward from Hall and arrived at Matrei on the 6th and Sterzing on the 7th after
a tiring march (his guns were left at Hall with Oberndorff). His troops returned to hold the Brenner Pass on
the 8th with Rouyer's men (although Arco himself remained with Lefebvre who valued the colonel's counsel) and retired to Matrei on the 10th. Rouyer joined Lefebvre's march column as the Bavarians fell back on
the capital and Arco alone covered the retreat.

117: Quoted in Leyh, p. 167.

118: Some elements of the 1st Division did take part in the battle: 1st Light and II/2 relieved 5th Light and I/5 in
their positions north of the Inn and contributed to the successful repulse of the Tyrolian attempts to advance
from Zirl. The order to withdraw came as a surprise to the officers and men of the division, who expected to
resume the struggle on the 14th (Uebe, p. 74). Casualties are taken from Leyh, p. 167.

119: The logistical difficulties of mountain warfare made it almost impossible to concentrate a large force in a
particular valley or locale for more than a few days. With a low population density and thin agricultural
base, the region could not support troops who 'lived off the land' (even in the best of times, the Tyrolians
themselves had to import much of their own sustenance). Nor could an army rely on large provisions trains;
the poor roads, high passes, innumerable bridges and narrow valleys impeded the progress of ponderous
wagon convoys and made them extremely vulnerable to attack from the energetic partisans. Moreover, the
Innsbruck area had been crossed and recrossed by the combatants several times and its slim resources had
already been taxed beyond endurance.

120: Although the brave colonel had been killed on the 13th, it is convenient to use his name in refering to the
men he had commanded. After Arco's death, his corps and the Jäger continued on to Schwaz under GB
Montmarie, clearing several Tyrolian ambushes en route. Leaving Hauptmann Bauer with three light companies, three line companies, 60 mounted Jäger and a 3-pounder at Schwaz, Montmarie marched on to
Rattenberg, but returned to Schwaz the next day (14 August). Völderndorff, pp. 314-16.

121: See the Marshal's report on the retreat in Völderndorff, pp. 326-327.

122: The provisional companies of the 1st, 3rd and 5th Light were dissolved and the men distributed among the
consituent companies of their respective battalions; the same occurred with the detachments of the 1st
Dragoons and 1st Chevauxlegers from Lerchenberg's *ad hoc* squadron. The 1st Reserve and Vögler's company of the 2nd Reserve were reduced to supply replacements to their parent regiments but were not disbanded and retained their separate identities. Bezzel, 'Grenz', pp. 145-8.

123: Note that the two companies of the 14th Infantry and the gun left behind at Melleck when Deroy entered the
Tyrol rejoined their division on the 17th. They had been guarding the corps' communications at Lofer since
the end of July.

124: Lefebvre's route of march took him via St. Johann (18th) and Unken (19th) to Salzburg. The Bavarian 4th
Chevauxlegers remained with Rouyer's Division.

125: Quoted in Junkelmann, p. 272.

126: Napoleon himself vacillated between moderation and frighteningly draconian measures ('demand 150
hostages and plunder and burn at least six large villages as well as the homes of the leaders so as to make
clear that the entire region will go down in blood and iron if all firearms, a minimum of 18,000, are not
delivered up' - 30 July). Junkelmann, pp. 272-5; Köfler, *Bergisel,* p. 40.

127: In a 2 September letter to Max, the Marshal tried to recall his harsh words of 16 August, praising the performance of the Bavarians in 'a retreat of which history would speak' and attempting to argue that the events of
early August were 'not a defeat but a retrograde movement.'' Junkelmann, pp. 271-3; Völderndorff, pp. 328-
31.

128: As the Second Offensive got underway, Arco and Oberndorff marched south into the Tyrol and only a few
scattered detachments were left to defend the territory of Altbayern. When the offensive opened, however, a
number of replacement detachments en route to the Tyrol were halted and ordered to protect the traditional
borders of the kingdom. On 10 August, the defensive situation thus had 2nd Reserve Battalion at Murnau
(two companies only, one other was with Arco and the other was the 1st Division's staff company) with

about 206 replacements for the 1st Infantry, 7th Reserve (720 men) and 155 replacements for the 5th Infantry in and around Kreuth. Three days later, these troops were disposed to slightly better positions: 2nd Reserve in Benediktbeuren, 1st Infantry replacements at Habach, 7th Reserve pulled back to Tegernsee with the 5th Infantry replacements. The men from the 5th Infantry moved to Tölz and Lenggries on the 15th.

129: Siebein and Oberndorff assumed their positions on 21 August. Siebein: six companies of *Ysenburg*, a squadron and a battery at Benediktbeuren (relieved 2nd Reserve); two companies of the same regiment at Tölz and Lenggries (relieved 5th Infantry replacements); remains of 10th Infantry (about one weak battalion) at Miesbach. The 5th Infantry replacements joined their regiment at Kufstein on the 22nd. Oberndorff: 2nd Reserve moved from Bendiktbeuren to Tegernsee (relieved 7th Reserve); 7th Reserve moved back to Wolfratshausen; two companies of Jäger and the squadron of mounted Jäger at Murnau and Kohlgrub; one Jäger company at Weilheim, five companies of Jäger and Oberndorff's five guns at Habach with the 1st Infantry replacements. The 1st Reserve was also slated to join Oberndorff's corps.

130: Quoted in Bezzel, 'Grenz', p. 148.

131: II/5, I/14 and 5th Light in Rosenheim; I/5 about 10 kilometres south of the city in the Inn valley; II/14 at Traunstein; one squadron at Aibling; the other squadron probably also at Rosenheim. The 5th Reserve garrisoned Kufstein with three companies. The two 'new' companies of the 7th Light left on the 23rd for Salzburg where they were amalgamated with the two 'old' companies (previously garrison at Lueg) to bring the battalion up to strength.

132: The 1st Division's positions in late August were: I/2 in Berchtesgaden; II/2 in Reichenhall; 8th Infantry and 1st Chevauxlegers around Pass Lueg from Werfen to Hallein; 1st and 4th Infantry, 7th Light, 1st Dragoons, Rouyer's Division, probably 3rd Light (with the companies of the 2nd and 4th Light), 8th Reserve (forming) in Salzburg and vicinity; 4th Chevauxlegers at Neumarkt an der Wallersee.

133: The Landes-Defensionsbataillon remained in Kempten with Picard during Beaumont's expedition through the Tyrol to the Vorarlberg. Bezzel, 'Grenz', pp. 109-12.

134: Only the 97 men of the 11th Infantry remained in the Vorarlberg region. The depot troops of the other units all marched to their respective regiments/battalions or depots: 9th (254), 13th (187), 14th (167), 3rd Light (23), 6th Light (44), 7th Light (46).

135: General Beaumont was ordered to Munich on 28 August to assume responsibilities for Upper Bavaria; his place as commander of all Allied troops from Feldkirch to the Lech was taken by GD Joseph Lagrange.

136: The 1st Reserve occupied Habach and incorporated the regiment's replacements that had been in the area since 10 August. Vögler's Company joined the 2nd Reserve at Tegernsee, bringing the battalion to three companies. II/Jägers held a line from Steingaden to Murnau and I/Jägers with the mounted Jäger squadron moved back to a reserve position at Weilheim.

137: Beaumont's force included the 3rd (Diessen and Weilheim) and 4th (Ebersberg) Provisional Dragoon Regiments, a detachment of the 14th Ligne (Weilheim), a combined battalion at Holzkirchen, two French companies (17th and 26th Regiments), a Bavarian light company, von Xylander's company and two French horse guns. The Bavarian light company was probably the provisional company of the 2nd Light which left the 1st Division with the 4th Light's provisional company on 3 September.

138: Bezzel, 'Grenz', pp. 148-9, Völderndorff, pp. 347-8.

139: By 21 September, some slight changes had taken place in the positions occupied by the Bavarians: I/2 at Berchtesgaden, II/2 at Lofer and Strub, I/1 at Unken, II/1 at Reichenhall; GM Stengel had been reinforced by II/4.

140: Total Bavarian casualties in the area around Lofer were about 360. Leyh, pp. 168-9; Völderndorff, pp. 335-44.

141: For the engagement at Pass Lueg, see Köfler, *Lueg*, pp. 19-25; Leyh, p. 169; Völderndorf, pp. 343-8. Even Völderndorff comments (p. 348) that 'nothing had forced' Stengel to pull back; see also Uebe (p. 76).

142: 1st Division positions at the end of September and early October: 1st Light, 1st and 2nd Infantry, a squadron of 1st Dragoons, one battery at Reichenhall under Rechberg; II/4 and a squadron of 1st Chevauxlegers around Grödig; Stengel commanded I/4, a battery and the other three squadrons of 1st Chevauxlegers south of Salzburg; on the opposite bank of the Salzach from Stengel were I/8, I/14, a squadron of *Bubenhofen*, and two guns; the remaining troops were in Salzburg itself.

143: In addition to 14th Infantry, Montmarie's column consisted of a French company, Major Theobald's two companies of 3rd Light, II/8, two squadrons of *Thurn und Taxiz* and one squadron of *Bubenhofen*. Völderndorff, pp. 349-50.

144: Junkelmann, p. 273. Döderlein, on the other hand, defends Stengel, portraying him as wronged by Lefebvre and Napoleon.

145: Napoleon's 8 October letter included the following: 'I am dissatisfied with the Bavarian troops. Instead of fighting, they carp and intrigue against their chief...In the army there are no Princes. It may be that the Crown Prince has cause to complain about the Duke [of Danzig], but that has nothing to do with soldier's honour; rather he should march against the enemy when they insult the Bavarian flag and are on the verge of attacking it at the gates of Salzburg. I will bring order to your army...I have taken it upon myself to write to you because I value your talent and your courage. Speak with your comrades and see to it they do not dishonour themselves.' See Junkelmann and Uebe for descriptions of the correspondence among the various parties in this tangled dispute. Quotes are from Junkelmann, pp. 273-4.

146: Junkelmann, p. 274. See Uebe (pp. 47, 74-5) for Bavarian complaints against Lefebvre. Although Pierre Germain, Drouet's recent biographer, argues that the general was often hesitant in his later years, there is little evidence of indecision in 1809 (Pierre Germain, *J.-B. Drouët d'Erlon, Maréchal de France*, Paris: Lanore, 1985, pp. 325-6). Thanks to his good relationship with King Max, Drouet would find succor in Bavaria during fifteen years of exile after the Waterloo disaster. Lefebvre's admiring biographer, Joseph Wirth, simply ignores this entire episode (see his *Le Maréchal Lefebvre Duc de Dantzig*, Paris: Perrin, 1904).

147: Leyh, p. 170.

148: With a final peace treaty signed, there was no further need for Wrede to guard the Danube opposite Bohemia; his division (with the exception of a detachment under Minucci at Linz) was thus called south and arrived in Traunstein on the 15th. Here he was reunited with the 7th Infantry, which had arrived in Traunstein to reinforce Deroy on 29 September. Minucci's command consisted of 3rd Infantry, 4th Light, 3rd Chevauxlegers, a battery and the eight 12-pounders of Dietrich's and Dobl's batteries (total of fourteen guns); it remained around Linz until 30 October when it too was brought south to the Inn valley. The 4th Light had been reconstructed from its depot, returned prisoners and new recruits in late September and early October at Steyr (the depot sent 415 men to Steyr from Munich on 23 September). Zoller's force consisted of 4th Infantry, a squadron of 1st Chevauxlegers and a half-battery.

149: Rechberg attacked with 1st Light and elements of 1st, 2nd and I/8 Infantry. II/8 was at Berchtesgaden with a company of the 1st Regiment.

150: Heilmann, vol. 88, p. 276; Leyh, p. 170.

151: Völderndorff, p. 383.

152: The fortress had been encircled for the third time on 25 September. The only attempt to storm any part of the fortress complex was undertaken on the night of 10/11 October against the bridgehead redoubt across the Inn from the castle proper. The three efforts by about 500 Tyrolians cost them heavily but gained nothing. The rebels withdrew quickly on Deroy's approach. Schlagintweit, p. 37.

153: Zoller took the 4th Infantry and the 1st Dragoons, while Rechberg marched with the 1st and 2nd Infantry. The location and actions of the 7th Light in the opening stages of the Third Offensive are not clear: the battalion may have remained in Salzburg or accompanied the 1st Division into the Tyrol.

154: Hirn, p. 741; Völderndorff, pp. 388-9.

155: Oberndorff marched on the pass with both Jäger battalions, 1st and 2nd Reserve, the mounted Jäger squadron and six guns (he had received two 6-pounders from Munich on the 15th). The 800 French infantry had departed for Passau on the 19th, and three platoons of the 2nd Dragoons, attached to Oberndorff since the 16th, left to rejoin their regiment in the Tyrol on the 23rd. Oberst Oberndorff, however, apparently had a somewhat stormy relationship with Drouet (where Arco had been one of Lefebvre's favorites), and the French general at least once threatened to relieve the Bavarian (Germain, p. 107).

156: See Bezzel, 'Grenz', pp. 150-1, 179.

157: The insurgent leader, Martin Firler, was accused by his fellows of suffering the ill effects of too much drink imbibed the previous night. He and his men thus slept through the early morning and attacked too late in the day and with too little energy to have any appreciable impact on the struggle. Hirn, p. 752.

158: Losses for the day were 15 Bavarians dead and 87 wounded, approximately 50 Tyrolians captured (Leyh claims 'several hundred'); the number of dead and wounded rebels has never been clearly established. In a 1 November letter, Drouet expressed his satisfaction with the Bavarian troops, especially the artillery (Germain, pp. 108-9). Hirn, p. 753; Köfler, *Bergisel*, p. 45; Leyh, p. 172; Völderndorff, pp. 391-3.

159: The Crown Prince handed over command of his division to GM Raglovich on the 2nd.

160: The lack of fourage had also become a problem and many of the Corps' horses were sent back to Bavaria on the 12th: most of 2nd Division's artillery to Schongau, two squadrons of *König* to Weilheim, 1st Dragoons to Benediktbeuren, 2nd Dragoons to Rosenheim. Völderndorff, pp. 399-400, 404.

161: Generally, the 1st Division was deployed as follows: 1st Light at Prutz; 1st Infantry at Landeck; 2nd Infantry at Imst; 8th Infantry in the Pitze valley; 4th Infantry in the Oetz valley and Telfs; 3rd Light (returned to full strength by the arrival of Oberstlieutenant Bernclau and two new companies on 15 November) in Innsbruck; 1st Chevauxlegers scattered throughout the division's positions; 1st Dragoons at Benediktbeuren; three light guns at Landeck, three at Silz, a light battery at Imst; two foot batteries were still in Salzburg and the artillery park was at Innsbruck. The 3rd and 13th Reserve Battalions had been added to Oberndorff's corps on the 8th and 9th of November, while the 1st Reserve had provided over 400 replacements to its regiment and was preparing to return to Munich (departed 22 November). Under Raglovich's command from 13 November, Oberndorff had 3rd Reserve at Seefeld, the Jäger Regiment stretched from Mittenwald to Ehrwald to Reutte, 13th Reserve at Ehrwald, 2nd Reserve at Nassereith and the mounted Jäger at Ehrwald. Bezzel, 'Grenz', pp. 152-3; Völderndorff, pp. 404-5.

162: The attack was made by five regular companies and an adhoc company of combined Schützen from the 1st, 2nd and 4th Regiments under Major Seiboltsdorf; he was supported by Raglovich himself with three other companies and two guns. Völderndorff, pp. 409-10.

163: Metzen had I/5, two companies of II/5, two companies of 14th Infantry and one gun. Völderndorff, pp. 435-436.

164: In late November and early December, Wreden brought to the Vorarlberg: two companies of 11th Infantry, 14th Reserve, the rebuilt 2nd Light (only about 260 strong), two companies of 6th Reserve and a squadron of 3rd Chevauxlegers. The two companies of the 11th Infantry were united with their fellows to form a new 1st Battalion for the regiment. Dispositions in early December: 2nd Light in Lindau and Bregenz, 7th and 14th Reserve around Feldkirch, I/11 and the squadron around Bludenz, the two companies of 6th Reserve at Immenstadt. Bezzel, 'Grenz', pp. 113-116.

CHAPTER 8:

A Reputation for Bravery

In addition to large states like Bavaria with legitimate aspirations to royal status, Napoleon's German allies included a host of tiny 'Zwergstaaten' or dwarf states. Although not so numerous as the congeries of duchies, principalities, baronies and free cities that existed under the Holy Roman Empire, there were close to thirty German states with a population of less than 300,000 within the structure of the Rheinbund. Elevated in stature by Napoleon (from baron to prince, for example), the rulers of these minute countries now owed their allegiance and existence to the French Emperor. They also owed him troops. In its never-ending search for soldiers, the eye of the Imperial eagle encompassed even the smallest of the German princedoms within its stern regard. To receive the benefits of membership in the confederation, the Prince of Leyen was thus required to supply a contingent of 29 men for the common defence; the other participants in the alliance were similarly assessed contingents based upon their populations and territories. Too small in most cases to constitute viable independent units, these contingents were amalgamated into combined battalions and regiments not unlike the 'regional regiments' (Kreisregimenter) of the Holy Roman Empire. Some saw action in the 1807 campaign and by mid-1808 the gnawing Spanish war had consumed pieces from most of the contingents. Far from home and fighting a brutal war against an implacable enemy, the men rapidly lost any positive feelings they might have harboured for France and its Emperor, but in Central Europe in 1809 the Germans could still respond to Napoleon with enthusiasm. Called to take the field against an enemy they understood, an old oppressor, the officers and men of Napoleon's small allies went to war against Austria with visions of the glory to be won under the Battle Kaiser's mighty gaze.

From the bewildering myriad of miniature monarchies in the Confederation, Napoleon established seven 'Regiments of the Confederation of the Rhine' to serve with his Army of Germany:[1]

1st Rheinbund	Nassau (2nd Nassau Infantry)
2nd Rheinbund	Nassau (1st Nassau Infantry)
3rd Rheinbund	Würzburg
4th Rheinbund	Saxon Duchies
5th Rheinbund	Anhalt and Lippe
6th Rheinbund	Reuss, Schwarzburg and Waldeck
7th Rheinbund	Mecklenburg-Schwerin

The exigencies of the political-military situation in 1809 demanded the rapid mobilization of these regiments, but the smaller Rheinbund monarchies, having already contributed relatively large proportions of their militaries to the Iberian cauldron, experienced considerable difficulty in raising their new contingents. Officers and NCOs were in especially short supply and many of the leadership positions in the 5th and 6th Regiments were filled by expatriate soldiers from Prussia, Austria and the dissolved states of Hannover and Hesse-Kassel (for example, some $2/3$ of Reuss's officers were foreigners). Foreigners were also prevalent in the ranks, as were large numbers of green troops, recruited or conscripted in early 1809 as the tiny states struggled to meet their military commitments.[2] Nor were personnel problems the only impediment to the organization of these new regiments. Variations in drill, regulations and weaponry complicated co-operation and reduced efficiency. Napoleon thus stressed the introduction of French rank insignia and drill to improve the effectiveness of the Rheinbund units and facilitate their incorporation into the larger structure of his multi-national army.[3]

Plans for integrating the small Rheinbund contingents into the Army of Germany evolved rapidly as war approached. The French initially envisaged combining the first six regiments into a single reserve division (often called the 'Division Princière') as part of a larger 'corps d'armée de la Confédération du Rhin'. This corps was to consist of three German divisions with a total of approximately 30,000 men. While the Badeners formed the 1st Division and the troops of Hesse and Berg the 2nd, the six combined Rheinbund Regiments were to constitute the 3rd; a reserve brigade was to be established from the Mecklenburg contingents.[4] However, as many of the regiments, including the 1st (Nassau) and 3rd (Würzburg) Rheinbund Regiments, had already deployed for Spain,[5] the corps could not be formed and, in February it was decided to incorporate the troops of the small German states into Marshal Massena's 'Corps d'observation de l'armée du Rhin'. Just as the Baden and Hessian contingents were allotted to Massena's 1st (Legrand) and 2nd (Carra Saint-Cyr) Divisions respectively, the 4th Regiment of the Confederation (Saxon Duchies) was assigned to the 3rd Division (Molitor) and the 2nd, 5th and 6th Regiments were to reinforce the 4th Division (Boudet).[6] As the pace of events increased, however, expediency became the prime consideration and this plan too was slowly abandoned. On 4 March, Napoleon, aiming to speed the concentration of the army, ordered the smaller Rheinbund contingents to assemble at Würzburg by the 20th. Although still destined for Massena, the regiments were temporarily placed under the orders of Marshal Davout who was to 'press their arrival and the organization of the entire corps'.[7] Direct command of the four German regiments, still referred to as the 3rd Confederation of the Rhine Division, was entrusted to Général de Division Baron Marie-François Rouyer on 11 March. Riding into Würzburg some two weeks later, the general learned he had been formally attached to Davout's III Corps with the provision that his troops might be recalled by Army Headquarters at any time 'to furnish fortress garrisons and to escort prisoners'.[8]

MARCH/APRIL - SPECTATORS TO BATTLE

The troops of the smaller German states began to gather in the Würzburg area in late March, the contingents of the five Saxon Duchies being the first to arrive. Leaving their garrisons in Thüringen between the 13th and 16th of March, the soldiers of Sachsen-Weimar, Sachsen-Gotha, Sachsen-Meiningen, Sachsen-Koburg and Sachsen-Hildburghausen reached Würzburg on the 21st to be organized into the 4th Rheinbund Regiment.[9] The largest of the Rheinbund regiments, the 4th had participated in the 1807 campaign as a regimental formation ('Régiment des Duchés de Saxe') and its commander, Oberst von Egloffstein of Sachsen-Weimar, enjoyed the confidence of the Saxon Dukes and the French.[10] Like many other military organizations, however, it suffered from a surfeit of staff officers, having twice as many colonels (two) and majors (six) as were authorized. The regiment's 2,368 men were organized into three battalions, two line and one light, each comprising six companies in accordance with the standard French pattern (see Table 8-2).[11] With three different basic uniforms, these eighteen companies presented an interesting spectacle when formed for review. The men of Gotha and Meiningen wore dark-blue coats with red facings, white breeches and black bicorne hats. Whereas the Gotha soldiers had white leather equipment and coats of a French cut, however, the two companies from Meiningen were distinguished by their Prussian-style coats and black leather belting. Each of the line battalions also included a voltigeur company from Koburg dressed in dark-green coats with yellow collars and cuffs, red turnbacks, white belting and black shakos.[12] The members of the light battalion (Weimar and Hildburghausen), in consonance with long-standing light infantry tradition, were also issued dark-green coats with yellow collar patches and turnbacks. The uniform was completed by grey breeches, buff leather work and a large black bicorne hat.[13] These uniforms thus presented visible manifestations of the epoch and the prevailing military influences in central Germany in 1809. In the first case, the transition from the older, 18th-century modes of conflict to the newer, Revolutionary and Napoleonic style of warfare was symbolized by the mixture of old bicorne and modern shako.[14] In the second instance, the intermingling of French and Prussian uniform details indicated the shift in influence in central Germany as the trappings of defeated Prussia were gradually replaced by those of victorious, dominant France.

The men of the 4th Rheinbund thus shared a common cultural, political and military heritage. Moreover, thanks to their participation, albeit brief, in the 1807 war, most of the officers and many of the men had had recent successful combat experience under Oberst von Egloffstein. In contrast, the 5th and 6th Regiments were patchwork creations, combining contingents from diverse backgrounds which had not previously served together. The 5th Regiment, for example, was composed of troops from two distinctly different regions of Germany: the Anhalt Duchies of Thüringen and the Lippe Principalities of the North German Plain. The 6th Regiment was even more colourful, combining pairs of companies from Waldeck, the Reuss possessions and the Schwarzburg Principalities. Although these states had mobilized units for the 1807 campaign, their battalions had marched as separate entities and arrived too late to engage in combat. The component contingents of the 5th and 6th Rheinbund therefore had almost no field experience and had not been assembled as regiments prior to 1809.[15] As a result, the battalion and regimental officers found themselves commanding multi-national formations where many of their subordinates were unfamiliar and where they lacked the authority to impose discipline on the soldiers of the other states. The leadership of these two new regiments consequently had the unenviable task of organizing and training their calico units while they were marching to war.

The problems of organizing the 5th Regiment were exacerbated by delays in collecting all of its constituent companies around Würzburg. Where the entire 4th Rheinbund only missed its assembly date by one day, the first elements of the 5th did not appear until early April, more than two weeks behind schedule. To make matters worse, the contingents arrived in dribs and drabs. The first three companies of the Lippe Battalion (two from Lippe-Detmold, one from Schaumburg-Lippe), for example, did not march in until 8 April and the battalion would not be complete until early June. Destined to be the 2nd Battalion of the 5th Rheinbund, the men of Lippe were under the nominal command of Oberstlieutenant Friedrich von Campe (Lippe-Detmold), but that rather frail individual (60 years old) remained in Detmold and the battalion's quotidian affairs were managed by an able Detmold Hauptmann named Böger who simultaneously commanded the 1st Company. The soldiers of Böger's Battalion, regardless of origin, all wore the same handsome uniform of white, French-style coat trimmed in dark-green, white breeches and leather belting, black gaiters and shako.[16]

The three Duchies of Anhalt-Dessau, Anhalt-Bernburg and Anhalt-Köthen provided the regiment's 1st Battalion (six companies). The Anhalters were uniformed with tasteful simplicity and practicality: dark-green tunics with rose-coloured distinctions, grey breeches, black shakos. Departing Dessau on 23 March, an initial detachment of three companies (421 men) arrived in Würzburg on 6 April, well after the prescribed concentration date of 20 March. During the ensuing week of drills and reviews, they were combined with the three Lippe companies to form the basis of the 5th Rheinbund. Like the Lippe Battalion, however, I/5 could not immediately complete its organization as the other half of the Anhalt contingent (420 men) was across the Rhine in France with the designated regimental commander, Oberst Friedrich von Chambaud of Anhalt-Dessau. Having left Anhalt for Boulogne (and presumably Spain) on 3 February, Chambaud and his men reached Metz on 5 March and occupied themselves with garrison duties in that fortress until new orders arrived directing them to Strasbourg. Relieved not to be headed for the Spanish border, the Anhalters performed rear area escort and guard duties in Strasbourg from 13 March to 8 April, when they finally marched to unite with their comrades behind the battlefront in Bavaria (25 April).[17] Each battalion of the 5th Regiment thus counted only three companies (totalling about 840 men) when Rouyer put them on the road for the Danube on 13 April.

Simultaneous with the formation of the 5th Rheinbund, the 6th Regiment's constituent elements were also collecting in and around Würzburg. The contingent from the Princely Houses of Reuss departed Schleiz on 15 March with a strength of 254 men in two companies; additionally, each company was permitted four women to perform domestic chores on campaign. The soldiers of Reuss wore a white, single-breasted tunic with medium-blue facings, black shako and blue Hungarian breeches with yellow cord decorations. The garb of their female companions is not recorded. Arriving in the city on the 28th, the Reuss companies joined with the Waldeck contingent (two companies, 250 men), to form the 2nd Battalion of 6th Rheinbund on 1 April. The Waldeck companies had left their principality on the 19th and reached Würzburg the same day as their comrades from Reuss. Like the Reuss troops, the Waldeckers wore a simple white coat, but with dark-blue distinctions; for the rest of their uniform, they wore grey breeches and a black French shako. Together with its two companies, Waldeck also supplied the regimental commander, Grossmajor (lieutenant-colonel) von Heeringen; it was therefore only equitable that Reuss provide the commander of II/6, Hauptmann von Watzdorf.[18]

The 1st Battalion of the 6th Rheinbund was formed from the contingents of Schwarzburg-Rudolstadt and Schwarzburg-Sondershausen (approximately 460 men). Each principality was required to send two companies to Rouyer, but the contingents were not fully formed until late March and did not reach Würzburg until 8 April. Even then, the Rudolstadt companies were understrength, totalling only about 200 soldiers. The troops of both contingents wore similar uniforms: a dark-green Prussian-style coat with red collar and turnbacks, grey breeches, and a black shako; only in their tunic cuffs and the crests on the shako were the uniforms different.[19] Known as the Schwarzburg battalion (I/6), these four companies were commanded by Major Schumann of Sondershausen.[20] When Rouyer's Division was summoned to the Danube on the 13th, the Reuss, Waldeck and Schwarzburg troops were ready, but with a total of only eight companies, the entire 6th Rheinbund amounted to a mere 969 men, noticeably weaker than either the 4th or 5th Regiments.[21]

One other unit was temporarily associated with the Division Princière. Like the other Rheinbund states, the Grand Duchy of Würzburg was required to provide a federal contingent in time of war. Assessed a force of 2,000 men, Würzburg had already provided an infantry regiment (3rd Rheinbund) and a chevauxlegers squadron for the conflict in Spain, but Napoleon demanded more and received a 'division' (two companies) of sappers for the campaign against Austria. Formed from the infantry depot and a small artillery company, the sappers departed their home city on 8 April to join the army's 'parc du génie' at Donauwörth.[22] Later combined with a similar company from the five Saxon Duchies, they supported the army's manifold engineering labours throughout the campaign, helping to bridge the Inn at Burghausen in late April and contributing to the extensive fortifications constructed on Lobau Island from May to July.[23]

As the German contingents were gradually collecting around Würzburg, GD Rouyer was en route to the same goal from Boulogne to assume his new responsibilities. From the Vosges mountains of eastern France, Rouyer was forty-four in 1809 and spoke German, having served the Habsburgs as a junior officer prior to the French Revolution; his previous experience with Napoleon's German-speaking allies included command of the Hessians at Graudenz in 1807 and the Swiss in Spain. Arriving in Würzburg on 27 March, he took command and immediately conducted 'the usual musters' to inspect his men and prepare them for battle.[24] Ordered to Donauwörth late on the 13th, Rouyer set his men on the road to the Danube that very day. Moving south independently, the three regiments passed through Uffenheim, Ansbach and Nördlingen without incident to reach their destination early on the 18th after a tiring night march. Donauwörth was chock-a-block with of soldiers, horses and vehicles. Napoleon had established his headquarters here the previous day and the air was alive with earnest activity, punctuated by the sudden arrival and departure of harried couriers. While most of the men sought quarters and food in the bustling, troop-choked streets, the Weimar Light Battalion was sent on to occupy the Lech River bridgehead at Rain. Here they were inspected by the Emperor himself, who closely questioned both officers and men and personally examined the contents of several soldiers' cartouche boxes.[25]

In addition to his Emperor, Rouyer found his other regiment in Donauwörth. The Nassau Regiment (2nd Rheinbund) had reached the town on the 17th, having departed Wiesbaden on the 8th. It was perhaps an even more unusual creation than the other regiments of Rouyer's Division. Most of the small Rheinbund states of western Germany were grouped into a 'college of princes' headed by the Duke Friedrich August of Nassau.[26] As with all other adherents to the Rheinbund, the college's member states were required to provide contingents of troops in case of war; the states within the college, however, had an option: they could either supply soldiers to be completely integrated into a combined force under Nassau command or they could pay a subsidy to Friedrich August and Nassau would recruit and equip the requisite number of men from its own population.[27] Only three member states, Isenburg, Hohenzollern-Hechingen and Hohenzollern-Sigmaringen, elected to send troops in 1809, five others paid subsidies into Nassau's coffers according to painfully negotiated bilateral treaties.[28] The regiment that joined Rouyer in Donauwörth was thus called the 1st Nassau Infantry (2nd Rheinbund), but actually included a substantial number of men from three other principalities.[29]

Table 8-1: The 2nd Rheinbund Regiment (1st Nassau Infantry)

States Paying Subsidies to Nassau in Place of Supplying a Contingent of Troops:

Duchy of Aremberg	379
Principalities of Salm-Salm & Salm-Kyburg	323
Principality of Liechtenstein	40
Principality of Hohengeroldseck (Prince von der Leyen)	29

States Whose Contingents were Integrated into the 2nd Rheinbund

Principality of Isenburg-Birstein	350
Principality of Hohenzollern-Sigmaringen	193
Principality of Hohenzollern-Hechingen	97

Contingent sizes per treaty

Based on the 1st and 4th Battalions of the old Nassau brigade, the 1st Nassau Infantry was called into existence on 16 March in Wiesbaden. Commanded by

Oberst von Pöllnitz, the regiment was organized after the French pattern, consisting of two battalions, each comprising a grenadier company, a light company and four fusilier companies. The Nassau recruits were of high quality, but there were not enough of them and their leaders, a solid group of officers and NCOs, had almost no time to train and organize the regiment before it set out to join the Emperor's army. Although bolstered by the Isenburg contingent (two companies) on 18 March, the Hohenzollern troops had not yet appeared and the 2nd Rheinbund was thus understrength when it crossed the borders of its homeland and headed south-east on 8 April. All the soldiers of the regiment, regardless of origin, wore the same uniform: green coat with black collar and shoulder straps, grey breeches, buff leather belting and black shako. In addition to red epaulets, the grenadiers were supposed to be distinguished by their headgear, a leather helmet with a fur caterpillar crest similar to that worn by the Württemberg Army. Shortages of money, *matériel* and time precluded such luxuries, however, and only the the 1st Grenadier Company (1st Battalion) wore this distinctive, if somewhat burdensome, helmet in 1809.[30]

The Nassauers were finally united with their division at Donauwörth on 18 April, but they and the rest of Rouyer's men were soon on the move again. Given the mission of guarding the crossings over the Danube, the division left the incomplete 5th Regiment at Donauwörth on the 19th and slogged east through cold, drenching rain to Ingolstadt, depositing detachments at Rain (I/6), Neuburg (Nassau) and Gerolfing (II/6). Despite bottomless mud, exhausting marches, inadequate provisions and ceaseless downpours, the soldiers were thrilled and awed by the dull sound of cannon that rolled through the fog and rain from the struggles at Arnhofen and Abensberg.[31] Only a few short, damp miles from the battlefields, the crux of the early campaign, the division's camps were filled with anxious excitement as officers and men anticipated demonstrating their martial abilities under the eyes of the Emperor. Unfortunately, the division played no part in Napoleon's lightning victories south of Regensburg. Relegated to important but inglorious garrison duties along the swollen and sullen Danube, the multi-coloured battalions passed their days in the bland routine of fortress troops while the full might of the Army of Germany surged forward around them.

By the 24th, Rouyer's battalions had been stretched along the river from Ingolstadt (4th) through Neuburg (2nd), Gerolfing (II/6) and Rain (I/6) to Donauwörth (5th) to cover the army's line of communications. Now, as Napoleon advanced into Austria, the Rheinbund division was gradually shifted downstream toward Regensburg to guard the key bridge there. The Nassau Regiment thus departed Neuburg on 25 April to join Rouyer and the 4th Rheinbund at Ingolstadt, both regiments marching for Regensburg the following day. By this time the Austrians had been evicted from Bavaria and the French Army was pressing against the frontiers of the Habsburg monarchy, but the battlefields over which Rouyer's soldiers passed were strewn with the gruesome wrack of war: bloated corpses of man and beast, ruined villages, terrifying hospitals. A young Koburg lieutenant in Ingolstadt watched curiously from a bridge over the Danube as 'amputated arms and legs were given over to the river

Table 8-2: Composition of Rouyer's Regiments

2nd Rheinbund (1st Nassau)...........Nassau, Isenburg, Hohenzollern Princes
    1st Battalion: 1st Grenadier, 1st Voltigeur, Fusilier Companies 1-4
    2nd Battalion: 2nd Grenadier, 2nd Voltigeur, Fusilier Companies 1-4

4th Rheinbund.........Saxon Duchies
    1st Battalion : 1st Grenadier Company   ⎫
                Musketeer Companies 1-4   ⎬ Sachsen-Gotha
                1st Voltigeur Company..................Sachsen-Koburg
      2nd Battalion: 2nd Grenadier Company...............Sachsen-Gotha
                  Musketeer Companies 1&2...........Sachsen-Meiningen
                  Musketeer Companies 3&4..........Sachsen-Gotha
                  2nd Voltigeur Company.................Sachsen-Koburg
      3rd (Light) Battalion: Fusilier Companies 1-5........Sachsen-Weimar
                  6th Fusilier Company............Sachsen-Hildburghausen

5th Rheinbund.........Anhalt Duchies and Lippe Principalities
    1st Battalion: Companies 1-6 (men from all three Anhalt Duchies intermixed)
    2nd Battalion: 1st, 2nd, 4th and 6th Companies.....Lippe-Detmold
                3rd Company.................................Schaumburg-Lippe
                5th Company................................both principalities

6th Rheinbund.......Reuß, Waldeck and the Schwarzburg Principalities
    1st Battalion: 1st Company_ _ _ _ _ _ _ _ _2nd Sondershausen
                  2nd Company_ _ _ _ _ _ _ _3rd Sondershausen
                  3rd Company_ _ _ _ _ _ _ _2nd Rudolstadt
                  4th Company_ _ _ _ _ _ _ _3rd Rudolstadt
     2nd Battalion: 1st Company_ _ _ _ _ _ _ _2nd Reuß
                  2nd Company_ _ _ _ _ _ _ _3rd Reuß
                  3rd Company_ _ _ _ _ _ _ 2nd Waldeck
                  4th Company_ _ _ _ _ _ _ _3rd Waldeck

The 5th and 6th Regiments did not designate special grenadier or voltigeur companies.

Approximate Strengths (17 April)
2nd Rheinbund _ _ _ _ _ _ _c.1,550   [Hohenzollern contingent (181) joins 5 June]
4th Rheinbund _ _ _ _ _ _ _ _2,368
5th Rheinbund _ _ _ _ _ _ _ _c.840   [to 1,260 on 25 April; c. 1,360 by mid-June]
6th Rheinbund _ _ _ _ _ _ _ _ 969

from out of the windows of the hospitals along its banks'.[32] The ardour of many young Rheinbund recruits waned as they were exposed to these sights and desertion began to thin the ranks of the division on its move east. The 5th and 6th Regiments seem to have been particularly afflicted by this malady.[33] None the less, the entire division was finally assembled in the vicinity of Regensburg on the 29th when the 5th and 6th Regiments arrived from Donauwörth and Ingolstadt respectively.

It will be recalled that Rouyer had left the 5th Rheinbund behind in Donauwörth (19 April) to await the arrival of its commander and his three Anhalt companies from Strasbourg. On the 25th, Oberst Chambaud and the Strasbourg detachment reached Donauwörth where the regiment had also been reinforced by another company from Lippe-Detmold. Now ten companies strong, the 5th Rheinbund set out on the 27th to catch up with its division at Regensburg.[34]

One further German unit briefly crossed paths with Rouyer's Division in April. In addition to demanding an infantry regiment from the five Saxon Duchies, Napoleon required them to provide a company of sappers. Commanded by Hauptmann von Spiller, 138 Saxon sappers dutifully departed Gotha on 11 April to become part of the army's engineer park. Arriving in Ingolstadt on the 25th, they set out next day to join the long blue columns on the road to Vienna.

May-July - The Passau Garrison

The stay in Regensburg was brief. Having crossed the Salzach, Napoleon's drive on the Austrian capital was gaining momentum and the Archduke Charles was continuing his retreat into the heart of Bohemia with most of the Austrian army. To strike at the heart of his enemy, the Emperor characteristically decided to shift the entire weight of his effort to one point: the Danube valley. Davout was thus directed to cease his pursuit of Charles and move south to join the main army while Bernadotte's Saxon's were ordered to hurry behind the Duke of Auerstädt. The end of April therefore saw the French III Corps crossing the Danube at Regensburg and heading east; IX Corps was not far behind. Following the two Marshals' long columns as they sped toward Vienna were GD Dupas's weak French Division and Rouyer's Germans.[35] As the main army drove east by forced marches, these two divisions were brought forward to cover the line of communications along the Danube and to supplement the garrison of Passau. This city was crucial to Napoleon's strategic concept. Located on the Austro-Bavarian frontier at the confluence of the Danube, Inn and Ilz, Passau was not only the army's principal logistic centre, but also a bulwark against occasional Austrian incursions from Bohemia and a rallying point in the event of the army suffering a setback. From 1 to 3 May, Rouyer's Germans headed out of Regensburg and slogged through incessant rain to reach the town on the 4th and 5th of the month.[36]

Although their duty in Passau was demanding, the men passed the next three months in relative comfort. Napoleon was determined to make the city impervious to assault and had detailed GB Dominique Chambarliac to oversee the construction of a complex series of redoubts and other field fortifications. This massive effort required a large number of workers and Rouyer's men together with thousands of local inhabitants spent their days with shovels in hand, preparing the city to repel an attack that never came. Austrian Landwehr in the dark Bohemian hills periodically threatened the city, albeit impotently, and the resultant alarms kept the multi-national garrison alert, but there was never a serious danger to Passau and its vast stores. None the less, prudent precautions were instituted and each regiment kept half its men under arms from midnight till 4 a.m. in two 2-hour shifts. When not engaged in building redoubts or standing guard, the German units were occupied with drill. To promote uniformity within the army, the men were required to exercise twice daily according to the Westphalian translation of the French drill regulations. French commands remained unfamiliar, but the drill requirements were quickly learned and the German units were soon proficient. Construction work, midnight alerts and repetitive drill were arduous, but duty in Passau offered compensations. In addition to the supplementary pay the soldiers received for each day's labour, the troops' quarters were good and provisions were plentiful. Each man was issued two pounds of bread, a pound of meat, appropriate vegetables and a 'Bavarian measure' (quart) of beer per day, far better than the rations provided to many of the regiments engaged in the dreadful slaughter at Aspern-Essling. An envious IX Corps officer described a typical scene: 'Behind the newly-constructed fortifications, we recognized our close countrymen of Gotha, who had built themselves huts and were savouring the contents of a great tun which the nimble serving girl could hardly tap fast enough.'[37]

Pay was not regular for all the contingents, but the Germans were pleasantly surprised when the Emperor granted a special award of 100,000 francs to each French and Confederation regiment on 28 May. The Anhalters were the beneficiaries of further French largess. Having told this battalion that they 'would not regret fighting on the side of the French', Rouyer came to their aid with a loan of 2,800 francs when the contingent's pay fell into arrears; the conscientious Germans repaid the debt to Madame Rouyer some time later in Nancy.[38]

While it enjoyed the small pleasures of duty in the Passau garrison, the Lippe Battalion (II/5) was finally able to complete its organization. Joined by another Lippe-Detmold company on 8 June and later by a mixed detachment of 130 men, mostly from Schaumburg-Lippe, the battalion was formed into six similar companies. Four of these consisted of Detmold soldiers under Detmold officers and two were predominantly Schaumburg and thus commanded by Schaumburg captains. Unfortunately, the final Detmold company to arrive had got lost en route to the battalion and 61 of its 120 men deserted as it wandered around southern Germany from 13 April to 8 June. The other companies had also suffered losses from desertion and illness so that the battalion numbered only 564 effectives (rather than the required 840) when it reorganized.[39]

Their stay in and around Passau also brought the Germans several opportunities to engage the enemy. The most significant of several small encounters was an engagement fought near Zwiesel on 19 June. Austrian Landwehr from Bohemia had been conducting raids into Bavarian border towns since mid-May and Dupas ordered a detachment to this village on 8 June to monitor Austrian activity and deter further marauding. Commanded by Hauptmann Schierbrandt of the Weimar Light Battalion, this tiny force of about 120 Weimar light infantry (Schierbrandt's Company), 102 Bavarians (depot troops from the 6th and 9th Infantry out of the Oberhaus garrison battalion) and 21 French hussars reached Zwiesel on the 9th and had its first contact with the foe on 15 June. Reports from this little skirmish convinced Schierbrandt the Austrians were preparing to launch a foray into Bavaria and he ordered the roads around Zwiesel to be carefully outposted. His caution paid off. In the foggy pre-dawn hours of 19 June three Austrian columns totaling 620 men approached Zwiesel with the intention of surprising and annihilating Schierbrandt's detachment. The concealed Weimar and Bavarian pickets discovered the main Austrian column, however, and opened fire, surprising the Landwehr and forcing them to halt. This bold action by the outnumbered vedettes gave Schierbrandt time to rush to their assistance. With a force of approximately 60 men, the courageous Hauptmann advanced against some 320 Austrian Landwehr and a lively firefight ensued. At about this time, Leutnant Einsiedel with 40 other Weimar soldiers appeared on the scene. Acting on his own initiative, the lieutenant had marched toward the sound of the skirmish and now approached the Austrian left in the mist-shrouded moments just before sunrise. The Austrian commander, seeing the grey overcoats of the Weimar men, mistook them for one of his other two columns and hailed Leutnant Einsiedel, telling him he was not following instructions and was attacking too early. The quick-witted lieutenant replied 'No, we are not too early', and promptly took the Austrian leader and his small escort prisoner. Thrown into confusion by the loss of their commander and panicked by the sudden appearance of an enemy force on their flank, the Landwehrmen fled back to Bohemia pursued by the happy Schierbrandt.

The 100 Landwehr of the Austrian left column also retreated after losing their captain and several fellows in a brief exchange of fire with the riflemen of a Weimar outpost. The middle Austrian column (200 men) withdrew without firing a shot. At the cost of two wounded, the men of Sachsen-Weimar inflicted eighteen casualties on their prospective attackers and captured an additional fourteen of the enemy, including the Austrian commander. It was a small but bright success and when he reviewed the 4th Regiment in early July, Marshal Lefebvre promised to request the cross of the Legion of Honour for Schierbrandt in recognition of his victory; unfortunately, this capable officer would meet his death before he could receive his just award. This engagement at Zwiesel is minute in comparison to the titanic struggles waged around Regensburg and Vienna during this campaign, but it illustrates the courage, coolness and tactical ability of these German troops, particularly the 4th Rheinbund. They would need all their competence and bravery in the coming advance into the Tyrol.[40]

The Austrians persisted in probing toward Passau to unsettle its garrison, but there were no further serious battles. Hauptmann Schierbrandt, reinforced by an Anhalt company (23 June), remained in Zwiesel until 4 July when increasing Austrian activity decided the garrison commander, GD François Bourcier, to pull the German detachment closer to Passau. Indeed, there were repeated alarms during the first days of July. A reconnaissance by three companies of the 4th Rheinbund had revealed a force of approximately 5,000 Austrians near Wegscheid, only 25 kilometres east of Passau on the 1st of the month and the enemy soon launched a number of weak probes toward the fortified city, attacking the Hildburghausen company north of the Danube on the 2nd and causing constant alerts in Passau itself from the 3rd to the 8th. A raid across the Danube on 11 July proved to be the last Austrian attack; it was repelled and the armistice brought an end to active hostilities along the Bohemian border.[41]

Part of the Nassau Regiment also came into contact with the enemy in May, but under more unusual circumstances. Unlike the Isenburg troops, the Hohenzollern contingents had been unable to join the regiment prior to its departure from Wiesbaden. Finally marching from their home principalities in May, these two tiny contingents (totalling four officers and 177 men) had reached Eichstätt when they were halted by a French colonel named Marie-Antoine Reiset. This officer, leading a squadron of the 1st Provisional Dragoons, ordered the Hohenzollern troops to follow him in pursuit of a small band of Austrian soldiers who were attempting to escape from Vorarlberg to the safety of Bohemia by marching clear across Bavaria[42] The bold, if perhaps foolish, Austrians had managed to evade most of the Allied troops sent against them, but fate and Colonel Reiset caught up with them near Neumarkt in der Oberpfalz on 27 May. The French dragoons and Hohenzollern infantry made short work of the exhausted Austrians, capturing 63 of them and scattering the rest after a brief skirmish at the village of Pfeffertshofen. The remaining Austrian fugitives were rounded up by another squadron of the 1st Provisional Dragoons and the warriors of Hohenzollern marched to meet their regiment at Passau, the only men of the Nassau Regiment to engage in combat during the 1809 campaign.[43]

Strengthened by the incorporation of the Hohenzollern contingents, the 2nd Rheinbund departed Passau on 14 June en route for Vienna.[44] Arriving in the Austrian capital on the 22nd after impressive marches, the regiment was detailed to the city's garrison, providing more than 400 men per day to guard and police duties. These tasks occupied the Nassauers throughout the remainder of the campaign and the regiment took no part in the bloody struggle at Wagram. A detachment of 60 men under Lieutenant Rohm did escort 200 wagons loaded with bread and wine from Vienna on to Lobau Island, but the Nassauers faced more danger from potential Allied plunderers than from the enemy and the detachment did not become involved in the brutal combat on the Marchfeld. While Rohm's men and some French gendarmes exerted themselves to protect their convoy, most of the regiment watched the battle from vantage points in the city: 'The soldiers could not find words to express their wonder at the spectacle provided by the cannonade of over 1,000 guns firing from both banks that stormy night.'

The war soon came to an end, but the men faced a final challenge before departing Vienna to rejoin Rouyer: an Imperial Review. On 5 October, the Emperor appeared before the regiment, drawn up in the grand courtyard at Schönbrunn Palace. Approaching the silent ranks on foot, he had one of his adjutants, General Rapp, give a series of commands in French which Oberst Pöllnitz translated into German. After observing the manoeuvres of the 1st Battalion, Napoleon ordered the 1st Grenadier Company to step forward and personally inspected the men in detail, including the rucksack of one of the grenadiers. Although pleased with the appearance and bearing of the men, the Emperor was not satisfied with their drill techniques; still modelled on old Austrian regulations, the commands and manoeuvres of the regiment were incompatible with those of the rest of the army and Napoleon ordered the immediate introduction of French drill and exercises. Only two of the regiment's officers were familiar with the French techniques, however, and no German versions of the French manuals were available, so that the transition to the new drill became the 2nd Rheinbund's principal occupation for its remaining days in Vienna and during its long march back to Germany.[45]

A small group of Germans from the smaller states did stand in the ranks on the Marchfeld during the terrible days of Wagram. The *ad hoc* sapper battalion composed of men from Würzburg and the five Saxon Duchies arrived in Vienna on 21 May and remained in the city as part of the reserve park until called to the battlefield on 5 July. Although the sappers spent the 5th on Lobau Island and crossed over to the north bank of the Danube at 1 p.m. on the 6th, they did not participate in the slaughter and suffered no casualties from enemy action. There was a brief alarm that night when rumour of a body of Austrian cavalry caused the German sappers to take up their muskets in a former Austrian redoubt on the Russbach Heights, but the roving cavalry turned out to be a detachment of Württembergers and the men returned to their bivouac fires. The Germans spent the 7th burying the dead and clearing the scorched and bloody Marchfeld before following the army to Znaim. Contributing to a number of construction projects even after the armistice, the tiny German sapper battalion, much reduced by illness, was finally broken up late in the year, the Saxons returning to Rouyer's Division at Linz on 24 November and the Würzburgers marching home in February 1810 after completing the demolition of the fortifications at Klagenfurt and Raab.[46]

AUGUST - DISASTER AT OBERAU

When Napoleon directed Lefebvre to launch the Second Offensive into the Tyrol, he included Rouyer's German Division in the Marshal's command. Couriers were thus sent hurrying to the area around Passau to alert the Rheinbund Regiments and bring them to Salzburg. These new orders reached the regiments at 1 a.m. on 23 July and, within hours, their march columns were on the road to Salzburg where Lefebvre was gathering the Bavarian 1st Division in preparation for the invasion. The 6th Rheinbund arrived on the 25th and the other two regiments the next day after a series of punishing marches under the oppressive heat and dust of July; the 4th Regiment alone lost five men as heat casualties along the way. When the 4th entered Salzburg, it was immediately directed to the palace of the Prince-Bishop where it was reviewed by the Duke of Danzig and greeted with a speech in his Alsatian German: 'As we are about to enter the Tyrol, the Regiment of the Dukes of Saxony, as a sign of my special trust, will assume the role of avant-garde.' Then, turning to the men of the Light Battalion, he continued, 'And because this battalion is said to consist of good riflemen, it shall form the point of the division and thus of my entire corps, as I am firmly convinced it will preserve its honour and mine and maintain its notable discipline.'[47]

If the men had been subjected to choking heat and dust on the road from Passau, they would now be plagued by cloying mud and unending rain. Leaving the Schwarzburg Battalion in the Salzburg castle, the division marched out of the city at daybreak on the 27th and spent an unpleasant night in bivouac around Reichenhall before proceeding to Söll on the 28th. Here conditions were even worse. The meadows allotted to the men of Rouyer's Division were flooded, the few buildings were occupied and the soldiers were left with no place to sleep; only by collecting planks and doors from nearby homes and laying these atop

large stones could the men create relatively dry beds for the night.[48] The next
day brought better weather, but the empty houses and ashen ruins made the valley seem desolate, casting a shadow over the spirit of the troops and making the
march to Strass a sombre affair; moreover, provisions were already beginning to
run short and the men resorted to foraging to satisfy their hunger. The division
proceeded to the destroyed town of Schwaz on the 30th, but returned to the road
after a short break to conduct a forced march through Innsbruck to the foot of
Bergisel, leaving more heat casualties and numerous stragglers in its wake.
Fortunately, the 31st was decreed a rest day and most of the men who had fallen
out of the march columns rejoined their companies during the course of the day.

Having occupied the Tyrolian capital with little opposition, Lefebvre now
decided to send Rouyer south to open the way to Brixen while a Bavarian force
cleared the valley of the Upper Inn. Reinforced by the Bavarian 4th
Chevauxlegers and van Douwe's Battery, Rouyer marched toward the pass on 1

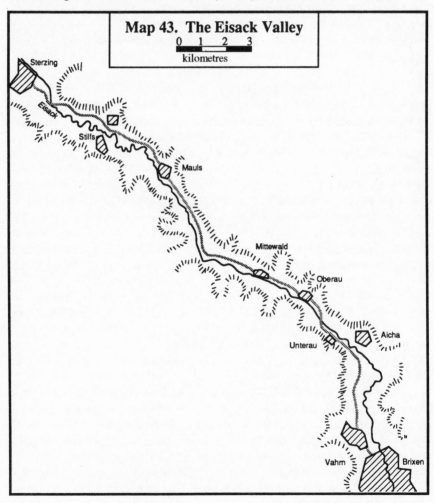

Map 43. The Eisack Valley

August, camping at Matrei and Steinach for the night. Although groups of insurgents had been visible in the hills along the route of march all day, no shots were fired and the advance proceeded without incident. The division crossed the Brenner Pass and entered Sterzing on the 2nd. Rouyer located his headquarters in this town, guarded by the two Gotha grenadier companies, while the remaining units bivouacked in the fields outside. Unfortunately, the devilish Tyrolians opened several floodgates and swamped the low ground where the men had established their meagre campsites, disturbing their rest and forcing them to withdraw to higher ground. With little sleep and less food, most of the division rested again on the 3rd. A reconnaissance detachment probing south along the road to Brixen, however, skirmished with the partisans and reported back that strong bands of insurgents had collected at Mauls and Mittewald.[49]

The road from the Brenner to Brixen follows the valley of the cold River Eisack, first on its eastern bank from Sterzing to Unterau, then crossing the river to continue down its western shore to Brixen. South of Sterzing the valley narrows dramatically. Rocky cliffs and steep, forested bluffs crowd together from both sides, in some places allowing only enough space for the river and the road. The Eisack itself runs deep and swift, presenting a formidable barrier despite its small size. In August 1809, swollen by heavy rains, the river was wide and treacherous, threatening to overflow its banks and flood the few tiny hamlets that huddled on the valley's floor. In all, the Eisack valley between Sterzing and Brixen was ideally suited to the type of irregular warfare practised by the Tyrolian insurgents, and, defended by these crafty and fanatic partisans with their intimate knowledge of the terrain, it formed a perfect trap.

Leaving one company at Sterzing to maintain contact with the Bavarian detachment at the Brenner Pass,[50] General Rouyer took his men south down the Eisack in the early morning hours of 4 August. Led by the Weimar Light Battalion, the column cleared a small abattis and reached Mauls without enemy contact but was forced to halt when it encountered a larger barricade north of Mittewald. As sappers removed this second obstacle, hundreds of concealed insurgents opened a terrific fire on Rouyer's leading units, cutting down numerous Germans with the initial fusillade. The way was opened in short order, but resistance only increased as the column resumed its march toward Mittewald. In addition to a hail of rifle bullets, the Tyrolians rolled monstrous boulders and logs down from the heights to bound amongst the hapless Saxons on the road below. To the unfortunate men of the 4th Rheinbund, the situation was horrifying. While the Tyrolians, protected by rocks, trees and unscalable heights, loosed dreadful barrages of lead and rock against their tightly packed columns, they could only march on helplessly, attempting to time their advances to avoid the deadly avalanches from above. Before long, the road was strewn with huge rock fragments and crushed corpses; the Light Battalion's advance guard alone lost 20 of its 50 men and had to be reinforced. None the less, the march proceeded and, aided by two Bavarian guns, the light infantrymen quickly stormed and cleared the little village of Mittewald.

At Mittewald, the two Koburg voltigeur companies crossed to the west bank of the Eisack by a slender footbridge to protect the main column's right flank and prevent the destruction of the important bridge at Unterau. At the same time, Oberst von Egloffstein, leaving two companies to hold Mittewald,[51] resumed his advance down the Brixen road. Coming within sight of Oberau, the Light Battalion, still leading the division's march column, was sent charging ahead in a vain effort to reach the all-important bridge.[52] The Tyrolians, however, retreated slowly, defending every foot of ground and inflicting heavy casualties on the advancing Saxons. Finally driven from the hamlet (it consisted of an inn and two homes), they set a torch to the bridge and withdrew to establish themselves in a position on the western bank from which their rifle fire raked the span and its approaches. Although the light infantrymen made several courageous attempts to gain the little bridge, this heavy and accurate fire prevented them from reaching it and dousing the flames. Several Bavarian chevauxlegers attempted to spring across the burning planks but the wood collapsed beneath them with a great groan and a shower of sparks, plunging men and mounts to violent deaths in the raging river. The Koburgers, inching forward on narrow footpaths, had no more success and were withdrawn to the east bank to rejoin their battalions.

The men of the Light Battalion, punished by a renewed rain of boulders and trees, were also ordered to assemble behind Oberau and reform. This signalled an impromptu attack by the insurgents, who mistook the movement for a retreat and surged forward with renewed vigour. Fortunately, help was at hand and the two line battalions of the 4th, aided by the Anhalt Battalion, counter-attacked to repulse the Tyrolians. Simultaneously, the seemingly inexhaustible Light Battalion was sent across a small footbridge in single file finally to sweep the enemy from the slopes on the western shore. The musketry persisted until evening when a heavy downpour put an end to the day's combat. The Light Battalion bivouacked on the west bank around Unterau (a popular tavern surrounded by a few buildings) with the Lippe Battalion behind it near the destroyed bridge. The line battalions of the 4th with their two Bavarian pieces held the high ground south of Oberau, while the remainder of the division camped around the village itself.

The day had been long and bloody, but the men had displayed courage, discipline and endurance despite heavy losses. Almost all the casualties had been borne by the 4th Regiment which had 207 men dead or wounded, 174 of those from the Light Battalion alone;[53] the soldiers of Weimar and Hildburghausen thus paid heavily for the honour of leading the way. Particularly tragic for the Light Battalion was the loss of two pairs of brothers from the families von Schierbrandt and von Hönning; the valiant and able Hauptmann von Schierbrandt would thus never receive the decoration he had earned at Zwiesel in June. Their casualties and exhaustion notwithstanding, a detachment was drawn from these stalwarts to conduct a dangerous night raid against a gathering of Tyrolians south of Unterau. Although the partisans departed before von Egloffstein and his men could catch them, the patrol convinced the colonel of the enemy's strength and his regiment's exposed position. General Rouyer, who had suffered a slight wound during the day's fight, had also concluded that his division's position was untenable: cut off in a narrow valley, his men were short of food and ammunition, far from assistance and facing an implacable foe. Retreat seemed the only logical option, but the general did not want to abandon the gains he had won. He settled on a half measure: the majority of the division would withdraw to Sterzing in the dawn hours of 5 August, but the 4th Rheinbund and its two Bavarian guns would remain at Oberau until Rouyer could organize its relief.[54]

Expressing the trust he placed in the Saxons' courage and promising to return by mid-morning with food, ammunition and transportation for the wounded, Rouyer marched north at 3 a.m. on the 5th. The Tyrolians attacked in force less than an hour later. The Light Battalion, dreadfully exposed on the west bank at Unterau, was soon forced to retire and crossed back over the footbridge to join its comrades on the eastern side of the river. From this position around Oberau, von Egloffstein and his men courageously held the insurgents at bay until the two Bavarian guns exhausted their ammunition at about 1 p.m. The regiment had now been in combat for seven hours and its situation was desperate. Crammed into a tiny area around the three structures of Oberau, all stuffed with the growing number of wounded, the men had been without food for more than 30 hours, were running short of cartridges and were even prevented from quenching their thirst by the heavy fire from the enthusiastic Tyrolians. All four of the messengers sent to beg for help had been captured or killed and the rebels were edging ever closer to the Saxon positions. As the Tyrolians outflanked his line and resistance began to crack, von Egloffstein ordered a retreat on Mittewald in the hopes of saving the guns entrusted to his regiment's honour, and as many of his foot soldiers as possible. All those living and able who could not reach the illusory safety of the village's buildings thus retired through Mittewald under constant pressure from the insurgents. But there was no rest at Mittewald and no sign of Rouyer or a reinforcing column. Retiring another three kilometres up the valley, the men hoped to gain a brief respite and refresh themselves with a small keg of wine dragged from a cellar. The wine cask, however, attracted bullets as well as thirsty Saxons and before long the little column was headed north again, a steady trickle of casualties dropping in its wake. Hastening to fill their canteens against the hot August sun, the sweating men did not seem to notice the dead drummer whose blood was slowly darkening the pale red wine in the cask.[55] The retreat thus continued through ambushes and barricades to Sterzing where Egloffstein begged in vain for a column to march to the aid of his entrapped troops.

Those left behind in Oberau resisted stubbornly as their ammunition dwindled and their casualties mounted. As darkness fell and the fire from these little fortresses diminished, the Tyrolians, shouting and wielding flaming brands, threatened to set the two houses aflame. The parties defending the homes had no choice but to surrender and the banners of both line battalions thereby fell into the hands of the enemy. The insurgents now closed in on the tavern, the last point of resistance, jammed tight with some 230 men. Attempts to negotiate with the exultant Tyrolians failed and the tiny garrison surrendered at about 8 p.m. after more than thirteen hours of battle.[56]

In the relative safety of Sterzing, the 4th Rheinbund counted its losses while the Tyrolians celebrated. The previous two days had cost the regiment 948 casualties, approximately 43 per cent of the 2,190 men who entered the Eisack valley on the morning of 4 August, almost half of these (406) from the Weimar-Hildburghausen Light Battalion. Lefebvre appeared in Sterzing the next morning, embraced von Egloffstein and addressed a stirring speech to the regiment, promising to 'avenge and deliver' their killed and captured comrades. The troops responded with a rousing cheer and fully expected to return to the Eisack valley, but the Marshal's efforts to drive through this valley of death to Brixen were no more successful than Rouyer's, and the entire VII Corps retired to Innsbruck several days later. To this day, the valley around Oberau is known as the 'Sachsenklemme' or 'Saxon Trap' and the little meadow near the bridge as the 'Saxon Grave'. Despite their horrendous losses, their privations and frustrations, however, the men had proved themselves under fire, earning 'a true reputation for bravery'.[57]

Instead of marching south as they had anticipated, the men of the 4th Rheinbund were sent north on the evening of 6 August to garrison the Brenner Pass while Rouyer's other three battalions remained at Sterzing. At the pass, von Egloffstein reorganized his much depleted regiment by combining the two line battalions into one battalion of six companies (about 800 men) and reducing the number of companies in the Light Battalion to four (total of 436 men). The 4th remained here for the next six days, occasionally skirmishing with small parties of insurgents and desperately foraging for food. Although their duties at the pass were relatively light, the men suffered from the cold mountain air and the pervasive lack of provisions (each man only received a quarter ration of *zwieback* and a small amount of meat per day). According to one Bavarian observer, these meagre rations had a particularly deleterious effect on the men of the 4th Regiment because 'a large percentage of the Saxon Jägers of Weimar lived on sausages and brandy which the foot messenger of each company had carried even up into the peaks of the Tyrol'.[58] The troops were thus in a poor physical state when they left the pass at 2 a.m. on the 11th. The remainder of Rouyer's Division had departed Sterzing some four hours earlier and the reunited division now marched back toward Innsbruck with the rest of Lefebvre's command. Tyrolians in the wooded hills on both sides of the route of march inflicted a few casualties on the Germans, but the division separated from the main column at Matrei and continued on to Hall, thereby escaping most of the repeated firefights that sapped the strength of the Bavarian battalions. The exhausted men finally reached Hall at about 9 p.m., hungry, thirsty and drained from their gruelling 18-hour march under the hot August sun.[59] Still suffering from the paucity of food, the division passed the 12th in peace, resting as well as it could from the exertions of the preceding ten days.

On the 13th, while their Bavarian allies were locked in the fierce struggle at Bergisel, Rouyer's Germans skirmished briefly with rebels south of Hall and Volders but were never subjected to serious attack. Beyond these insignificant firefights, Rouyer's men took no part in the day's action.[60] As darkness settled over the valley, however, the men remained watchful: for miles up and down the river, the hills were illuminated by Tyrolian bonfires and the clear night sky carried the rebels' wild, almost inhuman, cries to the ears of Rouyer's apprehensive men. The Germans were left undisturbed on the 14th, however, and, when the two Bavarian divisions stealthily evacuated Innsbruck that evening and withdrew to Hall, Rouyer's Division quietly joined the march column to slip out of the town under the cover of darkness. Retreating down the Inn, the battered Corps bivouacked at Schwaz on the 15th and 16th before proceeding to Wörgl the following day. From this town the Bavarian 3rd Division retired on Rosenheim while the 1st Division and Rouyer's men marched for Salzburg.[61] On 20 August, a little less than one month after the launching of the Second Offensive, the weary Rheinbund regiments returned to Salzburg, their honour increased, but their ranks sadly thinned.[62]

SEPTEMBER-OCTOBER - IN THE HABSBURG CAPITAL

Scattered in and around Salzburg, Rouyer's men expected any day to receive orders returning them to the 'Land of Murderers' for a renewed offensive against the intransigent rebels.[63] As with all armies, the coming and going of couriers and the mood of headquarters were the subjects of countless campfire conversations and the troops were much surprised when word arrived on 31 August that they were to be transferred to Vienna. With these orders, the division's active role in the the 1809 campaign came to an end. The regiments departed their quarters in the region around Salzburg on 1 September and marched via St. Pölten to arrive in the Austrian capital on the 21st.[64] Although pleasantly quartered in a variety of palaces, an Imperial review had been scheduled for 23 September with a pre-inspection to be held on the 22nd; the men were thus kept busy on the night of their arrival, polishing, buffing, straightening and sewing to prepare for their first meeting with Napoleon. Closely examined by one of the Imperial adjutants, General Dumas, the following morning, the regiments were pronounced ready and assembled at the Schönbrunn Palace early on the 23rd.

These Imperials reviews, for all their pomp and glitter, provide interesting insight into the leadership techniques of the era in general and the relationship between Napoleon and his soldiers, even the Germans of the Rheinbund, in particular. As was the norm, Rouyer formed his men early in the morning and awaited the Emperor. Napoleon soon appeared, followed by a brilliant collection of glittering marshals and showy staff officers but distinguished from them by the simplicity of his dress and the aura of command that surrounded him. Then the gates of the palace opened, the drum majors whirled their batons, the drummers beat a furious staccato, the musicians leaped to life with brazen calls and a thousand voices cried 'Vive l'empereur' as one.[65] Napoleon neared the serried ranks of anxious soldiery and the men shouldered their muskets, with the exception of those regiments which had been in combat; these latter were permitted the honour of keeping the butts of their weapons on the ground next to their feet. The Emperor then reviewed each company in considerable detail. The officers and men were faced with a barrage of potentially embarrassing questions: Were rations adequate? How many men in the company were sick? What were their ailments? Where were they quartered? The officer without a ready and accurate answer was unlikely to see promotion or reward in the near future. As he was questioning the regiment, Napoleon had individual soldiers called out of the ranks to remove their packs and display the contents. He was remarkably attentive to detail and noted each item of a man's belongings, especially such military necessities as shoes and ammunition. When he was satisfied with the appearance of the company or regiment and the administrative competence of its leadership, he would have a battalion or two execute some basic manoeuvres to prove their tactical ability. These exercises were particularly trying for the German regiments as the officers, still not completely familiar with French drill, had to comprehend the Emperor's commands and translate them almost instantaneously into German for the troops to execute. Fortunately for the 4th, 5th and 6th Rheinbund Regiments, the officers were sharp and the men well drilled; the manoeuvres were conducted without a hitch and Napoleon expressed his satisfaction with all concerned.

Expressions of the Emperor's satisfaction took a variety of forms. For the Anhalt Battalion of the 5th Regiment, it meant promotions. Napoleon, ever desirous of introducing homogenizing French practices in his German units, wanted to establish for each battalion the position of 'chef de bataillon'. He was prepared to name some lucky officer of Lippe when Oberst Chambaud intervened with the request that the battalion commander be an officer who shared the same homeland as the men. Napoleon agreed and asked for the name of the most able officer in the battalion. When Chambaud replied that all his officers were equally competent, the Emperor personally began to question each in turn. He seemed ready to select one fortunate captain when he learned that the officer had temporarily served the Duke of Braunschweig, one of Napoleon's arch enemies. Brusquely turning from the man, the Emperor put several questions to the next officer, was pleased to hear sensible answers in fluent French and elevated the gentlemen from captain to battalion commander on the spot. He was thus able to demonstrate simultaneously the penalties inherent in Imperial displeasure alongside the rewards that awaited those who basked in the 'sunshine of Imperial grace'.[66]

An Imperial gesture that had a salutary effect upon the men of all three regiments was the arrival of a new pair of shoes for each soldier; with long marches behind and ahead of them, the troops greatly appreciated this seemingly simple gift. In addition to footwear, the 4th Rheinbund received a pair of shining cannon and watched with pride while their commander and a number of others within the regiment were decorated with the cross of the Legion of Honour.[67] These measures, ordinary as many of them were, illustrate Napoleon's keen insight into the psychology of the soldiers of his age. He provided all the glory, splendour and regal loftiness any fawning servant could want, but also made himself real and familiar to the common men, spoke to them individually, inquired about their welfare, saw to their basic wants. He demanded a great deal and his penetrating eye missed no details, but he was equally quick to recognize and repay loyalty, courage and competence: the instant promotion of an officer or the distribution of Crosses of the Legion were immediate and tangible signs of Imperial largess that left a deep impression on officers and men alike. They were made to feel part of something greater than themselves, as though the Emperor's nimbus of victory encompassed even the rudest soldier within its glorious glow. Little wonder that these German troops, whose interests seem so distant from those of imperial France, yearned to fight at Napoleon's side, to earn the honour of his praise.

It is almost tragic to watch this glow fade. With October, however, Rouyer's Division passed up the Danube, stopping for a time at Linz before returning to Germany as December's snows began to gather. The troops expected to head for the warmth and comfort of their home hearths but instead found themselves bound for the barren hills of Spain and its fearful war. The officers, appalled at this prospect, tried to conceal their destination from the men, but word soon spread and desertion, previously almost unknown in the Saxon regiment, became rife. By the time they crossed the Pyrenees in March 1810, many of Rouyer's German battalions would be at half strength.[68]

If only dragged to Spain by their honour or the threat of punishment, the officers and men of Rouyer's German regiments seem to have been willing allies of Napoleon in the war against Austria in 1809. Although frustrated in their desire to fight a great battle under the eyes of the Emperor, they always performed their duties capably and behaved with admirable discipline and professionalism. The 5th and 6th Regiments certainly displayed some frailties, largely based on the circumstances of their creation and their lack of combat experience, but the 2nd and 4th Rheinbund left a positive impression with all contemporary observers. The stern Davout noted the sure military bearing of the 4th Regiment when he reviewed it on 31 April; complimenting Oberst von Egloffstein, he said, 'One certainly notices that these are the soldiers of a sovereign who is himself a general.'[69] The discipline of these soldiers could also be observed from the other end of the social spectrum. Although his cloister was occupied by a company from Sachsen-Gotha on 13 August, Prior Neunhäuserer of Volders in the Tyrol recorded that 'everyone, officers as well as privates, was so uncommonly courteous, that we have never encountered their like among soldiers'.[70] This discipline and a solid *espirit de corps* were evident throughout the campaign. Moreover, although generally relegated to rear area duties, the Germans were tactically competent and, in those few instances where they faced the enemy in combat, all ranks displayed bravery, determination and coolness under the most harrowing of circumstances. Finally, their *espirit de corps* never left them. They endured grinding privations with little complaint and even after the dreadful events in the Eisack valley, the survivors of the 4th Rheinbund cheered at the prospect of returning to rescue their comrades. Despite the heterogeneous composition of their units, the minuscule size of their homelands and the bewildering variety of their uniforms, these soldiers represented a competent, professional component of Napoleon's Army of Germany in 1809. They deserve a better reputation than history has accorded them.

NOTES

1:    The numeration of the Rheinbund regiments presents a problem for the historian, particularly with regard to the first three regiments. Original French documents (e.g., Saski and Napoleon's *Correspondence*) establish the numbering system cited in the text, but many other sources (e.g., Commandant Sauzey, *Le Régiment des Duchés de Saxe,* volume IV of *Les Allemands sous les Aigles Françaises,* Paris: Terana, 1988, p. 44) refer to the Würzburg Regiment as the 1st Rheinbund Regiment and ascribe the 2nd and 3rd Rheinbund designations to the two Nassau regiments. I have followed the original French designations (1st Rheinbund from Nassau, 2nd Rheinbund also from Nassau, 3rd Rheinbund from Würzburg).

2: The very place of the military in society differed from state to state. While most at least publically embraced the notion that it was each citizen's duty to serve in the defence of his country, Frederickian attitudes persisted in many of the little monarchies. The enlistment of foreigners continued to be common and, in some cases, military service was still used as a form of punishment for minor crimes. In the Hohenzollern principalities, for example, civil authorities were directed to enroll 'ahead of all others' a list of unsavoury sorts: fornicators, wastrels, gamblers, topers, field and garden thieves, poachers and those who distinguished themselves by resistance to authority. Other states had an entirely different approach. Princess Pauline, Regent of Lippe-Detmold, for one, was stern with deserters but emphasized the dignity of the individual and reduced corporal punishment in her little army. See Wilhelm Oesterhaus, *Geschichte der Fürstlich Lippischen Truppen in den Jahren 1807-1815,* Detmold: Meyer, 1907; and Major von Runkel, 'Zur Geschichte der Besatzung der Burg Hohenzollern und der Truppen der Fürsten von Hohenzollern von 1806 bis 1815', *Mittheilungen des Vereins für Geschichte und Altertumskunde in Hohenzollern,* XXXIII Jahrgang 1899/1900.

3: In addition to their field forces, most rulers kept some depot and constabulary troops in their home country. Isenburg, for example, had a small depot company, as well as a 'Landmiliz' (militia) and twelve hussars for internal security, while Lippe-Detmold retained a garrison company, a Landjäger 'Brigade' (probably no more than 50-100 men), a small gendarmerie and its 'Janitscharen', a twelve-man military band of which the Princess was evidently quite proud. For general comments on the military forces of the small states, see Oesterhaus and Runkel as well as: Martin Bethke, 'Das Fürstentum Isenburg im Rheinbund', *Zeitschrift für Heereskunde,* Nr. 302/303 (Jul/Oct), XLVI Jahrgang, 1982; Rittmeister Fiebig, 'Das Bataillon des Princes', *Zeitschrift für Heeres- und Uniformkunde,* Heft 61/63 (Jan 1934) and 'Das 4., 5. und 6. Rheinbund-Regiment', *Zeitschrift für Heeres- und Uniformkunde,* Heft 64/66 (Apr 1934); Hans Stahlberg, 'Reussisches Militär bis zum Ende der Befreiungskriege', *Zeitschrift für Heereskunde,* Nr. 269 (Jan/Feb), XLI Jahrgang, 1977; Wolf-Heino Struck, 'Die Gründung des Herzogtums Nassau', in *Herzogtum Nassau 1806-1866,* Wiesbaden, 1981.

4: Mecklenburg-Schwerin was to provide one regiment (7th Rheinbund) and Mecklenburg-Strelitz one battalion. *Correspondence* 14793; Pelet, vol. I, 179, 361-5. In one plan, the Mecklenburg-Strelitz and Oldenburg contingents were to be amalgamated into a 'Régiment de Holstein' (Bacher to Napoleon, 27 February, Saski, vol. I, pp. 119-21). See also Chapter 10.

5: Major Rheinbund units in Spain included 1st Rheinbund (2nd Nassau), 3rd Rheinbund (Würzburg Regiment), a battalion from Frankfurt, the 'bataillon princière' (one company each from Lippe-Detmold, Reuss, Waldeck, Schaumburg-Lippe, Schwarzburg-Rudolstadt, and Schwarzburg-Sondershausen), the Hessian *Gross- und Erbprinz* Regiment and the 4th Baden Infantry.

6: Imperial Decree of 23 February, Saski, vol. I, pp. 101-3. In fact, one of Massena's adjutants was waiting for the Germans when they arrived in Würzburg, informing the men of the Saxon Duchies that they would join the Marshal's Corps at Strasbourg in the near future; Rouyer's arrival with new instructions changed this situation (Gustav Jacobs, *Geschichte der Feldzüge und Schicksale der Gotha-Altenburgischen Krieger in den Jahren 1807 bis 1815,* Altenburg: Gleich, 1835, p. 53).

7: See Napoleon's and Berthier's directives of 4, 5, 11 and 18 March in Saski, vol. I, pp. 133, 140-1, 144-5, 228, 296-7.

8: Napoleon to Berthier on 30 March, Saski, vol. I, p. 430.

9: En route, the Koburg and Hildburghausen troops encountered a French regiment of Davout's Corps and a Koburg officer wrote that 'the sight of these veteran marchers and fighters was a good example for our young men and their heavy packs, carried without effort, astounded our soldiers' (Schauroth, p. 2).

10: In 1806, the Dukes of Sachsen-Weimar and Sachsen-Gotha, who provided the two largest contingents, had agreed that command of the regiment would alternate between staff officers of the two duchies; as Weimar's Oberst von Egloffstein had led the unit in 1807, it was now Gotha's turn to nominate a commander. Von Egloffstein's abilities had so impressed the Dukes, however, that they decided to leave him at the head of the regiment for the 1809 campaign. Ludwig Freiherr von Seebach, *Geschichte der Feldzüge des Herzoglich Sachsen-Weimarischen Scharfschützenbataillons im Jahr 1806 und des Infanterieregiments der Herzöge von Sachsen in den Jahren 1807, 1809, 1810 und 1811,* Weimar: Voigt, 1838, p. 132.

11: Seebach (p. 133) gives the following approximate figures for the various contingents in early April: Weimar 667, Gotha 1,031, Meiningen 265, Koburg 269, and Hildburghausen 136. The strengths of the battalions were: 1st Line 740, 2nd Line 741, Light 800, regimental staff 87 (Seebach, pp. 284-6).

12: Koburg's tiny army also included a grenadier company, but it was not counted as part of the Duchy's Rheinbund obligation and thus remained at home during the campaign (in peacetime, the three companies were considered a battalion). Georg Lantz, *Geschichte der Stammtruppen des 6. Thüringischen Infanterie-*

Regiments Nr. 95, Braunschweig: Sattler, 1897, p. v.

13: In the light battalion, the men of the third rank were issued rifles. Leo von Pfannenberg, *Geschichte des Infanterie-Regiments Grossherzog von Sachsen (5. Thuringisches) Nr. 94 und seiner Stammtruppen 1702-1912,* Berlin: Stilke, 1912, p. 57.

14: By the time of the 1812 campaign in Russia, all of the contingents would have shakos.

15: For the pre-1809 military experiences of the contingents, see Fiebig and a recent series of articles by Friedrich Herrmann ('Eine Bildersammlung aus dem Kriege in Spanien 1808-1813', *Zeitschrift für Heereskunde,* 1989-1990).

16: At this point, all Lippe companies were numbered sequentially, regardless of origin. Those arriving in Würzburg were the 1st, 3rd (both Detmold) and 4th (Schaumburg); the 1st and 3rd had left Detmold on 19 March, the 4th had marched out of Bückeburg on the 17th. The 2nd (Detmold) and 5th (mixed) Companies were in Spain with the Bataillon Princière. After the 6th and 7th Companies (Detmold) and a separate Schaumburg detachment joined the battalion, it was reorganized and its subordinate companies renumbered 1-6 in the conventional fashion. In December, Böger was elevated to the rank of OTL and battalion commander. See Oesterhaus, pp. 6-7, 19-22, 29; and Christian U. Freiherr von Ulmenstein, *Die Offiziere des Schaumburg-Lippischen Truppenkorps, 1648-1867,* Berlin: Verlag für Standesamtswesen, 1940, pp. 14-15.

17: Hans Küster, *Geschichte des Anhaltischen Infanterie-Regiments Nr. 93,* Berlin: Mittler & Sohn, 1893, pp. 41-4.

18: The four companies of the battalion were numbered as follows: 1st (2nd Reuss), 2nd (3rd Reuss), 3rd (2nd Waldeck), 4th (3rd Waldeck). For the Reuss and Waldeck troops see Freiherr von Dalwigk zu Lichtenfels, *Geschichte der waldeckischen und kurhessischen Stammtruppen des Infanterie-Regiments v. Wittich (3. Kurhess.) Nr. 83. 1681-1866,* Oldenburg: Littmann, 1909, pp. 66-7; Hans von Döring, *Geschichte des 7. Thüringischen Infanterie-Regiments Nr. 96,* Berlin: Mittler & Sohn, 1890, pp. 115-16; M. Meinhard, *Geschichte des Reussischen Militairs bis zum Jahre 1815,* Gera: Blachmann und Bornschein, 1842, pp. 366-7.

19: Schwarzburg-Rudolstadt: plain, round red cuffs. Schwarzburg-Sondershausen: red cuffs with green cuff flaps. Both had brass plates on their shako: Rudolstadt's was rhombic with the monogram 'FSR' (Fürstentum Schwarzburg-Rudolstadt) under a crown; Sondershausen's was octagonal with the initials 'FSS' surmounted by a crown.

20: The battalion's companies were: 1st (2nd Sondershausen), 2nd (3rd Sondershausen), 3rd (2nd Rudolstadt), 4th (3rd Rudolstadt). Döring, p. 116; Meinhard, p. 367.

21: Dalwigk, p. 67. It is worth noting that all four contingents (Reuss, Waldeck, Rudolstadt, Sondershausen) were made up of the 2nd and 3rd Companies of their respective forces. All four 1st Companies had marched for Spain with 'bataillon princière' (Fürstenbataillon) in late 1808.

22: Commanded by Hauptmann Freiherr von Waldenfels, the exact strength of the Würzburg sapper division is not known, but it probably numbered 150-300 men. It was originally intended to be part of the 3rd Confederation Division (*Correspondence* 14793, 17 February and Napoleon to Champagny, 21 February in Saski, vol. I, p. 116), but was ordered to the army's Engineer Park in Napoleon's 30 March instructions to Berthier (Saski, vol. I, p. 432). Since the Würzburg infantry wore white uniforms with red distinctions and its artillery wore brown with red trim, the sapper division may have been decked out in either colour or a combination of the two.

23: Würzburg's other contribution to the war effort against Austria was a small detachment of train personnel (22 men) picked up by GD Junot when his corps marched through the city en route to its defeat at Gefrees (see Chapter 7). The train troops probably wore brown uniforms similar to those of the artillery. Sources for the Würzburg sappers and train include Walter Kopp, *Würzburger Wehr,* vol. 22 of *Mainfränkische Studien,* Würzburg: Freunde Mainfränkischer Kunst und Geschichte, 1979, p. 128; and Hermann Helmes, 'Die Würzburger Truppen vor hundert Jahren', *Archiv des Historischen Vereins für Unterfranken und Aschaffenburg,* Nr. 55, 1913, p. 127.

24: Küster, p. 44.

25: Seebach, p. 138.

26: The members of the 'College of Princes' were Aremberg, Frankfurt (Prince Primate), Hohenzollern-Hechingen, Hohenzollern-Sigmaringen, Isenburg, Hohengeroldseck (whose ruler also bore the title Prince von der Leyen), Liechtenstein, Nassau, Salm-Kyrburg and Salm-Salm.

27: This is a brief simplification of a complex series of diplomatic manoeuvres that occurred between 1806 and 1809 whereby Nassau, with Napoleon's support, managed to increase its power *vis-à-vis* the other members of the college (it not only presided over the body, but also supplied the majority of the required military force). The other states initially attempted to retain separate military units, not unlike the old forces of the Holy Roman Empire, but their proposals were impracticable and all the troops of these little countries were fully incorporated into the Nassau regiments.

28: Ironically, the crowned heads of two Confederation states commanded *Austrian* corps during the 1809 war while their contingents were represented in the 2nd Rheinbund Regiment: Prince Johann of Liechtenstein led I Reserve Corps and Prince Friedrich Franz Xavier of Hohenzollern-Hechingen commanded III Corps (later switched to II Corps). To complicate matters further, the latter's son, Friedrich Anton, served on the staff of Bavaria's Crown Prince Ludwig and was captured on 22 April during the battle of Eggmühl. Such was the nature of dynastic politics and war in early 19th-century Europe.

29: As noted above, the State of the Prince Primate (Frankfurt) was also a member of the college, but the Prince was sufficiently independent to form a separate battalion which never came under Nassau command. The 1st and 2nd Isenburg Jäger Companies (the weak 3rd Company remained behind as a depot), on the other hand, were incorporated into the 1st Nassau (2nd Rheinbund). Although the companies were not broken up and distributed throughout the regiment, they lost their separate Isenburg identity and their officers were required to swear oaths of loyalty to the Duke of Nassau who granted them commissions as officers of his Duchy in return. When Princess Charlotte of Isenburg, acting on behalf of her absent husband, protested this action, she was rather shabbily dismissed by Friedrich August (see Bethke's article and August Woringer, 'Geschichte des Fürstlich Isenburgischen Militärs 1806-1816', 1953, pp. 85-6).

30: The strength of the 2nd Rheinbund can only be estimated. With 140 men in twelve companies, plus staff, the total strength should have been slightly over 1,700. Indeed, Woringer gives a strength of 1,729 for 8 April (Woringer, p. 86). At that date, however, the Hohenzollern contingent (about 181) had not yet arrived and Roessler that states the regiment lacked 175 men when it left Wiesbaden for Donauwörth. If the reasonable assumption is made that Woringer's figure applies to the entire regiment, including the Hohenzollern soldiers, its strength in April would have been approximately 1,550. The formation, organization and uniforming of the 1st Nassau are described in Alfred von Roessler, *Geschichte des Königlich Preussischen 1. Nassauischen Infanterie-Regiments Nr. 87 und seines Stammes des Herzoglich Nassauischen 1. Infanterie-Regiments 1809-1874*, Berlin: Mittler & Sohn, 1882, pp. 5-17; Ph. von Rössler, *Die Geschichte der Herzoglich Nassauischen Truppen*, Wiesbaden: Stein, 1863, pp. 52-3; Sauzey, *Les Soldats de Hesse et de Nassau*, vol. VI of *Les Allemands sous les Aigles Françaises*, Paris: Terana, 1988, pp. 55-7, 293-5; Peter Wacker, *Das Herzoglich Nassauische Militär 1806-1866*, Taunusstein: Schellenberg, 1985, pp. 2-6; and Woringer.

31: Our diarist in the 1st Battalion's Koburg Voltigeur Company wrote that since the regiment's 'young troops were unaccustomed to these extraordinary exertions and hunger, many lay completely enervated and some gave up the ghost'. For himself, he found on reaching Ingolstdt that his assigned quarters were full of French soldiers and he slept 'half-dead from hunger, cold and long marching' in a store room niche; on awakening, his breakfast consisted of 'a glass of bad brandy' (Schauroth, pp. 7-8).

32: Schauroth, p. 8. On the other hand, this officer recorded that he and his fellows were able to attend the theatre in Ingolstadt and ruined Regensburg 'despite the warlike scenes'.

33: The problem was apparently negligable in the 2nd and 4th Regiments, but the 5th and 6th lost a number of men. Exact figures are scarce but Oesterhaus (p. 21) says the highest number of desertions in II/5 was 17 men from one company (about 15 per cent), so the problem, while significant, clearly did not represent a massive exodus. Oesterhaus further claims that the Anhalt, Waldeck and Reuss companies also suffered from desertion, the latter losing the most.

34: The complex movements of the small Rheinbund contingents have been amalgamated from a variety of sources and are recapitulated here. Nassau Regiment: Donauwörth (17th), Neuburg (18th), Ingolstadt (25th), Neustadt (26th), Regensburg (27th). 4th Rheinbund: in Donauwörth (Line Battalions) and Rain (Light Battalion) on the 18th, then Ingolstadt on the 19th (entire regiment), departed on the 26th for Neustadt, reached Regensburg on the 27th. 5th Rheinbund: six companies in Donauwörth (18th), joined by Oberst Chambaud and other three Anhalt companies on the 25th, joined by Lippe-Detmold's 6th Company (exact date unknown), departed Donauwörth on the 27th, arrived Regensburg on the 29th. Saxon sappers arrived in Ingolstadt on the 25th, departed on the 26th to join main army. 6th Rheinbund: Donauwörth (18th), next day to Rain (I/6) and Gerolfing (II/6), both battalions in Gerolfing on the 27th, Ingolstadt (28th), Regensburg (29th).

35: Rouyer had been placed under Dupas's orders on 6 April (*Correspondence* 15021), but seems to have taken most of his instructions from army headquarters or Davout in the early stages of the campaign and the two divisions did not unite until 1 May at Regensburg (see Napoleon's and Davout's *Correspondence*, and Buat, vol. I). Dupas's Division comprised two single-regiment brigades, Gency (5th Léger, two battalions) and Veaux (19th Ligne, three battalions), for a total of 3,785 infantry and twelve guns. In early May, one of Rouyer's regiments was attached directly to Dupas (apparently the Nassau regiment) when he marched for Passau and, by the 5th of that month, each of Dupas's two brigades had been assigned one German regiment (4th Rheinbund to Gency and 2nd Rheinbund to Veaux). Neither of these regiments marched with Dupas when he left for Linz on 16/17 May; although the 4th Rheinbund was initially ordered to accompany the French division, the orders were rescinded before the battalions left their cantonments (Seebach, p. 153, Roessler, p. 20). See also letters by Neil Litten and Jean Lochet regarding Dupas's Division in issues 74 (September 1983) and 76 (December 1983) of *Empires, Eagles and Lions*.

36: The 4th Rheinbund left Regensburg on 1 May and reached Passau on the evening of the 4th. The Nassauers departed either late on the 1st or early on the 2nd and also arrived at the Division's destination on 4 May. I/5 and 6th Regiment marched out on the 3rd, the Anhalt battalion becoming part of the Passau garrison (arrived

5 May) and the men of the 6th being split between the latter city and Straubing. The Lippe Battalion (II/5) remained in Regensburg for several days and did not come into Passau until the 11th.

37: The German accounts of the stay in Passau are almost uniform in their descriptions of the duties and conditions, for example, Döring, p. 120; Meinhard, p. 368; Seebach, p. 150. Quote from Rühle in Kircheisen, p. 97.

38: Not unlike modern recruiters, the French general also told his Anhalt troops that they would 'see the world and have much to tell their families' (Küster, pp. 47-9).

39: Oesterhaus, p. 22. The last Detmold company to join the battalion was the 7th; the other detachment was apparently never designated as a company. With the reorganization, the previous numeration of the companies (1, 3, 4, 6 and 7 plus the unnumbered detachment) was abandoned and the companies were simply numbered 1-6 with the 3rd and 5th being the 'Schaumburg-Lippe' companies (actually, they seem to have been mixed but the commanders were from Schaumburg).

40: The engagement at Zwiesel is described in detail in Seebach, pp. 153-8. See also Chapter 7.

41: Küster, p. 49; Seebach, pp. 158-9.

42: This is the same Austrian detachment mentioned in Chapters 3 and 7.

43: Hohenzollern casualties were one dead and one wounded (Runkel, p. 101). Pfeffertshofen is about 7 kilometres north-east of Neumarkt in der Oberpfalz. Many sources, including Roessler and Sauzey, erroneously place this little affair at Pfaffenhofen on the River Ilm (probably due the the confusion arising from the profusion of places named Neumarkt and the coincidence of two Pfaffenhofens). Bezzel ('Grenz', pp. 101-2), Runkel (p. 101) and Wengen (p. 74), who provide the most detailed accounts of the chase and skirmish, clearly place the firefight near Neumarkt in der Oberpfalz: Bezzel (and Wengen who follows him) at Pfeffertshausen and Runkel at Kastl-Pfaffenhofen.

44: Like the Isenburg contingent, the men of the two Hohenzollern Principalities formed two, albeit understrength, companies of the regiment (Runkel, p. 100); they reached Passau on 5 June (Roessler, p. 22; Runkel, p. 101).

45: Roessler, pp. 22-6 (including quote in previous paragraph).

46: Although never engaged in combat, sickness had reduced the Saxon Sapper Company from 138 men (April) to 89 (November); Seebach, pp. 271-3. See also Jacobs, pp. 106-9 and Kopp, p. 129. Nassau was also supposed to provide a sapper company, but it is not clear that this unit was ever formed.

47: Quoted in Seebach, p. 160.

48: Döring, p. 127.

49: The reconnaissance force consisted of 2 officers and 60 men from the Light Battalion and an officer and 40 troopers of *Bubenhofen* (Seebach, pp. 215-16).

50: The company was the 2nd Musketeer Company, 1st Battalion, 4th Rheinbund. The Bavarian force at the pass was Oberstleutnant Wittgenstein's (see Chapter 7). The Light Battalion led the column of march, followed by the two line battalions of 4th Rheinbund, two squadrons of 4th Chevauxlegers, one cannon and one howitzer under Oberleutnant von Wittmann, 5th Rheinbund, the Waldeck-Reuss Battalion, the remaining guns of van Douwe's Battery and, finally, the other two squadrons of *Bubenhofen*. Seebach, p. 217.

51: The 1st and 2nd Musketeer Companies (Sachsen-Meiningen) of II/4.

52: A number of the Bavarian chevauxlegers, bored with watching the battle from their saddles, grabbed their carbines and joined the Saxon skirmish line.

53: Pfannenberg, p. 70. In contrast, the Anhalt Battalion lost about eleven men (only one dead), the Lippe Battalion 39 (six dead) (Küster, p. 52; Oesterhaus, p. 25).

54: Some authors (e.g., Döring, Jacobs) aver that a messenger arrived in the night with instructions from Lefebvre for Rouyer and his division to withdraw; they thus argue that the general had no choice but to obey his corps commander. The truth of this assertion can neither be clearly established nor denied and the fact remains that Rouyer left a significant portion of his division to face overwhleming odds with little hope of succour.

55: Jacobs, p. 85. See also Franz J. A. Schneidawind, *Das Regiment der Herzoge von Sachsen in den blutigen Tagen des 4. und 5. August 1809 in dem Kriege in Tirol*, Aschaffenburg: Wailandt, 1852, p. 32.

56: If the Saxon accounts are to be believed, the Tyrolians observed few of the accepted rules of war. The Germans at Oberau tried twice to negotiate with the insurgents but were mishandled and attacked in both cases. Even after they surrendered, the men were robbed and assaulted, the drum major of the 1st Battalion being almost beaten to death because the enraged Tyrolians mistook his gold-braided coat for a general's uniform (See, among others, Hauptmann von Otterstedt, *Das 8. Thür. Inf.-Regiment No. 153 und seine Altenburger Stammtruppen*, Altenburg: Bonde, 1898, p. 9).

57: Sauzey, vol. IV, p. 78.

58: Baur, pp. 109-10. Oberst Wittgenstein, temporarily commanding the Bavarians of Arco's corps, joined the 4th Rheinbund at the Brenner on the morning of the 8th with approximately 1,860 men and three guns.

59: Rouyer still had the two guns from van Douwe's Battery and two squadrons of 4th Chevauxlegers (Maretich, *vierte Berg Isel*, p. 64).

60: In his history of the Anhalt Regiment (p. 52), Küster states the 5th Rheinbund engaged in a short skirmish with the Tyrolians on the 14th (on the north bank of the Inn between Hall and Volders). Maretich (*vierte Berg Isel*, p. 317), however, argues that it is more likely this little affair occurred on the previous day as there was no other action on 14 August and Hofer himself had ordered the combat broken off.

61: Rouyer and the 1st Bavarian Division departed Wörgl on the night of 17/18 August and marched via St. Johann (18th) and Lofer/Unken (19th) to reach Salzburg.

62: The 4th Regiment alone lost an additional 60 men between the 6th and 20th of August (Seebach, p. 267). Losses for the other three battalions during the entire expedition had been minimal. The Lippe Battalion was fortunate enough to find a replacement detachment of about 70 men waiting for it when it returned to Salzburg (detachment arrived 17 August). The Schwarzburg Battalion (I/6) had spent these weeks in the fortress Hohensalzburg above the city. The only elements of the battalion to enter the Tyrol were a Rudolstadt company (the 4th), which temporarily occupied the Lofer Pass on 29 July (Döring, p. 141) and a mixed detachment which marched as far as Mittersill to disarm the Salzach Valley. This latter force had a somewhat less than honourable encounter with the foe. Having accomplished its mission over a period of several days with no opposition, the detachment was preparing to return to Salzburg. It was decided to take a brief rest in a local tavern before marching off, however, and most of the men, heartily entertained by the friendly Tyrolians, enjoyed themselves for a considerable time while one misfortunate fellow guarded their stacked muskets and provisions wagon. Suddenly, a shot interrupted their revelry. Rushing outside, the Schwarzburgers found their guard and muskets gone and their wagon emptied of all the weapons they had confiscated. Thoroughly embarrassed, but fortunately undisturbed by the Tyrolians, the detachment headed back to Salzburg armed only with staves (Schüler, *Geschichte des schwarzburg-rudolstädtischen Contingents in den Kriegsjahren von 1807 bis 1815*, Rudolstadt: Bock, 1883, p. 20).

63: Hauptmann Böger's words quoted in Oesterhaus, p. 27.

64: The march to Vienna did not encompass twenty days, the division stopped at St Pölten from the 8th to the 20th before continuing on to the capital via Sieghartskirchen (20 September) to enter Vienna on the 21st.

65: As one author described it: 'It was a splendid, imposing spectacle such as the men of Schwarzburg had never witnessed' (Schüler, p. 21).

66: Küster, p. 54.

67: Jacobs (99) claims the new shoes were a special gift to the 4th alone, but others (e.g., Dalwigk's history of the Waldeck contingent) also mention receiving this boon. The pair of guns, however, were a particular present for the 4th Regiment (curiously, these were initially crewed by Frenchmen).

68: Dalwigk, p. 76; Döring, p. 146; Küster, p. 56; Meinhard, pp. 387-8. Seebach avers that despite the dreadful tales they heard of Spain ('they were informed... that they were about to enter their open graves with no hope of rescue') the men held to the colours until the rumour spread that his regiment (the 4th) was to be fully incorporated into the French army, at which point (16/17 January 1810) over 200 men deserted in a single night (p. 274). The men of Reuss in the *bataillon princière* were horrified when they read in the French papers that their compatriots were en route for the Iberian Peninsula; they had hoped at least their countrymen would be spared this experience (Benno von Hagen, *Das Reussische Militär in den Kriegsjahren 1806-15*, Gera-Reuss: Lange, 1904, p. 12).

69: Pfannenberg, p. 60.

70: Ludwig Rapp, ed., *Schicksale des Servitenklosters bei Volders in Tirol in den Kriegsjahren 1703, 1805 und 1809*, Brixen: Weger, 1886, pp. 30-1.

CHAPTER 9:

The Merry Monarch's Men

In addition to defeating the Austrian regular forces and the Tyrolian insurgents, Napoleon in 1809 had to contend with the twin challenges of raid and rebellion in central and northern Germany. Combat in this theatre, stretching from Saxony to the Baltic Sea, fell principally on the shoulders of France's allies, particularly the Army of Westphalia.

KINGDOM AND KING

Westphalia was a new feature on the map of Germany. At the height of his power in the summer of 1807 after the defeat of the Russo—Prussian coalition, Napoleon sought measures to consolidate his position in Europe, especially his hegemony over western Germany. The Confederation of the Rhine was the linchpin of his consolidation strategy. While Bavaria and Württemberg provided solid bulwarks in the south against Austrian encroachments, there was a void in the north along the Confederation's border with Prussia. The territory in this area consisted primarily of English and Prussian holdings and states that had taken Prussia's side in the recently concluded war. To strip Berlin of its influence west of the Elbe and establish a buffer against any further Prussian expansion, Napoleon thus erased the duchies of Braunschweig and Hesse-Kassel, combined their lands with portions of the English possession Hannover, and added a host of small Prussian properties to create a new state, the Kingdom of Westphalia.[1] While defence considerations were paramount and would dominate the kingdom's brief existence, Westphalia was also to serve a second purpose in the Emperor's grand scheme for central Europe by providing an example for other members of the Rheinbund to emulate. Westphalia was thus to be a model state, an enlightened constitutional monarchy. Its citizens raised from the degradation and ignorance of the past by a constitution similar to France's own, the kingdom would light the path to the future for the other Rheinbund states and solidify French pre-eminence in central Germany.

At first, events seemed to accord with Napoleon's plans and the formation of the state progressed rapidly under French auspices. If the initial reaction of newly designated Westphalians was cool and cautious, they soon became receptive. The promulgation of the kingdom's constitution in December 1807 was particularly well received, planting hopes in the hearts of many Germans who had admired the accomplishments of the French Revolution and the early Empire from afar. This document not only abolished serfdom and other tyrannies of the petty princes, but also established a parliament, codified individual rights under the Code Napoleon (all were now to be equal under the law, for

example) and introduced numerous enlightened social, legal and political concepts (freedom of religion, an independent judiciary, etc.). Furthermore, the
new government followed the French model in providing a standardized system
of taxation and rationalizing the jumble of weights, measures and currencies that
had hampered commerce in the plethora of predecessor states. Although the
emphasis was on French precedents, almost all posts in the Westphalian departmental and national administrations were allotted to Germans (at Napoleon's
direction, the defence portfolio was an exception) and German was retained as
the language of the state, dispelling a deep suspicion that the young kingdom
was to be turned over to a ruling class of foreigners and gallicized into another
department of France.

Despite its auspicious beginnings, however, the Westphalian state ultimately
failed. The causes of its failure were manifold but may be compressed into four
general categories. First, while many new Westphalian citizens looked to the
future with hope, large numbers of their fellows turned their eyes to the past,
retaining old loyalties despite the backwardness and oppression that had characterized life under former rulers like Kurfürst Wilhelm of Hesse-Kassel.
Moreover, there soon developed a popular perception that 'the fattest positions
were in the hands of the French' and that the land was being overrun by all manner of unscrupulous 'adventurers'. Regardless of the inaccuracy of this impression, it was already evident in 1809 and gained in acceptance over time, souring
the Westphalians toward a regime they increasingly viewed as foreign and domineering.[2] Second, because of Napoleon's preoccupation with military matters,
the kingdom was plagued with all manner of French intrusions and exactions
from its inception. The provision of a military contingent under the Rheinbund
treaty was accepted, indeed, initial recruiting for the army proceeded surprisingly well, but Westphalia was also required to support sizable French forces on its
soil (most notably the garrison of Magdeburg) and eventually had to supply a
division for the fearful war in Spain. The cost of funding the French garrison
combined with other debilitating financial demands from Paris and the strictures
of the Continental System to cripple the Westphalian economy and discourage
German businessmen who had hoped to profit from the foundation of the kingdom. Aggressive harassment of the citizenry by the suspicious, French-domi-
nated police force created further resentment, the government's mistrust sowing
reciprocal mistrust within the populace. French actions thus stifled Westphalia's
growth and seemed to flout its fledgling independence, dashing hopes of
progress and profit from association with France. As one French historian has
remarked, Napoleon 'gave constitutions to nations as he gave crowns to princes
but did not require himself to respect either' and it is hardly surprising that the
French name was eventually made odious to most of the kingdom's citizens.
Third, the pressures of time and war hobbled Westphalia's development.
Harnessed to Napoleon's chariot from the moment of its birth, the government
was unable to establish itself and provide its diverse population with a new
focus of loyalty. It was a state that never had time to become a nation.[3]

The fourth factor in the failure of the Westphalian state was the character of
its king. When Napoleon established the kingdom in mid-1807, he reserved its

throne for his youngest brother, Jerome, and the new monarch duly arrived in Kassel in early December of that year to assume the reigns of government from a council of French regents.[4] Jerome is one of the many curious and controversial figures that populate the Napoleonic era. Born in 1784, he was fifteen years younger than his Imperial brother and had led a rather dissolute life which did little to prepare him for his royal seat. The Bonaparte patriarch, Charles, having died when Jerome was only fifteen months old, Napoleon assumed the paternal role and eventually brought his brother to France to gain an education. Young Jerome, however, evinced little interest in scholastic pursuits and Napoleon, now First Consul, decided that a career in the navy might instill some discipline and seriousness in the giddy adolescent. Jerome dutifully sailed with the fleet but changed little. Before long, he and some wastrel associates left their ship without permission and travelled to America where Jerome managed to outrage his older brother by badgering the French ambassador for cash and unexpectedly marrying a Baltimore woman in 1803. Forced to annul the marriage, Jerome returned to Napoleon's good graces and the sea, winning a small naval engagement during an unauthorized Atlantic cruise. Back on dry land, he was showered with Imperial honours and exchanged his sea legs for a general's rank to participate in the 1807 campaign as commander of IX Corps (Bavarians and Württembergers). Although he performed adequately in this, his first experience in land warfare, his earlier escapades had already established his reputation as an irresponsible youth who owed his position to his brother's over-indulgence.

Despite this dubious reputation, Napoleon was forgivingly fond of his youngest brother and thought to detect excellent qualities in his character: 'I am much mistaken if he does not have that within him out of which a man of the first rank may be made.' To give the family prodigal a measure of respectability in aristocratic circles and credibility with his new subjects, the Emperor arranged for him to marry Friedrich of Württemberg's daughter Katharina, who soon wrote of her husband as the 'bliss and delight of my life'. The erratic Jerome was thus sent off to Kassel to assume his royal robes, accompanied by his devoted German wife and armed with tomes of earnest advice on the role of Westphalia in the larger Imperial scheme and the consequent importance of winning the trust and loyalty of his new subjects:

Do not listen to those who tell you that your people, accustomed to serfdom, will regard your good deeds with ingratitude. People in the Kingdom of Westphalia are more enlightened than is generally accepted and your throne can only be truly founded on the trust and love of the population. The people of Germany impatiently wish that. . . every sort of subservience and obstruction between the sovereign and the lowest classes will be completely erased. . . . . Your people must enjoy a freedom, an equality and a prosperity unknown to the nations of Germany and this liberal regime must, one way or another, aim for the healthiest changes in the systems of the Rheinbund and in your monarchy. This regime will be a stronger barrier against Prussia than the Elbe, the fortresses or French protection.. . . . Be a constitutional king.[5]

Indeed, Jerome seems to have had the best of intentions when he began his reign, initially working hard, promising to learn German within three years and applying his considerable intelligence to the task of organizing the kingdom. Charming and courageous, he made himself popular by his generosity and sincere concern for the citizens of this realm. Bound to these positive qualities, however, were a collection of pertinacious negative characteristics and these rose to the surface as he began to lose interest in the complex affairs of state. Unlike his brother Louis in Holland, Jerome made little effort to forge a firm link between himself and his German subjects, neglecting his study of the language and allowing a hedge of sycophants to separate him from the population. He remained irresponsible and had no sense of economy, tapping his overburdened exchequer to support his taste for expensive extravagance, particularly the increasing harem of mistresses that accumulated around the palace in Kassel. Ineluctably attracted to gaudy show and hollow glitter, the neophyte king and his court soon acquired a reputation for licentiousness, excess and meretricious display. All manner of wild tales were in circulation: lascivious parties lasted till dawn, the King bathed in Bordeaux wine; his agents scoured the countryside for beautiful women to satisfy his desires. Scandalized Westphalians gave their sovereign the sobriquet that would bedevil his memory throughout history: 'König Lustig' (the 'Pleasure King' or the 'Merry Monarch'). The stolid North Germans were not alone in being shocked by the alien 'Asian' luxury that pervaded the capital and drained the royal coffers; Napoleon frequently and strictly admonished his sibling, asking why Westphalia could not meet its financial obligations to the French military when its king could afford to support worthless cronies and fund infamous soirées. Clearly, there was much exaggeration in these stories, but they gained considerable audience throughout the realm, weakening Jerome's credibility with his people and embarrassing the Emperor. For all his intelligence and good nature, it is clear that Jerome was undisciplined and frivolous, an overprivileged youth who often allowed his indulgences to drown his better potential.[6]

A number of critical weaknesses thus lurked within the structure of the Westphalian state and the nature of its monarch. Although these were not fully developed in 1809, they defined the environment in which the kingdom's army functioned and illuminate the character of its royal commander.

THE ARMY

One of Jerome's first tasks upon assuming the throne was the organization of a national army to meet Napoleon's expectations. Article 5 of the Westphalian constitution specified that the Kingdom would provide a field contingent of 25,000 men (20,000 infantry, 3,500 cavalry and 1,500 artillery) to fulfill its military obligations as a member of the Confederation of the Rhine. It was Napoleon's intent, however, that Jerome's army be carefully constructed over a period of years on a solid foundation, a model for other German states. Half of the Westphalian contingent was indeed to be raised rapidly and made ready for active campaigning, but the Emperor apparently believed that an over-hasty expansion of the nascent kingdom's military would only produce mediocre units, unmotivated, partially trained and lacking cohesion. To preclude this, an additional provision of the constitution stated that the kingdom would only be expected to supply 12,500 troops 'for the first years', the rest of its military obligation to be met by assuming the expense of supporting the 12,500 French soldiers garrisoning the fortress of Magdeburg. In theory, Jerome would thus have the time necessary to organize his forces and could hope to be relieved of the requirement to support French troops on his soil as his army grew in size and competence. But the young King's head was full of the glamour and the glories of war and an ambition to imitate his Imperial brother (albeit on a smaller scale). Like other Confederation monarchs, he also seemed to harbour the conviction that a large army would enhance his stature in Napoleon's eyes and grant him a greater role in Rheinbund affairs. He thus allowed martial dreams to overwhelm common sense, exceeding his realm's limited fiscal resources and frequently leaping the bounds of sartorial good taste in his effort to create an army worthy of his self-image.

Decreeing the formation of his initial line units, internal security forces and a fairly large and expensive royal guard in 1808, Jerome managed to irritate Napoleon. The Emperor found his brother's proposed military establishment pretentious and inappropriate to the size of the Westphalian kingdom; he was particularly annoyed by the size and composition of the royal guard and Jerome's intention to raise a regiment of cuirassiers. The King curbed his desires somewhat in response to Imperial disapproval and scepticism, but persisted in his general course and by late 1808 was able to organize his guard and line units into two small divisions totalling some 14,500 men.[7]

The premier element of the Westphalian Army was the Royal Guard. Writing to Jerome in January 1808, Napoleon had recommended that the Westphalian Guard should consist of about 1,200 men equally divided among light horse, grenadiers and Jägers; 300 German-speaking Frenchmen would serve as the cadre for this force, the remainder to be recruited from young, well-situated Westphalians of the middle classes who could afford to pay for their own uniforms and equipment.[8] It was the Emperor's hope that these young men would thereby attach themselves to their new king while the French cadre instilled in them the spirit of French military institutions and a broad loyalty to the Napoleonic Empire. Always focused on his long-term goal of binding western Germany to France, Napoleon's comments thus emphasized thrift and moderation combined with careful political—military calculation. Jerome, however, had his own ideas of what was appropriate to his royal status and the Westphalian Guard soon burgeoned far beyond Napoleon's restrained suggestions: by early 1809, it numbered almost 2,700 men in four squadrons of horse, three battalions of foot and an attached horse artillery battery.[9]

Two units provided the mounted component of the Guard. First and most prestigious was Jerome's Garde du Corps, an excess Napoleon derided as 'contrary to the etiquette' of the Bonaparte family.[10] Organized around a cadre of Polish cavalrymen donated by Napoleon and raised to a 'squadron' of 206 men (officially a single large company plus staff) by the recruitment of volunteers, the Garde du Corps was a palace guard much in the style of the *ancien régime*, its functions basically ceremonial: decorating the royal residence, dashing ahead of the King's carriage on his travels, escorting him on campaign. It never engaged in combat. Its brilliant uniform reflected its principal duties and Jerome's predilection for pomp and splendour: white coats with black lapels, collars and cuffs, all trimmed in red and sparkling with gold lace and tassels. White breeches, heavy cavalry jackboots, black bicornes with golden tassels and black leather equipment likewise trimmed in gold completed this impressive display to which Jerome later added a steel helmet and heavily emblazoned cuirass.

In addition to pleasing Jerome's ego, however, the glittering palace guard was also a training ground for the army's officer corps. Volunteers of the middle class who enrolled in the Garde du Corps not only enjoyed a number of privileges *vis-à-vis* the rest of the army but could hope to join line units as officers after several years' satisfactory service.[11] Similarly, outstanding NCOs of the line who were selected for the Garde du Corps could expect to return with lieutenants' epaulets on their shoulders. This small but steady exchange of personnel between the Garde du Corps and the line served several practical purposes. First, it provided the army's regular formations with experienced officers, thoroughly schooled in French tactics and military administration. Second, it extended Jerome's influence by creating a body of officers who were at least nominally obligated to their king for their present positions and future promotions. Finally, this arrangement provided an avenue of advancement for men previously excluded from the upper strata of society. The Garde du Corps, indeed the entire Westphalian Army, was thus an instrument of social change in northern Germany, allowing individuals of talent to improve their status regardless of the accidents of birth.

The other mounted formation of Jerome's Guard was the Chevauxlegers-Regiment der Garde, composed of three squadrons (188 officers and men each) and a depot company (strength of 97) for a total authorized strength of 680 officers and men. As with the Garde du Corps, the Polish lancers Napoleon had sent to escort Jerome to Kassel in December 1807 formed the cadre of the regiment, the rest of its saddles being filled by drafting promising soldiers from line units and adding picked conscripts and volunteers.[12] These efforts were only partially successful, however, and the regiment was considerably understrength when it took the field in 1809. Like many of the German light cavalry regiments of this era, the chevauxlegers wore a black leather helmet, bound in brass with a black comb. The base colour of their uniform was dark-green with red distinctions on the coat and yellow trim and lace in every conceivable location.

Three battalions comprised the infantry of the Guard: Garde-Grenadier, Garde-Jäger and Jäger-Carabinier. The Grenadier Battalion consisted of a staff, six field companies of 116 men each and a depot company (also 116) for a nominal strength of 841. Assembled from Hessian veterans, drafts from the line infantry grenadier companies and the better conscripts, the battalion was uniformed in white with red distinctions and the decorative yellow lace standard to the Westphalian Guard. The battalion was further distinguished by large bearskin caps hung about with red cords and other typical grenadier paraphernalia. The Garde-Jäger Battalion had originally been organized with four companies (486 men), but by 1809 it seems to have been expanded into an establishment similar to that of the grenadiers: staff, six field companies (119 each) and depot.[13] The 1st Company bore an honourary designation as the battalion's 'Elite' or 'Carabinier' Company. The Garde-Jägers wore the dark-green uniform typical of German light infantry with yellow collar, cuffs, turnbacks and trim, all highlighted by extensive white lace. Despite its Jäger title, the battalion carried the same musket as the line infantry and Guard Grenadiers, being distinguished from them only by its light infantry garb and its intended function on the battlefield.

The Jäger-Carabinier presented a different picture entirely. Recruited exclusively from trained hunters and foresters, it was the only unit other than the Garde du Corps to be composed entirely of volunteers and was also the only formation in the army armed with rifles. Although not officially part of the Guard but rather attached, it was élite in character and habitually brigaded with the rest of the Guard infantry to perform standard Jäger functions (skirmishing, scouting, etc.). With a tiny staff and four small companies of 103 men each, the entire battalion totalled only slightly over 400 officers and men. As with the Garde-Jäger, the 1st Company was considered the élite of the battalion and its members accordingly wore bearskin caps. The rest of the battalion wore a black shako atop a uniform of dark-green with black facings and red lace trim.

By February 1809, the line troops of Jerome's army comprised four infantry regiments, a light infantry battalion, two cavalry regiments and three foot artillery batteries. Two additional infantry regiments were being slowly assembled from new drafts. Like the rest of the army, these infantry regiments were organized exactly according to the French model, with two field battalions, each

---

Table 9-1: Westphalian Army Organization February/March 1809

1st Division - GD Reubell

1st Brigade - GB d'Albignac
  Garde-Grenadier Battalion
  Garde-Jäger Battalion
  Jäger-Carabinier Battalion*
  Garde du Corps
  Garde Chevauxlegers
  one horse artillery battery

2nd Brigade
  1st Infantry Regiment
  5th Infantry Regiment (forming)
  6th Infantry Regiment (forming)
  1st Cuirassier Regiment
  one foot artillery battery

2nd Division - GD Morio

1st Brigade - GB Boerner
  2nd Infantry Regiment
  4th Infantry Regiment

2nd Brigade - Adjutant Cmdt von Ochs**
  3rd Infantry Regiment
  1st Light Battalion

Division Artillery - von Heinemann
  two foot batteries

1st Chevauxlegers Regiment***

* The Jäger-Carabiniers initially marched to Metz with Morio's Division, but were recalled to Kassel before the division headed off to Spain.
** Promoted to Brigadegeneral (GB) in June 1809.
*** The 1st Chevauxlegers nominally belonged to Morio's Division, but never actually served with their compatriots.

---

of six companies, and a depot battalion of four companies; as with the French, there were no Inhaber, the line regiments being simply numbered. Field battalions included the normal French arrangement of four companies of fusiliers and one company each of grenadiers and voltigeurs, all companies with a strength of about 140 officers and men for a total of some 840 per battalion. An additional 560 men were found in the depot battalion's four fusilier companies, so a regiment with its staff might count as many as 2,282 in its ranks under ideal conditions. Conditions were hardly ideal, but most line infantry units seem to have taken the field with nearly a full complement of soldiers. In contrast with the extravagance of the Guard, the line infantry was uniformed in a simple, straightforward fashion: a white coat of French cut, white breeches, black shako.

Jerome's infantry also included a light battalion (the 1st) uniformed in light-blue. It was authorized some 870 men in the standard six-company organization (four chasseur companies, one carabinier and one voltigeur company) together with a depot of 140.

There were only two cavalry regiments, one light and one heavy, outside of the Royal Guard. The 1st Chevauxlegers Regiment was authorized 644 men for its four field squadrons and wore a dark-green uniform with orange distinctions. The organization of the heavy cavalry regiment, the 1st Cuirassiers, was almost identical with that of the Chevauxlegers: four squadrons each of two companies (79 men) plus staff gave a total authorized field strength of 652 officers and men. For both heavy and light cavalry, field companies were numbered 1 to 8, with the 9th Company forming the regimental depot. Westphalia was unique among the smaller nations of Europe in possessing a cuirassier regiment. True heavy cavalry, big men on big horses intended to perform decisive shock action on the battlefield, required extensive training and was extraordinarily costly to raise and maintain. Moreover, a nation needed multiple regiments formed into a mounted reserve if the heavy horsemen were to fulfill their role as battle cavalry, otherwise, their numbers would be insufficient to deliver the telling blow and their strength would be dissipated in the performance of typical light cavalry missions, scouting, screening and the like. Heavy cavalry was thus regarded as a luxury affordable only to larger states (France, Austria, etc.) and Napoleon was annoyed when he learned Jerome had formed the 1st Cuirassiers:

> I see that you have a regiment of cuirassiers. This arm does not seem to me appropriate for you. You are not a power large enough for a respectable body of heavy cavalry, what you should form is light cavalry. Your cavalry should be composed entirely of chasseurs.[14]

Jerome was not to be dissuaded, however, and the regiment was duly assembled and sent to Braunschweig, albeit without armoured breastplates. Wearing white coats with carmine distinctions, steel helmets and stiff black boots, the troopers rode into their new garrison with their overcoats rolled over their shoulders in place of the missing cuirasses.

Westphalia's artillery corps consisted of three foot companies, one horse company, a company of *ouvriers* (artificers who built and repaired artillery vehicles), a company of sappers and four train companies, all grouped under a single regimental headquarters for administrative purposes. Each company numbered about 100 men giving the regiment a total of approximately 1,000 gunners, sappers, *ouvriers*, train and staff. The lone horse artillery company was attached to the Guard together with a train company to form a battery of four 6-pounders, two howitzers, twelve ammunition wagons and a field smithy. The foot batteries were organized and equipped along similar lines.[15]

In addition to the field or mobile forces of the Guard and line, Westphalia also organized a number of paramilitary units for internal duties. The most important of these organizations was the Gendarmerie-Legion, a force of 144 carefully selected men who were distributed throughout the kingdom in small detachments as a form of national police.[16] Initially composed almost entirely of German-speaking Frenchmen, the gendarmes had their principal duty in the apprehension of deserters and draft evaders. The zeal with which they executed their onerous tasks quickly brought them an evil reputation and they were broadly hated in the countryside. As with their organization, their uniform followed the example of the French national gendarmes: dark-blue coat with red distinctions, buff breeches, black bicorne.

For more mundane duties, the police in each of Westphalia's eight departments were assisted by a Departmental Company (or Prefecture Guard) of fifty men.[17] Wearing a pike-grey uniform with red trim and bicorne hat, these men guarded armouries, gaols and other public buildings. Each department also had a Veteran Company of about 80 former soldiers in shako and a dark-blue uniform with red piping.[18] Together with these departmental units, major cities raised 'National Guard' formations. Unlike their French counterparts, however, the Westphalian National Guards had no fixed organization and no real military value, serving rather as honour guards (*Paradetruppen*) for festive occasions, posting the watch at city gates and otherwise reinforcing municipal police.[19] Lastly, a depot was established for the punishment of draft evaders (Depot für Refractäre); formed into companies of 100 men, the inmates of this cheery organization were sentenced to two years' hard labour, principally road construction.[20]

Filling the ranks of this plethora of units proved a major challenge for the new Westphalian administrative apparatus. The French had hoped to tap the supposedly rich reservoir of experienced and mercenary Hessian soldiery to create the kingdom's army, but the efforts of Westphalian recruiting officers were only moderately successful and about half of the army's personnel requirements had to be supplied through conscription.[21] From the start, there were problems with both volunteers and conscripts and some of the former seem to have been decidedly inferior to the draftees in military potential. The 1st and 2nd Infantry Regiments, for example, were based on two thin regiments of the old Franco-Hessian Legion, a lacklustre organization created when the French overran Hesse-Kassel in 1806. Much worse was the 1st Light, formed from non-Prussians who had been dragooned into Prussian service, captured in the Jena campaign and sent to Jerome by Napoleon; so egregious was its behaviour that Jerome had it transferred out of his capital to quieten the complaints of the city's residents. The 1st Chevauxlegers, consisting only of volunteer German cavalrymen, also earned a reputation for indiscipline.[22] Such units seem to have had a fairly mercenary demeanour and it is unlikely they were motivated by any nationalistic attachment to the new kingdom. The government in Kassel recognized the importance of generating at least a modicum of national sentiment, however, and enacted laws specifying that only Westphalian citizens could be conscripted and requiring that all Westphalians serving in foreign militaries return home or face confiscation of their property.

There were also problems with the conscription process. Evasion, desertion, bureaucracy, organizational inexperience and the incompetence of the Minister of War, Jerome's useless protégé GD Joseph Morio, all conspired to impede the initial formation of the army. Napoleon's frustration at delays in the preparation of a contingent for Spain eventually led to Morio's dismissal in August 1808 and his replacement by the tough and extraordinarily able GD Jean-Baptiste Eblé.[23] Eblé soon brought a degree of efficiency and energy to the War Ministry, providing the administrative experience necessary to put the Westphalian Army on its feet, but the attempt to expand the army rapidly in 1809 seriously strained the kingdom's resources, delaying the formation of many new units for months or even years.

Difficulties of a different nature attended Westphalia's attempts to create an officer corps. Where experienced soldiers were in short supply, the kingdom had to cope with an unexpected surfeit of officers. Initially, almost any applicant was granted a Westphalian commission and numerous 'adventurers and dubious personalities' apparently slipped into Jerome's service during the first few months of his reign. The dangers of this policy were soon obvious, however, and strict measures were enacted to ensure the Westphalian origin and military competence of prospective officers. Although Westphalia would gradually develop the ability to educate and train its own leaders, the officer corps of 1808-9 had to be built from scratch. Fortunately, the defeat of Prussia and its allies in 1806 had created a large pool of experienced but unemployed officers and these quickly migrated to the Rheinbund states. Former Hessian officers comprised 50 per cent of the Westphalian officer corps and another 24 per cent had previously served with the Prussian, Braunschweig or Hannoverian armies. French influence was also strong and former French officers made up another 15—20 per cent of the leadership, particularly in senior command and staff positions. Unfortunately, many of these Frenchmen were Jerome's feckless associates from his navy days or adjutants who had served on his staff during the 1807 campaign in Silesia; most had only limited combat experience and none had ever led large formations in battle.[24]

The motives of these officers varied widely. Many, such as Johann von Borcke posted to the 1st Light Battalion, were unhappy at leaving their former sovereigns and swore allegiance to Jerome 'with the greatest reluctance' for lack of any other source of income. Others welcomed the call to lead their countrymen. Jerome's announcement that all Westphalian natives serving in foreign armies were required to return 'was greeted with much jubilation', remembered Heinrich von Meibom, soon to don the uniform of the Garde-Jäger.[25]

There was indeed considerable cause for satisfaction, for the army these officers and men joined was fresh and modern, carefully following the dynamic French pattern and hence brash and alien to those emerging from the stiff old traditions of Prussia and the petty princes. If some officers grumbled at the amount of time they were expected to spend with their men, however, most were pleased by the good pay and unprecedented opportunities for advancement; a man of energy and ability, be he a humble cannoneer or an ambitious lieutenant, might hope for rapid promotion and other rewards.[26] The army was characterized by an enlightened outlook, punishments were made more humane, funds were established to care for veterans, widows and orphans, decorations were introduced to recognize individual bravery and every effort was made to draw the soldier into a greater national entity. The army was thus intended to function as an instrument of social change in Westphalia, gradually eroding old loyalties and class distinctions while providing a focus for national sentiment and forging durable bonds between the new citizens and their sovereign. Jerome, attempting

Table 9-2: The Westphalian Army in April 1809

Line Infantry Regiments

Organization: two field battalions per regiment; one grenadier company, one voltigeur company and four fusilier companies per battalion; one depot battalion of four fusilier companies per regiment; company strength 140 men.
Uniform: white coat with distinctive colour on collar, lapels, cuffs, turnbacks; white breeches; white belting; shako.

Number	Distinctive Colour	
1	dark-blue	
2	dark-blue	(in Spain)
3	light-blue	(in Spain)
4	light-blue	(in Spain)
5	yellow	(forming)
6	yellow	(forming)

Other Line Infantry and Cavalry Formations

1st Light Infantry Battalion (in Spain)
Organization: one carabinier, one voltigeur, four chasseur companies; one depot company.
Uniform: light-blue coat with orange distinctions; shako.

Jäger-Carabinier Battalion (attached to Guard)
Organization: four companies of 103 men each.
Uniform: dark-green coat and breeches; black facings with red trim; shako.

1st Chevauxlegers Regiment (in Spain)
Organization: four squadrons; one depot company.
Uniform: dark-green coat and breeches with orange distinctions; shako.

1st Cuirassier Regiment
Organization: four squadrons; one depot company.
Uniform: white coat with carmine distinctions; white breeches; steel helmet; no cuirass.

Royal Guard

Garde du Corps
Organization: one company of 206 men.
Uniform: white coat and breeches with black facings trimmed with red and gold lace; black bicorne hat.

Garde Chevauxlegers Regiment
Organization: three squadrons (188 men each); one depot company (97 men).
Uniform: dark-green coat and breeches with red distinctions and yellow trim; black leather helmet.

Garde-Grenadier Battalion
Organization: six field companies and one depot company; company strength 116.
Uniform: white coat with red distinctions and yellow lace; white breeches; bearskin cap.

Garde-Jäger Battalion
Organization: six field companies and one depot company; company strength 119.
Uniform: dark-green coat and breeches with yellow distinctions and white trim; shako.

Artillery

Organization: Artillery Regiment with three foot companies, one horse company (attached to the Guard), one *ouvrier* company, one sapper company, four train companies; company strength 100 men.
Artillery uniform: dark-blue coat with red facings; dark-blue breeches; shako. Train uniform: grey coat with red facings; grey breeches; shako.

to promote this process, personally lavished attention on his men, especially the Guard, speaking openly and caringly with the common soldiers, tasting their food, inquiring about their conditions. His concern naturally sparked a similar interest in his officers and even the diffident von Borcke had to admit that 'it would not be easy for any army to exhibit more internal order or more care for the soldier than this one'.[27]

While it had its promising, positive features, the Westphalian Army was also beset by several potentially debilitating weaknesses when it went to war in 1809. First, it was new and inexperienced, untested and stuffed full of raw conscripts. The men drilled eight hours a day,[28] but it was still forming when called to march; unit cohesion and *esprit* had not had time to develop. Second, the army possessed no national military tradition, indeed no national tradition of any sort

Map 44. North Central Germany

Insurrections: ✳

0   50   100
kilometres

to bind it together and inspire it to great deeds. The officers might fight to satisfy their notions of honour, oath and professionalism, but they and their men
were still Hessians and Braunschweigers, not yet Westphalians, and it remained
to be seen whether Jerome had had sufficient time to instill in them a sense of
citizenship and national duty. Third, the Westphalian Army's metamorphosis
into a true national military was hindered not only by the diversity of its soldiery
but by a strong lingering suspicion of French intentions. French influence was
nowhere more evident than in the army and the wholesale adoption of French
military practices (such as the 1791 drill regulation [29] and the detested conscription laws) combined with the prevalence of parvenus Westphalian generals of
French birth to generate latent concern if not resentment in the minds of many
new soldiers.[30] Finally, the military qualities of these expatriate Frenchmen,
now senior Westphalian leaders, were not readily apparent. The king, his chief
of staff and his division commanders were all relatively new to the business of
organizing and leading large formations in combat and it was not clear how they
would stand up under the test of fire.[31]

APRIL - THE INSURRECTIONS: KATTE AND DÖRNBERG

When the war with Austria opened on 10 April 1809, a large portion of the
Westphalian Army was headed for the Spanish cauldron, only about two-thirds
remaining available to protect the kingdom and support the operations of the
Armée d'Allemagne. The 1st Chevauxlegers had ridden for the Pyrenees in
September 1808 to join Marshal Victor's I Corps and General Morio's Division
departed for the Iberian Peninsula in February of the following year, eventually
coming under the command of GD Gouvion Saint-Cyr (VII Corps). Jerome was
thus left with only his Guard, the 1st Cuirassiers, three line infantry regiments,
two artillery batteries and his paramilitary organizations. Furthermore, of the
line infantry regiments, only the 1st had completed its formation, the 5th and 6th
were just beginning to assemble. Scattered about the realm in its garrisons and
incompletely organized, the army would therefore require several weeks, if not
months, of preparation before it could be considered ready to take the field.

KATTE'S RAID (2-4 APRIL)

Despite Austria's martial preparations, the first threat Westphalia faced in the
spring of 1809 was not external invasion but internal rebellion. Indeed, the initial sparks of unrest flew into the night sky near Magdeburg a week before the
Archduke Charles crossed the Inn to enter Bavaria.

Friedrich Karl von Katte had served as a lieutenant in the Royal Prussian
Army until he was pensioned off when the army was reduced in the wake of the
1806 débâcle.[32] Approached in the autumn of 1808 by an agent of a nascent
German nationalist movement, he was informed that Austria would soon take up
arms against France and that Germans living under French domination must
seize this opportunity to throw off the Napoleonic 'yoke'. Persuaded that he
could play an important role in this patriotic effort by capturing the fortress of
Magdeburg, he spent the next several months riding through the Westphalian
districts north of the city in disguise, recruiting potential rebels, primarily former

Prussian soldiers, and preparing for his moment. In a subsequent meeting with his mysterious contact from Berlin, it was decided that Katte would strike on 2 April. His success would be the signal for all Germany from the Elbe to the Rhine to rise in 'a general explosion'. Late on the afternoon of the appointed day, Katte and his band of followers crossed the Elbe near Havelberg and moved south to occupy Stendal, where they confiscated some money from surprised local officials and disarmed two gendarmes. The rebels, some 300 strong, pro-ceeded toward Magdeburg on the following evening, but French and Westphalian authorities had by now been alerted, a patrol of mounted Magdeburg National Guardsmen appeared, a brief scuffle ensued in which eleven rebels were apprehended, and Katte abandoned his plans, fleeing over the Elbe and sadly disbanding his little troop. On the 5th, Katte's thirty-ninth birth-day, the 1st Westphalian Infantry reached Magdeburg and secured the city. The half-formed 6th Infantry arrived three days later, while the frustrated von Katte, pursued by Prussian authorities, slipped over the border into Bohemia to join the Duke of Braunschweig's free corps.

Katte's raid was militarily insignificant, his only encounters with the 'enemy' being the capture of the two gendarmes at Stendal and seizure of one Magdeburg National Guardsman as the rebels were retreating. Hardly any shots appear to have been fired in anger and the intended insurrection collapsed almost before it started.[33] Nor is there any solid reason to believe the raid would have achieved its aim of rousing central Germany against Napoleon even if Magdeburg had been temporarily occupied. Despite Katte's sedulous prepara-tion and the supposed co-ordination of his act with other uprisings, the general plan was poorly conceived and never enjoyed any real hope of success. None the less, the incident is important for two reasons. First, it highlighted the dan-ger of insurrection in Westphalia, showing that there existed a group of dedicat-ed, if apparently unrealistic, men supported by outside powers who were willing to risk all to overthrow Jerome's throne. There was considerable panic in Kassel as the first reports arrived and the fear persisted that this was but the 'partial and premature explosion of a much more general plan'.[34] Second, it indicated that the Westphalian people were not yet ready to rise up *en masse* against their new king. While many might have grumbled complaints about the regime in Kassel and some would welcome Katte, very few actually joined the ranks of the rebels. The time was not yet right for insurrection.

DÖRNBERG'S UPRISING (22-24 APRIL)

Other hopeful rebel leaders, such as Wilhelm Freiherr von Dörnberg, might have profited from the lesson of von Katte's failure. Fifty-one years old, the musta-chioed Dörnberg was a competent and apparently charismatic figure, another former Prussian officer who had been one of the last to capitulate in 1806.[35] He was also a dedicated Hessian patriot. In communication with the German nationalists in Berlin as well as the deposed dukes of Hesse-Kassel and Braunschweig in their Bohemian exile, he accepted a commission in the Westphalian Guard in December 1807, evidently with the intention of using his position to infiltrate the army and unseat Jerome. He thus swore fealty to the

Westphalian king despite his deep aversion to the 'foreign' regime and rose rapidly in rank and responsibility, enjoying Jerome's complete trust. As Colonel and commander of the Jäger-Carabiniers at Marburg (April 1808 to February 1809), he sought to lay the foundation for insurrection, slowly and quietly gathering adherents, particularly within the Guard. Promoted to Royal Adjutant and commander of the Garde-Jäger in late February 1809, he swore a second oath of loyalty to Jerome and was brought to Kassel as his former battalion took the road to Spain.[36] The time for action was fast approaching, however, and Dörnberg did not wish to be deprived of the men he considered loyal followers, a reliable rebel cadre; he thus persuaded Jerome to recall the Jäger-Carabiniers and the battalion duly returned to Westphalia, this time as part of the capital's garrison.

By April 1809, therefore, all seemed auspicious for the undertaking. Within Westphalia, military support appeared widespread and dedicated, with Dörnberg's most trusted units strategically located in Kassel. There also seemed to be a broad base of popular support, the efforts of Dörnberg and others having brought together a disparate collection of discontented individuals from all elements of society—peasants, foresters, burghers and disgruntled minor gentry—all apparently eager to overthrow the French.[37] Beyond the kingdom's borders, the imminent war between France and Austria promised to distract French attention and bring Habsburg military intervention. The exiled dukes and a fervently nationalistic Prussian major named Schill were also expected to appear with small armies of patriots. Relying on this external assistance, the rebels concocted a vague plan to seize Jerome and his French generals, dramatically imprison them in a ruined castle and occupy the Westphalian capital. Beyond this, the plan became nebulous as the plotters were driven by widely different interests and could agree on little more than their hatred of the French. In fact, the entire enterprise was characterized by amateurism and if Dörnberg was a capable and dedicated officer, many of his co-conspirators could offer little more than self-importance and muddle-headed enthusiasm to the cause.

On the morning of 22 April as Napoleon was crushing Rosenberg's IV Corps at Eggmühl, Dörnberg's associates called the people of Hesse to arms and by afternoon two principal groups of insurgents were taking form, one west of Kassel, the other at Homberg to the south. There were two squadrons of the 1st Cuirassiers in Homberg and some of the troopers joined the insurrection, but the majority withdrew, holding themselves 'neutral' for the moment while many of the officers rode to the regimental headquarters at Melsungen to demand that their commander, Colonel Marschall, take action against the rebels. Acceding to this pressure, Marschall reluctantly headed toward Homberg with the regiment's other two squadrons and some fifty French infantrymen.

In Kassel meanwhile, all was hectic activity and confusion, but Dörnberg, believing himself betrayed (erroneously, as it happens), gave up his half-baked notions of seizing Jerome and fled to Homberg. Arriving in the town at about 5 p.m., the perspiring Oberst found a crowd of several thousand, a jumbled mixture of peasants, townspeople and former Hessian soldiers thrown together with little equipment and less discipline. The supply of brandy, however, was apparently plentiful. Colonel Marschall and his cuirassiers rode into town shortly thereafter, but Dörnberg persuaded the cavalry colonel to remain neutral until the next day and the troopers departed, many doubtless disgusted by their commander's pusillanimous conduct.[38] At about 8 p.m., the ragtag rebel cavalcade, probably numbering 4—5,000, moved off in the direction of Kassel to reach a tiny hamlet called Knallhütte (now Kirchbauna, some 10 kilometres south of Kassel) in the misty pre-dawn hours of the 23rd. Here they were surprised by a detachment of Garde Chevauxlegers who captured several of the insurgents and returned to the capital with intelligence on Dörnberg's strength and dispositions. GD Jean-Jacques Reubell[39] was quickly dispatched with two companies of Garde-Jägers (about 200 men), twenty-five Garde Chevauxlegers and two guns to oppose Dörnberg's further advance. Deploying on a hill, the Guardsmen were joined by Oberst Marschall and loyal elements of the 1st Cuirassiers. Together they watched the disorderly rebels approach. There were a few tense moments as Dörnberg attempted to cajole the Jägers into joining the insurrection, but when Reubell's order to fire was obeyed, the insurgent band dispersed in moments like a flock of panicked geese. In the words of a newly conscripted Westphalian gunner:

> We had hardly stood here [on the height] for several hours when the insurgents came up the highway in dense bunches, not ordered but wildly disorganized, screaming and yelling and firing their guns in the air. That a trained military would soon finish this mob was obvious. ... The command to fire, however, was not given until the mob had approached to within half-range and because we had had to load canister our gun did dreadful execution in the dense crowd of men. The business only required one volley, the sabring cavalry completed the defeat and scattered the mob with little effort. Thus did I at this opportunity experience my first combat action.[40]

Shocked at the resistance and pursued by eager chevauxlegers, Dörnberg flew south, disguised himself in tattered peasant garb and eventually made his way to Bohemia.

The western group of rebels, about 1,200 strong, displayed a similar lack of organization and met a similar fate. Reaching the town of Wolfhagen, they had just been joined by a group of like-minded cuirassiers when GB Philippe de Rivet Comte d'Albignac appeared at the head of the 1st Squadron of Garde Chevauxlegers. Lances lowered, the Poles stormed into the market-place, scattered the terrified insurgents and came upon the now furtive Westphalian heavy cavalrymen.[41] Demanded to explain his presence, the cuirassiers' commander claimed that he had been pretending to make common cause with the rebels in order to escape capture and d'Albignac accordingly sent him back to his regiment. The departure of the cuirassiers and the fearsome demeanour of d'Albignac's Guardsmen cleared the air of all rebellious ardour and most of the would-be rebels were back at their hearths by sunset. The cuirassier officer prudently disappeared during the night.

Another band of rebels, some 4,000 strong, was also closing on Kassel on the morning of 23 April. Organized by several officers and local foresters, this group approached from the north-west, halting about 8 kilometres outside the city and closing off several key roads. Like the other collections of rebels, however, organization and discipline were weak and the crowd rapidly disintegrated when the demoralizing news of Dörnberg's repulse and flight became known. Two other hopeful rebels were even less successful. Attempting to raise the flag of revolt east of Kassel, they found the population unreceptive and were promptly seized by local authorities, clapped in irons and sent to the capital as prisoners.[42]

By the evening of the 23rd, then, Dörnberg's insurrection had collapsed completely. The kingdom had weathered another crisis and calm gradually returned to the nervous court in Kassel. Several factors contributed to the failure of the revolt: poor planning and shoddy organization on the part of the rebels, the absence of outside assistance, lukewarm response from the general populace and prompt action by the Westphalian Army. But credit must also be given to Jerome for his coolness and courage. Surrounded by confusion and personally shocked by the rebellion—he at first refused to believe that the man he had honoured and trusted would turn against him—he was advised to leave the capital but clearly saw that flight would bring only ruin and shame. Instead, he stayed on, reviewed the troops of the Kassel garrison and addressed their officers, telling them that any who repented the oath of loyalty they had sworn to him would be released from its bonds to join the ranks of the rebels. 'I know the heart of the soldier,' he said. 'I do not know that of the traitor.' He gave them two hours to decide. 'By his words one could see that he was a brother of the great Emperor,' remembered a Lieutenant Wolf. 'The King won every heart.' and the hall resounded with a loud 'Vive le roi!' To a man, they returned after the allotted period and renewed their oaths to Jerome.[43] Like Lieutenant Wolf, many doubtless felt a strong conflict between their oaths to the king and their patriotic duty as Germans, but they stood by their vows and led their men against the insurgents even though 'hot tears' might rise in their eyes.[44] Despite the serious weaknesses in the planning and prosecution of the brief rebellion, the story might have been very different if any significant number of these men had deserted their king and followed Dörnberg's flag.

While Jerome was coping with internal challenges to his regime, Napoleon was prosecuting the campaign against the Austrian Main Army. To cover his lines of communications, the Emperor not only created a *corps d'observation* at Hanau under Marshal Kellermann but also placed his brother in command of an odd assortment of allied troops with the imposing title of 'X Corps of the Armée d'Allemagne'. To the elements of his own army remaining in Westphalia after Morio's departure, Jerome was to add a Dutch division, two French *demi-brigades de reserve* (composed of new recruits and depot troops), the garrisons of Küstrin, Stettin and Swedish Pomerania (French, Polish, Saxon, and Mecklenburg troops), the Erfurt garrison (a Frankfurt battalion) and a battalion from the Grand Duchy of Würzburg.[45] In all, Napoleon eventually hoped to provide Jerome with a mobile force of some 20,000 men exclusive of the

fortress garrisons to 'maintain tranquility from Hamburg to the Main', to oppose
any English landings on the German coast, to 'disperse insurgents', and to render all possible assistance to the Saxons should the need arise. This force would
be slow to gather, however, and Napoleon had limited confidence in its combat
capacity. He thus relied on deception to shield his rear area, giving his brother's
command its impressive title and telling him to spread the rumour that X Corps
numbered 40,000 or more soldiers.[46] The first of these troops began to arrive in
Westphalia in the days immediately following Dörnberg's abortive insurrection,
just in time to counter the next threat to the realm.[47]

Table 9-3: X Corps Initial Organization (May)
Commander: King Jerome Napoleon
Chief of Staff: GD Reubell

1st (Westphalian) Division - GD Graf Bernterode

Garde-Grenadier Battalion
Garde-Jäger Battalion
Jäger-Carabinier Battalion
Garde du Corps
Garde Chevauxlegers (three squadrons)
one horse artillery battery (6 guns)

2nd (Westphalian) Division - GB d'Albignac

1st Infantry Regiment
5th Infantry Regiment
6th Infantry Regiment
3rd Berg Infantry Regiment (two battalions)
1st Cuirassiers
one foot artillery battery (6 guns)

3rd (Dutch) Division - GD Gratien

1st Brigade - GM Anthing
   6th Dutch Infantry Regiment (two battalions)
   7th Dutch Infantry Regiment (two battalions)
2nd Brigade - GM van Hasselt
   8th Dutch Infantry Regiment (two battalions)
   9th Dutch Infantry Regiment (two battalions)
2nd Dutch Cuirassiers (three squadrons)
one foot battery (1st Company, 2nd Foot Artillery)
1st and 2nd Horse Batteries
   (4 guns per battery)

French Troops

IV/22 Ligne
Detachments of:
   28th Léger, 27th, 30th, 33rd, and 65th Ligne

Strength (approx.)

Westphalian -	8,000
Dutch -	5,300
Berg -	1,400
French -	1,300
Total --	16,000 men
	24 guns

NOTES:
1. This appears to have been an administrative organization because until Schill's defeat on the last day of May, these units were dispersed all over Germany and never actually fought as a Corps in this configuration. See text.
2. All three division commanders were Frenchmen who had taken service with Napoleon's brothers (Bernterode was one of Jerome's friends, a Frenchman named Ducoudras, who had been granted the title 'Graf Bernterode').
3. Garrisons nominally under Jerome's command were:
- Küstrin: I/22nd Ligne, 5th Polish Infantry, detachment of 4th Polish Chasseurs;
- Stettin: III/22nd Ligne, I/10th Polish Infantry, 4th Polish Chasseurs, II/von Dyherrn (Saxon);
- Swedish Pomerania: the Mecklenburg contingents (3 battalions).

MAY - SCHILL'S RIDE

The next figure to step on to the Westphalian stage was Major Ferdinand von
Schill, a Prussian cavalry officer who had gained wide renown by leading bold
partisan raids in the French rear during the 1807 campaign. Although daring,
charismatic and successful in a time of Prussian defeat, Schill was also romantically oriented, a dreamer of unrealistic plans, eager to disobey higher authority
when it conflicted with his personal vision of German glory. A fervent patriot,
he had been in contact with other nationalists from Berlin to the Rhine, including von Dörnberg, and now hoped that his talisman name would ignite rebellion
across northern Germany and force the Prussian king into war against France.
In late April, feeling pressured by fate and flattering pleas for action from all
corners of Germany and heartened by what seemed to be dramatic Austrian successes on the battlefield, Schill secretly decided it was time to move. On the

Map 45. Schill's Ride

rainy afternoon of 28 April, he marched his regiment, the 2nd Brandenburg Hussars, and a few odd detachments out of Berlin, ostensibly for manoeuvres. Several hours outside the city, however, he halted the men, announced his intentions, allowed those who were opposed to depart, and turned toward the Westphalian border in defiance of specific orders to the contrary.[48]

Schill's initial objective was Magdeburg, and he thus marched due east from Berlin, reaching Gross Kreutz on the night of the 29th. Here, however, he learned that the fortress had been alerted and rather than assault a prepared defender, he turned south toward Wittenberg, crossing the border into Saxony on 30 April and arriving under the walls of the ancient fortress on the morning of 1 May.[49] The appearance of the renegades at Wittenberg threw the Saxon court into a panic and it was only with the greatest exertion that General von Funck of the king's staff managed to impose order and orchestrate a military response. Wittenberg's garrison was small, the enemy's numbers were initially exaggerated and Schill apparently announced that he was the vanguard of the entire Prussian Army.[50] Moreover, most of Saxony's mobile troops had marched away to join Napoleon's main army in the Danube valley, leaving only scattered detachments available for home defence. The situation seemed grim. Fortunately, Saxony had two cool-headed captains on the scene and these men soon determined that the Prussian had no guns whatsoever, that his entire force amounted to little more than 500 men and that the Prussian Army was nowhere to be seen. They therefore refused Schill's demands for entrance and money, ignoring his threat to storm the city and informing him that a regiment of cuirassiers was en route to relieve them. Indeed, Schill had neither the strength nor the desire to assault Wittenberg and, after reducing his demand for coin from 500,000 to 2,000 talers without result, had to content himself with merely being permitted to cross over the Elbe undisturbed. Observed by the city's defenders, Schill and his band passed over the river, bivouacked on the southern bank and marched west for Dessau the next morning, pursued at a distance by elements of the *Zastrow* Cuirassiers.[51] The determination of the two Saxon captains and Funck's prompt action had not only preserved a fortress, a well-stocked armoury and their sovereign's honour, but also saved more than six million talers of the kingdom's treasury secured in the city when the Saxon government had evacuated Dresden.[52]

Departing Saxony, Schill entered the Anhalt Duchies on 2 May, spending the night in Dessau and sending a raiding party ahead to Köthen to spread the word of liberation.[53] The following day, he continued west to Bernburg, his rear guard confronting the pursuing Saxon cuirassiers at Dessau. The cuirassiers almost trapped Schill's men, but the Prussians made good their escape and the Saxons, now well beyond their own borders, gave up the chase and rode back to the east. Schill's men made their first foray into Westphalia that night, striking south to Halle which they claimed for the King of Prussia after disarming 150 hapless Westphalian invalids and other second line troops. Despite these little successes, it was already evident that Schill's appearance was not inspiring the mass of the populace to rise against the French. The Saxon peasants had fled in terror, fearing brigandage, and however much some might cheer, neither

Anhalters nor Westphalians seemed enthused about actually joining Schill's troops. More bad news came in on the night of 3/4 May: Dörnberg's revolt had failed, Napoleon had gained a major victory at Eggmühl and Prussian authorities had issued urgent condemnations of the insubordinate escapade. The atmosphere was gloomy but most of his officers still supported the venture and when Schill learned that a French—Westphalian force was marching south out of Magdeburg to attack him, he ordered his little command north to Borne and eagerly began to prepare for combat.

SKIRMISH AT DODENDORF (5 MAY)

Schill's advance excited considerable anxiety in Kassel and Jerome, mistrusting the loyalty of his own soldiers, was soon calling on Marshal Kellermann's Corps and GD Pierre-Guillaume Gratien's Dutch Division for help. Before any of these troops could reach the kingdom's eastern border, however, Westphalian

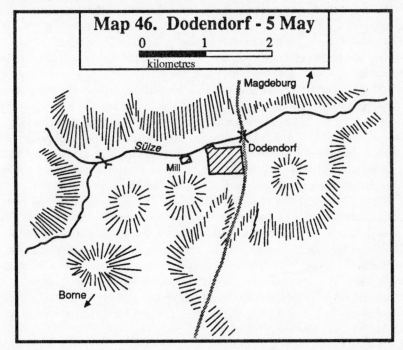

Map 46. Dodendorf - 5 May

and French troops met Schill's raiders in combat south of Magdeburg. The French commandant of that fortress, GD Claude Michaud, decided to send a detachment out of the city to discover Schill's strength and intentions and to bring the intruders to battle if a favourable opportunity presented itself. With a force of two French infantry companies, four Westphalian companies and two French guns, GB Leopold von Uslar, one of Jerome's adjutants, consequently moved south on 4 May and took up a fine defensive position near the village of Dodendorf.[54] Having no horsemen of his own and aware that the enemy disposed of some 500—600 cavalry but only about 50 infantry and no guns, Uslar deployed his men on high ground north of the village with a stream (the Sülze) to their front to negate Schill's superior mobility. Unfortunately, Michaud decided to replace von Uslar, who had fallen out of favour with Jerome, and, at about 11 a.m. on the 5th, Colonel Vauthier, commander of the 1st Westphalian Infantry, arrived at Dodendorf to assume command of the detachment.[55]

As the Oberst rode up, dust clouds off to the south-west signalled the approach of Schill's force. It hardly seemed the appropriate time to change dispositions, but Vauthier, ordered by Michaud to take the offensive, immediately began to move the little command south of the stream to attack the advancing Prussians. Things quickly began to go wrong. Vauthier had barely got two of the Westphalian companies (one company each of voltigeurs and grenadiers) across the Sülze when part of Schill's force swung north, evidently intending to cross the brook and cut the allies off from Magdeburg. Leaving the first two companies south of the stream, Vauthier hastily turned the others about and oriented them to the west, the French and the guns with their left on the stream, the two Westphalian fusilier companies to their right rear facing north toward Magdeburg.

The Allies were scarcely in position when Schill opened his attack. Two of his squadrons broke Vauthier's left south of the stream, scattering many of the Westphalian voltigeurs and grenadiers and forcing the remainder to take refuge in the town's churchyard. Prussian hussars pushed into the streets, but neither they nor Schill's feeble infantry could evict the Westphalians from their tiny strongpoint and the fight in the south degenerated into desultory musketry. Meanwhile, well-aimed fire from the French companies repelled a charge by the other two squadrons of Schill's regiment north of the Sülze. Some of the hussars, however, slid past the French, caught the Westphalian companies in the flank, charged them twice and shattered them, sending fugitives fleeing in all directions. This left the two French companies as the principal source of organized resistance. Schill cast about for a way to crush them but his troopers had been unable to make any impression on the determined men of the 22nd Ligne and, lacking infantry or artillery, he could not bring sufficient firepower against the French to dislodge them. He even dismounted his Jäger zu Pferd in an effort to improvise foot soldiers and twice sent them up the slopes against the French, but their attacks were repulsed and Schill decided to call off the battle, retiring to the west and leaving the mangled Allied detachment in possession of the field.

Tactically, the Allies had been handed a sharp little defeat. Although only one man had been killed, about 50, including Oberst Vauthier, were left wounded and another 200, one of whom was Vauthier's captain brother, were missing, mostly led off as prisoners by Schill's hard-riding hussars. Still, the 22nd had performed well and when Michaud arrived on the battlefield later in the afternoon, he found the troops calmly 'manoeuvring as if on exercise', the French demonstrating for their Westphalian allies the tactics and techniques employed to resist cavalry. The inexperienced Westphalian soldiers certainly stood in need of further training, their manoeuvres were slow and they displayed little endurance or tactical skill; the two fusilier companies north of the stream, for example, had neglected to form squares after Schill's first charge and had thus been overrun by the second attack. On the other hand, Michaud praised the 'good spirit and bravery' of the Westphalians, pointing out that the green fusilier companies had 'received the first charge with firmness' and that Jerome's men had generally exhibited 'a courage rare in young troops seeing combat for the first time.'[56]

As the Allies retired behind Magdeburg's walls, Schill at Wanzleben took stock of his position.[57] Although he had won a minor tactical success, the Westphalian soldiers had not deserted to him, he had been turned back from his objective and he had lost 12 officers, 70 men and numerous horses, losses that would be hard for the unsupported raiders to replace. Avoiding Magdeburg's large garrison, Schill thus continued north, passing through Haldensleben and Tangermünde to reach Arneburg on the banks of the Elbe on the afternoon of 8 May.[58] En route, a number of raiding parties struck out from the main body, disrupting the civil administration and spreading alarm. One of these disarmed the National Guard and Departmental Company in Halberstadt while capturing a few odd French, others occasionally seized Westphalian cash deposits, but the public was generally unresponsive and the small number of men recruited only sufficed to fill the gaps left by Dodendorf. Even many of these were of dubious character, more like brigands than liberators and destined to tarnish the reputation of Schill's band. Under these conditions, the raiders spent the next six days in Arneburg, undecided as to their next move and discouraged by the failure of Austrian arms and the Prussian king's undisguised condemnation of their venture. Finally, on the 13th, the band resumed its northwards progress, crossing into the Duchy of Mecklenburg-Schwerin and capturing the minuscule fortress of Dömitz on the Elbe two days later.

While Schill was making his way north along the river, Jerome's fearful government was hurriedly trying to gather forces to counter the incursion. Apparently in the grip of near panic, the Westphalian regime swallowed Schill's deceptions, believing him to be the harbinger of an invading Prussian army and habitually exaggerating his strength. The King, like Marshal Bernadotte, had limited faith in the loyalty ('I can only count on these troops up to a certain point') and preparedness ('The X Corps is totally lacking in organization,' wrote Reubell) of his own army and was particularly insistent that French troops be sent to reinforce him. Urgent messages therefore flew out of Kassel in all directions, the most egregious probably being one written on 4 May which claimed that General Blücher had crossed the Elbe at the head of 13,000 Prussians! Marshal Kellermann and the French War Ministry had begun to respond to these desperate cries for help when Napoleon intervened. 'The idea that Prussia would declare war is folly,' he wrote in a stern letter, adding that Kellermann was 'not to dispose of a single battalion' without his order. The Emperor, clearly tiring of his brother's incessant complaints, repeatedly pointed out that sufficient forces were already available to oppose Schill and refused to place any more men under Jerome's orders, telling Kellermann that 'all the French troops would not suffice for the King of Westphalia'.[59]

Jerome, sulky after this Imperial rebuff, began to organize his own defence. His X Corps resources were concentrated at three locations: the Westphalian

Guard, a combined battalion of French depot troops and the Berg infantry regiment at Kassel, the Westphalian line units and IV/22nd Ligne in Magdeburg, and GD Gratien's Dutchmen in the vicinity of Hamburg and Bremen. Principally concerned with the protection of his capital, Jerome brought the Dutch Division down to Göttingen by wagon to shield Kassel while elements of his Guard moved towards Halle under GB Jean Bongars. Slowly though, the intelligence picture improved. Schill's weakness became evident, the supposed threat to Kassel evaporated and Jerome sent two columns to the north-east in a clumsy effort to entrap the raiders. Gratien, with the bulk of his division, formed the left column, aimed at the Elbe north of Magdeburg, while the ambitious GB d'Albignac commanded the 4,000 men of the right column (two Dutch regiments and some Westphalian troops from Kassel) and marched for the fortress itself. The columns reached Haldensleben and Magdeburg respectively on 13 May, but an invidious rivalry existed between the two generals and, rather than co-ordinating their actions, they competed with one another to see who would garner the glory of capturing Schill. None the less, their disjointed movements slowly took them north toward Dömitz.

By this time, however, Schill was again on the move. Leaving a small garrison of 400 men at Dömitz, he struck north to Stralsund where he hoped to find a defensible fortress and succour from the Royal Navy.[60] Allied troops did not appear across the river from Dömitz until several days after Schill's departure. This was d'Albignac's force and, thinking he had won the race to find Schill, he put his Dutch infantry across the river to attack the tiny fortress on the late afternoon of 24 May. By that evening, Dömitz was in his hands, but he lacked cavalry to pursue the defenders and most escaped to rejoin their leader. Satisfied with the glory he felt he had won, d'Albignac remained at Dömitz for the next four days while Gratien set off in pursuit of Schill's main force.[61] With part of his own command and a Danish division under General Ewald, Gratien reached Stralsund on the last day of May, stormed the city and crushed Schill's defenders after a brutal fight.[62] Schill himself was killed, his head sent to Holland in a cask of wine, and Gratien's men were soon on the road back to Westphalia. Their return was timely because two small Austrian forces had pushed north out of Bohemia and X Corps was now needed in Saxony.

SKIRMISHES ON THE SAXON BORDER

On 15 and 16 April, Marshal Bernadotte led the Saxon IX Corps out of Dresden to the Danube valley, where Napoleon, following his clear strategic vision, was concentrating all his power for the decisive campaign against the Austrian Main Army. Lucid strategic thought offered little solace to King Friedrich August of Saxony, however, who saw his kingdom practically denuded of troops. Almost 75 per cent of his army had marched with Bernadotte and the remainder was scattered about in Prussian and Polish garrisons, leaving woefully few regular units to guard the kingdom's long border with Bohemia.

Saxon forces immediately available for the defence of the realm numbered only some 1,540 men in two depot battalions (hastily built from the depots of all twelve line infantry regiments), a squadron of *Zastrow* Cuirassiers, an additional detachment from *Zastrow*, a detachment from the *von Polenz* Chevauxleger Regiment and a small, newly organized horse battery of four guns.[63] Concentrated around Dresden by 2 May, these troops were placed under the command of Oberst Johann Adolf Thielmann, a capable, energetic and extraordinarily ambitious officer who enjoyed the king's favour but developed something of a reputation for self-promotion within the army.[64] The first threat to the realm came from the north, however, in the form of Schill's raiders and Thielmann was too distant to respond quickly. Fortunately, Saxony had been able to recall the *Zastrow* Cuirassiers from garrison duty in Danzig.[65] Arriving in Saxony in mid-April and quartered around Leipzig, this fine regiment was in time to play its ancillary role in the repulse of Schill at Wittenberg before being attached to Thielmann in early May.[66] More significant was the return of GM Ludwig von Dyherrn's command from Poland: one infantry battalion (I/*Oebschelwitz*), Major Kurt von Einsiedel's Grenadier Battalion (four companies), two other grenadier companies under Major Thomas von Wolan, two squadrons of hussars and two batteries for a total of some 1,800 men and fourteen guns.[67] Setting out from Warsaw on 20 April, Dyherrn's men had marched through Thorn and Torgau to unite with Thielmann around Dresden between 20 and 23 May.

Although GM von Dyherrn was placed in nominal command of Saxony's defence upon his arrival, he was required to consult with Thielmann and it quickly became apparent that the Oberst would be the creative, motive force behind Saxon operations on the border; Dyherrn faded into the background almost immediately. Thielmann had been active even before Dyherrn's return, shifting 1,000 of his men (800 infantry and 200 cavalry) to Chemnitz and Freiberg from 5 to 9 May in response to threatening Austrian concentrations across the border. King Friedrich August, however, had no desire to provoke the Austrians and issued specific instructions to Dyherrn and Thielmann that Saxon forces were not to cross the border into Bohemia. None the less, with his command more than doubled in size, Thielmann was determined to take the offensive and, according to his detractors, make a name for himself.[68]

Dyherrn's men had barely returned to Dresden when Thielmann decided to lead a reconnaissance to the Bohemian border. On the 24th, he marched to Pirna with 100 *Zastrow* cuirassiers, 100 hussars, Einsiedel's Grenadier Battalion and four guns, probing on towards Nollendorf the following day. Just north of Nollendorf, his men surprised a 12-man patrol from the Duke of Braunschweig's free-corps. The Saxons quickly captured eleven of the surprised intruders, but the patrol commander managed to flee, tearing his clothes to shreds in his flight. This was none other than the luckless Friedrich von Katte, promoted to Rittmeister in the Duke's miniature army and fortunate to escape with his life a second time. Thielmann continued south, seized an additional twenty prisoners in a brief skirmish with an enemy outpost and returned to Pirna that night with considerable satisfaction.

He marched back into Dresden on the 26th but was off again two days later, this time headed east to Zittau. The latter town, just within the Saxon border, had been occupied by Braunschweig's men since the 21st and their patrols had scouted as far as Löbau and Bautzen, almost 50 kilometres inside the kingdom. Thielmann found their boldness an affront to Saxon honour as well as a military danger and he moved out on the 28th with his entire cavalry plus 150 Schützen and four guns to teach the Braunschweigers a lesson. The town was held by only sixty-odd Braunschweig hussars and they were neglectful of their security. On the afternoon of the 30th, Thielmann's troopers, aided by local townspeople, cautiously approached Zittau from the west and achieved complete surprise, galloping through the streets and capturing more than forty of the Braunschweigers almost before they were alerted. Leaving his foot soldiers inside Zittau's walls, the pleased Oberst withdrew his cavalry to a bivouac slightly north of the town. That night, however, it was Thielmann's turn to be caught unawares. The Saxon infantry in the town were attacked at about midnight and, despite the intervention of 100 Saxon horsemen, Thielmann was forced to evacuate Zittau and retire to Löbau on the 31st with the loss of some thirty men. Both forces remained in the area for several days, but on 3 June Thielmann returned to Dresden and Braunschweig headed west towards Aussig two days later.

Thielmann's border scuffles raised new fears in Kassel, where Jerome's government was still recovering from the Schill episode. The worries of the nervous Saxon court were apparently infectious and the reaction in Westphalia as Friedrich August's breathless couriers arrived was typically excited: Braunschweig was threatening Dresden with 5,300 men, the King of Saxony was in dire straits and would have to flee to the west, Kellermann should put a division of his French troops on the road toward Erfurt at once. Even Blücher reappeared, this time in Bohemia to support the deposed princes with a corps of 10,000—15,000 Prussians! Napoleon, with a cooler head and better intelligence, dismissed his brother's anxious reports. 'The Duke of Braunschweig does not have 800 men and the former Elector of Kassel does not have 600,' he wrote on 9 June and old Marshal Kellermann responded to Jerome's heated messages with something like disdain: 'I believe, Sire, that the news and reports given to Your Majesty about the march a Prussian corps composed of 15,000 men are exaggerated.'[69] Saxony would be threatened soon enough, but the invading army would march under Habsburg banners, not Prussian.

JUNE/JULY - THE CAMPAIGN IN SAXONY

When Archduke Charles took the Austrian Main Army out of Bohemia to confront Napoleon across the Danube from Vienna, he left behind a small body of regulars and Landwehr to guard the province's mountainous borders. The aggressive actions of Thielmann and Braunschweig, however, drew Austrian attention to this tertiary theatre of war and, buoyed by the success at Aspern, Charles directed the Bohemian detachments to move north and east over the difficult passes into Germany. These limited thrusts were intended to achieve two goals. First, they would distract Napoleon's attention and perhaps some of his forces from the principal seat of conflict around Vienna. Second, the Habsburg monarchy had long harboured the largely illusory hope that Germany was on the verge of widespread insurrection. With news of Schill's apparent successes being trumpeted about (aided by Schill's embellished reports to Charles), it was imagined that the appearance of a few white-coated Austrian regulars with lofty proclamations would suffice to sound the tocsin of rebellion from one end of Germany to the other.

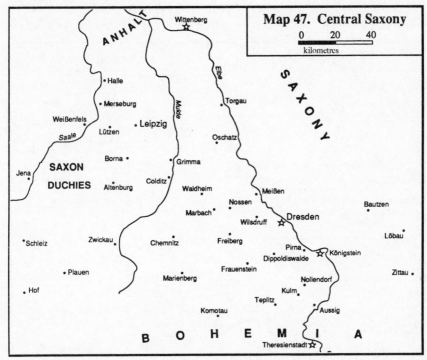

Map 47. Central Saxony

Under the overall control of General der Kavallerie Johann Graf von Riesch, two small commands were therefore assembled in Bohemia during the early days of June. The first of these 'divisions' was to create 'significant diversions' in Saxony where 'a large portion of the population desire [our] advance'. Gathered at Theresienstadt under the command of the cautious GM Carl Friedrich Freiherr Am Ende, its 8,600 men and ten guns included a core of regulars, six Landwehr battalions, the Duke of Braunschweig's little black-clad army and the even tinier band of ill-disciplined men who had enlisted under the banner of the deposed Kurfürst of Hesse-Kassel.[70] Entered on Braunschweig's muster rolls were Dörnberg, Katte and a number of their compatriots. FML Paul Radivojevich commanded the second 'division' at Eger, 7,428 men and four guns whose mission it was to push into Bayreuth and threaten Napoleon's communications.[71]

While these Austrian forces were numerically small when compared to the vast armaments arrayed on the plains east of Vienna, they greatly outnumbered the tiny Saxon defence forces. The Saxons, however, had not been idle and the corps assembled under Dyherrn and Thielmann by mid-June was noticeably superior to its predecessors in quality if not quantity. First, through Funck's persistent efforts as Inspector General of Cavalry, additional troopers from *Zastrow* and *Polenz* were mounted and sent to Dresden to raise each regiment's detach-

ment to squadron strength.[72] Second, on 10 June, the unfit men were culled
from the depot battalions, reducing each to two companies; these companies
were then combined with the two *von Rechten* grenadier companies into a single
mixed battalion under Major von Wolan. Finally, on 13 June, the little corps
was joined by three more recently mounted cavalry squadrons (two of *Zastrow*,

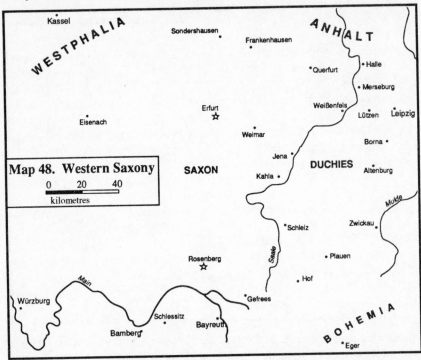

Map 48. Western Saxony

one of hussars), four more horse artillery pieces (to complete the horse artillery
battery under Hauptmann Grossmann) and a detachment of 101 men from the
depot of the *von Burgsdorff* Infantry.[73] By this time, however, Am Ende had
already invaded the kingdom and occupied the Saxon capital. Reinforcements
notwithstanding, Dyherrn and Thielmann were far too weak to offer serious
resistance to the Austrian incursion and couriers were soon pelting north toward
Kassel with pleas for assistance.

THE AUSTRIANS ADVANCE (9-23 JUNE)

On 10 June, Am Ende's mixed bag of Austrians, Hessians and Braunschweigers
crossed the border into Saxony and marched on Dippoldiswalde.[74] Hesitantly
resuming their advance the next afternoon, the invaders encountered no real
opposition and entered Dresden that evening under the fearful stares of its inhabitants.[75] Dyherrn and Thielmann, meanwhile, on learning that the enemy had
reached Dippoldiswalde, had recognized the impossibility of defending Dresden
with their meagre command and had instead chosen to evacuate the capital and
retire on Wilsdruff.[76] That night, however, intelligence seemed to indicate that
the enemy had not advanced beyond Dippoldiswalde and Thielmann, pressured

by Oberstlieutenant Heinrich Wolf von Gablenz of the hussars, decided to reoccupy Dresden. Von Gablenz's patrols soon brought the truth to the Saxon headquarters, but the energetic von Thielmann chose to 'alarm' the Austrian pickets outside the capital while attacking the enemy rear at Dippoldiswalde. Major Wolan consequently led two of his companies toward the latter town while a Major von Ryssel probed the capital's defences with two other companies of Wolan's *ad hoc* battalion.[77] Wolan turned back before reaching his objective, but Ryssel stirred up a hornet's nest at Dresden at about 3 a.m., stinging the Duke of Braunschweig into action. Braunschweig got his command out of bed and, reinforced by some Austrians and Hessians, set out after Thielmann at 5 a.m. Although numerically superior to the Duke's force, Dyherrn and Thielmann did not want to become engaged close to the capital where Am Ende's full weight might have been brought against them. They therefore retired to the west, fighting a series of running rear-guard actions against the persistent Duke. Braunschweig's appeals for reinforcements failed to move Am Ende, however, and an outflanking column got lost, allowing the Saxons to withdraw through Wilsdruff and Nossen with the loss of about 60 men.[78] Dyherrn and Thielmann continued west over the following two days, reaching Borna on the 14th where they were reinforced by three squadrons, a small infantry detachment and four horse guns.[79]

The Saxons remained at Borna for the next several days while the Austrians around Dresden awaited new orders from General Riesch in distant Prague. On the 17th, however, the little Saxon corps moved still farther west, assembling around Lützen on the 18th. From here, Thielmann sent a courier to request assistance from GB d'Albignac who was marching on Frankenhausen with Jerome's advance guard. The following day, a royal order resolved the anomalous command situation in the Saxon force: Dyherrn was removed from the field to oversee the recruitment and organization of new units, leaving Thielmann in sole command of the mobile troops.[80] The same day, news also arrived that Am Ende had finally stirred from Dresden and was moving on Meissen and Oschatz.

Leaving two Landwehr battalions in Dresden, Am Ende's division (about 6,000 men) entered Oschatz on 20 June, crossed the Mulde at Grimma on the 21st and advanced on Leipzig the following day, the restless Braunschweig hoping to catch the Saxons before they could unite with Jerome's Westphalians.[81] Approaching the city from the east, Am Ende's advance guard bumped into Saxon light cavalry and a lively fight ensued. That morning, Thielmann had sent von Gablenz with the light horse and Schützen to reconnoitre around Leipzig and report the enemy's dispositions. Gablenz deployed his troopers in a screen east of the city and fought a skillful delaying action in which his hussars suddenly turned on some over-eager Braunschweig pursuers and overthrew them, capturing about twenty. Heavily outnumbered, however, von Gablenz was forced to fall back on his supports (the Schützen) just west of the city and the entire Saxon reconnaissance force eventually retired toward the River Saale with a loss of only six men.[82] Upon Gablenz's return, Thielmann, who had been joined by still more reinforcements, decided to fall back to Weissenfels, thus moving closer to the approaching Westphalians and putting a river between himself and the Austrians.[83] The next day, d'Albignac duly appeared in Weissenfels with X Corps' advance guard. The danger to the outnumbered Saxon corps had passed and Thielmann could begin to think of returning to the offensive.

In contrast, Am Ende was considering withdrawal. Much to Braunschweig's irritation, the Austrian commander had decided not to pursue the Saxons until the morning of the 23rd. Even this advance was called off when the corps reached Lützen and Am Ende received the disturbing news that Thielmann had retreated behind the Saale and was expecting to link with the Westphalians very shortly. Uncomfortable so far from Bohemia, the Austrian commander outraged his subordinates and allies by ordering a retreat on Leipzig.

Meanwhile, the other Austrian diversionary division had been making its presence felt in Bayreuth and northern Bavaria.[84] Radivojevich crossed out of

Table 9-4: Saxon Forces within Saxony (April - June)

Mobile Troops (April) - Oberst Thielmann

1st Depot Battalion
2nd Depot Battalion
one sqdn of *Zastrow* Cuirassiers
detachment of *Zastrow* Cuirassiers
detachment of *Polenz* Chevauxlegers
horse artillery detachment (4 guns)
Strength = approx. 1,540 men

Other Troops (April, near Leipzig)

half-battalion of Leib-Grenadier-Garde
Schweizer Leib-Garde
bulk of *Zastrow* Cuirassiers

GM von Dyherrn en route from
Poland with approx. 1,800 men.

Mobile Troops (late May) - Dyherrn/Thielmann

Grenadier Battalion *von Einsiedel*
two grenadier companies (Major von Wolan)
I/*von Oebschelwitz*
1st Depot Battalion
2nd Depot Battalion
two squadrons of *Zastrow* Cuirassiers
two squadrons of the Hussar Regiment
squadron of *Polenz* Chevauxlegers
two foot artillery batteries (14 guns)
horse artillery detachment (4 guns)
Strength = approx. 3,300 men
(many unfit for field duty)

Other Troops (May--June with King)

half-battalion of Leib-Grenadier-Garde
Schweizer Leib-Garde

Mobile Troops (mid-June) - Oberst Thielmann

Grenadier Battalion *von Einsiedel*
Combined Battalion (Major von Wolan)
I/*von Oebschelwitz*
detachment of *Burgsdorff* Regiment (101 men)
two foot artillery batteries (14 guns)

Zastrow Cuirassiers (four squadrons)
three squadrons of the Hussar Regiment (OTL v. Gablenz)
one squadron of *von Polenz* Chevauxlegers
one horse artillery battery (8 guns)

Strength = approx. 2,800 men

Sedentary Troops

Königstein Garrison
Garrison Company
Provisional Infantry Battalion
Fortress Artillery
Strength = approx. 800 men

Wittenberg Garrison
Half-Invalids
Bürger-Schützen (paramilitary)
Strength = approx. 300 men

Dresden (no regular military)
Bürger-Garde
Mounted Gendarmes
Strength = 260-340 men

Cavalry/Artillery Depots (at Weißenfels)
dismounted cavalry squadrons:
Karabiniers - 2
Polenz - 4, to 3 in late May
    (one sqdn mounted and sent to Thielmann)
Herzog Albrecht - 3
Hussars - 3, to 2 in early June
    (one sqdn mounted and sent to Thielmann)
cavalry depots
artillery depot

Half-Invalid Companies
Torgau
Waldheim
Eisleben

Bohemia on 9 June, met no opposition and was able to enter the city of Bayreuth four days later. Austrian raiding parties ventured as far as Nuremberg and Bamberg, but by the end of the month, elements of the French reserve corps at Hanau were headed for Bayreuth by forced marches. Radivojevich's situation was becoming precarious.

X Corps Campaigns in Saxony (23 June - 15 July)

When d'Albignac joined Thielmann at Weissenfels on the afternoon of 23 June, he was several days in advance of the rest of X Corps. Indeed, Jerome was rather slow in responding to Saxony's repeated appeals for assistance, in large part due to the disposition of his forces following the pursuit of Schill. That enterprise and the requirements of internal security had left Jerome's troops dispersed all over northern Germany and mid-June found the king with his Guard and the Berg regiment around Kassel, d'Albignac at Braunschweig, and Gratien en route to Magdeburg to join that city's garrison of French and Dutch units. It was not until the evening of 20 June that all these troops could be brought together on the western fringes of Saxony, d'Albignac's men closing on Frankenhausen while Jerome assembled the bulk of the Corps around Sondershausen 23 kilometres to the west. D'Albignac, in close communication with Thielmann, managed to cover the 80 kilometres to Weissenfels in three days, but the main body, moving due east, did not arrive in Querfurt until the 24th (despite Jerome's assurances to the Saxons that he would be there on the 21st).[85] None the less, d'Albignac's timely appearance removed the immediate danger to Thielmann's Saxons and Am Ende, learning of their juncture, withdrew to Leipzig on 24 June. Thielmann and d'Albignac prepared to pursue that very day, but the inexperienced Westphalians were slow in assembling and the Allies only got as far as Lützen before halting for the night.[86] For the next two days, they chased after the retiring Am Ende, cutting to the south-east through Colditz and Waldheim in an effort to get ahead of the foe, who was presumed to be marching back to Dresden.[87]

Table 9-5: Troops under d'Albignac and Thielmann (24 June)

Westphalians - GB d'Albignac

1st Infantry Regiment (1,680)	1st Cuirassier Regiment (400)
6th Infantry Regiment (1,700)	Garde Chevauxlegers (550) [1]
Garde-Jäger Battalion (600)	artillery battery (6 guns)

Strength = approx. 5,030 men

Saxons - Oberst Thielmann

Grenadier Battalion *von Einsiedel*	*Zastrow* Cuirassiers (four squadrons)
Combined Battalion (Major von Wolan)	three squadrons of the Hussar Regiment (OTL v. Gablenz)
I/*von Oebschelwitz*	three squadrons of *von Polenz* Chevauxlegers [3]
detachment of Leib-Grenadiers (119 men)	one horse artillery battery (8 guns)
detachment of *Burgsdorff* Regiment (101 men) [2]	foot artillery detachment (4 guns)
two foot artillery batteries (14 guns)	

Strength = approx. 2,840 men

NOTES
1. Joined d'Albignac on 25 June in Leipzig.
2. Kortzfleisch gives this detachment a strength of 193 (would raise total strength to about 2,930).
3. Kortzfleisch gives only one squadron, but adding the cumulative number of personnel reinforcements gives about 362 men, or three weak squadrons.

Hoping to intercept the enemy, d'Albignac and Thielmann swung south and east the next day. Encountering Austrian skirmishers west of Marbach at about noon, Thielmann assumed that these were merely a flank guard for the main column further east and began to push them back toward the town. Topping a rise, however, he saw the majority of the Austrian force deployed in a strong position around Marbach facing west and immediately brought up some of his guns to take the enemy position under fire. Austrian and Braunschweig pieces replied in kind. An inconsequential artillery duel began at about 2 p.m., but the arrival of d'Albignac and the rest of the Allied advance guard initially seemed to herald the opening of a serious engagement. The Saxons and Westphalians moved energetically, Wolan's Battalion quickly deploying opposite the town in the centre of the Allied line, other Saxon infantry moving up in support and the Allied cavalry trotting south toward the Austrian left flank. But nothing resulted from these rapid movements. D'Albignac was apparently hesitant and seems to have received orders from Jerome not to commit his force to combat until Gratien was within supporting distance. Gratien did not appear, no real attack was ever launched and the nascent battle degenerated into a desultory skirmish. The Allies withdrew at about 8 p.m. and slipped north to Waldheim during the night.[88]

As the skirmish died away with the summer evening, a new Habsburg general rode up to Am Ende's headquarters. FML Michael Freiherr von Kienmayer, formerly commander of II Reserve Corps, had been appointed to take control of all Austrian, Braunschweig and Hessian forces in Saxony and Bayreuth as the new XI Corps of the Austrian army. Assessing the situation, Kienmayer saw the Austrian forces in Saxony and Bayreuth threatened by Jerome in the north and Junot in the west, each of whom seemed to outnumber the separated Austrian divisions. He thus decided to concentrate most of his force in Bayreuth, defeat Junot and then turn on Jerome, all the while shielding Bohemia with Am Ende. This strategy sent more than half of Am Ende's former division toward the west on the morning of 28 June while Am Ende himself headed for the Bohemian border at Nollendorf with the remainder of his command.[89]

Meanwhile, Jerome had finally united with d'Albignac and Thielmann around Waldheim. The Westphalian king, his troops and a rather large and unseemly train of supernumeraries had crossed the Saale at Merseburg on the 25th and made a pompously triumphant entry into Leipzig the following day. Lieutenant Wolf describes this curious spectacle:

> At this entrance [into Leipzig], I received for the first time an understanding of what a great train of horses, coaches, footmen and other such useless baggage the King dragged about. Yes, I leaned towards the opinion that besides the chamberlains and other court flunkeys, even a portion of the comedians and dancers had been brought along for this war.

An appropriately bombastic proclamation was duly issued to the army before it marched south to join d'Albignac and Thielmann at Waldheim on the 29th. Here again, Wolf provides an unflattering picture of Jerome's headquarters:

Table 9-6: X Corps In Saxony (24 June)
Commander: King Jerome Napoleon
Chief of Staff: GD Reubell

Westphalians - GD Graf Bernterode

  Garde-Grenadier Battalion (840)
  Jäger-Carabinier Battalion (360)
  Garde du Corps (140)
  two artillery batteries (12 guns)

Dutch - GD Gratien

  6th Dutch Infantry Regiment (two battalions)
  8th Dutch Infantry Regiment (two battalions)
  9th Dutch Infantry Regiment (two battalions)
  2nd Dutch Cuirassiers (three squadrons)
  one foot battery (4 guns)
  one horse battery (4 guns)

Other Troops - Colonel Chabert

Detachments of:
28th Léger, 27th, 30th, 33rd, and 65th Ligne

3rd Berg Infantry Regiment (part)

Strength (approx.)

Westphalian -	1,540
Dutch -	4,460
Berg -	800
French -	800
Total --	7,600 men
	20 guns

NOTES:
1. Remaining in Magdeburg: IV/22 Ligne, 5th Westphalian Infantry, 7th Dutch Infantry, one Dutch battery.
2. Approximately 400 Berg soldiers remained behind in Westphalia (Kassel and Marburg); in fact, Kortzfleisch lists only one battalion of the 3rd Berg Infantry as taking part in the campaign. He includes, however, a Berg battery (5 guns) and a half-squadron of Berg chasseurs in the X Corps order of battle.
3. Other garrisons nominally under Jerome's command as in Table 9-2.

When ... the main body bivouacked around Waldheim and the King and his generals were quartered in the town, where they are said to have engaged in a vigorous orgy of drinking, there arose during the night, brought on by I do not know what cause, a sudden alarm. A great fear overpowered the entire camp and the most dreadful rumours flew about. It was said the Duke of Braunschweig and his black hussars were already in the camp and aimed to kidnap the King. Everyone ran about in wild confusion, chamberlains in their gold trimmed coats and silk stockings left their shoes in the mud of the alleyways, women shrieked, shots sounded, the comedians wailed and lamented, a truly panicked terror had the whole town and camp in its grip. Nearly an hour must have passed before minds were calmed and one asked oneself what the cause of this unnecessary terror had been.[90]

The Corps' sad state of military discipline and organization was exacerbated by serious discord within the ranks of its senior leaders. Although Gratien and d'Albignac had come to respect each other after the expedition against Schill, Jerome had developed a negative impression of the Dutch Division's commander, telling Napoleon that Gratien was 'a worthless officer without activity'. For his part, the latter apparently tended to go his own way with little concern for Jerome's instructions. Reubell, frivolous and unconcerned, was proving to be a poor chief of staff, seeking excuses rather than solutions, and the tension between him and the hot-headed d'Albignac was such that they even quarrelled in the presence of the king. It is thus hardly surprising that the operations of X Corps were characterized by uncertainty, delay and disorganization.[91]

With this disorder and discord as a background, Jerome prepared to renew his advance. Apparently convinced that 'one must effect public opinion in Saxony positively and this is best achieved through the occupation of Dresden', Jerome chose not to pursue the main Austrian force and marched for the Saxon capital on 30 June. Only GB Bongars with two cuirassier regiments and two French companies headed west, but instead of following the enemy, he moved on Altenburg, 35 kilometres north of the Austrian route of march. Amidst the 'loudest and most indubitable jubilation of the people', Thielmann thus entered Dresden at 11 p.m. on the 30th with the Corps' advance guard: two hussar squadrons, the Saxon Schützen, I/*Oebschelwitz*, the Westphalian Garde-Jägers and four Saxon horse guns.[92] Jerome made his own elaborate entrance the following day with the rest of the army. Greeted by the city's bells, he was gracious and reassuring but displayed a degree of luxury that 'one certainly had not expected during a war'. In particular, his large and glittering court left a peculiar impression on the Dresdeners: the Westphalian king was surrounded by an aggregation of twenty-one superior officers, four senior court officials, numerous royal pages, some thirty royal servants, including eight cooks, plus a cloud of minions required by his military and civilian staff.[93]

Jerome and his court dallied in Dresden for the next two days, visiting the opera and picture galleries but undertaking no military activity. Not until the morning of 4 July did X Corps depart the Saxon capital, not in pursuit of Am Ende, who had retired to Nollendorf on the Bohemian border, but toward Hof with the intention of combining with Junot's French and Bavarian troops to defeat Kienmayer. This march, like the previous movements of X Corps, was conducted with little security and a plenitude of disorder. The frustrated Lieutenant Wolf recorded that:

> ...no army on the march has ever been so badly secured as ours now is. There is never any sign of any sort of march security and we officers know absolutely nothing about the enemy or the intentions of the King. We are like a herd [of cattle], simply driven about...

Furthermore, the atmosphere in Corps headquarters seems to have been characterized by confusion and indecision: 'no one could tell who was actually in command', complained Wolf.[94] Although he had stated his intentions to Junot as early as 29 June, Jerome moved slowly. He marched to Freiberg on 4 July, but wasted a day there before advancing to Chemnitz (6 July) and Zwickau (7th). His Corps finally reached Plauen on 8 July, only 25 kilometres from his planned juncture with Junot at Hof, but it was already too late. That very day, Kienmayer's united forces inflicted a defeat on Junot's command at Gefrees, throwing the French and Bavarians back to the west and south.[95]

The arrival of this news coincided with other dire reports. Thielmann, writing from the Bohemian border, erroneously announced that 1,000 Hessians under their dour monarch were advancing on Jerome's southern flank and messages from Westphalia informed the young king of yet another, albeit brief and abortive, attempt at rebellion within his realm.[96] Unable to decide on a course of action, Jerome remained at Plauen for the next three days, his cavalry skirmishing with little success against Austrian and Braunschweig troopers north-east of Hof. With Junot out of the way, Kienmayer gathered his command and moved to strike Jerome at Plauen on the morning of 12 July, but found the town empty except for a handful of deserters. The Westphalian king, seeing perils approaching from every quarter, had taken counsel of his fears and retreated to Schleiz at 2 a.m.

Meanwhile, Thielmann with most of the Saxon corps and the Westphalian Garde-Jägers protected Jerome's southern flank from any possible threats out of Bohemia. Moving out of Dresden on 3 July, the Saxon Oberst initially pushed south toward Nollendorf, skirmishing with Am Ende's patrols on the 3rd and 4th. Receiving reports that the Austrians were slipping to their left behind the mountain screen to join Radivojevich, Thielmann swung west and shifted to Fraunenstein on the 5th. Continuing west on 6 July, he dispatched Major von Wolan with his small battalion, 80 chevauxlegers from *Polenz* and two guns to occupy Dresden, now utterly denuded of troops.[97] Thielmann himself proceeded to Marienberg on the 7th and raided Komotau in Bohemia the following day, reducing the threat to Saxony by forcing Am Ende, whose position at Nollendorf was now known, to retire toward Theresienstadt. Recalled by the anxious Jerome, however, the Saxons marched swiftly north on the 9th and, badgered by continually changing orders from Corps headquarters, passed through Chemnitz and Zwickau to reunite with X Corps at Schleiz on the morning of 13 July.

Both corps rested on the 13th, although Jerome kept his men busy throwing up rude earthworks. The slipshod nature of command in X Corps was highlighted when the King decided to have a salute fired to celebrate the news of his brother's victory at Wagram: his staff, however, neglected to inform Thielmann, and the Saxons, who were posted in front of the rest of the Corps, were most alarmed to hear cannon fire suddenly erupt in their rear. Matters were soon explained to the Saxons, but the mood of Corps headquarters was skittish despite the good news from the Danube valley. Thus, when Kienmayer, still hoping to engage Jerome, approached Schleiz in the pre-dawn hours of 14 July, he found the Westphalian camp empty. Jerome had retreated again.

It is not clear what moved the Westphalian king to depart his prepared defences and fall back to Kahla on the night of 13/14 July: wild rumours of an English landing on the Dutch coast; news of the renewed Austrian advance on Dresden; grossly exaggerated reports of Braunschweig reinforcements (in fact, X Corps and the Saxons outnumbered the Austrians and their allies); or perhaps fears for the security of his own kingdom.[98] Whatever the cause, a disorderly retreat to the north was the result. Thielmann, who saw his nation completely exposed to the enemy by the withdrawal, protested vehemently but to no avail. He was able, however, to detach himself from X Corps on the 14th and march to the relief of Dresden which had again fallen into Austrian hands. Jerome continued north by fast, if disorganized, marches.

In the absence of Thielmann and Jerome, Am Ende had been roused to action and his men trudged north into Saxony for the second time on the afternoon of 12 July. Ever cautious and fearing powerful enemy forces in all directions, Am Ende halted at Dippoldiswalde and did not even send a patrol into Dresden until the morning of the 14th. Learning that Major Wolan had evacuated the city with his tiny force at 3 a.m. the previous day, the Austrian scouts reported back to Am Ende and two Landwehr battalions arrived to take possession of the Saxon capital late on the night of 14 July. The Austrian division remained in its positions for the next several days until an order from Kienmayer arrived on the 19th directing Am Ende to occupy Dresden with his main body and to send detachments north and east so that large portions of Saxony would be under Austrian control as the belligerents went to the peace table. Am Ende dutifully brought the rest of his division into Dresden on the morning of the 20th, a mere two hours before Thielmann's advance guard appeared at the city's gates.

The Saxon corps was apparently in an exhausted state when it reached Kahla on the 14th, 'the infantry goes almost barefoot and the horses can hardly move', but Thielmann pressed his men forward.[99] They were in Nossen on the 19th and they moved on Dresden the next morning, capturing several Austrian pickets and disarming an entire company of Landwehr despite its commander's protestations that an armistice had been declared. Thielmann, however, was not particularly interested in news of the agreement reached at Znaim and ordered his rear guard to delay any couriers until he had retaken the capital. With considerable bravado, Gablenz and later Thielmann himself conducted negotiations with Am Ende (or at least exchanged threats with the Austrian) and by the evening of the 20th the two parties had arranged a ceasefire. On the morning of 21 July, however, new instructions reached Am Ende from Archduke Charles directing an immediate return to Bohemia. Complying with celerity, the last of the Austrians departed Dresden at 3.30 p.m. on the 21st and Thielmann was able to make a second triumphal entry into his country's capital.[100]

Jerome had also returned to his capital. Departing Kahla on the 14th, he had marched via Jena and Erfurt to re-enter Kassel with his Guard on 19 July; GD Gratien and the Dutch Division were temporarily posted in the Erfurt fortress while GD Reubell took the Westphalian line troops and the Berg regiment to Hannover.[101] The people of Saxony were heartily glad to see their allies leave. The Westphalians and Dutch had achieved an unenviable reputation for coarseness, ill discipline and rapacity during their brief campaign in Friedrich August's kingdom. 'The Dutch and Westphalian troops behaved themselves in Saxony as if in enemy territory,' ran one report to the Saxon king. Thielmann wrote to his monarch as early as 23 June to repudiate the lack of discipline among 'the Westphalian and even more the Dutch troops', complaining that 'the excesses are so numerous, the land suffers much and it is not to be denied that the behaviour of the enemy, whose discipline is exemplary, stands in strong contrast'. Even Westphalians complained: 'The commissaries plunder whenever they can, a third of the soldiers remain behind as stragglers on the march, the generals drink and gamble or tow young ladies about...there are dreadful conditions in this our army.' Nor did matters improve. A report from Thielmann's headquarters at the conclusion of the campaign stated that

>   ...the way the Westphalian and especially the Dutch troops act is inconceivable. They plunder as a matter of course...Their pretensions in their quarters are unspeakable, no foe could demand more. Fortunately, our

troops do not participate, on the contrary, they behave with more civility and humanity than I have ever seen.[102]

Jerome's Saxon allies were also bitter about the conduct of the brief campaign, feeling that all their exertions as part of X Corps had been 'pointless', leading only to retreat, deprivation and exhaustion. Some of the Westphalian soldiers evidently agreed. A common gunner of Jerome's army may have provided the best summation of the campaign: 'our march was more like a stroll as we hardly ever saw the enemy'.[103]

The Saxons, however, were not the only ones displeased by the performance of Jerome and his Corps. On returning to Kassel, the young king was subjected to a blistering message from his Imperial brother:

> You make war like a satrap. Good God, did you learn that from me? From me, who ride at the head of my troops when I have an army of 200,000 men, and do not even allow my minister of foreign affairs to accompany me.
>
> What has happened? You have given nothing but cause for dissatisfaction. Kienmayer, with his 12,000 men, laughed at your silly pretensions, concealed his movements from your gaze and hurled himself at Junot. This would not have happened if you had been with your advance guard and issued your commands from there. You make great claims; you have a certain amount of talent and a few good qualities but these are overshadowed by your follies. Furthermore, you are insufferably conceited and know absolutely nothing about public affairs. If the armistice had not been signed, Kienmayer would have marched against you after he had settled with Junot.
>
> Quit these follies. Send the diplomatic corps back to Kassel, make war without followers and baggage, and keep no table other than your own! Make war like a young soldier who has need of glory and renown. Try to be worthy of the high position to which you have been called, of the respect of France and Europe, whose eyes are upon you, and have at least sufficient intelligence to express yourself properly in orders and speeches.

By mid-August, X Corps had been significantly reduced in strength and responsibility, the notification arriving in Kassel under Berthier's signature rather than Napoleon's as a final signal of the Emperor's ire.[104]

The campaign in Saxony was over and an armistice had been declared between the French and Austrian Empires, but one final act remained to be played out on the Westphalian stage in 1809. The Duke of Braunschweig, officially an 'ally' of the Habsburg monarchy, declared himself unbound by the terms of the armistice. Unwilling to 'bow before Napoleon like the other princes of Germany and to breathe the air where French command', he gathered his officers and announced his intent to 'set out for northern Germany' and strike a blow for the 'freedom and independence of the German nation'.[105]

JULY/AUGUST - BRAUNSCHWEIG'S MARCH TO THE SEA

When Prussia went to war with France in 1806, its largest army was placed under the command of Karl Wilhelm Ferdinand, the Duke of Braunschweig. Mortally wounded at Auerstädt that October, the aged Karl was to be succeeded by his fourth son, Friedrich Wilhelm. Unfortunately for the new Duke, his father's opposition to Napoleon led to the summary occupation of his lands by French forces and the eventual incorporation of much of his territory into the fledgling Kingdom of Westphalia. The Duchy of Braunschweig had thus been effectively erased from the map of Europe and Friedrich Wilhelm deprived of his throne. Nursing a bitter hatred of Napoleon and France's expanding influence in Germany, the dispossessed Duke formally allied himself with the Habsburg Empire as an independent monarch in 1809 and proceeded to raise a small army in Bohemia with Austrian assistance.

Clad almost entirely in black and bearing a death's head as its symbol, this army was raised from volunteers and was variously known as the 'Army of Vengeance' or the 'Black Corps'. Many of its soldiers and most of its officers had formerly served under Prussian banners, so there was a degree of military experience in its ranks. Moreover, not a few of its officers (such as Katte, Dörnberg and a few fugitives from Schill's band) had already proven their determination to oppose the French with arms. Leading these men with great enthusiasm and considerable ability during the campaign in Saxony and Bayreuth, the thirty-eight-year-old Duke had won their loyalty and confidence despite his continual clashes with the conservative Am Ende. Now, although deep in enemy territory and bereft of allies, he was determined to fight on, to march into his former lands in a last desperate attempt to raise the population of northern Germany against the French. He therefore gathered the Black Corps at Zwickau in late July as the Austrians retired into Bohemia and organized its 2,110 officers and men into three small battalions, a reinforced cavalry regiment and a mounted battery of four pieces.[106] Despite their apparently hopeless situation, these men now prepared to follow their ardent commander north to death, glory or the Royal Navy.[107]

To attain his former realm, the Duke had first to pass through Saxony and he set out from Zwickau for Leipzig on the morning of 24 July, a small patrol surprising and capturing part of Thielmann's war chest and its 52-man escort as the Black Corps proceeded north the following day. Learning that a Saxon cavalry detachment was blocking his path through Leipzig, the Duke sent his command ahead in a night attack. Unfortunately for the Braunschweigers, the inexperienced men of their advance guard, approaching the city from the south, ventured too far forward and were roughly treated by the Saxon light cavalry. The well-led Saxon troopers, 170 chevauxlegers and hussars en route from depots to join Thielmann, charged swiftly out of the darkness and inflicted about twenty casualties on the hapless Braunschweig Scharfschützen before withdrawing to the east.[108] At Grimma they linked with Thielmann who had hurried north out of Dresden with von Einsiedel's grenadiers (transported in wagons) and two horse artillery pieces on receiving reports of Braunschweig's march. The Saxons entered Leipzig the next day (27 July) and were joined by a detachment under

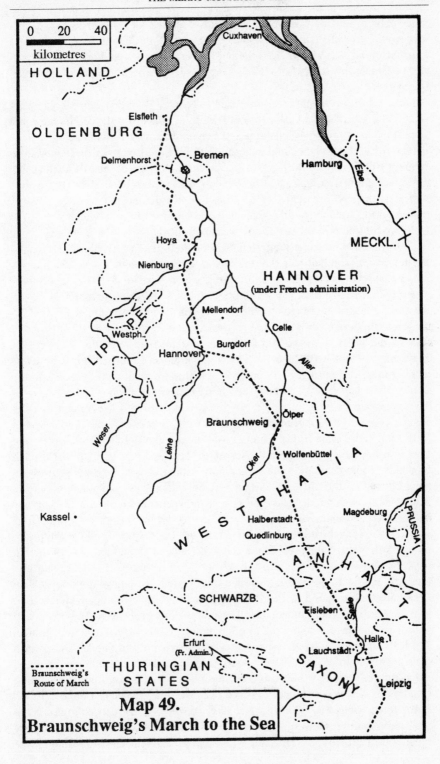

Map 49.
Braunschweig's March to the Sea

von Gablenz, but Braunschweig had already departed for Halle and Thielmann's men were too exhausted to pursue.[109] On the 28th, Thielmann marched to Lauchstädt but declined to cross the border out of Saxony and thus left the pursuit of Braunschweig and his Black Corps to Jerome's Dutch and Westphalian troops.[110]

Jerome's forces seemed well disposed to counter Braunschweig's bold enterprise. The Westphalian Guard was in Kassel, Michaud had the 5th Infantry and some French troops in Magdeburg and Gratien had moved his Dutchmen from Erfurt to Eisleben when Thielmann notified him of Braunschweig's march on Leipzig; the Duke would have to march through these forces to achieve his objective. Furthermore, Reubell's Division of Westphalian and Berg line troops was just south of Bremen, in a position to close off the route north. Jerome examined the situation with satisfaction and confidently told Michaud that the Duke would find himself caught 'between two fires'.

Unfortunately, Jerome's appreciation of the situation proved overly optimistic. Thielmann had halted at the Saxon border, Gratien was at least a day's march behind the Black Corps and Reubell's men were much too distant to provide any immediate assistance. The troops of the Magdeburg garrison, however, were in close striking range and the 5th Westphalian Infantry under Colonel P.-S. Meyronnet marched out of the fortress on the 28th with 1,980 officers and men to do battle with the Black Corps.[111] The plan apparently called for Meyronnet to link with Reubell's Division and crush Braunschweig with overwhelming power, but Reubell's men were still more than 150 kilometres to the north-west when the 5th Infantry reached Halberstadt at about 11 a.m. on 29 July. Two hours later, reports from gendarmes informed Meyronnet that the Black Corps was in Quedlinburg, about fourteen kilometres to the south. Seeing little immediate danger, the Colonel took no special defensive measures and seems to have been unpleasantly surprised when another gendarme galloped breathlessly into the market square at 5 p.m. with news that the Braunschweigers were closing on the town. Meyronnet quickly deployed his voltigeurs outside Halberstadt's walls and posted the rest of the regiment along with a company each of departmental troops and veterans to defend the town's numerous gates.[112] Braunschweig opened his attack at about 7 p.m. and by midnight, despite stiff Westphalian resistance, most of Halberstadt and the bulk of the 5th Infantry were in his hands. The raw Westphalian recruits had fought manfully, but with almost all their officers killed or captured, including Meyronnet, they eventually had to yield to the Black Corps. Last to surrender were the two Westphalian grenadier companies. These had barricaded themselves in several houses and managed to hold out through the night, but were forced to capitulate at 5 a.m. when Braunschweig brought up his howitzers and threatened to storm their position. In all, the Westphalians probably lost about 200 men dead and wounded and at least 1,500 captured; the remainder fled into the surrounding countryside with no semblance of order. The 5th Infantry had ceased to exist.[113]

His force swelled by 300 Westphalian prisoners who had chosen to desert the 5th Infantry, Braunschweig continued north towards his father's capital on the afternoon of 30 July.[114] His little victory at Halberstadt notwithstanding, the

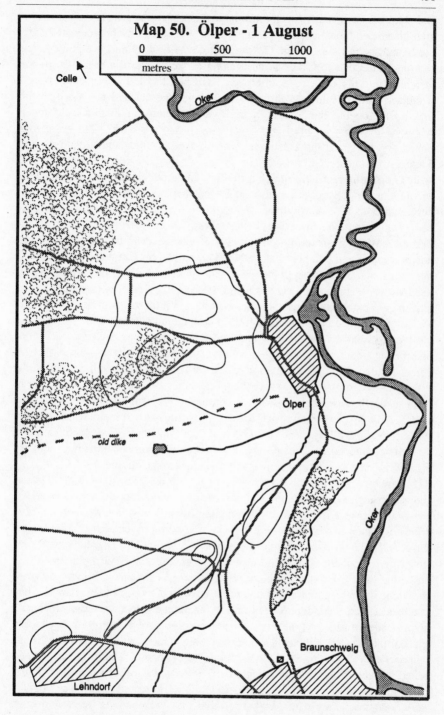

Map 50. Ölper - 1 August

Duke's position was critical: there was no evidence of a popular uprising even after he entered his ancestral lands, Gratien's Division was approaching from the south and Reubell's men were closing in from the north. Indeed, forced marches brought Reubell to Celle on the evening of the 31st as the Black Corps was marching into the city of Braunschweig. Reubell had left Hoya (south-east of Bremen) on the 29th with the 1st Cuirassiers, the 1st and 6th Westphalian Infantry Regiments, the 3rd Berg Infantry and ten guns, in all about 5,000 men. Allowing his troops a brief rest several kilometres beyond Celle, he requisitioned wagons to transport his infantry and moved his force south again at about 5 a.m. on 1 August.

Just north of Braunschweig, near the tiny village of Oelper, the Westphalians encountered enemy pickets and Reubell sent his cavalry forward to cover the deployment of his foot soldiers. They soon found the Black Corps arrayed before them outside the city. It was about 3 p.m. An hour earlier, Duke Friedrich Wilhelm, reacting to reports of Reubell's approach, had occupied a defensive position with his right anchored on the River Oker and his left extending about three kilometres to the west. The Duke had initially occupied Oelper itself with two companies, but during the afternoon, as his pickets were driven in and the Westphalians deployed, he withdrew his men from the village and pulled them back to the dominant hill several hundred metres to the south-west. The Westphalians were quick to take advantage of this unexpected good fortune and the 1st Infantry was soon in possession of Oelper, but it was almost 8 p.m. before Reubell attempted to exploit his gain. Forming an assault column in the village as the sun set, the Westphalian General sent the 1st Infantry forward against the Braunschweig position on the hill. The white-coated foot soldiers had hardly left the protection of the buildings when canister from two Braunschweig artillery pieces crashed into their ranks and forced them to recoil. A swift counter-attack by the Duke was repulsed in turn, however, and the Braunschweigers withdrew to their hilltop defensive position.

Meanwhile, the Westphalian right was in motion. The 1st Cuirassiers had moved through the large wood west of town and were forming for an attack on the Braunschweig right wing. Here again, however, well-aimed artillery fire from the other two Braunschweig guns created disorder in the Westphalian ranks and brought their forward movement to a halt. The Black Hussars were not slow to spot the discomfiture of their foes and boldly charged forward to strike the right front of the stationary cuirassiers. The heavy cavalry was overthrown in a short fight and sent streaming through the woods to the rear. In their panicked flight, the troopers overran the 6th Infantry and both regiments were soon headed north into the trees, disordered and useless. Fortunately, seven guns of the Westphalian artillery under an able French captain held their ground and opened a steady fire despite the rout of their supports. The Braunschweigers failed to exploit their advantage and the 3rd Berg soon marched up to stabilize the situation on Reubell's right. The Black Hussars retreated and the commander of Braunschweig's left, convinced that the Westphalians were advancing, decided on his own initiative to withdraw from the field. It was now about dusk and the Duke was endeavouring to organize another attack on Oelper when he learned to his disgust that half his army had retired. With no other option, he fell back as well and the fighting died out as full darkness settled over the field. Reubell, intimidated by the musket fire of a tiny Braunschweig rearguard detachment, allowed the Duke to retreat undisturbed, only sending two companies to follow the Black Corps to the city gates.

The little battle was a Westphalian victory. Although Reubell's Division lost about 200 men to the Braunschweiger's 100, the Westphalians had held the field and had halted the Black Corps' progress north. The discouraged Braunschweigers, short of ammunition, could only look forward to a renewed battle at far more unfavourable odds as Gratien's Dutchmen and other Allied reinforcements arrived.[115] Reubell, however, apparently saw the situation differently and on the night of 1/2 August, the Westphalian division conducted a disorganized retreat east over the Oker. Braunschweig's route to the sea was open.[116]

Reubell marched into Braunschweig late on 2 August, but the Black Corps had made its escape that very morning and was already well on its way to Burgdorf.[117] Reubell, however, believed the Duke to be still in the vicinity of his old capital and decided to wait for Gratien, whose troops had now reached Wolfenbüttel. The Dutch soldiers joined their Westphalian and Berg allies on the 3rd, only to learn that their enemies had flown and gained a day's march on them. Although the Allied soldiers were soon on the road to the coast, Reubell marching via Burgdorf (3rd) to Mellendorf (4th) while Gratien headed for Nienburg, the Braunschweigers kept well ahead of their pursuers.[118] Reubell almost caught up with the Black Corps' rear guard at Hoya on the 5th, but the Braunschweigers destroyed the bridge over the River Weser and again evaded the frustrated Westphalian general. Friedrich Wilhelm pressed his men hard and by the time Reubell reached Delmenhorst on the afternoon of 6 August, the Braunschweigers were in the process of crossing the River Hunte, 25 kilometres further north. The Westphalians could still catch up—it would take time for the Duke to assemble ships and embark his men—but Reubell was unsure of the Black Corps' direction of march. Had they gone due north toward Elsfleth, or east toward Bremen or north-west through the city of Oldenburg? His question seemed answered when a small Braunschweig detachment appeared from the direction of Bremen and pushed back the Westphalian tirailleurs east of Delmenhorst. This was a small detachment of about 120 men which Friedrich Wilhelm had sent to Bremen on the 5th for the express purpose of luring the Westphalians away from his true line of march.[119] In the brief skirmish which now ensued, the Braunschweiger hussars were broken, scattered and separated from their comrades, but the infantry made good their escape to the north-east. Convinced the Duke's main force was in Bremen, Reubell marched his division there on the 7th only to find the city empty of enemies. He returned to Delmenhorst on the 8th, but it was too late: a detachment sent to Elsfleth under GB Bongars learned that Duke and his Corps had taken ship for England the previous day.[120] For Jerome's men the 1809 campaign had finally come to an end.[121]

The brief campaign against the Duke of Braunschweig left Jerome feeling dishonoured and humiliated. Not only had the young troops of the 1st and 6th Infantry Regiments failed in the face of the enemy, but Reubell's poor military performance and inexcusable mistreatment of Westphalian citizenry had sullied the army's already damaged reputation at home and abroad. GB d'Albignac was thus sent north with orders relieving Reubell from command and directing him to report to Kassel for disciplinary action. Arriving in Bremen on 9 August, however, d'Albignac found the discredited Reubell gone, fled to the United States with his American wife; it would be eight years before he again saw the coastlines of Europe. As for Duke Friedrich Wilhelm and his men, they had been able to embark on requisitioned ships during the morning of 7 August, unhurried by their pursuers and molested only by the inclement weather. They had even had time to sell their horses. In October 1810, they arrived on the Iberian Peninsula, and for the next four years the Black Corps would fight alongside English troops in Spain and Sicily. The Duke himself, at the head of a new army, would find his fate on the field of Quatre Bras, laid low by a French bullet in the last campaign of the Napoleonic Wars, one of the French divisions to his front commanded by Napoleon's youngest brother, Jerome.

The year also held one final combat experience for the Saxon Army. On 10 August, as d'Albignac was moving the Westphalian division back to Bremen on the North Sea coast, a Braunschweig lieutenant in distant Bohemia led some 120 new Black Corps recruits from their depot into southern Saxony, apparently to avoid being enrolled in Austrian regiments. They were detected, however, and a detachment of twenty Saxon hussars caught them on the border 40 kilometres south-east of Dresden on the 11th. The Saxons attacked, killing the lieutenant and several of his men, capturing 31 other Braunschweigers and dispersing the remainder into the hills; one hussar lost his life. The hussars returned to Dresden, their small, successful skirmish providing an appropriate conclusion to Saxony's energetically extemporized defence of its borders in 1809.

The curtain thus fell on the campaign début of the Westphalian Army. It was hardly an auspicious opening and Jerome's military left the war with an unenviable reputation. The army's manifold problems can be distilled down to several basic deficiencies. First, as an immature kingdom, Westphalia lacked a national military tradition and the archaic martial background of some of its component states (e.g., Hesse-Kassel) did not immediately translate into a solid foundation for an effective army in the Napoleonic age. Aware of this problem, Jerome and his government made great efforts to instill a sense of nation in the population, but little could be done to effect such a massive change before the war opened. Unit cohesion and individual motivation suffered accordingly. Second, Westphalia's soldiers were thrown into war before they were ready. The formation of Jerome's regiments had proceeded slowly and there had been no time to develop the close bonds that link officers and men, no time to create resilient, cohesive combat organizations. Furthermore, although many of the officers were veterans of earlier wars, most of the men were new recruits, inexperienced, partially trained and poorly equipped when war came in 1809. Though many were courageous, they were not yet soldiers. The 5th and 6th Infantry

Regiments were particularly raw organizations but none of the other units had existed for more than a year and few were fully established before late 1808. This helps to explain the lacklustre performance of most Westphalian units (especially the 6th Infantry) and places the determined resistance of the 5th Infantry at Halberstadt in a more positive light.[122]

Lack of training and experience can be at least partly overcome by good leadership and a solid command structure, but in these areas X Corps and the Westphalian Army as a whole were grossly deficient. Generals such as d'Albignac and Reubell, the young king's cronies, had been promoted far beyond their levels of competence and were incapable of leading the large formations entrusted to their care. The indecisive movements of the army, its poor march security, the luxury of its headquarters and the abominable discipline of the Westphalian and Dutch soldiery are all symptoms of the feckless manner in which these men approached war.[123] Moreover, they seldom demonstrated any understanding of the German soldiers or citizens, alienating both by their suspicions and abuses. These problems were exacerbated by the inadequacies of the army and corps command structure. Inefficient and encumbered by a host of civilian functionaries, Jerome's headquarters seemed incapable of developing a plan and directing its execution. Instructions were vague, contradictory and frequently changed, leaving observers to cite the old military adage: order, counterorder, disorder.[124] It was impossible to determine who was in charge at the top and subordinate leaders constantly complained that they knew neither the enemy's dispositions nor their own king's intentions.

Indeed, the Westphalian king must bear the blame for many of his army's ills. By no means incompetent, Jerome none the less allowed his positive qualities to be swamped by fear, frivolity and love of luxury. He seems to have been unable or unwilling to focus on the military task at hand, preferring pleasure and pomp to the demands of a vigorous campaign. Despite a fairly satisfactory showing in 1807 and personal courage in the face of internal revolt, Jerome was clearly unfit for a major independent command in 1809 and his brave men were thus made to suffer an aimless, wandering campaign, full of privation and humiliation with no compensatory glory.

NOTES

1: The name 'Westphalia' (Westfalen), though termed 'absurd' by a German historian because the new kingdom was hardly located near the borders of the old duchy (Peace of Westphalia, 1648), satisfied Napoleon's penchant for evoking antiquity in the modern age. See Arthur Kleinschmidt, *Geschichte des Königreichs Westfalen*, Gotha, 1893, p. 3; and Alfred Rambaud, *L'Allemagne sous Napoléon Ier (1804-1811)*, Paris: Perrin, 1897, p. 200.

2: Quote from a letter written in early 1809 by a society lady of Kassel. For this and other contemporary observations, see Moritz von Kaisenberg, *König Jérome Napoleon, Ein Zeit- und Lebensbild*, Leipzig: Schmidt und Günther, 1899 (quote on p. 90). See also Stanislaus von Leszczynski, ed., *Kriegerleben des Johann von Borcke 1806-1815*, Berlin: Mittler & Sohn, 1888 (von Borcke was an expatriate Prussian officer who served in the Westphalian Army through 1813).

3: Quotation from an article by Rambaud in *Revue des deux Mondes* cited in Kleinschmidt, p. 19. In addition to Kleinschmidt and Rambaud, information on the foundation of the Kingdom of Westphalia and the seeds of its eventual demise taken from Owen Connelly, *Napoleon's Satellite Kingdoms*, New York: The Free Press, 1965, pp. 184-7, 193; and Herbert A. L. Fisher's thoughtful and balanced work *Studies in Napoleonic Statesmanship: Germany*, Oxford: Clarendon Press, 1903, pp. 240-1, 248-9, 274-5, 307.

4: Three exceptionally able French officials had been sent to Westphalia in August 1807 to prepare the way for Jerome. Jerome was the third of Napoleon's brothers to take a royal crown: Louis was King in Holland and

Joseph sat on the throne in Naples, which capital he would soon exchange for Madrid.

5: Napoleon to Jerome, November 1807, quoted in Kleinschmidt, pp. 13-14. Previous quotes also from Kleinschmidt: Katharina to her father (p. 6) and a letter Napoleon sent to Joseph in May 1807 (pp. 45-6).

6: German historians of the nineteenth century, caught in the hyperbole of untrammelled nationalism, frequently added to the libidinous legend of 'König Lustig', ignoring his abilities and exaggerating both Jerome's weaknesses and the disaffection of the Westphalian populace (see Connelly, p. 193). This brief background on Jerome drawn from accounts in Connelly; Elting (pp. 402-3); Fisher (pp. 240-9); Kaisenberg (pp. 88-98); Kleinschmidt (pp. 39-52); Williams, *Funck* (p. 144). Princess Pauline of Lippe-Detmold, visiting Kassel in 1808 wrote 'It was impossible not to think of the Harem of an oriental prince. . . . the surroundings with gardens, the luxury of the service and table, a certain soft, jaded essence, the absence of any serious word, the free jests - who could but think of the orient?' Quoted in Eckart Klessmann, ed., *Deutschland unter Napoleon in Augenzeugberichten*, Düsseldorf: Rauch, 1965, p. 292.

7: This figure includes field and depot elements of the guard and line but not internal security forces. Actual field troops probably numbered something over 12,000 (guard and line minus depots). See 'Die Armee des Königreichs Westfalen', *Beiheft zum Militär-Wochenblatt*, Heft 6, 1887 (hereafter 'Armee'); and W. Hewig, 'Die Armee des Königreichs Westfalen 1808-13', *Zeitschrift für Heeres- und Uniformskunde*, Nos. 142/143 (May/Jul 1955), 144/145 (Sep/Nov 1955) and 146/147 (Jan/Mar 1956). The Westphalian Constitution is given in *Correspondence* 13362.

8: *Correspondence* 13435, 5 January 1808. Typical of Napoleon's astounding attention to detail, this letter even proposed a pay scale for the Guard and suggested height requirements for entry into the élite corps.

9: The following information on the formation, organization, strength and uniforms of all elements of the Westphalian Army is drawn from a variety of sources: 'Armee'; Markus Gärtner and Edmund Wagner, *Westfälisches Militär*, Beckum: Deutsche Gesellschaft für Heereskunde, 1990; Hewig; Kleinschmidt; Fritz Lünsmann, *Die Armee des Königreichs Westfalen 1807-1813*, Berlin: Leddihn, 1935; Otto von Pivka, *Napoleon's German Allies (1): Westfalia and Kleve-Berg*, London: Osprey, 1975.

10: 'Ce n'est pas l'étiquette de notre famille', (*Correspondence* 13435, 5 January 1808).

11: In addition to lavish uniforms and the prospect of promotion, proximity to the royal court and other perquisites (troopers of the Garde du Corps were equal in rank to Unterlieutenants of the line) were intended to make enrollment as a guardsman an attractive proposition.

12: The Poles were concentrated in the 1st Squadron, apparently retaining the lances they had carried into the Westphalian capital ('Armee', p. 168). Although these Poles are generally described as 'lancers', their provenance may have been the short-lived 1st Polish Hussar Regiment of Colonel J. Kalinowski (see George Nafziger, Mariusz T. Wesolowski, and Tom Devoe, *Poles and Saxons of the Napoleonic Wars*, Chicago: The Emperor's Press, 1991, pp. 75-6).

13: Whether the unit had four, five or six companies in 1809 is unclear. I suspect it was complete in that year because one of its officers states in his memoirs that the 5th Company took part in the suppression of Dörnberg's rebellion in April (Heinrich F. von Meibom, *Aus napoleonischer Zeit*, Hans Jürgen von Gadow, ed., Leipzig: Koehler & Amelang, n.d., p. 91).

14: *Correspondence* 14809, 25 February 1809. Jerome responded to Napoleon's note by saying that the regiment was already formed and could not now be disbanded without creating an unpleasant effect. To mollify his brother, however, he said that he would arm the cuirassiers with musketoons so that they 'could properly render the same service as light cavalry'. Letter from Jerome to Napoleon, 1 March 1809, in Albert Du Casse, ed., *Mémoires et Correspondence du Roi Jérome et de la Reine Catherine*, Paris: Dentu, 1861-1868, vol. III, p. 383 (hereafter cited as Du Casse, *Jérome*).

15: Sappers and *ouvriers* wore uniforms like the foot artillery but with slightly different distinctions: the sappers had black collars and cuffs trimmed in red and the lapels on the *ouvriers'* coats were solid red.

16: These detachments, called 'brigades', consisted of a corporal and three gendarmes; an officer and a Sergeant-Major (Wachtmeister) were stationed in each departmental capital.

17: Westphalia's eight departments were: Elbe, Fulda, Harz, Leine, Oker, Saale, Werra, Weser. The Departmental Companies of the Werra and Fulda Departments were raised to a strength of 100 each during 1809.

18: The exact duties, if any, of the Veteran Companies are not known. It is probable they were used to supplement the Departmental Companies and perform other sedentary tasks.

19: Intended to include all men from 20 to 60 years of age, the National Guard wore dark blue coats and breeches, the former trimmed in red, black bicorne hats and black leather equipment. Only the National Guard of Kassel had any fixed organization: a battalion of five 120-man companies (four on foot and one mounted). During 1809, a second battalion was formed, this with eight companies, two of which were designated élites (one each of grenadiers and voltigeurs) with appropriate insignia.

20: This depot was initially formed in Paderborn, but had moved to Braunschweig by 1809; the number of companies in 1809 is unknown (possibly two). The men wore uniforms like those of the line infantry but made of cheap, rough cloth and lacking any regimental distinctions; for headgear, they were issued with brown cloth caps.

21: German authors (e.g., Kleinschmidt, Lünsmann) like to portray the recruiting effort as a complete failure, but more than half of the Westphalian Army in 1808 was made up of volunteers of one brand or another, only some 4,500 out of more than 10,200 were conscripts. That is not to say that all of these volunteers were superior soldiers or that Westphalians were wildly enthusiastic about serving Jerome, but only to indicate more realistically the role of conscription in building the kingdom's army. On the other hand, Connelly (p. 192) and Fisher (p. 302) seem rather too positive in their descriptions of the Westphalian government's recruiting successes.

22: Borcke, who was initially assigned to the 1st Light, had nothing but contempt for the battalion (Leszczynski, pp. 110-15). Napoleon himself complained to Jerome of the 1st Chevauxleger's indiscipline (*Correspondence* 14494, 19 November 1808).

23: Napoleon is said to have told Morio: 'You a general? In my army you would not even be a corporal!' (Connelly, p. 186). For other Napoleonic aspersions towards Morio see Ernest Picard, *Préceptes et Jugements de Napoléon*, Paris: Berger-Levrault, 1913, p. 495. Eblé's distinguished career was capped by extraordinary heroism during the retreat from Russia where his foresight, skill and determination saved the scarecrow remnants of the Grande Armée at the Berezina; drained by his superhuman exertions, he died several weeks later in East Prussia.

24: Quote and figures from Lünsmann (pp. 125-7). The percentages are for the 1810 officer corps but they generally reflect its composition in 1809.

25: Leszczynski, p. 112; Meibom, p. 81.

26: The continual and hasty expansion of the army naturally created a tremendous demand for new leaders, both officers and NCOs. See Leszczynski and Meibom (officers) as well as Heinrich Wesemann, *Kannonier des Kaisers*, Köln: Verlag Wissenschaft und Politik, 1971 (from conscript to NCO).

27: Leszczynski, pp. 118-119.

28: Wesemann, p. 15.

29: The Westphalian translation of these famous French regulations became the standard for the entire Rheinbund (*Reglement das Exercitium und die Manövres der Französischen Infanterie betreffend, vom 1sten August 1791*).

30: It should be noted that whereas the line units used German, the language of command in the Guard was French. The broad usage of both German and French also complicated the names of the Westphalian units and ranks. Thus the Jäger-Carabiner were also called the Chasseur-Carabinier d'Elite and a Général de Division might also be termed a Divisionsgeneral. To maintain consistency with the rest of this book, I have chosen to use the more commonly encountered designations, hence German titles for units (reflecting their composition) and French titles for ranks (most generals in 1809 being of French origin).

31: These comments apply to Jerome and his field commanders, specifically Reubell, d'Albignac, Morio and Ducoudras (Graf von Bernterode); Napoleon had little use for them. As Minister of War, the redoubtable Eblé did not campaign with the army; another artilleryman, GB Jacques-Alexandre- François Allix de Vaux, who would command X Corps' artillery in 1809, was also a capable and industrious officer (Kleinschmidt, pp. 432, 464). See also Picard.

32: This account of Katte's raid is taken principally from Rudolf von Katte, 'Der Streifzug des Friedrich Karl von Katte auf Magdeburg im April 1809', *Geschichts-Blätter für Stadt und Land Magdeburg*, No. 70./71., Jahrgang 1935/1936. Katte was recruited by the *Tugendbund*, a society formed in East Prussia in April 1808 for the purpose of arousing national consciousness in Prussia and, by extension, overthrowing French dominion. Though small in 1809, its agents were active in Prussia and Westphalia as Austria's intention to attack France became evident. The *Tugendbund* played an important role in shaping public opinion in the heady nationalistic days of 1813, but Prussian official circles had regarded it with mistrust from its inception and it was suppressed in 1815 because of its liberal inclinations. See Klessmann (pp. 338-48) and Hannsjoachim W. Koch, *Die Befreiungskriege 1807-1815*, Berg: Türmer, 1987 (pp. 268-73).

33: Some sources (e.g., Fisher and Kleinschmidt) mention a brief skirmish outside of Magdeburg, but according to von Katte's detailed account no real fighting took place.

34: Rambaud, p. 349.

35: He had fought under Blücher in what became the legendary retreat to and defence of Lübeck.

36: The English historian Fisher finds Dörnberg's behaviour thoroughly reprehensible: 'with a singular lack of honour [he] accepted the pay and the uniform of the prince whom it was his object to betray' (p. 250).

37: Like Katte, Dörnberg was linked with the *Tugendbund*.

38: When the rebellion fell apart, Marschall became one of many examples of Jerome's clemency, lucky to be merely relieved and assigned to a backwater administrative job.

39: Reubell's name is frequently spelled 'Rewbell'; I use the spelling in Georges Six, *Dictionnaire Biographique des Généraux & Amiraux Français de la Révolution et de l'Empire (1792-1814)*, Paris: Manutention a Mayenne, 1989.

40: Wesemann, pp. 17-18. Dörnberg's own account of the skirmish is very similar (Klessmann, pp. 352-5). As the Westphalian infantry and artillery were returning to Kassel, they met the Garde-Grenadiers who had also been sent to support Reubell; their presence no longer required, the grenadiers turned about and marched back to the city (Meibom, p. 92). Based on a detailed letter written by Lieutenant Fritz Wolf, it seems that part of the 2nd Infantry Regiment was also present at the Knallhütte affair; as the regiment had already marched off to France, it seems logical to conclude that all or part of the depot battalion was fielded to oppose Dörnberg (Wolf's letter is in Kaisenberg, pp. 104-13).

41: It will be remembered that the 1st Squadron of this regiment was formed from the Polish lancers who escorted Jerome into Kassel in 1807.

42: A subsequent attempt at revolt ran almost the same course. On the night of 23/24 June, an aged Hessian colonel (seventy-five!) named Emmerich with a virulently anti-French outlook led forty to fifty peasants into Marburg, disarmed a picket of veterans and tried desperately to rouse the inhabitants. But Marburg offered 'closed shutters instead of open arms' and the pathetic colonel with his hopeless band was soon driven from the city. See Fisher, p. 252.

43: Connelly, p. 202. Wolf, who also lauds General Eblé's calmness and organizational talent, claims that some twenty actually did turn in their epaulets; in any event, the number was small (Kaisenberg, p. 110).

44: Quotes from Wolf (see Kaisenberg). The account of the Dörnberg episode drawn from primarily Connelly, 200-3; Fisher, pp. 250-1; Kaisenberg, pp. 108-10; Kleinschmidt, pp. 232-57; Meibom, pp. 89-94; Rambaud, pp. 343-70; Wesemann, pp. 16-17.

45: Note that this Würzburg battalion was never formed. The only Würzburg units to take part in the campaign were a 'division' of sappers with the main army and a small detachment of train personnel with Junot.

46: *Correspondence*, 15042, 9 April 1809 and 15069, 15 April 1809. Kellermann would later (*Correspondence*, 15142, 29 April 1809) be placed at least nominally under Jerome's orders but Napoleon reserved troop deployment decisions for himself (see, for example, correspondence in Saski, vol. III, pp. 310-12) and eventually reversed his decision: 'The corps at Hanau is not under your orders and the Duke of Valmy [Kellermann] may not detach a single man without my orders' (*Correspondence*, 15269, 28 May 1809). The Westphalian King thus never exercised any real authority over the old marshal. The organization of X Corps shown in Table 9-3 is taken from Lünsmann (pp. 287-288) and was apparently an initial concept or possibly an early administrative organization. Other sources (e.g., Baut, vol. I, pp. 306-7) give a slightly different arrangement: all the Westphalian troops comprising one division, the Dutch a second and the French and Berg units combining to form a third. Strength is also a question, and the figures here are estimated from those provided in Buat, Lünsmann and Kellermann's April and May reports (in Saski, vol. III, pp. 76 and 405). The actual structure of the corps during the brief campaign in Saxony is shown in Tables 9-4 and 9-5.

47: A Dutch regiment (probably the 7th Infantry), an ad hoc French battalion from Kellermann (about 800 men in two companies of 28th Léger, one company each of 27th, 30th and 33rd Ligne and probably one company of 65th Ligne) and the 3rd Berg Infantry (over 1,200 men) with six guns (possibly a Berg battery) arrived in Kassel on 28 April (Kleinschmidt, p. 250). Westphalian units at this time were generally divided between Magdeburg (1st, 5th and 6th Infantry) and the capital area (Guard and 1st Cuirassiers). Other X Corps troops continued to arrive through May.

48: Schill's personality and background principally drawn from Rudolf Bartsch, *Die Schill'schen Offiziere*, volume VII of *Das Kriegsjahr 1809 in Einzeldarstellungen*, Wien: Stern, 1909, pp. 8-26.

49: On 29 April, the French commandant in Magdeburg, GD Michaud, was already notifying Berthier of Schill's departure (report reproduced in Klessmann, p. 357).

50: The garrison consisted of about 160 invalids and recruits from various regiments and 140 'Bürgerschützen' (municipal militia); some armed citizens joined the soldiers and militiamen as the day made its way into evening. The two captains were Siegmund von Wittern (fortress commandant) and von Förstel (an artillery-man in the city on other duty).

51: It was during his attempts to organize the relief of Wittenberg that von Funck had his exasperating encounter with the commander of the *Zastrow* Cuirassiers. See Chapter 6. The relief force consisted of 100 mounted cuirassiers and some 200 dismounted cavalrymen and it was the mounted element which rode off in pursuit of Schill, unfortunately under the same colonel who had bedeviled Funck the previous day.

52: The Saxon government had evacuated its capital, Dresden, and displaced to Leipzig for fear of Austrian raids over the border from Bohemia. The otherwise inexplicable fact that Schill was allowed to cross the Elbe may be accounted for by the following story: Schill may have known that a barge on the river contained much of the Saxon treasury; promising not to disturb it, he was permitted to use the bridge in peace (Bartsch, pp. 30-1). This account of the events at Wittenberg is compiled from Christian Binder von Kriegelstein, *Ferdinand von Schill*, Berlin: Voss, 1902, pp. 138-41; Exner, pp. 114-15; Williams, pp. 167-77.

53: In Köthen, the local duke's guard was disarmed and an NCO and fifty men were persuaded to join Schill's ranks.

54: French units: Grenadier Company and 1st Fusilier Company of IV/22nd Ligne, artillerymen from the 14th Company, 7th Foot Artillery Regiment with two 6-pounders. Westphalian units: 1st Grenadier, 1st Voltigeur, 1st and 4th Fusilier Companies of the 1st Infantry.

55: Von Uslar had been charged with overseeing the organization of the 5th and 6th Regiments. The task having proceeded slowly despite great efforts and he being unwilling to declare the units fit for action prematurely, he fell from grace and was dismissed from Jerome's service shortly after the events depicted here. Although removed from command, he remained with the detachment throughout the battle, had a horse shot out from under him and barely escaped capture. See Leszczynski, pp. 132-3.

56: This rendering of the fight at Dodendorf is taken from Binder von Kriegelstein's detailed rendition and Michaud's excellent 6 May battle report (Binder, pp. 147-56, 295-9). Note that some other historians have the Allies forming three large squares, the which Schill's riders proceed to break. Binder's detailed research and analysis puts this interpretation to rest.

57: Michaud sent 400 men (including some of the 8th Hussars) to reinforce Vauthier, but these only arrived after the battle. The old general himself rode out in advance of these reinforcements and thus appeared on the field to make his observations in the immediate aftermath of the fight. Vauthier's wound proved mortal and he was replaced at the head of the 1st Infantry by Colonel Legras.

58: At this time, the Magdeburg garrison consisted of the 1st, 5th and 6th Westphalian Infantry Regiments, two Westphalian artillery companies, IV/22nd Ligne, a small detachment of the French 8th Hussars, one company each from the French 7th and 8th Foot Artillery Regiments, and various detachments of sappers, workers, convalescents, etc. for a total of some 6,036 men (according to Michaud's report of 8 May in Binder, p. 299).

59: Napoleon to the Minister of War, 17 May 1809 (Saski, vol. III, pp. 312-13). Jerome's 4 May letter to Napoleon relating Blücher's apochryphal march is in Du Casse, *Jérome*, vol. IV, p. 38. Jerome's letters referring to his own men and his repeated requests for French reinforcements are in Du Casse, *Jérome*, vol. III, pp. 383 (1 March) and 411 (24 April); vol. IV, pp. 43 (5 May) and 54 (11 May). Reubell's comment is from a 15 May letter to Berthier (Du Casse, *Jérome*, vol. IV, p. 79).

60: Like many other German nationalists, Schill had great, and rather unrealistic, hopes for English support, eagerly anticipating the appearance of redcoats on the North Sea coast and relying on the Royal Navy to evacuate him in time of need. He likewise drew on the prevalent romantic images of Spanish guerrilla resistance to Napoleon and spoke of making Stralsund into a 'second Saragossa' (where Spanish insurgents held out against French siege for months).

61: There is little precise information on the actions of Jerome's forces during May. The composition of Bongars' force, for example, is not clear, nor is it certain which Westphalian forces marched out of Kassel with d'Albignac to pursue Schill (Lünsmann says it was part of the Guard). Based on Gratien's order of battle and later movements, it may be assumed that d'Albignac had the 7th and 8th Dutch Infantry Regiments (probably something over 2,000 men) and a Dutch battery plus some Westphalian troops; he apparently had no cavalry. On reaching Magdeburg on the 13th, Michaud reinforced him with three companies of IV/22nd Ligne, four companies of the 1st Westphalian Infantry and two howitzers with French crews, all commanded by Colonel Meyronnet. D'Albignac moved north from Magdeburg and reached Tangermünde on the 15th, but it is not clear when he actually appeared across the Elbe from Dömitz. Gratien's dispositions are equally mysterious. He seems to have been at Stendal on the 15th, and then moved to the vicinity of Lüneburg and had reached a village just south-east of Hamburg by the 23rd. He left on the 25th to move north-east toward Stralsund. When he attacked Stralsund on 31 May, he had with him the 6th and 9th Infantry Regiments, the 2nd Cuirassiers, a foot battery and a horse battery (Binder, *Schill*, p. 188); the remainder of his division was apparently with d'Albignac.

62: Ewald had come south to replace Gratien around Hamburg on 18 May. He marched his division east on the 25th to link with the Dutch on the 27th and headed toward Stralsund in the company of Gratien. In the assault, Ewald's force consisted of the *Oldenburg* Infantry Regiment minus its grenadier companies (not to be confused with the 800-man Rheinbund contingent from the Duchy of Oldenburg), III/*Holstein*, two companies of the Holstein Scharfschützenkorps, two squadrons of hussars, some Holstein cavalrymen and ten 3-pounders for a total of some 2,550 men (2,117 infantry, 214 cavalry, 139 artillery plus staff and others). Gratien's and Ewald's movements from Binder, *Schill*.

63: Approximate strengths: 1st Depot Battalion (683), 2nd Depot Battalion (654), *Zastrow* squadron (130), *Zastrow* detachment (51), *Polenz* detachment (45). Unfortunately, these numbers are deceptive as many of Thielmanns' men (over 50 per cent) were hardly fit for field duty; by June many of them would be dismissed, reducing the size of the force but generally raising its quality. Other Saxon forces within the realm included some 650 men in a dozen dismounted cavalry squadrons (having given up many of its steeds to the French in 1806/1807, Saxony could not put every trooper on a horse) as well as the depots of the cavalry regiments; these were located at Weissenfels with the artillery depot (see Table 9-4). Additionally, there were some 800 men in the fortress of Königstein south of Dresden: 205 in the Garrison Company, 449 in a provisional infantry battalion composed of yet more depot troops (from the *Prinz Anton, Prinz Friedrich August,* and *von Niesemeuschl* regiments), 104 artillerymen and several dozen fortress personnel. For this and other order of battle information, see Exner, pp. 14, 75-8; Schuster/Fancke, pp. 286-8; see also E. G. M. Freiherr von Friesen, 'Dresden im Kriegsjahre 1809', *Mitteilungen des Vereins für Geschichte Dresdens,* Heft 11, 1893, p. 12.

64: Thielmann later (1813) entered Prussian service and commanded III Corps of Blücher's Army in the Waterloo campaign.

65: Five Saxon line battalions and two grenadier companies remained on garrison duty: Regiment *von Rechten* (minus its grenadiers) at Danzig, Regiment *von Burgsdorff* (likewise without grenadiers) and the grenadier companies of *Prinz Max* at Glogau, and II/*von Dyherrn* at Stettin. Each fortress also held a small Saxon artillery detachment.

66: The saga of the *Zastrow* Cuirassiers is confusing. Upon its return from Danzig, the bulk of the regiment seems to have been in the area around Leipzig, only one squadron and a detachment serving initially with Thielmann. Another squadron did remain mounted and pursued Schill ineffectually from Wittenberg, but the rest of the regiment apparently languished around Leipzig as a result of ill will and inefficiency. Funck's account indicates that the regiment's Inhaber, apparently with the connivance of the commander and other senior officers, strove to keep the regiment from active campaigning, thereby increasing the amount of monetary profit they might hope to gain from the unit. Thus a large portion of the regiment seems to have been temporarily inactive from April through May and it was June before all four squadrons were in the field. Summary of estimated dispositions: from late April to early May, one mounted squadron and one detachment with Thielmann, one mounted squadron around Leipzig, the remainder inactive (reorganizing, men awaiting mounts, horses awaiting troopers, generally a bureaucratic Saxon mare's nest); by late May two mounted squadrons with Thielmann, no other mounted elements available; by mid-June four mounted squadrons with Thielmann. It should be noted that Funck specifically excluded the junior officers and troopers from his opprobrium, claiming that only the over-aged senior blunderers conspired to keep the cuirassiers in their garrisons. See Williams, pp. 270-1, 277-8.

67: Einsiedel's Battalion was composed of the grenadier companies from infantry regiments *König* and *von Dyherrn*; Wolan's two companies came from the *von Rechten* Infantry Regiment.

68: Thielmann was in the habit of issuing rather bombastic proclamations when he entered Austrian towns, telling sceptical villagers for example that 'the House of Habsburg has ceased to reign!' For interesting commentary on the ambitious Thielmann, see Franz J. A. Schneidawind, *Der Feldzug des Herzogs Friedrich Wilhelm von Braunschweig und seines schwarzen Corps im Jahre 1809,* Darmstadt: Leske, 1851, especially pp. 30-41.

69: Relevent correspondence: Jerome to Napoleon and Kellermann, 20 May 1809; Jerome to Kellermann, 27 May 1809; Napoleon to Jerome, 9 June 1809; Kellermann to Jerome, 21 May 1809. Cited in Du Casse, *Jérome,* pp. 69-73, 89, 119.

70: Quotes from Am Ende's orders as cited in Christian G. Ernst Am Ende, *Feldmarschall-Lieutenant Carl Friedrich Am Ende besonders sein Feldzug in Sachsen 1809,* Wien: Braumüller, 1878, p. 48; and Exner, p. 83. The alliance between the Austrians, Braunschweigers and Hessians was full of recrimination: the Braunschweigers were frustrated by what they perceived as lethargy on Am Ende's part whereas the Austrians found the Duke of Braunschweig's hot eagerness annoying; both decried the poor discipline of the Hessians. Note that the strength of the Braunschweig and Hessian detachments fluctuated widely during the war, often varying from day to day with accretions and desertions.

71: A former Prussian possession, Bayreuth was now under direct French administration.

72: This apparently occurred in late May or early June. The additional riders numbered 107 chevauxlegers and 90 cuirassiers (Exner, p. 84).

73: It should be noted that I/*Oebschelwitz* was apparently quite weak, numbering only some 250 men (H. von Schimpff, p. 145). Furthermore, von Holtzendorff states that Thielmann followed the normal Saxon practice of combining Schützen, forming a Schützen-Division for his tiny corps (Holtzendorff, p. 46).

74: The Austrians and Hessians had concentrated at Teplitz on the border on 9 June. The Braunschweigers moved from Aussig to Kulm the same day and united with Am Ende at Dippoldiswalde on the 10th. Am Ende's Austrian contingent consisted of two regular battalions: III/*Erbach*, III/*Mittrowsky* (these were depot battalions of only four companies each; the latter was probably from *Anton Mittrowsky*, Regiment No. 10); six Landwehr battalions: 2nd, 3rd, 4th and 5th Leitmeritz, 5th Königgrätz, 6th Bunzlau; a company of the 1st Jägers; one squadron each of *Schwarzenberg* and *Merveldt* Uhlans; a platoon from the reserve squadron of the *Klenau* Chevauxlegers; eight 3-pounders and two howitzers. The Duke of Braunschweig's army included two infantry battalions, a hussar regiment and a horse battery for about 1,000 men. The 340 Hessians were divided among three small companies (Garde-Grenadiers, Jägers, Füsiliers) and two miniature squadrons (Leib Dragoons, Hussars); an additional 280 Hessians joined the division from Bohemia on 1 July (Premier-Lieutenant Dechend, 'Das hessische Freicorps im Jahre 1809', *Jahrbücher für die deutsche Armee und Marine,* Band 54 (January-March 1885), pp. 252-3).

75: The only armed Saxons left in Dresden were the newly created Bürger-Garde and Mounted Gendarmes. Both were paramilitary formations intended to maintain public order. The foot guardsmen numbered about 165 in early June and rose to almost 250 by the end of the month; there were 98 Mounted Gendarmes. Neither formation had been uniformed by the time the Austrians arrived. See Friesen, p. 19 and Schuster/Francke, p. 288.

76: About 50 hussars were also posted at Nossen to watch the road north into the Saxon right (Süssmilch, p. 87).

77: Wolan also had about twenty cavalrymen of unspecified brand with him. It is not clear how many companies were in his combined battalion: accounts of the actions on the 12th imply there were only four, but it may be inferred from Exner that he had six (four from the reduced depot battalions plus the two grenadier companies from *von Rechten*).

78: Estimates of Saxon losses for the 12th range from 57 to 73 and include Major von Einsiedel (wounded); the enemy lost only about a dozen men. The Saxons halted for the night along a small river (the Strigis) about ten kilometres west of Nossen. This account of the skirmishes on 12 June is drawn primarily from Gustav von Kortzfleisch's detailed work: *Geschichte des Herzoglich Braunschweigischen Infanterie-Regiments und seiner Stammtruppen 1809-1867*, Braunschweig: Limbach, 1896, pp. 35-8. The fight was conducted principally by a rear guard under Thielmann (five squadrons, Einsiedel's Battalion, Ryssel's two companies and two guns) while Dyherrn took the rest of the corps to the west. Kortzfleisch mentions that the Saxon hussars were caught at a disadvantage outside of a village and suffered fairly heavy losses at the hands of the Austrian and Braunschweig cavalry; the Hussars' regimental history, however, states that only three men were wounded and generally passes over the skirmish with little comment (as does Exner).

79: These reinforcements (the same mentioned earlier) had arrived the previous day from the depots: two squadrons of *Zastrow*, one squadron of hussars, a detachment of 101 men from *von Burgsdorff*, four guns (see Table 9-4).

80: In addition to constructing new units, Dyherrn was to direct the rebuilding of the weak second battalions released from IX Corps when it was reorganized on 10 June (see Chapter 6).

81: Remaining in Dresden were the 5th Königgrätz and 6th Bunzlau Landwehr, the *Klenau* platoon and the Hessian infantry; they were joined by the 3rd Czaslau Landwehr on the 22nd. The same day, the 5th Bunzlau Landwehr was directed to Freiberg. See Kortzfleisch, p. 43.

82: The Saxon hussars apparently cut their infantry compatriots out of a tight spot when the foot soldiers advanced too boldly, but the retreat to Lützen was undisturbed by the Austrians. This action is generally known as the Skirmish at Holzhausen (a village east of Leipzig).

83: Some 210 mounted *Polenz* chevauxlegers, a detachment of Leib-Grenadier Guards (119 men) and four guns (see Table 9-4).

84: Radivojevich had the *Deutsch-Banat* Grenz Infantry Regiment (two battalions); the 1st and 2nd Tabor, 4th Königgrätz and 2nd Chrudim Landwehr battalions; the reserve squadron of the *Merveldt* Uhlans, a combined cavalry squadron (one platoon each from the reserve squadrons of the *Schwarzenberg* Uhlans, *Blankenstein* Hussars, and *Rosenberg* Chevauxlegers); and four 3-pounders for a total of 4,196 infantry and 213 cavalry. He left a squadron of *Merveldt* and five Landwehr battalions in Bohemia. See Welden, pp. 9, 98. Additionally, he supported the raising of a small Bayreuth free-corps under a Major Nostitz which numbered some 320 men by 3 July (Dechend, p. 246). See Chapter 7 for the actions in Bavaria during June and July.

85: Jerome sent the Berg infantry regiment and part of Guard to Eisenach on 16 June; following himself on the 18th with the remainder of the Guard, he linked with d'Albignac and Gratien on the 21st.

86: Two Saxon companies and a pair of horse guns were left at Weissenfels to guard the bridge; they rejoined Thielmann at Leipzig on the 25th.

87: It is extraordinarily difficult to arrive at a solid assessment of d'Albignac's and Thielmann's combat strengths. The figures given in Table 9-4 are estimated from Jerome's and Thielmann's correspondence (Du Casse, *Jérome*, vol. IV, pp. 134-5, 252-65) but there are numerous other interpretations. Kortzfleisch and Mayerhoffer give the Westphalians 2,750 men (without further definition), a figure which matches Schneidawind's: 1st and 6th infantry (together 2,050), 1st Cuirassiers (350), Jäger-Garde (350). These numbers generally seem too low, however, and I have developed my own estimate. Regarding the Dutch troops, note that the division numbered about 4,000 infantry, 260 cavalry and 200 (estimated) artillerists; the 7th Infantry and a battery apparently remained at Magdeburg with IV/22. As to other units, part of the Berg regiment (probably about 400) remained behind in Westphalia: one company (110 men) was stationed in Marburg (see note 42) and others probably garrisoned Kassel (Kortzfleisch says only one battalion was with X Corps). Jerome gives the strength of the Berg detachment with X Corps as 800. I have *estimated* Thielmann's strength to be 2,840 based on the following: *Einsiedel* (450), *Wolan* (400), I/*Oebschelwitz* (250), Leib Grenadiers (119), *Burgsdorff* detachment (101), *Zastrow* (400), Hussars (290), *Polenz* (360), artillery (420); my rules of thumb were about 100 men per company or squadron (most were far from full strength) and 100-120 per artillery battery. The *ad hoc* French battalion numbered about 800 men and was composed of two companies from 28th Léger, one company each from 27th, 30th and 33rd Ligne as well as (probably) one company from 65th Ligne; most of the battalion was in Magdeburg by 4 June, but the company from the 65th was apparently at Homberg (Michaud's report of 4 June in Du Casse, *Jérome*, vol. IV, pp. 134-5).

88: Saxon losses were about 100 (Exner). Westphalian casualties are not known, but must have been very light: of the Westphalian infantry only the 1st Regiment's voltigeurs even came within range of the Austrian position and the cavalry only skirmished with their Austrian and Braunschweig counterparts. Am Ende's losses were 10 dead and 60-70 wounded.

89: Austrian movements now become somewhat confusing because Kienmayer did not accompany his troops, rather rode off to Dresden on his own and from thence proceeded to join Radivojevich. The portion of Am Ende's force sent toward Bayreuth was under Oberst Rosener (also spelled Rosner or Rossner): III/*Erbach*, two companies of *Mittrowsky*, one company of the 1st Jägers, three Landwehr battalions (2nd Leitmeritz, 3rd

Czaslau, 5th Bunzlau), a squadron of *Schwarzenberg* Uhlans, four 3-pounders and two howitzers. This left Am Ende with two companies of *Mittrowsky*, five Landwehr battalions (3rd, 4th and 5th Leitmeritz, 5th Königgrätz, 6th Bunzlau), a platoon of *Klenau* Chevauxlegers and four 3-pounders. It is not clear whether the squadron of *Merveldt* Uhlans marched with Rosener or Am Ende. The Braunschweigers and Hessians (cavalry from Nossen and infantry from Dresden) made their way toward Bayreuth by different routes, the Hessians being joined by reinforcements along the way (see note 84 above).

90: This and previous quote taken from Kaisenberg, pp. 121-2.

91: Comments on d'Albignac, Reubell and Gratien from a report by Napoleon's minister in Kassel; Jerome's deprecations were in a letter to Napoelon dated 4 June, before the King learned of Stralsund's fall and Schill's death (Du Casse, *Jérome,* vol. IV, pp. 110, 212-13).

92: Quotes from Schneidawind (Jerome), p. 85; and Exner (Dresdeners), p. 97. Some sources state that the Austrians deceived Jerome regarding their true intentions so that he was unaware of the move toward Bayreuth; given the poor state of Westphalian reconnaissance, this is entirely possible. The troops GB Bongars took to the west on the 30th were the 1st Westphalian Cuirassiers, the 2nd Dutch Cuirassiers and two French companies; curiously, after reaching Altenburg, he seems to have turned north toward Leipzig (Kortzfleisch, p. 61).

93: Friesen, pp. 43-4.

94 Kaisenberg, p. 122. The command climate in X Corps was not improved by the rancor that existed between Jerome and Gratien. Napoleon valued Gratien and he certainly showed more energy and skill in the campaign than any of the generals Jerome had selected, particularly considering that he was constantly tugged this way and that by Jerome and Louis. See Du Casse, *Jérome,* vol. IV, pp. 13, 27, 110.

95: In Jerome's defence, it must be pointed out that Napoleon had neglected to appoint a single commander for the Allied operations in Bayreuth and Saxony; Jerome and Junot were simply expected to co-operate with one another. Without unity of command on the Allied side, Kienmayer enjoyed a tremendous advantage. Furthermore, Napoleon repeatedly expressed his desire that Jerome and Junot would be able to invade Bohemia; this project apparently annoyed and confused the Westphalian King, who felt he had his hands full dealing with Kienmayer. None the less, Jerome's inaction at Dresden and the torpor of his march west are hardly excusable.

96: This was the hopeless attempt of the septugenarian Oberst Emmerich to rouse the city of Marburg against Jerome on 23 June. It was put down the next morning with the assistance of a Berg company. See notes 42 and 87 above. This renewed attempt at rebellion prompted Jerome to detach the *ad hoc* French battalion, a squadron of the 1st Cuirassiers and two guns on 6 July, sending them north to Westphalia as a safeguard against further unrest (Jerome to Berthier, 7 July 1809 in Du Casse, *Jérome,* vol. IV, pp. 263-4).

97: The strength of Wolan's Battalion is variously given as 360 and 460 men. It should be noted that Thielmann's force did not include all the Saxon mobile troops; he had all of the Saxon infantry and light cavalry, but his artillery only amounted to the horse battery supplemented by two 4-pounder foot guns. The remaining artillery and the *Zastrow* Cuirassiers apparently remained with X Corps.

98: Some 700-800 redcoats had indeed come ashore at the mouth of the Elbe near Cuxhaven on the night of 7/8 July and these were apparently assumed to signal the start of the long-awaited British landings on the North Sea coast.

99: Quoted from a report sent to Funck by one of Thielmann's staff officers (Friesen, p. 51).

100: Curiously, another message reached Am Ende at 8 p.m. that night as he rested in his headquarters in Pirna south of Dresden. This instructed him to refrain from retreating until he received further orders; the withdrawal of the Dresden troops and others having already been effected, however, Am Ende felt justified in returning to Bohemia. See Am Ende, pp. 80-93.

101: By 6 July (the date Jerome sent the French battalion and one of his cuirassier squadrons back to Westphalia), GB Bongars and his detachment had evidently returned to X Corps from their inexplicable expedition to Leipzig (see notes 92 and 95 above).

102: First two Saxon quotes from official reports cited in Exner, pp. 94-95; Westphalian quote from the faithful Wolf (30 June letter in Kaisenberg, p. 122); third Saxon quote from a report of 15 July cited in Friesen, p. 45.

103: Saxon report of 15 July quoted in Friesen, p. 51. The gunner's comment is from Oberkannonier Wesemann (Wesemann, p. 17).

104: Quote is from a letter sent by Napoleon to Jerome, 17 July 1809, cited in Friedrich M. Kircheisen, *Jovial King: Napoleon's Youngest Brother,* H. J. Stenning, trans., London: Elkin Mathews & Marrot, 1932, pp. 186-187. Napoleon's August orders decreeing the formation of VIII Corps under Junot also limited X Corps in size and mission: Jerome was now only to 'guard his state and those lands that surround it' (*Correspondence,* 15644, Order of 11 August, and 15652, Napoleon to Berthier, 13 August).

105: The Duke's speech to his officers on 24 July quoted in Gutav von Kortzfleisch, *Des Herzogs Friedrich Wilhelm von Braunschweig Zug durch Norddeutschland im Jahre 1809,* reprint of 1894 edition, Krefeld: Olmes, 1973, pp. 8-9.

106: In addition to staff, the army was composed of the 1st and 2nd Light Battalions (500 men each), the 3rd

Jäger Battalion (only 150 men), a Scharfschützen Company (150), a Hussar Regiment (550) with an Uhlan Squadron (80), and a light battery of 80 men with two 6-pounders and two howitzers. Their chronology: 17 July - at Schleiz, learned of armistice, 19 July - Austrians receive orders to retire into Bohemia by 27 July, 21 July - Braunschweigers move to Zwickau, 24 July - the Duke informs his men of his intention to fight on. See Kortzfleisch, *Herzogs*, p. 11.

107: Braunschweig saw three possible outcomes for his expedition: (1) successful revolt, (2) defeat (hopefully glorious) and (3) rescue by the Royal Navy.

108: The detachment consisted of 130 *Polenz* chevauxlegers and 40 hussars under OTL Petzoldt. The Braunschweigers, from the Scharfschützen Company, were mostly green troops and had no bayonets with which to defend themselves against the Saxon horsemen.

109: Gablenz had been sent from Dresden toward Zwickau on the 24th when news of Braunschweig's move reached the Saxon capital; his force consisted of two hussar squadrons, five squadrons of cuirassiers and chevauxlegers (not further detailed), 200 Schützen and two guns. Thielmann sent new orders as the Black Corps approached Leipzig, however, and Gablenz reached the city almost simultaneously with Thielmann (Gablenz's route: Pirna, Dresden, Klein Waltersdorf near Freiberg, Penig, Leipzig). A portion of Gablenz's command continued on to Zwickau under Major von Mandelsloh (150 hussars and 120 Schützen); reaching the town on the 27th, they of course found it empty of Braunschweigers. See Süssmilch, pp. 91-2.

110: The order announcing Thielmann's promotion to General-Major was dated 17 July, but it did not catch up with him until the 27th in Leipzig. His command remained at Lauchstädt until 3 August when he returned to Leipzig to unite his forces. By the 11th, he was back in Dresden, where strenuous efforts were underway to reorganize the Saxon Army completely. An edict of 1 June had already decreed the recruitment of 6,000 new soldiers and these were now slowly becoming available; combined with the fit men returning from IX Corps, they were formed into five new infantry battalions. Major Wolan's Battalion was dissolved and the *von Rechten* grenadiers combined with those of *Prinz Max* (returned from Glogau) to form a new grenadier battalion (von Stutterheim). Two other battalions were also assembled, one from the infantry depots, the other from the infantry Schützen (20 August). Finally, a Jäger-Korps of 126 men was created from trained hunters on 31 August. The cavalry also improved as new mounts were obtained for the regiments in Saxony. By the end of August, the following Saxon forces were therefore available to defend the realm:
five new infantry battalions
I/*Oebschelwitz*
two grenadier battalions (*Einsiedel* and *Stutterheim*)
the new Schützen Battalion
the new Depot Battalion
the Jäger-Korps
Zastrow Cuirassiers (four sqdns)
Polenz Chevauxlegers (four sqdns and a detachment of *Herzog Albrecht*)
two hussar squadrons
one Karabinier squadron
$2^1/2$ foot artillery batteries and one horse artillery battery.
This gave a total of some 10,393 men, including 2,125 cavalry. Combined with the French 22nd Ligne (arrived Dresden mid-August), these Saxon troops were placed under the command of GD Carra St.-Cyr as the 3rd Division of Junot's new VIII Corps.

111: Meyronnet, another of Jerome's French friends from his seafaring days, had been raised to the nobility with the title Graf Wellingerode, by which name he is also known. Strength from Kortzfleisch, *Infanterie* (p. 87); note that one source gives the regiment a strength of only 1,700 (GL von Lossberg quoted in Schneidawind, p. 123) and Jerome supposed the regiment did not exceed 800 men (15 July letter to Berthier, Du Casse, *Jérome*, vol. IV, p. 272).

112: There were also about twenty gendarmes and thirty-five French soldiers in the town. One gate (facing north toward Braunschweig) was left unguarded for unknown reasons.

113: Braunschweig casualties numbered perhaps 150-200 dead and wounded. Those counted as wounded on both sides are only the more heavily wounded who ended up in the field hospitals; the number of light injuries is impossible to determine. This account is drawn from Kortzfleisch's two detailed histories and one of Lieutenant Wolf's letters (he was a participant in the battle) in Kaisenberg (pp. 130-3).

114: None of the Westphalian officers defected.

115: Gratien reached Halberstadt on the morning of 1 August. In addition to the Dutch, elements of General Ewald's Danish Division had crossed over the Elbe north of Hamburg and the 4th Polish Chasseurs departed Magdeburg on 2 August en route for Braunschweig (arrived 13 August). The Poles were from the Oder fortress garrisons and were in at least squadron, if not regiment strength; their lonely ride across Westphalia irritated Napoleon who felt they would be 'exposed to accidents' (*Correspondence* 15645, 11 August). The French 22nd Ligne (which Napoleon apparently held in high regard) was also ordered to unite at Magdeburg.

116: This account of the Battle of Oelper relies on Borcke, Kortzfleisch, Lünsmann, Müller and Schneidawind.

Reubell's motivation for (1) retreating and (2) chosing a route that opened the way for Braunschweig and his men has never been satisfactorily explained. One German historian, however, makes the persuasive argument that the Westphalian general was afflicted by numerous doubts: gross overestimation of Braunschweig's strength, rumours that Hessians and perhaps even Austrians had joined the Duke, the suspect loyalty of his own troops and fear of sharing the fate of the 5th Infantry. He thus believed his only safety lay in combining with Gratien. See Willi Müller, 'Das Gefecht bei Oelper am 1. August 1809', *Niedersächsisches Jahrbuch*, Band 1, 1924. Müller effectively destroys the fatuous notion that Reubell intentionally allowed Braunschweig to escape.

117: Some of Friedrich Wilhelm's men elected to abandon the cause on 2 August at Braunschweig. This small band made its way across Westphalia, escaping across the Elbe into Prussia before 200 men sent by Michaud from the Magdeburg garrison could intercept them.

118: The Dutch Division was recalled to Holland from Nienburg on 5 August.

119: The Braunschweig detachment consisted of about 60 hussars and 60 infantrymen (although figures vary somewhat) with two cannon.

120: Although the Black Corps embarked on the 7th, bad weather forced them to stop at the mouth of the Weser and they did not make the open sea until the 8th. This delay gave Ewald's Danes an opportunity to play a final part in the campaign: moving to the eastern bank of the narrow channel where the Weser lets out to the sea, the Danish artillery engaged the ships carrying the Black Corps; their efforts were unsuccessful, however, and they had to content themselves with a meagre number of hapless prisoners.

121: Decrees forming several new Westphalian units were issued in late July 1809: 7th and 8th Infantry (distinctive colour: black), 2nd Cuirassiers, 2nd Light Battalion. None of these organizations achieved any level of readiness during the actual campaign, however, and most would not be established until 1810 or even 1811. Likewise, the formation of a second chevauxlegers regiment was directed in December 1809 but delayed until the autumn of 1812.

122: Jerome himself denigrated the 6th Infantry and II/1st Infantry in a letter to Napoleon, saying that they had been 'intimidated by the enemy's fire' (Du Casse, *Jérome*, vol. IV, p. 198).

123: It is interesting to note that at least one historian (Schneidawind, p. 87) claims the Westphalians displayed fine discipline while under Thielmann.

124: As a small example of staff inefficiency, Meibom complained during the campaign that higher headquarters had twice failed to notify his company (on outpost duty) that the corps was moving out. See also Wolf's ascerbic comments in Kaisenberg (pp. 121-2).

CHAPTER 10:

The Peripheral Princess

While military operations inside Germany were conducted principally by soldiers of Bavaria, Württemberg, Westphalia and Saxony, several smaller states also contributed forces to combat insurgency, repress internal rebellion and repel Austrian incursions.

THE GRAND DUCHY OF BERG

Like Westphalia, the Grand Duchy of Berg was an artificial state, created by Napoleon from bits of territory ceded by Bavaria, Nassau and Prussia. Established in 1806, it was in many ways a precursor to Jerome's realm, a small monarchy heavily influenced by France and designed to shield its northern borders.[1] Also like Westphalia, Berg was to serve as an example of the benefits of French culture and administration, a showpiece country characterized by representative government (at least the beginnings of one), a modern bureaucracy, a unified financial structure, religious tolerance, abolition of feudal privileges and an enlightened civil code. Not all of these broad reforms fully met the inclinations of the first Grand Duke, Napoleon's vain brother-in-law Joachim Murat, but by the summer of 1808, the showy Marshal was headed for Naples to assume a royal throne and the ruling of Berg reverted to Napoleon himself. The situation changed in form if not in fact on 3 March 1809 when one of the Emperor's favourite nephews, Napoleon-Louis, Prince Royal of Holland, was declared the new Grand Duke of Berg. Napoleon-Louis, however, was only five years old and the Emperor continued to control the affairs of Berg through an able and industrious civilian commissioner named Jean-Claude Beugnot.[2]

Under the treaty establishing the Confederation of the Rhine, Berg was obligated to supply a contingent of 5,000 men in case of war. The 1st Infantry Regiment was formed in time to participate in several sieges during the 1807 campaign and, by 1809, Napoleon had increased the size of the army to around 7,000 men in three regiments of foot soldiers, a light cavalry regiment, a small artillery battalion and two companies of veterans.[3] There was also a small force of gendarmerie assumed from the old Duchy of Berg and a newly-organized militia (Bürgermiliz).[4] The infantry, uniformed in white with light-blue distinctions, was organized after the French pattern with two field battalions per regiment, each divided into six companies of about 140 men (one each of grenadiers and voltigeurs, four of fusiliers).[5] The first two regiments were combined into a brigade and sent to Spain in December 1808 where they soon acquired a curious reputation for courage, endurance and execrable discipline. Formation of the 3rd Infantry Regiment had begun in October of that year, but being only partially organized and trained, it remained behind in the Grand Duchy when its comrades departed for the Spanish war. It would soon find employment, however, in Saxony and Westphalia.

Berg's regiment of light horse, titled the *Chasseurs à Cheval de Grande Duché de Berg*, numbered slightly over 1,000 men in four squadrons, each squadron consisting of two companies. Part of the regiment had accompanied Murat to Madrid in 1808, but when the war with Austria opened, its squadrons had returned from the Iberian Peninsula and were split between Versailles (1st and 2nd) and Berg (3rd and 4th). The men were tastefully clad in the traditional dark-green of the light cavalry with rose-coloured trim and shako.[6] They too would soon be called to Germany to oppose the Austrian invaders.

The Berg artillery battalion numbered about 400 men in one foot company, one horse company, a train company and a combined company of sappers, miners and pontooneers. The foot company and part of the train, organized into a battery of six guns, had marched to Spain with the infantry brigade, leaving only the horse battery (six 4-pounders) in Berg by early 1809. The gunners wore standard artillery garb: dark-blue coat and breeches with red trim, the horse artillerists being distinguished from their foot comrades by their hussar-style breeches and boots. Uniforms of the train were similar but of light-grey with light-blue distinctions.[7] Being a modern army, artillery, infantry and train soldiers alike were issued with a black shako, grenadiers being the only exception; to denote their special status, these men received an imposing bearskin cap like their French counterparts.

The modernity of the Berg Army derived from its newness and its close adherence to French organizational and tactical precepts. When the Grand Duchy was established, the only trained soldiery available consisted of elements of the Bavarian *Kinkel* Infantry Regiment and a battalion of Nassauers. These were duly turned over to the Berg government (they went with the territory) and formed the basis of the 1st Berg Infantry Regiment.[8] The rest of the army had to be built from scratch and rapidly. This was primarily accomplished through the introduction of conscription, a new phenomenon for most of Berg. Conscription was broadly hated in the Grand Duchy as elsewhere, inspiring 'invincible repugnance' and widespread evasion. It proved particularly difficult to administer in the former Prussian districts where such practices had been previously unknown. Moreover, the soldiers produced by this process were not always reliable and desertion almost instantly developed into a major problem, leading to strict regulations, tight curfews and increasingly harsh punishments. These nostrums failed to curb the disease, however, and, by 1809 the apprehension of deserters and draft evaders had become the primary function of the gendarmerie. Beugnot and his administration seem to have been acutely aware of the problem and the commissioner repeatedly advised Napoleon not to employ the Berg troops in Germany against rebellious populations as the men would thus be exposed to all manner of dangerous temptations.[9]

The lack of a national military base and the rapidity with which the army was organized also effected the nature of Berg's officer corps. Forced to expand from almost nothing to a force of 7,000 in the space of two years, the army had to accept officer material from a variety of sources, sometimes less than desirable. The lack of junior officers was a particularly grave shortcoming which could only be addressed by the hasty promotion of newly recruited sergeants, lieutenants and captains. As a result, a major in a Berg battalion might be a man with no formal military schooling and little experience, perhaps only as much as six months as a captain. Frenchmen who spoke German (Alsatians, etc.) provided a significant part of the army's leadership, constituting about one-fifth of the infantry and one-third of the cavalry officers, but these men were often practically insubordinate toward their German superiors and did not necessarily contribute to unit cohesion. In any case, Napoleon preferred to equip his Berg formations with propertied native officers, but these were in short supply and many of those who came forward were little better than unscrupulous mercenary adventurers. Beugnot had very harsh words for the German officers, especially those of Prussian origin: 'The German officer, a species of decorated vagabond, has neither sovereign nor fatherland; he attaches himself to the prince who hires him and passes indifferently from one camp to another for a few coins more or less...he is a composition of presumption and ignorance, boasting and baseness, licentiousness and cupidity.'

The 'ignorance and indiscipline' of the officer corps determined the comportment of the men and Berg units quickly became infamous for their poor behaviour. The officers plundered freely and seemingly did little to curb the excesses committed by their troops. Allies and enemies alike were subjected to the same maltreatment, the soldiers of the Grand Duchy leaving tales of drunkenness, debauchery, pillage and abuse in their wake. In combat, however, the story was different. Despite the apparent lack of order within the Berg formations, they fought well, repeatedly winning generous praise from the French generals in Spain for their valour, determination and stoic stamina.[10]

While part of the army suffered the privations of Iberia, war with Austria loomed nearer and Beugnot was apprised of the Emperor's intention to employ the remaining Berg units in Germany. The formation of the 3rd Infantry was therefore hastened and by 15 April, the regiment was in a reasonable state of organization. Its training was still far from complete, however, and the conscripts in its ranks came predominantly from former Prussian lands, causing Beugnot to have serious misgivings about their loyalty to the Imperial cause. These concerns notwithstanding, the regiment, about 1,400 strong, was assigned to Kellermann's Reserve Corps when hostilities opened and consequently headed for Mainz on 17 April, possibly accompanied by the horse artillery battery.[11]

The regiment had only been in Mainz a few days when Dörnberg's abortive rebellion broke out in Westphalia and King Jerome called on Kellermann for assistance. Some French troops, the Berg regiment and six guns (possibly the Berg battery) were duly sent to Kassel, arriving in the Westphalian capital on the 28th. The Berg infantrymen remained here until the middle of June, garrisoning the city and training 'intensively' (according to Jerome). Their presence in Kassel allowed the King to send part of his Guard in pursuit of Schill in May but it also led to a certain amount of friction between Jerome and his Imperial brother. As the Grand Duchy's regent, Napoleon regarded the Berg soldiers as his own (sending instructions to Beugnot through the French Minister of War rather than the Foreign Minister for example) and he repeatedly directed the Westphalian king to return the regiment to the Reserve Corps at Hanau. Jerome consistently demurred, arguing that he needed reliable troops to counter the internal and external threats to his young realm. Supported in his arguments by his distance from the Emperor and the press of events, he sent 800 men of the 3rd Berg to Sondershausen with his Guard on 16 June as he concentrated X Corps for the little campaign in Saxony. The bulk of the regiment thus paraded through Saxony together with the rest of X Corps, participating in none of the sparse fighting but gaining an evil reputation for avid pillage and poor discipline.[12] With the close of active hostilities, it was assigned to Reubell's command and marched with that general through Hannover to Hoya, 40 kilometres south-east of Bremen.

While most of the Berg foot soldiers wandered around in Saxony, a significant part of the regiment remained behind to garrison key cities in Westphalia. A Berg company was thus on hand to quell an ill-timed and ill-conceived uprising in Marburg in late June. This pathetic episode, the vague scheme of a seventy-five-year-old retired Hessian colonel named Emmerich, was more quixotic than truly threatening: the ancient colonel, nursing a virulent hatred of the French, led some forty or fifty peasants into Marburg on the night of 23/24 June and succeeded in disarming a few members of the local veteran company. The population did not respond to his call to arms, however, and the Berg company in concert with Westphalian departmental troops evicted Emmerich and his little band the next morning after a brief scuffle. The incident cost the Berg troops one man dead and brought their commander the honour of a slight wound.[13]

Late July brought renewed instructions to send the 3rd Berg to the Reserve Corps (now under GD Junot), but the bulk of the regiment was still with Reubell when the Duke of Braunschweig began his perilous march to the sea. The Berg soldiers earned Jerome's respect for stabilizing the right of Reubell's line at Oelper (1 August) after the rout of the 6th Westphalian Infantry, but they apparently engaged in no serious fighting and took few casualties. Oelper was the regiment's first and last combat action in 1809.[14] In late September, it finally left Westphalia, marching to Dresden to enter Carra Saint-Cyr's Division of the new VIII Corps and heading to France to assume coastal protection duties when the final peace treaty was signed in October.

In Dresden, the 3rd Infantry was reunited with the Berg horse artillery battery. The battery had apparently remained in Westphalia for some time after April, but by July, it was back with the bulk of the Reserve Corps at Hanau, whence it departed to join VIII Corps as summer drew to a close.[15]

The third element of the Berg Army, the Chasseurs-à-Cheval, was also attached to Junot's Corps by late July. Split between Versailles and Berg when hostilities began in April and shuttled from command to command throughout the campaign, the regiment's peregrinations took it all over southern Germany but never brought it against the enemy. When Austria invaded Bavaria, the 1st and 2nd Squadrons of the Berg Chasseurs were ordered from Versailles to Strasbourg where they arrived on 7 May. Destined for Kellermann's Corps, however, they departed on the 8th for Frankfurt, reaching that city ten days later to unite with the 3rd and 4th Squadrons from Berg. The latter two squadrons were not yet fully trained ('sans instruction' said Kellermann) but the regiment headed south on the 19th, more than 1,000 troopers in all, evidently instructed to join the main army around Vienna.[16] Under the command of Oberst Graf von Goltstein, the chasseurs marched via Augsburg to arrive in Braunau on 24 June where new orders attached them to the French commandant in Passau, GD Bourcier. They remained with Bourcier for a few weeks before receiving yet another set of instructions, this time directing them north to join Junot.[17] Arriving in the Nuremberg area on the last day of July, the weary light cavalry-men were quartered on the population for several months, finally riding west for Paris and a new assignment as part of Napoleon's Imperial Guard on 16 September. Reorganized as a lancer regiment in November, they would later win great renown on battlefields from Spain to Russia.

FRANKFURT: THE STATE OF THE PRINCE PRIMATE

At the confluence of the Rhine and Main, several dozen kilometres south of Berg, lay the lands of Carl Theodor von Dalberg, the Prince Primate ('Fürstprimas') of the Rheinbund. Dalberg occupies a peculiar position in the history of the Confederation. Scion of an ancient knightly family and former Prince-Bishop of Mainz, he was the Archchancellor of the Holy Roman Empire when that institution was overthrown by Napoleon in 1806. He nevertheless became an enthusiastic supporter of the French Emperor and was chosen to pre-side over the councils of the Confederation as Prince Primate. In practice, the numerous kings and grand dukes of the Rheinbund proved too independent for Dalberg to control, but he retained his solemn position and lofty ideals to the end of the Napoleonic era in Germany. His lands in 1809 were centred around the defunct empire's traditional seats of power: Regensburg, home of the old Imperial Diet, and Frankfurt, commercial capital of southern Germany and site of the opulent imperial coronation ceremonies.

Dalberg's exalted rank did not exempt his state from military obligations to Napoleon. As a member of the Rheinbund, Frankfurt was expected to supply a regiment of 1,500 men and the Emperor had indeed ordered the contingent to Spain in 1808.[18] Fortunately, as Dalberg's military advisers struggled to comply with the Imperial demand, Napoleon changed his mind and reduced the require-ment to a single battalion. Much relieved, the Frankfurters dispatched a six-company battalion (853 men) to the Iberian Peninsula in August. In 1809, how-ever, the impending war with Austria brought more Imperial messengers and Frankfurt was notified in early April that a second battalion would be required, this one to reinforce the Armée d'Allemagne. A battalion of four companies was quickly raised under Major von Horadam and sent to garrison the fortress of Erfurt in May, its 600 men dressed in a simple uniform of white cloth with red distinctions, black shako and French badges of rank. Nominally under first Jerome's and later Junot's orders, the battalion remained in the fortress for the duration of the war, taking no part in the fitful campaign in Saxony and return-ing to Frankfurt at the end of the year.[19]

The Mecklenburg Duchies

Wedged between the Confederation of the Rhine, Prussia and the Baltic Sea on the sandy expanses of the North German Plain were two of Napoleon's most recent and reluctant German allies, the twin duchies of Mecklenburg-Schwerin and Mecklenburg-Strelitz. With close political ties to the Tsar and a strong cultural affinity to Prussia, these penurious realms were conservative and traditional, relics of a bygone age, antithetical toward revolutionary and Imperial France.[20] None the less, the two Dukes, Friedrich Franz I of Schwerin and Carl II of Strelitz, were also proud and staunchly independent, using their ties to St. Petersburg to resist domination by Berlin. When war clouds gathered in 1806, both tried to steer neutral courses, negotiating with Prussia but making no commitments. In the brilliant days of pursuit after the utter collapse of the creaky Prussian military machine at Jena-Auerstädt, however, Napoleon remembered their inclinations and ordered the occupation of both little monarchies. The stunned dukes were deposed, their armies disbanded and the two Mecklenburgs temporarily enjoyed the pleasures of French military government. The wishes of the Tsar returned both sovereigns to their thrones after the Peace of Tilsit in 1807, but they now came under heavy pressure from Paris and both felt compelled to join the Rheinbund in early 1808.

Membership in the Confederation obligated the larger of the duchies, Mecklenburg-Schwerin, to supply a contingent of 1,900 men for the common defence. Former soldiers were thus recalled to duty and new ones recruited to form a 'brigade' composed of four separate infantry battalions (each with its own distinctive colour) and a small artillery company. French organizational and tactical practices were introduced as Schwerin's Army was resurrected and each battalion was supposed to contain six companies of 98 men (one grenadier, one voltigeur and four musketeer companies), but manpower was inadequate for these sudden demands and the 'brigade' never reached full strength. Indeed, in the 4th Battalion, only the grenadier company was formed and it numbered a mere 80 men. The artillery company of 53 men was in equally wretched condition, lacking horses, vehicles and, above all, cannon. The infantrymen of Schwerin, reflecting their army's previous orientation, wore a Prussian-style uniform with dark-blue coat, grey breeches and black shako, the coat trimmed in yellow, white, red, and peach blossom for the 1st to 4th Battalions respectively. Except for their distinctive colour (black), the artillerists were similarly clad. French influence, however, was evident in badges of rank, sapper's distinctions and other small uniform details.[21]

In addition to his 'brigade,' Duke Friedrich Franz I disposed of some hussars for internal police duties, a company of personal guards (Leibgarde) and a small garrison company (65 men) whose mission it was to occupy the tiny fortress of Dömitz and guard the prisoners incarcerated there.[22]

As war with Austria approached in early 1809, a curious set of circumstances set the Mecklenburg troops on the road to an area of the Baltic coast called Swedish Pomerania, far from the dramatic struggles in the Danube valley. The only Swedish enclave on the south shores of the Baltic, Swedish Pomerania and its chief city, Stralsund, had been occupied by French and Rheinbund troops in 1807 after a series of skirmishes and sieges. The history actually goes back to 1805, when Sweden's unstable King Gustav entered the coalition against France. Despite the stunning French triumphs at Austerlitz, Jena-Auerstädt and Friedland, Gustav remained a belligerent and in the summer of 1807 the French were obliged to attack the only available Swedish forces, those in Stralsund and Pomerania. The city and province were eventually evacuated by the Swedes, but Gustav was not a party to the Peace of Tilsit and officially remained at war with Napoleon in 1809. The French Emperor, though he needed every possible bayonet along the banks of the Danube, was therefore required to maintain a garrison in the occupied Swedish territory and orders were sent directing the Mecklenburg contingents to 'march immediately to occupy without delay the city of Stralsund and Swedish Pomerania'.[23]

Mecklenburg-Schwerin's Army received its orders in early March and hastily underwent a major reorganization before departing its homeland. The old four-battalion 'brigade' was dissolved and its men consolidated into a regiment of two battalions very much along French lines. Designated the 7th Regiment of the Confederation of the Rhine, each of its battalions still contained six companies (two elite and four musketeer), but the authorized strength per company was increased to 147 men. In theory, this organization would have put some 1,800 infantrymen at Napoleon's disposal, which, when added to the artillery company (now equipped with six 6-pounders but still part of the regiment), would neatly fulfill the Duchy's military obligation to its 'Protector'. In reality, however, the companies rarely counted more than 100 men in their ranks and the 7th Rheinbund was seriously understrength when it headed for Swedish Pomerania. Moreover, it had little ammunition, its clothing and equipment, particularly its muskets, were in poor condition and the artillery had had no time to train the miserable animals it had procured from the local peasantry. None the less, the regimental commander, Major von Moltke, an uncle of Prussia's future Field Marshal, led the 2nd Battalion off to Stralsund on the 16th of March, the 1st Battalion following the next day. Although Stralsund would thus become the regiment's home for the next several months, three companies were detached to outlying positions, one to the town of Barth and two to Rügen Island.[24]

Left behind in Mecklenburg-Schwerin were the hussars, the garrison company (in Dömitz) and the 3rd Battalion of the regiment. This, however, was a battalion in name only. Formed to accept all those unfit to march with the mobile troops, the 3rd Battalion consisted of two weak companies with élite names— grenadier and voltigeur—but no élite troops. The 60-odd soldiers in each of these companies were the old and infirm, invalid troops with an average age of 53 for sergeants and 51 for common privates, the oldest NCO being 72, the oldest private 78! Nor was a single soldier truly fit, the long list of major and minor ailments including such debilities as gout, hernia, deafness, epilepsy and imbecility. Little wonder they remained as garrison in Rostock when their younger and healthier compatriots marched to war.[25]

The Strelitz contingent also moved to Swedish Pomerania in March. Required to provide 400 men for the Rheinbund, Carl II had his contingent organized into a small battalion of four companies, but suffered the same problems with recruitment as his larger neighbour. The men of Strelitz wore a uniform almost identical with that of their comrades in Schwerin: dark-blue Prussian coat with red distinctions, grey breeches and black shako. Although grossly under-strength (only about 200 officers and men), the battalion departed Strelitz on 10 March and reached its appointed station at Greifswald four days later. Only scant forces stayed behind in the Duchy: a depot detachment for the battalion (32 men), the Duke's personal guard (a grenadier company of 100), a company of veterans and 26 *Distrikthusaren* to perform police duties within the monarchy.[26]

Quartered on the population, the Mecklenburg troops now settled into the routine of garrison life: training, guard duty and more training. Integrated into the complex defence structure intended to shield northern Germany, they came under the immediate orders of GB Jacques-Lazare de Savettier de Candras, Baron de La Tour du Pré. Candras, who had formerly headed one of the brigades of GD St. Hilaire's Division, had been left behind to assume command in Swedish Pomerania when the division marched to the Danube. His superior was GB Jean-Jacques Liébert in Stettin, and Liébert was placed, at least nominally, under the command umbrella of King Jerome's X Corps. In addition to the Mecklenburg contingents, the forces available to Candras in Swedish Pomerania were meagre: a French artillery company and about 100 troopers of the Polish 4th Chasseurs-à-Cheval; the nearest French infantry was III/22nd Ligne in Stettin, more than 180 kilometres to the east.[27]

The Mecklenburgers evinced little love for their French commanders or Napoleon's cause. Indeed, their attitude was often closer to open hostility and Major von Moltke had to issue strict injunctions in an effort to maintain order and professionalism in the ranks. A frank and revealing order of 11 April demonstrates the seriousness of the situation as well as Moltke's perspicacity:

> Hauptmann von Schade will assemble the officers of the 1st Battalion and explain to them that complaints about the inappropriate behaviour of the common soldiers of our regiment toward the French officers are arriving daily. Specifically, numerous men of the 1st Battalion's Voltigeur Company yesterday allowed themselves to spit behind a French officer who was headed for the intendant's office and to repeat this upon his return. Such behaviour shows great animosity and leads unavoidably to ruin. Every proper and intelligent officer will comprehend that it is in our interest to generate a different spirit in our troops. I therefore challenge you to do everything possible toward this purpose. I demand that the soldiers be frequently instructed on this point especially, as well as regards morality, order and discipline.

> I assume it to be impossible that an officer would so forget himself as to make remarks against the French administration and army in the presence of his subordinates. Should this occur, however, I will have the officer immediately arrested and reported to the Duke. In this, I am responsible not only for the honour and safety of the regiment but also for the interests

of our gracious sovereign. A single unfavourable report to the Emperor could have disadvantageous results for our beloved Duke, which all of us, out of honest love and loyalty, certainly wish to avoid.[28]

Despite Moltke's orders, the true sentiments of the common soldiers and junior officers, many of whom had formerly served under Prussian standards, could not be fully disguised and the French were well aware of the enmity smouldering in the ranks of the Mecklenburg contingents. These were the troops who would now be called upon to defend France's interests against the depredations of the German national hero, Major von Schill.

When Schill found the fortress of Magdeburg too tough for his little band (despite his success at Dodendorf on 5 May), he decided to ride north, apparently with the intention of establishing a fortified base from which he could conduct raids as he had done in 1807. Such a move would also facilitate contact with the Royal Navy and possibly give him more time to rouse German popular will against the French. He thus headed for Mecklenburg-Schwerin and the fortress of Dömitz.

The Mecklenburg-Schwerin commandant of Dömitz, a Major von Röder, had only the tiny Garrison Company with which to hold the dilapidated fortifications, but he knew of Schill's approach and hurriedly attempted to put the miniature fortress in a proper state of defence. On 15 May, however, Schill's men surprised the garrison and captured von Röder before he had completed his preparations. With the gates of the fortress open and a pistol to his head, the major ordered his men to surrender. Thus fell Dömitz.

Schill now left a small garrison at Dömitz and continued north toward Stralsund, romantically determined to turn that city into 'a second Saragossa' if the French attacked. He arrived in Wismar on the 20th, and the next day sent a small force, commanded, ironically enough, by a Leutnant von Moltke, to scout the old fortress of Rostock. Appearing before the walls of the city, von Moltke demanded entrance, declaring that Schill's main body was close at hand and doubtless promising dire consequences should the defenders fail to yield. The Mecklenburg-Schwerin troops in Rostock consisted of the two invalid companies of the 3rd Battalion (about 120 men) and some constabulary hussars under the senior Schwerin officer, GL Otto von Pressentin. At Friedrich Franz's order, this little force had actually evacuated the city and retired to Ribnitz on 19 May, but, concerned about the possible French reaction, he had sent the men back the very next day to at least give the appearance of resistance. Incapable of actually defending Rostock, however, the aged GL von Pressentin opened its gates to Schill's advance guard on the 22nd and again retreated to Ribnitz, withdrawing the following morning across the Recknitz to join the 2nd Battalion at Damgarten.

The 2nd Battalion had been drilling outside Stralsund on the morning of the 20th when its commander, Major Georg von Pressentin (the general's son), received orders from GB Candras to send a company to Damgarten immediately and follow with the rest of the battalion as soon as possible. A company dutifully marched west under the noon heat and reached the little town in the pre-dawn

hours of the 21st. Major von Pressentin joined his advance force on the afternoon of 23 May with the remaining four companies of the battalion (the
voltigeur company remained on Rügen) and, reinforced by the Mecklenburg battery, began to organize his defence. Although Pressentin enjoyed the advantages of a fine defensive position, his plans were undermined from the start by
several crucial factors. First, his men were critically short of ammunition, both
infantry and artillery. The men of II/7, for example, had only about nine cartridges apiece and the invalids in the 3rd Battalion averaged a mere two!
Moreover, there were only horses and harness enough to make two of the little
battery's guns mobile. Second, Pressentin had no effective cavalry to provide
flank security or early warning, he would thus find himself reacting to Schill's
moves, unable to counter the bold Prussian horsemen.[29] Third and most important, however, was the poor morale of the Mecklenburg-Schwerin soldiers.
Sympathetic toward Schill's enterprise and hating the French, they had no
enthusiasm for the coming fight, many openly expressing their desire to join the
raiders in what they saw as the struggle for German freedom.

Candras made a brief appearance in Damgarten at about 6 a.m. on the 24th,
inspecting the position, issuing new orders and sending the four immobile
Mecklenburg guns back to Stralsund before riding off to join the 1st Battalion.
The commanding general was thus absent when Schill's skirmishers began to
edge toward the river around noon. The attack on the Mecklenburg position did
not really open until almost 5 p.m., however, when Schill's two cannon began to
fire and Prussian outflanking columns slowly made their way across the
Recknitz north and south of Damgarten. His ammunition almost exhausted and
his line of retreat endangered, Pressentin ordered his companies to withdraw at
about 7 p.m., but the retreat soon fell apart, men began to surrender and desert in
scores and all order was lost. Schill's happy raiders appeared to be everywhere
as Pressentin's battalion disintegrated, capturing the two guns, chasing fugitives
and rounding up the more or less willing Mecklenburg infantrymen. Losses in
the fight are difficult to determine, but of the 700—800 Mecklenburgers at
Damgarten, it is probable that about 50 fell killed or wounded and something
over 200 were captured, at least 80 of the latter choosing to join Schill's band.
Furthermore, over the next several days, as Schill made his way to Stralsund,
many more of the Mecklenburgers were seized or simply took the opportunity to
disappear. Schill's own losses are estimated at about 60 killed and wounded.
One bright spot for the Schwerin battalion was the courage of a young lieutenant
who saved the unit's standard by wrapping it about his body and fleeing north in
the wild confusion of the rout.

When he ordered the 2nd Battalion to Damgarten to cover the western
approaches to Stralsund, Candras had also taken measures to shield the city
against attack from the south-west. The 1st Schwerin Battalion under Major
Moltke was thus sent to Richtenberg on 23 May and pushed on toward Tribsees
late on the night of the 24th. Learning of the 2nd Battalion's disaster, however,
the French general recalled Moltke to Richtenberg and, as the extent of the
defeat became clear, continued his retreat to Anklam, picking up the Strelitz
Battalion en route.[30] Candras' little command (the two Mecklenburg battalions,

about forty-five Polish chasseurs and two French guns) finally reached the town at about 1 a.m. on the 27th, exhausted, demoralized and much reduced by desertion and straggling.[31]   Although Anklam lay within the borders of the Prussian Kingdom, Candras rested in the town for several days, finally returning north on the 31st when news of Gratien's successful assault on Stralsund reached him.[32]

All three Mecklenburg battalions spent most of June in Greifswald, recuperating from their trauma. Losses had been dreadful, GD Liébert reporting to Berthier on 30 May that the 2nd Battalion 'was nearly destroyed at Damgarten and, since that time, more than 500 men have deserted with arms and baggage'.[33] The high rate of desertion in Moltke's unit and the Strelitz Battalion had been particularly appalling to the French. Major von Pressentin and the captives of the 2nd Battalion arrived in Greifswald from Stralsund on 3 June and some stragglers were returned to the ranks, but the two Schwerin battalions only numbered 513 and 272 men respectively when they were mustered on the 9th.[32] The Mecklenburgers re-entered Stralsund on 26 June and remained in garrison there until the signing of a final peace treaty between France and Sweden in March 1810.

In the aftermath of the Damgarten débâcle, GD Liébert corresponded with both Mecklenburg dukes, praising their officers but complaining bitterly about the poorly trained sergeants and soldiers: 'mostly Prussian deserters who had already fought against France'. Citing 'the desertion of more than 600 men in two days, partly from the battalions that had not even been attacked', the French general brazenly recommended to Friedrich Franz of Schwerin that he compose his troops of loyal citizens 'who recognize their sovereign and who have a fatherland that holds their affections and their interests', further suggesting that 'it would be perhaps convenient to differentiate their uniforms from those of the Prussian troops'.[34] The haughty German duke evidently defended his men, but their performance in 1809 can perhaps be considered a prelude to 1813, when Mecklenburg-Schwerin would become the first country to desert the Confederation of the Rhine.

THE DUCHY OF OLDENBURG

The last and most unwilling German prince to join the Rheinbund was Duke Peter Friedrich Ludwig of Oldenburg. An uncle of the Tsar and no friend of France, Peter had no desire to join Napoleon's alliance, but Mecklenburg-Schwerin's adherence to the Rheinbund in March 1808 left him as the only non-aligned German monarch between Berlin and Paris. This precarious situation could not last. To protect his little realm from incessant Dutch encroachment and to retain at least a modicum of independence, Peter signed an agreement to enter the Confederation as its thirty-sixth member at the Erfurt Congress of Princes in October 1808.

Neither Duke Peter nor his subjects evinced much interest in military affairs and the little Duchy had chosen to expend money rather than blood as a member of the Holy Roman Empire during the Wars of the French Revolution. As a result, the only 'army' in Oldenburg in 1808 was a company of 100 infantrymen, predominantly foreigners, accustomed to garrison, guard and ceremonial duties. The demands of the Confederation of the Rhine were considerably more stringent. Required to supply a battalion of 800 men who might actually have to function as combat soldiers, Oldenburg initially tried to rely on volunteers, but the results were disappointing and more than half of the men had to be conscripted under a set of hastily composed and loosely administered regulations. The nature of the citizenry and the recruiting/conscription system meant that most of Oldenburg's soldiers continued to come from other lands and from the least desirable elements of the population. The result was a battalion with high desertion rates, low reliability and no discernible feeling of national loyalty. The lack of officers was particularly acute: there had been only three in the old company and the new spaces had to be filled with men who had previously served under Prussian, Hannoverian or other flags.

None the less, by 1809, Oldenburg had formed a battalion of 800 men under Oberstlieutenant von Arentschildt. Of its six companies, the 1st was the Grenadier Company, its men dressed in a dark-blue Prussian coat with red collar and cuffs, white breeches (grey in winter) and a tall bearskin grenadier cap; as an especially exotic touch, a black (a 'Moor' in 19th-century parlance) was recruited to be one of the company's drummers.[36] The rest of the battalion wore basically the same uniform as the grenadiers with the exception of the headgear: the 6th Company (Schützen) and the 2nd to 5th Companies (fusiliers) all wore a black Corsican hat with the left brimmed turned rakishly up.

The war of 1809 found two companies in the capital city and the remaining four scattered about the Duchy to enforce the strictures of Napoleon's Continental System of economic warfare against Great Britain. It was the Emperor's intention that the Oldenburgers join the Mecklenburg contingents under GB Candras in Swedish Pomerania, but in fact the battalion never stirred from Duke Peter's lands, perhaps due to a combination of incomplete organization, inadequate training and duchal recalcitrance.[37] Its single opportunity for martial glory as a French ally thus only came in early August when the Duke of Braunschweig's free corps approached Oldenburg's borders on its march to the coast. Indeed, Arentschildt's men were marching on Elsfleth on the 5th when Duke Peter, determined to avoid any contact with the Braunschweigers, ordered his companies to halt and withdraw to the west.[38] Patrols from the Black Corps encountered Oldenburg detachments over the next few days as the Braunschweigers made good their escape, but the Oldenburgers always retired obligingly and no attempt was made to interfere with the rebel duke's plans. Duke Peter even went so far as to extend a friendly welcome to a patrol of Braunschweig hussars who unexpectedly stormed into his residence. Only one Oldenburger seems to have attempted to fulfill the spirit of the alliance with Napoleon. This worthy, an Oldenburg *Landdragoner* (constabulary dragoon), rode up to the Black Corps detachment engaged in the skirmish near Delmenhorst on 5 August and indignantly demanded that the Braunschweigers cease firing. Friedrich Wilhelm's men were initially astonished but quickly recovered, plucked the white feather from the poor fellow's tricorne hat and sent him on his way escorted by peals of amazed laughter.[39] With the level of allied co-operation demonstrated by the Duchy of Oldenburg in 1809, it is hardly sur-

prising that Napoleon occupied the land and deposed the Duke in 1810 to seal
the North Sea coast against the English.[40]

THE HANSEATIC CITIES

In addition to the members of the Rheinbund, Napoleon's dominion in Germany
encompassed the semi-independent city states of the old Hanseatic League:
Hamburg, Bremen and Lübeck. Although not bound by the requirements of the
Confederation Treaty, these tiny entities had long retained military establishments for external defence and the maintenance of internal order.

Hamburg supported a small regular force of all arms numbering about 2,000
men. The largest component was a ten-company infantry regiment of some
1,800 soldiers clad in old-style red uniforms with light-blue distinctions, but the
city also boasted a dragoon company of 65 troopers and a small artillery company (about 100 gunners) to man fortress artillery and four field guns.[41] Beyond
these regular troops, Hamburg possessed a 'night watch' (*Nachtwache*) of
approximately 340 men to monitor the city's gates and maintain order within its
walls.

Bremen also had a force of municipal guards (Bürgerwehr or Bügermiliz) to
perform local police functions. Probably numbering some 30-50 men, the
Bremen Bürgerwehr was uniformed in dark-grey coat and breeches with red
trim. The city's regular military, under the command of Oberstlieutenant
Christian von Berchem, was limited to a small infantry battalion (one company
of grenadiers and two of musketeers) of about 550 men in red coats with white
distinctions.

Despite their rather long histories, none of these organizations could be considered truly combat-ready (the Bremen battalion drilled no more than once a
year and the city fathers wondered if that arduous schedule were not perhaps
excessive!) and none engaged in active fighting during the campaign. Some of
Bremen's troops did observe the entry of a small Braunschweig detachment into
their city on 6 August, but they offered only token resistance and Duke Friedrich
Wilhelm's men marched through the city gates to the cheers of the populace.[42]
Although they escaped the perils of war in 1809, the future held a far more terrifying prospect for the men of the Hanseatic cities: their municipalities incorporated into metropolitan France in 1811, they soon found themselves in French
uniforms en route to the horrors of the Russian campaign.

NOTES

1: The instrument actually establishing the Grand Duchy was signed in Schönbrunn Palace outside Vienna in
December 1805 after Napoleon's triumph at Austerlitz. This document provided for, among other things, a
complex exchange of lands among three nations: Prussia (for staying out of the war) was granted Hannover
by Napoleon and gave up some lands in southern Germany (such as Ansbach); these former Prussian properties were ceded to Bavaria (for siding with France) but that kingdom had to divest itself of its territories in
the north (the Duchy of Berg) and turn them over to France; Napoleon combined these Bavarian lands with
pieces from Prussia, Nassau and other monarchies to form the new Grand Duchy. The exchange was completed in early 1806. All in a day's work for a 19th-century diplomat!

2: Bonaparte family matters are convoluted in the extreme and the disentangling of them is complicated by the
frequency of names such as Napoleon, Louis and Jerome. Napoleon-Louis was the second son of the
Emperor's brother, Louis, whom Napoleon had placed on the throne of Holland. Louis (the father) was married to Hortense de Beauharnais, daughter of the Empress Josephine by a previous marriage. The eldest son
of the Dutch royal pair, Napoleon-Charles, had died in 1807. Their third son, Louis-Napoleon, would even-

tually become Napoleon III, Emperor of France. Murat was married to Napoleon's scheming and ambitious sister Caroline.

3: The decree expanding the size of the army was issued in August 1808 while Napoleon was formally the Grand Duke. Sources vary as to the actual strength of the army at this point: 6,600 according to Charles Schmidt, *Le Grande-Duché de Berg,* Paris: Alcan, 1905 (p. 151), and 7,120 by the reckoning of Karl Schröder, *Zwischen Französischer Revolution und Preussens Gloria,* Eitorf, Heimatsverein, 1989 (p. 175): 5,720 infantry, 1,000 cavalry, 400 in the artillery battalion. The veteran battalion consisted of 193 officers and men in 1809 (George Nafziger, *The Armies of Westphalia and Cleves-Berg 1806-1815,* privately published, 1991, p. 74).

4: The Berg gendarmes numbered about 90 when the Grand Duchy was formed, but grew in size over the ensuing years. Spread throughout the realm, they were organized into four companies of nonuniform size, with two companies forming a 'squadron' (the 1st and 3rd Companies comprised the 1st Squadron while the 2nd and 4th were under the 2nd Squadron). According to one account (Nafziger *Westphalia,* p. 66), the strengths of the companies were: 1st (135), 2nd (110), 3rd (103), 4th (135). Their uniform initially consisted of a dark-green coat with scarlet trim, a black bicorne hat and heavy black boots, but apparently changed to the dark-blue of the French gendarmes in later years (Hans Stahlberg, 'Das Sicherheitskorps im Bergischen Land', *Zeitschrift für Heereskunde,* 1978 and correspondence with Karl Schröder). The Bürgermiliz apparently comprised two infantry regiments, a Jägercorps, a Cavalleriecorps and an artillery company (Rudolf Goecke, *Das Grossherzogthum Berg unter Joachim Murat, Napoleon I. und Louis Napoleon 1806-1813,* Köln: DuMont-Schauberg, 1877, pp. 32-3, 46).

5: The Berg infantry experienced numerous reorganizations and sources consequently vary considerably regarding the number of battalions per regiment. While many want to allot three line battalions to each regiment, the relevant regimental histories and Schröder's detailed research clearly indicate the number was only two in 1809. In addition to Schröder, see W. Neff, *Geschichte des Infanterie-Regiments von Goeben (2. Rheinischen) Nr. 28,* Berlin: Mittler & Sohn, 1890; and Hauptmann Wellmann, *Geschichte des Infanterie-Regiments von Horn (3tes Rheinisches) No. 29,* Trier: Lintz, 1894. The provisions for regimental depots are also unclear. While there were only two regiments, a single depot battalion of four companies served both units, but when the fourth infantry regiment was raised in 1811, each regiment appears to have had its own depot company; interim arrangements (i.e., 1809) are not known.

6: This regiment underwent several changes in title and uniform during its career as a French ally. When first raised in 1807, it was called the *Chevaulégers de Grande Duché de Berg* and wore a rather garish outfit of pale-yellow with rose distinctions in keeping with Murat's sartorial taste. It included a company of Garde du Corps. Four companies (two squadrons) marched to the Spanish border in 1808 with their Grand Duke (only the Garde du Corps was mounted) and two of them accompanied him to Madrid (a second company having been mounted in Bayonne). Many individuals, particularly of the Garde du Corps, rode off to Naples with Murat in the summer of 1808, but the bulk returned to Berg (Münster) where they were united with four new companies and metamorphasized into the green-clad Chasseurs regiment of the 1809 campaign. The 1st Squadron (Elite and 5th Companies) journeyed to Paris in February 1809 followed by the 2nd (2nd and 6th Companies) in March; the 3rd and 4th Squadrons stayed in Berg to complete their training and there we find them when hostilities open in April. Note that the colour of the chasseurs' shako is variously given as black and rose; see Friedrich Herrmann, 'Bergische Reiter', *Zeitschrift für Heereskunde,* Nr. 287 (Jan/Feb 1980).

7: The location of the sappers, miners and pontooneers in 1809 is not certain. It may be assumed that part went to Spain with the brigade and part remained behind in Berg to support the forces at home. Their uniforms resembled those of the foot artillery but with black facings piped red for the engineer troops and blue facings piped red for the pontooneers.

8: An insignificant number of former Nassau hussars was apparently amalgamated into the Berg light cavalry.

9: The underlying causes of draft evasion and desertion were only partly political: many men attempted to avoid service for economic (e.g., some workers previously exempted from duty balked at donning uniforms) and personal reasons (distaste for the strictures of military life and simple homesickness). Self-mutilation, such as the amputation of a finger or two, was one of the most popular methods of escaping military service. See Fisher, pp. 215-16; Schmidt, pp. 156-63; and Schröder, p. 173. The phrase 'invincible repugnance' is quoted by Fisher from an official police report concerning the reactions of the industrial classes in the towns (March 1809).

10: This discussion of the personnel problems within the Berg Army is based primarily on Schmidt, pp. 164-72.

11: An initial plan to make the Berg troops and a Frankfurt battalion the 2nd Brigade of the 2nd Rheinbund Division (the 1st Brigade to be the Hessian contingent) never came close to fruition. See Chapter 8. The actual strength of the 3rd Berg is a matter of some conjecture: 1,400 is the approximate figure given in Kellermann's strength returns of 29 April and 17 May (Saski, vol. III, pp. 76, 405), and Napoleon's minister in Kassel says it was 1,500 strong (13 June letter in Du Casse, *Jérome,* vol. IV, p. 239), but on 11 May, Jerome claims the regiment only numbered 1,240 (Ibid., p. 53).

12: Comments by Napoleon's minister to Jerome's court, who had accompanied X Corps on the campaign (Du Casse, *Rois Frères,* p. 283).

13: Schröder, p. 176; Du Casse, *Jérome*, vol. IV, p. 254.

14: See Chapter 9 for a discussion of the little battle at Oelper. By early July, Jerome was complaining that Berg had only about 800 'in a state to fire a shot', but his statement is unclear and probably exaggerated (Du Casse, *Jérome*, vol. IV, p. 264). For Jerome's praise of the Berg troops see his early August report to Napoleon (Ibid., pp. 198-199); Napoleon evidently believed the Berg officers were superior to their Westphalian counterparts, thus accounting for the superior performance of the Berg infantry at Oelper (Napoleon to Berthier, *Correspondence*, 15645, 11 August 1809).

15: Little information is available on the Berg horse battery in 1809. It is clear that Napoleon originally demanded twelve guns from Berg and that the battery actually never had more than its normal six pieces. It is not clear, however, where they were disposed during most of the campaign (they do not appear, for example, in Kellermann's reports of 29 April and 17 May). A reliable report, however, announced the entry of six guns from Hanau into Westphalia on 28 April along with infantry of the reserve corps and it may be that these guns were from the Berg battery. Some historians (e.g., Kortzfleisch) place the Berg battery with X Corps during the campaign in Saxony, but I could find no evidence to substantiate this (it is not mentioned in any of Jerome's correspondence) and it seems unlikely the battery ever left Westphalia except to return to Hanau. What is certain is that by mid-July, the battery was at Hanau. See *Correspondence*, 15568 (21 July), 15597 (30 July), 15645 (11 August), and 15813 (14 September).

16: This version of events follows that provided in the two principal histories of the regiment: Freiherr von Ardenne, *Bergische Lanziers, Westfälische Husaren Nr. 11*, Berlin: Mittler & Sohn, 1877, pp. 6-8; and Rittmeister von Eck, *Geschichte des 2. Westfälischen Husaren-Regiments Nr. 11 und seiner Stammtruppen von 1807-1893*, Mainz: Militär-Verlagsanstalt, 1893, pp. 3-5. See also P. Zimmermann, *Erinnerungen aus den Feldzügen der bergischen Truppen in Spanien und Russland*, Düsseldorf: Stahl, 1840, pp. 95-7. Note, however, that the regiment's 4th Squadron may have been in Westphalia until as late as mid-June: in one of his several letters directing the return of the 3rd Berg Infantry, Napoleon also mentions the 4th Squadron (*Correspondence*, 15342, 12 June); in addition, Kellermann's return of 17 May (in Saski, vol. III, p. 405) lists only three squadrons (1st and 2nd at Metz, 3rd in Berg). Thus, although the regimental histories are quite specific, it is possible that Jerome had one Berg squadron under his command in Westphalia for several weeks; as with the Berg battery, however, it is unlikely the squadron took part in the campaign in Saxony.

17: The regiment may have engaged in some patrolling while attached to Bourcier but it had no significant contact with the Austrians; see Chapters 7 and 8 for combat around Passau and Nuremberg. Order attaching the regiment to Bourcier: Napoleon to Bourcier, *Correspondence*, 15445, 26 June 1809. Orders assigning the Berg troopers to Junot: Napoleon to Junot, *Correspondence*, 15568, 21 July 1809 and Napoleon to Berthier, *Correspondence*, 15597, 30 July 1809.

18: It is convenient to refer to Dalberg's territories by the name of his capital; moreover, the acquisition of new lands would bring him the title Grand Duke of Frankfurt in 1810 (as part of the deal, he lost Regensburg to Bavaria). Frankfurt also possessed a small artillery company and the normal array of constabulary troops and city guards, but none of these played a role in the 1809 campaign. Regensburg's tiny municipal guard likewise took no part in the vicious fighting around that unfortunate city (Jürgen Kraus, 'Das Regensburger Bürgermilitär in der fürstprimatischen Zeit: Infanterie', *Zeitschrift für Heereskunde*, Nr. 359 (Januar/Februar), LVI. Jahrgang 1992).

19: Heinrich Füchtbauer, 'Geschichte der Stammtruppen des k. b. 14. Infanterie-Regiments', part I of *Festschrift zur Jahrhundert-Feier des k. b. 14. Infanterie-Regiments Hartmann*, Nürnberg: Stich, 1914, p. 6. Füchtbauer further states that the Frankfurt contingent was 'formed as a Jäger Battalion', but I have found no information to confirm this. Note that the French expected the battalion to have six companies of 160 men each (Berthier to Napoleon, 5 March, Saski, vol. III, p. 155). The uniform description is based on the assumption that the new battalion had the same uniforms as the 1st Battalion when it headed for Spain in 1808. See also Guillaume Bernays, *Schicksale des Grossherzogthums Frankfurt und seiner Truppen*, Berlin: Mittler & Sohn, 1882, pp. 135-6; Martin Bethke, 'Frankfurter Soldaten...ein verlorener Haufen', *Zeitschrift für Heereskunde*, Nr. 284/285 (Jul/Oct), XLIII Jahrgang, 1979; Lt. Colonel Sauzey, *Le Régiment de Francfort*, vol. I of *Les Allemands sous les Aigles Françaises*, Paris: Terana, 1987; Alfred Umhey, 'Das Infanterie-Bataillon des Grossherzogtums Frankfurt 1808-1813', *Das Bote aus dem Wehrgeschichtlichen Museum*, Heft 17, Jahrgang 9, 1985; Peter Wacker, 'Grossherzoglich Frankfurtische, fürstlich Primatische Soldaten 1806-1813', *Zeitschrift für Heereskunde*, Nr. 304 (Nov/Dec), XLVI Jahrgang, 1982.

20: Serfdom and feudal privileges would be retained in the Mecklenburgs for many years yet to come. Troops from Schwerin had been sent to assist Holland in the repression of revolutionary unrest during the 1790's.

21: Although the French exerted considerable influence on the organizations and tactics of the Mecklenburg armies (the little artillery battery, for example, was commanded by a French major named Colleville and used French drill), it is noteworthy that Napoleon refrained from interfering with their outdated social and political forms. Other French military reforms introduced in Schwerin included care for veterans and conscription. Laws concerning the latter were promulgated just before the 1809 campaign opened, too late to provide soldiers for the campaign, but in time to rebuild the army that autumn.

22: The infantry battalions were garrisoned in Schwerin (1st), Wismar (2nd), Rostock (3rd), and Ludwigslust

(4th); the artillery was located in Rostock . Strength of the garrison company taken from Binder, *Schill*, p. 166. The Guard unit, though it had lost its horses in 1789, still bore the title 'Leibgarde zu Pferde'; it was uniformed after the fashion of Prussian heavy cavalry in straw-coloured tunics with carmine distinctions. The hussars wore red dolmans, blue pelisses and fur caps. See Ernst Schäfer, 'Mecklenburgs Militärwesen vor und in den Freiheitskriegen', *Jahrbuch des Vereins für mecklenburgische Geschichte*, vol. LXXX, 1915.

23: *Correspondence*, 14790, 20 February 1809; see also 14793 and 14794 (both 21 February), and 14975, 30 March ('Instructions pour le Major-Général'). Command and control arrangements (Candras, Liébert, etc.) are set out in a 22 February letter from Davout to St. Hilaire (Saski, vol. I, pp. 87-88).

24: II/7 arrived in Stralsund on the 18th, I/7 one day later; the unit in Barth was the Voltigeur Company of I/7, a musketeer company of this battalion and the voltigeurs of II/7 occupied Rügen. The regiment's strength was probably about 1,200-1,400 officers and men. Note that all members received new red distinctions for their uniforms before leaving Mecklenburg. Further note that German sources generally refer to the this unit as the Mecklenburg-Schwerin 'Kontingents-Regiment' rather than the '7e Régiment de la Confédération du Rhin'.

25: Sources for the Mecklenburg-Schwerin Army are: Oskar Haevernick, *Kurze Darstellung der Geschichte des Grossherzoglich Mecklenburgischen Füsilier-Regiments Nr. 90, 1788-1892*, Berlin: Mittler & Sohn, 1899; Klaus-Ulrich Keubke, 'Versuch einer formationsgeschichtlichen Betrachtung: Mecklenburg-Schwerin', *Zeitschrift für Heereskunde*, Nos. 350/351 (Jul/Oct) and 352 (Nov/Dec), LIV Jahrgang, 1990; Klaus-Ulrich Keubke, 'Otto Bernhard von Presentin', *Zeitschrift für Heereskunde*, Nos. 356/357 (Jul/Oct), LV. Jahrgang, 1991; Rudolph Freiherr von Langermann und Erlencamp and Werner von Voigts-Rhetz, *Geschichte des Grossherzoglich Mecklenburgischen Grenadier-Regiments Nr. 89*, Schwerin: Stiller, 1895; Christian Madaus, ed., *Beiträge Mecklenburgische Militärgeschichte von 1700 bis 1871*, Hamburg: Krüger & Nienstadt, 1980; Oberleutnant von Ondarza, *Geschichte der Grossherzoglich Mecklenburgischen Artillerie*, Leipzig-Dresden: Rissarth, 1913, pp. 5-8; P. von Wrochem and Oskar Haevernick, *Geschichte des Grossherzoglich Mecklenburgischen Füsilier-Regiments Nr. 90, 1788-1906*, M. von Below, ed., Berlin: Mittler & Sohn, 1907; Ernst Zipfel, *Geschichte des Grossherzoglich Mecklenburgischen Grenadier-Regiments Nr. 89*, Schwerin: Bärensprung, 1932.

26: The peacetime garrisons of the companies were: 1st and 4th in Neustrelitz, 2nd in Neubrandenburg, 3rd in Woldegk; the tiny depot at Alt-Strelitz was only formed on mobilization in April 1809. The strength of the four-company battalion was 201 when it headed north on 10 March; it later received some new recruits but it is not clear that these arrived before the Schill episode. Desertion was a constant problem. See Klaus-Ulrich Keubke, 'Versuch einer formationsgeschichtlichen Betrachtung, Teil 1: Mecklenburg-Strelitz', *Zeitschrift für Heereskunde*, No. 349 (May/Jun), LIV Jahrgang, 1990; General-Major von Puttkamer, *Kurze Geschichte des II. Bataillons Grossherzoglich Mecklenburgischen Grenadier-Regiments 89*, Neubrandenburg: Feller, n.d.; Gerhard Tarnow, 'Die Aufstellung des Mecklenburg-Strelitzer Rheinbundkontingents und des Vaterländischen Husaren-Regiments 1808-1817', *Mecklenburg-Strelitzer Geschichtsblätter*, Jahrgang X/XI, 1935. The hussars wore red dolmans and blue pelisses, see Paul Steinmann, *Die Mecklb.-Strelitzsche Landgendarmerie*, Schönberg: Hempel, n. d., p. 36.

27: Liébert, though supposedly part of X Corps, seems to have sent most of his reports directly to Berthier at Imperial Headquarters. The French artillery company was the 12th of the 7th Foot Artillery Regiment.

28: Quoted in Langermann und Erlencamp, pp. 43-44.

29: A Polish detachment (c. 40 chasseurs) and two French guns had initially marched to Damgarten on the 23rd, but these returned to Stralsund that evening (the latter replaced by the Mecklenburg battery). The four immobile Mecklenburg guns were loaded onto wagons for the journey back to Stralsund. The location of the Mecklenburg hussars is not clear. Wrochem/Haevernick (p. 41) say they had been withdrawn at the Duke's order to resume their constabulary duties, but Candras gave them orders to reconnoitre for Pressentin and Binder (p. 177) claims that Schill's men captured a detachment of 21 Mecklenburg hussars during the skirmish. Nor is their strength certain: figures vary from 20 to 60.

30: The precise movements of the Strelitz Battalion are not recorded, but it apparently joined the 1st Schwerin at Grimmen on the 26th.

31: In Anklam, Candras found about 100 additional Polish chasseurs ('all that I could send him', wrote Liébert) who had arrived from Stettin on the 26th.

32: The saga of the Mecklenburgers in late May was developed from Liébert's reports and Candras' orders (quoted in Du Casse, *Jérome*, vol. IV, pp. 15-25, 76-9, 96-100, 103-8, 113-17), Moltke's report (cited in Langermann und Erlencamp, pp. 45-7), Binder, *Schill*, pp. 174-8, and accounts in the regimental histories listed above.

33: Report from Liébert to Berthier, 30 May 1809, cited in Du Casse, *Jérome*, vol. IV, pp. 103-8.

34: Langermann und Erlencamp, p. 47. The strength of the Strelitz Battalion is not recorded but may be assumed to have been much reduced.

35: Quotations from Liébert's report (evidently from mid-June) quoted in Du Casse, *Jérome*, vol. IV, pp. 20-2.

36: The black drummers of Oldenburg later became a favourite of uniform artists, but it appears that there was only one of these unusual soldiers in 1809.

37: Duke Peter evidently responded very coolly to Napoleon's request for the Oldenburg contingent, 'astonishing' the Emperor with his insouciance (*Correspondence*, 14902, 15 March 1809).

38: The Braunschweigers surprised and disarmed a detachment of 20 Oldenburg soldiers in Elsfleth.

39: Another Landdragoner was pressed into service as a guide for the free corps on the 5th and 6th. For the actions of the Oldenburg contingent and their Duke in 1809 see: Kortzfleisch, *Zug durch Norddeutschland*, pp. 56-7, 59, 61, 64-6.

40: Oldenburg (along with Holland and the Hanseatic Cities) was declared a part of metropolitan France by a *senatus consultum* of 13 December 1810, with the French actually taking possession on 28 February 1811. Composition, organization and attitude of the Oldenburg contingent is derived from Eduard von Finckh, *Geschichte des Oldenburgischen Infanterie-Regiments Nr. 91*, Berlin: Mittler & Sohn, 1881, pp. 8-9; Wilhelm G. F. Wardenburg, 'Uebersicht der bewaffneten Macht und der kriegerischen Einrichtungen Oldenburgs, vom 15ten Jahrhundert bis auf die neuesten Zeiten, in chronologischer Ordnung', *Oldenburgische Blätter*, August 1826; and Louis von Weltzien, *Militärische Studien aus Oldenburgs Vorzeit und Geschichte des Oldenburgischen Contingents*, Oldenburg: Schulze, 1858, pp. 109-28.

41: The dragoons wore a red coat with blue distinctions, while the gunners had a standard artillery uniform of dark-blue cloth with red trim. The Nachtwache wore a long blue coat with red trim.

42: Information on the Hanseatic troops is taken from Johann Focke, 'Vom bremischen Stadtmilitär', *Bremisches Jahrbuch*, vol. 19, 1900; C. F. Gaedechens, *Das hamburgische Militär bis zum Jahre 1811 und die hanseatische Legion*, Hamburg: Gräfe, 1889; George Nafziger, *Napoleon's German Enemies*, privately published, 1990, pp. 92-96; Kortzfleisch, *Zug durch Norddeutschland*, pp. 58-59; and communication from Dr. Müller of the Bremen City Archives. Although Lübeck's regular military was apparently disbanded in 1806, it is reasonable to assume that some sort of municipal guard existed in 1809.

CHAPTER 11:

Conclusion:
Soldiers of the Empire

In January of 1809, Napoleon in Valladolid, Spain, had dictated a series of Imperial commands to his allies in the Rheinbund, directing that they prepare their contingents for war against Austria. Twelve months later, the Habsburgs once more defeated, most of the German troops finally returned home. It had been a major effort for the Rheinbund states. Every available man had been mobilized for the conflict and in most cases the only forces not engaged against the Austrians were those already committed to Spain. Additionally, most of the larger states raised new units during the course of the campaign; Württemberg, for example, eventually exceeded its Rheinbund requirement by nearly fifty per cent. In all, more than 100,000 German soldiers from thirty-one different states participated in the campaign, enduring brutal forced marches, horrifically grand battles and the dull loneliness of interminable picket duty in the service of their French Emperor. It had been a war broad in scope and the men of the Confederation had appeared in almost every theatre, from the Baltic to Lake Balaton, from Westphalia to Warsaw. From the opening guns along the Isar to the last rounds fired at Znaim, Napoleon's German allies had stood in the front ranks with their French comrades, playing a major role in the great struggles and paying a heavy price in blood.

Beyond the immediacy of the battlefield, however, it must be remembered that the early nineteenth century was a time of tremendous upheaval in Germany. The French Revolution and the subsequent progress of French arms across the face of Europe had awakened peoples and monarchs between the Rhine and the Elbe to new concepts of society, government and national identity. Militarily, these concepts were reflected in the changing nature of the German defence establishments as they made the transition from dynastic, mercenary forces into truly national armies. Heavily influenced, if not dominated, by France after their incorporation into the Rheinbund and exposed to Napoleonic warfare on the fringes of the 1805 and 1806-7 campaigns, the remodelled, national armies of the German states faced their first true test in 1809. The war with Austria thus provides an opportunity to assess the martial qualities of Napoleon's German allies within a context of dramatic social, political and military change.

THE HEROIC AND THE HAPLESS: ASSESSING THE RHEINBUND CONTINGENTS
Based on their battlefield performances in 1809, the Rheinbund troops can be placed into several categories. The best are relatively easy to select: the contingents of Württemberg, Baden and Hesse-Darmstadt all displayed superior val-

our, initiative, endurance and tactical skill during the course of the campaign. The light troops of these three states were particularly good. Von Hügel's crack Württemberg Light Brigade, for instance, nearly equalled the exertions of Davout's redoubtable veterans between 19 and 22 April and achieved a brilliant success in its daring night attack against the Pöstlingberg on 17 May. The Baden Jäger Battalion in the pursuit after Wagram and the Hessian fusiliers in the June expedition to Hungary provide further proof of the high quality of these hardy troops. The light horsemen matched their infantry comrades in courage and enterprise, earning the honest praise of such French cavalry heroes as Lasalle and Marulaz. Likewise, the light artillery batteries of Baden and Württemberg were noted for their proficiency and highly valued by the French. Nor should the line troops be neglected. The fighting at Linz, Aspern and Aderklaa gives testimony to the spirit, training and bravery of the line battalions, while their stamina was severely tested on numerous forced marches such as Massena's move from Augsburg to Eggmühl.

A key factor in the performance of these contingents was the excellence of their leaders. At all levels, officers in the three armies demonstrated energy, determination and tactical competence, training their men well and instilling in them the offensive spirit and drive characteristic of Napoleonic warfare. Among the senior leaders, the Württemberg generals von Hügel and von Wöllwarth were especially noteworthy, while men such as Oberstlieutenant von Francken, Major von Gall, Kapitän von Freydorf and Rittmeister von Bismark exemplified the fine qualities of the middle and junior grades.[1] Under leaders such as these, the troops of Baden, Württemberg and Hesse-Darmstadt represented the best the Rheinbund had to offer in 1809, providing Napoleon with superb troops easily equal to the majority of French soldiers.[2]

Just as best troops stand out, so do the worst, and it is a fairly simple matter to identify the Mecklenburg, Oldenburg and Westphalian units as the least reliable of Napoleon's German allies in 1809. The causes for their unreliability, however, were significantly different. Oldenburg and the two Mecklenburg Duchies were old states, unrepentantly clinging to the norms of a bygone age. Their armies, closely linked to Prussia's and imbued with Frederickian notions of military organization, were generally recruited from ne'er-do-well foreigners and consequently had no national spirit and little loyalty to their nominal monarchs. These weaknesses were compounded by the poor training, poor equipment and distinctly anti-French attitude that pervaded all three contingents. When Schill brought combat to the north German states, it is therefore hardly surprising that the Mecklenburgers broke and deserted *en masse*, while the Oldenburg troops, at the direction of their duke, carefully avoided any contact with Braunschweig's Black Corps. The French had every reason to be dissatisfied with these contingents.

The Westphalians, on the other hand, showed some potential. The men could be individually courageous—as at Dodendorf and Halberstadt—even as they went down to defeat and the army held together despite the tensions of divided loyalties and repeated internal rebellions. It was, however, a new army, there had been no time to develop unit cohesion, the troops were generally inexperienced and inadequately trained. Moreover, the army's leadership was conspicuously poor. Despite occasional moments of competence, Jerome and his senior commanders showed themselves confused, indecisive and far too fond of luxury, invariably setting a negative example for their subordinates on this their first campaign.[3]

Having defined the extremes among the Confederation contingents, the remainder may be placed in the middle. Bavaria supplied by far the largest body of German troops in 1809, its numbers approaching 47,000 when all the reserve battalions, volunteer formations and National Guard units are added to its corps of regulars. In general, the infantrymen of the regular and reserve battalions were steady, brave and competent, but unexceptional and rather slow, lacking something of the verve of the French and the determination of the better Rheinbund troops. When pressed, however, they could move with speed and decision, as Wrede's Division demonstrated in its admirable marches on Salzburg and Wagram. The cavalry and artillery were especially good, both branches repeatedly proving their courage and tactical skill on the road from Abensberg to Znaim. As with the armies of Württemberg, Baden and Hesse, leadership was a strong point of the Bavarian military. The divisional commanders and the cavalry brigade commanders stand out, but the entire officer corps performed well throughout the campaign, capable professionals who understood their missions and cared for their men.

A large part of the Bavarian experience of war in 1809 was in the Tyrol. The exigencies of combating tenacious insurgents in the mountains of that region posed significant challenges for the Bavarians at first, but they gradually learned to cope with this style of warfare and the opening of the Third Offensive was a model of careful planning and skillful execution. Unfortunately, the war in the Tyrol was also marked by all manner of excesses and cruelties which tainted the otherwise fine combat record of the Bavarian troops.[4]

Another unit to fight and bleed in the Tyrol was the 4th Rheinbund Regiment of the five Saxon Duchies. Like the Bavarian Corps, the 4th Rheinbund was a body of solid German troops, disciplined and professional. Though many were relatively new recruits, they trained hard, fought well, and exhibited excellent spirit under great adversity. The 5th and 6th Regiments, suffering somewhat from desertion, were apparently less stable and cohesive, but it is difficult to form a firm impression of their combat value as they were never involved in a serious engagement. The same applies to the 2nd Rheinbund, but this regiment, through its superior appearance and drill, managed to acquire a enviable reputation which it later substantiated in Spain.

The Saxons are the most controversial of the lot. Their cavalry was universally regarded as superb and, under leaders like von Gutschmidt, the mounted regiments added further lustre to their names in 1809 despite the lack of suitable horseflesh. The Schützen battalions, though new, also performed well. Battalion *von Metzsch*, for example, earned the respect of General Dupas for being the last unit of his division to withdraw from the Russbach Heights on the evening of 5 July. The remainder of the infantry, however, presented a different picture. Although the individual soldiers were brave enough, unit cohesion was weak and the line formations were plagued by ancient leadership, insufficient training, poor equipment and outdated attitudes. The situation improved slightly when much of the gerontocracy returned to Saxony in mid-June, but there was not time to revitalize the corps in the weeks before Wagram. Thrown into the centre of the line under Bernadotte's uncertain command, the infantry took heavy casualties on 5 and 6 July and had to be pulled out of the fight. The thorough reforms introduced in 1810 were long overdue, but the Saxon Army's reputation never recovered from the damage inflicted at Wagram.

The other contingents played only peripheral roles in the campaign. The Berg infantrymen seem to have been held in some esteem as combat troops when compared to the Westphalians, but shared the same evil reputation for misbehaviour and indiscipline. The cavalry regiment, on the other hand, had impressed Napoleon at Versailles and was considered a real asset although it saw no combat in 1809. The Würzburg sappers and train personnel were too small in numbers to excite any attention and were essentially excluded from combat by the nature of their tasks. Likewise, the Frankfurt battalion only saw easy garrison duty in Erfurt and its members returned to their hearths without firing a shot.

A BROADER PERSPECTIVE

Beyond the combat qualities of the various contingents, the 1809 campaign offers interesting insights into several other aspects of the Napoleonic era. First, the Rheinbund armies present the full spectrum of military modernization as Europe progressed from Frederickian to Napoleonic styles of warfare. At one extreme, stiff, traditional states like Saxony tenaciously clung to the forms of the past, while at the other, modern states such as Bavaria and Württemberg accepted the spirit of the new age and judiciously remoulded their armies within the framework of their military heritages and national loyalties. Fealty to the sovereign continued to be a major consideration, particularly for officers, but Württemberg's modern reserve system and Bavaria's truly national army pointed the way to the future.[5] The future was also evident in the details of the German armies in 1809. Influenced by the impressive triumphs of French arms as well as direct pressure from Paris, the Rheinbund states modified their organizations, their tactics and even their uniforms to meet the demands of modern war and alliance with Napoleon. In many cases, there was also a subtle change in attitude. Association with the impetuous, victorious Grande Armée infused in not a few Germans an expectation of glory and a bold offensive spirit, a desire, almost an urgency, to overcome all obstacles. The best of the Confederation forces thus drew close to the French model and fitted smoothly into the operational structure of the Grande Armée; the less capable were often bewildered, hastening to grasp changes they barely understood.

These changes in the military sphere, however, were only reflections of a much broader series of phenomena. The cataclysmic impact of the French Revolution and the Napoleonic Wars had destroyed the 'medieval detritus' trammelling Germany and had introduced a myriad of new ideas to fill the resultant vacuum.[6] One of the new ideas carried into central Germany on the bayonets of France's Revolutionary and Imperial armies was nationalism. Conjoined with concepts of equality and prosperity, it flooded across the patchwork of tiny German states. Where many German hopes of social and economic progress eventually withered into disappointment under French domination and exploitation, however, nationalism found fertile soil and flourished.

Ironically, military alliance with France and the exigencies of modern warfare accelerated the spread of German nationalism. To meet Napoleon's demands, the German states were forced to raise large armies from their populations, armies imbued with the idea that it was each citizen's duty to defend his fatherland. Participating in the great campaigns of the Empire, these new national armies were exposed to the patriotic fervour of the French and gradually began to acquire a national consciousness of their own. Furthermore, the French redrew the map of Germany, amalgamating many of the petty principalities, dukedoms and bishoprics into the larger monarchies or creating new realms such as Westphalia and Berg. Germans whose horizons had previously extended no farther than the next village suddenly found themselves conscripted into the large armies of large states. As allies of the French and enemies of the Austrians or Spanish, they began to think of themselves as Germans. In the words of one historian, it was a 'terrible but most prompt means of education', a 'different way of passing through a revolution'.[7]

Unfortunately for the Emperor, the brand of nationalism that evolved in the small German states soon evinced a distinctly anti-French tone. In part this was due to the competing interests and cultural differences inherent in any alliance like the Rheinbund, but French arrogance introduced additional frictions that angered and alienated many Germans. Ranging from serious affronts to minor quotidian irritations, these problems were already evident in 1809: discord stemming from the imposition of French commanders over German contingents; the forced introduction of French drill; the denigration of the German language; the looming terror of transfer to the Spanish hell. Regarded by Napoleon as minor aggravations in the victorious war with Austria, problems such as these grew more visible and more acute in the difficult campaigns to follow. To a certain degree, therefore, the Rheinbund held the seeds of the Empire's destruction, abetting as it did the spread of the virulent German nationalism that rose up against the French in 1813.

Paralleling the growth of nationalism, however, was an apparently contradictory trend among the German contingents: pride in their association with the Grande Armée. By transforming the Germans into allies and imposing upon them common tactics, doctrine and organization, Napoleon achieved a significant degree of standardization that raised the combat value of the German units and streamlined command and control in his multinational armies. Rheinbund units were thus full partners of the French in the great victories of 1809 and added bright streamers of glory to their regimental chronicles. Less tangible but equally important was the intimate link Napoleon thereby forged between himself and his German soldiers. The men and their commanders not only came to rely upon France for military support but also developed a personal attachment to the Emperor, and, before long, his appearance in front of a German regiment would evoke the same degree of enthusiasm he was accustomed to receiving from his French troops. Describing an Imperial visit to the Hessian camp on Lobau Island in late May, one Hessian historian commented:

He also sought out the Hessian troops, directed questions about the Battle of Aspern to officers and men, and expressed fulsome praise regarding the tough courage shown by the Hessians. It would be a falsification of history to deny that the personality and affability of the Emperor of Battles then, as later, made a powerful impression on the troops. Letters written at that time as well as the subsequent statements of officers who had participated in the campaigns from 1809 to 1813 confirm this. Furthermore, it is a generally acknowledged fact that Napoleon had a almost fascinating effect on other men, overwhelming friend and foe alike.[8]

To have fought under the eye of the great Emperor thus became a matter of lasting pride, a certification of martial prowess, a story for grandchildren undimmed even by the assertive nationalism of a later age.

In January of 1810, as chill winds hustled down the streets of Munich, Karlsruhe, Dresden and a dozen other Rheinbund capitals, the soldiers of Napoleon's German allies returned home to the cheers of their countrymen and the warm embraces of long-missed families. They had been absent from their homes for nearly twelve months, participating in a campaign that not only protected their own countries from Austrian designs, but also preserved French hegemony over central Germany for another four years. Marching with the glittering eagles of a magnificent army under the command of the greatest soldier of the age, they had fought frightful battles and won dramatic victories; they had been made to feel that they were an important part of something far greater than themselves. Memories of the hunger, privation, forced marches and cold bivouacs slowly faded, but the triumphs and honours remained fresh and German veterans sitting by their fires looked back on 1809 as their most glorious campaign. They had become true soldiers of the Empire.

NOTES

1: Francken was the Chief of Staff of the Baden Brigade, Gall commanded the Hessian 1st Leib Fusiliers, Freydorf commanded the Baden artillery, and Bismark led a squadron of Württemberg's *Leib-Chevauxlegers*. A dozen other names could easily be added to this list, see the relevant chapters.

2: It should be noted, however, that the Germans probably never matched their Gallic allies in impetuosity and élan. That, at least, was clearly the opinion of most contemporary observers, including Napoleon.

3: Considerable improvement was made by the time of the Russian campaign, but many of these ills continued to plague the Westphalian Army throughout its brief existence.

4: As with almost every conflict of this nature, the brutality and recrimination were mutual.

5: Siegfried Fiedler, *Kriegswesen und Kriegsführung im Zeitalter der Revolutionskriege*, volume III/2 of *Heerwesen der Neuzeit*, Georg Ortenburg, ed., Koblenz: Bernard & Graefe, 1988, pp. 102-103; Paul Sauer, 'Die Neuorganisation des württembergischen Heerwesens unter Herzog, Kurfürst und König Friedrich', *Zeitschrift für Württembergischen Landesgeschichte*, Jahrgang XXVI, 1967.

6: Herbert A. L. Fisher, *Studies in Napoleonic Statesmanship: Germany*, Oxford: Clarendon Press, 1903, pg. 223.

7: Charles Schmidt, *Le Grande-Duché de Berg*, Paris: Alcan, 1905, pp. 176-177.

8: A. Keim, *Geschichte des Infanterie-Leibregiments Grossherzogin (3. Grossherzogl. Hessisches) Nr. 117 und seiner Stämme 1677-1902*, Berlin: Mittler & Sohn, 1903, pg. 193.

Appendix:
Comparative Military Ranks

German Rank (Abbreviation)	French Rank (Abbreviation)	Modern British or US Equivalent
General-Leutnant (GL)	Général de Division (GD)	Major General
General-Major (GM)	Général de Brigade (GB)	Brigadier General
[staff] Oberst	Adjutant-Commandant	[staff] Colonel
Oberst	Colonel	Colonel or Brigade-Major
Oberst-Leutnant (OTL)	Major	Staff officer first class or Lieutenant-Colonel
Major (MAJ)	Chef de Bataillon or Chef d'Escadron	Major
Stabs-Hauptmann	Adjoint	[staff] Captain
Hauptmann, Rittmeister (cavalry), or Kapitän	Capitaine	Captain
Oberleutnant (OLT) or Premierleutnant (PLT)	Lieutenant	Lieutenant, First Lieutenant
Leutnant	Sous-Lieutenant	Subaltern, Second Lieutenant

NOTES

1. All comparisons are approximate, protocol and functions could vary widely.
2. Contemporary German sources frequently use "Lieutenant" vice "Leutnant" in all of the above (e.g., Oberst-Lieutenant). Additionally, "Obrist" was often used in place of "Oberst" (e.g., Obrist-Lieutenant).
3. The Austrians used three additional rank designations:

Austrian	British/U.S.
Feldzeugmeister (FZM) or General der Kavallerie (GdK)	Lieutenant General
Feldmarschall-Leutnant (FML)	Major General

4. In the French Army, the title "Major Général" indicated a function rather than an actual rank and was unique to Berthier.

Campaign
Participation Matrix

X Major proportion of contingent took part in combat in this theatre/battle.
(X) Major portion of this contingent was present in theatre but did not engage in serious combat.

Contingents	Bavaria	Danube Valley	Aspern	Hungary	Wagram	Tyrol[1]	Central[2] Germany	North[3] Germany	Poland
Bavaria	X	X			X	X	X		
Württemberg	X	X	X[4]			X	(X)[5]		
Baden	(X)	X	X	X	X	X			
Hesse-Darmstadt	(X)	X	X	X	X				
Saxony		X			X		X	(X)	X
4th, 5th, 6th Rheinbund	(X)	(X)[6]				X			
2nd Rheinbund	(X)	(X)							
Würzburg	(X)	(X)			(X)		(X)[7]		
Westphalia							X		
Berg							X		
Frankfurt							(X)		
Mecklenburg-Schwerin								X	
Mecklenburg-Strelitz								(X)	
Oldenburg								(X)	

1. Includes the Vorarlberg.   2. Includes combat against Austrian forces and the Braunschweig Black Corps.   3. Includes garrisons in northern and eastern Germany (e.g., Saxons at Stettin).   4. One cavalry regiment only.   5. Württemberg 'observation corps' posted near Ellwangen in late June and early July.   6. Some elements did take part in small skirmishes near Passau.   7. Small detachment of train personnel with Junot's Corps.

This matrix is intended to provide a broad overview of the Rheinbund troops in the 1809 campaign. The German contingents are listed on the vertical axis and the principal battles and theatres of war on the horizontal axis (Italy and Dalmatia are not included as no German units were involved in those theatres). Reading across from a contingent presents a picture of where it marched and fought. Likewise, reading down from a theatre of war or battle shows which contingents had forces present and which took part in that particular action. Note that the presence of an **x** does not mean that the entire contingent was present. Read horizontally, for example, the matrix shows that Hessian troops were present for the Bavarian phase of the war but did not fight (excepting some cavalry scuffles), while elements of the contingent actually fought in the Danube Valley, at Aspern, in Hungary and at Wagram. Read vertically, it can be seen that the Hessians shared the battlefield of Aspern with comrades from Württemberg and Baden.

Chronology

General

15 January - Napoleon in Valladolid, Spain sends mobilization orders to Rheinbund monarchs

23 January - Napoleon returns to Paris

Feb-March - Rheinbund states mobilize their contingents

March-April - Rheinbund troops begin to assemble in southern Germany; Austria masses forces on borders of the French Empire

Theatres of War

	Danube Valley	Tyrol	Central Germany	Other
2 April			Katte's insurrection	
10 April	Austrian Main Army invades Bavaria	Rebellion begins, Chasteler enters Tyrol		Archduke Johann invades Italy
13 April	Napoleon departs Paris	Kinkel and Bisson surrender at Innsbruck		
15 April				Archduke Ferdinand invades Poland
16 April	First Battle of Landshut			Battle of Sacile
17 April	Napoleon reaches Donauwörth	Kufstein besieged for first time		
19 April	Battle of Hausen-Teugn			Battle of Raszyn
20 April	Battle of Abensburg			
21 April	Second Battle of Landshut	Austro-Tyrolian raids into Bavaria (from late April into May)		
22 April	Battle of Eggmühl		Dörnberg's insurrection	
23 April	Capture of Regensburg			
24 April	Battle of Neumarkt			

Theatres of War

	Danube Valley	Tyrol	Central Germany	Other
28 April			Schill departs Berlin	Battles at Caldiero (28-30 April)
30 April			Schill enters Saxony	
1 May	Skirmish at Riedau		Schill reaches Wittenberg	Archduke Johann begins withdrawal
2 May		Vorarlberg raids begin		
3 May	Battle of Ebelsberg			
5 May	Urfahr seized by VIII		Dodendorf Skirmish	
8 May				
10 May		1st Offensive opens		Battle on the Piave
12 May		Kufstein relieved		
13 May	Vienna falls			
15 May			Schill takes Dömitz	
17 May	Battle of Linz			
19 May		Bavarians occupy Innsbruck		
21-22 May	Aspern-Essling			
24 May			Damgarten Skirmish	
25 May				Battle of St. Michael
25-31 May			skirmishes on Saxon border	
29 May	Baden Bde enters Hungary	2nd Bergisel Battle Action at Dornbirn		
31 May		Deroy retreats to Kufstein	Stralsund captured by GD Gratien	
1 June	Probe at Engerau			
3 June	Attack on Engerau			
9/10 June		Tyrolian and Vorarlberg rebels launch raids into southern Germany throughout June	Austrians invade Saxony	
11 June			Austrians enter Dresden	
12 June				Action at Papa
14 June				Battle of Raab
22 June				Raab falls
23/24 June			Marburg rebellion	
25/26 June			Marbach Skirmish	Actions at Graz
30 June	Wrede to Vienna		Saxons retake Dresden	
5-6 July	Battle of Wagram			
7 July	Action at Korneuburg			
8 July	Action at Stockerau		Battle of Gefrees	

Theatres of War

	Danube Valley	Tyrol	Central Germany	Other
9 July	Actions at Hollabrunn and Staatz			
10-11 July	Battle of Znaim			
12 July	ARMISTICE			
13 July	Action at Stampfen		Austrians reoccupy Dresden	
13-17 July		Last major rebel raids into Germany		
21 July			Saxons regain Dresden	
24 July			The Black Corps marches north	
27 July		2nd Offensive begins		
29 July			Action at Halberstadt	
1 Aug		Innsbruck taken	Battle of Oelper	
4-5 Aug		Battle of Oberau		
7 Aug			Black Corps escapes	
11 Aug				British land at Walcheren
13 Aug		3rd Bergisel Battle		
20 Aug		Bavarians again evicted from the Tyrol		
25 Sep		Clashes around Salzburg		
30 Sep				British evacuate Walcheren
11 Oct		Lefebvre relieved		
14 Oct	PEACE OF SCHÖNBRUNN			
17 Oct		3rd Offensive begins		
25 Oct		Bavarians enter Innsbruck		
1 Nov		Final Bergisel Battle		
11 Nov		French and Bavarian troops link at Brixen		
early Dec		Rebellion ends		

Jan 1810   Most Rheinbund contingents return to their homes.

Glossary

Brief explanations of special terms are provided to assist the reader.

artillery organization - In many countries, artillerymen, their guns and the equipment to transport their guns were not brought together except for training or war. Artillery *companies* contained the men, guns were stored in armouries and train organizations took care of limbers and other equipment. Artillery *batteries* were thus only formed at need by combining gunners, guns, train personnel and equipment. Usually one company manned six to eight guns with appropriate limbers, horses and drivers to form a battery.

Bürgermilitär, Bürgermiliz, Bürgergarde - Home guard organizations (literally citizen military, citizen militia, citizen guard) designed to perform simple police and security tasks within the confines of the town or district. Often little more than armed and uniformed neighbours with little or no military training.

carabiniers - a. Elite heavy cavalry (e.g., Saxon Karabiniers, French 1st Carabiniers-à-Cheval). b. Elite light infantry (e.g., French carabinier companies, Westphalian Jäger-Carabiners).

chasseurs (à-cheval) - Regular light cavalry, literally 'mounted hunters' (e.g., French 14th Chasseurs). Term also applied to certain French light infantry and was often used by the French to refer to German Jäger units (chasseur = Jäger = hunter).

chevauxlegers - Light cavalry, literally 'light horse' (e.g., Württemberg *Herzog Heinrich* Chevauxlegers). Many variant spellings.

cuirassiers - Elite heavy cavalry, 'big men on big horses', usually equipped with metal breast armor (a 'cuirass') and steel helmet (e.g., Saxon *Zastrow* Cuirassiers).

depot - When a unit deployed for a campaign, it usually left behind a 'depot' commanded by a major or lieutenant-colonel to train new recruits, organize replacements and generally conduct the unit's administrative matters while it was away. German depot troops (especially Baden, Bavarian and Württemberg) were often called upon to take the field themselves in 1809.

dragoons - Standard line or medium cavalry, capable of performing most any cavalry task.

eagle - The standard issued to French regiments, consisted of brass eagle atop a pole to which the unit's flag was attached. The eagle was more important than the flag and was entrusted to a regiment by the Emperor himself in an emotional ceremony. No worse fate could befall a regiment than to lose its eagle to the enemy.

fusilier - a. Designation for standard line infantry. b. In Hesse-Darmstadt and Prussia, fusiliers were élite light infantry (e.g., Hessian Leib-Garde Fusiliers).

Fuss (zu Fuss) - Literally 'foot' ('on foot'), indicates foot soldiers (infantry, artillery) as opposed to mounted men. French: 'à pied'.

Garde du Corps - Literally 'body guard', special formations usually with showy uniforms to perform palace guard duty and other ceremonial functions associated with 19th-century monarchs. Seldom had a combat role (e.g., Westphalian Garde du Corps).

garrison units - Units thus *named* (as opposed to any other unit that may simply be assigned to garrison duty) were designed to perform relatively easy functions in fortresses, prisons and similar locales (guard duty, etc.), generally composed of less capable soldiers, either by reason of their training, age or physical fitness. Usually not suitable for active campaigning (e.g., Württemberg Garrison Battalion).

Graf - count.

grenadiers - a. Elite infantry (grenadier à pied or Grenadier zu Fuss), usually the larger, stronger men of an organization; selected for their courage, they were normally assigned the most dangerous battlefield missions. Often issued with imposing bearskin caps (e.g., Baden Grenadier Guards). b. Elite heavy cavalry (grenadier à cheval or Grenadier zu Pferd), also wore tall bearskin hats (e.g., Württemberg's mounted grenadiers of the Guard cavalry).

Grenzer - Peculiar brand of Austrian light infantry. Raised among border tribes in what is now Yugoslavia, they shielded the fringes of the Habsburg Empire from Turkish raids when they were not on campaign and were named for their districts (e.g., *Peterwardeiner* Grenzer). Gunther Rothenburg has written the classic English language study of this odd institution.

Herzog/Grossherzog - duke/grand duke.

horse artillery - Artillery units where every man rode a horse. Light, flexible, bold and fast. Some countries (e.g., Austria) chose to have their men ride on limbers and caissons rather than horses, but this was not as rapid as true horse artillery.

hussars - Elite light cavalry. By reputation, the quintessential light troopers, rakish, daring and wild. Uniforms harked back to Hungarian freebooters of earlier centuries and featured a *dolman* (a short, tight jacket), a *pelisse* (a fur-trimmed outer jacket) and profuse braiding (e.g., Baden Hussar Regiment).

Inhaber - The patron or sponsor of a unit (literally the 'owner'). In many monarchies, it was traditional to honour high-ranking aristocrats by granting them a regiment, in some cases this was no more than a ceremonial function, in others, the Inhaber would play a role in selecting officers, uniforms, etc. Many units thus bear only a name (Württemberg *von Camrer* Infantry Regiment) or a name and a number (e.g., Bavarian 3rd Infantry Regiment

Prinz Karl). Example: Austrian Uhlan Regiment Nr. 3 *Erzherzog Karl* was Archduke (Erzherzog) Charles's regiment of Uhlans. Where no Inhaber had been designated, armies would usually annotate a regiment's number with the word 'vacant'.

Insurrection troops - The name given to Hungarian military levies raised at the direction of the parliament in Pest during national emergencies; most were poorly equipped, indifferently trained and nearly worthless in combat.

invalid or **half-invalid** - Units made up of personnel who could perform light duties but were not fit for active campaigning, similar to garrison units (e.g., Saxon half-invalid companies).

Jäger - a. Jäger zu Fuss: type of German and Austrian light infantry, literally 'hunter on foot' (e.g., Württemberg Jäger Battalion *König*). Often equipped with rifles (slower to load but featuring greater accuracy and range than the smoothbore muskets carried by most troops). Many such units were specially recruited from official foresters and hunters. Traditionally wore dark-green, often with grey breeches and black leather gear (Austrians wore grey). b. Jäger zu Pferd: standard German light cavalry, equivalent to French chasseurs-à-cheval (e.g., Württemberg *Herzog Louis* Jäger zu Pferd Regiment).

König - king.

Kurfürst - prince-elector, a title associated with the Holy Roman Empire.

lancers - Medium cavalry equipped with lances, a Polish specialty. Also called Uhlans. The only Rheinbund lancers in 1809 were the Westphalian Garde Chevauxlegers.

Landwehr - Austrian or German militia, usually raised on a local basis (e.g., Austrian 2nd Chrudim Landwehr Battalion).

Léger - Designation of French light infantry regiments (e.g., French 13th Léger).

Leib - Literally 'body', term indicates a unit with special association to the reigning monarch ('the King's own'). Often used in German units as an honorary title for the 1st company of each battalion or the 1st squadron/battalion of each regiment. Examples: Württemberg *Leib-Chevauxlegers* Regiment or the Leib (1st) Squadron of each Bavarian cavalry regiment. Note: in Württemberg's case this caused considerable confusion to Frenchmen trying to translate the names of the *König* Jäger zu Pferd (literally the 'King's Mounted Hunters') and the *Leib-Chevauxlegers* (literally the 'King's own Light Horse') as both were light cavalry and both regimental titles were tied to the ruling sovereign.

light - Indicates units (infantry, cavalry, artillery) that were supposed to be more rapid, agile and independent than line troops by virtue of their training and (at least theoretically) lighter equipment. Usually assigned missions that required speed, flexibility and initiative: skirmishing, screening, combat in close terrain (mountains, forests), etc. Often considered élite or semi-élite, but not all light formations lived up to their title. Traditionally associated with hunters (chasseurs, Jägers) and foresters, their uniforms frequently featured various shades of green. Signals were passed by hunting horns rather

than the drums used by line infantry units (hence the need for hornists) and
light infantry sometimes carried special weapons (e.g., rifles).

light dragoons - Standard light cavalry (e.g., Baden Light Dragoons).

Ligne - Designation of French line infantry regiments (e.g., French 57th Ligne).

line - The bulk of an army, regular infantry or cavalry as opposed to light units
or élite guard formations. Usually fought in strictly ordered columns and
lines, but many French line infantry units and some German troops were
also capable of skirmishing (moreover, each French line infantry battalion
contained a specially selected and trained company of light troops - see
'voltigeurs').

march units - In the French Army, replacements being sent to the front were
combined into *ad hoc* formations for their journey from the homeland to
their regiments; these were known as 'march battalions' or 'march
squadrons' (*bataillons de marche, escadrons de marche*) and not infre-
quently found themselves in combat (e.g., some of the units under GD
Bisson in the Tyrol in April).

musketeers - Usually indicates the regular line soldiers of an infantry battalion
(as distinguished from the élite light and grenadier companies).

parole - a. Pair of passwords used to distinguish friend from foe in response to
the picket's challenge 'who goes there?' (e.g., *Bravoure, Bavière*). b. word
of honour.

Pferd (zu Pferd) - Literally 'horse' ('on horse'), indicates mounted men (cavalry, artillery) as opposed to foot soldiers. French: 'à cheval'.

pioneers - Soldiers of engineer labour units, constructed fortifications, bridges,
etc.

pontooneers - Engineer soldiers equipped with pontoons and other materiel to
construct bridges on campaign.

sappers - Combat engineers. In infantry battalions organized along French
lines, these were a hand-picked élite who marched at the head of the column
(by regulation, only four sappers per battalion). Sapper companies, on the
other hand, were specially trained engineer troops equipped with tools and
skills to erect bridges, raise or demolish fortifications, repair roads, etc. It is
unlikely, however, that the Duchal Saxon and Würzburg 'sappers' of the
1809 campaign had any special training or equipment; they probably served
simply as a labour force.

Schützen - Loose term describing different types of German light infantry.
Generally analogous to French voltigeurs: intelligent, agile men capable of
operating independently (e.g., the Schützen in Bavarian infantry battalions).
Unlike the French, German Schützen were often armed with rifles. Also
used to designate a variety of irregular formations (e.g., Bavarian
Gebirgsschützen).

train troops/units - The army's transport troops. Indicates men, horses and
vehicles used to move artillery pieces, engineer equipment and supplies.
An artillery battery, for example, could not move its cannon without adequate train troops. Usually clothed in simple grey or brown uniforms.

troopers - In this work, the term 'troopers' refers exclusively to cavalrymen.

Uhlans - Another term applied to lancers (e.g., Austrian *Schwarzenberg* Uhlans).

uniforms - The soldier of the Napoleonic era generally covered his head with a hat or helmet, his torso with a coat or jacket over a waistcoat, his legs with tight breeches (or sometimes loose trousers), and his feet with either boots or a combination of shoes and gaiters. The coat or jacket would have a 'base colour' (e.g., the unusual cornflower blue of the Bavarians) and would often be decorated with a distinctive colour of cloth for the collar, cuffs, lapels and coattail turnbacks (the distinctive colour of the Bavarian 7th Infantry Regiment, for example, was pink); there were innumerable combinations of these colours, further complicated by differences in piping (e.g., another Bavarian infantry regiment, the 13th, had black distinctions trimmed in red) and button colour (white or yellow metal). Generally speaking, German line infantry and cavalry sported base colours of white or blue, while the light troops most often donned the traditional green associated with the hunter forebears. Artillerymen almost always wore dark-blue. Guard units were often distinguished by further trim on their collars or around the button holes on their lapels and cuffs (e.g., Württemberg and Westphalian units enjoying Guard status). Breeches tended to be either white or grey for line troops, green or grey for light and dark-blue for artillery; officers and cavalrymen wore boots while foot soldiers of all varieties usually fit their feet into simple shoes. Headgear is a study in itself. Three general types predominated: leather or felt shakos, old-style bicornes, and a multitude of helmets, casques and morillons. Additionally, élite troops and particularly fashionable staff officers often wore fur bonnets (e.g., the famous tall bearskin caps worn by the French Imperial Guard and the Baden Guard Grenadiers). This book endeavors to provide a general description of each contingent's uniforms, thereby imparting to the reader a sense of the colourful pageantry that accompanied battlefield bloodshed in the age of Napoleon. The subject of uniforms is enormously complex, however, and those wishing further details are referred to authorities such as Umhey, Haythornthwaite and the Knötels.

units - The following is an overview of the hierarchy of military units in the Napoleonic era. Note that it is general and could vary greatly from army to army; the French model is emphasized as it served as the norm for many of Napoleon's German allies.

company: usually commanded by a captain, 100—200 men, French standard was 140 soldiers.

division (first definition): a tactical term indicating two companies operating in concert.

battalion: generally four to six companies, basic tactical formation, usually commanded by a major or lieutenant-colonel, a full strength French battalion would have more than 840 men in four line companies (fusiliers) and two élite companies (one of grenadiers and one of voltigeurs). The analogous cavalry unit was the squadron (strength generally from 100 to 200 men).

regiment: two to four battalions or squadrons (note that some battalions, such as the Baden Jäger, were 'independent' and did not belong to a regiment), usually commanded by a colonel.

brigade: two or more similar regiments, commanded by a GB or GM.

division (second definition): two or more brigades, usually of the same type (e.g., two infantry brigades) with attached artillery, some divisions were composed of a mixture of arms (Austrian light divisions had infantry, artillery and cavalry), commanded by a GD or GL.

corps: in the French system, several infantry divisions with light cavalry, artillery, sappers and other supporting troops attached, commanded by a marshal or GD.

voltigeurs - Designated men of the élite light infantry company contained in each French infantry battalion (both Ligne and Léger). Usually smaller, lighter men chosen for their independence, agility and marksmanship, intended to work closely with light cavalry and provide each infantry battalion commander with his own specially selected and trained skirmishers. Taken over into German usage when French organization was adopted (e.g., Baden voltigeurs), but note that the Badeners were armed with rifles while their French counterparts carried smoothbore muskets.

Bibliography

Bibliographies, Dictionaries, Encyclopedias

Bellangé, Joseph Louis Hippolyte. *Die Generale der französischen Republik und des Kaiserreichs*, Leipzig: Lorck, 1846-47.

Bernhardt, Walter and Seigel, Rudolf. 'Bibliographie der Hohenzollerischen Geschichte', *Zeitschrift für Hohenzollerische Geschichte*, vol. 97/98, 1974/75.

Chandler, David G. *Dictionary of the Napoleonic Wars*, New York: Macmillan, 1979.

Haythornthwaite, Philip J. *The Napoleonic Source Book*, New York: Facts on File, 1990.

Horward, Donald D., ed. *Napoleonic Military History: A Bibliography*, London: Greenhill, 1986.

Kircheisen, Friedrich M. *Bibliographie des Napoleonischen Zeitalters*, Hildesheim: Olms, 1977.

Martinien, Aristide. *Tableaux par Corps et par Batailles des Officiers Tués et Blessés pendant les Guerres de l'Empire (1805-1815)*, Paris: Editions Militaires Européennes, 1984.

Palmer, Alan. *An Encyclopaedia of Napoleon's Europe*, New York: St. Martin's Press, 1984.

Schröder, Bernd Philipp. *Die Generalität der deutschen Mittelstaaten 1815-1870*, Osnabrück: Biblio Verlag, 1984.

Six, Georges. *Dictionnaire Biographique des Généraux & Amiraux Français de la Révolution et de l'Empire*, Paris: Manutention a Mayenne, 1989.

Tulard, Jean, ed. *Dictionnaire Napoléon*, Paris: Fayard, 1987.

Wurzbach, Constant von. *Biographisches Lexikon des Kaiserthums Oesterreich*, Wien: Zamarski, 1856.

General Works

Baden und Württemberg im Zeitalter Napoleons, Stuttgart: Cantz, 1987.

Bartsch, Rudolf. *Der Volkskrieg in Tirol 1809*, vol. 2 of *Das Kriegsjahr 1809 in Einzeldarstellungen*, Alois Veltzé, ed., Wien: Stern, 1905.

——. *Die Schill'schen Offiziere*, vol. 7 of *Das Kriegsjahr 1809 in Einzeldarstellungen*, Alois Veltzé, ed., Wien: Stern, 1909.

Baur, C. *Der Krieg in Tirol während des Feldzugs 1809*, München: Baur, 1812.

'Beiträge zur Geschichte des Schillischen Zuges durch Nord-Deutschland von einem Augenzeugen', *Minerva*, Bänder I and II, 1810.

'Berichtigung zweier in dem württembergischen Jahrbuche erzählten

Anekdoten', *Oesterreichische militärische Zeitschrift*, Heft 7, 1818.

[Bianchi, Friedrich Freiherr von]. *Vertheidigung des Brückenkopfes vor Pressburg, im Jahre 1809,* Pressburg: 1811.

Binder von Kriegelstein, Christian Freiherr. *Der Krieg Napoleons gegen Oesterreich 1809,* Maximilian Ritter von Hoen, ed., Berlin: Voss, 1906.

——. *Ferdinand von Schill,* Berlin: Voss, 1902.

Bismark, General Graf Friedrich Wilhelm von. *Bismark's Ideen,* part I of the *Reuter-Bibliothek,* Karlsruhe: Müller, 1825.

——. *Ideen-Taktik der Reuterei,* Karlsruhe: Müller, 1829.

Bleibtreu, Carl. *Die Grosse Armee,* Stuttgart: Krabbe, 1907.

Bond, Gordon C. *The Grand Expedition,* Athens, GA: University of Georgia Press, 1979.

Bonnal, Henry. *La Manœuvre de Landshut,* Paris: Chapelot, 1905.

Bornemann, Karl. *Napoleon bei Znaim,* Geislingen/Steige: Verlag des Südmährischen Landschaftsrates, 1975.

Bowden, Scotty & Tarbox, Charlie. *Armies on the Danube 1809,* Arlington: Empire Games Press, 1980, and Revised and Expanded edition, 1989.

Buat, E. *1809 De Ratisbonne à Znaïm,* Paris: Chapelot, 1909.

Chandler, David G. *The Campaigns of Napoleon,* New York: Macmillan, 1966.

Chelminski, Jan V. and Malibran, A. *L'Armée du Duché de Varsovie,* Paris: Leroy, 1913.

Christoph, Franz. 'Die Isar-Uebergänge der Oesterreicher bei Landshut am 16. und 21. April 1809', *Verhandlungen des Historischen Vereins für Niederbayern.*

Connelly, Owen. *Napoleon's Satellite Kingdoms,* New York: The Free Press, 1965.

Durieux, J. 'Soldats d'Essling et de Wagram', *Carnet de la Sabretache,* No. 200 (August), 1909.

Elbing, Hanswerner. 'Die hessische Politik in der Rheinbundzeit 1806-13', *Archiv für hessische Geschichte und Altertumskunde,* Neue Folge, Band XXIV, Darmstadt 1952/3.

Elting, John R. *Swords Around a Throne,* New York: The Free Press, 1988.

Empires, Eagles and Lions, issues 57 (Jul/Aug 81), 74 (Sep 83), 76 (Dec 83), 77 (Jan 84), 78 (Mar 84), 80 (Jun 84), 83 (Oct 84), 84 (Dec 84), 88 (Jun 85), 99 (Mar/Apr 87), 100 (May/Jun 87), Ontario: RAFM.

Engel, Friedrich. *Geschichte der oberösterreichischen Landwehr,* Linz: Akad. Pressverein, 1910.

Fedorowicz,Wladyslaw de. *1809 Campagne de Pologne,* Paris: Plon, 1911.

Der Feldzug von 1809 in Bayern, prepared by the Generalstabssektion des königlichen bayerischen Generalquartiermeisterstabes, 1865.

Fiedler, Siegfried. *Kriegswesen und Kriegsführung im Zeitalter der Revolutionskriege,* volume III/2 of *Heerwesen der Neuzeit,* Georg Ortenburg, ed., Koblenz: Bernard & Graefe, 1988.

Fisher, Herbert A. L. *Studies in Napoleonic Statesmanship: Germany,* Oxford: Clarendon Press, 1903.

Friesen, E. G. M. Freiherr von. 'Dresden im Kriegsjahre 1809', *Mitteilungen des Vereins für Geschichte Dresdens,* Heft 11, 1893.

'Gedanken über die beiden Schlachten auf dem Marchfelde bei Wien', *Pallas,* Band 2, 1809.

'Die Gefechte zwischen Riedau und Neumarkt-Kallham am 1. und 2. Mai 1809', *Linzer Volksblatt,* May 1914.

'Geschichte des Feldzugs an der Weichsel im Jahre 1809', *Minerva,* Band 1, 1810.

Glaser, Hubert, ed. *Krone und Verfassung, König Max I. Joseph und der neue Staat,* volume III/1 of *Wittelsbach und Bayern,* München: Hirmer, 1980.

Goecke, Rudolf. *Das Grossherzogthum Berg unter Joachim Murat, Napoleon I. und Louis Napoleon 1806-1813,* Köln: DuMont-Schauberg, 1877.

Gruber, Max. *Bruneck und das westliche Pustertal im Jahre 1809,* Schlern-Schriften No. 86, Innsbruck: Wagner, 1952.

Gunz, Johann. 'Der Krieg der Vorarlberger im Jahr 1809', *Militair-Wochenblatt,* Nos. 206, 210, 211, 212, 3 June-15 July 1820.

H., M. 'Ueber die Verwendung der Kavallerie in den Schlachten und Gefechten des Feldzuges 1809 in Süd-Deutschland', *Neue Militärische Blätter,* vol. LIV, Berlin, 1899.

Harder, Hans-Joachim. *Militärgeschichtliches Handbuch Baden-Württemberg,* Stuttgart: Kohlhammer, 1987.

Haythornthwaite, Philip J. *Napoleon's Military Machine,* New York: Hippocrene, 1988.

Heilmann, Johann von. 'Der Feldzug von 1809 in Tirol, im salzburgischen und an der bayerischen Südgrenze', *Jahrbücher für die deutsche Armee und Marine,* vols. 68 and 69 (1888), vol. 88 (1893).

Heller von Hellwald, Friedrich. *Der Feldzug des Jahres 1809 in Süddeutschland,* Wien: Carl Gerold's Sohn, 1864.

Hirn, Ferdinand. *Vorarlbergs Erhebung im Jahre 1809,* Bregenz: Teutsch, 1909.

Hirn, Josef. *Tirols Erhebung im Jahre 1809,* Innsbruck: Haymon, 1983.

Hoen, Maximilian Ritter von. *Aspern,* volume 3 of *Das Kriegsjahr 1809 in Einzeldarstellungen,* Alois Veltzé, ed., Wein: Stern, 1906.

———. *Wagram,* volume 8 of *Das Kriegsjahr 1809 in Einzeldarstellungen,* Alois Veltzé, ed., Wein: Stern, 1909.

Höfler, Edmund. *Der Feldzug des Jahres 1809 in Deutschland und Tirol,* Augsburg: Rieger, 1858.

Hölzle, Erwin. *Württemberg im Zeitalter Napoleons und der Deutschen Erhebung,* Stuttgart: Kohlhammer, 1937.

[Hormayr, Joseph]. *Das Heer von Innerösterreich unter den Befehlen des Erzherzogs Johann im Kriege von 1809 in Italien, Tyrol und Ungarn,* Leipzig and Altenburg: Brockhaus, 1817.

Johnson, David. *Napoleon's Cavalry and its Leaders,* New York: Holmes & Meier, 1978.

———. *The French Cavalry 1792-1815,* London: Belmont, 1989.

Johnson, Ray, *Napoleonic Armies,* London: Arms & Armour Press, 1984.

Junkelmann, Marcus. *Napoleon und Bayern,* Regensburg: Pustet, 1985.

Just, Gustav. *Der Friede von Schönbrunn*, volume 9 of *Das Kriegsjahr 1809 in Einzeldarstellungen*, Alois Veltzé, ed., Wein: Stern, 1909.

Katte, Rudolf von. 'Der Streifzug des Friedrich Karl von Katte auf Magdeburg im April 1809', *Geschichts-Blätter für Stadt und Land Magdeburg*, No. 70./71., Jahrgang 1935/1936.

Kerchnawe, Hugo. *Bei Linz und Ebelsberg Anno Neun*, Wien: Stern, 1910.

Kirschmaier, Fritz. *Die Gefechte an der Pontzlatzer Brücke 1703 und 1809*, Militärhistorische Schriftenreihe Heft 48, Wien: Bundesverlag, 1983.

Kleinschmidt, Arthur. *Geschichte des Königreichs Westfalen*, Gotha, 1893.

Koch, Hannsjoachim W. *Die Befreiungskriege 1807-1815*, Berg: Türmer, 1987.

Köfler, Werner. *Die Kämpfe am Bergisel 1809*, Militärhistorische Schriftenreihe Heft 20, Wien: Bundesverlag, 1983.

——. *Die Kämpfe am Pass Lueg im Jahre 1809*, Militärhistorische Schriftenreihe Heft 41, Wien: Bundesverlag, 1980.

Kortzfleisch, Gustav von. *Des Herzogs Friedrich Wilhelm von Braunschweig Zug durch Norddeutschland im Jahre 1809*, reprint of 1894 edition, Krefeld: Olmes, 1973.

Krieg 1809, prepared by the staff of the k. und k. Kriegsarchiv as part of the series *Kriege unter der Regierung des Kaisers Franz*, Vienna: Seidel & Sohn, 1907-10.

Kuckenburg, Heinz. *Soldat in Ulm*, Biberach an der Riss: Höhn, 1985.

Kurz, Franz. *Geschichte der Landwehr in Oesterreich ob der Enns*, Linz: Haslinger, 1811.

Litschel, Rudolf W. *Das Gefecht bei Ebelsberg am 3. Mai 1809*, Militärhistorische Schriftenreihe Heft 9, Vienna: Bundesverlag, 1968.

Maretich von Riv-Alpon, Gedeon Freiherr. 'Die Gefechte in der Umgebung von Salzburg in den Jahren 1800, 1805 und 1809', *Streffleur's Oesterreichische Militärische Zeitschrift*, XXXIV Jahrgang, Band I, Heft II (February), 1893.

——. *Die zweite und dritte Berg Isel-Schlacht*, Innsbruck: Wagner, 1895.

——. 'Josef Struber und die Kämpfe in der Umgebung des Passes Lueg im Jahre 1809', *Mittheilungen der Gesellschaft für Salzburger Landeskunde*, vol. XXXVII, 1897.

——. *Die vierte Berg Isel-Schlacht am 13. August 1809*, Innsbruck: Wagner, 1899.

Martens, Karl von. *Geschichte der innerhalb der gegenwärtigen Gränzen des Königreichs Württemberg vorgefallenen kriegerischen Ereignisse vom Jahr 15 vor Christi Geburt bis zum Friedensschlusse 1815*, Stuttgart: Königliche Hofbuchdruckerei, 1847.

Mayerhoffer von Vedropolje, Eberhard. *Oesterreichs Krieg mit Napoleon I*, Vienna: Seidel u. Sohn, 1904.

Mortonval. *Die Feldzüge in Teutschland*, Leipzig: Leske, 1831.

Ortenburg, Georg. *Waffe und Waffengebrauch im Zeitalter der Revolutionskriege*, volume III/1 of *Heerwesen der Neuzeit*, Georg Ortenburg, ed., Koblenz: Bernard & Graefe, 1988.

Otto, Friedrich. 'Schlacht bei Landshut am 21. April 1809', *Verhandlungen des Historischen Vereins für Niederbayern*, Band 33, 1897.

Pelet, Jean-Jacques. *Mémoires sur la guerre de 1809 en Allemagne*, Paris: Roret, 1824-26.

Pergler, Adolf. *Selbst- und Landesverteidigung der vereinten Pinzgauer und Tiroler in den Jahren 1800, 1805 und 1809 an den Pässen Botenbühel, Strub und Luftenstein*, Lofer, 1906.

Petre, F. Lorraine. *Napoleon and the Archduke Charles*, London: Lane, 1909.

Pivka, Otto von. *Armies of the Napoleonic Era*, New York: Taplinger, 1979.

Pritz, Franz Xaver. *Geschichte des Landes ob der Enns von der ältesten bis zur neuesten Zeit*, Linz: Haslinger, 1847.

Rambaud, Alfred. *L'Allemagne sous Napoléon Ier (1804-1811)*, Paris: Perrin, 1897.

Rapp, Ludwig. *Schicksale des Servitenklosters bei Volders in Tirol in den Kriegsjahren 1703, 1805 und 1809*, Brixen: Weger, 1886.

Rauchensteiner, Manfried. *Die Schlacht von Aspern am 21. und 22. Mai 1809*, Militärhistorische Schriftenreihe Heft 11, Wien: Bundesverlag, 1986.

——. *Die Schlacht bei Deutsch Wagram am 5. und 6. Juli 1809*, Militärhistorische Schriftenreihe Heft 36, Wien: Bundesverlag, 1977.

Reglement das Exercitium und die Manövres der Französischen Infanterie betreffend, vom 1sten August 1791, published in Braunschweig in 1812, reprinted Starnberg: LTR-Verlag, 1988.

R. [Rothenburg], F. R. von *Die Waffentaten der Oesterreicher im Jahre 1809*, Wien: Hirschfeld, 1838.

Sapherson, C. A. *A Year at War 1809*, Leeds: Raider Books, 1986.

Saski, Charles. *Campagne de 1809 en Allemagne et en Autriche*, Paris: Berger-Levrault, 1899-1902.

Sauer, Paul. *Napoleons Adler über Württemberg, Baden und Hohenzollern*, Stuttgart: Kohlhammer, 1987.

Schels, Johann B. 'Die Schlacht bei Aspern am 21. und 22. Mai 1809', *Oesterreichische militärische Zeitschrift*, Heft 1, 1843.

——. 'Der Feldzug 1809 in Polen', *Oesterreichische militärische Zeitschrift*, Heft 3, 1844.

——. 'Das Gefecht an der Isar bei Landshut am 16. April 1809', *Oesterreichische militärische Zeitschrift*, Heft 5, 1845.

Schemfil, Viktor. 'Das k. k. Tiroler Korps im Kriege 1809', *Tiroler Heimat*, XXIII Band, 1959.

Schikofsky, Karl. 'Die Vertheidigung des Brückenkopfes von Pressburg im Jahre 1809', *Organ der militär-wissenschaftlichen Vereine*, XLVI Band, 1893.

Schlagintweit, Maximilian. 'Kufsteins Kriegsjahre (1504, 1703, 1809)', *Darstellungen aus der Bayerischen Kriegs- und Heeresgeschichte*, Heft 12, München: Lindauer, 1903.

Schmidt, Charles. *Le Grande-Duché de Berg*, Paris: Alcan, 1905.

Schneidawind, Franz J. A. *Der Krieg Oersterreich's gegen Frankreich, dessen Alliirte und den Rheinbund im Jahre 1809*, Schaffhausen: Hurter, 1842.

——. *Der Feldzug des Herzogs Friedrich Wilhelm von Braunschweig und seines schwarzen Corps im Jahre 1809*, Darmstadt: Leske, 1851.

Schröder, Karl. *Zwischen Französischer Revolution und Preussens Gloria,* Eitorf: Heimatverein Eitorf, 1989.

Schulz, Uwe, ed. *Die Geschichte Hessens,* Stuttgart: Theiss, 1983.

Soltyk, Roman. *Relation des Opérations de l'Armée aux Ordres du Prince Joseph Poniatowski pendant la Campagne de 1809 en Pologne contre les Autriciens,* Paris: Gauthier-Laguione, 1841.

Stato Maggiore Dell'Escerito, Ufficio Storico. *L'Escerito e i Suoi Corpi,* Rome, 1971.

Staudenrauss, Alois. *Chronik der Stadt Landshut in Bayern,* Landshut: Thomann, 1832.

Struck, Wolf-Heino. 'Die Gründung des Herzogtums Nassau', in *Herzogtum Nassau 1806-1866,* Wiesbaden, 1981.

[Stutterheim, Karl Freiherr von]. *Der Krieg von 1809 zwischen Oesterreich und Frankreich,* Wien: Strauss, 1811.

Thonhauser, Josef. *Osttirol im Jahre 1809,* Schlern-Schriften No. 253, Innsbruck: Wagner, 1968.

Tranie, Jean & Carmigniani, Juan Carlos *Napoléon et l'Autriche - La Campagne de 1809,* Paris: Copernic, 1979.

'Das Treffen von Ebelsberg am 3. Mai 1809', *Oesterreichische militärische Zeitschrift,* Heft 7, 1832.

U., J. A. *Der Feldzug Frankreichs und seiner Verbündeten gegen Oesterreich im Jahre 1809,* Meissen: Goedsche, 1810.

'Ueber den Volkskrieg mit Bezug auf den Tyroler Krieg 1809', *Militair-Wochenblatt,* No. 107, 11 July 1818.

Veltzé, Alois. *Kriegsbilder aus Polen, Steiermark und Ungarn,* volume XI of *Das Kriegsjahr 1809 in Einzeldarstellungen,* Wien: Stern, 1910.

Wachtel, Wilhelm. 'Die Division Jellacic im Mai 1809', *Mitteilungen des K. und K. Kriegsarchivs,* dritte Folge, Band VIII, 1911.

Wagner, Anton H. *Das Gefecht bei St. Michael-Loeben am 25. Mai 1809,* Militärhistorische Schriftenreihe Heft 51, Wien: Bundesverlag, 1984.

Wanner, Gerhard. *Kriegsschauplatz Bodensee 1799/1800 und 1809,* Militärhistorische Schriftenreihe Heft 59, Vienna: Bundesverlag, 1987.

Welden, Ludwig Freiherr von. *Der Krieg von 1809 zwischen Oesterreich und Frankreich von Anfang Mai bis zum Friedensschlusse,* Wien: Gerold, 1872.

Wierichs, Marion. *Napoleon und das 'Dritte Deutschland' 1805/1806,* Frankfurt: Lang, 1978.

Wise, Terence. *Artillery Equipments of the Napoleonic Wars,* London: Osprey, 1979.

Wisnar, Julius. 'Die Schlacht bei Znaim im Jahre 1809', *Jahresbericht des k. k. Gymnasiums in Znaim für das Schuljahr 1909 1910,* Znaim: Lenk, 1910.

Xylander, Rudolf von. 'Zum Gedächtnis des Feldzugs 1809 in Bayern', *Darstellungen aus der Bayerischen Kriegs- und Heeresgeschichte,* Heft 18, München: Lindauer, 1909.

Memoirs, Correspondence, Biographies

Am Ende, Christian Gottlob Ernst. *Feldmarschall-Lieutenant Carl Friedrich*

Am Ende besonders sein Feldzug in Sachsen 1809, Wien: Braumüller, 1878.

Angeli, Moritz Edlen von. *Erzherzog Carl von Oesterreich als Feldherr und Heeresorganisator*, Wien: Braumüller, 1897.

Augustin-Thierry, A. *Masséna*, Paris: Albin Michel, 1947.

Barton, Sir Dunbar Plunket. *Bernadotte and Napoleon 1799-1810*, London: Murray, 1921.

——. *The Amazing Career of Bernadotte*, London: Murray, 1929.

Bonnefons, André. *Un Allié de Napoléon, Frédéric-Auguste Premier Roi de Saxe et Grand-Duc de Varsovie*, Paris: Perrin, 1902.

Comeau de Charry, Baron Sébastien Joseph de. *Souvenirs des Guerres d'Allemagne pendant la Révolution et l'Empire*, Paris: Plon, 1900.

Corti, Count. *Ludwig I of Bavaria*, Evelyn B. Graham Stamper, trans., London: Thornton Butterworth, 1938.

Criste, Oskar. *Erzherzog Carl von Oesterreich*, Wien: Braumüller, 1912.

[Czetteritz und Neuhaus, von.] 'Erinnerungen eines Kavallerie-Offiziers', *Zeitschrift für Kunst, Wissenschaft und Geschichte des Krieges*, Band 44, 1838.

Davout, Marshal Louis-Nicolas. *Correspondence de Maréchal Davout*, Charles de Mazade, ed., Paris: Plon, 1885.

Deifl, Josef. *Infanterist Deifl. Ein Tagebuch aus napoleonischer Zeit*, Eugen von Frauenholz, ed., München: Beck, 1939.

Dormann, Hasso. *Feldmarschall Fürst Wrede*, München: Süddeutscher Verlag, 1982.

Du Casse, Albert. *Opérations du Neuvième Corps de la Grande Armée en Silésie, sous le commandement en chef de S. A. I. le Prince Jérome Napoléon, 1806 et 1807*, Paris: Corréard, 1851.

——. *Mémoires et correspondence politique et militaire du Prince Eugène*, Paris: Lévy, 1859.

——. *Mémoires et Correspondence du Roi Jérome et de la Reine Catherine*, Paris: Dentu, 1861-1868.

——. *Le Général Vandamme et sa Correspondence*, Paris: Didier, 1870.

——. *Les Rois Frères de Napoléon Ier*, Paris: Baillière, 1883.

Dumas, Count Mathieu. *Memoirs of His Own Time*, Philadelphia: Lea & Blanchard, 1839.

Epstein, Robert M. *Prince Eugene at War*, Arlington, TX: Empire Press, 1984.

'Friedrich Wilhelm Graf von Bismark', *Militair-Wochenblatt*, No. 340, 28 December 1822.

Gachot, Edouard. *1809 Napoléon en Allemagne*, vol. VI of *Histoire militaire de Massena*, Paris: Plon, 1913.

Gallaher, John G. *The Iron Marshal*, Carbondale & Evansville: Southern Illinois University Press, 1976.

'General-Lieutenant Rühle von Lilienstern', *Beiheft zum Militair-Wochenblatt*, Berlin: Mittler, 1847.

Gersdorff, General-Lieutenant von. 'Zwei Schreiben veranlasst durch eine Stelle in den *Notes et mélanges, redigis par le Comte Montholon*', *Militair-Wochenblatt*, No. 353 (29 March 1823).

Heere, Johann Gottlob. *Erinnerungen des Schlossaufsehers - aus den Feldzügen der Jahre 1806, 1809, 1813, 1814 und 1815,* Mergentheim, 1847.

Heilmann, Johann von. *Feldmarschall Fürst Wrede,* Leipzig: Duncker & Humblot, 1881.

Hourtoulle, F. G. *Le Général Comte Charles Lasalle 1775-1809,* Paris: Copernic, 1979.

J., M. 'Zur Erinnerung an den Königl. bayerischen General der Infanterie und General-Quartiermeister der Armee, Clemens v. Raglovich', *Jahrbücher für die deutsche Armee und Marine,* vol. 63 (April-June 1887), Berlin: Wilhelm, 1887.

Kaisenberg, Moritz von. *König Jérome Napoleon, Ein Zeit- und Lebensbild,* Leipzig: Schmidt und Günther, 1899.

Keubke, Klaus-Ulrich. 'Otto Bernhard von Pressentin', *Zeitschrift für Heereskunde,* Nos. 356/357 (Jul/Oct), LV. Jahrgang, 1991.

Kircheisen, Friedrich M. *Jovial King: Napoleon's Youngest Brother,* H. J. Stenning, trans., London: Elkin Mathews & Marrot, 1932.

Kircheisen, Friedrich M., ed. *Feldzugserinnerungen aus dem Kriegsjahre 1809,* Hamburg: Gutenberg, 1909.

Klessmann, Eckart, ed. *Deutschland unter Napoleon in Augenzeugberichten,* Düsseldorf: Rauch, 1965.

Koch, Général. *Mémoires de Massena,* Paris: Paulin et Lechevalier, 1850.

Kummer, August. *Erinnerungen aus dem Leben eines Veteranen der Königlich Sächsischen Armee,* Dresden: Meinhold & Söhne, n.d.

[Larisch, Ferdinand von]. 'Meine zweite Campagne (Aus dem Tagebuche eines Verstorbenen)', *Bautzener Nachrichten,* Nos. 21-25, 1883.

Lejeune, Louis-François. *Memoirs of Baron Lejeune,* Felling: Worley, 1987.

Leszczynski, Stanislaus von, ed. *Kriegerleben des Johann von Borcke 1806-1815,* Berlin: Mittler & Sohn, 1888.

Liverpool, Lord Russell of. *Bernadotte,* London: Ascent Books, 1981.

Madroux, Ludwig von. 'August von Floret', *Archiv für Offiziere aller Waffen,* Jahrgang 3, Band 2, 1846.

Mändler, Friedrich. *Erinnerungen aus meinen Feldzügen,* Franz J. A. Schneidawind, ed., Nürnberg: Lotzbeck, 1854.

Marbot, Jean-Baptiste-Antoine-Marcelin. *The Memoirs of Baron de Marbot,* Arthur J. Butler, trans., London: Longmans, Green, and Co., 1905.

Marmont, Marshal Auguste-Frédéric-Louis Viesse de. *Mémoires du Maréchal Duc de Raguse de 1792 a 1832,* Paris: Perrotin, 1857.

Marshall-Cornwall, James. *Marshal Massena,* London: Oxford University Press, 1965.

Meibom, Heinrich Friedrich von. *Aus napoleonischer Zeit,* Leipzig: Koehler & Amelang, n.d.

Napoléon I. *Correspondence de Napoléon Ier publiée par ordre de l'Empereur Napoléon III,* Paris: Imprimerie Impériale, 1858-1870.

Obermüller, Karl F. *Aus der Zeit der Fremdherrschaft und der Befreiungskriege,* Karlsruhe: Müller, 1912.

Obser, Karl, ed. *Denkwürdigkeiten des Markgrafen Wilhelm von Baden,*

Heidelberg: Winter, 1906.

Pajol, Comte. *Pajol: Général en Chef*, Paris: Didot, 1874.

Palmer, Alan. *Bernadotte: Napoleon's Marshal, Sweden's King*, London: John Murray, 1990.

Picard, Ernest. *Préceptes et Jugements de Napoléon*, Paris: Berger-Levrault, 1913.

Pingaud, Léonce. *Bernadotte et Napoléon 1797-1814*, Paris: Plon, 1933.

Reithofer, Franz D. *Die Kriegsereignisse in Landshut am 16. und 21. April 1809 als die ersten in diesem Kriegsjahre*, Leipzig: Baumgartner, 1810.

Rühle von Lilienstern, Otto August. *Reise mit der Armee im Jahre 1809*, Rudolstadt: Hof- Buch- und Kunsthandlung, 1810.

Savary, Anne-Jean-Marie-René. *Mémoires du Duc de Rovigo*, Paris: Bossange, 1828.

Schauroth, Wilhelm Freiherr von. *Im Rheinbund-Regiment der Herzoglich Sächsischen Kontingente Koburg-Hildburghausen-Gotha-Weimar während der Feldzüge in Tirol, Spanien und Russland 1809-1813*, Alexander Freiherr von Schauroth, ed., Berlin: Mittler & Sohn, 1905.

Schlossberger, August von, ed. *Politische und Militärische Correspondez König Friedrichs von Württemberg mit Kaiser Napoleon I. 1805-1813*, Stuttgart: Kohlhammer, 1889.

Sommerock, H. 'Kriegserlebnisse im Jahre 1805 und 1809 bei Landshut und insbesondere zu Berg ob Landshut', *Verhandlungen des Historischen Vereins für Neiderbayern*, Nr. 47, 1911.

Stoll, Franz Xaver. 'Kriegsberichte aus den Jahren 1800 und 1809, was sich in der Stadt und im Landgerichte Abensberg ereignet', J. Schuegraf, ed., *Verhandlungen des Historischen Vereins für Niederbayern*, Nr. 7, 1860.

Suckow, Karl von. *Aus meinem Soldatenleben*, Stuttgart: Krabbe, 1862.

Vaudoncourt, Frédéric G. de. *Histoire politique et militaire du Prince Eugène Napoléon*, Paris: Mongie, 1828.

Walter, Jakob. *A German Conscript with Napoleon*, Otto Springer, ed. and trans., Lawrence: University of Kansas, 1938.

Watson, S. J. *By Command of the Emperor. A Life of Marshal Berthier*, Cambridge: Trotman, 1988.

Wesemann, Heinrich. *Kannonier des Kaisers*, Köln: Verlag Wissenschaft und Politik, 1971.

Williams, Oakley, ed. *In the Wake of Napoleon, Being the Memoirs (1807-1809) of Ferdinand von Funck, Lieutenant-General of the Saxon Army and Adjutant-General to the King of Saxony*, London: Lane, 1931.

Wirth, Joseph. *Le Maréchal Lefèbvre Duc de Dantzig (1755-1820)*, Paris: Perrin, 1904.

Würdinger, Josef. 'Das Leben des königl. bayerischen Generallieutenants Maxim. Grafen v. Preysing-Moos', *Verhandlungen des Historischen Vereins für Niederbayern*, Band 9, 1863.

Zimmermann, P. *Erinnerungen aus den Feldzügen des bergischen Truppen in Spanien und Russland*, Düsseldorf: Stahl, 1840.

Zwiedineck-Südenhorst, Hans von. *Erzherzog Johann von Oesterreich im*

Feldzuge von 1809, Graz: Styria, 1892.

Contingent Histories

Abriss der Grossherzoglich Hessischen Kriegs- und Truppen-Geschichte 1567-1871, Darmstadt & Leipzig: Zernin, 1886.

'Die Armee des Königreichs Westfalen', *Beiheft zum Militär-Wochenblatt*, Heft 6, 1887.

Badischer Militär-Almanach, 1 December 1854.

Badisches Staatsarchiv, Karslruhe, Kriegs-Archiv des Grossen Generalstabes, Feldzug 1809 gegen Oesterreich, Verz. 10, 48/4283.

Bernays, Guillaume. *Schicksale des Grossherzogthums Frankfurt und seiner Truppen*, Berlin: Mittler & Sohn, 1882.

Bethke, Martin. 'Frankfurter Soldaten...ein verlorener Haufen', *Zeitschrift für Heereskunde*, Nr. 284/285 (Jul/Oct), XLIII Jahrgang, 1979.

——. 'Das Fürstentum Isenburg im Rheinbund', *Zeitschrift für Heereskunde*, Nr. 302/303 (Jul/Oct), XLVI Jahrgang, 1982.

Bezzel, Oskar. *Geschichte des Königlich Bayerischen Heeres unter Max I. Joseph von 1806 (1804) bis 1825*, volume VI/1 of *Geschichte des Bayerischen Heeres*, München: Schick, 1933.

——. 'Die Massnahmen Bayerns zum Grenzschutze im Feldzuge 1809', *Darstellungen aus der Bayerischen Kriegs- und Heeresgeschichte* Heft 14, München: Lindauer, 1905.

Brabant, Artur. 'Die Sachsen in früheren Kriegen von 1740 bis 1871', in volume I of *Sachsen in grosser Zeit*, Edmund Hottenroth, ed., Leipzig, 1923.

Bucher, H. 'Die Theilnahme der sächsischen Truppen an den Kriegsereignissen vor hundert Jahren', *Dresdener Anzeiger*, 179 Jahrgang, Nos. 185 and 186 (6-7 July 1909).

Bumiller, A. 'Nassauer und Hohenzoller, Eine Erinnerung an die napoleonischen Kriegen 1809-1813', *Verbo Hohenzollerische Volkszeitung*, Nr. 218, 11 Sep 1935.

Darbou, René. 'Die Infanterie des Grossherzogtums Berg 1806/1813', *Zeitschrift für Heereskunde*, Nr. 128 (Jan 1953), Jahrgang 1953/I.

Dechend, Premier-Lieutenant. 'Das hessische Freicorps im Jahre 1809', *Jahrbücher für die deutsche Armee und Marine*, Band 54 (January-March 1885).

Düsseldorf als Garnisonstadt, Schriften des Historischen Museums und des Archivs der Stadt Düsseldorf Heft 6, Düsseldorf: Strucken, 1933.

Duvernoy, Hauptmann. *Württembergischen Heeresgeschichte*, Berlin: Eisenschmidt, 1893.

Exner, Moritz. *Die Antheilnahme der Königlich Sächsischen Armee am Feldzuge gegen Oesterreich und die kriegerischen Ereignisse in Sachsen im Jahre 1809*, Dresden: Baensch, 1894.

Fabrice, F. von. 'Nochmals die bayerische Reiter-Brigade Seydewitz bei Eggmühl', *Jahrbücher für die deutsche Armee und Marine*, vol. 65 (October-December 1887), Berlin: Wilhelm, 1887.

'Feldzug der 2ten Division 4ten Armeecorps der Armee von Teutschland im

Jahr 1809', *Pallas,* Jahrgang 2, Stück 6, 1810.

Focke, Johann. 'Vom bremischen Stadtmilitär', *Bremisches Jahrbuch,* vol. 19, 1900.

Gaedechens, C. F. *Das hamburgische Militär bis zum Jahre 1811 und die hanseatische Legion,* Hamburg: Gräfe, 1889.

Gärtner, Markus and Wagner, Edmund. *Westfälisches Militär,* Beckum: Deutsche Gesellschaft für Heereskunde, 1990.

Gerber, Kurt. 'Sigmaringen als Garnison, Sigmaringer als Soldat', in *900 Jahren Sigmaringen 1077-1977,* Sigmaringen, 1977.

Haffner, J. D. *Geschichtliche Darstellung des Grossherzoglich Badischen Armee-Corps,* Karlsruhe: Malsch und Vogel, 1840.

Hagen, Benno von. *Das Reussische Militär in den Kriegsjahren 1806-15,* Gera-Reuss: Lange, 1904.

Hauthal, Ferdinand. *Geschichte der Sächsischen Armee in Wort und Bild,* Leipzig: Schrader, 1859.

Hellrung. 'Die Organisation der Westphälischen Armee', *Minerva,* Band 4, 1840.

Helmes, Hermann. 'Die Würzburger Truppen vor hundert Jahren', *Archiv des historischen Vereins von Unterfranken und Aschaffenburg,* Nr. 55, 1913.

Hermes, Sabina and Niemeyer, Joachim. *Unter dem Greifen: Altbadisches Militär von der Vereinigung der Markgrafschaften bis zur Reichsgründung 1771-1871,* Karlsruhe: Braun, 1984.

Herrmann, Friedrich. 'Bergische Reiter', *Zeitschrift für Heereskunde,* Nr. 287 (Jan/Feb 1980).

——. 'Eine Bildersammlung aus dem Kriege in Spanien 1808-1813', *Zeitschrift für Heereskunde,* 1989-1991.

Hessisches Staatsarchiv, Darmstadt, file E8C, Nr. 17/12.

Hewig, W. 'Die Armee des Königreichs Westfalen 1808-13', *Zeitschrift für Heeres- und Uniformskunde,* Nos. 142/143 (May/Jul 1955), 144/145 (Sep/Nov 1955) and 146/147 (Jan/Mar 1956).

J., M. 'Die bayerische Reiter-Brigade Seydewitz bei Eggmühl', *Jahrbücher für die deutsche Armee und Marine,* vol. 63 (April-June 1887), Berlin: Wilhem, 1887.

Jacobs, Gustav. *Geschichte der Feldzüge und Schicksale der Gotha-Altenburgischen Krieger in den Jahren 1807-1815,* Altenburg: Gleich, 1835.

Kattrein, Ludwig. *Ein Jahrhundert deutscher Truppengeschichte dargestellt an derjenigen des Grossh. Hessischen Kontingents 1806-1906,* Darmstadt: Schlapp, 1907.

Kessler, St. 'Das hohenzollerische Militär vor 150 Jahren im Dienste Napoleons', *Hohenzollerische Heimat,* 12 Jahrgang, Nr. 3 (Jul 1962).

Keubke, Klaus-Ulrich. 'Versuch einer formationsgeschichtlichen Betrachtung: Mecklenburg', *Zeitschrift für Heereskunde,* Nos. 349 (May/Jun), 350/351 (Jul/Oct) and 352 (Nov/Dec), LIV Jahrgang, 1990.

Kolb, R. *Unter Nassaus Fahnen,* Wiesbaden: Bechtold, 1904.

Kopp, Walter. *Würzburger Wehr,* vol. 22 of *Mainfränkische Studien,*

Würzburg: Freunde der Mainfränkische Kunst und Geschichte, 1979.

Kösterus, Martin. *Geschichtliche Darstellung der Entwicklung der Militär-Verfassung der Hessen-Darmstädtischen Truppen seit Phillip dem Grossmüthigen bis auf unsere Tage. Nebst den Feldzügen welchen dieselben von 1792 bis 1815 beigewohnt haben,* Darmstadt: Brill, 1840.

Kraft, Heinz. *Die Württemberger in den Napoleonischen Kriegen,* Stuttgart: Kohlhammer, 1953.

Kraus, Jürgen. 'Das Regensburger Bürgermilitär in der fürstprimatischen Zeit: Infanterie', *Zeitschrift für Heereskunde,* Nr. 359 (Jan/Feb), LVI Jahrgang, 1992.

'Die leichte württembergische Brigade Hügel in dem Gefechte bei Linz, im Jahre 1809', *Archiv für Offiziere aller Waffen,* Jahrgang 4, Band 3, 1847.

Leyh, Max. *Die Feldzüge des Königlich Bayerischen Heeres unter Max I. Joseph von 1805 bis 1815,* volume VI/2 of *Geschichte des Bayerischen Heeres,* München: Schick, 1935.

Lipowsky. *Bürger-Militär-Almanach für das Königreich Bayern 1809,* München: Fleischmann, 1809.

Lünsmann, Fritz. *Die Armee des Königreichs Westfalen 1807-1813,* Berlin: Leddihn, 1935.

Madaus, Christian, ed. *Beiträge Mecklenburgische Militärgeschichte von 1700 bis 1871,* Hamburg: Krüger & Nienstadt, 1980.

Madroux, Ludwig von. 'Die bayerische Kavallerie-Brigade Seydewitz in der Schlacht von Eggmühl (22. April 1809)', *Archiv für Offiziere aller Waffen,* Jahrgang 2, Band 2, 1845.

Meinhard, J. M. *Geschichte des Reussischen Militairs bis zum Jahre 1815,* Gera: Blachmann und Bornstein, 1842.

Münich, Friedrich. *Geschichte der Entwicklung der bayerischen Armee seit zwei Jahrhunderten,* München: Lindauer, 1864.

Nafziger, George. *The Wurttemburg Army,* Leeds: Raider Books, 1987.

——. *The Bavarian and Westphalian Armies 1799-1815,* Cambridge: RAFM, 1981.

——. *The Armies of Kingdom of Bavaria and the Grand Duchy of Würzburg 1792-1815,* privately published, 1991.

——. *The Armies of Westphalia and Cleves-Berg 1806-1815,* privately published, 1991.

Nafziger, George; Wesolowski, Mariusz T.; and Devoe, Tom. *Poles and Saxons of the Napoleonic Wars,* Chicago: The Emperor's Press, 1991.

Nettesheim, Oberstleutnant. 'Studie zur Geschichte der Garnison und Festung Düsseldorf', 1941, manuscript in the collection of the Zentralbibliothek der Bundeswehr, Düsseldorf.

Oesterhaus, Wilhelm. *Geschichte der Fürstlich Lippischen Truppen in den Jahren 1807-1815,* Detmold: Meyer, 1907.

Paulus, G. 'Bayerische Kriegsvorbereitungen, Mobilmachung und Einleitung zum Feldzuge 1809', *Darstellungen aus der Bayerischen Kriegs- und Heeresgeschichte,* Heft 2, München: Lindauer, 1893.

Pfaff, Karl. *Geschichte des Militärwesens in Württemberg von der ältesten bis auf unsere Zeit*, Stuttgart: Schweizerbart, 1842.

Pilzecker, Carl. 'Scenen aus dem Feldzuge der Sachsen in Oesterreich, und zwar vor, während und nach der Schlacht bei Deutsch-Wagram; vom 2. bis mit dem 27. Juli 1809', *Sachsenzeitung*, No. 233 ff., August-September 1830.

Pivka, Otto von. *Napoleon's German Allies (1): Westfalia and Kleve-Berg*, London: Osprey, 1975.

——. *Napoleon's German Allies (2): Nassau and Oldenburg*, London: Osprey, 1976.

——. *Napoleon's German Allies (3): Saxony*, London: Osprey, 1979.

——. *Napoleon's German Allies (4): Bavaria*, London: Osprey, 1980.

——. *Napoleon's German Allies (5): Hessen-Darmstadt & Hessen-Kassel*, London: Osprey, 1982.

——. *Napoleon's Polish Troops*, New York: Hippocrene, 1974.

Rattelmüller, Paul E. *Das Bayerische Bürgermilitär*, München: Süddeutscher Verlag, 1969.

Rawkins, W. J. *The Armies of Naples & Kleve-Berg 1806-1814*, Rawkins, 1978.

——. *The Armies of Baden and Württemberg 1806-1814*, Rawkins, 1984.

[Roessler]. *Tagebücher aus den zehen Feldzügen der Württemberger unter der Regierung König Friedrichs*, Ludwigsburg: Nast, 1820.

Rössler, Ph. von. *Die Geschichte der Herzoglich Nassauischen Truppen*, Wiesbaden: Stein, 1863.

Runkel, Major von. 'Zur Geschichte der Besatzung der Burg Hohenzollern und der Truppen der Fürsten von Hohenzollern von 1806 bis 1815', *Mittheilungen des Vereins für Geschichte und Altertumskunde in Hohenzollern*, XXXIII Jahrgang 1899/1900.

'Das 2. sächsische Schützenbataillon in der Schlacht bei Wagram am 5. Juli 1809', *Sachsen-Post*, 14 July 1909.

'Die sächsischen Husaren im Feldzuge von 1809 in Oestreich', *Zeitschrift für Kunst, Wissenschaft und Geschichte des Krieges*, Heft 7, Jahrgang 1847.

Sauer, Paul. 'Die Neuorganisation des württembergischen Heerwesens unter Herzog, Kurfürst und König Friedrich', *Zeitschrift für Württembergischen Landesgeschichte*, Jahrgang XXVI, 1967.

Sauzey, Commandant. *Les Allemands sous les Aigles Françaises*, 6 vols., Paris: Terana, 1987-88.

Schäfer, Ernst. 'Mecklenburgs Militärwesen vor und in den Freiheitskriegen', *Jahrbuch des Vereins für mecklenburgischen Geschichte und Altertumskunde*, Jahrgang LXXX, 1915.

Schmelzing, Julius. *Darstellung der mobilen Legionen oder der Nationalgarde IIter Klasse im Königreich Bayern aus den Gesetzes-Quellen*, Nürnberg: Zeh, 1818.

Schüler, *Geschichte des schwarzburg-rudolstädtischen Contingents in den Kriegsjahren von 1807 bis 1815*, Rudolstadt: Bock, 1883.

Schuster, O. and Francke, F. A. *Geschichte der Sächsischen Armee von deren Errichtung bis auf die neueste Zeit*, vol. II, Leipzig: Duncker & Humblot, 1885.

'Skizze zur Organisations- und Formations-Geschichte der Bayerischen Artillerie', Bavarian Kriegsarchiv, *Darstellungen aus der Bayerischen Kriegs- und Heeresgeschichte,* Heft 10, München: Lindauer, 1901.

Stadlinger, Leo I. von. *Geschichte des Württembergischen Kriegswesens,* Stuttgart: Guttenberg, 1856.

Stahlberg, Hans. 'Reussisches Militär bis zum Ende der Befreiungskriege', *Zeitschrift für Heereskunde,* Nr. 269 (Jan/Feb), XLI Jahrgang, 1977.

——. 'Das Sicherheitskorps im Bergischen Land', *Zeitschrift für Heereskunde,* 1978.

Steinmann, Paul. *Die Mecklb.-Strelitzsche Landgendarmerie,* Schönberg: Hempel, n. d.

Tarnow, Gerhard. 'Die Aufstellung des Mecklenburg-Strelitzer Rheinbundkontingents und des Vaterländischen Husaren-Regiments 1808-1817', *Mecklenburg-Strelitzer Geschichtsblätter,* Jahrgang X/XI, 1935.

Theilnahme der Grossherz. Hess. Truppen an dem Kriege zwischen Oestreich und Frankreich im Jahre 1809, (written in October 1809), Darmstadt: Auw, 1850.

Treitschke, Eduard von. 'Die königl. sächsischen Truppen in der Schlacht bei Wagram, am 5. und 6. Juli 1809', *Zeitschrift für Kunst, Wissenschaft und Geschichte des Krieges,* Band 34, Jahrgang 1838.

Uebe, Kurt. *Die Stimmungsumschwung in der Bayerischen Armee gegenüber den Franzosen 1806-1812,* München: Beck, 1939.

Ulmenstein, Christian Ulrich Freiherr von. *Die Offiziere des Schaumburg-Lippischen Truppenkorps 1648-1867,* Berlin: Verlag für Standesamtswesen, 1940.

Veling, Captaine. *Nos Alliés Allemands,* Paris: Frères, 1909.

Verlohren, Heinrich A. *Stammregister und Chronik der Kur- und Königlich Sächsischen Armee von 1670 bis zum Beginn des Zwanzigsten Jahrhunderts,* Leipzig: Beck, 1910.

Völderndorff und Waradein, Eduard Freiherr von. *Kriegsgeschichte von Bayern unter König Maximilian Joseph I.,* 4 vols., München, 1826.

Wacker, Peter. 'Der württembergische Feldzug gegen die Vorarlberger 1809', *Die Zinnfigur,* 8. Jahrgang, 1959.

——. 'Das nassauische Militärwesen', in *Herzogtum Nassau 1806-1866,* Wiesbaden, 1981.

——. 'Grossherzoglich Frankfurtische, fürstlich Primatische Soldaten 1806-1813', *Zeitschrift für Heereskunde,* Nr. 304 (Nov/Dec), XLVI Jahrgang, 1982.

——. *Das Herzoglich Nassauische Militär 1806-1866,* Taunusstein: Schellenberg, 1985.

Wardenburg, Wilhelm G. F. 'Uebersicht der bewaffneten Macht und der kriegerischen Einrichtungen Oldenburgs, vom 15ten Jahrhundert bis auf die neuesten Zeiten, in chronologischer Ordnung', *Oldenburgische Blätter,* August 1826

Wengen, Freiherr von der. *Der Feldzug der Grossherzoglich Badischen Truppen unter Oberst Freiherrn Karl v. Stockhorn gegen die Vorarlberger und Tiroler 1809*, Heidelberg: Winter, 1910.

Werlhof, Generalmajor von. 'Bernadotte und die Sachsen bei Wagram. 5. und 6. Juli 1809', *Beiheft zum Militär-Wochenblatt,* Heft 1, 1911.

Wilhelm Gustav Friedrich Wardenburg (1781-1838). Oldenburgischer Soldat, Altertumsforscher und Sammler. Eine Austellung zum 200. Geburtstag im Oldenburger Stadtmuseum, Oldenburg, 1981.

Wolf, Gustav. *Der Eilmarsch Wrede's von Linz bis Wagram,* Innsbruck: Wagner, 1909.

Woringer, August. 'Geschichte des Fürstlich Isenburgischen Militärs 1806-1816', 1953.

Württembergisches Militärarchiv, Stuttgart, files D64, E270b, E270e, E271a, E271e.

Zech, Karl von and Porbeck, Friedrich von. *Geschichte der Badischen Truppen 1809 im Feldzug der Französischen Hauptarmee gegen Oesterreich,* Rudolf von Freydorf, ed., Heidelberg: Winter, 1909.

Regimental Histories

Ardenne, Freiherr von. *Bergische Lanziers, Westfälische Husaren Nr. 11,* Berlin: Mittler & Sohn, 1877.

Aubier, Lieutenant. *Un Régiment de Cavalerie Légère,* (20th Chasseurs) Paris: Berger-Levrault, 1888.

Auvera, Premierlieutenant. *Geschichte des Kgl. Bayer. 7. Infanterie-Regiments Prinz Leopold von Bayern,* Bayreuth: Ellwanger, 1898.

Bahls, G. *Das 3. badische Dragoner-Regiment Prinz Karl Nr. 22,* Berlin: Bernard & Graefe, 1934.

Barsewisch, Theophil von. *Geschichte des Grossherzoglich Badischen Leib-Grenadier-Regiments 1803-1870,* Karlsruhe: Müller, 1893.

Beck, Fritz. *Geschichte des Grossherzoglich Hessischen Gendarmeriekorps 1763-1905,* Darmstadt: Hohmann, 1905.

Beck, Fritz; Hahn, Karl von; and Hahn, Heinrich von. *Geschichte des Grossherzoglichen Artilleriekorps 1. Grossherzoglich Hessischen Feldartillerie-Regiments Nr. 25 und seiner Stämme,* Berlin: Mittler & Sohn, 1912.

Berg, Franz. *Geschichte des königl. Bayer. 4. Jäger-Bataillons,* Landshut: Rietsch, 1887.

Bezzel, Oskar. *Das K. B. 4. Infanterie-Regiment König Wilhelm von Württemberg vom Jahre 1806-1906,* München: Lindauer, 1906.

Bigge, W. *Geschichte des Infanterie-Regiments Kaiser Wilhelm (2. Grossherzoglich Hessisches) Nr. 116,* Berlin: Mittler & Sohn, 1903.

Bonie, A. *Historique du 3e Régiment de Chasseurs,* manuscript, 1875-1876.

Bray, Graf von. *Geschichte des 1. Badischen Leib-Dragoner-Regiments Nr. 20 und dessen Stammregiments des Badischen Dragoner-Regiments von Freystedt von 1803 bis zur Gegenwart,* Berlin: Mittler & Sohn, 1909.

Buxbaum, Emil. *Das königlich Bayerische 3. Chevaulegers-Regiment 'Herzog Maximilian' 1724 bis 1884,* München: Oldenbourg, 1884.

Caspary, E. *Geschichte des dritten Grossherzoglich Hessischen Infanterie-*

Regiments (Leib-Regiments) Nr. 117, Darmstadt: Lange, 1877.

Castillon de Saint-Victor, M. de. *Historique du 5ᵉ Régiment de Hussards,* Paris: Lobert/Person, 1889.

Champvallier, H. de. *Historique du 9ᵉᵐᵉ Régiment de Chasseurs à Cheval,* manuscript, 1890.

Chavane, J. *Histoire du 11ᵉ Cuirassiers,* Paris: Charavay, 1889.

Chevillotte, Lieutenant. *Historique du 16ᵉᵐᵉ Chasseurs à Cheval,* manuscript, 1887.

Dalwigk zu Lichtenfels, Freiherr von. *Geschichte der waldeckischen und kurhessischen Stammtruppen des Infanterie-Regiments v. Wittich (3. Kurhess.) Nr. 83. 1681-1866,* Oldenburg: Littmann, 1909.

Dauer, Joseph. *Das königlich Bayerische 10. Infanterie-Regiment Prinz Ludwig,* Ingolstadt: Ganghofer, 1901.

d'Ivry, Ogier. *Historique du 9ᵉ Régiment de Hussards,* Valence: Ceas, 1891.

Döderlein, Oberstlieutenant. *Geschichte des Königlich Bayerischen 8. Infanterie-Regiments (Pranckh),* Landshut: Rietsch, 1898.

Döring, Hans von. *Geschichte des 7. Thüringischen Infanterie-Regiments Nr. 96.,* Berlin: Mittler & Sohn, 1890.

Dupuy, Raoul. *Historique du 12ᵉ Chasseurs de 1788 à 1891,* Paris: Person, 1891.

Eck, Rittmeister von. *Geschichte des 2. Westfälischen Husaren-Regiments Nr. 11 und seiner Stammtruppen von 1807-1893,* Mainz: Militär-Verlagsanstalt, 1893.

Fabrice, F. von. *Das Königlich Bayerischen 6. Infanterie-Regiment Kaiser Wilhelm, König von Preussen,* München: Oldenbourg, 1896.

Feill, Heinrich. *Das 3. Badische Infanterie-Regiment Nr. 111 im Feldzuge 1870/71 nebst einer kurzen Vorgeschichte der badischen Truppen von 1604 bis 1850 und von der Errichtung des Regiments 1852 bis 1870,* Berlin: Mittler & Sohn, 1884.

Felder, R. M. *Der schwarze Jäger oder Württembergs Krieger in den Jahren 1805-1816,* Cannstatt: Ruckhäberle, 1839.

Ferber, A. *Geschichte des 1. Badischen Feldartillerie-Regiments Nr. 14,* Karlsruhe: Müller, 1906.

Fiebig, Rittmeister. 'Das Bataillon des Princes', *Zeitschrift für Heeres- und Uniformkunde,* Heft 61/63 (Jan 1934).

——. 'Das 4., 5. und 6. Rheinbund-Regiment', *Zeitschrift für Heeres- und Uniformkunde,* Heft 64/66 (Apr 1934).

Finckh, Eduard von. *Geschichte des Oldenburgischen Infanterie-Regiments Nr. 91,* Berlin: Mittler & Sohn, 1881.

Formanek, Jaromir. *Geschichte des k. k. Infanterie-Regiments Nr. 41,* Czernowitz: Czopp, 1887.

Friedel, Hauptmann. *Geschichte des 7. Infanterie-Regiments 'König Georg' Nr. 106,* Leipzig: Jacobsen, n.d.

Fromm, Hauptmann. *Geschichte des Infanterie-Regiments König Wilhelm I (6. Württ.) Nr. 124.,* Weingarten: regimental, 1901.

Füchtbauer, Heinrich. 'Geschichte der Stammtruppen des K. B. 14. Infanterie-

Regiments', part I of *Festschrift zur Jahrhundertfeier des k. b. 14. Infanterie-Regiments Hartmann*, Nürnberg: Stich, 1914.

Gerneth, Major and Kiessling, Premierlieutenant. *Geschichte des Königlich Bayerischen 5. Infanterie-Regiments,* Berlin: Mittler & Sohn, 1893.

Geschichte des Königl. Sächs. Königs-Husaren-Regiments No. 18, Leipzig: Baumert & Ronge, 1901.

Geschichte des Königlich Sächsischen 3. Infanterie-Regiments Nr. 102 'Prinz-Regent Luitpold von Bayern' 1709-1909, Berlin: Mittler & Sohn, 1909.

Geschichte des Königl. Sächs. Schützen-Regiments 'Prinz Georg' No. 108, Leipzig: Jacobsen, n.d.

Geschichte des 8. Thüringischen Infanterie-Regiments Nr. 153 und seiner Stammtruppen, Leipzig: Jacobsen, n.d.

Geschichte des 3. Württ. Infanterie-Regiments No. 121 1716-1891, Stuttgart: Kohlhammer, 1891.

Geschichte des Ulanen-Regiments 'König Karl' (1. Württembergisches) Nr. 19., n.d.

Gessler, Tognarelli, and Strobl. *Geschichte des 2. Württembergischen Feldartillerie-Regiments Nr. 29*, Stuttgart: regimental, 1892.

Gleich, Rittmeister. *Die ersten 100 Jahre des Ulanen-Regiments König Wilhelm I. (2. Württemb.) Nr. 20.*, Stuttgart: Uhland, n.d.

——. *Ulanen-Regiment 'König Wilhelm I.' (2. Württ.) Nr. 20.*, Sammlung kurzer Regimentsgeschichten Nr. 5., Stuttgart: Moritz, n.d.

Greisinger, Theodor. *Geschichte des Ulanenregiments 'König Karl' (1. Württembergischen) Nr. 19 von seiner Gründung 1683 bis zur Gegenwart*, Stuttgart: Deutsche Verlags-Anstalt, 1883.

Grosch, Feodor; Hagen, Eduard; and Schenk, Albert. *Geschichte des K. B. 12. Infanterie-Regiments Prinz Arnulf und seiner Stammabteilungen*, München, 1914.

H., M. *Kurze Darstellung der Geschichte des Königlich Bayerischen 4. Chevaulegers-Regiments 'König' von 1744 bis zur Gegenwart*, Berlin: Mittler & Sohn, 1895.

Haevernick, Oskar. *Kurze Darstellung der Geschichte des Grossherzoglich Mecklenburgischen Füsilier-Regiments Nr. 90, 1788-1892*, Berlin: Mittler & Sohn, 1899.

Heinze, E. *Geschichte des Kgl. Bayer. 6. Chevaulegers-Regiments 'Prinz Albrecht von Preussen'*, Leipzig: Klinkhardt, 1898.

Hermannsthal, Friedrich von. *Geschichte des Tyroler Feld- und Land-, später 46. Linien-Infanterie- Regiments*, Krakau: Czas., 1859.

Herrman, Pfarrer Heinrich. *Geschichte des Königlich Sächsischen Leibgrenadier-Regiments Nr. 100*, Zittau: Mönch, n.d.

Histoire du 1er Régiment de Cuirassiers, Angers: Lachese & Dolbeau, 1889.

Histoire Militaire: 5eme de Cuirassiers, manuscript.

Historique du 19e Chasseurs à Cheval, manuscript, 1878.

Historique du 10e Régiment de Cuirassiers, manuscript, 1892.

Holtzendorff, Albrecht von. *Geschichte der Königlich Sächsischen Leichten Infanterie von Ihrer Errichtung bis zum 1. October 1859*, Leipzig: Geisecke

& Devrient, 1860.

'Das k. k. Husaren-Regiment Palatinal im Feldzuge 1809', *Oesterreichische militärische Zeitschrift*, Heft 6, 1847.

Hutter, Herman. *Das Königlich Bayerische 1. Chevaulegers-Regiment 'Kaiser Alexander von Russland' 1682 bis 1882*, München: Oldenburg, 1885.

Johann, Erzherzog von Oesterreich. *Geschichte des K. K. Linien-Infanterie-Regiments Erzherzog Wilhelm No. 12*, Wien: Seidel & Sohn, 1877.

Käuffer, Hauptmann. *Geschichte des königlich bayerischen 9. Infanterie-Regiments Wrede*, Würzburg: Ballhorn und Craner, 1895.

Keim, A. *Geschichte des Infanterie-Leibregiments Grossherzogin (3. Grossherzogl. Hessisches) Nr. 117*, Berlin: Bath, 1903.

Klingelhöffer, Hauptmann. *Geschichte des 2. Grossherzoglich Hessischen Infanterie-Regiments (Grossherzog) Nr. 116*, Berlin: Mittler & Sohn, 1888.

Kneussl, Hauptmann. *Geschichte des K. bayer. 2. (vormals 3.) Jäger-Bataillons*, Würzburg: Stürtz, 1899.

Köberle, Rudolf. *Geschichte des 4. Württemb. Infanterie-Regiments Nr. 122 von seiner Gründung 1806 bis 1874*, Ludwigsburg: regimental, 1881.

Kortzfleisch, Gustav von. *Geschichte des Herzoglich Braunschweigischen Infanterie-Regiments und seiner Stammtruppen 1809-1867*, Braunschweig: Limbach, 1896.

Kretschmar, A. von. *Geschichte der kurfürstlich und königlich Sächsischen Feld-Artillerie von 1620-1820*, Berlin: Mittler & Sohn, 1876.

'Das Kürassier-Regiment Kronprinz Ferdinand in der Schlacht bei Wagram am 5. und 6. Juli 1809', *Oesterreichische militärische Zeitschrift*, Heft 6, 1844.

Küster, Hans. *Geschichte des Anhaltischen Infanterie-Regiments Nr. 93.*, Berlin: Mittler & Sohn, 1893.

Langermann und Erlencamp, Rudolph Freiherr von and Voigts-Rhetz, Werner von. *Geschichte des Grossherzoglich Mecklenburgischen Grenadier-Regiments Nr. 89*, Schwerin: Stiller, 1895.

Lantz, Georg. *Geschichte der Stammtruppen des 6. Thüringischen Infanterie-Regiments Nr. 95*, Braunschweig: Sattler, 1897.

Larrass, Johannes Anton. *Geschichte des Königlich Sächsischen 6. Infanterie-Regiments Nr. 105 und seine Vorgeschichte 1701 bis 1887*, Strassburg: Kayser, 1887.

Legde, Adolf. *Geschichte des 2. Badischen Dragoner-Regiments Nr. 21*, Berlin: Mittler & Sohn, 1893.

Lichterfeld, M. S. von. *Regiments-Geschichte des Königlich Sächsischen Garde-Reiter-Regiments*, Berlin: Vobach, 1904.

Lommatzsch, Carl. *Geschichte des 4. Infanterie-Regiments Nr. 103*, Dresden: Heinrich, 1909.

Louvat, Captaine. *Historique du 7ème Hussards*, Paris: Pairault, 1889.

Margon, Comte de. *Historique du 8e Régiment de Chasseurs*.

Marx, Karl. *Geschichte des Infanterie-Regiments Kaiser Friedrich, König von Preussen (7. Württembergischen) Nr. 125. 1809-1895*, Berlin: Mittler & Sohn, 1895.

Masse, P. *Le 19e Régiment d'Infanterie à travers l'Histoire 1597-1923*, Paris:

Morlaix, 1923.

Moine de Margon, Lieutenant-Colonel le. *Historique du 11e Régiment de Chasseurs,* Vesoul: Bon, 1896.

Muff, Karl and Wencher, Hauptmann. *Geschichte des Grenadier-Regiments König Karl (5. Württembergischen) Nro. 123.*, Stuttgart: Metzler, 1889.

Müller, Herbert. *Füsilier-Regiment Kaiser Franz Joseph von Oesterreich, König von Ungarn (4. Württemb.) Nr. 122.*, 'Die Achselklappe' Sammlung kurzer Regimentsgeschichten Nr. 6, Stuttgart: Uhland, n.d.

——. *Geschichte des 4. Württembergischen Infanterie-Regiments No. 122 Kaiser Franz Joseph von Oesterreich, König von Ungarn 1806-1906,* Heilbronn: Scheuerlen, 1906.

Neff, W. *Geschichte des Infanterie-Regiments von Goeben (2. Rheinischen) Nr. 28,* Berlin: Mittler & Sohn, 1890.

Neubronner, Oberleutnant von. *Geschichte des Dragoner-Regiments König (2. Württ.) Nr. 26.*, Stuttgart: regimental, n.d.

Niethammer, Georg von. *Geschichte des Grenadierregiments Königin Olga,* Stuttgart: Kohlhammer, 1886.

Nübling, Oberleutnant. *Geschichte des Grenadier-Regiments König Karl (5. Württembergischen) Nr. 123.*, Berlin: Eisenschmidt, 1911.

Obpacher, Josef. *Das k. b. 2. Chevaulegers-Regiment Taxis,* München: Bayerisches Kriegsarchiv, 1926.

Ondarza, Oberleutnant von. *Geschichte der Grossherzoglich Mecklenburgischen Artillerie,* Leipzig-Dresden: Rissarth, 1913.

Oré, C. *1er Régiment de Chasseurs,* Chateaudun: Laussedat, 1903.

Otterstedt, Hauptmann von. *Das 8. Thür. Inf.-Regiment No. 153 und seine Altenburger Stammtruppen,* Altenburg: Bonde, 1898.

Petermann, Premierlieutenant. *Geschichte des Infanterieregiments Kaiser Wilhelm König von Preussen (2. Württ.) Nr. 120.*, Stuttgart: Kohlhammer, 1890.

Pfannenberg, Leo von. *Geschichte des Infanterie-Regiments Grossherzog von Sachsen (5. Thüringisches) Nr. 94 und seiner Stammtruppen 1702-1912,* Berlin: Stilke, 1912.

Pfeffer, J. *Geschichte des K. bayer. 15. Infanterie-Regiments König Friedrich August von Sachsen von 1722 bis 1907,* Neuburg a. Donau: Griessmayer, 1907.

Pfister, Albert von. *Infanterie-Regiment 'König Wilhelm I.' (6. Württ.) Nr. 124.*, 'Die Achselklappe' Sammlung kurzer Regimentsgeschichten Nr. 7., Stuttgart: Moritz, n.d.

——. *Denkwüdigkeiten aus der württembergischen Kriegsgeschichte des 18. und 19. Jahrhunderts im Anschluss an die Geschichte des 8. Infanterieregiments,* Stuttgart: Grüninger, 1868.

——. *Geschichte des 1. württ. Infanterieregiments,* Stuttgart: Kirn, 1875.

——. *Das Infanterieregiment Kaiser Wilhelm, König von Preussen (2. Württ.) No. 120.*, Stuttgart: Metzler, 1881.

[Prielmeyer, Max von]. *Geschichte des k. b. I. Infanterie-Regiments König,* München: Huttler, 1881.

Puttkamer, General-Major von. *Kurze Geschichte des II. Bataillons Grossherzoglich Mecklenburgischen Grenadier-Regiments 89,* Neubrandenburg: Feller, n.d.

Quinemont, Commandant de. *Historique du 2ᵉ Régiment de Chasseurs à Cheval,* manuscript, 1888.

Rau, Ferdinand. *Geschichte des 1. Badischen Leib-Dragoner Regiments Nr. 20 und dessen Stamm-Regiments von Freystedt von 1803 bis zur Gegenwart,* Berlin: Mittler & Sohn, 1878.

Reichert, Moritz Ritter von. *Das Königlich Bayerische 2. Infanterie-Regiment 'Kronprinz',* München: Oldenbourg, 1913.

Renschler, Adolph. 'Die badischen Husaren', 1978, unpublished manuscript in the collection of the Wehrgeschichtliches Museum Rastatt.

Röder, Fritz. *Geschichte des bisherigen K. B. 4. Jäger-Bataillons und seiner Stamm-Abteilungen,* Landshut: Rietsch, 1890.

Röder von Diersburg, Carl Christian Freiherr von. *Geschichte des 1. Grossherzoglich Hessischen Infanterie- (Leibgarde-) Regiments Nr. 115,* Fritz Beck, ed., Berlin: Mittler & Sohn, 1899.

Roessler, Alfred von. *Geschichte des Königlich Preussischen 1. Nassauischen Infanterie-Regiments Nr. 87 und seines Stammes des Herzoglich Nassauischen 1. Infanterie-Regiments 1809-1874,* Berlin: Mittler & Sohn, 1882.

Ruith, Max. *Das k. bayerische 10. Infanterie-Regiment 'Prinz Ludwig',* Ingolstadt: Ganghofer, 1882.

———. *Das K. Bayer. 12. Infanterie-Regiment 'Prinz Arnulf',* Ulm: Ebner, 1902.

Ruith, Max and Ball, Emil. *Kurze Geschichte des K. B. 3. Infanterie-Regiments Prinz Karl von Bayern,* Ingolstadt, 1890.

Schäfer, Ernst. 'Mecklenburgs Militärwesen vor und in den Freiheitskriegen', *Jahrbuch des Vereins für mecklenburgische Geschichte,* LXXX.

Schimpff, Georg von. *Geschichte des Kgl. Sächs. Garde-Reiter-Regiments,* Dresden: Baensch, 1880.

Schimpff, H. von. *Geschichte der beiden Königlich Sächsischen Grenadier-Regimenter: Erstes (Leib-) Grenadier-Regiment Nr. 100 und Zweites Grenadier-Regiment Nr. 101, Kaiser Wilhelm, König von Preussen,* Dresden: Höckner, 1877.

Schneidawind, Franz J. A. *Das Regiment der Herzoge von Sachsen in den blutigen Tagen des 4. und 5. August 1809 bei Ober- und Unter-Au in dem Kriege in Tirol,* Aschaffenburg: Wailandt, 1852.

Schönberg, Georg von. *Geschichte des Königl. Sächsischen 7. Infanterie-Regiments 'Prinz Georg' Nr. 106,* Leipzig: Brockhaus, 1890.

Schubert, Franz und Vara, Hans. *Geschichte des K. B. 13. Infanterie-Regiments,* vol. I, München: Lindauer, 1906.

Schwarzbach, Moriz. *Gedenkblätter aus der Geschichte des k. k. 3. Dragoner-Regimentes Johann, König von Sachsen,* Wien: Hof- und Staatsdruckerei, 1868.

Seebach, Ludwig Freiherr von. *Geschichte der Feldzüge des Herzoglich Sachsen-Weimarischen Scharfschützenbataillons im Jahr 1806 und des*

Infanterieregiments der Herzöge von Sachsen in den Jahren 1807, 1809, 1810 und 1811, Weimar: Voigt, 1838.

Sichlern, Oskar von. *Geschichte des königlich bayerischen 5. Chevaulegers-Regiments 'Prinz Otto',* München: regimental, 1876.

Spiess, Karl and Ritter, Hans. *Geschichte des Dragoner-Regiments Königin Olga (1. Württ.) Nr. 25.,* Ludwigsburg: regimental, n.d.

Starklof, R. *Geschichte des Königlich Württembergischen Zweiten Reiter-Regiments ehemaligen Jäger-Regiments zu Pferde Herzog Louis,* Darmstadt & Leipzig: Zernin, 1862.

———. *Geschichte des Königlich Württembergischen vierten Reiterregiments Königin Olga 1805-1866,* Stuttgart: Aue, 1867.

Steinmann, Paul. *Die Meckl.-Strelitzsche Landgendarmerie, ihre Vorgeschichte, ihre Gründung im Jahre 1798 und ihre weitere Entwicklung,* Schönberg: Hempel, n.d.

Strack von Weisenbach, Hauptmann. *Geschichte der Königlich Württembergischen Artillerie,* Stuttgart: Kohlhammer, 1882.

Strobl von Ravelsberg, Ferdinand. *Geschichte des k. und k. 12. Dragoner-Regiments seit seiner Errichtung bis zur Gegenwart 1798-1890,* Wien: regimental, 1890.

Süssmilch gen. Hörnig, M. von. *Geschichte des 2. Königl. Sächs. Husaren-Regiments 'Kronprinz Friedrich Wilhelm des Deutschen Reichs und von Preussen' Nr. 19,* Leipzig: Brockhaus, 1882.

Umhey, Alfred. 'Das Infanterie-Bataillon des Grossherzogtums Frankfurt 1808-1813', *Das Bote aus dem Wehrgeschichtlichen Museum,* Heft 17, Jahrgang 9, 1985.

Walz, Hauptmann. *Geschichte des Linien-Infanterie-Regiments Grossherzog Nro. 1.,* 2 vols., 1843-44, manuscript in the collection of the Wehrgeschichtliches Museum Rastatt.

Wellmann, Hauptmann. *Geschichte des Infanterie-Regiments von Horn (3tes Rheinisches) No. 29,* Trier: Lintz, 1894.

Weltzien, Louis von. *Militärische Studien aus Oldenburgs Vorzeit und Geschichte des Oldenburgischen Contingents,* Oldenburg: Schulze, 1858.

Wenz zu Niederlahnstein, Rolf von; Hentz, Heinrich; and Abt, Otto. *Dreihundert Jahre Leibgarde Regiment (1. grossherzoglich Hessisches) Nr. 115,* Darmstadt: Kichler, 1929.

Wetzel, Georg H. *Die Hessischen Jäger,* Kassel: George, 1987.

Wrochem, P. von and Haevernick, Oskar. *Geschichte des Grossherzoglich Mecklenburgischen Füsilier-Regiments Nr. 90, 1788-1906,* M. von Below, ed., Berlin: Mittler & Sohn, 1907.

Xylander, Rudolf Ritter von. *Geschichte des 1. Feldartillerie-Regiments Prinz-Regent Luitpold,* Berlin: Mittler & Sohn, 1909.

Zechmayer, Georg. *Geschichte des Königlich bayerischen 14. Infanterie-Regiments und seiner Stammtruppen,* Nürnberg, 1885.

Zimmermann, Karl von. *Geschichte des 1. Grossherzoglich Hessischen Dragoner-Regiments (Garde-Dragoner-Regiments) Nr. 23.,* Darmstadt: Bergsträsser, 1878.

Zipfel, Ernst. *Geschichte des Grossherzoglich Mecklenburgischen Grenadier-Regiments Nr. 89,* Schwerin: Bärensprung, 1932.

Zoellner, Hauptmann. *Geschichte des K. B. 11. Infanterie-Regiments 'von der Tann' 1805-1905,* München: Lindauer, 1905.

Index

Entries in italics refer to geographic locations; the numbers indicate maps featuring these locations (thus the River Abens may be found on Maps 12, 13, 14 and 15).